New Communities U.S.A.

New Communities U.S.A.

Raymond J. Burby, III
Shirley F. Weiss

With

Thomas G. Donnelly
Edward J. Kaiser
Robert B. Zehner

And

David F. Lewis
Norman H. Loewenthal
Mary Ellen McCalla
Barbara G. Rodgers
Helene V. Smookler

Lexington Books
D.C. Heath and Company
Lexington, Massachusetts
Toronto   London

Library of Congress Cataloging in Publication Data

Burby, Raymond J   1942-
   New Communities U.S.A.

   Bibliography: p.
   Includes index.
   1. New towns—United States. I. Weiss, Shirley F., joint author.
II. Title.
HT167.B87   301.36'3'0973   75-34575
ISBN 0-669-00371-9

NSF-RA-E '75-023

All of the material incorporated in this work was developed with the financial
support of National Science Foundation grant number APR 72-03425. However, any opinions, findings, conclusions or recommendations expressed
herein are those of the authors and do not necessarily reflect the views of the
National Science Foundation.

Published simultaneously in Canada

Printed in the United States of America

International Standard Book Number: 0-669-00371-9

Library of Congress Catalog Card Number: 75-34575

HT
167
.B87
1976

Contents

List of Figures

List of Tables

Prologue

Title VII, The Urban Growth and New Community Development Act, was designed to meet four specific areas of need: the creation of a national urban growth policy; the establishment of a program to encourage the development of a variety of new communities; the preparation of a planning program to assist states and regions in achieving more rational patterns of urban growth; and the provision of capital subsidies for land write-down to cities to undertake development of new-towns-in-town.

The purpose of Title VII was to require the executive branch to assume responsibility for defining goals, setting policy to be followed by the bureaucracy, and recommending as a priority part of the presidential program the coordinated strategies to be implemented by Congress, the states, and other governmental units. The idea was to cause comprehensive and functional planning for all the components of growth and development—transportation, education, environment, housing industrial location, etc.—to supplement each other in achieving specific national objectives, as distinct from the no-goal, program-oriented system that had characterized the federal approach up to that date.

Moreover, those of us who were actively involved in the creation of Title VII, and in seeking support for it in the Congress, felt that the legislation, if enacted, would stimulate new interest and involvement on the part of the private sector and state and regional public authorities in large-scale, mixed-use development, which we believed should be encouraged as a substitute for the aimless, haphazard, and piecemeal development that had characterized the growth process in the past.

To accomplish this, Title VII included tangible dollar incentives for planning, land acquisition, infrastructure development, and the provision of necessary public services. It was hoped that through these incentives, some new partnerships and alliances between the public and private sectors would be created and that these new institutional arrangements would build more stable, more attractive, and more open neighborhoods and communities in the United States. We were looking for more than improved ways to develop communities physically. We were interested, to be sure, in increasing efficiency in physical development generally, in achieving economies of scale, and in providing better quality housing; but, equally important, the idea was to focus on the development of the whole community to set high standards for community development, and to encourage the building of better overall communities and livable neighborhoods. We were interested in making it possible for local governments and regional planning agencies to take a much stronger and more affirmative hand in managing community growth and development and the renewal process.

Our basic objective was, in the words of the act, to "encourage and support development which will assure our communities of adequate tax bases, community services, job opportunities, and well balanced neighborhoods in socially, economically, and physically attractive environments."

We also intended that the new law would encourage more interest and action in the revitalization of inner cities through the use of large-scale new-towns-in-town. We went to considerable effort to make that objective very clear in the committee report.

We also wanted to provide opportunities in rural areas for the creation of freestanding new towns and to help existing smaller communities outside of major metropolitan areas develop any potential they might have for needed economic growth. While we were quite aware of the fact that satellite new towns seemed to be the most popular, at least to private developers, of the variety of new towns with which we were concerned, we did not seek the emphasis on satellites that eventually resulted.

It is also fair to say that the more realistic among us did not see the program, at least in terms of the resources that Congress allocated to it, as one of great dimension. Nor did we expect that the new communities program could be instantly implemented. We knew it would take time to staff up and organize to move ahead. But we did have a law approved by the Congress. It was the result of intense and hard bargaining between Congress and the executive—and we did bargain with the administration for Title VII in good faith. It was signed by the president and as such represented a commitment by the executive branch to implement it to the best of its ability.

But the result in terms of commitment and effort on the part of the administration was considerably less than we bargained for. Once the new law was passed, the administration simply refused to take seriously the mandate of trying to develop a national urban growth policy, even though the president has requested growth policy authority in his most recent State of the Union message. In spite of some good effort on the part of HUD staff to implement the new communities program as authorized in Title VII, the administration remained indifferent. Moreover, it must be acknowledged that the rest of the public sector—state and local governments, with one or two notable exceptions—also showed little or no interest in large-scale development and even less concern about the need to develop a national growth policy.

The program attracted far more interest in the development of satellite new towns that we expected, and that emphasis dominated the program from the beginning and continues to dominate it even now. Although the program attracted a long procession of potential private applicants for assistance under Title VII, many of these developers completely missed the point of the legislation and saw it only as a convenient vehicle for more large-scale, homogenized housing tract development for middle-class America.

The kind of disregard for the social objectives of the program on the part of many prospective Title VII developers tended to reinforce the nascent antideveloper bias, which already existed within governmental circles and particularly within HUD. Unfortunately, this made it difficult for legitimate Title VII developers, those of high caliber with a good public orientation and with substantial devotion to the objectives of the legislation, to be treated by HUD with the trust and confidence they deserved.

Clearly, the new communities program has produced less than we hoped for, at least in terms of homes and neighborhoods completed. Most now face serious financial problems in the form of capital shortages. Other shortcomings of Title VII new communities, as well as other large-scale, private developments in the United States, have been documented by this study as well as other research and evaluation projects recently underway or completed.

Nevertheless, I firmly believe the overall product of the last five years has been one that basically supports the underlying concepts of Title VII: the need for growth policy, the need for a new towns program, the need for more rational patterns of growth at the local and regional levels, and certainly much more large-scale revitalization of inner city neighborhoods. But because many Title VII developers are facing serious financial constraints, it may prove necessary for the executive to take over some of the faltering new communities and learn to manage them into the stage of stability called for under the law. In my judgment, this course would be far preferable to a foreclosure, which likely would involve dismantling the project and selling off the land.

The program still has considerable potential. Our primary task is to demonstrate that potential to others, in particular the executive branch, but also to the many members of the Congress who have doubts about the program's usefulness. State, regional, and local government officials must also become more positively involved and committed to the need for continuing governmental participation in projecting and managing growth and renewal. Unless we succeed in developing the support necessary to strengthen the involvement and commitment of the executive branch and of state, regional, and local governments, we will lose our chance to build on the experience of the last five years and to provide the basic validity of Title VII.

There are, at a minimum, two ways in which this higher order of involvement will have to be achieved: The first involves the designation process itself and the governance of the new community; the second involves the need for local governments to finance acquisition and infrastructure development of the land (in all forms of eligible new communities) in order to insure economical and orderly development by the private developers and to insure that the community will benefit from the land values created by the process of developing the new town.

No new town ought to be approved for federal assistance without a full-scale public hearing and the approval of all affected local general-purpose governments. Finally, local governments ought to be willing to insure that the citizens of any new community will have a continuing opportunity to be heard and their views taken into account on any proposed changes in the community plan in the course of its development.

If publicly controlled development (including renewal) is accepted as a method to achieve open, balanced, racially and economically integrated communities, then the long-term, front-end investments in land and infrastructure are going to have to be made increasingly by government. Local governments, which want to control growth, protect the environment, and make certain there are jobs and housing for their citizens, will have to buy and hold land for future development. Once the land is banked, the local government can, by carefully staging the infrastructure development, manage growth and renewal consistent with the economic, social, and environmental needs of the community.

With local or regional governments assuming the responsibility for financing the capital costs of land and infrastructure (which they should be able to do less expensively than private developers), private developers will be able to construct and finance the market rate housing and commercial and industrial facilities necessary to give the community its full complement of social, educational, and employment opportunities.

Planned, mixed-use, large-scale development as envisaged by the Title VII new community development process is one of the very few ways we can ever achieve economically and racially integrated neighborhoods and communities. But no community can ever be expected to provide its necessary and fair share proportion of low- and moderate-income housing without commensurate levels of federal government subsidy. There simply is no way the private sector can assume this function.

The new communities program did not set rigid limits on the scale or term of development that had to be undertaken in the course of completing the community. Emphasis was on the completed product, that it be whole, balanced, open, and offer a full range of housing, educational, and economic opportunities. In the future the program should be used for infilling in existing communities, for supplementing existing development, which needs to be augmented through the provision of facilities and/or services that will help them achieve a proper mix of housing types, commercial and industrial uses, and public facilities.

New Communities U.S.A. should prove enormously helpful in helping us make a better case for a national growth policy and a new communities program to the executive branch, to members of Congress, and to the American people. For it is only through the sober and objective evaluation of our past effort that we can progressively refine our policies and programs and make them more helpful, useful, and responsive to the citizens they are intended to serve.

THOMAS LUDLOW ASHLEY, M. C.
Ranking Member
Subcommittee on Housing and
Community Development
of the
Committee on Banking, Currency
and Housing
U. S. House of Representatives

Washington, D.C.
June 26, 1975

Foreword

It is reliably reported that Adam and Eve took the environmental quality of the Garden of Eden for granted—until they were exiled. All of us take the familiar for granted, and the environment in which we spend our lives is quintessentially familiar.

In recent years the natural environment has been taken less for granted, perhaps because it has become less and less familiar. The wilderness, where most of us can spend but a tiny fraction of our time, has enlisted an army of defenders. The environment built by man for his own shelter, succor, and stimulation—the environment of human settlements where almost all of us spend almost all of our time—continues to be taken for granted.

Settlements are founded and grow because of the common interests of settlers. Trade requires that traders come together and industry requires that workers and managers come together. Living in proximity, both individuals and enterprises find that their needs may be served more conveniently and efficiently. Human interchange born of the same proximity stimulates ideas and the creative instinct.

We appropriately call a settlement serving the full range of common interests of its inhabitants a "community." And we have come to the conclusion that as our cities grow—by bringing rural land into urban use at the periphery or urban land into higher densities at the core—the desirable pattern for organization of growth is the community pattern. Both city and suburb work best when composed of community elements, each bringing within reasonable compass a range of diverse but complementary human activities and habitats.

Planners whose duty it is to chart in advance the growth of our metropolitan centers have therefore been projecting communities on the urbanizing fringes of the cities. But the communities have not been built. Instead, vast areas of uniform, relatively low-residential densities dominate the suburbs, punctured at irrational intervals by enormous shopping centers, strip commercial development, and occasional industrial parks. This haphazard pattern of growth is wasteful of energy, environmental, and economic resources, and has reinforced polarization of city and suburban populations by income, race, and geography.

Many students of urban growth believe that these haphazard patterns are the inevitable result of piecemeal development of land. For a project of subdivision scale at the periphery of urbanization, the market invariably dictates the same low-density development. The long-term vision of the planner may call for high-intensity use of such land as a community core, but the small-scale builder is at work in today's market. A small-scale project is not built over the long term and cannot respond to the long-term vision of the planner or the long-term interest of the public.

A developer of land at community scale working over 15 to 20 years is concerned not only with today's market but the market 15 to 20 years hence. He has the flexibility to build around acreage earmarked for high-intensity use while the market evolves. He is obliged to respond to the long-term interests of residents since his development schedule is long term. His objective is not to "get in and out fast" but to improve the value of residual land holdings through the quality of initial and subsequent development stages.

No one argues that community-scale development will insure high quality in the living environment or achievement of other public objectives in the urbanization process. New community advocates do contend that community scale offers an opportunity to achieve such public objectives.

But theory aside, what in fact has been achieved in community-scale projects? The Center for Urban and Regional Studies of The University of North Carolina has made the first systematic effort to provide a comprehensive answer to that question. The results of its national study, undertaken over a three-year period with the well-directed support of the National Science Foundation, are summarized in this book.

The new community concept as we know it today in the United States has evolved over time with the steady accretion of public objectives. In the 1950s and earlier, it was enough that a project achieve community scale and a communitywide range of uses of land located in accordance with sound planning principles. In the 1960s other objectives were added: excellence in the design of structures, landscaping, and other visual elements conceived as a piece with land use planning (Reston, Va.); planning for a mix in income levels of residents and for improved delivery of health and educational services (Columbia, Md.); emphasis on sound environmental planning for a hierarchy of open space and recreational resources mounting from cluster gardens to neighborhood swimming pools and tennis courts to village lakes and golf courses to community forest or agricultural preserves (Irvine, Cal.); and the attempt to achieve more equitable distribution of population at regional and national scale (Lake Havasu City, Ariz.).

In the 1970s the diverse public objectives of new community development were refined and codified in standards set by the Department of Housing and Urban Development for its new communities assistance programs. The range of public interests reflected in these standards is now generally accepted as the current definitional basis for the new community concept. The authors of this book accurately portray the current concept in chapter 2 and summarize in the 11 chapters of parts III and IV their investigation of the variety of public interests contributing to the concept.

It is hardly surprising that the new communities begun in the 1960s, particularly those pioneering projects responsive to new public objectives in land development, should more closely reflect the current new community concept than projects initiated in the 1950s or earlier.

For the new communities initiated in the 1970s, either influenced by or subject to federal standards, our expectations of achievement should be even greater. As indicated by the authors in chapter 18, this new "federal" generation of projects is as yet too immature for more than a baseline evaluation. It is not too early, however, to predict some measure of disappointment, for the federally imposed objectives have been supported by only a fraction of the assistance authorized by Congress.

On January 14, 1975, the secretary of Housing and Urban Development announced that no additional new communities would be approved for assistance and that available resources would be devoted instead to assisting the 14 projects already approved. No indication has been given, however, that the numerous unfunded grant programs would be activated even for this limited purpose. Controversy has surrounded the role that preliminary findings of The University of North Carolina study may have played in the HUD secretary's decision to abandon federal encouragement for new community development.

Based on aggregate data from all projects studied, headlines appeared in the press in mid-1974 announcing much disappointment with new communities: residents of the new communities studied were only marginally more satisfied than residents of paired conventional communities resulting from incremental growth. No differentiation was made in these press reports among the communities conceived in the 1950s, the pioneering projects of the 1960s, and the immature generation of the 1970s. Disaggregated, the data in fact often show greater satisfaction with such communities as Reston, Columbia, and Irvine than with paired conventional communities. In short, the data reveal resident appreciation of the benefits inherent in the evolving new community concept.

It is hardly rational to conclude that, because projects conceived in the 1950s do not meet the full expectations of the 1970s, the new community concept of the 1970s should be abandoned. Since the decision makers responsible for abandonment of the new community assistance programs are rational and reasonable federal servants, I can only conclude that their decision was taken not as a result of, but in spite of, the findings of The University of North Carolina. This conclusion is supported by the university's public statement released on November 17, 1974 calling for more, not less, federal assistance for new communities based on findings of the study summarized in this book.

Under crossfire from new community advocates and detractors, members of the research team at The University of North Carolina have worked quietly and professionally to achieve a rigorously objective product. With the publication of this book, they have made a major contribution to public understanding of the realistic benefits and problems associated with new community development.

There is scarcely a subject worthy of greater public attention and understanding than the process by which we create the physical and social environment in which our lives are spent. This book should go far to combat the current lack of attention born of familiarity. When the consciousness of the public is aroused, our rational and reasonable federal servants may be awakened as well.

New communities are not portrayed here as Gardens of Eden. But, exiled by our federal servants, we may yet come to appreciate their virtues as well as their limitations. This book offers the beginning of understanding.

WILLIAM NICOSON

Washington, D.C.
June 10, 1975

Preface

This book summarizes the results of an extensive study and evaluation of the concepts and realities of new community development in the United States. The study was initiated in May 1972 under the direction of Dr. Shirley F. Weiss, principal investigator, and co-principal investigators Dr. Raymond J. Burby, III, Dr. Thomas G. Donnelly, Dr. Edward J. Kaiser, and Dr. Robert B. Zehner, at the Center for Urban and Regional Studies of The University of North Carolina at Chapel Hill, with support from the Research Applied to National Needs Directorate of the National Science Foundation.

When the original prospectus for the study was prepared, new community development was riding atop a wave of expansion in community building and of high hopes that new communities would serve as the central focus of an emerging national urban growth policy. Private investment in new communities was at an all-time peak. Federal involvement in new community development had been significantly expanded by passage of the Urban Growth and New Community Development Act of 1970. Officials were confidently projecting that ten new communities per year would be assisted under the federal program. With the population of the United States then expected to increase by some 75 million between 1970 and the year 2000, new communities were widely hailed as a promising solution to America's urban growth problems.

Although the national economic recession beginning in 1973 has severely crippled the community building industry, the central question that stimulated this study is as valid today as it was three years ago. At that time, we pointed out that, "The critical question for new community policy in the 1970s is not whether new communities will be built, but how well they will perform in improving the quality of life for new community residents." The level of public resources devoted to community building, though never large, has fluctuated with the persuasiveness of hypothetical arguments put forward by new community proponents and opponents. In light of the grave concerns many have expressed for the character of metropolitan expansion, the extent to which the benefits of new community development are real or imagined is crucial to the public interest. Publication of this book should contribute to more informed decisions regarding public investment in community building and to new community projects that are more responsive to the revealed needs of all residents.

The study is the most comprehensive investigation of new community development ever undertaken. However, it would have been folly to approach the study as an effort to provide a complete analysis of the new community phenomenon. Such a goal is illusive under ideal circumstances, and it is clearly unrealistic given the immense number of topics that could have been addressed. Instead, our objective has been to provide a carefully conducted study that comprehends the major benefits and problems claimed for new communities so that reasonable judgments about their value to the nation may be reached.

The Study Team

This book is the product of the two senior authors, three collaborating colleagues who joined with them in formulating the research design and conducting the study, a number of capable research associates who devoted their efforts to special analyses, and a supporting research staff. The authors are responsible for the content of the study and assume full liability for inadvertent errors and for matters of interpretation.

A number of manuscripts prepared by members of the study team and the authors were combined for this book. In the process of integrating these materials and to avoid duplication and excessive length, it was necessary to condense the original manuscripts and fit them into the overall concept of the study. Seven books will be subsequently published for readers who would like to pursue particular topics in greater depth.[a] These monographs include:

Access, Travel, and Transportation in New Communities: Results of a Nationwide Study, by Robert B. Zehner

Economic Integration in New Communities: An Evaluation of Factors Affecting Policies and Implementation, by Helene V. Smookler

Health Care in New Communities, by Norman H. Loewenthal and Raymond J. Burby, III

Indicators of the Quality of Life in New Communities, by Robert B. Zehner

Recreation and Leisure in New Communities, by Raymond J. Burby, III

Residential Mobility in New Communities: An Analysis of Recent In-movers and Prospective Out-movers, by Edward J. Kaiser

Schools in New Communities, by Raymond J. Burby, III and Thomas G. Donnelly

---

[a] Forthcoming from Ballinger Publishing Company, Cambridge, Mass., Spring 1976.

This study would not have been possible without the major contributions of the following colleagues:

Dr. Thomas G. Donnelly, who assumed responsibility for the extensive data processing required for the study, including editing of the data tapes, preparation of special computer programs, computation of data weights, and advice on analysis strategies that were used in the course of the study.

Dr. Edward J. Kaiser, who helped to formulate the original research design and research management strategy. He offered invaluable advice throughout the study and contributed to the analyses of new community population characteristics and residential mobility summarized in chapters 5 and 6.

Dr. Robert B. Zehner, who assumed primary responsibility for the design and conduct of the household survey. He participated in all phases of the data analysis, developed the study of transportation and travel in new communities reported in chapter 14, and contributed to the analyses of community livability reported in chapter 16 and the quality of life reported in chapter 17.

The research associates who participated in the study included:

David F. Lewis, who prepared a comparative analysis of the population characteristics of new communities, their host counties, and host SMSAs, and contributed to the anlaysis of housing and the neighborhood reported in chapter 9.

Norman H. Loewenthal, who undertook a major portion of the professional personnel survey design and field work and contributed to the analysis of health and medical care reported in chapter 11.

Mary Ellen McCalla, who assumed responsibility for immediate supervision of the household survey sampling, field work, and coding operations and supervision of the community inventory, map measurement, and professional personnel survey coding. She contributed to the analysis of social life presented in chapter 15 and to the description of the study methodology presented in appendix A.

Dr. Helene V. Smookler, who assumed primary responsibility for the decision study of subsidized housing in new communities, which is reported in chapters 5 and 19.

Invaluable assistance throughout the study was provided by Barbara G. Rodgers, who served as administrative aide, research assistant, and publications manager.

The research work was supported by a staff of technical specialists, research assistants, interviewers, coders, and office personnel too extensive for a complete listing. In particular, the efforts of the following persons should be recognized: research assistants Jerry L. Doctrow, Mary C. Edeburn, Leo E. Hendricks, Christopher G. Olney, and Raymond E. Stanland, Jr.; and secretaries Cathy A. Albert, Lisa D. McDaniel, Linda B. Johnson, Lucinda D. Peterson, and Diana Pettaway.

The National Science Foundation

The study reported in this book was made possible by research grant APR 72-03425 from the Research Applied to National Needs Directorate of the National Science Foundation. Throughout the course of the study, the research team benefited greatly from the continuing interest and constant encouragement of Dr. George W. Baker, the project's program manager. Dr. Baker worked with the research team to achieve scientific excellence in each phase of the study.

Of course, the findings, opinions, conclusions or recommendations arising out of this research grant are those of the authors and it should not be implied that they represent the views of the National Science Foundation.

Site and Advisory Committees

The process of refining the initial research design was aided by the expert advice of the Site Visit Committee and the panel of anonymous reviewers whose ideas were synthesized by Dr. George W. Baker.

An important source of guidance and consultation was made possible by the project's Advisory Committee, drawn from experts in new community development, city planning, economics, political science, and sociology. Jonathan B. Howes, director, Center for Urban and Regional Studies, The University of North Carolina at Chapel Hill, ably served as chairman of the Advisory Committee, which included: Dr. George W. Baker, National Science Foundation; Professor F. Stuart Chapin, Jr., The University of North Carolina at Chapel Hill; Dr. Amos H. Hawley, The University of North Carolina at Chapel Hill; Morton Hoppenfeld, The Rouse Company (resigned March 5, 1975); Dr. Richard M. Langendorf, University of Miami; Floyd B. McKissick, McKissick Enterprises, Inc.; Dr. Frederick A. McLaughlin, Jr., New Communities Administration, Department of Housing and Urban Development (appointed in 1973); Dr. Peter H. Rossi, University of Massachusetts; Dr. Joseph J. Spengler, Duke University; Dr. Lawrence Susskind, Massachusetts Institute of Technology; Dr. Dorothy S. Williams, Department of Housing and Urban Development (1972-73); and Dr. Deil S. Wright, The University of North Carolina at Chapel Hill.

While their collective and individual contributions to the conduct of the study are gratefully acknowledged, it goes without saying that neither the Site Committee, the Advisory Committee, nor any individual members bear responsibility for the findings and interpretations in this book.

New Communities Policy Applications Workshop

A New Communities Policy Applications Workshop was held in Chapel Hill at The University of North Carolina from November 17 to 19, 1974. The workshop brought together invited representatives of federal, state, local, private, and academic user communities to review the methodology and preliminary findings of the study. The workshop was structured to insure that critical feedback to the study team would be secured from formal and informal discussion sessions and to provide a forum for the consideration of broad issues in new community development.

The Policy Applications Workshop was an invaluable part of the research process. The following participants offered many astute observations and critical comments, which were helpful in preparing this book.

Representing the federal government: Dr. Harvey A. Averch, National Science Foundation; Dr. George W. Baker, National Science Foundation; Bernard P. Bernsten, U.S. Postal Service; Larry W. Colaw, Tennessee Valley Authority; Dr. James D. Cowhig, National Science Foundation; Dr. Frederick J. Eggers, U.S. Department of Housing and Urban Development; Richard L. Fore, U.S. Department of Housing and Urban Development; James L. Gober, Tennessee Valley Authority; George Gross, House Budget Committee, U.S. House of Representatives; Charles A. Gueli, U.S. Department of Housing and Urban Development; Benjamin McKeever, Subcommittee on Housing of the Committee on Banking and Currency, U.S. House of Representatives; Dr. Frederick A. McLaughlin, Jr., U.S. Department of Housing and Urban Development; Paul W. Rasmussen, U.S. Department of Transportation; Dr. Salvatore Rinaldi, U.S. Office of Education; Ali F. Sevin, Federal Highway Administration; Dr. Frederick T. Sparrow, National Science Foundation; Otto G. Stolz, U.S. Department of Housing and Urban Development; Jack Underhill, U.S. Department of Housing and Urban Development; Margaret L. Wireman, U.S. Department of Housing and Urban Development; and Theodore W. Wirths, National Science Foundation.

Representing state, local, and community government: D. David Brandon, New York State Urban Development Corporation; W.C. Dutton, Jr., The Maryland-National Capital Park and Planning Commission; Brendan K. Geraghty, Newfields New Community Authority; James L. Hindes, Office of Planning and Budget, State of Georgia; Mayor Gabrielle G. Pryor, City of Irvine, Calif.; Roger S. Ralph, Columbia Park and Recreation Association; Anne D. Stubbs, The Council of State Governments; and Gerald W. von Mayer, Office of Planning and Zoning, Howard County, Md.

Representing new community developers: James E. Bock, Gerald D.

Hines Interests; Dwight Bunce, Harbison Development Corporation; David J. Burton, Harbison Development Corporation; Gordon R. Carey, Warren Regional Planning Corporation; David Scott Carlson, Riverton Properties, Inc.; Eva Clayton, Soul City Foundation; Mark H. Freeman, League of New Community Developers; Morton Hoppenfeld, DEVCO— The Greater Hartford Community Development Corporation; Joseph T. Howell, Seton Belt Village; Floyd B. McKissick, The Soul City Company; Richard A. Reese, The Irvine Company; Jeffrey B. Samet, Harbison Development Corporation; Elinor Schwartz, League of New Community Developers; Michael D. Spear, The Rouse Company; and Francis C. Steinbauer, Gult-Reston, Inc.

Representing public interest groups and new community-urban affairs consultants: Mahlon Apgar, IV, McKinsey and Company; Evans Clinchy, Educational Planning Associates; Ben H. Cunningham, The Hodne-Stageberg Partners; Harvey B. Gantt, Gantt/Huberman Associates; John E. Gaynus, National Urban League, Inc.; James J. Gildea, Barton-Aschman Associates; Nathaniel M. Griffin, Urban Land Institute; Guy W. Hager, Planning and Management Consultant; William H. Hoffman, National Corporation for Housing Partnerships; Jack Linville, Jr., American Institute of Planners; Hugh Mields, Jr., Academy for Contemporary Problems; William Nicoson, Urban Affairs Consultant; Dr. Carl Norcross, Advisor on New Communities; Robert M. O'Donnell, Harman, O'Donnell and Henninger Associates; Donald E. Priest, Urban Land Institute; Edward M. Risse, Richard P. Browne Associates; George M. Stephens, Jr., Stephens Associates; Eugene R. Streich, System Development Corporation; and Doris Wright, REP Associates.

Representing the academic community: Dr. Allen H. Barton, Columbia University; Professor David L. Bell, North Carolina State University; Professor Richard D. Berry, University of Southern California; Donald W. Bradley, Michigan State University; William A. Brandt, Jr., University of Chicago; David J. Brower, The University of North Carolina at Chapel Hill; Lynne C. Burkhart, University of Massachusetts; Professor F. Stuart Chapin, Jr., The University of North Carolina at Chapel Hill; Dr. Lewis Clopton, The University of North Carolina at Chapel Hill; Dr. Robert H. Erskine, The University of North Carolina at Chapel Hill; Dr. Sylvia F. Fava, Brooklyn College of The City University of New York; Dr. Nelson N. Foote, Hunter College of The City University of New York; Russell C. Ford, The University of North Carolina at Chapel Hill; Dr. Gorman Gilbert, The University of North Carolina at Chapel Hill; Dr. David R. Godchalk, The University of North Carolina at Chapel Hill; Dr. Gideon Golany, The Pennsylvania State University; Professor Philip P. Green, Jr., The University of North Carolina at Chapel Hill; Dr. George C. Hemmens, The University of North Carolina at Chapel Hill; Dean George R. Holcomb, The University of North Carolina at Chapel Hill; Jonathan B.

Howes, The University of North Carolina at Chapel Hill; Frederick K.
Ickes, The University of North Carolina at Chapel Hill; Dr. Suzanne
Keller, Princeton University; Joseph E. Kilpatrick, The University of
North Carolina at Chapel Hill; Professor Alan S. Kravitz, Ramapo College
of New Jersey; Dr. Richard M. Langendorf, University of Miami; Dean
Claude E. McKinney, North Carolina State University; Dr. Robert W.
Marans, The University of Michigan; Susan L. Marker, Bryn Mawr College; Dr. Michael J. Minor, University of Chicago; Professor Roger
Montgomery, University of California, Berkeley; Daniel W. O'Connell,
Harvard University; Dean Kermit C. Parsons, Cornell University; David
R. Paulson, The University of North Carolina at Chapel Hill; Dr. Francine
F. Rabinovitz, University of California, Los Angeles; Dr. Peter H. Rossi,
University of Massachusetts; Dr. Arthur B. Shostak, Drexel University;
Dr. Michael A. Stegman, The University of North Carolina at Chapel Hill;
Dr. Robert Sullivan, Jr., Duke University; Dr. Lawrence Susskind, Massachusetts Institute of Technology; Professor Maxine T. Wallace, Howard
University; Dr. William A. Wallace, Carnegie-Mellon University; Kenneth
Weeden, The University of North Carolina at Chapel Hill; Professor Warren J. Wicker, The University of North Carolina at Chapel Hill; Dr. Deil S.
Wright, The University of North Carolina at Chapel Hill; and Dr. Mary
Wylie, The University of Wisconsin-Madison.

Representing the press: Barry Casselman, *Appleseeds and Many Corners* newspapers; Thomas Lippman, *The Washington Post*; William B.
Richards, *The Washington Post*; and Barry Zigas, *Housing and Development Reporter*.

Foreign observers: Åsel Floderus, The National Swedish Institute for
Building Research; and Hans Floderus, Building and Town Planning Department, Avesta, Sweden.

To list all the people who contributed to this study is impossible. Among
others, these would include 6,485 residents who spent time responding to
the household survey interview, the 577 professionals who shared their
knowledge and opinions about the study communities, and the 173 informed individuals who were interviewed in connection with the developer
decision studies.

A final note of thanks is due the new community developers and their
staffs who were generous in making available their time and expert knowledge to the study team. In reciprocation, this book is offered as an aid in
their continuing efforts to realize better communities and a more livable
environment.

RAYMOND J. BURBY, III AND SHIRLEY F. WEISS
The University of North Carolina at Chapel Hill

Chapel Hill, N.C.
June 26, 1975

**Part I
The New Communities
Movement**

1

Introduction and Summary

The form, processes, and outcomes of metropolitan expansion are major policy issues in the United States.

In 1970 Congress found that new patterns of development and, in particular, new communities, were needed to house future population growth, prevent further deterioration in the nation's physical and social environment, and to make positive contributions to improving the overall quality of life in the country. Seventeen new communities have been approved for federal assistance under the provisions of the Urban Growth and New Community Development Act of 1970 and its immediate predecessor, Title IV of the 1968 Housing and Urban Development Act. Loan guarantee commitments by the federal government now total $361 million. When completed in about 20 years, these 17 new communities will house almost one million persons. Private investments will total in the billions of dollars. Yet, in 1972 no systematic evaluation of this major and costly effort had been undertaken. Accordingly, it seemed appropriate for such an evaluation to be proposed and funded.

In spite of a promising beginning, new community development is in trouble. Faced with mounting financial problems with assisted projects, on January 14, 1975, the Department of Housing and Urban Development suspended further processing of applications for assistance.

Attention within the federal government and the new communities industry has shifted away from the outputs of the program to more pressing concerns for the economic viability of assisted new community ventures. In the long run, however, continuance of the federal presence in new community development must rely on more than financial considerations. New communities not only must survive as financially viable undertakings, but must also produce benefits that could not be readily achieved through conventional urban growth.

The purpose of *New Communities U.S.A.* is to provide federal, state, and local officials, as well as public and private developers, with: (1) an improved base of information to use in judging the merits of new community development as an urban growth alternative; and (2) an indication of the critical factors affecting the success or failure of new communities in meeting the needs of all of their residents.

In pursuing these two goals, the research was designed to provide answers to the following major policy questions:

3

1. Are federally guaranteed new communities contributing more to residents' quality of life than nonguaranteed new communities and less planned environments?
2. Which characteristics of housing, neighborhood design, community facilities, and governmental mechanisms contribute most to the quality of life of new community residents, including minorities, low-income families, the elderly, and teenagers?
3. Which factors in the developer decision process lead to new community characteristics that contribute most to the quality of life of new community residents?
4. How has the federal new community development program influenced developer decisions regarding housing, neighborhood design, community facilities, and governmental mechanisms?
5. How can the federal new community development program be applied most effectively to produce communities that promise to improve the quality of life of their residents?

These questions focus on new community housing, neighborhood design, community facility, and governmental characteristics; the contributions of these characteristics to the satisfactions and quality of life of new community residents; and the decision factors that lead to their production.

This chapter, which provides a concise overview of the study, is presented in three parts: The first describes the research methods and their limitations; the second reviews the major findings of the study, together with the study team's conclusions about the implications of the findings for state and federal new community policy; and the third presents a quick digest of the contents of *New Communities U.S.A.*

Methods of the Study[a]

Answers to the research questions are based on information gathered in 36 communities. Seventeen are new communities, including 13 developed by the private sector without federal assistance, two that are participating in the federal new communities program, and two specifically designed for the elderly.

The nonfederally assisted new communities are Columbia, Md., Reston, Va., and North Palm Beach, Fla., on the East Coast; Forest Park, Oh., Elk Grove Village, Ill., and Park Forest, Ill., in the Midwest; Sharpstown, Tex., and Lake Havasu City, Ariz., in the Southwest; and in California, Foster City, outside San Francisco, and Valencia, Westlake Village, Irvine, and Laguna Niguel, in the Los Angeles area.

---

[a]Appendix A, Methods of the Study, provides a detailed description of data collection procedures.

The federally assisted new communities are Jonathan, Minn., and Park Forest South, Ill., two of the first three new communities to be approved for assistance. The retirement communities include Rossmoor Leisure World, Laguna Hills, Calif., and Sun City Center, Fla.

In order to evaluate new communities in comparison with less planned traditional modes of urban development and to control for contextual factors, such as climate, data were gathered in a sample of conventional communities. Each of the nonfederally assisted and federally assisted new communities was paired with a significantly less planned conventional community. The paired conventional communities were similar to the new communities in terms of the age, price range and type of housing available, and location. Because the conventional communities did not have sufficient black and low- and moderate-income populations for comparison with the new communities, information was gathered in four additional conventional communities. These included four suburban communities, two with subsidized housing and two with predominantly black residential areas.

The study results summarized below are based on analyses of four types of data. These include: (1) the plans and activities of developers, governments, and other institutions involved in the development of new communities and conventional communities; (2) characteristics of housing, neighborhoods, and community service systems produced during the development process; (3) the responses of professional personnel operating in and serving the study communities; and (4) the responses of residents living in the communities in 1973.

Data on developer activities were secured during preliminary reconnaissance interviews in each community and subsequently through two waves of interviews with developer personnel. Additional information was obtained from accounts in newspapers and other published secondary sources, from visits to local governmental offices, and from the professional personnel survey.

Data on community characteristics were obtained from community inventories completed for all 36 sample communities and from the professional personnel survey. Objective data gathered included the number, accessibility, and quality of facilities, services, and programs offered. Also, the characteristics of individual housing clusters and neighborhoods were recorded.

Interviews were conducted with 577 professional personnel in the 36 communities. These included interviews with school district superintendents and principals, health officials and practitioners, recreational administrators, and community association leaders.

Finally, data on people's responses to their living environments, including attitudinal data (what people say they feel) and behavioral data (what people say they do), were collected through a 90-minute household interview. A total of 3,395 interviews was conducted with the adult residents of the nonfederally and federally assisted new communities, including special subsamples of black and subsidized housing residents; 1,522 with paired conventional community adult residents; 204 with adult residents of the retirement new communities; and 390 with adult residents of the two conventional communities where subsidized housing samples and two conventional communities where black samples were obtained. Young adults' responses were obtained from the return of 974 questionnaires that were left by interviewers with a randomly selected person 14 to 20 years old (excluding family heads and their spouses) in all sample households where such persons were residing.

The findings of the study have all of the limitations of the methods by which they were reached. For example, most of the data were collected at one point in time. They represent a cross-sectional view of new community development in the United States as of 1973. Although the results of earlier studies and post-1973 changes were taken into account where data were available, longitudinal analysis and monitoring of new communities over time will be required for a dynamic view of new community development processes.

It should also be stressed that the new communities studied were by no means completed communities. Some new communities had gone farther in the development process than others; for example, Park Forest had achieved about 90 percent of its target population, but on the average, the study new communities were only about one-fifth completed. Thus, this is a study of developing communities and not one of completed communities. Particular circumstances in individual new communities and conventional communities will change over time as their populations grow and the provision of more community facilities and services becomes possible.

The two federally assisted new communities and their paired conventional communities were in the very initial stages of development. The findings for them provide an early empirical picture of the results of the federal new communities program and benchmarks for comparison with later studies of these two and other federally assisted communities. They should not, however, be used to judge the entire federal new communities program.

One other caveat is in order. This study has produced the most significant and comprehensive set of information ever collected for new communities in the United States. However, not all aspects of new community development have been covered. Subjects of importance to new community policy that were not treated in the study include, among others: the question of national growth policy and the location of new communities; the impact of new and conventional communities on the natural environment; the economics of private new community development; the costs of new community development in comparison with incremental suburban sprawl; industrial development and employment (except as they influence travel behavior); and some community services, such as, public safety and public utilities. Research on each of these topics is needed for a complete evaluation of new community development.

Major Findings and Their Implications for Public Policy

New communities share some common elements. They are large. They are planned (though sometimes to varying degrees). Their growth has been guided by a unified development organization. Beyond this, new communities differ in the motivation and social consciousness of their developers, regional contexts for development, stage and pace of growth, and governmental structure. These and other differences make generalization difficult and even somewhat risky. The shining success of one new community may be the faltering stepchild of another. Nevertheless, common threads run throughout the new community experience and form the basis for conclusions about both the strengths and weaknesses of new community development.

What New Communities Are Doing Best

The outputs of new community development processes were in many respects superior to those of conventional community growth. The advantages in favor of new communities included: (1) better land use planning and access to community facilities; (2) reduction in automobile travel; (3) superior recreational facilities; (4) enhanced community livability; and (5) improved living environments for low- and moderate-income households, blacks, and the elderly.

Orderly growth and the careful arrangement of land uses have been keystones of the new community concept since the first large-scale community development projects emerged after World War II. Based on objective measures, and from the residents' perspectives, better land use planning is a major benefit of new community development. Compared with conventional suburban communities, new communities provided an increased choice of housing types for purchase or rent. Neighborhoods were designed with more amenities and with greater attention to the provision of safe modes of access to them. A variety of community facilities and services—from elementary schools to doctors' offices—were more conveniently located. Almost without exception, new community residents rated the planning of their communities more highly than the residents of conventional communities.

Major transportation and travel benefits resulted from new community development. New communities provided more alternative modes of travel than conventional communities. New community residents gave higher ratings to the ease of getting around their communities. They were also less likely to use their automobiles. New community residents drove 7.5 percent fewer miles, on average, than conventional community residents, a significant saving in light of the nation's diminishing energy resources.

Centralized direction of the community development process and the use of new forms of community governance enabled new communities to provide better recreational services than conventional suburban communities. In turn, more abundant recreational resources were reflected in residents' evaluations. Recreational facilities and services were rated much higher in new communities than in conventional communities.

Community planning, the convenience of facilities, and generally high quality of new community environments contributed to very high resident assessments of overall community livability. In addition, new community residents were more likely than the residents of conventional communities to rate their communities as excellent or good places to live and to say that they would advise others that their communities were particularly good places to which to move.

Finally, although only a few new communities made significant progress in achieving income, class, and racial balance, new communities provided highly desirable living environments for target populations. Low- and moderate-income residents of subsidized housing were more likely to improve the quality of facilities and services available to them by moving to new communities than were nonsubsidized housing new community residents. They also tended to be more satisfied with their living environments than subsidized housing residents living in conventional communities. Black residents of new communities rated a number of aspects of their homes, neighborhoods, and communities as highly as nonblack residents and were more satisfied with their living environments than black residents of conventional suburban communities. Elderly residents of new communities were generally more satisfied with their living environments than younger residents or elderly persons living in conventional communities. However, older persons living in retirement new communities that were specifically designed with the needs of the elderly in mind tended to be even more satisfied and experienced significantly less isolation from the mainstream of community life.

What New Communities Are Doing Well–But Often Not
Better Than Conventional Communities

For a variety of reasons—many of which were beyond the control of developers—there were a number of aspects of community development in which the performance of new communities was little different from that of conventional communities. These included: (1) satisfaction of many of the key goals families hoped to achieve in moving to new communities and conventional communities; (2) evaluations of housing and neighborhood livability; (3) residents' social perspectives and participation in community life; (4) satisfaction with the quality of life; (5) the provision of some community services; and (6) community governance.

New and conventional community residents gave similar reasons for their choice of a community, and in both settings were likely to feel that their move led to improvements over their previous communities. Perceptions of improvements were equivalent for: (1) the community as a good place to raise children; (2) convenience to work; (3) layout and space of the dwelling and lot; (4) appearance of the immediate neighborhood; and (5) nearness to the outdoors and natural environment.

Both new and conventional community residents tended to be attracted by characteristics of the home and immediate environment around the home. Satisfaction with the overall livability and various characteristics of the home were similar. Although overall neighborhood livability was also rated the same in new and conventional communities, new community residents were more satisfied with some aspects of their neighborhoods. This was particularly so in new community rental apartment neighborhoods, which were rated more highly than conventional community apartment neighborhoods in terms of appearance, privacy, quiet, safety, maintenance, and places for children's outdoor play.

New community development generally had much less impact on social perceptions and participation than many planners had anticipated. Community identity, satisfaction with family life and the community as a place to raise children, neighboring, and participation in community organizations were not much different in new than in conventional communities. Although the availability and quality of facilities had a moderately strong effect on participation in recreational activities, participation rates were only marginally higher in new than in conventional communities. Finally, residents' perceptions of their quality of life—both in terms of improvements gained from the move to a new or conventional community and in terms of overall life satisfaction—were equivalent in both settings.

New communities have had particular difficulties with community service systems that are highly dependent on the presence of a substantial market for their financial support or that entail political approvals or support from local governments. The disjointed character of health care delivery in the United States, developers' unfamiliarity with social services and lack of interest in aspects of community development that are not self-supporting, and political difficulties in securing approval of health care projects often resulted in inadequate health care and social service facilities and programs in new communities. This situation, however, was no better in conventional suburban communities, where health care facilities and services were even less accessible than in new communities. Inadequate health care resources were reflected in residents' attitudes. A sizable proportion of new and conventional community residents felt that health and medical services were not as good in their present communities as where they had lived before.

Based on perceptions that families want public schools that are easily accessible to their homes, many new community developers contributed to the provision of schools through donations of staff time, land, and funds for school construction. Based on their experience with both new community and more conventional forms of urban development, school officials often recognized the advantages to the educational system from the advanced planning that was possible in new communities. Nevertheless, the outcomes of school development processes were similar in new and conventional communities. Although new community schools tended to be more conveniently located than schools in conventional communities, there was little difference in terms of availability of schools, degree of crowding, use of innovative techniques, community school programs, student performance, parents' perceptions of their children's attitudes toward school, and parents' overall evaluations of the schools.

New communities have been caught between the financial risk involved in premature shopping center development and the risk of losing opportunities to competing centers outside of the new community if shopping centers are delayed too long. As a whole, new communities were doing little better than conventional communities in providing shopping and commercial services. Shopping facilities tended to be somewhat more accessible to users, but the per capita number of establishments was similar. Compared with conventional community residents, those living in new communities were somewhat more likely to patronize a shopping center within their own community, but were somewhat less likely to shop for convenience items and at supermarkets in the community. Although residents of some new communities rated shopping facilities better than the residents of conventional communities, the advantage in favor of new communities was small.

Finally, new communities often did not succeed in centralizing the provision of public services. User satisfaction with services and political participation in planning and governance decisions were similar in new and conventional suburban communities. Local governments serving new communities faced the same problems as governments serving any rapidly developing suburban area. They were called on to make substantial "front-end" investments in public facilities and services before property values and economic activity produced sufficient revenues to support such expenditures. The developer faced the same problem—initial capital outlays far exceeded initial revenues in new community development—but the developer was not limited by often rigid state debt limitation laws, which circumscribed debt financing by local government. The new community political problem was further compounded by the number of competing and politically independent jurisdictions that tended to serve new community development sites. Each jurisdiction pursued its own interests, which were not necessarily those of the new community, and answered to its own constituency. While new community development offered the opportunity for installing superior public service systems, many local governments found it politically impossible to favor one section of their jurisdiction over another.

Some of the limitations experienced in new community development in the United States may be overcome as new communities embrace more aspects of the new community concept and as developers incorporate more public objectives into their development programs. In particular, Columbia stands out for the breadth and depth of its attention to population balance, innovation in governance, planning for the provision of better educational, recreational, health care, and transportation service systems, and the development of a variety of shopping facilities at an early stage of community development. At the same time, however, Columbia residents often thought that community expenditures for public services were inadequate and shared other new community residents' cynicism about the developer and local officials. Columbia residents were not overly satisfied with housing, neighborhood, and community livability, and were no more likely to be satisfied with their quality of life than other residents of new and conventional communities. Irvine and Reston, along with Columbia, generally subscribed to more aspects of the new community concept than other privately developed new communities. However, like Columbia, they also had a mixed record.

Can Public Policy Make a Difference?

New community development, while producing substantial benefits, has fallen short of achieving the full potential of the new community concept for solving urban problems and making possible a better life. In some cases, such as social and political participation, satisfaction with family life, and with the quality of life as a whole, this gap is probably due to unrealistic expectations about the degree of influence of the physical environment on people's activities and personal satisfactions. Clearly, these expectations have to be trimmed back.

Given the weak influence of community characteristics on satisfaction with housing and neighborhood livability, it is also unreasonable to expect that new communities will uniformly improve on these aspects of community development. In fact, given the importance of housing and neighborhood characteristics in families' selection of a new home, the key will be to maintain a competitive position with conventional development, while at the same time producing a better overall community environment.

In many cases, however, including population balance, education, health care, recreation, shopping, transportation, and other public-private community services, the gap between concept and reality can be traced to a variety of factors subject to change through public policy. These principally include: (1) the private sector's limited ability to assume public sector responsibilities without corresponding increase in cash flow; (2) the inability of local governments to overcome the debilitating effects of continuing decentralization with accompanying fragmentation of public service responsibilities and insufficient financial capacity; (3) the lack of priority received by new communities in metropolitan planning, state public investment decisions, and the allocation of federal grants-in-aid funds and new capital improvements.

Implications for State and Local Governments

At this writing the Council of State Governments is exploring the role of state government in new community development. A number of states have individually examined their policies toward new communities and some states have already enacted legislation to aid and regulate new community ventures. Full realization of the potential of the federal new communities program will require an even greater state commitment to the objectives of new community development and to formulating and implementing strategies for overcoming the weaknesses of local government.

For example, although the federal new communities program calls for the achievement of population balance in new communities, in the absence of state directives for nonexclusionary land use policies, local governments may, and actually have, discouraged the development of low- and moderate-income housing in new communities. While new community development is predicated on the balanced phasing of growth, local governments may, and have, reneged on commitments toward planned allocations of land uses and densities so as to threaten the financial viability of new community projects. If private investors' enthusiasm for new community development is to be renewed and the social objectives of the federal new communities program are to be uniformly realized, state assumption or monitoring of the administration of land use controls in new communities may be essential. Whether the states are ready to assume this responsibility, however, is a question yet to be answered.

The key to successful governance of new communities lies in improving the tools for financing community services and in developing a system of shared power for the expenditure of funds. If new communities are to provide superior public services and at the same time to keep housing prices at reasonable levels, long-term financing of public facilities at moderate rates of interest is required. Because general-purpose governments—counties and municipalities—often have limited debt carrying capacity and are politically constrained from giving favored treatment to new communities, developers have been forced to turn to special districts to finance some facilities, while loading the costs of others onto land prices and forming homes associations to maintain them.

One promising alternative to the currently unsatisfactory modes of governing new communities may be the formation of transitional new community authorities. Created by joint action of state governments and new community developers, authorities would centralize governmental powers for a new community development site and would be authorized to issue bonds sufficient to cover the capital and initial operating costs of the public infrastructure required by the development program. Local governments, of course, are the creatures of the states. Any reorganization or reform of local governmental structure, such as the proposed new community authorities, will require, at the least, new state legislation, and, in some cases, revisions in state constitutions. Achieving positive results in many cases will involve a herculean effort.

Additional state policy revisions are needed. They include modifying state debt limitation laws, so that local government can play a more effective role in preservicing new communities, and revising state school development regulations, to allow for community use of school facilities and participation of educational officials in the planning, financing, and construction of shared-use facilities. Public participation in financing and operating centers that include both commercial and public facilities should be encouraged, together with state or metropolitan regulation of regional shopping center location and development. Both of these innovations would require changes in the planning and land use regulation enabling statutes of most states.

Implications for the Federal New Communities Program

The mixed performance of the 13 nonfederally assisted new communities and two federally assisted new communities studied indicates that federal participation in new community development is needed. Privately developed new communities are not likely to achieve population balance and cannot be expected to give attention to the full variety of community service systems called for in the new community concept and federal new community standards. At the same time, it seems clear that if the federal new communities program is operated solely as a loan guarantee program, assisted new communities will stand little better chance of fully achieving federal new community standards than new communities developed without federal assistance.

Whether under these circumstances the level of public benefits forthcoming is adequate to justify the federal presence in the new communities field is a difficult question. The benefits from successful income, class, and racially balanced communities, together with the significant benefits from new community development enumerated above, argue for resumption of the federal new communities program, particularly if the costs of new community development are no greater than those incurred in conventional suburban development.[b]

If the full intent of the 1970 Urban Growth and New Community Development Act is to be realized, however, more than a loan guarantee program is necessary. The federal new communities program has required that developers devote a considerable amount of attention to environmental and community service system planning. However, there was little evidence that such planning provided a commensurate return to the developers of Jonathan and Park Forest South for the resources invested. These are public functions. Requirements for public planning by the private sector can be expected to result in perfunctory efforts, as was the case for educational and health care planning in Jonathan, or to so divert the developer from the fundamental task of producing a marketable product, as in Park Forest South, that the new community venture faces financial ruin. As often as not, both results may occur. If the federal new communities program is to produce a truly new generation of new communities, some means must be found to match the private sector's capacity to design and produce high quality housing and neighborhood environments with an improved capacity of the public sector to plan for and provide equally high quality community service systems.

The need for better performance from the public sector was clearly anticipated in the Urban Growth and New Community Development Act of 1970. Section 715 of the act authorized public service grants to enable local governments and school districts to provide services during the first three years of development when the lag between demands generated by residential development and increases in the tax base are most acute. This section of the act was never funded. Funding of Section 718, which provided

---

[b] In fact, this is suggested by two recent studies: Real Estate Research Corporation, *The Costs of Sprawl: Environmental and Economic Costs of Alternative Residential Development Patterns at the Urban Fringe: Detailed Cost Analysis,* Washington, D.C.: U.S. Government Printing Office, April 1974; and James Lee Short, *Total New Town Building Costs and Comparisons with Alternative Development.* Ph.D. Dissertation, University of California, Los Angeles, Ann Arbor, Mich.: University Microfilms, 1973.

supplemental grants to the federal share of existing categorical grants-in-aid programs, was limited to $25 million and was terminated in 1973. Section 719 of the act was to provide technical assistance to developers and public agencies, but was never funded. Finally, Section 720 was designed to provide special planning grants for public service planning in new communities, but it also was never funded. Thus, public agencies that served Jonathan and Park Forest South were little better equipped to respond to new community development opportunities and problems than agencies serving nonfederally assisted new communities. The performance of the federally and nonfederally assisted new communities revealed in the preceding sections indicates that there is a need for these unimplemented sections of the federal new communities legislation or equivalent aid from state governments.

In addition, administration of the federal new communities program should take into account another lesson revealed by the development of Jonathan and Park Forest South. Public officials serving both communities complained that they had had minimal contact with federal new community administrators. To insure that federal aid is made available to local governments and developers in a timely and effective manner, the Department of Housing and Urban Development could station a project liaison officer at each new community site with adequate administrative support in Washington. In addition, attention should also be given to establishing standards and monitoring the performance of social, physical, and environmental systems in assisted new communities.

It is difficult to predict whether these policy initiatives will be sufficient to insure that federally assisted new communities do not suffer the same shortfalls as have been experienced by nonfederally assisted new communities. Much will depend on the location of newly assisted projects, the severity of local governmental financial problems, and the sophistication of existing local governments and community service institutions. However, even when conditions are most conducive to the provision of ''new-community level'' services, such as when development is undertaken in an urban county, a variety of local political factors may limit the capacity of governmental units to take advantage of the opportunities new communities provide for qualitatively better services than have previously been offered.

In many cases the establishment of new community authorities would substantially improve the capacity of local government to serve as an effective partner with the developer in realizing the goals of the federal new communities program. If and when a comprehensive reevaluation of the 1970 Urban Growth and New Community Development Act is undertaken, careful thought should be given to how the federal government can foster state and local initiatives to establish new governmental structures for new communities. One obvious step in this direction would be to guarantee not only the debt instruments of developers, but to guarantee also the bonds of local governments-new community authorities so that they are as capable as developers of meeting the front-end costs imposed by new community development. Guarantees could be made contingent on state establishment of mechanisms for regulating and assisting new community development and state approval of local governmental new community investment programs.

New Communities U.S.A. in Brief

The major findings and policy implications of the study were drawn from the 20 chapters of *New Communities U.S.A.* The following summaries highlight the findings and conclusions presented in each chapter and provide a quick review of the contents.

The New Community Concept (chapter 2)

Although the geneology of American community building extends back through many generations and has involved most sectors of our national life, new community development has not been an evolutionary process. Instead, it has emerged and reemerged as each generation has perceived the new community as an opportunity for profitable investment in real estate or as an answer to the various ills besetting society at the time.

The new community concept as we know it today is in large part a response to the suburban critique. This term summarizes four separate lines of criticism—aesthetic, environmental, functional, and social—that have been directed at metropolitan growth outside of central cities. The appeal of new communities stems from the prospect of combining the solutions to many problems in one package developed from scratch and unconstrained by past errors and built-in institutional practices that have limited the effectiveness of planning in established areas. Numerous opportunities for improvements in the pattern and process of suburban development have been attributed to the new community concept. They run the gamut from better planned and more orderly growth to elimination of social stratification and racial conflict.

Unfortunately, much more has been written about the potential accomplishments of new communities than about the new community concept itself. Nevertheless, a set of characteristics that are widely accepted as elements of the new community concept has gradually emerged. These include: unified ownership of the development site; master planning; self-sufficiency and self-determination; housing choice and social diversity; environmental preservation and protection; a commitment to urban design; and easy access to facilities and services. With the exception of unified ownership, when incremental suburban development is aggregated, it may encompass most of the components of new communities.

New Community Development Since 1947 (chapter 3)

The resurgence of the new community movement following World War II produced a great expansion in community building in the United States and renewed interest in new communities at all levels of government. New community development began to attract capital from a variety of sources. Entrepreneurs who were concerned with the character of conventional suburban growth saw opportunities to combine social goals with the profit motive through community building. City planners renewed their longstanding advocacy of new communities as a means of channeling metropolitan expansion. A variety of national commissions, organized to investigate the consequences of urban growth and to propose new courses of action for the public sector, recommended increased support of large-scale new community development, and the federal government subsequently entered the field.

Now, after more than a quarter century of sustained activity, community building has come close to a standstill. The national economic recession beginning in 1973 has shaken the foundations of the new community movement and led many observers to recommend retrenchment through smaller-scale planned neighborhoods and villages. However, the slowdown in community building also offers an opportunity to take stock of this important phenomenon in American urbanization before another phase of the new community movement gets underway.

Private New and Conventional Communities (chapter 4)

Criteria used to identify and select new communities for the study were established. These included: (1) development of the community under the direction of a single entrepreneur or development company to insure unified and coordinated management of the development process; (2) sufficient size—2,000 or more acres planned for target populations of 20,000 or more persons—to allow for social diversity and to support a variety of urban functions; (3) development programmed in accordance with an overall master plan; (4) provision for a variety of urban functions through the reservation of land for residential, commercial, industrial, public, and institutional uses; (5) provision of a variety of housing choices, including at a minimum opportunities for owning and renting and for single-family and apartment life-styles. Additional criteria used to select new communities for the study included requirements that active development be underway after 1960, that a minimum of 5,000 persons be in residence on January 1, 1972, and that the community be located in the continental United States. Based on these criteria, a sample of 13 new communities was selected for the study through a stratified random sampling procedure. Each new community was paired with a significantly less planned conventional community.

Vignettes describing each new community illustrate the diverse character of new community development in the United States. Based on their performance on 19 indicators, a rank order index of adherence to the new community concept was calculated. In descending order of adherence to the new community concept, the sample nonfederally assisted new communities ranked as follows: first, Columbia, Md.; second, Reston, Va.; third, Irvine, Calif.; fourth, Valencia, Calif.; fifth, Park Forest, Ill.; sixth, Westlake Village, Calif.; seventh, Elk Grove Village, Ill.; eighth, Foster City, Calif.; ninth, Laguna Niguel, Calif.; tenth, Lake Havasu City, Ariz.; eleventh, Sharpstown, Tex.; twelfth, Forest Park, Oh.; and thirteenth, North Palm Beach, Fla. With one exception (Forest Park) each new community ranked higher on adherence to the new community concept that its paired conventional community.

Who Lives in New Communites? (chapter 5)

New community development has not stimulated the flight of middle-income residents from central cities. For 10 of the 13 nonfederally assisted new communities studied, only 30 percent or less of the respondents had moved from a central city. New community residents were no more likely than the residents of the paired conventional communities to be former central city dwellers.

New community residents, like many others living in suburban areas, tend to be young families who are raising children. Almost 50 percent of the household heads were under 40 years old; 61 percent of the households contained children. Only 12 percent were single persons without children, while 27 percent of the new community households were childless couples. Recent inmovers to new communities were not significantly different in life cycle characteristics from conventional community in-movers, or what might be termed the general metropolitan mover profile.

Both recent and earlier in-movers to new communities tended to have much higher family incomes (median of $17,500 for 1972) and much more formal education than the average person in the metropolitan housing market. In contrast to the expectations for population balance embedded in the new community concept, private new communities provided relatively few housing opportunities for lower income and working class people. Only 12 percent of the new community respondents had family incomes of less than $10,000; only 28 percent had not attended college; and only 22 percent were employed in blue collar occupations. Lake Havasu City was the only new community to have attained socioeconomic balance.

Just over 3 percent of the new communities' population was black, while the conventional communities had a black population of just over 1/2 of 1 percent. Only two new communities—Columbia and Reston—had consciously sought racial balance.

Attainment of socioeconomic balance through subsidized housing was influenced by a combination of three factors: (1) developers' attitudes and commitments to population balance; (2) the attitudes of community residents; and (3) local, state, and federal governmental policies. Analysis of these factors indicates that income and racial integration in new communities is feasible, both politically and economically, but it does not occur automatically. Favorable developer policies are essential to successful integration.

Why People Move In–Why They Move Out (chapter 6)

Key factors attracting residents to new communities (mentioned by 20 percent or more of the respondents) were: (1) perceptions of the community as a good place to raise children; (2) layout and space of the dwelling and lot; (3) appearance of the immediate neighborhood; (4) nearness to the outdoors and natural environment; and (5) community planning. The cost of the dwelling and convenience to work were often mentioned as reasons for moving to new communities, but were not factors that households necessarily expected to improve as a result of the move. Community planning and the availability of recreational facilities were the only factors that differentiated the appeal of new communities from that of conventional communities.

The type of housing selected in new communities varied substantially by household income and life cycle characteristics. Higher income households and families with children overwhelmingly preferred single-family detached ownership units. Moderate-income families, single persons, and childless married couples under age 40 were those most likely to have selected a new community rental townhouse or apartment. The reasons households gave for moving to new and conventional communities varied significantly by the type of housing selected. Single-family detached homes were more often selected by households concerned with child-related factors, while multifamily dwellings were more often selected by persons concerned with leisure facilities and convenience to work.

Prospective out-mobility from new communities was comparable to that for metropolitan areas in general. New community households were no more likely to be planning to move than conventional community households. Renters, apartment dwellers, younger housseholds, those living in less well maintained dwellings, and those who had moved in more recently were more likely to be planning to move than other new community residents. The most frequently given reasons for planning to move were expected job changes and the need for a larger home.

Community Planning from the Residents' Perspective
(chapter 7)

The importance of community planning in persuading consumers to settle in new communities was closely associated with the extent to which communities adhered to the new community concept. The character of community planning was mentioned by more than a third of the respondents as one of the three most important reasons for their move to Columbia, Reston, Irvine, Valencia, and Westlake Village. In contrast, less than a fifth of the respondents moved to Elk Grove Village, Laguna Niguel, Lake Havasu City, Sharpstown, Forest Park, North Palm Beach, or Park Forest because of the character of community planning. In many cases residents viewed planning as a form of insurance against detrimental neighborhood changes. Persons who valued this insurance and who were most likely to have moved to a new community because of its planning tended to have higher family incomes and to be moving to single-family detached homes. The character of community planning was less important in the moving decisions of renters and persons with moderate incomes.

A majority of the residents who were aware of neighborhood development plans when they moved to new communities felt that the plans had been subsequently followed. Although differences were not statistically significant, new community residents were somewhat more likely than conventional community residents to feel that plans had been followed in the development of their communities. Perceptions of deviations from community master plans tended to be highest in new communities that had changed ownership.

As a rule, new community residents did not feel confident of their ability to influence community planning and development decisions. In all but one new community less than a majority of the respondents thought that they would have a good or very good chance of preventing a harmful project from being built in their neighborhood. However, conventional community residents were also unlikely to believe that they could prevent a threatening development. Factors associated with greater citizen feelings of competence to influence development decisions included: (1) the presence of a municipal government; (2) the availability of citizen's associations that represented the residents' views before the developer and local government; and (3) a developer who made it a practice to consult with the residents on a regular basis.

Three fourths of the new community respondents, versus just over one half of the conventional community respondents, rated the planning of their communities as better than that of the communities from which they had moved. Planning was rated highest in those new communities and conventional communities characterized by landscaping of public and common areas, preservation of environmental corridors, existence of architectural controls, and the grouping of all commercial facilities in centers. Planning was also rated better in communities that provided walking paths, a greater degree of pedestrian-vehicular separation, and greater accessibility of community facilities and services. Better community planning has been one of the most successful aspects of new community development in the United States.

Governing New Communities (chapter 8)

The contrast between the orderly and rational planning of new communities and their fragmented governance is striking. Each new community used a number of institutions to provide services and to accommodate citizen participation in decision making. The patchwork approach to new community governance was the result of a complex set of factors. These factors included: (1) the weakness of local governments in the jurisdictions where new communities were initiated; (2) developers' lack of attention to the long-term implications of the institutions they established; and (3) the ease of forming special districts and homes associations that could be controlled initially by the developer.

On average, 7 out of 10 new community residents were satisfied with community expenditures for fire and police protection, public health, public transportation, recreation, schools, and community upkeep and maintenance. However, there was no difference in new community and conventional community residents' composite satisfaction with service expenditures.

New community and conventional community residents tended to be cynical about the responsiveness of local government officials. In 11 of the 13 nonfederally assisted new communities a majority of the respondents thought that local officials were more likely to respond to the wishes of a few influential citizens or to act independently, than to do what a majority of the citizens wanted. Political cynicism was equally great in the paired conventional communities. Although a majority of the new community respondents were not convinced that local officials were responsive to the citizenry, a majority did believe that local government was conducted in an open and aboveboard fashion. Satisfaction with service expenditures and with the responsiveness and openness of local government tended to be highest in incorporated new communities and lowest in new communities served by more politically distant county or large-city governments.

Some critics of new communities have argued that because of monopolistic economic control by the developer, new community development will stifle citizen political participation. In fact, however, there was no difference in participation in local political activities among new community and conventional community residents. Dissatisfaction with services and distrust of the benevolence of local officials and the developer tended to stimulate residents to get involved in local government.

The inability of new communities to centralize governmental institutions or to provide more effective public services than conventional suburban communities indicates that there is a clear need for new modes of new community governance. One promising alternative to the currently unsatisfactory means of governing new communities may be the creation of transitional new community authorities chartered by state governments and assured of adequate financing through state or federal guarantees of authority debt instruments.

Housing and the Neighborhood (chapter 9)

New communities offered consumers a wider range of housing in the same community than did conventional communities. Net residential densities were often higher than are typical of suburban areas, thus offering the possibility of savings in the costs of various community facilities. However, neighborhood densities (including nonresidential land uses) were about the same as conventional suburbs. Thus, new communities may be able to achieve some economic and environmental cost savings by clustering dwelling units in townhouse and apartment projects, but not the very large savings that would be possible through much higher than usual overall neighborhood and community densities.

On the whole, new communities came much closer to achieving neighborhood self-sufficiency than the paired conventional communities.

The advantage in favor of new communities was greatest for the provision of bus stops, walking and bicycle paths, nursery schools and day care centers, neighborhood-community centers, playgrounds and totlots, and elementary schools, all of which were available significantly more often in new community residents' neighborhoods.

Residents' satisfaction with the livability of their homes depended on a variety of characteristics of the home, neighborhood, and community, and how these characteristics were perceived and interpreted. For all dwelling unit types the most important factors influencing housing satisfaction were characteristics of the dwelling unit itself. Owning instead of renting was of overriding importance. After tenure, both the amount of indoor and outdoor space and the way it was perceived in relation to family needs had a strong influence on satisfaction with housing livability. Privacy from neighbors was also critical, particularly among persons living in multifamily dwellings.

Neighborhood characteristics had less influence on housing satisfaction than did characteristics of the dwelling. The most important neighborhood attributes were the perceived attractiveness of the immediate neighborhood and maintenance levels. The number of dwelling units per acre (density) had very little influence on housing satisfaction; but, persons who perceived their neighborhoods as crowded, noisy, or lacking in privacy were less satisfied with their homes.

Although satisfaction with the community as a place to live was associated with satisfaction with housing livability, the availability of community facilities and satisfaction with them had less influence on housing satisfaction than either dwelling unit or neighborhood factors. In part for this reason, only minor differences were apparent in the housing livability evaluations of new community and conventional community residents.

Recreation and Leisure (chapter 10)

Preservicing recreational facilities challenged the ingenuity of new community planners and developers. Basic problems were caused by: (1) county governments' bias toward regional recreational facilities; (2) the uncertainties involved in the timing of school construction and joint community and educational use of school grounds and facilities; and (3) the inability of municipal governments to finance heavy recreational front-end costs during the initial stages of development when property values and economic activity did not produce enough revenue to support such expenditures. Developers have sometimes overcome these problems through the commercial provision of recreational facilities and the use of homes associations to operate facilities financed through increased lot prices.

Overall, new community recreational service systems were much more successful than recreational service systems in the paired conventional communities. Recreational resources, including sites for outdoor recreation, the variety of facilities available, access to facilities, recreational programs, and recreational operating expenditures per capita, were far greater in new communities. The superiority of new communities in providing recreational resources was not reflected in recreational participation rates, which tended to be only marginally higher in new communities than in conventional communities. It was reflected, however, in residents' evaluations of the recreational system. New community residents were significantly more likely than conventional community residents to rate recreational facilities as better than those of their previous communities, to rate facilities as excellent or good, and to feel that community expenditures for outdoor recreation were adequate. The strong associations between a number of objective characteristics of the recreational system and residents' ratings indicate that their evaluations were not arbitrary. More and better recreational facilities resulted in more satisfied residents.

Health and Medical Care (chapter 11)

In contrast with the considerable amount of attention devoted to recreation, health and medical care have often been on the periphery of new community developers' interests. This may be a reflection of residents' general lack of concern for community health matters. Residents rarely moved to new communities because of health and medical care facilities and services, even when they were readily available. Health care was a relatively insignificant aspect of their quality of life or the factors residents felt were important in making their communities good places to live. Few respondents cited health care as a major community problem and the availability of facilities had little influence on the use of health care services. Nevertheless, as balanced and self-contained residential settlements, new communities have been expected to provide basic health care resources.

In 8 of the 13 nonfederally assisted new communities, health professionals thought that developers' attention to health care planning was inadequate. Two related problems often hindered such planning. First, as real estate entrepreneurs, new community developers were not necessarily the most appropriate agents to engage in such planning. Health care was not their area of expertise and there was little incentive in terms of consumers' market behavior to devote company staff time and funds to community health care. Second, the highly decentralized, free-enterprise character of health care delivery in the United States discouraged preplanning at the community level.

Many new communities faced a shortage of physicians—a problem that was frequently noted by health care professionals. However, the accessibility of the nearest general practitioner, nearest hospital, and nearest public health clinic was better in new communities than in the paired conventional communities. The fact that health care seeking behavior (use of physicians, annual checkups, failure to see a doctor when the need was felt) was not associated with either the relative availability or accessibility of doctors explains why there was little difference in the use of medical care services among new community and conventional community residents.

Three new and three conventional communities had community hospitals. In addition, hospitals were in the planning or construction stage in a number of other new communities. New community residents who were familiar with a nearby hospital tended overwhelmingly, to recommend its use. Health care professionals, on the other hand, were often critical of available hospital facilities and of emergency service to them.

Social services have been a serious problem in new communities. In addition to a general lack of many services, the variety of sources from which services were offered compounded problems of coordination. Health professionals often described services as "fractured" and called for more effective social service delivery systems in new communities.

Facilities offering public health services were not only absent from most of the new and conventional communities, but were also quite distant from them. The combination of large distances to public health facilities and the sometimes negative attitudes of residents toward them meant that these facilities could not be considered a significant health care resource for community residents. This situation contributed to the lack of variety of types of health care available in new communities, with few alternatives to traditional fee-for-service practice.

On an aggregate level, new community residents tended to give somewhat higher ratings to community health care facilities and services than did residents of the paired conventional communities. However, as many new community respondents thought that their move to a new community had given them poorer health and medical services as those who thought that services were better than where they had lived before.

Schools (chapter 12)

The characteristics of existing school districts, their staffs, and methods of financing the development of educational systems often limited the ability of new communities to serve as vehicles for new, different, or better approaches to the provision of schools or education of children than have generally characterized suburban development in the United States. The major challenge of educational development in new communities has instead been actually getting schools constructed on time to serve the educational needs of children who occupy each new increment of housing. New community developers' participation in school development processes was often essential in successfully meeting this challenge. On the whole, school superintendents tended to be highly pleased with developers' contributions to the educational process.

In spite of the best efforts of many new community developers, however, the conventional communities had been somewhat more successful in constructing schools. School sites and plants, including design capacity and number of students enrolled, were similar in the new and the conventional communities. There was also little difference in various indicators of overcrowding. Although the number of elementary schools and middle schools per capita tended to be greater among the conventional communities, new community developers' attention to school siting resulted in somewhat better accessibility of schools. Reflecting the greater convenience of the schools, new community children were more likely than conventional community children to walk to school.

Schools serving new communities have adopted many of the ideas that are currently in vogue among professional educators. However, the adoption of innovative programs was no greater in new communities than in the conventional communities. Also, an equal proportion of school principals, and a somewhat higher proportion of conventional community school superintendents, rated their programs as highly innovative.

Parents' evaluations of whether their children liked going to school and objective indicators of student performance, including the proportion of students reading at grade level, drop-out rates, and the proportion of students who went on to college, were similar in new communities and conventional communities.

Less than a majority of the new and conventional community respondents rated schools in their communities as better than the schools in the communities from which they had moved. Although new community parents rated the quality of the public schools highly, their ratings were not significantly higher than ratings given by conventional community parents.

Shopping Facilities (chapter 13)

The goal of preservicing in new community development—where homes and facilities are provided simultaneously—implies that residents' shopping needs are accommodated at all stages of the community development process. For the new communities studied, every development plan designated sites for shopping facilities. However, not all new communities were equally successful in their development. Factors that have worked against the provision of shopping centers have included the economics of their development (an adequate base population is essential) and external developments that have diluted the market.

The number of shopping centers located in the new and the conventional communities and the number of individuals shopping and service establishments were strongly associated with the size and affluence of a community's trade area. Because of the dependence of commercial centers and establishments on the market, it is understandable why the majority of new communities did not have a greater number of shopping centers or establishments per 10,000 population than the conventional communities.

The greater attention to land use planning that characterized new communities led to better accessibility of centers to the consumers they served. New community residents traveled about 20 percent less distance than conventional community residents to the shopping centers or malls they used most frequently. The choice of the shopping center used depended on the variety of goods and services offered, convenience, and the attractiveness of the stores. New community residents were more likely than conventional community residents to use a shopping center located within their own community. However, shopping centers in only three new communities regularly captured two thirds or more of the local households. Each of these communities had a regional mall.

Less than a majority of the new and conventional community respondents rated shopping facilities as better than those available in the communities from which they had moved. New community residents, however, were significantly more likely than conventional community residents to rate facilities as better than their former communities and, overall, to rate shopping facilities as excellent or good. The highest ratings tended to be given to new communities with a regional mall located within the community or a short distance from it.

Transportation and Travel (chapter 14)

A central premise of new community development has been that through comprehensive planning better relationships can be attained among many of the key variables that influence travel behavior. A variety of community facilities (13 of 15 facilities inventoried) were more accessible to the residents of new communities than to the residents of the conventional communities. However, most of the conditions required for employment self-sufficiency and reduced commutation to work did not characterize the nonfederally assisted new communities. Only 1 of the 13 new communities was freestanding; many had yet to develop sufficient ratios of jobs to residents; and housing prices and rents were often beyond the means of blue-collar and clerical workers employed in the communities.

As a result, relatively few new community (14 percent) or conventional community (16 percent) employed household heads lived and worked in the same community. In addition, median trip times, distances traveled, and the mode of the journey to work were nearly identical in both settings.

The use of buses was significantly higher among new community respondents, but the proportion who reported ever using a bus (8 percent and 4 percent) was very low in both settings. New and conventional community residents indicated little interest in the location of a bus stop within their neighborhoods.

Both new and conventional community residents overwhelmingly used their cars to travel to work, and to convenience stores, supermarkets, and shopping centers. Striking differences emerged in the case of trips to school, however. In new communities with more than one neighborhood pathway, the proportion of children walking to school doubled over that of communities without path systems.

Although automobile ownership rates were similar in new and conventional communities, total automobile mileage per household was 7.5 percent less in new communities. Key factors associated with lower automobile mileage included living in multifamily housing, living closer to work, the absence of teenagers in the household, a nonemployed spouse, and the use of closer shopping centers and schools.

New community residents were significantly more likely than conventional community residents (48 percent versus 35 percent) to rate the ease of getting around their communities as better than that of the communities from which they had moved.

The Social Life of New Communities (chapter 15)

In addition to housing and service systems, an important component of community development is the emergence of social networks and social ties among the residents. A number of aspects of new community development have led to heightened expectations regarding community social life. In contrast with these expectations, however, new community development has had little effect on: (1) residents' perceptions of belonging to their communities (community identity); (2) satisfaction with family life and the community as a place to raise children; (3) perceptions of the friendliness of neighbors and ease of calling on neighbors in time of need; (4) frequency of neighborhood social contacts; and (5) participation in community voluntary organizations.

Nevertheless, the environment had some influence on social perceptions and behavior. The use of neighborhood and community homes associations tended to promote a sense of belonging to the community. Residents tended to be happier with the community as a place to raise children when highly regarded neighborhood parks were available, their homes were located on cul-de-sac streets, and they felt safe from criminal activities. Interaction with neighbors and perceptions that neighbors were friendly were heightened when neighborhood privacy was adequate; when residents felt that the neighborhood was socially homogeneous; and when facilities that increased the potential of meeting neighbors, such as parks, playgrounds, and paths, were available. Location on a cul-de-sac street was also associated with more interaction among neighbors. People living in more highly planned communities with more neighborhood facilities, paths, newspapers, meeting rooms, and other features that eased community participation were most likely to feel that opportunities for participation in community life were better than those of the communities from which they had moved.

Community Livability (chapter 16)

A majority of the new community respondents rated 7 of 19 community attributes as better in their present new communities than in the communities from which they had moved. Five of these 7 attributes—the community as a good place to raise children, layout and space of the dwelling and lot, appearance of the immediate neighborhood, nearness to the outdoors and natural environment, and community planning—were also among the most frequently given reasons for moving to new communities. However, while new communities tended to satisfy the objectives residents expressed in their moving decisions, they had no greater success in this regard than the conventional communities.

Among community features that were less important in residents' moving decisions, new communities had a decided edge in perceptions of improvements gained from the move. These features included recreational facilities, shopping facilities, ease of getting around the community, opportunities for participation in community life, and health and medical services.

New community residents were slightly, but significantly (statistically), more likely than conventional community residents to rate their communities as excellent or good places to live (90 percent versus 86 percent). They were also significantly more likely to say that they would recommend their communities to friends and relatives as particularly good places to which to move (81 percent versus 75 percent). The quality of the environment, including perceived lack of crowding, nearness to nature and the outdoors, and the attractiveness of the community, was mentioned most often as a reason for rating community livability highly. Other factors that were mentioned by 10 percent or more of the respondents included, in order, the convenient location of community facilities, quality of community facilities, friendliness and social status of community residents, and quality of community planning.

The reasons residents gave for moving to new communities, the improvements they achieved as a result of the move, and the statistical correlates of their overall community livability ratings suggest that four factors are key elements of community livability. These include satisfaction with: (1) dwelling unit livability; (2) neighborhood livability; (3) the proximity of the natural environment and countryside; and (4) the convenience of community facilities, particularly recreational facilities. In general, new communities met these conditions for a livable environment and an overwhelming proportion of residents rated each new community as an excellent or good place to live.

The Quality of Life in New Communities (chapter 17)

Residents living in new and conventional communities mentioned virtually the same factors as contributors to their quality of life. Most frequently mentioned was economic security. Beyond that, family life, personal strengths and values (such as honesty, fortitude, and intelligence), and friendships were mentioned by over a fifth of the respondents. Living in an attractive physical environment ranked fifth. The quality and accessibility of community facilities and services ranked eleventh among new community respondents and thirteenth among conventional community respondents. Based on their individual definitions of the quality of life, two thirds of both the new and conventional community respondents said that their life had been improved by the move to their present community.

In addition, new and conventional community residents tended to be highly satisfied with their lives as a whole. In both settings only about one out of ten residents indicated that they were neutral or dissatisfied with their lives. However, various groups of new community residents found their lives significantly less satisfying than others. Least satisfied with their lives were persons who were not married, who had below average family income, who rented their homes, and who were living in apartments.

Residents also tended to be very satisfied with various aspects of their lives. For example, over 90 percent of the respondents reported that they were satisfied with their marriages. Between 80 percent and 90 percent indicated that they were satisfied with their communities, neighborhoods, personal health, family life, dwelling units, standard of living, and jobs. The least satisfaction was expressed with the use of leisure time (72 percent were satisfied) and with housework (71 percent were satisfied).

Residents' satisfaction with aspects of the physical environment had less influence on their overall satisfaction with life than satisfaction with those domains that were more personal in nature or that reflected their economic well-being. In the strength of their influence on overall life satisfaction, among ten life domains considered, satisfaction with the livability of the home ranked seventh; satisfaction with the livability of the immediate neighborhood ranked ninth; and satisfaction with overall community livability ranked tenth.

Since the quality of life was found to depend on many factors not greatly influenced by community planning and adjustments in the physical environment, there are obviously limits to the extent to which new community development should be or can be expected to produce a better quality of life than could be experienced in other settings.

Federally Assisted New Communities: Two Case Studies
(chapter 18)

Jonathan and Park Forest South illustrate the commitment to balanced development required of participants in the federal new communities program. Goals for community service systems, industrial development, low- and moderate-income housing, and environmental protection summarized in their Project Agreements with the Department of Housing and Urban Development (HUD) far surpass most nonfederally assisted new communities. On the other hand, development experience and residents' responses to these communities do not suggest that their accomplishments will be much different than those achieved by new communities that are not participating in the federal program.

Compared with nearby conventional communities that were also in early stages of the development process, both Jonathan and Park Forest South provided a somewhat broader range of housing types. Housing costs, however, while lower in Jonathan than its paired conventional community, were higher in Park Forest South than in its paired community. While Jonathan had been successful in constructing a substantial amount of subsidized housing, Park Forest South secured HUD approval for a delay in income integration and had to withdraw a major mixed-income project when it was opposed by residents of the community.

Although Jonathan was more likely than its paired community to offer a variety of neighborhood facilities and amenities, this was not the case in Park Forest South. The record of the two federally assisted communities was also mixed in terms of the provision of community facilities. Both communities were more successful than their paired conventional communities in preservicing open space and providing recreational facilities. Much greater difficulties, however, had been experienced with schools, health care facilities, shopping, and transportation. These problems stemmed from a variety of factors, including their small population bases, slower than expected paces of development, difficulties encountered in dealing with local government, and the failure of anticipated federal aid to materialize.

In spite of these problems, residents who moved to Jonathan and Park Forest South noted a number of improvements over their former communities. In both federally assisted new communities a majority of the respondents reported improvements in overall community planning, layout and space of their homes, opportunities for participation in community life, appearance of the immediate neighborhood, nearness to the outdoors and natural environment, and the community as a place to raise children. A majority of the Jonathan, but not Park Forest South, respondents also rated recreational facilities, the type of people living in their neighborhood, ease of getting around the community, and safety from crime as better than their former communities.

The major factors residents gave up in achieving these gains were the quantity and convenience of shopping facilities and convenience to work. More respondents in each community rated shopping and convenience to work as worse than in their former communities than rated them as better. In addition, Park Forest South respondents were highly critical of the cost of housing in the community and health and medical care.

About a third of the respondents in both Jonathan and Park Forest South felt that they had not been adequately informed about future community development. Few residents in either community listed the developer as their most reliable source of planning information. Only about a third of the residents felt that they would have more than a limited chance of preventing development that might seriously harm their neighborhoods. In addition, residents were highly critical of local governmental officials. Less than a third of the Jonathan and Park Forest South respondents thought that local municipal officials did what a majority of the residents wanted and barely a majority thought that local governmental affairs were carried on in the open, rather than "behind closed doors."

Reflecting similar ratings given to housing livability, the neighborhood, and recreational facilities, Jonathan residents were just as likely to rate their community as an excellent or good place to live as the residents of the more fully developed nonfederally assisted new communities. The overall livability of Park Forest South received lower ratings than either Jonathan or most of the nonfederally assisted communities. Nevertheless, Park Forest South received significantly higher livability ratings than its paired conventional community, and ratings that were equivalent to the more mature new community, Park Forest, that was located adjacent to its northern boundary.

Residents of Jonathan, Park Forest South, and their paired conventional communities were highly optimistic about the future livability of their communities. Half or more of the respondents in each community thought that the community would be a better place to live in five years.

Experiences of Target Populations (chapter 19)

Special samples of subsidized housing residents were interviewed in five new and two conventional communities. A majority of the new community subsidized housing residents reported that their move to a new community had resulted in improvements over their former communities in 11 of 19 selected community characteristics. In contrast, a majority of the conventional community subsidized housing residents reported improvements in only 3 of the 19 community characteristics.

New community development offered subsidized housing residents a better community than they could achieve in other suburban locations. However, cost constraints on housing and federal regulations governing housing and neighborhood design resulted in housing satisfaction that was distinctly lower than that of the residents of nonsubsidized housing in new communities and not much different than that of subsidized housing residents living in conventional communities. What is more, subsidized housing residents' strikingly lower ratings of the reputation of their immediate neighborhoods suggest that new community development has yet to succeed in diminishing the stigma attached to residence in subsidized housing projects.

Occasional concern has been expressed that lower income residents living in the midst of affluent, high social status communities may achieve the benefits of superior community facilities and services funded by their more affluent neighbors at the cost of extreme social isolation. However, subsidized housing residents living in new communities were not all isolated. They had more interaction with friends and neighbors than nonsubsidized housing new community residents or persons living in subsidized housing in the conventional communities.

Special subsamples of black residents were also interviewed in five new and two conventional communities. Black persons living in new communities differed in very few respects from nonblacks and tended to be living in the same proportions in ownership and rental housing and in single-family detached, townhouse, and apartment units.

Black households who had moved to new communities were more likely to have improved more aspects of the residential package than nonblack households who had moved to the same new communities and black households who had moved to conventional communities. The advantage of new communities over conventional communities for black households was greatest for perceptions of improvements in community planning, recreational facilities, the community as a good place to raise children, safety from crime, ease of getting around the community, the public schools, and shopping facilities. Achieving these advantages involved some costs. Black residents of new communities were significantly less likely than black residents of the conventional communities to feel that the cost of housing and the cost of living was better than the communities from which they had moved.

Compared with nonblack new community single-family homeowners, black homeowners were significantly more satisfied with the livability of their homes. Greater black housing satisfaction extended to a number of aspects of the immediate neighborhood, including neighborhood attractiveness, lack of crowding, privacy, quiet, and reputation. In the case of rental apartments, there were virtually no differences in housing and neighborhood satisfaction among black and nonblack renters.

Blacks appeared to be about as well integrated into new community life as nonblacks. In fact, a significantly higher proportion of black respondents said they felt a part of what went on in their communities. Thus, at least for black persons who have been willing to move to and live in affluent, predominatantly white communities, minority status in the community did not seem to have created special hardships.

Because elderly persons (age 65 and over) are much less residentially mobile than younger households, it is not surprising that the elderly comprised a significantly smaller proportion of the residents of new and paired conventional communities than would be indicated by their numbers in the general population. In addition, compared to older persons in the United States as a whole, those living in new communities, paired conventional communities, and retirement new communities (Rossmoor Leisure World, Laguna Hills, Calif. and Sun City Center, Fla. were studied) tended to be much more affluent.

Although new and conventional community elderly residents mentioned about the same reasons for moving to their communities, new community elderly residents were more likely to believe that they had improved their living situations as a result of the move. These differences were most notable for perceptions of improvements in the appearance of the immediate neighborhood, community planning, opportunities for participation in community life, and the type of people living in the neighborhood.

The facilities at Rossmoor Leisure World designed specifically for the elderly were reflected in residents' perceptions of improvements gained by moving there. Compared to new community elderly residents, those living in Rossmoor Leisure World were significantly more likely to feel that they had gained improvements in health and medical services, recreational facilities, safety from crime, and ease of getting around the community. Sun City Center residents were more likely than new community residents to have perceived improvements in recreational facilities, safety from crime, and the ease of getting around the community.

In general, there was little difference in the housing and neighborhood livability evaluations of new and conventional community elderly persons. Elderly residents of both retirement communities tended to be more satisfied with the livability of their homes and neighborhoods than elderly persons living in either new or conventional communities. These differences in favor of the retirement communities extended to satisfaction with overall community livability, which also tended to be higher.

Based on three indicators of social integration, the age-segregated retirement communities provided more opportunities for social contact and the avoidance of social isolation than age-integrated new communities or conventional communities.

The Future of New Communities U.S.A. (chapter 20)

This study has traced the efforts of myriads of individuals and institutions seeking to produce better communities, documented their successes and failures, and indicated how community development influences people's lives. The results have undoubtedly disappointed many observers who have expounded the virtues of new communities over conventional forms of suburban expansion. The results, however, show that while new communities have encountered their fair share of problems, the promise of new community development is by no means a chimera. Behind the image is the real potential for more rational patterns of urban growth, more effective community service systems, and more livable residential environments. Fully achieving this potential will require a greater commitment of state and local governmental resources to new communities and expanded federal assistance.

Even in the absence of public sector support, new communities are being planned and built in the United States, and continue to follow a better approach to new urban growth than conventional suburban development. Although the new communities will not have a major impact on metropolitan expansion—too few will be built to accommodate more than a fraction of anticipated suburban population gains—they may be expected to demonstrate significant improvements in the ways in which rural land is converted to urban use. Innovations tested in new communities are likely to be applied in other development contexts so that, overall, the quality of community service systems and the livability of the urban environment in the United States are enriched.

Spontaneous new communities—areas of rapid growth through incremental development—will continue to occur in metropolitan regions that are still experiencing substantial in-migration. With improved planning and a greater commitment of public resources toward the preservation of open space and provision of public services, they may offer a means of achieving some of the benefits of new communities without the enormous financial risks that have slowed community building in an adverse economy. In addition, smaller scale new communities, ranging from development of several hundred acres to villages of more than a thousand acres will be built. These small-scale new communities will encompass many of the benefits from improved environmental planning and a broader range of residential amenities that characterize full-scale new communities. However, neither spontaneous new communities nor planned unit developments offer a total approach to urban growth problems.

After all is said and done, only full-scale new communities have the potential for a quantum improvement in the form and processes of community development. The findings of this study open the way toward understanding the necessity for strengthening public-private partnerships needed to translate the new community concept into the new community reality.

2 The New Community Concept

Few aspects of modern urbanization have captured the public's imagination more intensely than the concept of large-scale new communities. Thousands of column inches in newspapers, popular magazines, trade publications, and academic journals have chronicled the new community's promise of a better way of life, and, more recently, the trials and tribulations of the entrepreneurs and public servants at the forefront of the new community movement. Like the winning of the West, new community development captures a basic urge in our national character to start afresh, free from the constrictions and constraints of established patterns of urban life.

Origins of the New Community Concept in America

The origins of the new community concept can be traced to the first settlements in America. Many early colonial communities—Annapolis, Williamsburg, Savannah, and the villages of New England among others—were built according to carefully drawn plans. Even major metropolitan centers of today, such as Philadelphia and Washington, began with a master plan.

Continual westward expansion of the United States brought with it a host of planned communities, though many were laid out on the basis of a simple gridiron pattern by land speculators and the railroad companies. Rapid industrialization throughout the nineteenth century prompted the development of a number of company towns. One of the first, Lowell, Mass., was begun in 1832. Altogether some 52 company towns, including Gary, Ind.; Pullman, Ill.; and Kingsport, Tenn., were built. America's new community heritage also had its idealistic elements. Religious and utopian movements produced Salt Lake City in Utah, the Salem of Winston-Salem, N. C., Oneida in New York, and the three Harmony Society towns in Pennsylvania and Indiana.

The profit-motivated and idealistic new community strains were both active during the first part of the twentieth century. As Americans began to follow the trolley tracks out to the suburbs, entrepreneurs created several suburban planned communities designed to insulate residents from the undesirable aspects of industrialized cities. The County Club District in Kansas City (1906), Forest Hills Gardens on Long Island, New York (1911): and Palos Verdes Estates near Los Angeles (1923) are examples of the first privately-sponsored, large-scale planned communities in this century. Following a more idealistic bent, the English garden city movement espoused by Ebenezer Howard in 1898, and the prototype towns of Letchworth and Welwyn Garden City, influenced American entrepreneurs and planners to design and develop suburban communities based on garden city principles. Many current urban design ideas, including superblocks and pedestrian-vehicular separation, were incorporated in the design of Radburn, N.J., begun by Clarence S. Stein and Henry Wright in 1928. The Radburn concept was utilized by Stein, Wright, and others in several projects started during the following decade. "At Baldwin Hills Village in 1941," Stein wrote, "the Radburn Idea was given its most complete and most characteristic expression" (1957, p. 189).

The Great Depression of the thirties caught most of the American attempts to replicate the English garden city idea, and as a result they could not be completed. Out of the Depression, however, came the first large-scale federal involvement in community building. During the 1930s the Federal Resettlement Administration built three new communities: Greenbelt, Md., near Washington, D.C.; Greenhills, Oh., north of Cincinnati; and Greendale, Wis., near Milwaukee. Other federal enterprises during the 1930s and 1940s also spawned new communities. Large power projects led to the development of Boulder City, Nev., as a town for construction workers building Boulder Dam; and the Tennessee Valley Authority built Norris, Tenn., between 1933 and 1935 on a site 21 miles north of Knoxville. The final federal involvement in community building during this period originated with the first development of atomic energy. Using Boulder City and Norris as examples, the Atomic Energy Commission first built Los Alamos, N.M., followed by Oak Ridge, Tenn., and Hanford (now Richland), Wash., to house workers and their families who were employed at isolated AEC plants.

Although the geneology of American community building extends back through many generations and has involved most sectors of our national life, new community development has not been an evolutionary process. Instead, it has emerged and reemerged as each generation has perceived the new community as an opportunity for profitable investment in real estate or as an answer to the various ills besetting society at the time. The upsurge in popular interest in new communities during the past 15 years has its origins in the mass markets created by the unprecedented metropolitanization of the population following World War II, in addition to a growing concern with the predominant character of suburban growth around large metropolitan centers.

The Suburban Critique

The new community concept as it is known today is in large part a response to the suburban critique. This term summarizes four separate lines of criticism—aesthetic, environmental, functional, and social—that have been directed at metropolitan growth outside of central cities.

The aesthetic critique of suburban development focuses on suburbia's lack of urban design, its drab architecture, the clutter and ugliness of strip shopping streets with their jumble of competing signs and tangles of utility poles and lines, and its look-alike subdivisions and tracts thrusting outward from the central city to the ever receding countryside. Lacking both order and beauty, suburban America has been viewed as "God's Own Junkyard."

Metropolitan growth is the end product of millions upon millions of individual decisions. The environmental critique centers on those of the merchant builders, aided and abetted by the Federal Housing Administration, and the process of converting rural land to urban use. This critique holds that because of the incremental nature of suburban growth, the small size of individual development tracts, the stifling character of FHA and local development regulations, and the overwhelming importance of the profit motive and consequent exclusion of other values, metropolitan growth has been unconscionably destructive of our natural environment. Gridiron streets are platted with no attention to natural contours. Woods are cleared. Streams and rivers are converted to storm sewers. Separation of homes from places of work leads to massive commutation and gagging air pollution.

The functional critique centers on the inefficiencies created by incremental suburban development and the tremendous costs involved in providing necessary public services. Large lots and the single-family detached home require more miles of street and longer water and sewer lines, and also necessitate longer trips to shop and work than would occur if development were more orderly and more dense. Separation of homes from work and extensive political fragmentation create imbalances in the distribution of fiscal resources, so that once identified, problems cannot be adequately solved but continue to mount until they reach crisis proportions.

A final aspect of the suburban critique points up the social consequences of suburban development. Lacking schools, churches, and other social institutions, tract development is believed to produce personal isolation, disorientation, and other psychological problems. A sense of community and community identity are more difficult to achieve. Human needs and the livability of the environment are ignored in the development process, while tracts composed of a single housing type and built within narrow price ranges are viewed as promoting economic and racial segregation.

Although the picture of metropolitan development painted by the suburban critique is a stereotype, it is one that has motivated a continuing search for better ways to accommodate growth and to manage the environment. Cluster development, land banking, suburban development districts, and metropolitan government are but a few of the many proposals that have been put forward. None of these, however, has been as popularly received as the concept of building wholly new communities to house suburban growth and to divert migration away from overcrowded metropolitan areas.

New Communities as One Answer

The appeal of new communities stems from the prospect of combining the solutions to many problems in one package developed from scratch and unconstrained by past errors and built-in institutional practices that have limited the effectiveness of remedial planning in established areas. Numerous opportunities for improvements in the pattern and process of suburban development have been attributed to the new community concept. They run the gamut from better planned and more orderly growth to elimination of social stratification and racial conflict.

New community development is often viewed as providing real opportunities to plan better for and to accommodate urban growth. Through development of large tracts of land and development staging, new communities are expected to match the pace of development to the growth of job opportunities and to the availability of public facilities and services, transportation networks, and commercial establishments. Parks and open spaces, as well as cultural opportunities, can be located so that they reflect anticipated population densities and needs. Better relationships between homes, shopping facilities, and employment areas, together with the provision of alternative transportation modes and pedestrian-vehicular separation in new communities, are seen as ways to ease internal movement, lessen congestion, and reduce commutation. Preplanning and architectural controls exercised for the entire development acreage should produce a better aesthetic environment, while careful attention to site planning can minimize environmental damage. In short, new community development has been viewed as an ideal means of avoiding most of the land use problems associated with urban sprawl.

New community development has also been seen as a solution to many housing and social problems accompanying suburban growth. By acquiring lower priced land and using various housing subsidy programs, new communities may provide opportunities to furnish a broad range of housing types at prices affordable by a broad spectrum of the population. Since new communities are by definition new urban places, they may also be able to transcend social and racial segregation patterns that characterize established communities. The availability of a range of housing choices and prices together with the lack of established social stratification patterns have also been seen as facilitating the diminution of urban ghettos.

New communities have been expected to contribute to improved governmental organization and more efficient use of public resources. The new community is planned and developed as a whole; therefore, it should encourage centralization of governmental organization to regulate and serve the development site. Elimination of fragmented government and disjointed incremental development decisions are expected to increase the efficiency of governmental operations. Through planning and staged development, the scale of public investments can also be optimized. Not only should government be more efficient, it should also be more innovative. For example, more flexible approaches to land use regulation are seen as possible with new community development. Newness is expected to extend to public services, such as health care and education, which can be imaginatively planned and implemented from the ground up. Finally, by focusing attention on one site and one development plan, new communities are viewed as a way to make the public more aware of urban growth problems and the range of choices for future metropolitan area development.

Although a number of other benefits have been attributed to new community development, the point has been amply made. Almost every societal ill identified with metropolitan growth is susceptible to solution, and the best solution is most likely when urban growth is planned from start to finish; this is made possible when development occurs in wholly new communities.

Defining New Communities

Unfortunately, much more has been written about the potential accomplishments of new communities than about the new community concept itself. In fact, there has been a strong tendency to define new communities in terms of the end results expected; that is, a new community is simply one that lacks all of the problems associated with the suburban critique. In spite of the common practice of confusing ends with means, a set of characteristics that are widely accepted as elements of the new community concept has gradually emerged.[a]

---

[a] This section draws on a pioneering effort of John B. Lansing, Robert W. Marans, and Robert B. Zehner (1970, pp. 3-9) to define the characteristics of planned residential environments, new communities, and new towns.

Size and Unified Ownership

One of the principal elements of the new community concept is size. New communities are larger than other forms of new urban growth. This facilitates comprehensive planning of the development site and the provision of a more complete range of urban services. Although how large a project must be to become a new community has never been answered to everyone's satisfaction, few communities developed on less than 2,000 acres are labeled new communities. It should be noted that under the federal new communities program there is no prescribed size.

Not only must a new community be large, it must also be held in some form of single ownership or control during the development process. In this manner it is possible to achieve integrated planning of the entire development site and to have some assurance that the plans will actually be followed.

The Master Plan

Many of the benefits attributed to new communities are viewed as products of planning and the orderly staged development of the new community site. Therefore, a master plan is an essential component of the new community concept. This is not to say that all new communities follow the same plan. Obviously, they do not. But whatever the development scheme, a document that establishes categories of land use and circulation and allocates them to various sections of the site is critical.

While land use planning is a key component of the new community concept, functional planning for community services cannot be ignored. New communities are usually viewed as creating opportunities for planning all aspects of community life. Since the provision of many public and institutional services is not controlled by the developer, their advance planning requires close cooperation between the developer and responsible local government agencies.

Self-sufficiency and Self-determination

There is general agreement that new community plans should include a variety of land uses so that provision is made for most of the necessities of urban life. That is, rather than depending on the surrounding region for employment opportunities and services, the new community should be as self-sufficient as possible. Self-sufficiency is attained through size. The community must be large enough to support complex service systems and maintain balance, by consciously setting aside land for industrial, commercial, public, recreational, and institutional functions that are appropriate to the expected population.

In addition to being self-sufficient, the idea of self-determination is also commonly associated with the new community concept. Self-determination involves the provision of governmental mechanisms that enable residents to become involved in the operation of their community and to participate in decisions about its future.

Housing Choice and Social Diversity

The idea of a complete community embodied in the notion of self-sufficiency implies that provision is made for a variety of alternative life-styles. Most discussions of the new community concept call for a variety of housing types—single-family detached, townhouses, and apartments—as well as variation in housing costs and arrangements for purchase or rental. These provisions of the new community concept are designed to promote social diversity—mixtures of differing social, economic, and racial groups—and to create the potential for greater interaction among residents than is characteristic of conventional suburban development.

Environmental Preservation and Protection

The development plan for a new community is often expected to reflect a conscious effort to protect and preserve the natural environment. Environmental corridors may be established to preserve streams and eliminate the excessive siltation that is a common by-product of conventional urban growth. Encroachment on water bodies should be minimized, and sufficient open space should be designated so that unique natural areas may be set aside and protected from damage by urban intrusions.

Commitment to Urban Design

The man-made environment should be conceived in accordance with sound principles of urban design. It is generally agreed that new community master plans should not only meet the technical requirements of comprehensive planning, but should also reflect the application of modern planning and design concepts. These concepts, of course, change with each generation. Currently, new communities are expected to group commercial activities in attractively designed centers; provide for pedestrian-vehicular separation; place utility lines underground; include landmarks and visual symbols to identify facilities and to increase community awareness; use curved streets and cul-de-sacs to increase pedestrian and traffic safety and add to the attractiveness of the environment; and, establish a hierarchical form of residential units—from dwelling units to neighborhoods to villages—to provide logical service areas and increase interaction among the residents. The plan and subsequent development should at all times reflect a concern for the creation of an aesthetically pleasing environment.

Ease of Access and Movement

Finally, facilities and services provided in new communities are expected to be placed so that they are in close proximity to each other and convenient to all residents in the community. This is intended to reduce vehicular trips and to facilitate contacts among the residents. To further reduce dependence on the automobile, the new community concept also calls for the provision of a variety of modes of travel, including walking paths connecting homes with facilities and some form of community transit.

The New Community Continuum

In the absence of a widely accepted single definition of new communities, the elements that comprise the new community concept have been frequently used to distinguish new communities from more conventional forms of urban growth. The problem this creates, however, is that with the exception of unified ownership, when incremental suburban development is aggregated, it may encompass most of the components of new communities. Many suburban communities attempt to guide growth through master planning and land development regulations. Self-sufficiency is relative—most communities make provision for public and commercial facilities and many eagerly seek to attract industry to increase their tax bases. The veritable explosion in suburban apartment and townhouse construction during the past ten years has increased housing choice. Shopping center development has also mushroomed in the suburbs.

Few suburban communities remain unincorporated long after their initial settlement. In fact, the fragmentation of governmental units created by residents' desires for self-determination has been one of the principal components of the suburban critique. While the environment was long disregarded in the course of suburban growth, the environmental movement of the past several years and more stringent state and local legislation have forced developers and builders to exercise greater care in the conversion of rural land to urban use.

In sum, the distinction between new and conventional urban growth might be more usefully thought of as one of degree rather than one of kind. In this light, both new and conventional communities can be viewed in terms of their place on a continuum of new community characteristics. Both types of growth can encompass most of the elements of the new community concept and both can vary in the degree that they achieve any given element. Self-sufficiency, housing choice, social diversity, ease of access, and other aspects of the new community concept are all relative terms. No community can be entirely self-sufficient, but some communities can be more self-sufficient than others. Similarly, communities can achieve varying degrees of housing mix, accessibility to facilities and services, and social integration. They can occupy a low place on the new community continuum, if relative to other communities they do not perform well in terms of the components of the new community concept; or, they can place higher on the continuum as they adhere to more of the elements and/or perform particularly well on one or more given elements.

Difficulties in defining new communities and sharply distinguishing new from conventional suburban growth have not restrained the widespread enthusiasm that has characterized the new communities movement in the United States. Chapter 3 traces the increasing acceptance of new community development since 1947 as a solution to the problems raised by the suburban critique and describes the private and public participants involved. Chapter 4 then provides a series of vignettes that summarizes the characteristics of a sample of new and conventional communities and shows how they rate on the new community continuum.

3

New Community Development Since 1947

The resurgence of the new community movement following World War II produced a great expansion in community building in the United States and renewed interest in new communities at all levels of government. Beginning with a number of large-scale community development projects initiated by the residential building industry during the late 1940s through the 1950s, the 1960s saw a significant multiplication in both the number of new communities under development and the participants in the community building process.

New community development began to attract capital from a variety of sources. Entrepreneurs who were concerned with the character of conventional suburban growth saw opportunities to combine social goals with the profit motive through community building. City planners renewed their longstanding advocacy of new communities as a means of channeling metropolitan expansion. A variety of national commissions, organized to investigate the consequences of urban growth and to propose new courses of action for the public sector, recommended increased support of large-scale new community development, and the federal government subsequently entered the field.

Now, after 25 years of sustained activity, community building has come close to a standstill. The national economic recession beginning in 1973 has shaken the foundations of the new community movement and led many observers to recommend retrenchment through smaller scale planned neighborhoods and villages. However, the slowdown in community building also offers an opportunity to take stock of this important phenomenon in American urbanization before another phase of the new community movement gets underway.

The New Community Movement in the Private Sector

Unlike the new community movement in other countries, where new community development has been an integral aspect of national growth policies, community building in the United States has largely been a product of entrepreneurial initiative. Although profit has not been their only motive, the potential for large returns through large-scale community development has been the principal reason behind developers' enthusiasm for this type of enterprise.

The profitability of new community development may come from one or more of four sources of income generated during the development process. One of the key objectives of developers is to create urban values on nonurban land as quickly as possible. In essence, developers add value to their land in the course of preparing it for prospective users and in attracting urban activities to the new community site. Capital appreciation of land holdings is thus a major incentive for private sector involvement in community building. In addition to marketing finished lots to builders, commercial developers, industrial firms, and local governments, developers may actually engage in residential home building. In this way they may profit not only from the increased value of the land, but also from the seller's markup on completed homes. A third source of income from community development comes from cash flows generated by investments in income-producing properties, such as apartment projects, shopping centers, and office buildings. Finally, negative cash flows, which are typical of new community development in the early years, may be used to offset income from other sources, thus producing considerable tax savings for new community investors.

Profit, of course, has not been the sole reason for the private sector's participation in new community development. Many developers seem to have been strongly influenced by various aspects of the suburban critique and by the examples of new community development offered by the new towns of Great Britain and Scandinavia. Developers universally believe that they are providing consumers with a better product than can be obtained in conventional suburban communities. In addition to pride in their product, some developers have been characterized as social visionaries. They believe that new community development is the best way for new urban growth to occur in the United States and have widely espoused the new community cause.

Large-scale Development of the 1950s

Large-scale community development projects started after World War II capitalized on the pent-up housing demand created by the war and related housing shortages, easy financing offered by the Veterans Administration and the Federal Housing Administration, and highway construction, which opened up peripheral areas for residential settlement. Two of the first large-scale communities of the modern era, Park Forest, Illinois, and Levittown, New York, were begun by builders who had been involved in various federal housing programs during the war.

Park Forest, which is described more fully in chapter 4, was the sole new community enterprise of American Community Builders, Inc. The company was formed in 1946 for the express purpose of building a new community in southeastern Cook County. Construction of the community began in 1947 and continued through 1959, at which time the development team disbanded. American Community Builders was a complete community-building enterprise. The company acquired the development site, prepared the master plan, constructed the infrastructure required to serve the community, including schools and shopping facilities, and built and marketed rental units and homes.

The firm of Levitt and Sons began building small suburban subdivisions on Long Island during the 1930s. Based on experience gained in building navy housing during the war, the Levitt's developed a mass production system, which they applied in the development of their first large-scale community—Levittown, New York. Begun in 1947, Levittown was not preplanned. Instead, the company designed each neighborhood just prior to the start of construction. Nevertheless, Levittown contained many of the elements of a new community. Residential subdivisions were planned around village greens, which consisted of a playground, swimming pool, and shopping facilities. The market success of this initial venture led the Levitt's to start another large-scale development in Bucks County, Pennsylvania, in 1951. This community followed the neighborhood design principles established in the New York Levittown, but also included a large regional shopping center. However, like their first community-building venture, the Levitt's continued to build entire neighborhoods composed of a single housing type. A third Levitt project, Levittown, New Jersey, was established in 1958 as a model new community. Unlike its predecessors, the New Jersey Levittown began with a general plan, which designated land uses, the circulation system, and utilities. The Levitt's also provided a variety of housing types in each neighborhood and built neighborhood schools, playgrounds, and swimming pools. The cost of these facilities was incorporated into the prices of individual homes. Already renowned for the housing value it offered, in its third Levittown the Levitt firm sought to establish a reputation for also building a superior community.

While Park Forest and the Levittowns are the best known large-scale development projects underway during the 1950s, many others were begun in different parts of the country. Four of them—Sharpstown, Texas; North Palm Beach, Florida; Forest Park, Ohio; and Elk Grove Village, Illinois—are described in some detail in chapter 4.

The new communities of the 1950s were built and merchandised to the broad middle- and lower middle-income segment of the housing market. Because of financial constraints dictated by the market, developers paid relatively little attention to neighborhood livability and community amenities (in addition, the 1950s was a seller's market for the housing industry). The planning principles pioneered in Radburn, the Greenbelt communities, and the British garden cities were not continued in these large-scale developments, partly because of financial considerations, partly because of developers' reliance on planning engineers who may not have embraced the advanced planning concepts, and partly because local governmental land use regulations inhibited innovations, such as cluster development.

Blossoming of the New Community Concept: The Record of the 1960s

During the 1960s the scope of new community development in the United States broadened considerably. New sources of capital were located. Entrepreneurs, from a variety of backgrounds, initiated new community projects. Both the development process and resulting new community product became increasingly sophisticated, and new methods of land use regulation were adopted, in part, to accommodate new community development.

While large-scale developments begun during the 1950s were almost universally products of firms that had expanded their home building operations to community building, the home builder became the exception in new community development of the 1960s. One of the first of the new breed of entrepreneurs was the large landowner whose properties began to ripen for urban development. In Arizona, The Goodyear Tire and Rubber Company's Goodyear Farms (initially acquired as a source of cotton fiber) became the site of Litchfield Park. New communities were begun on a number of large ranch properties in California, including the 88,000-acre Irvine Ranch (the new community of Irvine), 44,000-acre Newhall Ranch (Valencia), and 50,000-acre O'Neill Ranch (Mission Viejo). Other landowners turned community builders included the Janss Corporation, which built Janss/Conejo on a 10,000-acre site initially acquired in 1911, and the Humble Oil & Refining Company, which succeeded the Del E. Webb Company in developing Clear Lake City, Texas, on a 23,000-acre site originally acquired in 1938 for gas and oil production.

Humble Oil is also an example of a second type of new participant in new community development, namely, large corporations with available cash for diversification into large-scale real estate projects. When Humble Oil assumed control of Clear Lake City, it formed the Friendswood Development Company as its land development-management subsidiary. Friendswood has since become a major developer in the Houston area and is building a second new community—Kingwood—on a 14,000-acre site, 25 miles north of downtown Houston. Other oil companies, which diversified into new community development, included the Gulf Oil Corporation (Reston), Sunset International Petroleum (Sunset City, San Marin, and San Carlos in California), Mobile Oil Company (Redwood Shores), and McCulloch Oil Company (Lake Havasu City).

In addition to providing an outlet for corporate cash, several other factors induced companies to become involved in real estate ventures. For example, Westinghouse Electric Company bought an interest in Coral Ridge Properties, Inc., and joined in the development of Coral Springs, Florida, in part, to provide a testing ground and showplace for new company products. Gulf Oil Corporation's initial participation in financing Reston was obtained in exchange for a first option on all of the service station sites in the community. General Electric Company established a Community Systems Development Division and spent some three years exploring possible company participation in new community development, in part, to serve as demonstration sites for new products and technology. Companies with product lines related to the building industry, such as American Cement and U.S. Gypsum, became partners in new community ventures. Other large corporations, which entered the new community field during the 1960s and early 1970s, included: Phillip Morris (Mission Viejo); Illinois Central Industries (Park Forest South); Pennsylvania Railroad Company (Porter Ranch); Kaiser Aluminum and Chemical Corporation (Hawaii-Kai, Rancho California, Rancho Ventura, and Warner Ranch); and Marshall Field & Company, Sears, Roebuck & Company, and the Burlington Northern Railroad (Fox Valley East).

Large amounts of capital injected into new community development by these and other large corporations were accompanied by increasing investments in new communities by banks and insurance companies. The Chase Manhattan Bank, Teachers Insurance and Annuity Association, and Connecticut General Life Insurance Company financed the development of Columbia, Maryland. John Hancock Mutual Life Insurance Company helped finance Reston. The Prudential Insurance Company provided capital for Westlake Village. The Aetna Life and Casualty Company joined Kaiser in developing a number of new communities, and was a member of the consortium formed to develop Fox Valley East. In many cases insurance companies not only loaned money to new community developers, they also assumed equity investment roles.

The increasing corporate presence in new community development during the 1960s went hand in hand with increasing sophistication of both new community planning and the management of new community enterprises. At the same time, however, there was a decline in developer involvement in many phases of the community building process. In particular, the new developers often lacked home building experience, and, as a result, tended to confine their activities to land acquisition, planning, and preservicing the land with roads, water, sewer, and various community amenities.

Since appreciation in land values often formed the primary source of profit for developers, rather than proceeds from home sales, community development plans were designed to create an attractive environment, which would encourage a rapid rise in values. Most new communities made extensive use of open space and invested heavily in the early provision of recreational amenities, such as golf courses, swimming pools, lakes, and tennis courts. Neighborhood site planning was emphasized. Homes were often clustered and related to adjacent open space networks and path systems. Provision was made for higher density (and more profitable) apartment development, and community circulation systems were designed to feed traffic into high value village and community core areas, where a variety of office and shopping facilities were planned, and, quite frequently, actually built by the developer.

The return to garden city planning principles and the greater attention to the interrelationships among land uses that characterized new communities were made possible by the advent of planned community zoning. Under the traditional zoning ordinances, which governed new community development during the 1950s, residential, commercial, and industrial land uses were strictly segregated; detailed lot-size, height, and yard requirements limited site design options; and little incentive was provided to preserve open space and protect natural features of the landscape. Special planned community district ordinances, such as those adopted by Fairfax County, Virginia, Howard County, Maryland, and Orange County, California, on the other hand, allowed much greater flexibility in new community planning and design. Cluster development on smaller lots was allowed in exchange for greater amounts of community open space. Land uses could be mixed on the same site. In return for this greater planning and site design flexibility, the planned community regulations required the developer to secure approval of a master plan for the entire community and subsequently to submit rather detailed site and engineering plans for each section of the community to be developed.

More sophisticated new community plans were accompanied by much greater attention to market research, financial analysis of the development project as a whole, and careful monitoring of the financial performance of each development phase. In this regard, the development of Columbia, Maryland, was particularly noteworthy. The Columbia Economic Model projected cash flows over the entire development period, and identified the peak debt, length of exposure, and return on investment associated with various development alternatives. It introduced economic discipline into the development process and was extensively used to test the financial consequences of planning and design decisions. As the 1960s came to a close, many felt that the capital and management expertise offered by the large corporations who were entering the new community field, the accumulation of experience and new community development know-how during the decade, and the application of economic models to community building heralded a golden age of community development in America.

Persistent Problems

In spite of the optimism that pervaded the new community development industry, a number of serious problems threatened the successful future of community building. Most of these were related to the scale of new communities and unique financial and marketing problems, which were a consequence of scale.

Large-scale new community development requires exceedingly large initial investments in land, community infrastructure, and amenities. These investments are heaviest at the start of the development process, and, as a result, it is not unusual for a number of years to pass before incoming revenues exceed annual developer expenditures on the project. The relatively long turnaround time for investments in new communities has meant that patient capital, which must wait for an eventual return, is required. The number of investors with long-time horizons is never large and may fluctuate radically depending on national economic conditions.

A second consequence of scale is that developers often have to leap beyond the developing urban fringe to assemble large tracts of land at low enough prices to enable them to realize a return from land value appreciation. The remote location of many new communities places them at a competitive disadvantage with smaller scale projects located in more established areas. This may be an acute problem, since the heavy debt service load caused by extremely large front-end investments usually necessitates a rapid pace of development through capture of a significant proportion of the market for new homes and rental units. If the new community is to succeed, it must attain a critical urban mass as quickly as possible. If the projected capture rate and annual pace are not achieved, the developer may experience serious cash flow problems. An additional consequence of scale and remote location is the inability of rural local governments to finance needed community facilities and services. This may cause the developer to internalize costs that are often assumed by public agencies, leading to further increases in the front-end costs of the development project. Additional subsidies may also be required for commercial services during the early years of development if the surrounding population density is too low to support needed shopping facilities.

The scale of new community projects, their extended development periods, and the large capital investments required create an enlarged risk for private investors. This risk is compounded by the uncertainty surrounding local governments' commitment to and participation in new community projects. While one set of officials may approve the development plan and agree to provide needed services, their successors may not be as supportive of the new community project. Delays in securing site plan approvals, sewer moratoriums, and other unforeseen circumstances beyond a developer's control can play havoc with development pace projections and the financial viability of the undertaking.

The risk involved in new community development may be further compounded if an experienced and competent development team cannot be assembled. Although increasing corporate participation in new community development promised to upgrade management skills, new community development is a relatively new business enterprise in the United States. Developers, planners, and new community managers have learned the business through trial and error. However, when the difference between profit and loss is cut as fine as it is in many new community ventures, the margin of error is often alarmingly small.

Mounting Public Interest in New Communities

Throughout the 1960s the accelerating pace of new community development in the private sector was matched by mounting public interest in new communities as one solution to the many problems exposed by the suburban critique. New community development began to occupy a prominent place in metropolitan growth plans; state legislation to foster new community development began to be enacted; and a national movement calling for federal support of new communities gathered strength. By the end of the decade the first federal new community program since the New Deal had been enacted.

Metropolitan Perspectives

The new community concept has been particularly appealing to planners as a means of structuring metropolitan growth. For example, in 1961 *A Policies Plan for the Year 2000: The Nation's Capital* was published by the National Capital Planning Commission. The plan organized the future growth of the National Capital Region into a series of radial growth corridors with intervening fingers of open space. The following year it was supplemented by the Maryland-National Capital Park and Planning Com-

mission's plan, ...*on Wedges and Corridors* (1962), for the Maryland suburbs of the District of Columbia. Both plans called for the channeling of all
new growth into corridors served by rapid transit and for the development
of new communities as the focal points of corridor development. At about
the same time, the Baltimore Regional Planning Council and Maryland
State Planning Department proposed a plan for the Baltimore region,
Metrotowns for the Baltimore Region–Stages and Measures (1963), which
recommended that new communities serve as growth points at the intersections of the regional highway grid. By 1967, 13 metropolitan planning
agencies had developed plans that included provisions for new community
development and another 26 agencies had such plans under development or
consideration (Advisory Commission on Intergovernmental Relations
1968, p. 83).

Metropolitan interest in new community development continued strong
into the early 1970s. In response to the widespread rioting that swept the
country in 1968, and that was particularly severe in Detroit, Metropolitan
Fund, Inc. (1970; 1971) proposed a unique plan for pairing urban redevelopment in Detroit with peripheral new communities to provide residents
with the widest possible choice of living environments and to promote
understanding and communication among the races. Also prompted by
racial strife and center city decay, the Greater Hartford Corporation was
formed in 1969 by some 26 businessmen in order to develop a total approach to the region's redevelopment and growth. The corporation created
two instruments—the Greater Hartford Process, Inc., and the Greater
Hartford Development Corporation—to plan and carry out a process of
regional revitalization. Among its other recommendations, the Greater
Hartford Process proposed the development of suburban new communities
with racially and economically balanced populations. In 1973 the Greater
Hartford Community Development Corporation acquired 1,600 acres in
the small suburban town of Coventry to actually carry forward its commitment to new community development, and proposed construction of a new
town of 20,000 residents. Finally, the Lucas County (Ohio) Renewal Department proposed in 1971 that a new community (later named Oak Open-
ings) be developed for 20,000 residents on a 5,000-acre site located in the
predominantly black Spencer Sharples Township. All of these projects,
however, have yet to be implemented.

New Communities and the States

Although interest in new communities from state governments trailed
behind that of metropolitan areas, by the early 1970s a number of states had
become involved in the new community movement. One of the first ac-

tivities of many state governments, including Connecticut, Delaware, Florida, Massachusetts, Michigan, New York, North Carolina, and Wisconsin, was to sponsor studies and symposiums to explore possible state roles in new community development.

Legislation to aid and regulate new community ventures was passed by four state legislatures. The Arizona General Improvement District Act of 1970 authorized the establishment of special districts that could finance up to two thirds of the major development costs of new communities. A State Community Development Council was established to administer the legislation. Kentucky's 1970 New Communities Act provided for the establishment of new community districts that would operate as nonprofit public membership corporations. The districts, whose formation had to be approved by county courts, were to be exempted from all land use regulations by surrounding governments, and were authorized to exercise general governmental powers, including zoning and eminent domain. Tennessee's Prospective New Community Certification Act, passed in 1971, was designed to protect new community projects from premature annexation by neighboring municipalities. In 1972, the Ohio New Communities Act was passed to provide an improved method of furnishing certain public facilities in new communities. The act authorized the establishment of new community authorities that could sell bonds and charge user fees to finance recreational, educational, health, social, vocational, cultural, beautification, and amusement services for the residents of an authority's service district. However, new community authorities were not allowed to exercise police powers and could provide water and sewer services only if they could not be obtained from existing political subdivisions.

Five states also became actively involved in specific new community projects. In 1968, New Jersey established the Hackensack Meadowlands Development Commission to undertake the 30-year, $10 billion development of a new city for 200,000 people on 20,000 acres in the Hackensack River Basin "at the hub of the New York-New Jersey Metropolitan Area." The Missouri Department of Community Affairs began planning for a new town pilot project at Pattonsburg, where an existing rural community was to be inundated by a large reservoir in the late 1970s. Ohio's State Department of Urban Affairs, with funding from the Appalachian Regional Commission, prepared a development plan for a new community in Scioto County. Following an intensive study by the University of Minnesota, the state legislature created the Minnesota Experimental City Authority in 1971. The 11-member authority, appointed by the governor, was charged with the responsibility of (1) selecting a site in the state for an experimental city; and (2) preparing a plan for the development of the new city.

Of all the states, New York showed the greatest interest in new communities and the greatest commitment to their development. The foundation for New York's involvement in community building was established in 1968, when the state legislature created the New York State Urban Development Corporation. This unique state agency was given $1 billion in bonding authority, which allowed it to participate in a variety of housing, land, civic, and industrial development projects. It was also given the power to override local zoning and building codes, and was exempted from certain local property taxes and other local and state taxes.

In 1970 the Urban Development Corporation and State Office of Planning Coordination submitted a report to the governor, *New Communities for New York,* proposing that new communities play a predominant role in accommodating a projected population increase of five million persons in the state by the year 2000. The report included a policy statement recommending that 25 percent of the population requiring new housing during the 1970s be housed in new communities, 50 percent in the 1980s, and 75 percent in the 1990s. To support this recommendation, estimates of the costs and benefits from new community development were presented, as well as the initial steps required to establish a new communities program in New York State. As a first step, the Urban Development Corporation began planning and development on three new communities: Audubon, adjacent to a new state university campus in Amherst, outside of Buffalo; Radisson, located 12 miles northwest of downtown Syracuse; and Roosevelt Island, a new-town-in-town being developed on land leased from New York City.

The Call for a National New Community Program

Within a three-year period in the latter half of the 1960s five major reports were issued that called for greater federal involvement in planning for future urban growth and the establishment of new federal programs to see that the plans were actually carried out. In 1967 the President's National Advisory Commission on Rural Poverty issued its report, *The People Left Behind,* and proposed that the growth of existing small towns be encouraged in those parts of the country, such as Appalachia, the South, and the Midwest, which were experiencing rapid outmigration to the cities. The next year two reports, *Building the American City* by the National Commission on Urban Problems and *Urban and Rural America: Policies for Future Growth* by the Advisory Commission on Intergovernmental Relations, presented exhaustive analyses of the problems caused by metropolitan growth. Both reports argued for increased public intervention in land development processes and the encouragement of large-scale planned communities. Also in 1968, the American Institute of Planners released a report, *New Communities: Challenge for Today,* recommending that the nation launch a massive drive to create integrated new communities. The report urged the federal government to make a major resource commitment to develop a national new communities program and a national settlement policy. Both the Democratic and Republican party platforms of 1968 spoke of the need for new communities as one response to the "crisis of the cities."

Building on these recommendations, in 1969 the National Committee on Urban Growth Policy (sponsored by the National Association of Counties, National League of Cities, United States Conference of Mayors, and Urban America, Inc.) recommended that federal assistance be extended to create 100 new communities averaging 100,000 population each and 10 new communities of at least one million each by the year 2000. According to the committee's report, *The New City,* the cost of the program would be relatively small compared with the costs caused by the inefficiencies in current approaches to urban growth and the lack of coordination among existing federal urban programs.

Public-Private Partnership: The Federal New Communities Program

The drive for an expanded federal role in new community development was capped by hearings before the House of Representatives Ad Hoc Subcommittee on Urban Growth (Ashley Committee) in 1970. The committee's report, *The Quality of Urban Life,* made a strong case for a variety of types of federal assistance to new communities and led directly to the enactment of the Urban Growth and New Community Development Act of 1970 (Title VII of the Housing and Urban Development Act of 1970), which provides the legislative basis for the current federal new community program.

Early Legislation

The Urban Growth and New Community Development Act of 1970 also represented the culmination of a long effort within the federal government to enact new communities legislation. The first new communities bill of the modern era was drafted by the Housing and Home Finance Agency in 1964 and presented to Congress as Title II of the Housing Act of that year. Title II authorized up to $50 million in mortgage insurance for land acquisition and development for large-scale new community projects, but died in committee when it failed to receive support from new community proponents and was actively opposed by the National Association of Home

Builders and National Association of Real Estate Boards. In addition, the bill was coolly received by central city mayors, who opposed increased federal support of suburban development and feared the effects of new communities on the competitive position of central cities.

In 1965 virtually the same bill was introduced again as Title X of the Housing and Urban Development Act, but the maximum mortgage guarantee was reduced to $10 million. The same doubts about the bill as appeared in 1964 were voiced again, and though it passed, assistance was limited to smaller scale subdivision development. However, in 1966 the administration secured favorable testimony from a number of new community developers and diluted opposition from various groups by calling for an experimental new community program. It was successful in mustering sufficient support to amend Title X to provide mortgage insurance of up to $25 million for new community land acquisition and site improvements. Although the administration was successful in securing passage of new communities legislation, the provisions of the act were not sufficiently attractive to the development industry, and no new community projects were ever supported under Title X.

Title X did serve, however, to resolve many of the legislative obstacles to a more effective federal role in new community development. Thus, when an expanded new community program was introduced as Title IV of the 1968 Housing and Urban Development Act, it passed with much less difficulty. Title IV provided a number of inducements for developer involvement in the program which were missing from the earlier Title X program. Where Title X provided mortgage insurance guarantees on loans to developers, Title IV authorized the secretary of Housing and Urban Development to guarantee the bonds, debentures, notes, and other obligations issued by new town developers for land acquisition and development.

Title IV pledged the full faith and credit of the United States Government to pay the guaranteed obligations in the event that developers could not meet the scheduled payments. In addition, the act authorized supplemental grants of up to 20 percent of the required local costs of federal grants for water, sewer, and open space. In return for more attractive federal aid, Title IV stiffened eligibility requirements, with much greater emphasis on the planning and land use characteristics of assisted projects, and tied the supplemental grants to an assisted project's provision of a substantial number of housing units for low- and moderate-income persons. Initial administration of the program was shifted from the Federal Housing Administration, which had responsibility for Title X, to the assistant secretary for metropolitan development of the Community Resources Development Administration within the Department of Housing and Urban Development.

The mortgage insurance and loan guarantees offered by Title X and Title IV were designed to overcome one of the major obstacles to expanded new community development, that is, the difficulty in obtaining patient money over a long period at interest rates that are sufficiently low to make the development project economically feasible. With the federal guarantee offered by Title IV, it was expected that developers could obtain financing without turning over control of their projects to equity investors and at interest rates well below those that would have been required without the guarantee of federal repayment of the developer's obligations.

In spite of these advantages, several factors delayed the implementation of the Title IV program. As noted by Robert M. Paul (1971), national economic conditions during 1968-69 limited developers' ability to borrow money at reasonable rates, with or without a federal loan guarantee. In addition, the Johnson Administration between August 1968 and January 1969 did not have time to set up the complex organization required to process applications from developers. After nine months of uncertainty and debate, the Nixon Administration eventually decided to implement the program. On February 13, 1970, the first loan guarantee commitment was made to Jonathan, Minnesota. On July 1, 1970, commitments were announced for St. Charles Communities, Maryland, and Park Forest South, Illinois.

The Urban Growth and New Community Development Act of 1970

The 1970 new communities legislation (Title VII) was designed to overcome many of the financial difficulties experienced by new community developers, and to achieve a much broader array of federal goals for new urban growth. Congress found that new patterns of development, and, in particular, new communities, were needed to accommodate future population growth, prevent further deterioration in the nation's physical and social environment, and to make positive contributions to improving the overall quality of life in the country.

To be eligible for federal assistance under the provisions of the legislation, private developers had to show that they had the background and management capability to undertake a new community project and that their proposed new communities were financially sound undertakings. In addition, proposed projects had to meet eight specific eligibility criteria. In brief, Congress specified that assistance should only be extended to those new communities that: (1) provided alternatives to disorderly growth and enhanced the natural and urban environment, or improved economic conditions in existing communities so as to reverse migration from them;

(2) would create sound economic bases and the potential for economic growth; (3) would contribute to the welfare of surrounding areas; (4) would be consistent with comprehensive plans for surrounding regions; (5) had received all necessary governmental reviews and approvals; (6) would contribute to good living conditions through balanced and diversified land use patterns and adequate public services; (7) made substantial provision for housing within the means of persons of low and moderate income; and (8) proposed significant advances in design and technology with respect to land utilization, construction materials and methods, and the provision of community facilities and services.

To achieve new communities with these characteristics through maximum private involvement in their long-term development, Title VII greatly expanded the scope of federal assistance to approved projects. The aggregate of outstanding obligations that could be incurred through loan guarantees was increased from $250 million under Title IV to $500 million. Although the limit of $50 million per project was retained, the guarantee could include 80 percent of the value of real property before improvements and 90 percent of land development costs.

To enable developers to get through the initial years of development when project revenues might not be adequate to cover the carrying costs on the large indebtedness required in new community development, the secretary of Housing and Urban Development was authorized to loan developers up to $20 million for a period of 15 years after the start of development so that they could make interest payments on their debts.

Public service grants to enable local agencies to provide educational, health, safety, and other services during the first three years of development were authorized. Up to two thirds of the cost of special planning studies was authorized so that developers could plan programs that were fully responsive to social and environmental problems and that supported the use of new and advanced technology. The secretary of Housing and Urban Development was authorized to provide technical assistance to developers. The 20 percent supplemental grants initially authorized by Title IV were extended to 13 federal grants-in-aid programs. Coverage of new community development sponsors eligible for assistance was expanded to include public bodies; urban renewal legislation was amended to encourage development of new-towns-in-town; and the federal government itself was authorized to plan and carry out large-scale new community projects as demonstrations.

Although administration of the legislation was to remain within the Department of Housing and Urban Development, provision was made for a separate Community Development Corporation within HUD to assure that the program would be highly visible, would have its own identity, and could be readily monitored by Congress.

Passage of the Urban Growth and New Community Development Act promised to expand the number of new communities that were participating in the slowed down federal new communities program. In 1970 officials of the Department of Housing and Urban Development estimated that ten new communities a year would be approved for assistance. A number of factors, however, seriously limited the number of new communities actually assisted.

The Fate of the Federal Program

As of January 1, 1974, new community project guarantees had been extended to ten new communities (including two approved under Title IV) involving guarantee commitments by the federal government of $240.5 million. The communities were located in seven states, and had projected populations at completion of development ranging from a low of 26,000 (Riverton, New York) to 150,000 (The Woodlands, Texas). Two projects of the New York State Urban Development Corporation, Radisson and Roosevelt Island, had also been approved for assistance, but had not requested federal loan guarantees. Five other projects had been offered loan guarantee commitments (one subsequently dropped out of the program), but had not issued bonds or debentures guaranteed by the federal government. During 1974 no new loan guarantee commitments were made by the Community Development Corporation, and on January 14, 1975, the Department of Housing and Urban Development suspended further processing of applications for assistance.

From the beginning, the new communities program faced a number of serious difficulties. One of the most basic was the program's lack of political support within the executive branch. Passage of the Urban Growth and New Community Development Act, which was opposed by the president, had been engineered by a Democratic coalition in the House of Representatives and the Senate. Among other provisions, the Office of Management and Budget was opposed to the interest loan program because it feared it would increase the size of the budget, and it disliked both the public service grants and the authority of the Community Development Corporation to undertake demonstration projects. As a result, the Office of New Community Development (which became the New Communities Administration with the activation of the Community Development Corporation) was understaffed during the first years of the program and a number of provisions of the legislation were never implemented. For example, the Department of Housing and Urban Development never requested funds from Congress to make interest loans to developers, public service grants, or to provide technical assistance or undertake the development of demonstration new communities. Although $168 million in supplementary grants for public facilities was authorized by Congress through 1973, only $25 million had actually been appropriated for this purpose. In June 1973, this provision of Title VII was terminated by the administration. The Title VII program also suffered when administration priorities resulted in delays in the release of funds for some categorical grant programs and the suspension of other federal aid programs. For example, Title VII eligibility requirements pointed to the provision of substantial amounts of housing in new communities for low- and moderate-income families. However, a January 1973 moratorium on federal subsidized housing programs eliminated the major federal tool for achieving this goal.

Another set of difficulties arose from the newness of the program, its complexity, and the need for both the Office of New Communities Development and participating private developers to learn the new community business. Throughout the initial years of the program each new community project seeking assistance was processed on a highly individualized basis, which typically involved two to three years of negotiation before a loan guarantee could be consummated. The publication of final regulations governing the administration of the program and accompanying handbooks were delayed for a number of years and produced developer complaints about the idiosyncratic treatment of their projects and the lack of coordination and consistency within the government. In some cases, developers also lacked new community experience. Initial projections of start-up costs were often too low, while forecasts of the pace of development to be achieved were too high. Some developers suffered from various management weaknesses, which further compounded their problems.

Many of the initial difficulties with the Title VII program might have been overcome with time and the accumulation of experience, knowledge, and techniques for managing both the new community program and individual new community projects. A combination of factors beyond the control of the participants in the program prevented this from occurring. First, steadily rising interest rates and the scale and suddenness of inflation and energy shortages sharply increased developers' front-end costs and in turn, the size of their interest payments on borrowed funds. In order for projects to remain economically viable, an accelerated pace of development was required. However, high interest rates, difficulties in securing mortgage money, materials shortages, and the recession beginning in 1973 led to a drastic drop in new home construction throughout the country. With builders' inventories at record levels, it became increasingly difficult to market land in new communities, or, for that matter, in new developments in any setting.

External hazards and internal problems within the federal new communities program were felt in two ways. First, there was a steady drop in private developers' interest in the program. The number of preapplications received by the Office of New Communities Development dropped from 23 preapplications in 1972, to five in 1973, to only one in the first six months of 1974. When processing of new applications was suspended in early 1975, only four full-scale applications were pending. Second, new communities that had already received loan guarantees and issued bonds and debentures began to experience severe financial problems. Jonathan, the first federally assisted new community under Title IV, failed to make a $468,000 interest payment, which HUD was forced to cover, when it found it had a two and one-half year inventory of lots and homes for sale. Park Forest South was placed in default on its loan guarantee when HUD had to make a $1.05 million interest payment. HUD subsequently allowed the developer to raise additional capital by selling land used as collateral for its federally guaranteed loans. The Department of Housing and Urban Development was also forced to make an interest payment out of its new communities revolving fund for St. Charles, and it increased the loan guarantee to Riverton by $4 million after the developer had suspended operations and laid off the project's staff. A number of other federally assisted new communities were reported to be in precarious financial straits. Begun as a program to greatly increase the production of new communities in the United States, as 1975 approached, the Department of Housing and Urban Development's New Community Administration was devoting all of its resources to insure the survival of the new communities it had previously assisted.

Retrenchment or Regeneration: Taking Stock of New Communities

With private entrepreneurs' interest in new community development waning and the federal new communities program at a standstill, the new community movement is currently at a crossroad. Three options for the future course of new community development have been proposed.

In 1972 the American Institute of Architects (AIA) rejected new communities as the major thrust of future urban growth in the United States and, instead, proposed that the development of highly planned neighborhood "growth units" of from 500 to 3,000 residential units be encouraged. The AIA felt this scale of development was more in keeping with the capabilities of the balkanized home building industry and the vast majority of small planning and architectural firms. By 1974, the development of smaller scale planned neighborhoods and communities was also being proposed by several new community developers and consultants, who felt that the adverse economic climate, immense management problems, and difficulty in securing long-term commitments from local government precluded a recurrence in the 1970s of the new communities boom of the previous decade. Additional support for retrenchment through smaller scale neighborhood and community development was offered by the general manager of the Community Development Corporation (Trevino 1974), who suggested that smaller developments and noncontiguous holdings would be able to produce some of the benefits of new communities at lesser costs.

A second suggested course for future development has emphasized the experimental benefits that can be derived from new communities. From this perspective a full-scale new community production program may be impossible to achieve under present economic and governmental conditions, but much can be learned from the experimentation with urban facilities, services, and social programs that is possible in new community settings. Supporters of the experimental new communities approach feel that new community development will never occur at a large enough scale to capture a preponderance of national growth and thus will have a limited effect on the patterns of metropolitan expansion. However, through continuation of the modest scale of new community development achieved by the federal new communities program, new ideas, concepts, and techniques can be generated and applied in other urban settings.

A third perspective on the future of new communities views present difficulties as a temporary stoppage in the long-term trend toward increasing concentration of new growth in new communities. Pointing to the lack of administration support of the Title VII program as a major deterrent, proponents of expanded new community development envision new communities as the major instrument of a long-awaited national growth policy. What is needed, they argue, is a regeneration of new community development through full implementation of Title VII, rather than retrenchment through smaller scale development or continuation of a reduced or experimental federal new communities program.

Whatever course the new communities movement takes in the future, much can be learned from those new communities that are already being developed. They provide laboratories in which many of the claims made for the new community concept can be evaluated and in which many of the problems facing developers and public administrators can be more accurately defined. By taking stock of new communities at this critical point in the new community movement, it should be possible to work toward the achievement of many of the goals embodied in this innovative approach to urban growth and development.

Part II

Places and People: New Communities and Conventional Urban Growth

4

Private New and Conventional Communities

Identifying new communities has been a favorite pastime of new community buffs over the past decade. This game began in 1964 when *House & Home* magazine published a list of 50 "big new towns" then under development in the United States. Over the years the number of participants in the game and the number of new communities found to exist have both multiplied with the growing national interest in large-scale development. At last count 175 new communities had been identified in 32 states, the District of Columbia, and Puerto Rico ("New Community Checklist Update" 1974).

How New Communities Were Identified and Selected

Early in 1972 the study team began to winnow through various lists of new communities to select a representative sample for intensive study. At that time the most reliable compilation of new communities in existence was a list prepared by the Department of Housing and Urban Development's (HUD's) New Communities Division in 1969. However, the list had one obvious flaw. It did not distinguish between the 63 new communities and large-scale developments listed.

To remedy this deficiency the study team first identified five criteria that are basic to the new community concept: (1) Development of the community must be under the direction of a single entrepreneur or development company to insure unified and coordinated management of the development process; (2) the community must be of sufficient size to allow for social diversity and to support a variety of urban functions. This criterion is met by projects of 2,000 or more acres planned for populations of 20,000 or more persons; (3) development must be programmed in accordance with an overall master plan; (4) the community plan must provide for a variety of urban functions by reserving land for residential, commercial, industrial, public, and institutional uses; and (5) the community must provide a variety of housing choices, including at a minimum opportunities for owning and renting and for single-family and apartment life-styles.

Adoption of these criteria automatically narrowed the number of projects that were eligible for inclusion in the study. Most notably, all special-purpose communities, such as recreation and retirement developments, were eliminated from consideration.[a] Also eliminated were suburban planned unit developments, which could not meet the acreage, population, or land use diversity criteria, and urban redevelopment projects—sometimes called new-towns-in-town—which could not meet the acreage criterion.

The remaining new communities were screened against three additional criteria. First, because of the study team's interest in analyzing community development decisions, new communities that had ceased all active development before 1960 were eliminated from consideration to avoid insurmountable problems in identifying and interviewing key decision makers. Second, to insure that new communities had progressed sufficiently to provide enough dwelling units, facilities, and services for the proposed evaluation, new communities that had fewer than 5,000 residents on January 1, 1972 were also eliminated from further consideration.[b] Third, new communities outside the continental United States were excluded from the study in order to avoid excessive field survey costs.

These screening processes eliminated 36 of the 63 communities on the HUD list. From the 27 remaining new communities, 13 were selected for intensive study.

Five new communities were selected because they contained various features of particular interest to the study team. Columbia, Md., was known to have a large black population. Reston, Va., was widely recognized for its outstanding urban design. Lake Havasu City, Ariz., was the only freestanding new community not dependent upon an existing large urban area. Irvine, Calif., was projected to become the largest new community in the United States. Park Forest, Ill., was the only eligible new community in which development had been substantially completed by 1972.

Eight additional communities were then randomly selected to insure that the full variety of new communities in the United States was adequately represented. New communities selected at this stage included: Elk Grove Village, Ill.; Forest Park, Oh.; Foster City, Calif.; Laguna Niguel, Calif.; North Palm Beach, Fla.; Sharpstown, Tex.; Valencia, Calif.; and Westlake Village, Calif.

The study team next solicited the help of county planning officials and local realtors to find conventional communities that could be compared to the selected new communities. Ideally, the conventional communities would represent alternative housing possibilities for people who had cho-

[a] Special studies conducted in two retirement new communities are reported in chapter 19.

[b] The requirement of 5,000 residents automatically eliminated the seven new communities that were participating in the federal new communities program at that time. Special studies conducted in two of these communities (Jonathan, Minn. and Park Forest South, Ill.) are reported in chapter 18. Jonathan and Park Forest South were the only federally assisted new communities with sufficient populations and facilities for a baseline evaluation.

sen to settle in new communities. Discussions with knowledgeable local officials and businessmen were designed to help locate communities that offered the home buyer or renter approximately the same choice of location, housing type, and housing cost as the new community, but in a distinctly less planned setting. One conventional community was paired with each of the 13 new communities.

The locations of the new and conventional communities selected are shown in figure 4-1. The new communities all meet the basic criteria for new community status. At the same time, they differ in a number of important ways.

Five Older New Communities

Five new communities—Park Forest, Sharpstown, North Palm Beach, Forest Park, and Elk Grove Village (table 4-1)—began development during the late 1940s through the mid-1950s. Their developers were major home builders, apartment developers, and real estate entrepreneurs who saw the economic potential of large-scale community building. The five new communities represent some of the best planning thought of their era. However, they do not include some innovative aspects of community design, such as cluster development, which were introduced by new communities initiated during the following decade. With roots in the home building and real estate industries, their developers' attention focused on building and marketing housing, plus capturing returns from the commercial development attracted by the market they had created. Minimal attention was given to many of the amenities and features—open space corridors, neighborhood centers, and swimming pools—that are common in later new communities. With the exception of Sharpstown, the residents played major roles in shaping these communities. They incorporated early in their development (Sharpstown was annexed to the City of Houston) and municipal governments assumed responsibility for land use control and most community facilities and services.

Park Forest, Illinois

Park Forest was begun in 1947 on some 2,200 acres of Illinois prairie in southeast Cook County. It was developed by American Community Builders, a partnership consisting of Nathan Manilow, Phillip M. Klutznick, and Jerrold Loebl. Manilow was a large Chicago home builder; Klutznick was a lawyer with extensive experience with federal housing programs, most recently as commissioner of the Federal Public Housing Authority; and Loebl was an architect. Land planning was under the direction of Elbert

Figure 4-1. Location of the Study Communities

Peets, who had earlier designed the town of Glendale for the United States Housing Authority.

Park Forest's developers had two major goals. One was to show that private entrepreneurs could design, develop, and build a new town for profit. The second was to create a better way of life for people who settled in their community.

The developer's first goal dictated many of the decisions that shaped Park Forest. Because of the vast housing market created by returning war veterans and the availability of financing for rental housing for veterans, initial residential building consisted of 3,010 rental townhouses grouped in courts near the center of the community. Several years later these courts received national publicity as the home of William Whyte's "organization man." Families who occupied the rental housing units and the single-family subdivisions, which were subsequently built, provided customers for a large shopping center located at the geographical and population center of Park Forest. The shopping center was one of the first open malls in the country and made a major contribution to Park Forest's economic success.

The developer's concern for people is partly reflected in the early incorporation of Park Forest. Four months after the first families moved into the rental townhouses the developer encouraged formation of a provisional town government. In February 1949 the settlement was incorporated

Table 4-1
Five Older New Communities

Community	Developer	Initial Occupancy	Target Population	Target Acreage	Paired Conventional Community
Park Forest, Ill.	American Community Builders	1948	35,000	3,182	Lansing, Ill.
Sharpstown, Tex.	Frank W. Sharp	1954	35,000	4,100	Southwest Houston, Tex.
North Palm Beach, Fla.	North Palm Beach Properties	1956	30,000	2,362	Tequesta, Fla.
Forest Park, Oh.	Kanter Corporation	1956	35,000	3,725	Sharonville, Oh.
Elk Grove Ill.	Centex Construction Company	1957	58,500	5,760	Schaumburg, Ill.

as a village. Widespread and intense citizen participation in village government characterized Park Forest from the first. In addition to providing an outlet for citizen interest in the community, incorporation allowed the developer to shift major responsibility for police and fire protection, recreation, and road maintenance to the village government. Coping with these responsibilities was not an easy task. The village government found that establishing and maintaining public services from scratch required a budget equivalent to a much larger community. Revenues and needs never seemed to be in balance, in part because the tax yield was always one year behind initial residential occupancy and revenues from licenses and fees were restricted by the developer's total control of commercial growth (Meltzer 1953). As a result, heavy subsidies from the developer were required during Park Forest's formative years.

Although industrial land was set aside in Park Forest, industrial development was not a factor in the community's growth. The industrial sites had good rail access, but poor highway access limited their appeal to prospective firms. Park Forest's location at the end of the Illinois Central's commuter rail line to the Loop meant that the developer did not have to rely on local employment as a source of housing demand. In fact, most of the community's early residents worked 29 miles away in downtown Chicago.

By 1959 Park Forest was mostly completed and American Community Builders disbanded. In 1960 the community had a population of 30,000, just short of current numbers. During the next 12 years development was limited to a public housing project for the elderly, an apartment project, and a partially subsidized planned unit development. Park Forest is generally considered to be the first private new community developed in the United States since World War II. It is one of the few new communities that has achieved financial success for its developers.

Lansing, Illinois. Park Forest was paired with the Village of Lansing, located adjacent to the Indiana state line in southeastern Cook County, 26 miles from Chicago's Loop. Although Lansing was incorporated as a village in 1893 (with a population of 200), major residential growth did not occur until after World War II. In 1950 both Lansing and Park Forest had a population between 8,000 and 9,000 residents. Both communities more than doubled in population during the 1950s. However, while Park Forest's growth was guided by a single developer, Lansing's growth resulted from a series of disjointed residential subdivisions. Commercial growth was limited to shopping centers in Park Forest. In Lansing, on the other hand, commercial establishments spread up and down three major shopping streets. Lansing has had somewhat greater success than Park Forest in attracting industrial development. In 1970 there were 30 manufactuing establishments and a total of 1,000 manufacturing employees in the community. Major amenities in Lansing include a community park and swimming pool operated by the Lan-Oak Park District, a number of small neighborhood parks, and a section of the Cook County Forest Preserve adjacent to the community's southwest boundary. The population of Lansing was 25,218 in 1970.

Sharpstown, Texas

Frank W. Sharp began building homes in the Houston area during World War II, including the largest subdivision—some 2,000 acres—developed to that time. He acquired 4,100 acres 10 miles southwest of Houston in 1953. Road access to this site was very poor. However, by giving $500,000 worth of right-of-way to the State Highway Commission, with the provision that highway construction start within one year, Sharp succeeded in changing the route of the Southwest Freeway to bisect the proposed new community of Sharpstown. To attract customers during the early years, Sharp built an 18-hole golf course and swimming club and offered membership in the facility to all who purchased homes.

Sharpstown's design followed traditional patterns, with single-family subdivisions surrounding neighborhood elementary schools and small parks. Little emphasis was placed on architectural merit, but homes were built and marketed at prices within the means of a broad spectrum of consumers.

During the past two decades Sharpstown has acquired all of the trappings of a new community. In 1960 ground was broken for the Sharpstown Center. This regional shopping complex occupies a 77-acre site in the heart of the community and includes major department stores and a 10-story office building. Surrounding the center are a number of apartment complexes, including Texas' first condominium project (an 18-story high rise), and an 11-story apartment building opened in 1964 as a home for senior citizens.

Institutional development has kept pace with housing and commerce. The Society of Jesus opened a boys' preparatory school in 1961. In 1963 Houston Baptist College opened classes on a 196-acre site in Sharpstown. A branch of the Houston Public Library opened in the spring of 1965. Sharpstown has attracted two hospitals. The Memorial Baptist Hospital's Southwest Branch began operation in 1962, followed by Sharpstown General Hospital in 1964.

The Sharpstown Industrial Park is a 755-acre, highly restricted industrial subdivision with sites for many types of industry. The industrial park has been rapidly developing in recent years and includes the regional offices of the Allstate Insurance Company. Cultural facilities in Sharpstown include a drive-in theater, 2,100-seat movie theater, and 3,000-seat professional theater.

Sharpstown is now within the city limits of Houston. Twenty years after initial residential occupancy the community has over 11,000 homes and apartments. With its location at the heart of the rapidly expanding southwest sector of the Houston-Galveston metropolitan region, continued growth and development well past the developer's original target of 35,000 people seem inevitable.

Southwest Houston, Texas. This conventional community consists of three large subdivisions located southwest of Sharpstown at the edge of the Houston city limits. The subdivisions were developed gradually over a period of years and are tied together by a major thoroughfare and series of strip-commercial shopping centers. Major amenities and recreational facilities include the Braeburn Country Club, Southwest Branch of the Houston YMCA, and the city of Houston's Southwest Tennis Center.

North Palm Beach, Florida

North Palm Beach is a 2,362-acre waterfront community located along the intercoastal waterway, seven and one-half miles north of West Palm Beach. The land was formerly part of the estate of Sir Harry Oakes. It passed successively through the hands of industrialist Ralph Stolkin and then to John D. MacArthur, the insurance magnate. North Palm Beach

Properties, owned by Herbert A. and Richard E. Ross, John A. Schwencke, and Jay H. White, bought the site for $2,870,000 in 1955 and began development of a planned community. Early land development operations included the dredging of a series of canals and the bulkheading of all waterfront properties. Almost half of the homesites in the community are on a waterway. The overall planning of North Palm Beach was honored by the National Association of Home Builders for its design, layout, restrictions, and facilities.

Shortly after the development site was acquired and before the first homes were built the Ross brothers incorporated North Palm Beach as a village and hired a village manager. Originally restricted to public safety and housekeeping activities, the village has gradually increased its functions. Its most ambitious undertaking was the purchase of the North Palm Beach Country Club from the developer in 1961 for $1,025,000. In addition to the country club, the village operates a public marina, library, art center, and a small park system. The water supply and distribution system was retained in private ownership. North Palm Beach Properties sold its last parcels in 1967 and is no longer active in the community's development.

The area in which North Palm Beach is located has, in recent years, been one of the best housing markets in the country and the village has the highest growth rate in Palm Beach County. During the past five years condominium apartment construction has soared. Commercial development is located in a series of shopping centers along U.S. Highway 1, the major north-south artery through the town. A small area is zoned for industrial use, but has not been occupied. In 1972 the population was estimated to be 12,500, 42 percent of the 30,000 population projected at full development.

Tequesta, Florida. North Palm Beach was paired with the small incorporated village of Tequesta, located nine miles to the north on the Loxahatchee River at Jupiter Inlet. Tequesta began to develop in 1956 when United Aircraft Corporation located its Pratt & Whitney Research and Development Center ten miles to the west. The community consists of a patchwork of small subdivisions and condominiums. Community amenities include the Tequesta Country Club, the Community Public Library, and a small art institution, the Lighthouse Gallery. In 1970 the population of Tequesta was 2,576 with 4,323 persons living in adjacent unincorporated areas.

Forest Park, Ohio

Forest Park is located in Hamilton County, 15 miles northwest of the City of Cincinnati. The community site was once part of a 6,000-acre parcel acquired by the federal government in the early 1930s for the Greenbelt Program. Six hundred acres were developed and became the City of Greenhills. The Corps of Engineers used part of the original tract for a flood control project, and some 2,000 acres were given to Hamilton County for a regional park. When the remaining acreage was declared surplus in 1952, the government began searching for a buyer.

Several concerned leaders in Cincinnati learned of the government's intentions and resolved to prevent development of the land into typical suburban housing tracts. They formed the Cincinnati Community Development Corporation to acquire 3,725 acres from the federal government for a planned community. In 1954 the land was sold to the Warner-Kanter Corporation with the proviso that the Community Development Corporation would retain the right to approve development plans for a period of five years. Victor Gruen Associates prepared a community plan and in 1956 the first residents moved into Forest Park.

Gruen's plan featured a series of residential neighborhoods surrounding neighborhoods parks and elementary schools. A regional shopping center was to serve as the central core of the community. However, when a large regional center located several miles to the east, the plan had to be altered. Today, a central park, high school, and municipal center are located in the heart of Forest Park. Residents' shopping needs are accommodated at three satellite neighborhood centers. Several hundred acres have been reserved for the Northland Industrial Park in Forest Park. Twelve manufacturing firms were located in this park in 1972. In addition, the Union Central Life Insurance Company maintains its corporate headquarters and home office in the community.

Joseph H. Kanter purchased Marvin Warner's interest in Forest Park in 1959. Since that time the Kanter Corporation, whose interests also include apartment construction and management, has coordinated development. Forest Park incorporated as a municipality in 1961 to ward off annexation by neighboring Greenhills. By 1972 the community's population was estimated to be 17,000, almost half of its target population of 35,000.

Sharonville, Ohio. Forest Park was matched with the conventional town of Sharonville, located several miles to the east and 12 miles north of Cincinnati. Although the town was originally platted in 1818, it had barely 1,000 residents in 1950, when it began a period of steady growth. Between 1950 and 1960, 200 acres of residential land were subdivided and the population increased to 2,600 persons. Since 1960, several hundred additional acres have been developed, and the population has passed 10,000. Sharonville was in the path of major industrial growth out the Mill Creek Valley from Cincinnati. By the early 1970s over 30 manufacturing plants with over 7,000 employees had located in the community. This strong industrial base has enabled the city of Sharonville to establish a park system, two community swimming pools, and a community recreation center. An additional amenity is the adjacent Sharon Woods Regional Park with a golf course, boating facilities, hiking and picnic areas. Nevertheless, the Sharonville General Plan prepared in the late 1960s noted that rapid growth had created many problems—bad land use relationships, traffic congestion, and inadequate recreation—which all required solution.

Elk Grove Village, Illinois

In 1956 the Centex Corporation acquired 1,300 acres adjacent to O'Hare International Airport, 26 miles northwest of the Loop, and began development of a major housing project with a small light industrial park and neighborhood shopping center. Between 1956 and 1960 an aggressive land acquisition program quadrupled the company's land holdings. Elk Grove Village was then replanned as a full-scale new community. The original new community plan was prepared by the Dallas firm of Phillips, Proctor, Bowers, and Associates.

With room for over 450 establishments, Elk Grove Village contains one of the largest and most successful industrial parks in the country. Employment in the park now exceeds 27,000. Residential development has not matched the pace of industrial expansion. Unlike most new communities, Elk Grove Village's developer is also the community's major homebuilder. The first home was sold in 1957 and within three years 6,608 persons were living in the community. However, the pace of development slowed down during the 1960s. Elk Grove Village's population was 22,900 in 1972. By 1980 a population of 58,500 is expected.

The original Centex plan and the Village's own 1967 comprehensive plan envision a community of neighborhood schools and parks surrounded by single-family subdivisions and apartments. A major regional shopping center was not planned for Elk Grove Village; instead, shopping needs are met by a series of smaller centers within easy access of residential neighborhoods.

In order to free itself of Cook County zoning and subdivision control and also meet the need for municipal services, Centex incorporated Elk Grove Village in 1956, fully 13 months before the first homes were occupied. The incorporated village has largely restricted its activities to public safety, municipal housekeeping, and land use regulation. Difficulty in developing park lands set aside by the developer led to the formation of the Elk Grove Village Park District in 1966. The district operates recreational programs at 19 park sites, including a major community recreational center and swimming pool complex. Village residents also have access to the adjacent 3,800-acre Ned Brown Forest Preserve.

Schaumburg, Illinois. Lying just west of Elk Grove Village, the Village of Schaumburg has one of the most sophisticated municipal planning processes among the conventional communities included in this study. Beginning in 1954 when the area was farmland and had less than 200 residents, citizens began a comprehensive planning process that culminated in 1961 with the adoption of the Schaumburg General Plan and nine supporting functional plans and development ordinances. Each plan and ordinance contained performance standards detailing the type of community the citizens desired. In addition, the plans reserved some 4,000 acres for regional commercial and industrial development.

By 1970 the population of Schaumburg had grown to 18,830 persons housed in a series of residential subdivisions, apartments, and condominium complexes. The Woodfield Mall opened in Schaumburg in 1971 with three levels, 215 shops, three department stores, and over two million square feet in its initial phase. A number of strip commercial shopping centers are also located in the community. Industrial development has centered on five industrial parks ranging in size from 160 to 675 acres. Sixteen plants with a combined employment of over 4,000 had located in them by 1970. Commuter bus service is provided by the Schaumburg Transportation Company.

Schaumburg incorporated as a village in 1956. The village government prides itself on not levying any taxes. As a result, however, its activities have been limited to planning and land use regulation, public safety, and housekeeping. The separate Schaumburg Park District operates recreational programs at ten neighborhood and community parks. Schaumburg residents also benefit from Cook County Forest Preserve district lands, which surround the community on three sides and provide some 10,000 acres for recreational use.

A Freestanding New Community

A peninsula juts into Lake Havasu, a 45-mile long reservoir formed by Parker Dam on the Colorado River. In 1958 the peninsula contained an airstrip left over from a World War II air force rest and rehabilitation center. The surrounding land, some 3,530 acres, was owned by a group of ex-servicemen who operated a fishing and boating resort from the barracks, which still stood on the site. On St. Patrick's Day, Robert P.

McCulloch, a Los Angeles oilman and manufacturer, flew over the peninsula while looking for an outboard motor testing site. He landed on the airstrip and shortly thereafter acquired the land and built a $250,000 testing facility. Two years later when McCulloch's outboard motor plant in Los Angeles was unable to expand its facilities, he turned to Lake Havasu and conceived the idea of building a new city in the Arizona desert 150 air miles northwest of Phoenix and 235 miles east of Los Angeles. (See table 4-2.)

With C.V. Wood, the former general manager of Disneyland, McCulloch went about acquiring the adjoining 12,990 acres of desert in a complex series of transactions, which required release of the federally owned land to the state of Arizona and its subsequent sale at a public auction. McCulloch was the only bidder, paying approximately $73 an acre. In 1963 he acquired 3,000 additional acres at $300 an acre to form the initial site for his new city.

The general plan for Lake Havasu City was drawn up by Wood. Some 22 miles of lakefront were set aside for community use and are part of Arizona's Lake Havasu State Park. The rest of the land was divided into some 40,000 residential, commercial, and industrial building sites. Minimum building restrictions were established, but architectural decisions were left to individual homeowners, builders, and investors. Although 36 lots were set aside for parks, no mechanism was established to insure park construction and operation. Pending urban pressures, the state park, lake, and surrounding desert environment were counted on to provide adequate recreational opportunities.

Land sales have been conducted on a nationwide basis. McCulloch runs a private airline to transport prospects to the community and has sold over 30,000 lots.

By 1972 Lake Havasu City had about 8,500 residents and most of the elements of a complete community. To bolster the economic base McCulloch transferred his chain saw manufacturing operation (which has since been sold) to the community. To provide a tourist attraction that would stimulate the recreational industry he bought the historic London Bridge for $2,460,000 and reassembled it over a canal dredged between the peninsula and the mainland. Water and major roads are provided by the Lake Havasu Irrigation and Drainage District; limited sewer service is provided by a sanitary district. Schools were provided by organizing an elementary school district from scratch and by persuading the Mohave County Union High School District to build a community high school. To augment the natural recreational opportunities of the site McCulloch built (and later sold) a bowling alley and movie theater. Two developer-owned golf courses are also in operation. Public and developer investments in the community have stimulated private investment in a variety of commercial enterprises and services, including a weekly newspaper.

Table 4-2
A Freestanding New Community

Community	Developer	Initial Occupancy	Target Population	Target Acreage	Paired Conventional Community
Lake Havasu City, Ariz.	McCulloch Properties, Inc.	1963	60,000	16,630	Kingman, Ariz.

Kingman, Arizona

Located 56 miles across the desert from Lake Havasu City, Kingman is the closest comparably-sized community on the Arizona side of the Colorado River. Kingman was founded in the early 1880s, but was not incorporated as a city until 1952. Over the years the community has developed laterally along U.S. Highway 66 and the Atchison, Topeka, and Sante Fe railroad tracks, which run through the heart of town. It has a small downtown clustered near the Mohave County Courthouse, a long strip commercial section running along the highway, and a series of residential neighborhoods following a grid pattern of development. The economy centers on government, transportation, and commercial services, with a small manufacturing sector. A golf course, three city parks, and a municipal pool provide recreational amenities within the community. Kingman's population was 7,312 in 1970.

The California New Communities

California has been an especially fertile area for new community development. In 1974, 38 of the 175 existing and proposed new communities in the nation were located in this one state. A number of factors account for the community building phenomenon in California. Certainly the existence of many large tracts under single ownership has played a major role. Land assembly has been much less difficult than in regions with fragmented land ownership patterns. Rapid population growth has been a major contributor. The state's rapidly expanding freeway and interstate highway system has provided ready access to previously isolated land holdings. Every new community in California is bisected by or adjacent to a freeway. Finally, the ready availability (and easy formation) of special districts to provide water, sewerage, and other improvements made large-scale development feasible in areas far removed from existing urban service systems. (See table 4-3.)

Table 4-3
The California New Communities

Community	Developer	Initial Occupancy	Target Population	Target Acreage	Paired Conventional Community
Foster City	T. Jack Foster & Sons/ Centex West, Inc.	1964	36,000	2,600	West San Mateo
Laguna Niguel	Cabot, Cabot & Forbes/ Avco Community Developers, Inc.	1962	40,000	7,936	Dana Point/ Capistrano Valley
Valencia	Newhall Land and Farming Company	1966	25,000	4,000	Bouquet Canyon
Westlake Village	American-Hawaiian Steamship Company (Daniel K. Ludwig)/ Prudential Insurance Company	1967	50,000	11,709	Agoura/Malibu Junction
Irvine	The Irvine Company	1966	338,000	64,000	Fountain Valley

The California new communities represent a sharp departure in community building technique from the older and freestanding new communities described above. California community builders were among the first to recognize the market for the "amenity-packed" community. Early new community developers were steeped in the lore of homebuilding. They marketed the home first and the community second. Land was reserved for various community functions, but its actual development was often left to the vagaries of municipal government and the market. In contrast, the California community builders have taken an alternative approach. They have sought reputable home builders who were able to market their own products and have concentrated on producing and marketing their community's image.

California new communities pay much closer attention to landscaping and architectural style than is common in the older new communities or Lake Havasu City. Community facilities—particularly recreational facilities, which contribute to community image—have been provided earlier in the development process. Quality has been a guiding principle. The major trade-off the California developers have made is housing price. While older new communities and Lake Havasu City provide homes within the means of a broad segment of the population, California community builders have stuck largely to the middle- and upper middle-income markets, which could afford elaborate community amenity packages.

Foster City, California

With his three sons, T. Jack Foster in 1959 acquired 2,600 acres of low-lying land along the west shore of San Francisco Bay, 25 miles south of San Francisco. Known as Brewer's Island, the property had been used as pasture by a dairyman early in the century and was later partially converted to evaporating ponds by Leslie Salt Company. In the late 1950s Foster and Richard D. Grant, another highly successful Bay Area developer, took an option on the land for $200,000. They eventually paid $13 million for the property and Foster subsequently bought out Grant.

Foster envisioned the creation of a complete community with homes, apartments, industry, and shopping centers. Before development could begin, however, the land had to be reclaimed from San Francisco Bay. In order to finance the reclamation effort and certain municipal services, the developer retained a bond counsel to draft state legislation that would create the first municipal improvement district in California. The enabling act gave the district most of the powers of a municipality (certain police powers were not included) and allowed it to issue tax-exempt bonds. The Estero Municipal Improvement District was organized on September 8, 1960, with the first Board of Directors appointed by the San Mateo County Board of Supervisors. The three men selected were chosen by the Foster's. On June 18, 1961, the Board of Supervisors approved the General Plan for Foster City and ground was broken that August. Three years later the first residents occupied homes in the community.

The 1961 General Plan, prepared by the firm of Wilsey, Ham and Blair, set forth a series of goals and policies to guide development. These included housing a cross-section of the county population, providing a balance between working and residential areas so that residents could find employment within the community, and offering a wide range of convenient and attractively grouped community facilities. A highlight of the plan and subsequent development was a series of lagoons for boating and other aquatic activities. Between the lagoons nine residential neighborhoods, a town center, satellite shopping centers, and an industrial park were laid out. Land was also reserved for schools, churches, parks, and a municipal center.

Partially because of the high tax rate required to support the Estero District's indebtedness ($63.86 million at the time), a petition drive for incorporation began in August 1970. In April 1971 the citizens overwhelmingly approved incorporation of Foster City and made the district a subsidiary of the new city government.

Five days before the Local Agency Formation Commission approved the circulation of incorporation petitions, the remaining 1,500 acres of undeveloped land in Foster City was sold to Centex West, Inc., a wholly-owned subsidiary of the Centex Corporation of Dallas, for approximately $15 million. Centex is also developing Elk Grove Village.

By 1972 Foster City had grown to a community of 15,000 people housed in six of the projected nine residential neighborhoods. Three shopping centers were in operation and a professional theater made its home in the community. However, the location of a nearby regional shopping center had slowed growth of Foster City's town center. The 378-acre Foster City Industrial Park had begun to develop. Initial occupants were primarily warehousing and distribution operations. School construction was far behind schedule, but the citizens had organized a concerted effort to push for construction of the long awaited Marina High School in the heart of the community.

West San Mateo, California. Foster City was paired with two residential subdivisions and adjacent apartment complexes located 30 miles south of San Francisco, at the western edge of the city of San Mateo. San Mateo had experienced its most rapid growth during the 1950s. While Foster City was growing during the 1960s on bayfill just to the east, much of the remaining undeveloped land in the community developed in the hills to the west. San Mateo is an established city of 79,000 persons. It has a well developed downtown, regional shopping center, and an extensive municipal park system. Other amenities and facilities include the Bay Meadows Race Track, Peninsula Golf and Country Club, College of San Mateo (two-year junior college), and the San Mateo County Hospital. Most of these facilities are as accessible to Foster City residents as the residents of the conventional subdivisions in West San Mateo.

Laguna Niguel, California

Laguna Niguel is being developed within and on the hills overlooking a valley extending seven miles from the Pacific Ocean to the San Diego Freeway in southern Orange County. The 7,936-acre development site, once part of the Moulton Ranch, was acquired in 1960 by the Boston firm of Cabot, Cabot & Forbes. The publicly-held Laguna Niguel Corporation was then formed to finance and manage the development process and the firm of Victor Gruen Associates was retained to do the master plan. Gruen's plan called for the construction of a major parkway to serve as the spine of the community, with a series of residential neighborhoods located on either side. Nineteen schools and six neighborhood shopping centers were envisioned for an ultimate population of 80,000. An industrial park was planned at one end of the community, adjacent to the freeway, and a major hotel and resort complex at the other, adjacent to the Pacific Ocean. A major civic and town center was planned for a site midway between the industrial and resort areas. Two artificial lakes, the Pacific beaches, and a golf course were to provide major recreational amenities.

Throughout the 1960s the pace of development fell well below expectations. When the community was sold in 1971 to the Avco Corporation, a conglomerate with roots in the aerospace industry, only 2,300 homes had been completed. Avco merged the Laguna Niguel Corporation with its own new community enterprise, Rancho Bernardo, Inc., to form Avco Community Developers, Inc. Although Avco has invested heavily in Laguna Niguel to speed development, it has been caught up in the California environmental and antibuilding movement. At one point in 1972, 43 projects worth $300 million were stalled by the California Environmental Quality Act's requirement for developer environmental impact statements. Later, in spite of day and night grading for a planned adult village along the coast the project was halted by the California Coastal Commission pending environmental studies. Concern for the fragile environment of the coastal hills and soaring development costs have cut Laguna Niguel's projected population in half to 40,000 residents by 1983.

In spite of these setbacks Laguna Niguel is a functioning new community. In 1972, 8,500 people were in residence. Three shopping centers and a medical complex had been completed, along with the golf course, a tennis club, and a beach club. County investments in the community include the South Coast Regional Civic Center, located adjacent to the town center; Niguel Regional Park, which occupies a 167-acre site surrounding Niguel Lake; and a county beach park. The Laguna Niguel Industrial Park had attracted 55 firms with a total of 500 employees. In a second industrial area the Autonetics Division of North American Rockwell (now Rockwell International) built a 1,000,000-square foot building designed to house 7,500 employees. Because of changes in the market and company policy the building was never occupied. It was acquired by the General Services Administration in 1974 to house a branch of the National Archives. A coaxial cable system, owned by Storer TV, was also in operation in Laguna Niguel.

Dana Point/Capistrano Valley, California. This conventional community just to the south of Laguna Niguel includes several subdivisions and a small shopping area located next to the Pacific Coast Highway. Original residential development occurred on the bluffs overlooking the Pacific Ocean and then extended inland toward the nearby town of San Juan Capistrano. Major amenities in the area include the Dana Point Harbor and Marina, Doheny State Park and Beach, and a neighborhood park operated by the Capistrano Bay Park and Recreation District. The community, like Laguna Niguel, is an unincorporated portion of Orange County. In 1972 its population was estimated to be 6,600.

Valencia, California

The land on which Valencia is located was purchased by Henry Mayo Newhall in 1875. The Newhall Land and Farming Company was established in 1883 to administer Newhall's land holdings.

Valencia is 32 miles northeast of downtown Los Angeles, seven miles north of the San Fernando Valley. The area is surrounded by mountains and is located on the Golden State Freeway, a major California north-south interstate highway. It has been one of the fastest growing regions of Southern California.

By the early 1960s the 44,000-acre Newhall ranch seemed ripe for development. Urbanization from the San Fernando Valley was approaching to the south and the Palmdale International Airport had been proposed for nearby Antelope Valley. After two years of study, a general plan prepared for the new community of Valencia by Thomas L. Sutton and Victor Gruen Associates was adopted by the Los Angeles County Regional Planning Commission in October 1965. The first phase of the plan covered a 4,000-acre section at the eastern end of the ranch adjacent to the rural town of Newhall, California. Initial projections saw a population of 25,000 by 1975, and a city of 173,000 by 1985. However, several factors have slowed the pace of development. The plans for the airport—to be the largest in the United States—have been suspended pending environmental and legal considerations. A 1971 earthquake occurred near Valencia and the widespread publicity of fallen freeway overpasses and bridges hurt sales. These factors and periodic layoffs in the aerospace industry resulted in a 1972 population of only some 7,000 persons.

Valencia's plan follows a neighborhood-village pattern. Individual neighborhoods with schools and parks are combined to form a series of planned villages, each with its own shopping and recreational centers, high schools, library, and church. Paseos (pathways) connect superblocks of homes with neighborhood schools and parks. An open space system separates the villages. At the heart of the community a major regional shopping and civic center is planned. Employment opportunities are provided at the 1,000-acre Valencia Industrial Center.

Initial development has proceeded on a number of fronts. As of 1972, some 15 companies had located in the Industrial Center, thus creating an employment base approaching 3,000 jobs. Although residential development was slower than expected, over 2,000 homes and garden apartments had been constructed. The first village shopping center opened in 1965 and planning was underway on a second center. Two educational institutions had located in Valencia. The California Institute of the Arts, a four-year art and music school conceived by Walt Disney, occupied a $54 million campus on a 60-acre site in the community. Nearby, a community college, known as College of the Canyons, had also begun operation. Grading had begun for the $7 million Henry Mayo Newhall Memorial Hospital in Valencia and the Los Angeles County Administration Center had opened as the first element of the town center.

In order to attract potential residents to Valencia the Newhall Land and Farming Company has invested heavily in regional recreational and entertainment facilities. Three golf courses are located in Valencia. A $30 million family ride park called Magic Mountain opened in 1971 and received well over a million visitors. A public riding stable was opened in 1969. Other facilities included a travel trailer park and dune buggy-motorcycle park.

Bouquet Canyon, California. The hills and valleys northeast of Valencia began to develop several years before Valencia's master plan was approved. The Bouquet Canyon community consists of a series of single-family residential subdivisions on the canyon floor. Shopping facilities are available at two centers located near the mouth of Bouquet Canyon and its junction with San Francisquito Canyon. The community is also served by a small park operated by the Los Angeles County Park and Recreational Department. The community contains no medical or major employment facilities.

Westlake Village, California

Westlake Village is surrounded by mountains in the picturesque Conejo Valley, 40 miles northwest of the Los Angeles Civic Center. The community occupies a site that has been used extensively by the motion picture and television industries—movies such as *King Rat, Tobacco Road*, and *Robin Hood* and television series such as "Gunsmoke," "Rawhide," "The Fugitive," "The FBI," and "Mod Squad" were filmed on the property.

After one year of litigation over title to the 11,709-acre Albertson Ranch, shipping magnate Daniel K. Ludwig finally acquired the land in 1964 for $32 million. Ludwig's American-Hawaiian Steamship Company, which was being converted from shipping to finance and real estate, was to manage the development process. During 1964 and 1965 the Bechtel Corporation conducted exhaustive master plan studies for a community projected to house 70,000 persons. Earthmoving began in 1966 and the first families moved into Westlake Village in 1967.

Westlake's original plan was based on interrelating a series of neighborhood clusters. Each cluster was to include schools, parks, recreational facilities, and shopping for its own residents. A major regional shopping facility was planned for a site adjacent to the Ventura Freeway close to the center of the community. Approximately 500 acres along the freeway were set aside for industrial development. Unique among American new communities, a 170-acre tract was also set aside as a cemetery at the community's southern border. The theme for Westlake Village was established by a 150-acre artificial lake, which cost $10 million to construct.

By 1972, five years after its opening, Westlake Village had attracted 13,000 residents. A community shopping center, two satellite centers, a motel-restaurant complex, and a commercial automotive center were in operation.

An 18-hole, night-lighted executive golf course and tennis club were being used by community residents, as well as neighborhood swimming pools and recreational centers. Other amenities and facilities included two riding stables, a marina at Lake Westlake, a fire station, and a community hospital. A number of nationally known firms had located in the town's industrial parks. These included Bunker-Ramo Corporation, Burroughs Corporation, Control Data Corporation, the Federal Systems Division of IBM, and a computer service center for State Farm Mutual Automobile Insurance Company. Over 4,500 people worked in Westlake Village.

Throughout its history management and political problems have caused serious difficulties in Westlake Village's development. The Los Angeles-Ventura County boundary bisects Westlake so that the developer has had to comply with two different sets of planning and land use regulations, arrange fire and police service from two jurisdictions, and school construction from three. Even telephone service is divided, with different companies serving the Ventura and Los Angeles county portions of the community. To compound these problems Ventura County's City of Thousand Oaks annexed a portion of Westlake Village in 1967. Although the developer did not oppose this initial annexation, later annexation and rezoning of the North Ranch section of Westlake Village resulted in greatly reduced housing densities from those projected in the master plan.

In 1966 the American-Hawaiian Steamship Company obtained a $30 million land loan from Prudential Insurance Company. The loan was renegotiated in 1969 with Prudential becoming a general partner in the project. During that same year a slump in the housing market resulted in an unsold housing inventory of 800 units in Westlake. By late 1972 disagreements between American-Hawaiian and Prudential led to dissolution of the partnership. Prudential kept the undeveloped acreage in Westlake Village, and American-Hawaiian retained the income property. American-Hawaiian is now liquidating its Westlake Village holdings. Prudential has completed a second golf course and is beginning development of the North Ranch properties with a staff greatly reduced from the peak of 400 employees attained in 1972 before the partnership was dissolved.

Agoura/Malibu Junction, California. The Malibu hills and canyons between Westlake Village and the new community of Calabassas Park several
miles to the south have been steadily developing since the late 1960s. This
conventional community of some 5,000 residents consists of a series of
unrelated and widely separated subdivisions located on either side of the
Ventura Freeway. Shopping facilities are provided at a small convenience
center located just off the freeway. A 12-acre park is owned by the Simi
Valley Recreation and Park District and several subdivisions have
neighborhood recreational facilities operated by homes associations. A
movement to incorporate the area as the new city of Las Virgenes has been
active for several years. The land proposed for incorporation includes the
Los Angeles County portion of Westlake Village.

Irvine, California

The present-day 88,000-acre Irvine Ranch encompasses three Mexican
land grants located 40 miles south of Los Angeles in Orange County. The
land was acquired by James Irvine in the latter half of the nineteenth
century for an estimated 35 cents an acre. Irvine and his son ran a large
cattle and farming operation on the ranch for many years, but sold off some
parcels along the coast to finance agricultural irrigation facilities. Several
peripheral tracts were also developed on a lease-hold basis. In order to
keep the ranch property intact, James Irvine, II formed the James Irvine
Foundation in 1937. When he died in 1947, he left majority control of The
Irvine Company, the operating entity for the ranch, to the foundation.

By the late 1950s urbanization of Orange County was approaching the
Irvine Ranch from the north and the company began to receive offers from
developers interested in acquiring various portions of the property. Two
major freeway routes were planned through the ranch and taxes on the
property began to reflect its potential for urban development. Rather than
sell the property in a piecemeal fashion, as proposed by some of James
Irvine's descendents, the foundation decided to restructure The Irvine
Company and develop the property itself.

The major stimulus to plan a new community on the Irvine Ranch
occurred in 1959 when 1,000 acres were donated to the University of
California for a new campus at Irvine. William Pereira was retained by the
university to plan the campus, but he also saw the need for a supporting
community. Pereira proposed this to the company and subsequently prepared a plan for a 10,000-acre university-oriented community. It soon
became apparent that plans for the orderly development of the entire Irvine
Ranch were also needed. Pereira proposed a three-tier approach. Initial
development was to occur on the 34,000 acres comprising the southern

sector of the ranch bordering the Pacific coast. The 32,000-acre central sector, which had the best soils and was being intensively farmed, was given second priority, and the mountainous areas to the east were to be developed last. The South Irvine Ranch General Plan, including Pereira's proposed University Community, was approved by the Orange County Board of Supervisors in February 1964. Initial developments in the area between the coast and the San Diego Freeway included the villages of Eastbluff and University Park, two neighborhood shopping centers to serve the villages, a regional shopping and office complex at Newport Center near the coast, and the Irvine Industrial Complex adjacent to the Orange County Airport several miles inland.

In 1970 plans for the southern sector were incorporated into recently completed plans for the central sector and the new Irvine General Plan was submitted to Orange County for approval. A major component of the plan was the proposal that a new city of 53,000 acres be incorporated in the central portion of the ranch. The city was to include the 10,000-acre University Community, first proposed by Pereira, the industrial complex, and the central valley of the Irvine Ranch. A population of 430,000 residents was projected by The Irving Company. In mid-1970 the city of Newport Beach proposed to annex a portion of the Irvine Industrial Complex and touched off an incorporation drive spearheaded by the Council of the Communities of Irvine and supported by the developer. In December of the following year the citizens overwhelmingly voted to approve incorporation and the city of Irvine came into being.

This new community in the central portion of the Irvine Ranch was selected for the present study. Originally encompassing 18,300 acres and a population of about 20,000 persons, the city has since annexed over 7,000 additional acres. It has also embarked on its own planning program, with the aid of the consulting firm of Wilsey and Ham. In 1973 the City Council adopted a general plan for the city, its sphere of influence, and a 10,000-acre coastal zone south of Newport Beach. The plan includes three development options for this 64,000-acre section of the Irvine Ranch. Option 1 follows Irvine Company plans for a series of villages and environmental corridors, with an additional industrial complex and a new regional commercial center at the juncture of the Santa Ana and San Diego freeways. A midrange population of 337,800 is projected. Option 2 assumes maximum urbanization and projects a midrange population of 453,000. Option 3 is based on minimum urbanization assumptions, including reservation of the entire 10,000-acre coastal hills section as open space, and projects a midrange population of 194,000. Each of the options is compatible with the short-term development plans of The Irvine Company.

When Irvine was selected for study in 1972, work was underway on five villages within the city limits: Walnut, Valleyview, New Culver, University Park, and Turtle Rock. The villages were composed of individual neighborhoods with neighborhood recreational facilities run by homes associations. A neighborhood shopping center was completed adjacent to University Park and another was ready for construction next to Walnut Village. A 345-acre site had been donated by The Irvine Company for the William R. Mason Regional Park (the $750,000 first phase, 45 acres, opened in 1974). The University of California at Irvine was in full operation, and a small town center building was open adjacent to the university. A public golf course had been constructed by The Irvine Company. Over 16,000 employees were working in the highly successful Irvine Industrial Complex.

Fountain Valley, California. Fountain Valley is located on the flat coastal plain along the San Diego Freeway four miles north of the Irvine city limits. Although this conventional community incorporated in 1957, residential tract development did not begin until January 1962 when the first 100 acres of land were approved for residential use. During the next 10 years approximately 2,500 acres were zoned or developed for single-family homes and apartments. Population growth has been equally spectacular, increasing from 597 persons when the community was incorporated to 31,826 in 1970 and an estimated 49,000 in 1972. Substantial industrial development has taken place. In 1972, 315 acres were zoned industrial and an additional 320 acres were planned for future industrial occupancy. A number of neighborhood and community shopping centers were located in the community. Major recreational facilities included a county park, golf course, and a community center.

New Communities in the East

Two new communities in the Washington-Baltimore region—Reston and Columbia (table 4-4)—have been at the forefront of the new communities movement in the United States. Both have attracted extensive nationwide publicity and have served as models for later new community development. Reston and Columbia match the California new communities' concern for environmental design and residential amenities, but add a concern for population balance and diversity, which is missing from the western communities. In a sense, the California new communities represent suburban development at its zenith; Columbia and Reston are first efforts to create new cities in the suburbs. In Reston, urbanity is achieved through urban design and a conscious effort to create a true urban atmosphere. In

Table 4-4
New Communities in the East

Community	Developer	Initial Occupancy	Target Population	Target Acreage	Paired Conventional Community
Reston, Va.	Simon Enterprises/ Gulf-Reston, Inc.	1964	75,000	7,400	West Spring-field, Va.
Columbia, Md.	Howard Research and Development Corp.	1967	110,000	18,000	Norbeck-Wheaton, Md.

Columbia, urbanity is reflected in the developer's humanistic efforts to create a total community that responds to present-day urban ills through a variety of innovative community institutions.

Reston, Virginia

Lying 18 miles northwest of Washington, Reston is being built on the site of a defunct new community founded in the late nineteenth century by Dr. C.A. Max Wiehle. This early community-building effort failed after only a few homes had been sold. The property reverted to farmland and was later the location of the distillery used to make Virginia Gentleman bourbon. Reston's founder, Robert E. Simon, Jr., bought the land in March 1961 for $13.15 million after he and his family had sold Carnegie Hall in New York City.

Simon established seven goals for the development of the 6,750 acres of Virginia countryside he had acquired. These included providing wide opportunities for the use of leisure time; making it possible for people to remain in a single neighborhood throughout their lives; giving priority in planning to the dignity of the individual; making it possible for people to live and work in the same community; providing a variety of recreational, cultural, and commercial facilities from the beginning of development; preserving and encouraging beauty; and insuring financial success of the enterprise. To achieve these goals Simon hired the New York architectural firm of Whittlesey and Conklin to prepare a master plan and to design the initial village center at Lake Anne.

The Reston master plan assigned about 23 percent of the site for recreational areas, provided for a 970-acre industrial park, and for a variety of housing types and commercial areas. These land uses were organized in a series of seven villages, each with a projected population of 10,000 to

12,000 people. The town center was designed to serve Reston's projected 75,000 residents plus 50,000 people in the surrounding region. A key feature of the plan was Simon's concept of mixed land uses in which apartments, townhouses, and commercial facilities were designed and built as a unit.

The master plan was approved by the Fairfax County Board of Supervisors in June 1962 when they established Residential Planned Community (RPC) zoning in the county. The RPC zone allowed Reston to be divided into three density areas (high, 60 persons per acre; medium, 14 persons per acre; and low, 3.8 persons per acre) as long as overall density of the community did not exceed 13 persons per gross residential acre. With zoning approval, Simon secured a major loan from the Gulf Oil Corporation and started construction of the Lake Anne Village Center in the spring of 1963. The first residents moved into Reston in December of the following year.

Throughout its early years Reston was plagued by a slow development pace and financial difficulties. Without access to the four-lane freeway that connects nearby Dulles Airport to downtown Washington, Reston residents faced an arduous commuting trip to work in the nation's capital. Simon achieved architectural success with a variety of avant-garde dwellings, but did not succeed in attracting many home buyers. By the end of 1966 the residential population of Reston was only 2,500, far short of expectations.

Following the initial Gulf Oil loan, Simon obtained additional financing from the John Hancock Mutual Life Insurance Company ($24 million), the State Planters Bank of Commerce ($5.4 million), and the Empire Trust Company ($2.4 million). With annual debt service running $2.5 million and continuing slow sales, Gulf Oil moved to protect its investment. On September 28, 1967 Gulf took over full financial and operational responsibility from Simon and formed Gulf-Reston, Inc., headed by Pittsburgh real estate consultant Robert H. Ryan. Ryan then moved to accelerate the pace of development. Gulf invested another $35 million in Reston; and $10.5 million in additional financing was obtained from the Metropolitan Life Insurance Company.

By 1972 Reston was able to report a positive cash flow. The population had increased to 20,000 residents living in two villages, Lake Anne and Hunters Woods. Over 50 tenants occupied the Lake Anne Village Center. Two golf courses were operating, as well as a series of neighborhood swimming and tennis facilities and a riding stable. Medical and day care centers were functioning. Virginia Polytechnic Institute and State University's Graduate Studies Center had located in the community. Ground had been broken for a major hotel and conference center, and an adjoining Center for Associations and Educational Institutions had welcomed its first occupants. Over 2,000 persons were employed in Reston and construction was underway on a $54 million headquarters building for the U.S. Geological Survey.

West Springfield, Virginia. This conventional community in Fairfax County is located 18 miles southeast of Reston and 13 miles southwest of downtown Washington. With almost 35,000 residents in 1972 the West Springfield community was served by four neighborhood and community shopping centers, but made no provision for industrial development. Recreational facilities were provided at Lake Accotink, Cardinal Forest, and West Springfield parks, in addition to the Springfield Golf and Country Club and facilities provided by individual tract and apartment developers.

Columbia, Maryland

Probably more has been written about Columbia than any other new community in the United States. Columbia was conceived by Baltimore mortgage banker and shopping center developer James Rouse in mid-1962. At that time he began secretly acquiring approximately 15,000 acres (13,690 were to be included in the new community) in rural Howard County midway between the beltways surrounding Baltimore and Washington. Land acquisition was managed by the Howard Research and Development Corporation, a company jointly owned by Community Research and Development, Inc. (now The Rouse Company) and Connecticut General Life Insurance Company. Connecticut General advanced $23.5 million to acquire the more than 140 separate parcels assembled for Columbia's development. The average cost of these initial land purchases was $1,450 an acre, well below the $1,900 an acre Robert Simon paid for the Reston acreage a year earlier.

On October 29, 1963 Rouse announced that he had acquired a tenth of the land in Howard County and proposed the building of an entirely new city. Five main goals were to guide the planning of Columbia. These included the development of a complete and self-sustaining city; good design; respect for the land; creation of a social and physical environment that would nourish human growth; and financial success of the venture. From these primary goals a number of other principles were derived. Columbia was to provide a job for every residence, a dwelling for every job in the community, and a full spectrum of housing types and community services for a diverse population.

One year was allocated to prepare a development plan and financial program for Columbia. A highlight of the planning process was the creation of a number of work groups. Over a period of six months distinguished social scientists were assembled twice monthly to propose new ideas for community institutions and systems and to evaluate alternative sketch plans prepared by the resident planning staff headed by Morton Hoppenfeld. From these efforts the basic concepts for Columbia's development emerged.

The Columbia plan starts with a neighborhood of 2,000 to 5,000 people built around a neighborhood center consisting of an elementary school, park and playground, swimming pool, community center building, and in some cases a convenience store. Two to four neighborhoods are then combined to form a village of from 10,000 to 15,000 people. Village centers provide convenience shopping, community meeting facilities, land for middle and high schools, and major recreational facilities. Seven villages were planned around a downtown core, which was to contain a major regional shopping and office complex. More than 20 percent of the development acreage was set aside for open space, with another 20 percent reserved for business and industry.

Throughout 1964 Rouse and his planners went about selling the Howard County residents and their county commissioners on the Columbia idea. They were successful. In mid-1965 the plan was approved and the entire development site was rezoned in accordance with a recently completed new-town section of the zoning ordinance. Overall density of Columbia was set at the prevailing density in the county, a relatively low 2.2 dwellings per gross acre (with a maximum of 2.5 dwelling units allowed by the new town provisions of the Howard County zoning ordinance). However, like the RPC zone governing Reston's development, the Howard County ordinance allowed clustering of dwelling units on lots that were smaller than those allowed in conventional subdivisions.

Construction of Columbia began in June 1966 and the first homes were offered for sale the following year. By 1972 Columbia's population had grown to 24,000 of a projected 110,000 residents at full development. The growth of the community had been marked by a number of institutional innovations. When Howard County officials balked at the creation of a special service district, the unique Columbia Park and Recreation Association was created to build, operate, and maintain a broad range of community facilities. The Protestant Columbia Cooperative Ministry was formed in 1966 to seek out new opportunities for mission and service. Catholics, Jews, and Protestants share common religious facilities in The Interfaith Center, located in Wilde Lake Village. The Columbia Medical Plan, a prepaid group practice health care program provided by the Columbia Hospital and Clinics Foundation in affiliation with The Johns Hopkins Medical Institutions, was formed to meet health needs in the community. Innovation in the schools has drawn national attention, as have the early childhood educational programs organized by the Columbia Association.

By 1972 Columbia provided a variety of facilities to accommodate residents' leisure time interests: an indoor hockey-sized ice rink, two lakes for boating, an indoor pool and eight outdoor neighborhood pools, two golf courses, an indoor tennis club and numerous outdoor courts, an athletic club, a horse center, miniature golf, a professional dinner theater, an outdoor concert pavilion, several restaurants and lounges, and hundreds of acres of parks and open space. The Howard County Public Library had opened a branch in Columbia. Shopping facilities included the Columbia Mall, a regional center with two department stores, and three village centers with supermarkets, banks, drug stores, gas stations, and assorted specialty shops. Four college-level institutions were operating in Columbia—the two-year Howard Community College, the new four-year Dag Hammarskjold College, a branch of Antioch College, and Loyola College of Baltimore. Columbia also provided numerous employment opportunities. Over 65 firms had located in the Columbia industrial parks. General Electric, which located its Appliance Park-East in Columbia, had completed the first phase of construction—2.4 million square feet of space in three buildings. Total employment in the community was more than 15,000.

Norbeck-Wheaton, Maryland. Columbia was paired with the conventional community of Norbeck-Wheaton, located on the urban fringe of Montgomery County 15 miles northeast of downtown Washington. Major facilities serving the community's 20,000 residents included the Aspen Hill and Rock Creek Village neighborhood shopping centers, Manor Country Club, four neighborhood parks, sections of the North Branch and Rock Creek (regional stream valley) parks, ten schools, and a public library. There were no hospitals or medical facilities in Norbeck-Wheaton and only one major employment facility, Vitro Laboratories, which employed about 3,600 persons.

The Study Communities and the New Community Continuum

The preceding vignettes illustrate the diverse character of new community development in the United States. The communities differ in location, size, stage of development, design features and amenities, developer types and motivation, and local governmental structure. They also differ in the degree that they meet the specifications of the new community concept discussed in chapter 2. There it was noted that in addition to the basic notions of size, unified ownership, planning, and diversity of land uses and housing, new communities have often been expected to encompass a

Table 4-5
Index of New Community Characteristics

New Community	Index Value	Paired Conventional Community	Index Value
Columbia, Md.	6.1	Norbeck-Wheaton, Md.	13.9
Reston, Va.	7.3	West Springfield, Va.	12.3
Irvine, Calif.	8.2	Fountain Valley, Calif.	15.6
Valencia, Calif.	10.2	Bouquet Canyon, Calif.	19.7
Park Forest, Ill.	10.6	Lansing, Ill.	14.5
Westlake Village, Calif.	11.0	Agoura/Malibu Junction, Calif.	18.8
Elk Grove Village, Ill.	11.3	Schaumburg, Ill.	15.0
Foster City, Calif.	11.4	West San Mateo, Calif.	14.0
Laguna Niguel, Calif.	12.9	Dana Point/Capistrano Valley, Calif.	18.1
Lake Havasu City, Ariz.	13.0	Kingman, Ariz.	17.8
Sharpstown, Tex.	13.7	Southwest Houston, Tex.	18.1
Forest Park, Oh.	14.4	Sharonville, Oh.	14.2
North Palm Beach, Fla.	14.7	Tequesta, Fla.	16.6

Note: Lower index values indicate greater adherence to the new community concept.

number of other planning principles. Since new communities were likely to vary in the degree to which they adhered to these principles—for example, varying degrees of self-sufficiency seemed likely—the concept of a new community continuum was introduced.

The study new communities and their paired conventional communities were scored in terms of their performance in 19 indicators of adherence to the new community concept.[c] The rank of each community on each indicator was determined and an index of average rank across all of the indicators was computed. Although this measure is crude—for example, it assumes that each component measure has equal weight—it provides a way to sort communities into a continuum ranging from high to low adherence to the new community concept.

The results of this exercise are illustrated in table 4-5. The lower the index number the greater was a community's adherence to the new community concept. The two eastern new communities—Columbia and Reston—ranked first and second, followed closely by Irvine. Of the older

[c]The following indicators of adherence to the new community concept were used: (1) architectural controls; (2) bus service; (3) commercial facilities grouped in centers; (4) communications media; (5) ease of access to facilities; (6) environmental protection; (7) housing choice; (8) landscaping of public and common areas; (9) master plan; (10) open space preservation; (11) pedestrian-vehicular separation; (12) self-government; (13) self-sufficiency; (14) income mix; (15) racial mix; (16) underground utilities; (17) unified development by single entrepreneur; (18) preservation or creation of water bodies; and (19) variety of land uses.

developments, Park Forest and Elk Grove Village ranked in the center of the continuum. On the other hand, three other older new communities—Sharpstown, Forest Park, and North Palm Beach—were at the bottom of the continuum.

For 12 of the 13 paired comparisons the new communities indicated greater adherence to the new community concept than did the paired conventional communities. The one exception was Forest Park where the paired community of Sharonville ranked slightly higher in terms of new community characteristics even though it had urbanized through conventional subdivision development. Several other conventional communities also ranked higher than some of the older new communities. This suggests that new community development principles have had an impact in other development contexts, particularly in areas with relatively strong local governments with a high commitment to community planning, such as Montgomery and Fairfax counties in Maryland and Virginia and the City of San Mateo in California.

5 Who Lives In New Communities?

Social stratification has long been a pervasive aspect of American society. It has been particularly dominant in suburban areas, where a variety of factors have inhibited class and racial integration. These include: suburban residents' desires for neighbors whose values and life-styles are much like their own; simple snobbery and racial prejudice; fears of rising property taxes, declining property values, and lower quality schools if poor or black people live nearby; and exclusionary housing and zoning policies pursued by local governments under the veil of promoting the health, safety, morals, and general welfare of the community.

The consequences of suburban class and racial segregation have been well documented. Poor school performance and high crime rates in ghetto neighborhoods are said to be caused to a great extent by economic deprivation and segregation. Concentrations of low-income families are purported to reinforce deviant behavior patterns and create neighborhoods that are neither economically nor socially viable. Additionally, the movement of industry to outlying areas may create severe hardships for workers who are least able to afford the costs of an extended journey to work. These and other negative results of segregation have led many to the conclusion that dispersal of black and working class people to outlying areas is needed.

The Goal of Population Balance

One of the most persistent elements of the new community concept has been the belief that new communities, as microcosms of larger cities, will promote social diversity—including class and racial integration. This view has achieved some credibility because of the many unique advantages new communities enjoy: (1) their large scale; (2) unity of planning and development, with the site owned or controlled by a single firm; (3) comprehensive planning, with facilities and services provided at an early stage of development; and (4) a degree of self-sufficiency through commercial facilities and industry, which provide job opportunities.

Added to these characteristics are two key factors that can facilitate integration. Most new communities in the United States are being constructed on the fringes of metropolitan areas where there are few existing neighborhoods with entrenched social and political prejudices. In addition,

99

the high quality of amenities offered may help overcome the objections of middle- and high-income residents to a certain amount of mixing.

These unique characteristics of new communities and the resulting potential for innovation have led many to look to new communities as "laboratories for cities." They are seen as vehicles for social as well as technical experimentation. As the former secretary of the Department of Housing and Urban Development, Robert C. Weaver, has said, because new communities offer possibilities "to experiment with new approaches to housing for low- and moderate-income households . . . they should demonstrate how families and individuals of a wide variety of incomes and ethnic attributes can live together" (1964, p. 280).

The potential for population balance in new community development, however, is also limited by several key considerations. First, as Herbert J. Gans (1973) has noted, new communities are likely to be truly new in only certain selected respects, most notably site planning and some public services. They are not new in terms of political relations. The new community site and development process will most likely be governed, at least initially, by an existing political entity. Furthermore, since development is highly dependent on private financing and must show a return on the capital invested, developers must adapt their projects to the expected preferences of consumers, who may have "old" ideas about the social composition of the communities to which they will move.

On the other hand, because new communities are new settlements, the social diversity they can attain, at least in the short run, is constrained by the mobility characteristics of the population. Who moves to new communities largely determines who lives there. In a free soicety the stream of residents flowing into a community results from the accumulation of residential mobility decisions of individual households. There are two semi-independent but linked mobility decisions involved—the decicion to move from the previous residence, which puts a household into the housing market, and then a second decision, the choice of a new residence, which takes the household out of the market and brings it to a new community.

The first mobility decision—the decision to move—almost always precedes the residential selection decision. Very few households are pulled out of their previous residence by the discovery of a better alternative, including the new community alternative. The implication for the goal of population balance is that new communities can be expected to draw only from the mobile population who have already decided to move and are in the housing market. They cannot be expected to draw residents in large numbers from the more residentially stable portion of the market area population, such as the elderly and the more satisfied homeowners. Thus, it is unreasonable to expect new community residents during the initial

stages of development to mirror the host metropolitan or host county population distribution, since in each case the referrent group consists mostly of nonmoving households.

New Community Residents

Where They Came From

At one time it was feared that by increasing the residential attractiveness of suburban areas, new communities would stimulate the flight of middle-income residents from central cities. However, this has not occurred. For 10 of the 13 new communities studied, only 30 percent or less of the respondents had moved from a central city. Furthermore, as the paired comparisons illustrated in figure 5-1 show, new community residents were no more likely than the residents of conventional communities to be former central city dwellers.

Most new and conventional community residents simply moved from one metropolitan suburb to another. They were not fleeing from anything, but instead were looking for homes that offered adequate space, and that were convenient to work and located in a pleasant environment (see chapter 6). Very few new community residents moved from locations outside of metropolitan areas, although a fairly sizable proportion (about 40 percent) came from a metropolitan community located in another part of the same state or from out of state.

By offering a range of housing types, new communities have been expected to give households the option of moving within the same community when their housing needs change. For example, a young couple might initially settle in a small apartment, then move to a larger townhouse or a single-family detached home as their family grew, and then back to an apartment after their children had left home. In this way a household could move through its entire life cycle without the social and psychological disruption of changing communities every time its housing needs changed. In three new communities—Sharpstown, Park Forest, and Lake Havasu City—there was some evidence of this process at work. Fifty-six percent of the Sharpstown respondents, 27 percent of those in Park Forest, and 22 percent in Lake Havasu City had moved to their present residence from another dwelling unit in the same community. For the other new communities, many of which were too young for the process to be observed, 15 percent or less of the households interviewed had moved within their community.

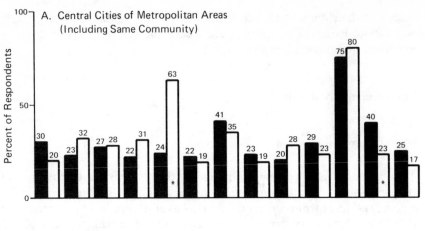

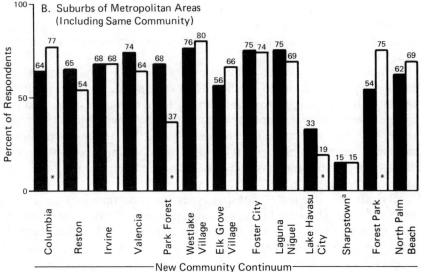

- ■ New Community
- □ Conventional Community
- * Statistically Significant Difference

[a]Sharpstown and its paired community were located within central city (Houston).

Figure 5-1. Location of Previous Residence

Life Cycle Characteristics

New community residents, like many others living in suburban areas, tend to be young families who are raising children. Almost 50 percent of the household heads were under 40 years old; 61 percent of the households contained children. More than a fourth of the households (28 percent) had children of preschool age; 37 percent had children in the primary school age group (six to 13); and 24 percent had older children living in their homes. Only 12 percent were single persons without children, while 27 percent of the new community households were childless couples.

The three new communities that had the highest proportion of rental housing units—Reston, Columbia, and Sharpstown—had attracted a somewhat younger population with a higher proportion of single persons than was characteristic of new communities as a whole. These were the only new communities where the median age of household heads was 35 or less (Sharpstown, 35; Reston, 34; Columbia, 32), and with more than 15 percent single persons without children. On the other hand, four other new communities had attracted a distinctly older population profile. The median age of household heads was 53 in North Palm Beach, 50 in Lake Havasu City, 44 in Laguna Niguel, and 43 in Westlake Village. The first three communities offered climates and natural surroundings that were particularly attractive to persons looking for a place to retire. Between 21 and 27 percent of the household heads and their spouses in these communities were no longer working. Westlake Village, on the other hand, had an average proportion of retired persons (13 percent), but had the highest median family income ($21,600) and the second highest median home value ($47,500) among the new communities. Apparently, expensive housing attracted an older, more established population.

When persons who had moved to new communities within the previous two years are compared to earlier in-movers, several notable differences in life cycle characteristics are evident. The recent in-movers were significantly more likely to have younger household heads, fewer or no children, to be single, in earlier stages of career development and were more likely to be changing jobs and to be renters. As a result, while new communities are undergoing active development, there is likely to be a constant infusion of families in earlier life cycle stages, which may balance off the natural aging of the nonmobile population.

It should also be noted that recent in-movers to new communities were not significantly different in life cycle characteristics from conventional community in-movers, or what might be termed the general metropolitan mover profile. In other words, families who were moving to new communities were similar in life cycle characteristics to families who were moving to other metropolitan locations.

Socioeconomic Characteristics

Although recent in-movers to new communities did not differ in life cycle characteristics from other residentially mobile households in metropolitan areas, they did differ in socioeconomic status. Both recent and earlier in-movers to new communities tended to have much higher family incomes and much more formal education than the average person in the metropolitan housing market. For example, while up to 18 percent of the residentially mobile metropolitan population have been found to be college graduates, 47 percent of the recent in-movers to new communities had that much formal education; while about 15 percent of the mobile metropolitan population have reported family incomes of $15,000 or more, 62 percent of those who recently moved to new communities were in that income bracket. The median income of all new community households was $17,500 for 1972, well above that of the host counties and metropolitan areas in which they were located.

In contrast to the expectations for population diversity embedded in the new community concept, private new communities have yet to provide many housing opportunities for lower income and working class people. Only 12 percent of the new community respondents had family incomes of less than $10,000. Only 28 percent had not attended college, and only 22 percent were employed in blue-collar occupations. Individual new community comparisons are included in figure 5-2. The new community with the most socioeconomic mixing was Lake Havasu City—58 percent of the household heads had a high school education or less, 33 percent had family incomes of less than $10,000, and 52 percent of the household heads were employed in blue-collar occupations. Because Lake Havasu City is a freestanding new community, housing opportunities had to be provided within the community for persons employed in its industrial plants and service jobs.

Class Integration. Using education and occupation as rough indices of social class, figure 5-2 shows that four new communities—Lake Havasu City, Elk Grove Village, Park Forest, and Forest Park—have come closest to achieving a modicum of class mixing. In each case 25 percent or more of the respondents were employed in blue-collar occupations and 25 percent or more had only a high school education or less. With the exception of Lake Havasu City, which, as mentioned above is freestanding, these communities were initially settled in the late 1940s and 1950s. Tastes in housing were less elaborate then; smaller housing units were built than are characteristic of later new communities; and a good bit of filtering of the older housing stock has occurred.

Income Integration. A modest amount of income integration has been achieved in new communities through both filtering of the housing stock and participation in federal housing subsidy programs. With the exception of Elk Grove Village, each of the older new communities had a somewhat

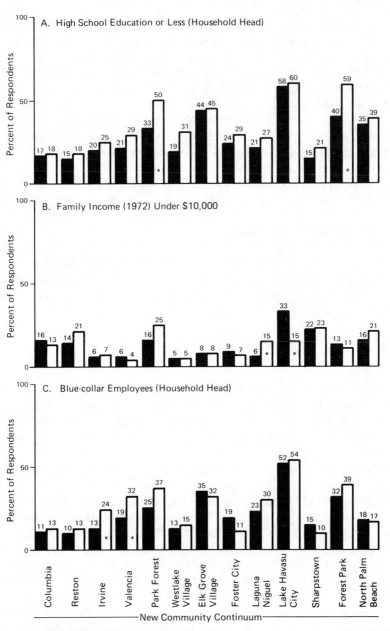

Figure 5-2. Selected Socioeconomic Characteristics

higher than average proportion of families with incomes under $10,000—Sharpstown, 22 percent; Park Forest, 16 percent; North Palm Beach, 16 percent; and Forest Park, 13 percent. This was also true of the five new communities with some form of subsidized housing—Lake Havasu City, 33 percent; Columbia, 16 percent; Park Forest, 16 percent; Reston, 14 percent; and Forest Park, 13 percent as noted above. On the other hand, among the newer new communities where filtering has not taken place and subsidized housing was not available—Irvine, Valencia, Westlake Village, Foster City, and Laguna Niguel—less than 10 percent of the families were in the lower income bracket.

The degree of class and income integration attained in new communities was not associated with a community's place on the new community continuum. Thus, the provision of community amenities and other elements of the new community concept does not necessarily induce socioeconomic mixing. Figure 5-2 also shows that the socioeconomic characteristics of the conventional communities, with few exceptions, were very similar to those of their paired new communities. Since conventional communities were matched to new communities, in part, on the basis of housing price and type, this result is to be expected.

Race

New communities have had even less success in achieving racially balanced populations than they have had with class and income integration. Just over 3 percent of the new communities' population were black, while the conventional communities had a black population of just over 1/2 of 1 percent.

Racial integration (and nonintegration) in new communities has generally followed one of three patterns. In some new communities, and in particular Columbia, the developer's goal for the construction of a complete city implied social and racial balance. Black models were consciously used in advertising the community and this nonexclusionary ethos attracted a substantial proportion of black residents. As shown in figure 5-3, 19 percent of the Columbia households were black. Reston appears to have attained a slightly higher than average black population through a similar process.

In the usual case, however, developers have not viewed black households as an important enough segment of the market to direct their advertising to them. Thus, while developers have not engaged in exclusionary practices (other than pricing homes above the means of many black families), they have also not encouraged black in-migration. The end result

107

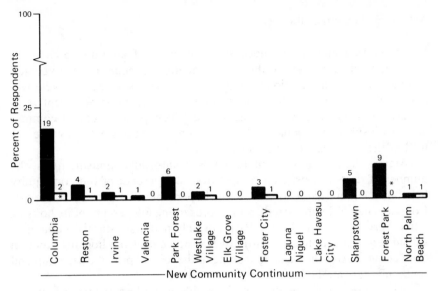

Figure 5-3. Black Households in New Communities

in communities such as Irvine, Valencia, Westlake Village, Elk Grove Village, Foster City, Laguna Niguel, Lake Havasu City, and North Palm Beach has been the attainment of negligible black populations.[a]

A third pattern of racial integration has been the in-migration of blacks into previously white single-family and apartment housing units. This has been particularly noticeable in three of the oldest new communities—Park Forest (6 percent black), Sharpstown (5 percent black), and Forest Park (9 percent black)—where blacks did not begin to move to them in large numbers until well after initial residential settlement had occurred.

Comparisons of recent arrivals (during past two years) with earlier in-movers shows that the proportion of blacks moving to new communities has been increasing. Among homeowners, the proportion of blacks increased from 1.5 percent of those who moved to new communities prior to 1971 to 3.9 percent of those who moved in between 1971 and 1973. Among renters the increase was from 2.4 percent to 4.1 percent.

[a] In 1973, Irvine and Westlake Village were served with racial bias suits for failure to comply with Section 804(c) of Public Law 90-284 (racial bias in advertising). As a result of these suits, their developers agreed to use minority models in advertising and to advertise in publications read by minority groups.

Achieving Population Balance

While filtering and racial succession are ways of attaining population balance, most supporters of the new community concept have advocated income and racial integration from the outset. If this is to occur, developers must build lower priced housing units and residents must be receptive to living in proximity to lower income people. The experience of new communities with subsidized housing illustrates some of the obstacles involved as well as the real opportunities for achieving this end.

Among the five new communities with subsidized housing units, the number of units constructed ranged from 2.9 percent of the community housing stock in Lake Havasu City to 11 percent in Reston. See table 5-1. Columbia had 532 subsidized units, representing 6.9 percent of its housing units. Park Forest and Forest Park not only had a substantial number of subsidized housing units—a little over 4 percent of the housing stock in each community—they also had some of the lowest priced ownership and rental market rate housing.

Why were some new communities able to build subsidized housing, while others were not? The answer lies in a combination of factors, including developers' attitudes and commitments to population balance, the attitudes of community residents, and local, state, and federal governmental policies.

Developers' Attitudes and Policies

The housing industry in the United States has typically responded to perceived market demand, rather than to the housing needs determined for particular population groups. This situation is not much changed by new community development. In fact, the economics of the development process lends itself even less to the production of lower priced housing than development in other settings. As noted in chapter 3, one of the primary sources of profit from new community ventures is appreciation in land values. Development strategies are designed to escalate values as rapidly as possible. Not only may housing for lower income persons be seen as threatening necessary appreciation in land values, but rising prices themselves make it exceedingly difficult to build moderately priced housing units. Because the arithmetic of new community development does not naturally lead to the production of lower priced housing units, their attainment is highly dependent on developers' attitudes and policies.

In 3 of the 13 new communities—Columbia, Reston, and Lake Havasu City—developers were openly receptive to the goal of income integration

Table 5-1
Moderate-Income Housing in New Communities

	Subsidized Housing		All Housing[b]	
New Community	*Number of Units*[a]	*Percent of Total Units*	*Median Home Value*	*Median Rent*
Reston	926	11.0	$58,000	$226
Columbia	532	6.9	44,100	183
Park Forest	354	4.1	24,800	150
Forest Park	201	4.4	27,300	148
Lake Havasu City	64	2.9	31,800	149
Sharpstown	0	0.0	31,200	141
North Palm Beach	0	0.0	35,500	182
Valencia	0	0.0	37,500	202
Elk Grove Village	0	0.0	38,400	187
Laguna Niguel	0	0.0	40,300	255
Irvine	0	0.0	42,800	204
Foster City	0	0.0	46,100	215
Westlake Village	0	0.0	47,500	186

[a]As of December 1973.
[b]Data supplied by household survey respondents, spring 1973.

and the provision of housing opportunities for people working in their communities.

Columbia. James W. Rouse of Columbia was the first new community developer to begin to operationalize socioeconomic goals and facilitate their attainment. He saw housing for lower income families as necessary for a "complete and balanced city." It is important to note, however, that when Rouse talked of lower income households and balance, he was not referring to occupants of public housing. Instead, he saw subsidized housing as nonprofit, community owned, and serving as a way station for young people moving up. For example, in Columbia the income limits of its subsidized housing range from approximately $5,000 for a family of one to $11,000 for families of five or six.

As soon as plans for Columbia began to be formalized, Rouse announced that the major strategy to be employed for achieving a balanced community would be the reservation of a minimum of 10 percent of all dwelling units for low- and middle-income housing. Since announcing this goal, he has taken a number of steps that have facilitated the provision of low-cost housing in Columbia. These include: (1) recruitment of key personnel who also have a commitment to socioeconomic integration; (2) early solicitation of strategies for implementation of income integration objectives; (3) early public announcements of income and racial integration goals; (4) facilitating construction of low-cost housing by writing down the cost of land; (5) development of alternative strategies not dependent of federal subsidy programs for the provision of low-cost housing; and (6) working with organizations and residents of the community to establish the credibility of income integration policies.

Reston. Like Columbia, Reston is often cited as an example of a successfully integrated community. Robert E. Simon, Jr., the original developer, did not formalize his concern for social structure in Reston as Rouse did in Columbia. Through his actions, however, he made it known that changes in persons' living circumstances, including age, family composition, or financial situation, should not make it necessary for them to move from the community. One of Simon's first actions in support of this philosophy was to propose that subsidized housing for elderly residents be built in each village center.

When Gulf-Reston, Inc. took over development it felt obligated to fulfill Simon's commitment, even though its own marketing studies indicated that construction of low- and moderate-income housing should be terminated. Gulf-Reston completed construction of Reston's first subsidized housing project, Cedar Ridge. Although it has not sponsored on its own additional subsidized projects, it has fully cooperated with other sponsoring groups. For example, land write-downs for subsidized housing in Reston have thus far amounted to $1.087 million. In addition, Gulf-Reston has continued to advertise the economic and social mix in Reston (though citizen pressure and a formal complaint were required before it began using minority models in its advertisements and tour guides).

Lake Havasu City. Although income integration goals were less explicit than they were in Columbia and Reston, Lake Havasu City has been developed from the start as a complete community for a balanced population. The provision of subsidized housing was prompted by the developer's perception of a need for low-cost housing units. In 1969 the community had reached a stage of development where there were many workers and few inexpensive places to rent or purchase. When an opportunity arose to experiment with an innovative housing system, Robert P. McCulloch invited the originator, Shoreline Development Company, to come into the community. Sixty-four housing units, selling from $17,000 to $19,000, were completed. The first ones were occupied in the spring of 1970.

Park Forest and Forest Park. Development of both of these communities was guided by a nonexclusionary ethos. In the case of Park Forest, however, American Community Builders, Inc., did not encourage black in-migration, reputedly because of investors' fears of integrated neighbor-hoods during the period of its most active development (1948-59). As shown in table 5-1, housing in Park Forest and Forest Park is moderately priced.

Although developer policies made acceptance of subsidized housing possible in these communities, its construction did not result from their concern with housing needs, as in Columbia, Reston, and Lake Havasu City. In Park Forest, subsidized housing was built after the developer was no longer active. It was a direct result of citizen concerns for elderly housing and a private builder's conclusion that multifamily housing for moderate-income families would be the most profitable use of his land. In Forest Park, the developer salvaged a market-rate subdivision whose builder went bankrupt by converting the project to federally subsidized ownership housing units.

New Communities Without Subsidized Housing. Developers' attitudes and policies in new communities without subsidized housing have ranged from active concern for the provision of moderate-income housing to outright hostility.

On three occasions The Irvine Company attempted to gain approval for housing projects aimed at moderate-income families. In each case, how-ever, the proposal was turned down—once by the Federal Housing Admin-istration, once by Orange County, and once by the City of Irvine. The company's interest in producing a balanced community, however, may be questioned. It has never offered to write down land costs, as was done in Columbia and Reston, and its advertising has never mentioned balance or openness as a community goal. Instead, since its inception, Irvine has been marketed as a high-income, homogeneous place to live.

Laguna Niguel's builder, Avco Community Developers, Inc., was the only other new community developer to indicate any interest in subsidized housing. The community's general plan projects that 25 percent of the market with incomes under $8,600 will be housed on scattered sites in Laguna Niguel. However, Avco has taken no action to implement this goal, and, like Irvine, has advertised the community as an upper middle-income residential settlement.

In other new communities developers have never seriously considered the question of income integration. For example, Frank Sharp has said that Sharpstown "is not that kind of community," and that there is no need for lower cost housing. The developers of Valencia have not planned to pro-vide subsidized housing because, "cash flow problems of new town de-velopment conflict with social goals." In a similar vein, American-Hawaiian Steamship Company has stated that the front-end costs of

Westlake Village were so large that housing could not feasibly be developed for the low-income owner.

Residents' Attitudes Toward Moderate-income Housing

One of the rationales for a policy of nonintegration is the commonly held belief that people prefer to live in socially homogeneous communities. Among new community residents as a whole, there is some evidence that this conclusion is correct in the case of integration by low-income households. When respondents were asked whether housing for low-income families (under $5,000) would harm their neighborhood (the area within one-half mile of their homes), over two thirds of the new community respondents thought that it would.[b] However, there was considerably less resistance expressed for neighborhood income integration by low-income retired families or moderate-income families with annual incomes between $5,000 and $10,000. In fact, in the latter case 65 percent of the respondents felt that housing for moderate-income white families would not harm their neighborhoods, and almost a majority, 49 percent, felt the same way about moderate-income black families.

What determines new community residents' attitudes toward neighborhood income and racial integration? The key variables that consistently accounted for the variance in attitudes were: (1) the existence of subsidized housing in the community; (2) the value of the respondent's dwelling unit; (3) whether the respondent owned or rented; and (4) the respondent's concern with his or her own social status.

Figure 5-4 shows the impact of the existence of subsidized housing on attitudes toward neighborhood income integration by families with annual incomes between $5,000 and $10,000. Residents of the communities with subsidized housing were significantly more receptive to income integration than were residents of new communities without such housing.[c] Although it is difficult to determine whether this striking difference in attitudes was due to contact with low-cost housing and its occupants within the community or self-selection of residents with more tolerant attitudes, the implications for

[b]There were two new communities in which less than a majority of the respondents thought that integration by low-income families would harm their neighborhoods. In Columbia, 38 percent of the respondents thought that their neighborhood would be harmed by low-income white families and 39 percent perceived harm from low-income black families. In Reston, 49 percent of the respondents thought that low-income white families would harm their neighborhood, while 53 percent perceived harm from low-income black families.

[c]Religious groups composed of Columbia and Reston residents were instrumental in securing the first subsidized housing projects in each community. Fifty percent of the Columbia respondents and 44 percent of those in Reston felt more money should be spent in their communities for low-income housing.

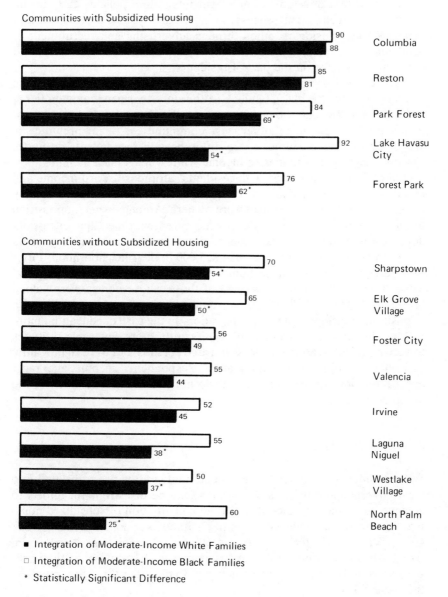

Percent of Respondents Who Feel That Housing for Moderate-Income
($5,000–$10,000) Families Would Not Harm Their Neighborhood

Communities with Subsidized Housing

90 / 88	Columbia
85 / 81	Reston
84 / 69*	Park Forest
92 / 54*	Lake Havasu City
76 / 62*	Forest Park

Communities without Subsidized Housing

70 / 54*	Sharpstown
65 / 50*	Elk Grove Village
56 / 49	Foster City
55 / 44	Valencia
52 / 45	Irvine
55 / 38*	Laguna Niguel
50 / 37*	Westlake Village
60 / 25*	North Palm Beach

■ Integration of Moderate-Income White Families
□ Integration of Moderate-Income Black Families
* Statistically Significant Difference

Figure 5-4. Attitudes Toward Neighborhood Income Integration of White
Families and Black Families

developer policies are clear-cut. If income integration is to be successful it is important that developers implement integration policies early in the community development process, or alternatively, make decisions that create a nonexclusionary ethos through advertising and recruitment of residents. As explained below, delay in implementation often leads to obdurate resistance on the part of residents.

Figure 5-4 also shows that residents were highly tolerant of integration of moderate-income black families in the only two new communities—Columbia and Reston—which had consistently advertised their open occupancy policies. In many other new communities, racial prejudice is suggested by the sometimes sharp differences in respondents' attitudes toward integration of moderate-income white versus black families.

Other factors associated with residents' attitudes toward income and racial integration should also be mentioned. Renters were more favorably inclined toward integration than were owners. Among owners, opposition to moderate-income housing sharply increased with the value of respondents' dwelling units. For example, respondents were asked if they would object to homes selling for less than $25,000 in their neighborhood. Fifty-two percent of those whose homes were valued between $25,000 and $30,000 objected, versus 74 percent of those whose homes were valued between $45,000 and $80,000. Status concern also correlated highly with opposition to income and racial integration. In the case of education, more highly educated respondents had significantly more favorable attitudes toward racial integration than less educated persons, but were significantly more likely to oppose class integration. Respondents' income, age, race, and occupation, on the other hand, do not account for as much of the variance in attitudes.

Governmental Policies

When residents' attitudes toward income integration are translated into local governmental policies, the results may be disastrous for efforts to achieve population balance through the construction of subsidized housing. In five of the eight communities without subsidized housing—Elk Grove Village, Foster City, Irvine, Laguna Niguel, and North Palm Beach—local government was instrumental in defeating or stifling proposals to build moderate-income housing. In the other three communities, the issue had not even arisen.

In November 1971, a housing commisission was established in Elk Grove Village after a series of shack fires had left a number of families homeless. It reported to the Village Board of Trustees that there was a need for 1,055 low- and 922 moderate-income housing units in the community. In January 1972, the trustees declared that the community had no responsibility for families who had lost their homes and no responsibility to provide housing within the means of persons employed in Elk Grove Village's large industrial complex. Two years later the chairman of the planning commission was not reappointed after he initiated discussions with the developer regarding the provision of moderate-income housing.

An Irvine Company proposal for moderate-income market housing was rejected by Orange County in 1970 on the grounds that proposed densities were too high. After Irvine incorporated, virtually the same proposal was submitted to the City Council. After a storm of resident protests, the City Council rejected the proposal, again because of the high density. Although Irvine's mayor has indicated that there is a need in the community for low-cost housing, the City Council has been adamantly opposed to participation in federal housing programs. Instead, it has insisted that The Irvine Company provide some nonsubsidized moderate-income housing in new villages.

Three proposals to build moderate-income housing in Foster City were rejected, first, because of poor soil conditions and second, because of cost restrictions due to the high tax rate in the community and zoning-density requirements. In order to increase the tax base, the city government has repeatedly stiffened building code requirements, and has also shifted proposed rental apartments to condominium units.

A proposal by the building firm of Kaufman and Broad for a 298-unit, moderate-income planned unit development in Laguna Niguel was amended out of existence by the Orange County Board of Supervisors after both the residents and Avco Community Developers, Inc. vigorously protested the construction of the units, which were to sell for $21,000 to $25,000. In 1971 a church group approached the North Palm Beach city government with a proposal for a subsidized housing project. The city responded that it did not want to get involved in any federal program.

Of course, not all local governments are opposed to moderate-income housing. Park Forest's city council took a leading role in securing an elderly housing project and did not oppose the second subsidized project built in the community. Local governments serving Columbia, Forest Park, and Lake Havasu City have generally not interfered in efforts to build subsidized units, and Fairfax County, which serves Reston, has taken an active role in promoting such housing. The Fairfax County Housing and Redevelopment Authority is sponsoring 50 units in Reston for families with incomes just above those who could qualify for public housing, and the County Board of Supervisors at one time required subdividers to reserve a certain proportion of their projects for low- and moderate-income housing. The key point, however, is that when a majority of the residents are opposed to subsidized housing, local government has usually accommodated their wishes.

State and federal policies also influenced the provision of subsidized housing in new communities. The most notable example of state involvement was the Illinois Housing Development Authority, which helped finance one of the subsidized housing projects in Park Forest. Acceptance of the project was eased by the agency's policy of combining monies from bonds floated on a statewide level with FHA Section 236 rental housing subsidies. Because of this method of financing, townhouses and apartments subsidized by IHDA offer better construction and a wide range of amenities not usually available under straight federal subsidy programs.

The federal government of course, played an instrumental role in achieving income integration in each of the new communities with subsidized housing. Without federal subsidy programs, below market rate housing would never have been constructed. In addition to this direct and obvious involvement, the relocation of federal facilities also provided a stimulus for the provision of moderate-income housing. Executive Order No. 11512 requires that sites for federal installations have an adequate supply of decent and nonsegregated housing within the area of expected residency and within price ranges affordable by an agency's employees. When the U.S. Geological Survey announced its proposed relocation to Reston, the Washington Metropolitan Housing Authority and the Housing Opportunities Council brought a class-action suit against the General Services Administration (GSA) and Gulf-Reston for noncompliance with this order. The suit resulted in an agreement by Gulf-Reston to provide 688 more subsidized housing units in the community. On the other hand, when the Department of Housing and Urban Development objected to GSA's acquisition of the North American Rockwell building in Laguna Niguel on similar grounds, GSA ruled that housing 20 to 25 miles away in Santa Ana was within commuting distance to the facility. It is conceivable that if the Orange County Fair Housing Council or some other group had brought suit against GSA, as was done in Reston, some moderate-income housing in Laguna Niguel might have resulted.

In summary, income and racial integration in new communities is feasible, both politically and economically, but it does not occur automatically. If integration is to occur, developers must incorporate integration policies into the initial plans for their communities. As Irvine and Laguna Niguel show, however, planning is not enough. In order for integration policies to be implemented successfully, resident support is vital. It is important that residents are aware of integration goals, and if possible, involved in the decisions regarding integration. If developers incorporate integration policies into their planning efforts, make public statements as to these goals, recruit a staff committed to them, and honestly market the community, they can create a viable integrated community. If they do not, the goal of population balance is no more likely to be achieved in new communities than in any other suburban setting.

6 Why People Move In—Why They Move Out

Why do people move to new communities? The answer to this question is of more than academic interest. If new communities are to thrive in the United States, they must capture significant proportions of the households in their primary market areas who are looking for new homes. To penetrate the market, developers have to know what consumers are looking for when they move to a new house or apartment, and then must provide a product that is at least as good as that offered by the competition.

New community development has been predicated on the belief that consumers can differentiate the new community product from housing in conventional communities and that such perceived differences will provide a competitive edge. Whether, and in what ways, consumers view the choice offered by new communities as different, however, has not fully been determined.

Screening Housing Alternatives

Before finally making up their minds about the home and community they will move to, many households examine a number of alternatives. The reasons respondents gave for not moving to these other places provide a glimpse as to why a new or conventional community was selected.

Four reasons were given by over 80 percent of the respondents for not choosing a home in other communities they had seriously considered during the housing search process. The most frequently given reason was that the cost of living, particularly the cost of housing and taxes, was too high in the other community. This was followed by, second, complaints about the housing; third, perceptions that the environment was crowded and unattractive; and fourth, feelings that the community was inconvenient to place of work or that it lacked job opportunities. Other reasons lagged far behind these four.

As shown in table 6-1, there was virtually no difference in the reasons given by new community respondents for rejecting conventional communities from those given by conventional community respondents for rejecting either new or other conventional communities. Thus, characteristics of the housing search do not suggest that consumers viewed new communities in a different light from other suburban alternatives.

117

Table 6-1

Reasons for Not Moving to Alternative Communities Considered During the Housing Search

| | *Percent of Households Who Cited Reason*[a] | | |
| | | *Conventional Communities* | |
Reasons	*New Communities*	*Considered New Community*[b]	*Total Sample*
Cost of living was too high—housing costs, taxes, prices generally	30	35	34
Housing—poorly constructed or designed, wrong types	26	23	28
Environment—crowded, unattractive, dirty, lack of amenities	13	19	15
Employment/work—inconvenient, lack of opportunity	12	13	13
Other facilities poor or inconvenient	5	3	5
Schools poor or inconvenient	4	8	4
Other reasons[c]	21	18	16

[a]Percents in each column may add to more than 100 percent because multiple responses were recorded for this open-ended question.

[b]Fifteen percent of the conventional community respondents who seriously considered another housing alternative had considered housing in a paired new community.

[c]Nine other reasons were each cited by 3 percent or less of the respondents in each group. These included: poor transportation; residents' racial, economic, or age composition, either too heterogeneous or too homogeneous; negative child-related factors; inconvenient recreational, shopping, or health facilities; and unsafe.

Choosing a Community

To determine which housing and community features were most important in households' decisions to move to a new or conventional community, respondents were given a list of 19 features and asked, "Thinking of what attracted you to this place, could you tell me which three of these factors were most important in your (family's) decision to move to this community (originally)?"

Key Reasons for Selecting a New Community

Surprisingly, there was no prevailing agreement among respondents about the features that attracted them to either the new or the conventional communities. In the aggregate, there was no single factor that attracted a majority of the respondents. In fact, not even a third of the new community households shared the same reason for choosing their community. Perhaps this can be expected, given the variation in community characteristics discussed in chapter 4. Nevertheless, even among individual new communities, it is noteworthy that there were only three cases in which a majority of the respondents cited at least one of the 19 features in common among the three most important factors that attracted them to the community. In short, even the same new community product tended to attract consumers for different reasons.

In spite of this variation, five features—the community as a good place to raise children, layout and space of the dwelling and lot, appearance of the immediate neighborhood, nearness to the outdoors and the natural environment, and community planning—may be viewed as the driving forces in attracting residents to new communities. They were associated with respondents' screening of alternative housing choices, and, as shown in table 6-2, were important in the final selection of a community. In addition, over 60 percent of the respondents said these features were better in the new community than the community from which they had moved.

The cost of the dwelling and convenience to work were frequently mentioned as reasons for having moved to a new community, but were often not improved as a result of the move. The pattern of responses for housing cost is easily interpreted. Improvements gained in other aspects of the community and dwelling, plus inflation, were likely to have resulted in a higher cost. Nevertheless, in selecting a new residence, each household had a budget constraint, which was used to eliminate some alternatives and to guide the final selection of a home.

Previous research has indicated that convenience to work is not an important motivation in households' decisions to move out of their previous residences and that people are willing to give up some convenience to work in order to achieve improvements in their dwelling and neighborhood (Lansing 1966; Thibeault, Kaiser, Butler, and McAllister 1973). At the same time, while being tolerant of some inconvenience, many households have a threshold limit beyond which they are not willing to commute to work, and which may be used to eliminate otherwise attractive housing choices. Thus, households use convenience to work in weighing the advantages and disadvantages of alternative housing choices, but evidently do not necessarily expect to improve their access to work as a result of the move.

Climate was a third factor cited by over 20 percent of the households as a reason for selecting a new community. However, it also was not improved by a majority of the households as a result of the move. The reason for this is that climate was an important consideration in choosing a new home only in the Southern California new communities, where respon-

Table 6-2
Reasons for Moving to New Communities

Reasons	New Community Households	
	Percent Who Mentioned Feature	Number of New Communities in Which Feature Was Mentioned by 20 Percent or More
Good place to raise children	31	13
Convenience to work	30	11
Layout and space of the dwelling and lot	28	10
Appearance of the immediate neighborhood	26	9
Nearness to the outdoors and the natural environment	26	7
Cost of buying (and financing) the dwelling or renting	24	6
Overall planning that went into the community	23	6
Climate	21	6
Public schools	15	3
Recreational facilities	12	2
Type of people living in the neighborhood	12	1
Shopping facilities	9	1
Construction of the dwelling	7	0
Ease of getting around the community	7	0
Safety from crime	6	0
Opportunities for participation in community life	5	0
Finding a job in the community	4	0
Cost of living in the community	2	0
Health and medical services	2	0

dents moved to get beyond the smog belt, and in Arizona and Florida new communities. Respondents living in these communities overwhelmingly felt that the climate was better than in their previous communities. On the other hand, very few respondents moved to new communities in Texas, the Midwest, or the East because of the climate, and very few felt the climate was any better than in their previous communities.

Other Reasons for Selecting a New Community

Several other features assumed some importance in respondents' decisions to move to particular new communities. For example, community recreational facilities were mentioned by 30 percent of the households who had moved to Lake Havasu City and by 21 percent of those who had moved to Irvine. Although only 12 percent of the new community respondents as a whole selected a community for this reason, recreation may be of more than marginal importance to prospective residents.

Recreational facilities ranked fifth among the features respondents reported they had improved as a result of the move to a new community (mentioned more often were overall planning of the community, layout and space of the dwelling and lot, appearance of the immediate neighborhood, and the community as a place to raise children). It is noteworthy, however, that recreational facilities was one of only two features (the other being community planning) that strongly differentiated the appeal of new communities from that the conventional communities.

Community schools were particularly important as a basis for the appeal of three older new communities—Elk Grove Village, Forest Park, and Park Forest—which had well developed school systems. Over 20 percent of the respondents in each community had moved there because of the character of the public schools. Although less than 10 percent of the new community households were attracted by community shopping facilities, 32 percent of those who moved to Sharpstown and 19 percent who had moved to Park Forest cited shopping as one of their reasons. Both communities have large regional shopping centers. In sum, while they must perform well on the five key factors that form the primary attraction of communities to consumers, new communities can strengthen their marketing appeal if they also develop other outstanding characteristics.

*What Distinguishes the Appeal of New Communities from
That of Conventional Communities?*

Overall, there was little difference in the key features that formed the appeal of new and conventional communities. With the exception of community planning, 20 percent or more of the conventional community respondents cited the same 8 features that were cited by 20 percent or more of the new community respondents. In fact, only 2 of the 19 housing and community characteristics—planning and recreational facilities—were mentioned significantly more often by new community respondents. Conventional community respondents, on the other hand, were significantly more likely to have moved to their communities because of layout and space of the dwelling, construction quality of their home or apartment, and cost of buying or renting. Except for community planning, which was mentioned by 16 percent more new community households, none of these differences was greater than 10 percent.

The lack of differentiation in the appeal of new and conventional communities was also apparent from comparisons of each new community with its paired conventional community. Planning and recreation were the only features mentioned significantly more often, on net, in new communities for more than two of the 13 paired comparisons. Layout and space of the dwelling and lot was the only feature mentioned significantly more often, on net, in the conventional communities for more than two of the paired comparisons.

It has often been assumed that consumers will be able to differentiate the new community product from the competition, but in most respects it does not appear that they are regarded by consumers as being very much different from other suburban communities offering housing in the same price ranges. The only major feature that distinguishes the new community product, planning, was not one of the top five reasons for moving to new communities as a whole. It was not mentioned by a majority of the respondents from even a single community as one of the three most important reasons for their housing selection. Thus, it does not appear that developers can rely on slogans, such as "New America" and "Tomorrow's City Today," to sell their products. Instead, they must offer consumers the same features they are looking for in conventional communities and, in these terms, provide a better housing and community product for the price charged.

Life-style and the Choice of a Home

The types of dwelling selected in new communities and reasons for the choice varied among households with differing life-styles. By taking into account what different types of household are likely to be looking for in a new home, planners can better match the housing mix and design features of a new community with the preferences of the households in its market area. In this way they can maximize the appeal of the community to prospective residents, and, hopefully, the pace of development and the financial success of the new community venture.

Who Moves to What Type of Housing?

The two factors with the strongest influence on the choice of housing type and tenure (whether to own or rent) were family income and life cycle-

Table 6-3
Family Income and Type of Housing Selected

Housing Type Selected	Income Group (Percent)			
	Below Average Under $10,000	Average $10,000-14,999	Above Average $15,000-24,999	Affluent $25,000+
Ownership	35	62	80	85
Single family	74	79	86	83
Townhouse	14	16	10	14
Apartment	12	5	4	3
Rental	65	38	20	15
Single family	5	11	15	27
Townhouse	20	18	30	27
Apartment	75	71	55	47

family type.[a] As shown in table 6-3, when families' incomes increased, they had a greater tendency to move to ownership units. For example, 65 percent of the households with below average (under $10,000) incomes moved to rental units. Sixty-two percent of those with average incomes ($10,000-$14,999), on the other hand, chose an ownership unit. The proportion of households who moved to ownership units increased to 80 percent of those households with above average incomes ($15,000-$24,999) and to 85 percent of the affluent (income of $25,000 or more) households.

For both owning and renting, higher family incomes were associated with selection of single-family detached homes. Seventy-four percent of the owners with incomes of less than $10,000 acquired a single-family home versus 86 percent of the homeowners with incomes of $15,000 to $24,999, and 83 percent of those with incomes of more than $25,000 had done so. Among renters, only 5 percent of the households with incomes of less than $10,000 moved to a single-family rental unit versus 27 percent of the households with incomes of $25,000 or more.

Lower income owners and renters were the households most likely to select a condominium or rental apartment. For example, 12 percent of the homeowners with below-average incomes, but only 3 percent of the affluent owners, chose to live in a condominium (ownership) apartment. While 75 percent of the renters with below-average incomes were living in rental apartments, only 47 percent of the affluent renters were occupying apartments. Finally, in the case of townhouses, there was little association

---

[a] In order to minimize changes in household characteristics after moving, analyses in this section are limited to those households who had moved to new communities during the three-year period prior to the household survey in the spring of 1973.

between income and selection of an ownership townhouse, between 10 percent and 16 percent of the households in each income bracket had done so, but renters with incomes of $15,000 and above were more likely to have occupied a rental townhouse than less affluent renters.

As illustrated in table 6-4, the choices of whether to own or rent and whether to move to a single-family detached dwelling, townhouse, or apartment were also associated with the stage of the households' life cycle and whether children were living at home. Single persons under age 40 without children were the most likely group to have selected a rental unit, and, when tenure is controlled, to have selected an ownership townhouse or a rental apartment. In contrast, married couples in the same age bracket and without children were much more likely to have chosen an ownership rather than a rental dwelling. Those who chose to own were probably anticipating children, since an overwhelming proportion (85 percent) moved to single-family detached homes. On the other hand, other young married couples who chose to rent overwhelmingly (79 percent) moved to rental apartments.

The influence of children in the household on the choice of tenure and housing type was striking. Eighty-five percent of the married couples with children living in the household selected a new community ownership unit, and of this 85 percent, 92 percent selected a single-family detached dwelling. Also, although relatively few married couples with children selected a rental unit, they had a higher proportion than any other group of renters in selecting single-family detached rental units. Single persons (usually divorced, separated, and widowed women) with children living in the household were less likely to own, probably because they had insufficient income to attain home ownership. Of those that did own, a relatively high proportion (77 percent) had moved to single-family detached dwellings. They were also the second most likely group of renters (after married couples with children) to have moved to rental single-family homes.

As with persons without children living in the household who were under age 40, the choice of owning or renting for those aged 40 and above was highly dependent on marital status. Eighty-one percent of the 40-and-over group who were married chose to own versus only 51 percent of the single persons in this age group. Among owners, married couples were more likely to have selected a single-family detached dwelling (62 percent) or condominium apartment (18 percent) than single persons, while the single persons were more likely to have moved to a townhouse (45 percent). Among the renters, the married couples were more likely to have selected a rental townhouse (42 percent versus 16 percent), while the single persons were more likely to have selected a rental apartment (84 percent versus 53 percent).

Table 6-4
Life Cycle-Family Type and Housing Type Selected

Housing Type Selected	Life Cycle-Family Type[a] (Percent)					
	Type 1	Type 2	Type 3	Type 4	Type 5	Type 6
Ownership	22	53	85	48	81	51
Single family	41	85	92	77	62	45
Townhouse	45	11	8	13	20	45
Apartment	14	4	0	10	18	10
Rental	78	47	15	52	19	49
Single family	3	0	27	17	5	0
Townhouse	15	21	27	25	42	16
Apartment	82	79	46	58	53	84

[a]Life cycle-family types:
Type 1—single persons under age 40 without children living in household
Type 2—married couples under age 40 without children living in household
Type 3—married couples of any age with children living in household
Type 4—single persons of any age with children living in the household
Type 5—married couples age 40 and over without children living in household
Type 6—single persons age 40 and over without children living in household

Reasons for the Choice

In many cases, the reasons households gave for moving to new communities varied by the type of dwelling unit selected. The exceptions were layout and space of the dwelling and lot, nearness to the outdoors, and appearance of the neighborhood, which were important in decisions to move to all types of housing; and opportunities for participation in community life, safety from crime, and the type of people living in the neighborhood, which were relatively unimportant, regardless of the housing type selected. The statistically significant differences in reasons for moving are enumerated in table 6-5.

Since households with children were most likely to have moved to single-family detached homes, it is not surprising that the community as a good place to raise children was given more often as a reason for having moved to a new community by households who selected a single-family ownership or rental unit. This factor was of somewhat less importance to townhouse owners and renters, though it was mentioned by 20 percent or more of the households in each case, and was of little importance to households who moved to condominium and rental apartments.

The tendency of single-family homeowners and renters to be involved in (or anticipating) child rearing is also related to the role of the public

Table 6-5
Reasons for Moving to New Communities by Housing Type Selected

Reasons for Moving to Community[a]	Percent of New Community Households					
	Own			Rent		
	Single Family	Town-house	Apart-ment	Single Family	Town-house	Apart-ment
Good place to raise children	38	20	0	33	24	11
Convenience to work	28	28	27	26	33	43
Cost of buying (and financing) the dwelling or renting	24	19	7	21	16	20
Overall planning that went into community	25	27	13	14	14	16
Climate	23	21	46	25	19	15
Public schools	16	6	0	28	6	6
Recreational facilities	9	17	22	13	22	18
Shopping facilities	6	5	19	8	11	13
Construction of the dwelling	6	3	17	5	6	7
Ease of getting around the community	4	7	22	1	13	11
Finding a job in the community	3	2	3	7	7	9
Cost of living in the community	1	5	0	0	1	3
Health and medical services	1	3	8	4	2	4

[a]Includes only those features for which differences among housing types were statistically significant. No significant differences were found for layout and space of the dwelling and lot, nearness to the outdoors and natural environment, appearance of the immediate neighborhood, opportunities for participation in community life, safety from crime, and the type of people living in the neighborhood.

schools in moving decisions. Sixteen percent of the single-family homeowners and 28 percent of those who moved to single-family rental units in new communities gave the public schools as a reason. In contrast, the schools were mentioned by 6 percent or less of the households who moved to ownership or rental townhouses and apartments.

The only community feature that tended to distinguish the reasons for moving of owners as a group from renters as a group was community planning (see chapter 8). Households who had moved to single-family and townhouse ownership units were almost twice as likely as renters to have done so because of the planning that went into the new community. This seems to be mainly due to the added security that planning brings to the housing investment. However, planning was not particularly important to the condominium apartment owners, who tended to be concentrated in North Palm Beach and Laguna Niguel. The tendency of condominium owners to live in these two communities, though, helps explain condominium owners' concern for the climate—they moved to North Palm Beach for the Florida sun and to Laguna Niguel for its lack of smog. Also, the somewhat older age of respondents living in Laguna Niguel and North Palm Beach may account for the greater concern with health and medical services revealed by condominium apartment owners.

Shopping and recreational facilities tended to be given much more consideration in the moving decisions of households who selected higher density housing than in the decisions of households who moved to single-family detached dwellings. This also tended to be the case for the perceived ease of getting around the community as a reason for moving to a new community. These attractions were anticipated, since in giving up the privacy and personal outdoor space associated with single-family homes, households moving to rental townhouses and apartments would likely expect to achieve greater convenience. Also, rental townhouses and apartments were most likely to be selected by households without children, who might naturally be expected to pursue more leisure-oriented life-styles than the child-centered families who tended to move to single-family detached housing.

Finally, renters in general and households who had moved to rental townhouses and apartments, in particular, were those most likely to have moved to a new community because of its convenience to their place of work or because they thought there would be jobs available in the community. Convenience to work was cited most often by apartment renters who were single persons under age 40 without children (50 percent) and by married couples under age 40 without children (62 percent) as a reason for moving to a new community. For these two groups, apartment living was probably viewed as a temporary situation prior to moving to an ownership single-family detached home or townhouse or out of the community; hence, their overriding concern with convenience. Ease of finding a job was cited most often by households with below-average family incomes—15 percent—as a reason for selecting a new community rental apartment. This group might naturally be expected to be more concerned about the availability of jobs, and, of course, had few other housing choices outside of rental apartments.

The preceding discussion clearly shows why there was so little agreement among respondents as to the key reasons for their move to a new community. Different types of households moving to different types of housing had specific needs they hoped to meet in the selection of a home and community. By taking these revealed preferences into account, new community developers should be more able to optimize community design and marketing decisions.

Moving Out of New Communities

To this point, the discussion here and in the preceding chapter has focused on people moving into new communities. However, the characteristics of people moving out and their reasons for moving are also important. The population profile of a new community is affected by the characteristics of out-movers as well as by those moving into the community. Thus, those concerned with population balance must attend to departing households being lost to new communities as well as new arrivals and permanent settlers.

It has also been hypothesized that new communities will tend to attract highly transient populations. For example, in a Rand Corporation report, Peter Morrison has suggested that,

By attracting both young and hypermobile residents, a new city would develop a markedly transient population base composed precisely of the most likely candidates for further movement. . . . and it is probable that new cities would function more as migratory way stations than as permanent settlements (1970, p. 24).

If this hypothesis is correct, it has serious implications for the formation and maintenance of stable institutions in new communities.

The Rate of Prospective Mobility

While the actual rate of out-mobility cannot be determined from a survey taken at one point in time, estimates can be derived by examining households' moving intentions. The rate of moving intentions in the 13 new communities is shown in table 6-6, where it is compared with the 13 conventional communities.[b]

Moving intentions were only slightly higher in new than in the conventional communities. In fact, the difference between households in these two settings disappears altogether once differences in tenure and age of household heads are taken into consideration. This lack of difference in

[b]To determine their moving intentions, respondents were asked, "How likely are you to move from this place in the next two or three years? Are you certain to move, will you probably move or do you plan to stay here?" Whether respondents planned also to move out of the community, as opposed to moving out of "this place" (dwelling unit) was not determined.

Table 6-6
Moving Intentions

Reported Likelihood of Moving Within Two to Three Years	Percent of Respondents	
	New Communities	Conventional Communities
Certain to move	17 ┐	14 ┐
Probably move	19 ──┤42	17 ──┤38
Don't know	6 ┘	7 ┘
Plan to stay	58	62

the rate of prospective mobility also obtained when each new community was individually compared with its paired conventional community. The only exceptions were the Park Forest-Lansing pair, where 23 percent more Park Forest residents were probable movers in the next two to three years; and the Sharpstown-Southwest Houston pair, where 16 percent more Sharpstown residents planned to move.

Both the new and conventional community findings are comparable to the findings of metropolitan mobility research conducted during the 1950s and 1960s. The two- to three-year prospective mobility rate of 42 percent among the new community households is bracketed by the 48 percent five-year prospective mobility rate found by John B. Lansing, Eva Mueller, with Nancy Barth (1964) and Lansing (1966) in two national metropolitan area samples in 1963 and 1965; and the average of 24 percent in one-year prospective mobility rates found by Peter H. Rossi (1955), Maurice Van Arsdol, Jr., Georges Sabagh, and Edgar W. Butler (1968), Butler, F. Stuart Chapin, Jr., George C. Hemmens, Edward J. Kaiser, Michael A. Stegman, and Shirley F. Weiss (1969), and David P. Varady (1973). Thus, there is no evidence of Morrison's prophecy that new communities will serve only as migratory way stations rather than as permanent settlements. New community residents were no more transient than the conventional community residents or metropolitan area residents in general.

Based on the moving intentions of respondents and findings from past metropolitan mobility research, the actual rate of residential mobility can be estimated. It has been established that somewhere between 70 percent and 80 percent of the households who say that they are going to move actually match their intentions by subsequently moving. On the other hand, 20 percent to 30 percent of those who think they will stay in their dwellings have been found to subsequently move over a two- to three-year period. Using these figures, it appears that about 38 percent of the new community households interviewed in 1973 will actually move by 1976.

Who Is Planning to Move Out?

Households who intended to move were not representative of the new community population as a whole. Renters, apartment dwellers, younger households, those living in less well maintained dwellings, and those who had moved in more recently were more likely to be planning to move than other residents. These findings are consistent with other research on residential mobility.

However, the relationship between dwelling type and plans to move is spurious. It is totally due to tenure, which happens to be associated with dwelling type as well as with plans to move. With dwelling type eliminated, tenure is clearly the most significant factor associated with moving intentions. Renters were four to five times more likely than owners to be planning a certain move within two to three years, regardless of whether they were renting a single-family detached house or apartment, and regardless of the age of the head of the household.

When both tenure and age were controlled, several other household characteristics were associated with moving intentions. For example, black owners and young blacks were significantly more likely to plan to stay than nonblack owners and young nonblacks. Combined with the increasing rate of black in-migration to new communities noted in chapter 5, this may result in somewhat greater racial integration in new communities than has been experienced to this time.

Duration of residence was not associated with the prospective mobility of owners, but was an important factor in the mobility intentions of renters. That is, renters who were more recent in-movers were the most likely to plan on moving again; longer term renters were next most likely; and owners were the least likely to plan on moving, regardless of how long they had lived in their current residence. Finally, the inclination to move of the single person, the young, and those living in more poorly maintained buildings was dampened among owners, though it remained strong among renters.

Why Households Were Planning to Move

The reasons people gave for planning to move were generally the same as those given by potential movers among the conventional community respondents. In order of the frequency mentioned, they included: (1) expected change in job situation (33 percent of the new community respondents); (2) more space in the dwelling was needed (26 percent); (3) desired tenure change—especially the desire to own instead of rent (17 percent); (4) dissatisfaction with characteristics of the physical environment (16 percent); and (5) expected changes in family composition, such as marriage, divorce, or additional children who required more space (8 percent). The only reason cited significantly more often by conventional community respondents was dissatisfaction with characteristics of the environment (mentioned by 22 percent of these respondents).

Reasons for planning to move were in some cases associated with household characteristics and housing type. For example, nonblacks were almost twice as likely as blacks to cite employment reasons; owners and dwellers in single-family detached dwellings were more likely than others to cite the need for a large place; owners, nonblacks, and those less satisfied with the community as a place to live were more likely to mention the quality of the environment; and, of course, renters, especially apartment dwellers, most commonly cited the desire to own their home.

In addition to examining the reasons households gave for their moving intentions, 29 variables measuring residential satisfaction and ratings of the dwelling, neighborhood, and community were considered in relation to prospective mobility. As expected, households least satisfied with their residential situation were most likely to have moving intentions. However, dissatisfaction with some aspects of the residential package and community led more directly to prospective mobility than did others. In general, summary expressions of dissatisfaction were better predictors of mobility intentions than were dissatisfactions with specific aspects of the dwelling, neighborhood, and community. Dissatisfaction with the dwelling had the strongest effect on mobility intentions, followed by dissatisfaction with the neighborhood, which, in turn, was more important than dissatisfaction with various aspects of the community.

In the case of dwelling unit satisfaction, dissatisfaction with outdoor privacy had the strongest relationship with prospective mobility, followed by dissatisfaction with indoor space and dissatisfaction with outdoor space. Respondents' rating of their dwelling as a financial investment was less important. A number of neighborhood characteristics were also associated with prospective mobility. The most important were respondents' assessments of the pleasantness, privacy, reputation, attractiveness, and maintenance of their immediate neighborhoods. Finally, among the communitywide factors, ratings of the community as a place to raise children and expectations regarding young adults' ratings of the community were most associated with respondents' moving intentions. Other community variables, such as satisfaction with church and religious facilities, ratings of recreational facilities, schools, shopping facilities, and homes associations, were much less important.

When tenure, housing type, respondents' personal characteristics, and their ratings of their home, neighborhood, and community were analyzed together, tenure emerged as the strongest factor in moving plans. The relationship between tenure and moving was undiminished by respondents' satisfaction with various aspects of their home and community. Furthermore, tenure seems to have an effect on the relationship between the other strong correlates of prospective mobility. Age of head, life cycle-family type, duration of residence, dissatisfaction with neighborhood and community, and conditions of the dwelling all had a lesser influence on prospective mobility for owners than for renters.

Beyond tenure, the young were more mobile, as well as those who were dissatisfied, especially with the dwelling itself. Job changes were the most likely reason for moving, being cited by one out of three prospective movers. It is noteworthy that these are all factors in which new communities do not differ much from other communities. Developers, however, may reduce out-migration to some extent by increasing housing and neighborhood satisfactions and providing more job opportunities.

Part III

Planning and Governance

7

Community Planning from the Residents' Perspective

One of the reasons for the widespread appeal of new communities is the opportunity to plan for the orderly growth of large tracts of suburban and rural land. Unlike conventional urban growth, where planning often follows and is shaped by initial settlement patterns, a distinguishing feature of new communities is preplanning. Before the first home is sold and the first residents arrive, the new community exists on paper. A master plan has been prepared, which organizes land uses into a system of hierarchical units—clusters, neighborhoods, and villages—and provides a blueprint of the community 20 or more years in the future when development had been completed.

The Central Role of Planning in New Community Development

New community development has been described as the "master plan's last stand" (Godschalk 1973b). This comment not only illustrates the crucial importance of new community plans, but also the periodic criticism that has been directed toward the concept of developer-controlled, long-range, comprehensive planning. Why, when the future is generally unknown, has the master plan played such a central role in new community development? To answer this question it is useful to look at the functions the master plan serves in the development process.

A number of acts of faith are involved in building a new community (Simon 1971). The developer must believe that he can assemble land for his community, arrange financing, secure the necessary approvals from local government, manage the development process, market the product, and in the end make a profit. Financing new community development involves a considerable risk. Investors who provide the front-end money and long-term capital, which make development possible, must believe that a proposed new community venture will succeed and that they will get an acceptable return on their investment. Local officials, who must approve vast land use changes and commit the resources of their jurisdictions to provide public services, must have faith that a proposed new community will offer a better future for their citizens than alternative modes of growth. They must also have faith that projected property tax revenues to finance

135

the principal and carrying charges on public investments will actually materialize. Finally, the consumer who moves to a new community, which in the initial stages may be little more than a sea of mud and a cacophony of grinding earth-moving machinery, must believe that out of this beehive of activity and landscape disarray a desirable place to live will emerge.

All these professions of faith are made easier by the existence of a comprehensive plan for the new community's future. The plan embodies the developer's concepts for the product he is about to create, and provides a link between characteristics of the site and market on the one hand, and the economic models that guide actual development decisions on the other. In combination, the master plan and economic models indicate how development can be most efficiently staged and allow the developer to program housing in different price ranges and for different life-styles for specific areas of the community. The phasing of development and projected cash flows offer investors assurance (on paper) that the proposed new community is economically viable.

The new community master plan provides local officials and consumers with an image of the completed product. This image is often of critical importance in convincing officials to rezone large land areas. Development phasing embodied in the master plans and economic models also gives officials the opportunity to base future public actions on the developer's performance, as well as on the cumulative experience gained during successive stages of the community's growth. Finally, the master plan has proven to be an invaluable tool in new community marketing. The plan usually describes the advantages of the proposed community in appealing terms. It assures the consumer that he is making the right choice by moving to a new community and that his housing investment will be protected.

In spite of its many advantages, the concept of a new community master plan has been subjected to occasional criticism. It has been observed that,

Proponents of planning have come more and more to see planning as a dynamic process, which enables decision-makers to be better prepared to cope with exigencies as they arise. Too often the planning process for new communities has been the opposite. It has been an attempt to bind the community builder and the occupants of new communities to a preconceived set of notions about what suburban life ought to be (Eichler and Kaplan 1967, p. 10).

Building on the concept of planning as a process rather than the projection of optimal end states, David R. Godschalk (1973b) has proposed that an adaptive planning procedure be substituted for the traditional new community master plan. As most planners and developers realize, the life span of new community master plans tends to be rather short. Changing circumstances lead to continual revisions and modifications in the plan. Not the least of these changing circumstances is the increasing number of residents living in a new community. As soon as the residents gain control of local land use regulations and planning mechanisms, they are likely to develop their own plan for the future development of their community.

The remainder of this chapter explores citizens' perspectives of new community planning. Four broad topics are addressed. The first is the master plan's role in attracting residents to live in new communities. Next, residents' awareness of community planning is explored, including their knowledge of neighborhood development plans and their sources of information about community planning matters. Two alternative concepts of citizens' relationship to the master plan are then examined. One views the master plan as an informal contract between the developer and community residents, which assures the residents that the future community they contracted for in their home-purchase or rental agreements will actually be built as planned. An alternative viewpoint distinguishes between residents' roles as passive consumers of planning and their roles as active participants in the planning process. The activists' point of view rejects the static consumer contract concept in favor of a dynamic planning process based on the mutual exchange of ideas and information between the developer's planners and the residents. New perspectives on both viewpoints, based on new community residents' actual perceptions, are offered. The chapter then concludes by contrasting residents' assessments of the quality of planning in new and conventional communities.

Planning and the Attraction of New Communities

New community developers' marketing efforts are often designed to make consumers aware of the planned character of the community. However, as shown in the preceding chapter, overall community planning was not one of the top five reasons for consumers' decisions to move to new communities. Mentioned by 23 percent of the respondents, planning ranked behind perceptions of the community as a good place to raise children, convenience to work, layout and space of the dwelling and lot, appearance of the immediate neighborhood, nearness to the outdoors and natural environment, and the cost of buying or renting.

The importance of community planning in persuading consumers to settle in a new community is closely associated with a community's place on the new community continuum. As illustrated in figure 7-1, consumers were more likely to move to a new community because of its overall planning if the community embraced more aspects of the new community concept.[a] Community planning also sharply distinguished the appeal of

---

[a] Park Forest is an exception. However, a large proportion of this community's present population moved there after active development had been completed.

new communities from that of conventional developments. For 10 of the 13 paired comparisons shown in figure 7-1, consumers were significantly more likely to have moved to a new community because of its planning than to its paired conventional community. Schaumburg (paired with Elk Grove Village) was the only conventional community that attracted more than 15 percent of its residents because of its overall community planning. As noted in chapter 4, Schaumburg had a very active and well-publicized community planning program.

What accounts for the importance consumers attach to community planning? One hypothesis is that planned communities are seen by consumers as the modern-day equivalent of restricted communities. According to researchers at the University of California, consumers view the amenities provided as part of the new community package as a way to add physical symbols of socioeconomic status to the appearance of the community. Consumers are said to view community planning as a technique for preventing these symbols from being destroyed or contaminated by the addition of lower priced residential developments or by the intrusion of unsightly commercial and industrial facilities (Werthman, Mandel, and Dienstfrey 1965). This view of planning emerged from a study of residents who had moved to Foster City and Janss/Conejo (now Thousand Oaks) in California.

Among the broader sample of new communities used in the present study there is some evidence that residents value planning as a means of insuring the stability of their neighborhoods. For example, consumers who moved to a new community because of its planning were significantly more likely than others to agree strongly with the statement, "The major advantage of living in a highly planned community is that you don't have to worry that the character of your neighborhood will change for the worse." Thus, to some consumers planning is a form of insurance against an unknown future. Persons who valued this insurance and were most likely to move to a new community because of its planning tended to have higher family incomes and to be moving to higher priced single-family homes. Planning was less important in the moving decisions of renters and persons with lower incomes.

There is also some indirect evidence that planning may be valued for its social class connotations. Persons who moved to new communities because of their overall planning were more likely than persons who moved for other reasons to say that they cared what kind of housing was built within one-half mile of their homes. In the California new communities only, they were also more likely to say that they preferred neighbors with the same levels of education.

However, it should be noted that countervailing evidence also exists. Planning was most often cited as a reason for having moved to a new

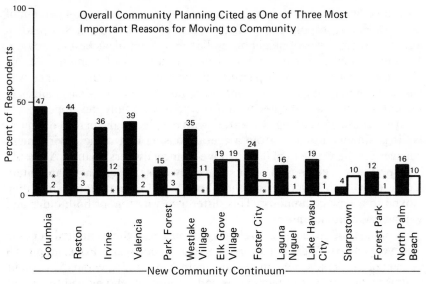

● New Community
□ Conventional Community
* Statistically Significant Difference

Figure 7-1. Importance of Planning in Decision to Move to Community

community by younger persons with more years of formal education, who were also more tolerant of neighborhood racial integration than persons who moved to new communities for other reasons. In addition, persons who moved to new communities because of their planned character were no more likely than other in-movers to be overly concerned with their own social status.

Residents' Awareness of Planning

Although less than half of the residents of new communities moved there because of the character of community planning, a majority said they were aware of neighborhood development plans when they moved. Consumers' attention to planning before moving was strongly related to a community's stage of development. For example, 77 percent of the Valencia respondents and 74 percent of those living in Westlake Village and Foster City claimed that they knew about neighborhood plans when they moved to these communities. Sixty percent or more of the respondents living in other new communities in earlier stages of the development process, such as Columbia, Reston, Irvine, and Laguna Niguel, also claimed to have been aware of neighborhood plans. On the other hand, people who moved to older, more fully developed new communities were less concerned. Only 14 percent of the Park Forest respondents and 22 percent of those living in Sharpstown informed themselves of neighborhood development plans before moving. This again seems to relate to the insurance function of planning. People were more concerned with planning if the area around their homes was vacant or undergoing development, since the threat of adverse changes in the environment was greater than if the area were fully developed.

Awareness of planning also varied with people's stake in the community. It is simpler to move from a rental housing unit if the environment changes for the worse than it is to move from an ownership unit. As would be expected, a much higher proportion of owners (58 percent) than renters (36 percent) were aware of neighborhood development plans when they moved to a new community. This difference was true of both older and younger new communities.

A number of other factors related to tenure also differentiated persons who were and who were not aware of neighborhood plans. For example, 58 percent of the persons who moved to single-family units, versus 52 percent of those who moved to townhouses and 36 percent who moved to garden apartments, informed themselves of plans before moving to their homes. Higher proportions of persons who had family incomes of $30,000 or more (68 percent) than those with incomes under $12,500 (37 percent); who acquired homes valued at $40,000 or more (71 percent) than those whose homes were worth less than $25,000 (33 percent); and who were between 35 and 54 years old (59 percent) than those under 25 years old (34 percent) were aware of neighborhood plans.

These differences in residents' concern for planning have serious implications for efforts to secure greater citizen participation in the planning process. Unless planners make a particularly strong effort to involve renters and less affluent residents, their interests may not be represented in mutual exchanges with the developer.

How Well Have Residents Been Informed?

Once people have settled in a new community, their awareness of planning depends on both their interest in community planning matters and the efforts of the developer, local government, and the media to keep the citizens informed. In every new community studied except Sharpstown a majority of the respondents felt they had been kept adequately abreast of plans for future developments in the vicinity of their homes. It is also noteworthy that new community residents were significantly more likely than residents of conventional communities (66 percent versus 57 percent) to feel that they had enough information about plans for future community development.

Nevertheless, the fact that a sizable proportion of the respondents in every community, ranging from 53 percent in Sharpstown to 14 percent in Park Forest, indicated a desire for more information about future plans, indicates that planners and developers could be a better job of keeping the citizens up to date. How they might do this is suggested by residents' current sources of planning information.

Where Residents Get Their Information

In 10 of the 13 new communities a majority of the residents felt local newspapers were the most reliable source of information about neighborhood development plans. See table 7-1. Papers that were particularly effective in keeping their readers informed included *The Columbia Times* and other papers in that community, *Park Forest Star, Elk Grove Village Herald, Foster City Progress,* and *Forest Park News.* In all of these communities 61 percent or more of the residents said that the local paper was their best source of planning information. In new communities without a community paper, such as North Palm Beach, Laguna Niguel, Sharpstown, Valencia, and Westlake Village, fewer residents saw the news media as their best source of information.

Homes and community associations were another important source of planning information. For example, Irvine community association leaders met regularly with city officials and with representatives of the developer to discuss planning and other matters of interest to their members. It is noteworthy that 31 percent of the Irvine respondents cited their homes association as the best source of planning information. Other communities in which homes associations played a major role in keeping residents informed about planning matters included Laguna Niguel, North Palm Beach, Westlake Village, and Valencia. All of these communities have well developed systems of neighborhood homes or condominium associations. On the other hand, the developer-controlled associations in Columbia and Reston were not relied upon as heavily. In those communities where relatively few residents cited homes associations as their best source of information very few associations were in existence.

Surprisingly few new community residents nominated the developer as their best source for information about neighborhood plans. This seems to indicate rather low direct efforts by developers to plan with their residents. On the other hand, the developers' efforts may be understated, since planning meetings with local governmental and homes association leaders would normally be reported in the news media and association newsletters.

A final source of information residents relied on was their family and friends. Word of mouth is well known to developers as an important basis for home sales. As shown in table 7-1, it also plays a role in informing residents about planning.

Table 7-1
Sources of Information About Planning

New Community	Most Reliable Sources of Information (Percent of Respondents)					
	Newspaper	Family and Friends	Homes Association	Developer	Radio/TV	Other
New communities	61	14	14	6	2	3
Conventional communities	55	18	15	3	2	7
Columbia	71	7	9	10	1	2
Reston	58	17	13	7	2	3
Irvine	54	8	31	2	0	4
Valencia	53	19	18	6	1	3
Park Forest	83	10	3	1	1	2
Westlake Village	48	16	21	8	1	6
Elk Grove Village	76	14	3	4	2	1
Foster City	80	12	3	2	0	3
Laguna Niguel	40	18	31	7	0	4
Lake Havasu City	57	17	4	10	5	7
Sharpstown	64	13	5	5	6	7
Forest Park	74	12	3	6	3	2
North Palm Beach	47	10	28	11	3	1

In sum, there appear to be a number of ways of getting planning matters before a new community's residents, though two seem particularly relevant for planners interested in maintaining closer contact with the citizens. Encouraging the establishment of a community newspaper and providing the paper with up-to-date information about the status of planning decisions is one. A second promising approach, as demonstrated by the Irvine experience, is to form neighborhood homes associations and meet regularly with their leaders. Direct developer contacts with residents through community forums and other such devices is a third possible approach. However, they suffer from the likelihood of citizen apathy—so that the majority of residents remain uninformed—and from logistical problems as a community's population grows.

The Illusive Goal of Citizen Participation

Several years ago the Twentieth Century Fund formed a task force to study the social and political issues involved in new community planning and development. In its report, *New Towns: Laboratories for Democracy,* the task force challenged the conventional wisdom that planning and development come first, followed by citizen participation. In fact, the task force recommended that "New towns should experiment with different and novel means of broadening and strengthening participation by people in planning, developing and governing their urban environment" (Twentieth Century Fund Task Force on Governance of New Towns 1971, p. 12).

Citizen participation, as a basic democratic principle, has had few detractors. Nevertheless, citizen involvement in new community planning decisions has been an illusive goal. During the initial stages of development there are few residents on the scene to share decisions with the developer and his planners. Having gained approval from local authorities for the community's initial master plan, the developer is anxious to get started with construction and land sales. Time and cost factors both weigh against initiating a planning dialogue with the early residents. Also, there is a difficult philosophical question: What standing do the first residents, who comprise a small portion of a community's ultimate population, have to make irrevocable decisions that will shape the living environment of succeeding residents?

Later in the development process, of course, public participation in at least some planning decisions is difficult to avoid. Increasing confidence in the market success of the community and desires for involvement voiced by residents led Columbia's developer to consult with residents in planning the Village of Owen Brown. In Reston the citizens participated in the planning of the Hunters Woods Village Center. In other communities, incorporation has shifted control of land use decisions from county government to the residents. Formal interaction between the developer and the residents' elected representatives assures the citizens some voice in planning. For example, in chapter 4 it was noted that The Irvine Company's 1970 general plan for a projected 430,000 residents was revised by the city of Irvine's 1973 general plan, which proposed three options for future development of the community. Other new communities whose municipal governments have adopted their own plans for future development include: Elk Grove Village, Forest Park, Foster City, Park Forest, and Westlake Village (the Thousand Oaks portion of the community).

The Planning Contract versus Citizen Involvement

Residents' participation in new community planning can be evaluated from two perspectives—the resident as a consumer of plans prepared by the developer and local government and the resident as a citizen and potential participant in planning processes.

Much of the conventional thought about the residents' place in new community development centers on their roles as consumers of developer-planned and packaged communities. Royce Hanson has described the market-oriented, consumer view of resident participation as follows:

In the new town as a market, the consumer votes with his money on whether to ratify the developer's and parent government's zoning and building decisions. He has no responsibility, moral or political, for the initial construction. He has no previous stake in the community. He purchases a dwelling unit, and as a consumer he is entitled to receive what he bought—a house plus other amenities. His homeowner's dues are a part of the market transaction, and he is still engaged, as an association member, in a producer-consumer contract. If his home or the amenities prove unsatisfactory, as a consumer he can first complain and seek to demonstrate that it is the producer's responsibility to improve his product. He ultimately retains the right of selling out, probably at a profit, and seeking a better place elsewhere. As a consumer he is not responsible for the future development of his community, and he has little or no direct and official responsibility for the decisions made about development, population mix and other matters affecting the community at large (Hanson 1971, pp. 61-62).

This view of resident participation is essentially consistent with the master plan approach to new community development and with the function of the plan as insurance against unforeseen and undesirable changes in the community. Resident-initiated efforts to change the plan, as Richard Brooks (1971) has noted of Columbia, may be viewed by consumers as unwarranted tampering with the product they purchased. From the consumers' perspective the key evaluative question is whether the developer has kept his part of the bargain and followed through with the plan.

Of course, not all residents see themselves as passive consumers of the developer's planning efforts. About 5 percent of the new community respondents, and over 10 percent of those who moved to Columbia and Reston, settled in a new community specifically for the opportunities it afforded for community participation. These residents would no doubt argue that they purchased the right to take part in planning decisions. From the activists' point of view citizenship should take precedence over consumership. In this case, the key evaluative question is not whether the plan has been followed, but whether community residents feel that they can successfully influence land development decisions.

Residents' Perceptions of the Planning Contract

A majority of the residents who were aware of neighborhood development plans when they moved to new communities felt that the plans had been subsequently followed. As shown in figure 7-2, new community residents were also somewhat more likely than those living in conventional communities to feel that the planning contract had been kept, though none of the differences quite reaches statistical significance at the 0.05 level of confidence.

Perceptions of deviations from neighborhood development plans were greatest in six new communities—Foster City, Laguna Niguel, Valencia, Westlake Village, Sharpstown, and Reston—where 25 percent or more of the respondents reported that changes had occurred. These six include every one of the new communities in which ownership of the development company changed after completion of the original master plan.[b] In addition to changes initiated by new developers, residents might have been upset by the failure to complete promised or master plan-designated facilities. For example, school construction fell far behind schedule in Foster City, Laguna Niguel, and Reston (see chapter 12). Some residents who moved to these communities expecting to live in close proximity to schools were disappointed when construction was delayed.

Also, the slower than anticipated pace of development due to sales problems in Laguna Niguel, Valencia, and Westlake Village led their developers to cut back on the provision of some facilities and to delay the completion of others. Contributing to a third cause of discontent were overt actions by the developers, which were bound to arouse the residents' ire. In

---

[b] New communities that have changed ownership (and the year of the change) include: Reston (1967); Foster City (1970); Laguna Niguel (1971); and Westlake Village (1973). The circumstances surrounding these changes are described in chapter 4.

Believe Neighborhood Has Been Developed
in Accordance with Plans

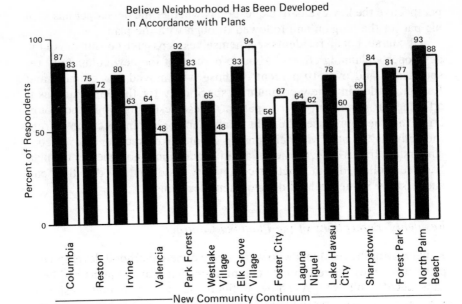

■ New Community
□ Conventional Community
* Statistically Significant Difference[a]

[a]None at the 0.05 level of confidence in this figure.

Figure 7-2. Residents' Perception of the Planning Contract

Sharpstown, for instance, the developer attempted to convert the community's golf course to multifamily housing. In Westlake Village and Laguna Niguel the proposed and actual construction of smaller and lower priced housing units led to some resident outcries.

New communities that scored best in terms of residents' perceptions that plans had been followed tended to be older communities and communities in which the developer had given careful attention to consultations with the citizens before launching new projects. For example, four of the five new communities in which development began prior to 1960 were among those where 80 percent or more of the respondents felt that neighborhood plans had been followed. The greater stability of these communities probably accounts for this result. The other two new communities that scored that highly, Columbia and Irvine, have both devoted a considerable amount of attention and staff time to working closely with the residents on the location and design of new housing projects and facilities.

Residents' Perceptions of Their Ability to Influence
Development Decisions

In general, new community planning processes have not been designed to give the residents a feeling of confidence that they can affect development decisions. Likening new communities to company towns, Godschalk has written,

Behind the semi-democratic facade, the new-town development corporation seeks to control both the economics and politics of the development. This is a variant of the unitary power system that has characterized American company towns, where pluralistic democracy never got started because residents never could accumulate enough of a stake to get into the civic game. While the new-town developer does not directly control most residents' jobs as in a company town, it could be argued that influence over the economics of new-town development takes on a similar importance in shaping the educational, recreational, cultural, and civic activities of the family. To protect the investment of the new-town developer and his financial backers, including the federal government in some cases, the balance usually gets tipped toward unitary corporate power and away from active citizen participation (Godschalk 1973, p. 199).

To evaluate residents' ability to influence community development decisions respondents were asked whether they could do anything to prevent a project that would seriously harm their neighborhood, and, if so, what they thought of their chances of success. The results summarized in figure 7-3 give some credence to the unitary power hypothesis. In only one of the 13 new communities, North Palm Beach, did more than half of the respondents feel that they would have a good or very good chance of preventing a harmful project from being built in their neighborhoods.

On the other hand, if new communities have not encouraged citizen competence to influence development, the same can be said for conventional urban development. As figure 7-3 shows, there was little difference in the proportions of new and conventional community respondents who felt they could prevent a threatening development. Apparently the impotence of citizens when they confront private developers is not a product of new community development, or their company town features, but is instead a more broadly based phenomenon in our society.

Residents' perceptions that they could successfully influence development decisions varied among new communities. At the high end of the spectrum were North Palm Beach, Irvine, Park Forest, Reston, and Westlake Village. Both North Palm Beach and Park Forest are older new communities in which the developer was no longer active. Also, both had municipal governments that controlled land use decisions. Irvine, as noted above, was characterized by a strong municipal planning operation, very

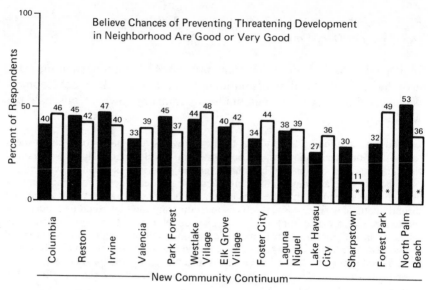

Figure 7-3. Residents' Perception of Their Ability to Influence Development Decisions

active community associations organized at the neighborhood level, and a developer who worked closely with the residents. Westlake Village was partially incorporated and also had a series of neighborhood homes associations that represented their residents' interests. In addition, the Westlake associations had formed the Westlake Joint Board to present a united front in lobbying with the developer and local government. Although Reston did not have a municipal government that controlled land use decisions (the Fairfax County Board of Supervisors had this power), an effective citizen interest group maintained a careful watch over the developer's activities. Formed in 1967 when Robert Simon, Jr. was replaced by Gulf-Reston, Inc., the Reston Community Association gained recognition from the county as a legitimate spokesman for Reston residents and was also periodically consulted by the developer.

The experience of these communities suggests several elements that may give new community residents greater confidence that they can participate in shaping their community's future. These include: (1) a municipal government that regulates land use and is close to the residents, as in North Palm Beach, Park Forest, and Irvine; (2) citizens' associations that represent the residents' interests before the developer and local government, as in Irvine, Westlake Village, and Reston; and (3) a developer who is no longer active, as in North Palm Beach and Park Forest, or who makes it a practice to consult with the residents, as in Irvine and to a lesser extent in Reston and Westlake Village.

Columbia, Elk Grove Village, and Laguna Niguel occupied intermediate levels in the spectrum of citizen confidence. Columbia has been characterized by its developer's willingness to work with the residents, but land use regulations were controlled at the county level and independent citizen action has been slow to develop. Elected village boards provided a medium for citizen participation in Columbia and met as the Columbia Combined Board to speak out on some issues. However, neither the village boards, Columbia Combined Board, nor the developer-controlled Columbia Association were active in lobbying before the Howard County Commissioners. Land use decisions in Laguna Niguel were also controlled at the county level. Neighborhood homes associations kept residents informed about planning matters, but they lacked political power in dealing with the Orange County Board of Supervisors. A communitywide voluntary organization, the Laguna Niguel Homeowners Association, which had been organized to provide a more effective vehicle for citizen influence, had not yet achieved standing as a spokesman for the community before the county government. In the case of Elk Grove Village, land use controls were in the hands of municipal government; however, the developer did not make it a practice to consult with residents and citizen participation in municipal government was not encouraged.

Finally, five new communities—Lake Havasu City, Sharpstown, Forest Park, Valencia, and Foster City—were characterized by relatively low levels of citizen confidence in their ability to influence development decisions. Citizen impotence in Sharpstown and Lake Havasu City is not difficult to understand. Both had been subject to rather free-wheeling land development activities. Located in the city of Houston, which lacked a zoning ordinance, Sharpstown residents had to rely on deed restrictions to maintain the integrity of the community master plan. The Sharpstown Civic Association was formed to enforce compliance with the restrictions, but it attracted little support from the residents. Land use regulations in Lake Havasu City were enforced by Mohave County, which maintained Arizona's traditional reliance on the operation of the free market and reluctance to interfere in market decisions. The most vocal citizen organization in Lake Havasu City, the Chamber of Commerce, represented commercial interests in the community and worked closely with the developer.

Three factors worked against greater citizen confidence in Valencia. Land use regulations were controlled by Los Angeles County. The county supervisor from Valencia's district worked closely with the developer and, in fact, was later unseated when his pro-developer sympathies became a campaign issue. Second, the Newhall Land and Farming Company did not have a consistent record of close contacts with residents with regard to planning and land use matters. Third, although a series of neighborhood homes associations were active in Valencia, they had not formed a combined front to represent the residents, but instead tended to act independently. As a result, only a third of the Valencia respondents thought they would be successful in preventing a project that threatened their neighborhood.

Although Forest Park's municipal government controlled land use regulations, the City Council was controlled by a faction that worked closely with the developer (in fact, upon leaving office the mayor was hired by the developer). In addition, little had been done in the community to encourage citizen contact with either elected or appointed city officials. In contrast, Foster City seemed to have most of the ingredients for greater citizen confidence in their capacity to influence development decisions. The community had incorporated after a lengthy battle with the developer over control of the Estero Municipal Improvement District; widespread citizen participation in municipal government was encouraged; and the Foster City Community Association, which had formed shortly after the first homes were sold in the community, provided an independent forum for citizen activism. However, Foster City was also characterized by higher than average feelings of citizen impotence. Two factors may account for this apparent anomaly. First, after initially building planned single-family neighborhoods in the community, the developer was increasing construction in neighborhoods planned for higher density townhouse and apartment units. Residents may have felt the character of the community was changing for the worse.[c] Second, as noted in chapter 4, Foster City was incorporated with a staggering debt inherited from the Estero District. There was a strong feeling in Foster City that increased development was urgently needed to bolster the tax base and provide additional revenues to help pay principal and interest charges. Residents might have felt that in the face of the community's need for accelerated growth, it would be difficult to prevent unwanted development activity.

In spite of the variation that has been described, the overall picture is not one that suggests that new communities will be the sites of a renaissance in citizen participation in planning. Even where conditions were most conducive to citizen involvement, a majority of the residents did not feel that they could have an effective voice in community development decisions. Obviously, before new community planning is reformed by

[c]Although some facilities were behind schedule (particularly schools), Foster City's development has closely followed the developer's original master plan. However, as shown in figure 7-2, Foster City's residents were the least likely to feel that neighborhood plans had been followed.

abolishing the master plan in favor of an open planning process based on full-scale citizen participation, some means must be found to instill greater resident confidence in their own power to influence development authorities.

Residents' Assessment of Community Planning

Planners' concern with the character of the planning process sometimes causes them to lose sight of one of the ultimate goals of new community planning—to produce a better planned community than is characteristic of conventional urban growth. However, this is one area in which new communities have done quite well. When asked to compare the overall planning of their communities with the communities they had moved from, 75 percent of the new community respondents said that the new community was better. In contrast, only 53 percent of the conventional community respondents felt that the communities they were living in were better planned than their previous communities.

The paired comparisons illustrated in figure 7-4 show that in each case new community respondents were more likely than those living in their paired conventional community to rate planning better. For 11 of the 13 comparisons the difference is statistically significant. Residents' assessments of community planning were associated with their community's place on the new community continuum. As a rule, planning was rated more highly among communities that placed higher on the continuum of new community characteristics. For example, among the six new communities to the left of center in figure 7-4 (the higher end of the continuum), from 79 percent to 91 percent of the respondents said that planning was better in their present communities than the communities from which they had moved. Among the six new communities to the right of center in figure 7-4 (the lower end of the continuum), community planning was rated better by only 55 percent to 71 percent of the respondents. In short, new community residents seem quite capable of distinguishing and appreciating more sophisticated planning efforts on the part of new community developers and planners.

The reasons residents gave for rating planning better run the gamut of planning principles embodied in the new community concept. The 10 most frequently given ones are shown in table 7-2. Two reasons for rating planning better in new communities stand out. The availability and quality of recreational facilities was mentioned most often (by 27 percent of the respondents). Close behind was the organization of land uses and orderly layout of the community (mentioned by 25 percent of the respondents). Other components of the new community concept were mentioned less

152

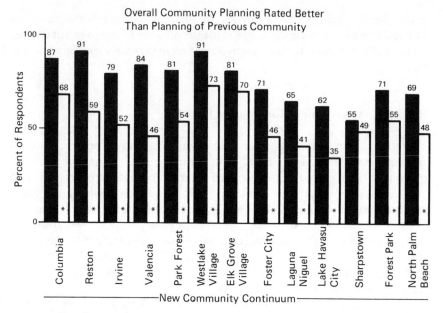

Figure 7-4. Residents' Assessment of Community Planning

often. The same 10 features were also mentioned most frequently by respondents living in conventional communities, though the order was somewhat different. In these settings the organization of land uses was most frequently given as the reason for rating planning better, with open space and the lack of crowding in the community a close second.

To provide further insights into components of good planning from the residents' perspective, ratings of planning were compared to objective characteristics of the new and conventional communities. The most striking associations were between ratings of planning and environmental design. Planning was rated highest in those new and conventional communities characterized by landscaping of public and common areas, preservation of environmental corridors, existence of architectural controls, and the grouping of all commercial facilities in centers. The actual per capita amount of land preserved in open space, preservation and protection of water bodies, and the proportion of a community served by underground utilities were also associated with higher ratings, but not as strongly as the previously mentioned environmental features.

Next in importance were the accessibility-transportation characteristics of the communities. Planning was rated better in communities that provided walking paths, a greater degree of pedestrian-vehicular separa-

Table 7-2

Ten Most Frequently Given Reasons for Rating Community Planning as Better Than Planning of Previous Community

Reason for Rating Planning Better	Percent of Respondents[a] (Rank)			
	New Communities		Conventional Communities	
Recreational facilities	27[b]	(1)	17	(3)
Organization of land uses	25	(2)	23	(1)
Attractiveness of community	16[b]	(3)	12	(5)
Street design	16	(3)	14	(4)
Shopping facilities	15[b]	(5)	10	(7)
Open space/lack of crowding	15	(5)	22[b]	(2)
Preservation of natural features	14	(7)	12	(5)
Schools	12	(8)	10	(7)
Social programs and citizen participation	5	(9)	5	(9)
Variety of housing types	3	(10)	5	(9)

[a]Adds to more than 100 percent owing to multiple responses.
[b]Difference is statistically significant at 0.05 level of confidence.

tion, and greater accessibility of community facilities and services. The availability of community bus service was positively related to assessments of community planning, but was of less importance.

Relatively strong associations were also found between objective manifestations of two other components of the new community concept and planning assessments. Planning tended to be rated better in communities that provided a greater choice of housing types, as indicated by the proportion of multifamily housing units in the community, and in communities that had local newspapers, thus providing an organized means of communication among the residents.

Although residents' perceptions of good planning were associated with many aspects of the new community concept, there were three notable exceptions. First, the achievement of population diversity had little influence on ratings of planning. Although communities with a higher black population received somewhat higher ratings, communities with a higher proportion of residents with incomes under $10,000 received somewhat lower ratings. Second, the achievement of employment self-sufficiency had no influence on ratings of planning. In fact, communities in which a higher proportion of respondents lived and worked in the same community tended to receive somewhat lower ratings. Third, the achievement of a higher degree of self-governance was also not associated with ratings of overall community planning.

Before concluding, one further question should be addressed, namely,

What is the association between citizens' awareness and participation in planning and their overall assessment of community planning? Not surprisingly, new communities in which residents were more aware of neighborhood development plans and in which they felt the developer was more responsive to their wishes tended to receive higher ratings of the quality of community planning. Thus, aspects of both the planning process and resulting product influenced residents' satisfaction with planning.

8

Governing New Communities

Although long neglected, governance is more and more being recognized as a critical factor in new community development. Existing and newly organized institutions must make decisions regarding plans for future growth, formulate appropriate land use regulations, provide adequate public facilities and services, and offer opportunities for citizen participation in decision making. Of course, these functions are not unique to new communities. They are performed by most general-purpose governments in the nation. The new community context, however, is unique. The scale and rapid pace of development, together with the higher level of expectations embodied in the new community concept, create special problems for new community developers and citizens alike. This chapter examines the approaches that have been followed in governing new communities and how they have affected new community residents.

The Structure of New Community Governance

When a new community project is initially conceived, most local governmental functions are usually performed by county government. Over time, however, the governmental structure tends to become more complex as the developer seeks ways to finance the infrastructure needed for his project and the residents seek new and improved public services and a voice in community decision making. Governmental and quasi-governmental forms that have been frequently used include: county government and county subordinate service districts; incorporated municipal government; multi- and single-function special districts; and various types of homes associations. In addition, if they are adequately capitalized, developers occasionally choose to provide some community services on a commercial basis.

County Government

The typical pattern of new community development in the United States has been for the developer to acquire the community site with no help from local government and then to petition county government for approval of the master plan and for appropriate zoning to carry out the plan (Hanson 1971, p. 38). Although securing such approval sometimes involves a lengthy political struggle, particularly if the county is frightened at the prospect of increasing urbanization, most counties have welcomed new community development as a preferable alternative to incremental suburban sprawl. Having secured a commitment from the county to support their project, many developers have understandably avoided early creation of a municipality for fear that they may suffer at the hands of an unpredictable political entity.

Facilities and services provided in new communities by county governments tend to vary with the extent of urbanization of the county. In a rural jurisdiction, such as Mohave County, Arizona (which served Lake Havasu City), county services to the new community were limited to police protection from a sheriff's substation and minimal public health and welfare services. The inability of Mohave County to provide urban services in Lake Havasu City led the residents to conduct a $10,000 incorporation feasibility study. Although incorporation was favored by the developer, the idea was dropped because of local businessmen's opposition to paying municipal license fees.

One step up the ladder of urbanization, as in Howard County, Maryland (which served Columbia), county government has been able to provide a broader array of services. In 1968 Howard County adopted a charter form of government in order to manage better the urban service systems required by the rapid population growth projected for Columbia and other sections of the county. By 1972, its services to Columbia included schools, libraries, police and fire protection, sewer and water supply, recreation, refuse collection, road maintenance, public health and welfare, and land use and building regulation.

Four other unincorporated new communities—Reston, Laguna Niguel, Valencia, and Westlake Village (part)—were served by urban county governments. Fairfax County, Virginia (which served Reston), had an urban county executive form of government with an organizational structure similar to that of a large municipality. Reston's place in the county resembled that of an urban neighborhood. With no direct representation on the County Board of Supervisors, however, Reston residents have periodically chafed at their community's lack of political identity.

In 1972, a study team of Reston residents concluded that local governance was necessary to maintain a sense of community, bring government closer to the people, and to provide a broader range of community facilities and services (The Study Team on RHOA Role and Structure 1972, p. 13). However, the study team rejected incorporation in favor of a proposed community council, which would serve in an advisory capacity to the Fairfax County Board of Supervisors. Several years later, continuing resident discontent with county services led the Fairfax County Board of Supervisors to create a task force to study the formation of a multipurpose tax district to finance improved services in Reston. Early in 1975 the task force's mandate was enlarged to include the possible incorporation of the community, even though Virginia statutes prohibited further municipal incorporation in Fairfax County after 1966. While Fairfax County provided a broad range of urban services, those actually located in Reston were limited to fire protection, library, and educational services. To provide a base for additional services in the community, the county agreed in 1974 to purchase a 50-acre site for a governmental subcenter.

Laguna Niguel and Valencia are both examples of the benefits that can accrue to new communities from close political ties between their developers and county officials. Laguna Niguel's 1972 population was only about 8,500, but Orange County had already located a regional civic center there to serve the southern half of the county. In addition, the county opened two parks in the community, established a county subordinate service district for road maintenance and neighborhood park development, acquired a site for a branch of the county library system, and helped complete construction of the parkway connecting the Pacific Coast Highway with the San Diego Freeway.

With a 1972 population of about 7,000, the Newhall Land and Farming Company persuaded Los Angeles County to build a Regional Administration Center in Valencia's City Center. Facilities located there included a regional library, sheriff's office, courts, and offices of the county engineering, health, and assessor's departments. Other county services were provided through subordinate service districts for road maintenance and fire protection, and through the county park and recreation department, which operated three parks in Valencia. Because of their developers' successes in negotiating for county services, residents of Laguna Niguel and Valencia have expressed little interest in incorporation. Both, however, have been included in incorporation movements originated by the residents of the surrounding region.

In comparison with Valencia, the American-Hawaiian Steamship Company had little success in persuading Los Angeles County to locate county facilities and services in Westlake Village. Los Angeles County operated a five-acre park and a fire station, but refused the developer's request to build a second county park. The county's reluctance to provide other public facilities stemmed from Westlake Village's location at the extreme edge of the county (most of the community was in the Ventura County town of Thousand Oaks). In recent years the residents of the area south of Westlake Village have explored the incorporation of the Los Angeles County portion of the Conejo Valley, including a portion of Westlake Village, into a new city to be known as Las Virgenes. By late

1974, citizen discontent with county services and county control of land use had also produced a movement to secede from Los Angeles County by forming a new County of Las Virgenes.

Municipal Government

The Twentieth Century Fund Task Force on the Governance of New Communities did not feel that all new communities should be governed in the same way, but it did recommend "that the ultimate establishment of a general purpose government should be encouraged for all public functions, since such governments provide a comprehensive political system within which conflicting interest can openly contend for power and resources" (1971, pp. 10-11). For a number of new communities the establishment of a municipal government has met this need, as well as the residents' desires for municipal-type services.

The normal course taken by unincorporated communities is to seek incorporation after their populations and tax bases have grown sufficiently to support city services. Some new communities, however, incorporated before, or shortly after, actual development began. Developers may favor early incorporation if satisfactory zoning cannot be obtained from county government. For example, in order to build on smaller lots than was allowed by Cook County's zoning ordinance, the Centex Construction Company incorporated Elk Grove Village in July 1956 with an initial population of only 116 persons. The corporation was able to dominate the initial village government and began development more or less as it pleased. Because Elk Grove Village had an inadequate tax base to finance needed community facilities, such as the community's water system, Centex built storage and distribution facilities and later sold them to the village government. A similar strategy was followed by the developers of North Palm Beach and Park Forest, both of which incorporated very early in the development process.

Another route to incorporation has been through annexation and defensive incorporation because of the threat of annexation. The new community of Janss/Conejo, developed by the Janss Corporation just north of Westlake Village, incorporated as the City of Thousand Oaks in 1964. Three years later the city extended its southern boundary to the Ventura County line and annexed 1,000 acres of Westlake Village, including the town center and half of Lake Westlake. In exchange for several million dollars worth of road construction promised by Thousand Oaks, Westlake's developer did not oppose annexation. One other new community, Sharpstown, was annexed when the City of Houston's southwestward growth encompassed the development site.

Two new communities incorporated when annexation was threatened by neighboring jurisdictions. The City of Greenhills sought to annex Forest Park; however, the day before annexation proceedings were filed, Forest Park residents filed for incorporation. Forest Park became a city under Ohio law on July 6, 1961, and in 1969 adopted a charter establishing a council-manager form of government. As noted in chapter 4, Irvine's incorporation was touched off by threatened annexation of a portion of the Irvine Industrial Complex by the City of Newport Beach, and the attempted annexation of industrial lands by the City of Santa Ana. In this case, incorporation took almost a year and one half to complete because of a series of petitions and law suits filed in opposition to incorporation by Santa Ana. The basis of the suits was a 1963 Irvine Company agreement that Santa Ana would one day annex a 938-acre section of the Industrial Complex. When The Irvine Company changed its plans and enlarged the size of its university-centered community from 10,000 acres to 53,000 acres, it recommended that a new city government, encompassing almost the entire Industrial Complex, be created and also abrogated its previous agreement with the City of Santa Ana. The Local Agency Formation Commission and the California courts denied Santa Ana's petitions and Irvine residents voted to approve incorporation in December 1971.

Incorporation of Foster City followed a long battle between residents of the community and the developer over control of the Estero Municipal Improvement District (see below). By 1970 the citizens had gained a majority of the seats on the district board of directors, but were faced with a staggering debt and the highest property taxes in San Mateo County. The citizens reasoned that various revenues accruing to San Mateo County could be captured by an incorporated government and used to reduce their tax burden. Centex West, Inc., which had recently purchased the undeveloped land in Foster City from T. Jack Foster & Son, testified in favor of incorporation. Because of the community's large bonded indebtedness, incorporation was not opposed by neighboring cities, such as San Mateo, which otherwise might have considered annexation. Lacking any significant opposition, the incorporation question was put to a vote of Foster City's residents on April 20, 1971 and was passed by an overwhelming majority.

The new communities that were annexed to neighboring cities— Westlake Village (part) and Sharpstown—were in similar positions as communities governed by urban counties. They received municipal-type services, but had little direct voice in the way resources were allocated. Sharpstown had no representatives on the Houston City Council, and it was 1974 before Westlake Village residents succeeded in electing one representative to the Thousand Oaks City Council.

On the other hand, in the six new communities that incorporated—Elk

Grove Village, Forest Park, Foster City, Irvine, North Palm Beach, and
Park Forest—residents had more control over their municipal government.

The incorporated communities have developed two distinctive styles of
municipal governance. After initial flurries of resident participation, the
older incorporated new communities of Elk Grove Village, Forest Park,
North Palm Beach, and Park Forest developed stable governments whose
operation stirred little local controversy. In the 1973 municipal elections
voter turnout was less than 30 percent in each community. The older
municipal governments contrast sharply with the volatile, participant-
oriented governance styles of Irvine and Foster City. Shortly after they
incorporated both communities established a broad range of citizen committees and commissions to advise elected officials and city staff members.
Numerous controversies have arisen over proposed municipal activities,
government's relationship with the developer, and the most appropriate
methods of conducting municipal business. Voter turnout has been exceptionally high (over 70 percent) and a number of candidates have typically
vied for each available city council position.

In addition to varying styles of governance, the scope of governmental
activities also varied among the incorporated new communities. Per capita
municipal expenditures for 1972-73 were highest in two new communities—Irvine ($158) and Elk Grove Village ($140)—which had very
large industrial tax bases. Although Foster City lacked a strong commercial
and industrial base, citizen interest in expanded services led to relatively
high general fund expenditures per capita ($122). Per capita municipal
expenditures were somewhat lower in North Palm Beach ($114), and were
lowest in Park Forest ($83) and Forest Park ($81).

Special Districts

After determining what form of general-purpose government—county or
municipal—will be most advantageous, new community developers must
consider how to arrange the most favorable financing of public facilities.
Although some developers have secured private financing of facilities, for
many developers public financing has a number of advantages: interest
paid on public bonds is exempt from the federal income tax; public financing frees the developer's capital for other purposes; and if the development
project is particularly risky, it may be the only way to raise large amounts of
capital to be repaid over a long period. One means of arranging public
financing is through the issuance of municipal bonds. However, most state
debt limitation laws restrict municipal government's capacity to carry a
heavy debt load during the early years of development when assessed
valuation is still relatively low. As a result, new community developers
have made extensive use of special districts.

In some cases developers were able to have their property annexed to an existing special district. For example, the development of Park Forest was made much easier when American Community Builders, Inc. discovered that the nearby Bloom Township Sanitary District had excess capacity that could be used. Laguna Niguel tapped into the Moulton Niguel Water District and South Coast Sanitary District, and park development in Westlake Village was facilitated by the community's annexation to the Conejo Park and Recreation District. In other cases, such as Elk Grove Village and Forest Park, developers were able to use metropolitanwide sanitary districts.

If an existing special district was not available, developers often had little difficulty forming their own districts and issuing revenue bonds to finance the construction of various types of infrastructure. For example, the Los Angeles Sanitary District No. 32 was formed expressly to build sewage treatment facilities and major trunk lines for Valencia. Similar services were provided in Lake Havasu City by the Lake Havasu City Sanitary District, and in Irvine by the Orange County Sanitation District No. 7 and Irvine Ranch Water District. In addition to financing the capital costs of public facilities, special districts have also been formed to perform maintenance activities. Parkway landscaping in Westlake Village was kept up by a parkway maintenance district; the paseos in Valencia were maintained by a subordinate service district controlled by Los Angeles County; and an Orange County subordinate service district was responsible for road maintenance in Laguna Niguel. Other types of districts that provided services to new communities included: community college districts, street lighting districts, mosquito abatement districts, flood control districts, soil conservation districts, forest preserve districts, hospital districts, library districts, fire protection districts, and drainage districts. In addition, most new communities were served by one or more independent school districts.

Two of the most interesting, and controversial, examples of the use of special districts to aid in new community development are the Estero Municipal Improvement District in Foster City and the Lake Havasu Irrigation and Drainage District.

As noted in chapter 4, the Estero District was established at the request of T. Jack Foster by a special act of the California legislature in 1960. The primary purpose of the district was to reclaim low-lying land adjacent to San Francisco Bay so that development of Foster City could proceed. However, the enabling act also gave the district the power to collect and treat sewage, garbage and refuse, erect and maintain street lighting, produce, store, and distribute water, construct parks and playgrounds, and provide fire protection. Thus, with the exception of land use regulation and police protection, the district had most of the powers of a municipality. Unlike a municipality, it was organized so that the Fosters could maintain control of the district board of directors throughout the development period. Voting rights were distributed on the basis of one vote for every one dollar of assessed valuation in the community. To insure developer control, undeveloped land was assessed on a benefits-to-be-received basis, that is, as if it had been fully improved and was ready for sale to builders.

The Estero Municipal Improvement District worked well enough until the first residents moved to Foster City. Quite naturally, the citizens objected to being saddled with a large public debt over which they had no control. They also objected to the Fosters' practice of capitalizing interest. In order to keep taxes low when they owned most of the land in Foster City, as well as to encourage home and commercial land sales, the Fosters used part of the proceeds of bond sales to make interest payments on earlier bonds.

The first challenge to the Estero District came just two years after the first homes were occupied, when a Foster City resident went to the San Mateo County Superior Court with a suit charging that the formation of the Estero District was unconstitutional and amounted to a wrongful use of a public agency for private purposes. The suit also requested that some $30 million in bond funds that had already been spent on development be restored to the district treasury. Although the suit was eventually denied in a 4-3 decision by the California State Supreme Court in 1969, the dissenting view seriously questioned the legitimacy of developer-controlled governmental institutions. In writing the dissenting opinion, Justice Stanley Mosk noted,

The effective political and economic power rests not with the residents of the district, but with a regency, like a vicarious government during a monarch's childhood, this district is ruled as if the people require a protective guidance during their minority. However tolerable in another time, such paternalism is undesirable in this year 1969. The U. S. Supreme Court "one-man, one-vote" command is not satisfied by the "one-man, three-fifths-of-a-vote" practice. To wholly or partially deprive more than 8000 residents of their constitutional right to an equal vote is unjust. That the injustice is to be cured in the future makes it no less unjust today (cited in Van Beckum, Jr. 1971, p. 73).

However, the U.S. Supreme Court did not concur and refused to hear an appeal of the State Supreme Court decision.

Where the judicial route did not succeed in modifying the Estero District, political action by Foster City residents was effective. In 1967 the Foster City Community Association reached a compromise with the Fosters. The Estero board of directors was expanded from three to five members. The election of board members was staggered to assure that by November 1971 all five directors would be directly elected by the residents. By the time Foster City incorporated in 1971, the residents had succeeded in replacing the district manager with a person of their own choosing. After incorporation, the Estero District was made a subsidiary of the city and the

City Council simultaneously sat as the district Board of Directors (because of its large debt it was impossible to merge the district into the city government).

While Foster City probably would not have been built without the Estero District, this form of development financing has had an number of serious repercussions. For one, the controversy over control of the district and court challenges of its constitutionality caused so much adverse publicity that the district had difficulty marketing bonds and the pace of development was crippled for a number of years, eventually resulting in the sale of the project. Second, in order to keep property taxes within reasonable bounds, Foster City must be developed to the fullest extent. While other Californians have been fighting developers, Foster City residents have pushed for an accelerated pace of development to increase the city-district tax base. They have also sought to increase the market value of new housing, in part by requiring that planned apartments be converted from rental to condominium units. Finally, the ability of the city to finance desired public improvements has been limited by the immense debt service payments that must be made every year. In 1972, bonded debt service expenditures were over twice as large as Foster City's general fund expenditures.

Development financing of Lake Havasu City was greatly aided by the Lake Havasu Irrigation and Drainage District, which was formed in 1963 to provide domestic and irrigation water, storm drainage works, and streets for the community. As of 1972, the district had authorized over $10 million in bonds. As with the Estero District, the payment of bond principal and interest was structured so that most of the burden would be shifted from the developer to the residents. For example, district taxes increased from $21.60 per acre in 1968 to $60.64 in 1973, by which time most of the undeveloped lots in Lake Havasu City were sold. However, unlike the Estero District, Lake Havasu City's developer did not have to contend with a citizen revolt and has easily maintained control of the three-man district board of directors. Although Lake Havasu City had about 8,000 residents in 1972, only 148 persons registered to vote in the district elections of that year, and only 16 actually voted.

Homes and Community Associations

Many of the innovations in environmental design fostered by new community development have been made possible by the use of homes and community associations to finance the maintenance of open space and to enforce architectural controls. Some homes associations perform a much broader array of functions, including planning and conducting cultural, recreational, social, and educational activities, and, in the case of Columbia, actually financing the capital costs of many community amenities and services.

Homes associations are nonprofit corporations established by developers through recorded deed restrictions and covenants. Residents automatically become members of an association when they purchase a home. They have the right to use the association's property and to vote for association officers, and, in return, are obligated to pay the association's assessments and follow its rules. Failure to do so can result in suspension of the right to use association facilities, and ultimately in foreclosure of the member's home to recover unpaid dues.

Three approaches to homes association governance have characterized new community development. These might be termed the Irvine, Reston, and Columbia homes association models.

The Irvine Model. Following experimentation with the homes association concept in its earlier coastal developments, The Irvine Company used homes associations as the primary form of internal governance for neighborhoods and villages in the new community of Irvine. Unlike Reston and Columbia, which have large centralized associations, the Irvine approach is based on the creation of small associations that can be turned over to the residents shortly after the first homes in a new neighborhood are sold. The boundaries and size of an association are set so that it encompasses a coherent area in terms of street patterns and open space, and also one in which development will be completed within three years. In this way The Irvine Company believes that it can maximize neighborhood identity and resident participation in association affairs. In 1973 the 11 Irvine Company homes associations in the city of Irvine ranged in size from 129 to 971 dwelling units and had annual expenditures ranging from $23,000 to $290,000. The original capital costs of association open space and amenities were recovered through additions to individual home prices.

The Irvine model of small neighborhood homes associations was closely followed in the development of Valencia and Westlake Village, where almost all neighborhoods had a homes association to maintain common property and to enforce architectural controls. Neighborhood associations were used quite extensively in Laguna Niguel, but a number of neighborhoods were also developed without open space and amenities that required maintenance by an association. Architectural controls were enforced by a communitywide architectural committee. Even more limited use of neighborhood homes associations characterized Foster City, Elk Grove Village, Lake Havasu City, Park Forest, North Palm Beach, and Sharpstown. In these communities homes associations (or equivalent condominium associations and cooperatives) were only used for multifamily ownership projects, such as townhouses and condominium apartments. Homes associations were not used in Forest Park.

The Reston Model. To maintain the extensive open spaces and recreational amenities planned for Reston, Fairfax County required the developer to provide an organization that would own and maintain them. Robert Simon intended to meet this requirement by establishing a homes association for each of the community's seven villages. Two associations were set up when construction began on Lake Anne Village and the Village of Hunters Woods. In order to achieve economies of scale and to simplify the homes association structure, they were combined in 1970 to form the Reston Home Owners Association.[a]

The Reston approach to homes association governance is similar to the Irvine model in several ways. The capital costs of open space and amenities are paid for by the developer and are then recovered by adding them to the price of individual homes and apartments. Voting in association affairs is allocated on the basis of one vote per housing unit, with apartment units voted by building owners rather than tenants. Also, the association is financed by dues, which are assessed for each housing unit (commercial and industrial properties are not assessed).

The Reston approach differs from Irvine in two important respects: First, one centralized association, rather than a series of smaller neighborhood associations, is used. Second, the central association vests control of association affairs with the developer rather than the residents. Gulf-Reston, Inc., has a vote for each unit it owns (developer-owned apartment buildings) and for each unsold platted lot. It is assured of at least one third of all votes in the association until 1985, with control of the Board of Directors maintained until over half of the units planned for Reston have been built and are occupied. Developer control of the Reston Home Owners Association, and resulting resident discontent with their voice in association affairs, has led to the development of an elaborate citizen participation structure in the community.

Village councils were created in 1970 to provide a forum for citizen participation within the newly consolidated Reston Home Owners Association. Originally, the village councils were to represent village residents within the Reston Home Owners Association structure by advising the association about village affairs and by participating in an advisory Town Council composed of three resident-elected members of the Reston Home Owners Association Board of Directors and the village council chairmen. The resident members of the Board of Directors were nominated by an

---

[a] A number of townhouse (cluster) associations have also been used in Reston. These associations have very limited responsibilities associated with exterior building, parking lot, and street light maintenance. They do not own recreational amenities.

advisory ballot of all homeowners and elected by the developer who had a majority of the votes. The village councils were elected by a vote of all residents age 16 and over, including renters. Because of the stigma of developer control of the Reston Home Owners Association, since 1972 the village councils have been looked upon as totally autonomous bodies with no official connection with the Home Owners Association. The Town Council was also dropped in 1972. It was replaced by an Advisory Council composed of the three resident representatives on the Home Owners Association board, representatives of the village councils, and the executive director of the Home Owners Association. Friction between the village council representatives and the resident members of the Home Owners Association board of directors led to a further change in 1973, when the Advisory Council was replaced by the Reston Home Owners Association Council, and voting power was limited to the three resident representatives on the Reston Home Owners Association Board of Directors. The council together with the Home Owners Association staff jointly recommend to the developer-controlled board of directors the proposed annual budget of the association. In 1972-73 annual expenditures of the Reston Home Owners Association were almost three quarters of a million dollars.

The difficulties produced by the Reston model of homes association governance were summarized by a resident study team in 1972 as follows:

There is little evidence that RHOA was considered as a potential government when the planners first conceived of Reston as a new town. Its structure demonstrates that the control of land was paramount. . . .

In terms of community participation, there is no evidence that it was considered at all until the pressures of the community demanded it, in part due to the residents' expectations of local self-determination. Reston was touted and viewed as an entity, yet local government was precluded by law. The distant County did not fit the visions many had of a local government. . . .

While there is little disagreement that RHOA had a fundamental responsibility for the care of common lands . . . it is an inappropriate vehicle for local governance in a broader sense for a number of reasons (The Study Team on RHOA Role & Structure 1972, pp. 14-15).

These reasons included the exclusion of renters—who would ultimately comprise a majority of Reston's households—from voting for the board of directors, developer control of the board of directors, and the association's inability to expand its scope of activities because the dues structure was set too low.

The Columbia Model. The Columbia Park and Recreation Association represents a third model of homes association governance. Formed on December 10, 1965, the Columbia Association, as it is commonly called, has a number of key features that distinguish it from the Irvine and Reston models.[b] First, the front-end costs of open space and community amenities are not loaded onto home prices and apartment rents, but are directly financed by the association. Second, voting for association officers is not limited to homeowners, but includes renters, though votes are allocated on the basis of one vote per unit, rather than one man, one vote. Third, association activities are financed through a permanent lien on all taxable property in the new town zone, including commercial and industrial property. The enormous General Electric complex in Columbia, however, lies outside the new town zone and is not assessed. Fourth, the lien takes precedence over purchase money mortgages (VA and FHA approval of this provision has never been repeated), so that the association has been able to borrow substantial amounts of money in commercial money markets. Fifth, rather than flat-rate assessments, those of the Columbia Association are tied to Howard County property tax assessments and may go as high as $0.75 per $100 assessed valuation. This provides that some equity in assessments is achieved as well as a hedge against inflation. Sixth, the association has a unique federal structure. In addition to the Columbia Association, each village in Columbia has its own village association. While residents can be members of their village association, they are not legally members of the Columbia Association, whose only members are its board of directors. For every 2,000 dwelling units completed in Columbia, the residents are entitled to one-half vote on the seven-member board.[c] However, residents do not select board members directly. Instead they elect village representatives to the Columbia Council, which in turn nominates members of the Columbia Association Board of Directors. The Board of Directors selects its members from the list of nominees.

The rationale for the Columbia Association, as opposed to alternative methods of providing amenities and services, was described by one of its founders in the following manner:

First of all, we wanted to stay away from the company town kind of thing where the developer provides everything. That way wasn't economically feasible if things were to go the way we wanted them to. The only way we could have provided these amenities would have been to add their costs into the costs of land, and with something like $30 million in capital costs to be expended and a maximum of just over 30,000 dwelling units to absorb the cost, we quickly saw that no one could afford to buy a lot.

Formation of a special tax district was attractive until we looked at it closely. Under the district, we could issue bonds for long term, low interest.

But, we believed that the time would come when the citizens might vote down our

[b] As is the case with Reston, Columbia has also used a number of townhouse associations with limited property maintenance responsibilities.

[c] Half votes were adopted to give recently developed villages some representation on the Columbia Association Board of Directors. Each village is limited to a maximum of one vote on the board.

bond issues. Back then, that kind of thing hadn't happened, but it has happened since, and if it happened to us, there wouldn't be any Columbia or new city. . . . (John M. Jones, Jr., quoted in "The Nebulous Art of New Community Management" 1971, p. 13).

Thus, the basic genius of the Columbia Association is that it provides a way to avoid front-end loading of amenity costs onto home prices and insures developer control of association investments in community amenities. In addition, by including commercial and industrial property in the assessment base and by tying assessments to property tax assessments, the association has had adequate revenues to fund a number of community service programs. In 1972, the Columbia Association's operating expenditures were in excess of $2 million and its debt was approximately $21 million.

Because the Columbia Association is controlled by the developer (complete resident control will not come before 1981), it has had to contend with residents' discontent over their lack of voice in association affairs. In August 1971 the village boards and the Columbia Association formed the Columbia Roles Study Committee to find ways to increase resident participation. One outcome of this process was the formation of a Goals Council, which in 1973 recommended a set of goals and operating policies for the association. A final draft, which included recommendations of the Columbia Combined Boards (an organization composed of village board representatives) was approved by the Columbia Association's Executive Committee in 1974.

A number of other methods of increasing citizen participation have also been used. Over 30 committees and advisory groups have been formed to work with the Columbia Association's professional staff. Provision was made for one-half votes on the association Board of Directors in order to provide greater representation to Columbia's villages. Meetings of the association Board of Directors and Executive Committee were opened to the public. Community forums were begun to air plans for future development. Resident representatives were included on planning teams for future areas of development. Finally, the village associations, which are similar in many respects to civic associations, since residents are not obligated to provide financial support for village association activities, have offered an important vehicle for resident participation in Columbia. The village boards of directors have been increasingly used in an advisory capacity by both the developer and the Columbia Association.

Developer Provision of Public Facilities

Some developers have themselves undertaken the construction of public facilities. Their involvement usually follows one of three patterns. First, developers may plan and construct various amenities and recover their cost through land sales prices. As discussed above, such amenities are typically turned over to homes associations for operation and maintenance. Second, developers may construct public facilities with the understanding that they will subsequently be purchased by a public entity. For example, in the early development of Elk Grove Village and Park Forest the developers built community water systems for later purchase by the village governments. In addition, a number of developers have also financed and constructed school buildings. Finally, some developers have viewed the construction and operation of public facilities as a sound investment. This is most often the case with certain types of recreational facilities, such as golf courses and tennis clubs. However, as exemplified by the North Palm Beach Utilities, Inc., Westlake Water Company, and Valencia Water Company, some developers have also found utilities to be a potentially profitable enterprise.

The Patchwork Approach to New Community Governance

When the different institutions discussed in the preceding pages are arrayed according to the new communities that use them, the result illustrated in figure 8-1 resembles a patchwork quilt. The contrast between the orderly and rational planning of new communities and their fragmented governance is striking. Each new community has used a variety of institutions to provide services and to accommodate citizen participation in community decision making, and each has evolved into a unique governance structure.

The patchwork approach to new community governance is the result of a complex set of factors. A basic cause is the absence of adequate local governmental organization where the new communities were initiated. Each began in an unincorporated area and county governments were simply unable to finance necessary community facilities and services. Thus, in every new community new governmental arrangements were essential. Unfortunately, with the exception of Columbia and Irvine, new community developers gave little thought to the long-term implications of the institutions they established. Instead, developer decisions seem to have been based on their financial position during the early years of development and the imperative of getting construction started as quickly as possible. In addition, the ease of forming special districts and homes associations, both of which could be initially controlled by the developer, opened the door to a proliferation of governmental and quasi-governmental institutions.

Although new community developers played a large role in the patchwork approach to governance, in most cases they have simply adapted to

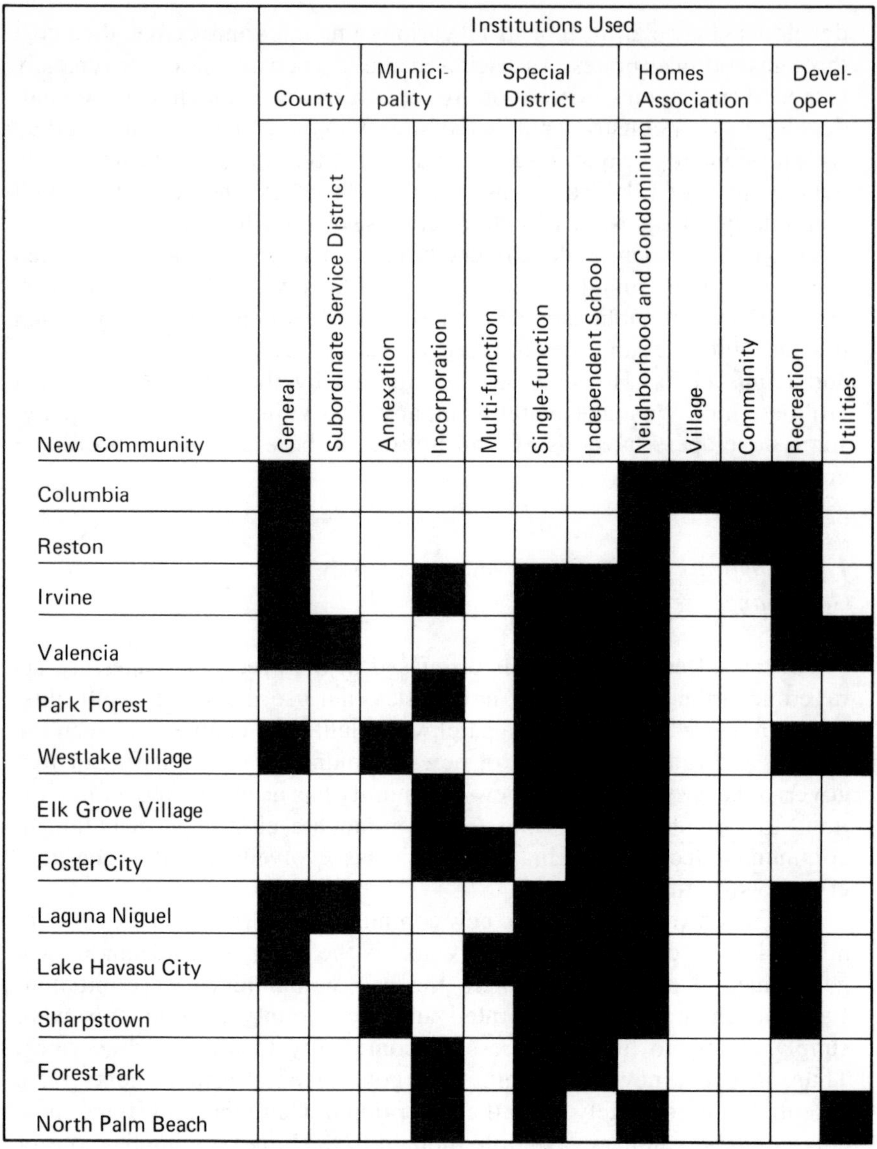

Figure 8-1. Structure of New Community Governance

New Community	County — General	County — Subordinate Service District	Municipality — Annexation	Municipality — Incorporation	Special District — Multi-function	Special District — Single-function	Special District — Independent School	Homes Association — Neighborhood and Condominium	Homes Association — Village	Homes Association — Community	Developer — Recreation	Developer — Utilities
Columbia	■							■	■	■		
Reston	■						■	■		■		
Irvine	■	■		■		■	■	■		■		
Valencia	■	■		■	■	■	■	■				
Park Forest			■	■	■		■	■			■	■
Westlake Village	■	■	■	■	■		■	■			■	■
Elk Grove Village			■	■	■		■	■			■	
Foster City			■	■		■	■	■			■	
Laguna Niguel	■	■			■	■	■	■				
Lake Havasu City	■	■		■	■	■	■	■			■	
Sharpstown		■		■	■	■	■	■				
Forest Park				■	■		■	■	■			
North Palm Beach				■	■		■	■				■

local circumstances. Finding themselves in a fragmented governmental system, they have usually had no other choice but to continue that system. Developers were not responsible for the weaknesses of county governments. They did not originate the practice of organizing independent school districts, nor did they pass stringent state debt limitation laws that encouraged the formation of single-function special districts. What is more, before new community development was far advanced, the residents began to have a voice in governance decisions. Their desires for local self-determination and improved public services added additional impetus to the already strong forces pushing toward governmental fragmentation.

Evaluating New Community Governance

Three questions guided the evaluation of new community governance structures. First, how well have the structures satisfied residents' desires for public services? Second, do the residents feel that local officials are responsive to their wishes and that local governance is conducted in an open and above board fashion? Third, to what extent have new community residents actually participated in local governance? Answers to these questions provide partial evidence as to the best approaches to new community governance.[d]

Residents' Satisfaction with Public Services

Satisfaction with public services was gauged by computing the average of respondents' satisfaction with community expenditures for fire protection, police protection, public health, public transportation, recreation, schools, and community upkeep and maintenance.[e] On average, 72 percent of the new community respondents were satisfied with expenditures for these public services. Individual community comparisons are shown in figure 8-2.

Of the seven new communities that scored above the average for all new communities, six—Elk Grove Village, Irvine, Westlake Village, Park Forest, North Palm Beach, and Foster City—were incorporated municipalities. The only high scoring unincorporated new community—Valencia—was served by an urban county and, as important, had been very successful in negotiating for public services.

Elk Grove Village and Irvine, which ranked first and second in terms of

---

[d] A complete determination, of course, would include consideration of the full costs of providing local public services. However, in view of the fragmented governmental structures found and the extended time periods over which investments were made, the ferreting out of this information from the multitudinous public and private agencies fell outside the limits of this study.

[e] Other measures of residents' satisfaction with health and medical care, transportation, recreational facilities and services, and schools are provided in chapters 10 through 14. These measures include ratings of the quality of facilities and services on five-point scales (excellent, good, average, below average, and poor) and comparisons of the quality of facilities and services with residents' previous communities, in addition to satisfaction with service expenditures.

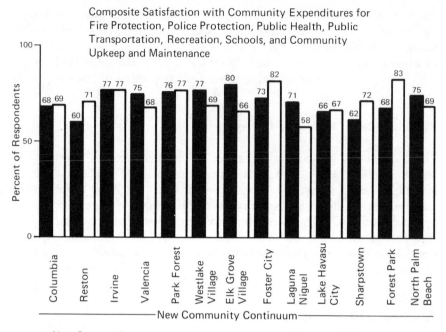

Figure 8-2. Satisfaction with Public Services

residents' satisfaction with public services, had the highest per capita municipal expenditure levels among the incorporated new communities. Park Forest and North Palm Beach, along with Elk Grove Village, were the oldest incorporated new communities and may have had a greater opportunity to develop well established public service systems. In spite of a complex governance system, which included services provided by municipal, county, and special district governments, as well as homes associations, Westlake Village residents were also highly satisfied with public service expenditure levels.

In general, residents were less satisfied with public services if their new community relied heavily on county government. For example, only 60 percent of the Reston respondents were satisfied with public service expenditures in their community. As noted above, they have been actively seeking a means to improve services received from Fairfax County, and are beginning to consider incorporation as one alternative. Lake Havasu City's reliance on Mohave County, Columbia's on Howard County, and Laguna Niguel's on Orange County are also reflected in somewhat lower resident satisfaction. Annexation to a large metropolitan city, as with Sharpstown's annexation to Houston, placed its residents in a position similar to that of residents living in new communities served by urban counties. The result has also been similar—only 62 percent of Sharptown's residents thought public service expenditures in their community were adequate.

Figure 8-2 clearly shows that residents' satisfaction with public services had little to do with a new community's adherence to the new community concept. New communities at the upper end of the new community continuum scored no better than those at the lower end. In addition, new community residents were no more satisfied with public service expenditures than residents living in conventional communities. Whatever its other benefits, new community development has not yet proven to be a vehicle for a more rational organization of local governance, or one that produces higher overall satisfaction with public services.

Residents' Attitudes Toward Local Officials

In addition to meeting residents' needs for public services, governance structures should be responsive to the citizenry. Unfortunately, most residents of both the new and conventional communities were rather cynical about local government. When asked whether local officials did pretty much what the majority of the citizens wanted, as opposed to doing what a few of the more influential citizens wanted or what they themselves thought best, relatively few respondents thought officials put the wishes of the citizens first. As figure 8-3 shows, there was little difference between new community and conventional community residents' attitudes about the responsiveness of local government.

Local official's responsiveness to the wishes of the citizenry was judged best by the residents of five new communities—North Palm Beach, Elk Grove Village, Park Forest, Irvine, and Forest Park—which had incorporated municipal governments. In each case, 40 percent or more of the respondents thought local officials did "pretty much what the majority of the citizens want." The responsiveness of more politically distant county and large city governments was not judged nearly as well—31 percent or less of the respondents living in Reston, Laguna Niguel, Columbia, Lake Havasu City, Sharpstown, and Valencia thought local officials usually did what the majority wanted. Westlake Village, which was served by a municipality on whose city council residents had little representation and county government, scored rather poorly, as did Foster City, which was characterized by intense factional politics.

Although a majority of the new community respondents were not convinced that local officials were always responsive to the citizenry, a major-

174

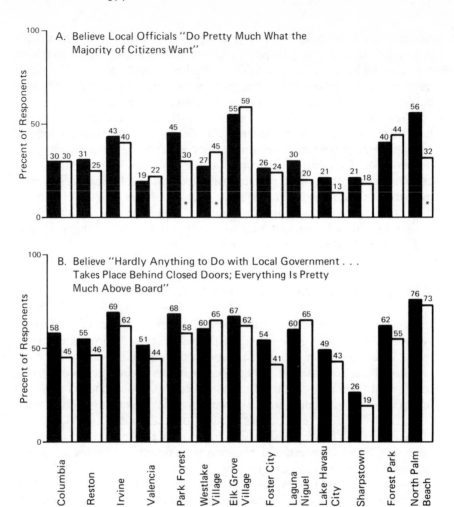

Figure 8-3. Attitudes Toward Local Governance

ity did believe that local governance was conducted in an open and above-board fashion. As with their attitudes toward the responsiveness of local officials, residents of five new communities with municipal governments—North Palm Beach, Irvine, Park Forest, Elk Grove Village, and Forest Park—scored highest in terms of respondents' perceptions of the openness of local government. On the other hand, less than a majority of the residents expressed confidence in the open conduct of governance in Lake Havasu City, which was governed by a county and developer-dominated special districts, and Sharpstown, which was governed by the city of Houston.

Residents' Participation in Local Governance

A third test of the governance structure is whether it encourages citizens to participate in local politics. Some critics of new communities, such as William Alonso and Chester McGuire (1973), have argued that because of monopolistic economic control by the developer, new community development will limit citizen political participation. As shown in figure 8-4, however, residents of conventional communities, as well as those living in new communities, tend to be politically inert. When asked about their participation in ten local political activities, ranging from talking about community policy matters with other people to actually holding office, the average resident had taken part in less than two during the previous year.[f]

In contrast with residents' satisfaction with public services and their beliefs about the responsiveness of local officials, which tended to be highest in incorporated communities, political participation rates were highest in the unincorporated new communities. Columbia ranked first, followed closely by Lake Havasu City and Reston. Political participation rates were also relatively high in the two other unincorporated new communities, Valencia and Laguna Niguel. Although Elk Grove Village ranked first in terms of citizen satisfaction with services and confidence in the responsiveness of local officials, it ranked last in terms of citizen political participation. Thus, up to a point it may well be that dissatisfaction with services and distrust of the benevolence of local officials and the developer actually stimulate residents to get involved in local government. As Sharpstown demonstrates, however, if alienation becomes too great, citizen participation may suffer.

The most successful model of new community governance appears to be Irvine. The combination of a municipal government and neighborhood homes associations used in that community resulted in very high resident

---

[f]Respondents were asked about their participation in the following activities during the previous year: (1) discussing local policy matters with other people; (2) writing to local political leaders or officials; (3) writing to a local newspaper about a community problem; (4) attending a meeting at which local policy matters were a major subject of consideration; (5) giving money to help in a local political campaign or issue; (6) speaking to a local political leader or public official; (7) contributing time in a local political campaign; (8) contributing time in support or opposition to a local issue; (9) serving in a local appointive office; and (10) being a candidate for or serving in a local elective office.

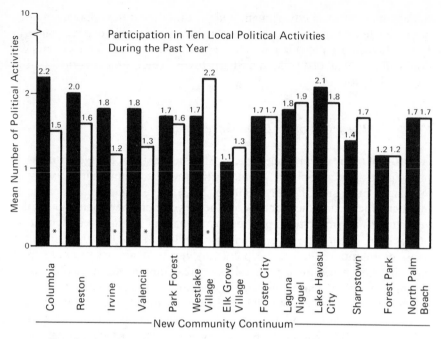

Figure 8-4. Local Political Participation

satisfaction with public services and confidence in local officials. In addition, Irvine ranked among the top six new communities in terms of citizen participation in local governance. As noted earlier, both city officials and The Irvine Company encouraged residents to take part in their homes associations and in city government. Also, Irvine's small resident-controlled neighborhood homes associations provided an incubator where residents could test their wings before becoming involved in larger political arenas. Four of the five members of Irvine's first City Council were homes association board members at the time of their election.[g]

Homes Associations: How Well Have They Worked?

The increasing use of homes associations in new community governance

---

[g] Homes association leadership has also been a stepping stone to higher political office in other new communities. For example, Westlake Village's first representative on the Thousand Oaks City Council had previously served as chairman of the Westlake Joint Board, an organization composed of homes association leaders.

and the variety of types of associations that have been developed prompted a special analysis of this unique quasi-public institution. The advantages of homes associations were spelled out earlier in this chapter. They offer developers a means to insure that open space and community amenities are maintained and that architectural controls are enforced. They are sometimes viewed as fostering neighborhood and community identity, and in at least two new communities—Irvine and Westlake Village—they have provided a training ground for community leaders. Although most homes associations do not relieve developers of the capital costs of community amenities, which must be recovered through increased lot and home prices, the Columbia Association has performed this function as well.

In spite of their well established role in new community development, homes associations have been the targets of much criticism. Because they involve a period of initial developer control, Albert A. Foer (1969) speculated that homes associations might breed too much developer paternalism, which he saw as being unhealthy in a vital and growing community. Foer also felt that by tying voting rights to property ownership, associations violated the principle of one man, one vote. Stanley Scott (1967) objected to the private character of homes associations and argued that local governments would be more appropriate custodians of developer-financed and resident-paid-for recreational property. Scott also pointed out that homes associations' open space and recreational facilities are almost always designed by the developer, but that the public interest in such facilities is so great that the public should have a role in their planning, even before the first residents move to a new community. Without public participation he felt that developers' concerns with profitability and residents' concerns with property values might obscure other important goals to which open space and recreational facilities contribute. Finally, Hugh Mields, Jr. (1973) suggested that homes associations might not be appropriate for large-scale new community development, because the services required by a heterogeneous population differ from those required in the homogeneous planned unit developments for which the homes association concept was originated.[h]

The philosophical arguments surrounding the homes association concept have raised some serious questions about the appropriateness of this governance institution, but have not touched the questions of how well associations work from their members' perspectives or which of the three homes association models—Irvine, Reston, and Columbia—work best.

---

[h] A number of other criticisms have been directed toward the use of homes associations in new communities. These include: (1) limited capacity to resolve conflicts among diverse groups in the communities; (2) lack of coordination with public agencies in the provision of services; (3) inability to float tax-exempt bonds or to receive intergovernmental transfer payments; (4) regressive character of association dues and assessments; (5) inability of residents to deduct association dues from state and federal income taxes; and (6) difficulty in changing the covenants to reflect changing circumstances that could not be foreseen by the developer.

Satisfaction with Association Performance

For the most part, homes association members were satisfied with the services their associations performed. As shown in table 8-1, this was particularly true for the maintenance of common areas, provision of recreational facilities, and social activities. In each case, over 80 percent of the respondents reported that they were satisfied with their associations' activities. Satisfaction with these services did not vary significantly among the three homes association models.

In the case of architectural controls and representation of residents' views to the developer and local government, however, members of the Columbia Park and Recreation Association and Reston Home Owners Association tended to be less satisfied with their associations' performance than were members of neighborhood associations based on the Irvine model. The reason for lower satisfaction levels in Columbia and Reston was due to the prominent role of the new community developer in both associations. Thirty percent of the Columbia respondents and 44 percent of those from Reston thought their developer had too much control of association affairs. In contrast, only 7 percent of the Irvine respondents and 4 percent of the Valencia respondents felt their developers' roles in association affairs were excessive. Other new communities, which followed the Irvine model, but which had somewhat lower resident satisfaction with architectural controls and representation of residents' views, were also characterized by higher perceptions of excessive developer control. Ten percent of the Foster City respondents, 27 percent in Westlake Village, and 31 percent in Laguna Niguel felt their developer exercised too much control over association affairs.

Residents' misgivings about the developers' roles in their associations carried over to their evaluations of overall association performance. While 86 percent of the Irvine respondents and 85 percent of the Valencia respondents were satisfied with their homes associations' overall performance, 69 percent or less of the Columbia, Reston, Westlake Village, Foster City, or Laguna Niguel association members were satisfied. In general, the larger the association and the larger the developer's role in association affairs, the less members felt they could have a personal voice in governance decisions and the less satisfied they were with their associations' overall performance. Satisfaction with various association services was positively associated with residents' evaluations, but of less importance than assessments of their voice in association affairs, developer control, and their association's performance in representing residents' views to the developer and local government.

Table 8-1
Satisfaction with Homes Associations

Associations[a]	Percent of Respondents Who Were Satisfied with:					Representation of Residents' Views to:	
	Overall Association Performance	Architectural Controls	Maintenance of Common Areas	Provision of Recreational Facilities	Social Activities	Developer	Local Government
Columbia Model							
Columbia Park and Recreation Association	62	75	89	91	86	65	77
Reston Model							
Reston Home Owners Association	51	78	91	86	90	73	73
Irvine Model							
Irvine (11 neighborhood associations)	86	93	92	92	95	93	96
Valencia (7 neighborhood associations)	85	92	96	93	92	94	95
Westlake Village (13 neighborhood associations)	69	83	88	91	93	83	85
Foster City (3 neighborhood associations)	65	81	95	100	100	81	77
Laguna Niguel (5 neighborhood associations)	63	77	82	77	86	86	81

[a]Includes only new communities with ten or more respondents who were members of automatic homes associations and excludes condominiums and cooperatives.

Members' Participation in Homes Associations Governance

A major concern with homes associations has been the possibility of citizen apathy, particularly with the affairs of small associations with limited responsibilities. For the most part, however, these fears have been unfounded. In fact, when gauged by voting in association elections, attending meetings, and serving on committees or holding office, participation tended to be much greater in the smaller neighborhood associations based on the Irvine model than in the larger Columbia Park and Recreation Association or Reston Home Owners Association. For example, while less than 40 percent of the Columbia and Reston association members had voted in the last elections of association officers, over 60 percent of the neighborhood association members had demonstrated this minimal level of interest in their association.

Over two thirds of the Columbia and Reston association members had not bothered to attend an association meeting during the previous year; in contrast, a majority of the members in each of the new communities with neighborhood associations reported that they had been to one or more association meetings. Serving on committees and holding office involve a much greater personal commitment than voting or attending meetings, and most association members—well over 80 percent—did not get this involved in the workings of their association. Again, however, almost twice as many neighborhood association members as those in Columbia and Reston had served in such a capacity.

Thus, in terms of both satisfaction with overall association performance and citizen participation in association governance, the Irvine model of small neighborhood associations seems preferable to the developer-controlled, communitywide associations, which have been used in Columbia and Reston. However, these advantages must be weighed against certain liabilities. If a general-purpose government is not able to provide community-level amenities, as it has in Irvine, a communitywide association may be the only means of accomplishing this end. Furthermore, since neighborhood associations require that the capital costs of amenities be recovered from lot prices, their use may not be suitable to a new community that seeks to accommodate low- and moderate-income households.

Toward New Modes of New Community Governance

Through the inventive use of a wide variety of governmental and quasi-governmental institutions new community developers have generally succeeded in producing high levels of resident satisfaction with public services. In doing so, however, they have further contributed to the extreme level of governmental fragmentation that characterizes metropolitan areas, and have usually not succeeded in producing greater than usual citizen confidence in public institutions or participation in community politics. Consequently, there seems to be a clear need for new modes of new community governance.

The key to successful governance of new communities lies in improving the tools for financing community services and in developing a system of shared power for the expenditure of funds. If new communities are to provide superior public services while at the same time keeping housing prices at reasonable levels, long-term financing of public facilities at moderate rates of interest is required. Because general-purpose governments—counties and municipalities—often have limited debt carrying capacity, developers have been forced to turn to special districts to finance some public facilities, while loading the costs of others onto land prices and forming homes associations to maintain them. The Columbia Park and Recreation Association's financial system provides an alternative to "front-ending" amenity costs, but the excessive amount of developer control associated with large associations alienates a significant proportion of the residents.

One promising alternative to the currently unsatisfactory modes of governing new communities may be the creation of transitional new community authorities. In outline form, such authorities would work as follows. After acquiring the development site and preparing preliminary plans, new community developers would petition a designated state agency for preliminary approval of the proposed community and for creation of a new community authority. Once an authority was established, the development site would be sterilized, so that administration of land development regulations would be transferred to the state agency and annexation by neighboring jurisdictions would be prohibited. The state agency would then appoint a board of public trustees to work with the developer on devising a final community development plan and a series of plans and financial models for public facilities and community service systems. (Initial planning costs might be financed by state or federal grants.) After reviewing these documents, the state would make a commitment involving approval of proposed land uses for the first stage of development and state guarantees of development authority bonds to finance public facility capital costs and initial operating deficits incurred by the authority.

As residents moved to the new community, they would at first elect representatives to an authority advisory council, and later, members of the new community authority board of directors. Replacement of public trustees by new community residents could be timed to coincide with the staged development of the community. The new community authority could remain as a new type of general-purpose local government, or could be phased into a municipal government, with transfer of land use regulatory power from the state to the municipality.

The concept of new community authorities is not new. Many aspects of this proposal have been discussed for a number of years and some have already been enacted by state legislatures.

For example, in 1960 Marion Clawson proposed a new independent form of local government—the suburban development district—as a response to many of the criticisms of urban growth. In addition to performing local government functions, including education, the districts would manage the suburban development process through either land use regulation or land acquisition and sale to private developers. Clawson suggested that the districts be organized as public-private corporations so that the full range of interests involved in suburban development could be represented on a district's board of directors. These might include representatives of county and central city governments, local landowners, real estate developers, and citizens who owned "stock" in the corporation. Sources of funds for the district would include borrowing, profits obtained from the purchase, improvement, and sale of undeveloped land, and property taxes.

Variations on Clawson's suburban development district proposal were recommended as vehicles to implement the Baltimore Regional Planning Council's "metrotown" growth proposal and The Maryland-National Capital Park and Planning Commission's concept of growth corridor new communities. In the former case, public-private development corporations modeled on the Communications Satellite Corporation were suggested (Baltimore Regional Planning Council 1963, p. 15). In the latter case, Henry Bain (1968) recommended that county-sponsored development districts be used to expedite and coordinate new community development along radial corridors extending outward from Washington, D.C. Although the districts would be authorized to acquire land for development, they were not viewed as a means of providing public services, which would be furnished by county government.

In its background paper on new communities, the American Institute of Planners (1968) offered two proposals for local governmental action in support of new communities. These included: (1) the formation of local public-private development corporations with power to acquire raw land, add improvements, and sell it for development in accordance with detailed plans; and (2) the creation of a new unit of general local government, which would be responsible for providing public facilities.

Also reporting in 1968, the Advisory Commission on Intergovernmental Relations recommended a larger state role in new community development. Among other proposals, the commission proposed that states enact legislation to authorize the creation of state and local land development agencies to undertake land acquisition and improvement for new communities. The commission also indicated that state or local review agencies could assume an interim trusteeship during the development and transitional stages of new community growth.

Some states have already responded to the need for new governmental institutions for new communities, although none has yet established an institution with the breadth of responsibility envisioned for the proposed new community authorities. For example, while the New York State Urban Development Corporation was given a broad array of powers to undertake land development and to construct housing, it was not designed to provide local public services to its housing projects or new communities. Arizona's General Improvement District Act of 1970 allows districts created under the act to finance up to two thirds of the major development costs of new communities and to provide various municipal services, but districts do not have eminent domain or other public powers. The Arizona legislation does provide, however, for state review and approval of applications for the establishment of general improvement districts and for state application of more stringent land use controls than those of a proposed new community's host county. California has also provided a mechanism for the review and approval of new community development by a state agency, in this case through the California local agency formation commissions. A similar function is performed in Tennessee under the 1971 Prospective New Community Certification Act. In the Tennessee case, the State Planning Commission is authorized to certify areas as prospective new communities and to prohibit their annexation by neighboring jurisdictions.

The public-private partnership dimensions of the proposed new community authorities are encompassed in the 1972 Ohio New Communities Act. The act enables a new community district and a new community authority to be established to undertake joint new community development with a private entrepreneur. However, the formation of a district and authority is subject to the approval of local governmental agencies, rather than the state, and authority functions are rather limited.

To date, the closest approach to the proposal for new community authorities is the 1970 Kentucky New Communities Act. Under the Kentucky legislation, a new community district may be established by county courts upon petition of an organization that controls 75 percent of the land in a proposed district, which must encompass a minimum of six square miles of territory. Once certified, districts must attempt to acquire all of the land within the district boundaries. Land for public uses can be acquired by eminent domain. Districts are also empowered to provide municipal services, establish independent school districts (with the consent of existing school governments), levy taxes, issue licenses, and impose fines. Once a district has been established, land use control shifts from existing jurisdictions to the district. Operation of districts is overseen by district commissioners, who are appointed by the governor. Finally, when the population of a district reaches 3,000 persons, it may incorporate as a municipality.

Although the basic ideas behind new community authorities have drawn widespread support, certain limitations of the concept should also be recognized. First, new community authorities are viewed as a more rational means of financing and staging the provision of public services in new communities and of insuring that regional and state interests are recognized in land use decisions. Land acquisition, some aspects of land improvement, such as neighborhood streets and utilities, and home building would continue to be private sector functions. While public land acquisition has drawn support from a number of commentators, the willingness of private entrepreneurs to assume this burden serves to test the economic feasibility of a proposed new community venture and, through appreciation in land values, provides a major incentive for private investment.

Second, the creation of new community authorities would involve a large financial commitment by state government, since authority bonds would require backing by the full faith and credit of the state to assure their marketability during the initial stages of development. Even though a state might never incur a loss, since authority bonds would be redeemed from the revenues of property taxes and special assessments, the potential exists if a new community venture should fail. This possibility and the many problems encountered by New York State's moral obligation bonds and the financing of the New York State Urban Development Corporation may create active resistance to state participation in new community ventures.

Third, existing local governments may not approve of the removal of a portion of their tax bases through the creation of a new community authority, or the transfer of land use regulations to state government. On the other hand, existing local jurisdictions inevitably lose control of new community development when new communities incorporate or are annexed to nearby municipalities (as has already occurred in 8 of the 13 new communities in this study), and in some cases may feel that new community development is more of a liability than an asset. Since the creation of new community authorities would remove the fiscal burden of development from existing jurisdictions, their establishment may, in fact, be welcomed.

Fourth, on the surface it may appear that new community authorities would add to the existing fragmentation of governmental units in metropolitan areas. However, unlike single-function special districts, authorities would be empowered to act as general units of local government. They would limit the proliferation of special-purpose districts and homes associations that now accompany new community development. In addition, they could help achieve economies of scale in the provision of public services: (1) by contracting with existing service providers for the performance of areawide functions, such as water supply and sewage disposal; and (2) during the early years of development, by contracting for local functions such as education, police and fire protection, and library services until the critical population mass is reached.

Finally, new community residents would be certain to chafe under a trusteeship arrangement, even though their views were represented through an authority advisory council and they were assured of eventual control of the authority board of directors. As the residents' numbers and political power increased, there would undoubtedly be pressure to speed up the transfer of power to the citizenry. However, the timing and degree of residents' interests in self-determination cannot be accurately predicted. Therefore, pressure for premature transfer of power must be anticipated, but it cannot be fully dealt with until it emerges as an issue and demands a political solution.

In sum, many of the apparent drawbacks of the new community authority proposal may not be as serious as they at first appear. The Twentieth Century Fund Task Force on the Governance of New Communities (1971) noted that new communities should serve as laboratories for testing new forms and processes of local government. The new community experience revealed in this chapter has shown this to be a pressing need if new communities are to match more rational planning with a more rational and effective system of governance.

Part IV

The Community

9 Housing and the Neighborhood

Housing and the character of the immediate neighborhood were major factors in families' decisions to move to both new and conventional communities. In fact, it can almost be said that people do not move to communities—they move to a house and the block on which it is located. The reason for households' greater interest in the home and neighborhood is easily understood. Purchase of a home is usually the greatest investment most households will ever make. The quality of the home and attractiveness of the neighborhood in large part determine the soundness of this investment. In addition, while people make use of community recreational, shopping, educational, and health facilities, the greatest proportion of their discretionary time is spent in and around their homes. The home and block are the centers of daily living from which people venture out into the extended community.

The Concept of Housing Choice

A key feature of the new community concept has been the provision of a range of housing alternatives within the same community. Planners have long held that our attachment to the single-family detached home—which has resulted in suburban sprawl—is to some extent due to the lack of other suburban housing choices. To be an effective antidote to sprawl, new community development must provide consumers with the option of living in a variety of housing types, including types such as townhouses and apartments, planned and developed at higher densities than are typical of detached housing.

New community ideology stresses a number of other benefits from a wider choice of housing. For one, new communities should be able to accommodate a broader range of life-styles. As shown in chapter 6, the single-family detached home was overwhelmingly preferred by families with children, but single-person households and married couples without children often chose to live in attached housing and apartments. If a broad range of housing prices as well as housing types can be offered, new communities should also be able to attain greater social and racial diversity than has been characteristic of suburban development in the United States.

189

Types of Housing Offered

In fact, new communities offered consumers a wide range of housing in the same community than did the conventional communities. The distribution of housing types is shown in figure 9-1. Two new communities at the upper end of the new community continuum—Columbia and Reston—had the greatest variety of housing types. They were two of only three new communities, the other being North Palm Beach, in which single-family detached units comprised less than half of the housing stock. In four other new communities—Irvine, Westlake Village, Foster City, and Sharpstown—over 40 percent of the housing stock consisted of duplexes, townhouses, and apartments. On the other hand, new communities such as Valencia, Elk Grove Village, Laguna Niguel, and Forest Park were developed with a relatively high proportion—over 75 percent of the housing stock—of single family detached units. This reflected their developers' perceptions of the market and, in the case of Laguna Niguel and Valencia, an attempt to establish a solid middle-class image of the community during the early stages of development. Both communities, however, have shifted an increasing proportion of new housing starts to townhouses and multi-family dwelling units.

Opportunities to Own or Rent

New communities also tended to give consumers the opportunity to live in either ownership or rental housing units. With over 40 percent of their housing stock in rental units, Columbia and Reston again offered the greatest choice. Other new communities with a relatively high proportion of rental units included Sharpstown (38 percent), Lake Havasu City (32 percent), and Foster City (29 percent). Rental opportunities in other new communities are shown in table 9-1. Since conventional community respondents were matched to the paired new communities by housing type, in most cases they did not vary in tenure.[a]

Housing Prices

Table 9-2 summarizes the distribution of current home values and rents reported by new community respondents in 1973. It can readily be seen that housing prices or values were not within the means of many moderate-

[a]The exceptions were Reston, with 15 percent more owners than West Springfield; Valencia, 13 percent more renters than Bouquet Canyon; Westlake Village, 18 percent more renters than Agoura/Malibu Junction; and North Palm Beach, 10 percent more renters than Tequesta.

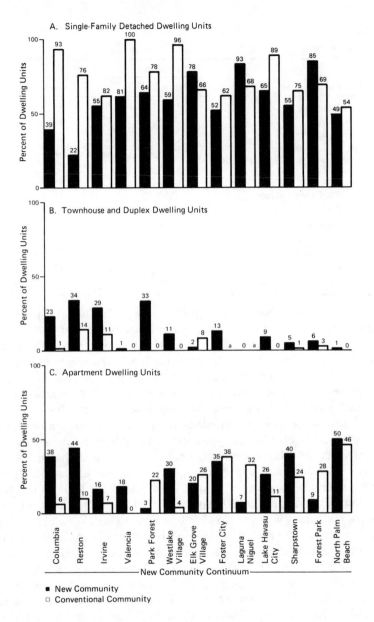

A. Single-Family Detached Dwelling Units

B. Townhouse and Duplex Dwelling Units

C. Apartment Dwelling Units

New Community Continuum

■ New Community
□ Conventional Community

Note: Dwelling unit mix includes all dwelling units in new and conventional communities. Conventional community respondents were sampled from each dwelling unit type in proportion to the distribution of dwelling unit types in their paired new communities.

[a]Data for townhouses and duplexes are included in the apartment dwelling unit figures.

Figure 9-1. Dwelling Unit Mix

Table 9-1
Housing Tenure

| Communities | Percent of Respondents | |
	Own or Buying	Rent
Columbia	57	43
Reston	52	48
Irvine	80	20
Valencia	82	18
Park Forest	78	22
Westlake Village	81	19
Elk Grove Village	83	17
Foster City	71	29
Laguna Niguel	96	4
Lake Havasu City	68	32
Sharpstown	62	38
Forest Park	88	12
North Palm Beach	88	12

income persons. Less than 10 percent of the single-family detached units, and less than 25 percent of the ownership townhouses and apartments, were valued at under $25,000. There were also proportionately few rental units for less than $150 a month. On the other hand, new communities have not provided very much housing aimed at the affluent and rich consumers. Under 10 percent of the ownership units were valued at $60,000 or more and a quarter or less of the rental housing was priced at $300 or more a month. Thus, while new communities have provided consumers with a variety of choices of housing types and tenure, housing prices cover a narrower spectrum. New communities bave tended to price housing within the means of middle- and upper middle-income consumers, and to ignore the low-, moderate-, and upper income segments of the housing market.

Of course, the range of housing prices varied among new communities. Median home values were over $45,000 in Foster City, Westlake Village, and Reston, and were under $35,000 in Forest Park, Lake Havasu City, Park Forest, and Sharpstown. Median values in the remaining new communities were between $35,000 and $45,000. Also, developers have varied in the extent of their efforts to provide housing for moderate-income persons. As reported in chapter 5, subsidized housing units were available in Columbia, Reston, Lake Havasu City, Park Forest, and Forest Park.

Neighborhood Design

Two neighborhood design principles have dominated the ideology of new communities. The first concerns density. In order to achieve greater effi-

Table 9-2
Housing Prices in New Communities and Conventional Communities, 1973

	Tenure and Housing Type[b] (Percent of Respondents)											
	Own						Rent					
	Single-family Detached		Townhouse		Apartment		Single-family Detached		Townhouse		Apartment	
Housing Prices[a]	NC	CC	NC	CC	NC	CC	NC	CC	NC	CC	NC	CC
Low	9	9	13	26	23	7	10	3	12	22	15	11
Moderate	28	33	23	32	36	51	19	19	26	15	36	48
Average	33	33	42	19	27	7	21	27	31	6	32	27
Above average	22	14	18	7	10	14	26	40	15	25	13	13
High	8	11	4	16	4	21	24	11	15	32	4	1
Percent of dwelling units	69	75	7	4	3	5	2	2	5	3	14	11

[a]Price categories:

	Ownership	Rental
Low	Under $25,000	Under $150/month
Moderate	$25,000-$34,999	$150-$199/month
Average	$35,000-$44,999	$200-$249/month
Above average	$45,000-$59,999	$250-$299/month
High	$60,000 and over	$300 and over/month

[b]NC = New communities
CC = Conventional communities

ciency in the provision of community facilities and services and to minimize environmental damage from development, new communities have been expected to build at higher than usual residential densities.[b] Second, new community planning has been strongly influenced by the neighborhood unit principle first espoused by Clarence Perry (1929) and used in the design of Radburn and the federal Greenbelt communities of the thirties.

According to Perry, community development should be organized into a series of relatively self-contained and socially homogeneous neighborhoods. An elementary school should be located near the center of each neighborhood, together with a church, a library, and a community center. Access to facilities should be made easier through provision of an internal pathway system. The neighborhood unit concept also calls for the reservation of a considerable amount of land for neighborhood parks and playgrounds. In order to increase safety, through traffic is to be discouraged by the provision of a series of collector roads, which lead traffic to major thoroughfares at the edge of the neighborhood.

Although the neighborhood unit concept was endorsed by the American Public Health Association and used in its influential publication, *Planning the Neighborhood* (1948), the disjointed character of suburban growth has limited its application.[c] However, the unified planning for large land areas made possible by new community development, and the adoption of neighborhood planning principles by many of the new communities under development since 1947, has led to renewed interest in this planning concept.

Housing Density

Housing density was measured at two geographic scales—the housing cluster and the neighborhood. The former measures the density of groups of five to seven single-family detached housing units and entire townhouse and multifamily projects; the latter generally includes the areas within one-half mile of housing clusters, and encompasses nonresidential land uses, such as schools and parks.

As shown in table 9-3, average densities at both scales were similar in new and the paired conventional communities (where housing units were sampled to match those provided in the new communities). On the other hand, average densities varied considerably among new communities.

[b] Potential cost savings through higher density development are detailed in the Real Estate Research Corporation's report, *The Costs of Sprawl* (1974).

[c] The neighborhood unit concept has had its share of critics, as well as proponents. For a fuller discussion of its history and application in new community development, see John B. Slidell (1972).

Table 9-3
Housing Density

Communities	Mean Units Per Acre		Mean Persons Per Acre	
	Housing Cluster[a]	Neighborhood[b]	Housing Cluster[a]	Neighborhood[b]
New communities	7.6	4.1	25	14
Conventional communities	6.7	4.4	23	15
Columbia	8.8	2.4	28	8
Reston	8.1	3.9	28	14
Irvine	4.6	4.1	14	13
Valencia	7.3	5.3	26	19
Park Forest	5.8	4.1	20	14
Westlake Village	8.2	5.8	26	19
Elk Grove Village	5.5	3.3	20	12
Foster City	10.2	4.0	33	13
Laguna Niguel	4.5	3.0	14	10
Lake Havasu City	2.0	0.3	6	1
Sharpstown	14.4	4.3	45	13
Forest Park	4.7	3.4	18	13
North Palm Beach	8.9	5.4	26	16

[a]Cluster density was calculated on the basis of groups of five to seven single-family detached dwelling units and entire attached and multifamily housing projects.

[b]Neighborhood density was calculated on the basis of the area within one-half mile of respondents' dwellings, or a smaller area if bounded on one or more sides by a major thoroughfare, a major body of water, undeveloped land of five or more acres, or the community boundary.

Cluster densities, both in units and persons per acre, were highest among the new communities that provided the greatest proportion of attached and multifamily housing. Columbia, Reston, North Palm Beach, Westlake Village, Foster City, and Sharpstown all averaged over eight dwelling units and 25 persons per acre. However, in large part because of public officials' concern with maintaining overall community densities at rather low levels,[d] average neighborhood densities did not vary as greatly among new communities, and were not too much higher than the 3.0 to 3.5 dwelling units per acre typical of many suburban areas. Thus, new communities may be able to achieve various economic and environmental cost savings by clustering dwelling units in townhouse and apartment projects, but it is doubtful that very large savings would be possible through much higher than usual overall neighborhood and community densities.

[d]For example, as pointed out in chapter 4, the overall density of Columbia was limited to a very conservative 2.2 dwelling units per acre, while in the case of Reston, overall density was not to exceed 13 persons per acre.

Table 9-4
Availability of Neighborhood Amenities and Facilities

| Facility[a] | Percent of Respondents Having Facility Within Their Neighborhood | |
	New Communities	Conventional Communities
Playground/tot lot	61[c]	49
Bus stop[b]	43[c]	22
Swimming facility	39[c]	33
Elementary school	35[c]	24
Walking-bicycling path	34[c]	15
Church	34	35
Tennis court	25	24
Convenience store	24	28[c]
Nursery school/day care center	21[c]	8
Supermarket	20[c]	16
Neighborhood/community shopping center	19[c]	15
Gas station	18	34[c]
Restaurant	16	14
Neighborhood/community center	15[c]	2

[a]The following facilities, in order of their availability, were found in less than 15 percent of the new community and conventional community respondents' neighborhoods: picnic areas, general practitioners/internists, middle schools, post offices, laundromats, libraries, hospitals, bars/taverns, movie theaters, golf courses, regional shopping centers, billiard parlors, bowling alleys, high schools, teen centers, public health facilities, roller skating rinks, and ice skating rinks.
[b]Defined as within a ten-minute walk of respondents' homes.
[c]Difference statistically significant at 0.05 level of confidence.

Neighborhood Amenities and Facilities

On the whole, new communities have come much closer to achieving neighborhood self-sufficiency than have the paired conventional communities. Fourteen facilities and amenities were available in 15 percent or more of the new community respondents' neighborhoods.[e] See table 9-4. Of these 14 facilities, 9 were available significantly more often in new community neighborhoods, 2 were available significantly more often in conventional community neighborhoods, and for 3 facilities the difference in availability was not significant.

[e]Neighborhood was defined as the area within one-half mile of respondents' homes, or a smaller area if bounded on one or more sides by a major thoroughfare, a major body of water, undeveloped land of five or more acres, or the community boundary.

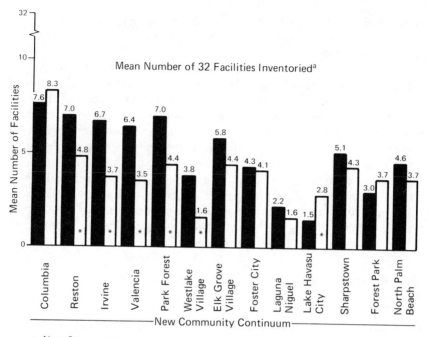

aThe 32 facilities inventoried are listed in table 9-4.

Figure 9-2. Facilities Available in Neighborhoods

The advantage in favor of new communities was greatest for bus stops (21 percent difference in availability), walking and bicycling paths (19 percent difference), nursery schools and day care centers (13 percent difference), neighborhood-community centers (13 percent difference), playgrounds and tot lots (12 percent difference), and elementary schools (11 percent difference). On the other hand, conventional community respondents were significantly more likely to find a gas station (16 percent difference) and convenience store (4 percent difference) in their neighborhoods.

Although new communities have done a better job than conventional communities in providing various neighborhood facilities, very few communities approached the degree of neighborhood self-sufficiency envisioned by the neighborhood unit concept. Of 32 facilities inventoried, the average new community respondent had about 5 in his neighborhood and the average conventional community respondent had about 4. As shown in figure 9-2, however, the difference among individual new communities was about as great as that between new communities and conventional communities.

New communities toward the upper end of the new community continuum generally provided a fuller array of neighborhood facilities and amenities than did new communities toward the lower end of the continuum. For example, using elementary schools as an organizing element in neighborhood design, Columbia's planners also viewed the provision of nursery schools and day care programs, community meeting rooms, pathways, parks and playgrounds, swimming pools, bus stops, and initially, neighborhood convenience stores as desirable neighborhood facilities to achieve their goals of efficiency, convenience, and social integration. Other new communities that provided their residents with a greater than average number of neighborhood facilities included Reston, Irvine, Park Forest, Valencia, and Elk Grove Village.

What Was Provided versus What the Residents Most Wanted

When new and conventional community respondents were asked which three neighborhood facilities they most preferred within one-half mile of their homes, a number of discrepancies between what had been provided and what the residents most wanted became evident.[f] The most striking deficiencies (in terms of residents' preferences) in new community neighborhood design were in the provision of libraries, teen centers, supermarkets, and post office substations. While 6 percent of the respondents had a library within their neighborhoods, 30 percent mentioned a library as one of the three facilities they most wanted. Although only 1 percent of the new community respondents' neighborhoods had teen centers, they were desired by 15 percent. Both post office substations and supermarkets were desired by 10 percent more of the respondents than actually had them in their neighborhoods. Among the conventional communities, differences between facilities most preferred by respondents and those actually provided were greatest for these same four facilities.

Conversely, there were many neighborhood facilities provided more frequently than would be indicated by respondents' preferences. Differences in the proportions of respondents who most wanted and actually had various facilities in their neighborhoods were greatest for playgrounds (19 percent vs. 61 percent), bus stops (10 percent vs. 43 percent), nursery school/day care centers (6 percent vs. 21 percent), swimming facilities (24

---

[f]Respondents were asked to disregard the facilities they actually had in their neighborhoods in indicating their preferences. Thus, the question was aimed at uncovering preferences as opposed to additional facilities needed. Needs, however, became evident when preferences were compared to the neighborhood facilities, which were available in new communities.

percent vs. 39 percent), tennis courts (13 percent vs. 25 percent), and convenience stores (14 percent vs. 24 percent). With the exception of bus stops, swimming facilities, and nursery school/day care centers, and the addition of gasoline service stations, the above facilities were also those provided in greater abundance in the conventional communities than indicated by respondents' preferences.

The Building Blocks of Housing Satisfaction

The importance of satisfaction with dwelling unit livability should not be underestimated. As noted in previous chapters, dwelling unit characteristics have a strong influence on households' original decisions to move to new communities and their subsequent decisions to move out. What is more, it will be shown in a later chapter that housing satisfaction is a key element in evaluations of new communities as good places to live.

Much of the previous discussion of housing satisfaction and its relation to public policy has centered on the association of housing type and people's apparent preference for the single-family detached home. Although it has often been demonstrated that higher density development is more efficient and less harmful to the environment, policy makers have been reluctant to authorize more dense development because of their belief that it will not provide a satisfying living environment for many types of families. This section examines factors that contributed to new community residents' overall satisfaction with the livability of their homes. Satisfaction with housing livability was measured by responses to the question: "Now, overall how do you feel about the (house/apartment) as a place to live?" The respondents were asked to answer using a seven-point scale ranging from "completely satisfied" to "completely dissatisfied."

Owning versus Renting

Home ownership is the most consistent factor associated with housing satisfaction. Regardless of their race, income, education, life cycle-family type, and satisfaction with neighborhood design and community facilities, new community owners were more satisfied with their dwellings than were new community renters. Ownership also transcended the often observed association between housing type and housing satisfaction. As shown in table 9-5, there was little difference in the satisfaction levels of new community respondents who owned single-family detached, townhouse, and apartment dwelling units. But for each housing type, renters were significantly less likely to be satisfied with their homes.

Why is home ownership so important? It is apparently not due to

Table 9-5

Influence of Ownership on Housing Satisfaction in New Communities

Housing Satisfaction	Tenure and Housing Type (Percent of Respondents)					
	Own			Rent		
	Single-family Detached	Townhouse	Apartment	Single-family Detached	Townhouse	Apartment
Completely satisfied	44	43	44	20	24	23
Satisfied	45	45	51	45	55	52
Neutral or dissatisfied	11	12	5	35	21	25

characteristics of the dwelling unit or neighborhood. When respondents who were most satisfied with the indoor and outdoor space of their homes, privacy, and a variety of neighborhood characteristics were compared, homeowners were always more satisfied than renters. Thus, ownership did not seem to be a proxy for some other housing or neighborhood factor that might influence satisfaction. It was also not a proxy for family type or income. When both of these factors were held constant, owners were again consistently more satisfied than renters, regardless of the type of dwelling unit. Instead, ownership seems to tap more basic goals of the family and the society. It implies security and stability, provides a visual symbol of social status, and may be viewed as a good investment—a way to save money and increase capital, which is not possible by renting. Additionally, home ownership allows the household to do as it pleases with its dwelling unit and, in the case of single-family detached units, the yard and grounds as well. Home ownership has been a traditional goal of families moving to suburban locations and it is clearly reflected in the housing satisfaction and dissatisfaction of new community residents.

Characteristics of the Dwelling Unit

When tenure and housing type are held constant, the influence of a number of other characteristics of the dwelling unit on housing satisfaction can be identified. These include the value of the dwelling and amount of rent, age of the dwelling, the amount of indoor and outdoor space, and privacy.

Home Value and Rent. New community residents' satisfaction with ownership units steadily increased with the value of the unit. For example, while 26 percent of the respondents living in single-family detached dwellings valued at less than $25,000 were completely satisfied with their homes, 68 percent of those living in homes valued at $60,000 or more were completely satisfied. The breaking point in complete satisfaction occurred for ownership single-family detached houses, townhouses, and apartments in the $35,000 to $44,999 price range. A lower than average proportion of respondents who owned homes valued at less than $35,000 and a higher than average proportion of those with homes valued at $45,000 or more were completely satisfied with their dwellings. Except for houses and apartments renting for less than $150 a month, whose tenants were much less likely to be satisfied with their dwellings, the amount of rent paid per month was not associated with higher dwelling unit satisfaction.

Age of the Dwelling. The age of individual housing units was not strongly associated with housing satisfaction. Households who occupied ownership units that were over ten years old were less likely to be completely satisfied with their homes, but up to ten years increasing dwelling unit age had little effect on satisfaction. Respondents who occupied newly constructed rental apartments were less satisfied than the occupants of older apartments. On the other hand, satisfaction with rental single-family detached homes and townhouses was lowest for units that were over ten years old.

Dwelling Unit Space. The physical size of dwelling units had little effect on housing satisfaction. However, when dwelling unit space was combined with household size, space did make a difference. For example, complete satisfaction with single-family detached homes increased from 18 percent of the respondents living in homes with less than one room per person to 59 percent of those living in units with three or more rooms per person. A similar relationship was also true for other types of ownership housing units and for rental units.

Housing satisfaction was also influenced by people's perceptions of the space they had available. The proportion of respondents who were completely satisfied with their homes was very low among those who reported that they had less indoor space than their families needed—ranging from 19 percent of the single-family detached homeowners to 7 percent of the rental apartment dwellers and 2 percent of those occupying rental townhouses. The proportion of respondents who reported they had too little indoor space for their families' needs did not vary greatly by housing type, but did vary by tenure. For example, only 8 percent of the condominium apartment dwellers reported they had too little space versus 40 percent of those living in rental apartments.

Respondents' perceptions of outdoor space and privacy were also related to housing satisfaction. Those who reported that they had enough or more than enough outdoor space for their families' needs were more than twice as likely to be completely satisfied with their homes as those who reported that they had too little outdoor space. The negative effects of too little outdoor space were most severe for renters. Less than 10 percent of the renters of single-family detached, townhouse, and apartment units who thought they had too little outdoor space were completely satisfied with their dwellings. Perceptions of insufficient outdoor space were about the same for owners and renters of single-family detached homes (18 percent and 20 percent). Owners of townhouses and apartments were less likely to feel that they had too little outdoor space (14 percent and 12 percent, respectively), and were about half as likely as townhouse and apartment renters (33 percent and 25 percent) to think that available outdoor space was insufficient for their families' needs.

Perceptions of the adequacy of outdoor privacy from neighbors also influenced housing satisfaction. About two thirds of the single-family detached homeowners, over 70 percent of the townhouse owners, and 48 percent of the condominium apartment owners thought they had sufficient outdoor privacy from their neighbors. In contrast, 51 percent of the townhouse renters, 49 percent of the single-family home renters, and 27 percent of the apartment renters said they had a place outside where they had privacy from their neighbors.

Neighborhood Attributes

The two aspects of neighborhood design that have received the most attention in planning and design literature, density and the neighborhood unit concept, had little effect on housing satisfaction. The apparent association between density and housing satisfaction was completely spurious, and disappeared when tenure was held constant. Apartment and townhouse residents appeared to be less satisfied with their dwellings, but this was only because they were more likely to be renters than owners.

Objective Characteristics of the Neighborhood. Neighborhood self-sufficiency was only moderately associated with housing satisfaction. For example, the only neighborhood facility associated with respondents' satisfaction with single-family detached ownership units was the existence of a swimming pool. Five percent more single-family owners with a neighborhood pool were completely satisfied with their home than owners whose neighborhoods lacked a pool. The housing satisfaction of townhouse owners was somewhat more responsive to the presence or absence of neighborhood amenities. The proportion of completely satisfied townhouse owners was from 5 to 15 percent higher when elementary schools, convenience stores, parks and playgrounds, swimming pools, and tennis courts were available in their neighborhoods. Apartment owners' satisfaction increased somewhat with the availability of swimming pools, tennis courts, gas stations, and convenience stores in the neighborhood. Among renters, the availability of neighborhood swimming pools and parks and playgrounds were most consistently associated with housing satisfaction.

Street design had a modest effect on housing satisfaction, particularly among owners and renters of single-family detached homes. Fifty-one percent of the single-family owners and 52 percent of the single-family renters whose homes were located on a cul-de-sac street were completely satisfied with their homes. In contrast, only 37 percent and 19 percent, respectively, were completely satisfied with homes located on straight through streets.

Underground telephone and electric wires were associated with increased housing satisfaction. For example, the proportion of respondents who were completely satisfied with single-family detached homes increased from 28 percent to 47 percent if these utilities were placed underground rather than overhead along the street. Forty percent of the respondents with overhead lines running along the back lot lines of their homes were completely satisfied, suggesting that this location is preferable if lines cannot be buried.

Finally, maintenance levels also influenced housing satisfaction. Although most new community respondents lived in dwellings that were well maintained, upkeep levels tended to be somewhat lower for renters than for owners. Over 90 percent of the ownership housing units' building exteriors and grounds were rated as well maintained by household interviewers. In contrast, less than 80 percent of the building exteriors and grounds of rental single-family detached units were rated as well maintained, while between 85 percent and 90 percent of the rental apartment units received such ratings. Rental townhouses, on the other hand, tended to be as well maintained as ownership units. Depending on the type of housing and tenure, the proportion of respondents who were completely satisfied with their homes dropped between 7 percent and 30 percent if the buildings or grounds were poorly kept up.

Residents' Perceptions of the Immediate Neighborhood. Because not all new community residents see objective neighborhood characteristics in the same way, the associations between subjective perceptions and housing satisfaction provide some useful insights. For example, new community planners' careful attention to aesthetics may contribute to increased satisfaction. Respondents who thought their immediate neighborhoods were highly attractive were from two to four times more likely to be completely satisfied with their homes or apartments as those who rated their immediate neighborhoods as unattractive. The association between perceptions of other aspects of the immediate neighborhood and housing satisfaction tended to vary with housing type and tenure.

After attractiveness, perceptions of neighborhood privacy, upkeep, reputation, and homogeneity had the strongest influence on satisfaction with single-family detached ownership units. Among those who had purchased townhouses, perceptions of convenience, upkeep, and safety were important to housing satisfaction, in addition to perceptions of attractiveness. In the case of condominium apartment owners, housing satisfaction was most strongly related to respondents' perceptions that their immediate neighbors had characteristics similar to their own, as well as to perceptions of the neighborhood's attractiveness, privacy, and friendliness.

Neighborhood attractiveness was as important to renters' satisfaction with their homes as it was to owners'. Other factors of importance to renters' housing satisfaction, regardless of housing type, were perceptions that the immediate neighborhood was safe, well kept up, and that it had a good reputation. In addition to these factors, housing satisfaction was higher among single-family detached and townhouse renters if they felt their neighborhoods were not crowded, and among apartment renters if they felt their neighbors had similar characteristics to themselves, were friendly, and that the neighborhood gave them enough privacy.

Much has been written about the importance of similarity among neighbors as a factor encouraging greater neighborhood sociability and greater housing and neighborhood satisfaction. As noted above, respondents who felt that their neighbors were people much like themselves and that their neighbors were friendly tended to be more completely satisfied with their homes than respondents who perceived greater neighborhood heterogeneity and less friendliness. Among the owners of single-family detached homes and condominium apartments there was also a tendency for persons who had closer ties with their neighbors to be more satisfied with their homes. For example, 50 percent of the single-family owners and 62 percent of the condominium apartment owners who reported that they often visited with their neighbors were completely satisfied with their dwellings, versus only 32 percent and 25 percent of those who said they hardly knew their neighbors. However, in the case of townhouse owners and all renters, the association between neighboring and housing satisfaction went in the opposite direction. That is, the closer the ties people had with their immediate neighbors, the less satisfied they were with their homes.

Satisfaction with the Community as a Place to Live

A basic premise of new community development has been that provision of a better community increases housing satisfaction. For the most part, this seems to be true. Respondents who rated the community as an excellent or good place to live tended to be most satisfied with their homes. Clearly, the association between community satisfaction and housing works both ways. Satisfaction with the community may increase the pleasure people derive from their homes, but housing satisfaction may also contribute to perceptions of the community as a good place to live.

In addition to overall evaluations of the community, respondents' evaluations of several community components were also associated with their satisfaction with housing. The strongest and most consistent relationship across housing and tenure types was satisfaction with the performance of homes and community associations (see chapter 8). For example, 64 percent of the single-family homeowners who were completely satisfied with their homes association were also completely satisfied with their home, versus 47 percent of those who were dissatisfied with homes association performance. In the case of townhouse owners, those completely satisfied with their association were more than twice as likely (69 percent versus 32 percent) to be completely satisfied with their homes as those who were dissatisfied with homes association performance. This was also true of both townhouse and apartment renters who were served by homes associations, but not apartment owners and single-family home renters.

Housing satisfaction was also associated with perceptions that various aspects of the community were better than the respondents' previous communities. With the exception of apartment owners and renters, respondents who thought community planning was better than their previous community were one and a half to two times as likely to be completely satisfied with their homes as those who thought planning was worse. Single-family homeowners and renters and townhouse owners and renters, but not apartment owners and renters, were also more likely to be completely satisfied with their homes if they thought their community was a better place to raise children.

Perceived improvements in community recreational facilities were most associated with housing satisfaction among townhouse owners and renters and single-family homeowners. Recreational facilities were somewhat less associated with housing satisfaction among condominium apartment owners, and had no influence on housing satisfaction among those who were renting single-family homes. On the other hand, single-family renters were the only respondents whose housing satisfaction was systematically associated with perceptions of improvements gained in the quality of schools after moving, and, along with condominium apartment owners, with improvements gained in health and medical services. Finally, improvements in shopping facilities were universally associated with lower, rather than higher, satisfaction with respondents' homes and apartments, possibly because shopping facilities tended to be rated highest in the older new communities with generally smaller and older housing than was available in the newer new communities with less abundant shopping opportunities.

Residents' Personal Characteristics

In concluding this discussion of factors associated with housing satisfaction in new communities, it should be noted that a number of personal and situational characteristics were also related to respondents' evaluations of their homes as places to live. First, the length of residence in a dwelling sometimes influenced satisfaction, though the direction and strength of the relationship varied among housing-tenure types. For example, length of residence was not associated with satisfaction with single-family detached ownership or rental units. In the case of ownership townhouses and apartments, and, to a lesser extent, rental townhouses, the longer respondents had lived in them, the less satisfied they were. On the other hand, longer residence in rental apartments was associated with greater satisfaction with the dwelling. Since it is easier to move from a rental apartment than an ownership unit, it is likely that only those most satisfied with their apartments had remained in them over a number of years.

Households' family types and the stages of their life cycle were also associated with housing satisfaction. For both ownership and rental single-family detached homes and apartments, respondents who were in later life cycle stages (married couples and single persons over age 40 without children living in the household) were most satisfied with their homes. In the case of ownership and rental townhouses the association between life cycle-family type and housing satisfaction was not as strong. Possibly reflecting housing space problems, married couples with children were the least satisfied with all types of housing and tenure alternatives. Additionally, the difference in satisfaction between owners and renters was sharpest for this group. Only 13 percent (rental apartments) or less of these respondents were completely satisfied with rental housing. Younger single persons and married couples without children generally occupied an intermediate position on the spectrum of housing satisfaction. They tended to be more satisfied than married couples with children, but less satisfied with their housing than older married couples and single persons without children.

Education and income were not consistently associated with dwelling unit satisfaction. Persons with less formal education tended to be most satisfied with ownership units, particularly townhouses and apartments, while those with more education tended to be most satisfied with rental units, though, in the latter case, the strength of the association with education was rather weak. Respondents with higher family incomes tended to be those most satisfied with ownership single-family detached homes, which was also reflected in the strong association between home value and satisfaction reported above. For other types of housing and tenure, however, there was either no association between income and satisfaction, or, as in the case of ownership apartments and rental townhouses, persons with lower incomes were those most satisfied with their homes.

Black respondents were somewhat less satisfied than whites with single-family detached ownership and rental housing, but were somewhat more satisfied with ownership and rental townhouses. Black and nonblack respondents were equally satisfied with rental apartments.

Key Factors Influencing Housing Satisfaction

As the preceding discussion suggests, housing satisfaction depends on a variety of characteristics of the home, neighborhood, and community, and how these characteristics are perceived and interpreted by new community residents. Nevertheless, the approximate order of their influence on satisfaction can be determined through the use of multivariate analysis techniques.

For all dwelling types the most important factors influencing satisfaction were those associated with the dwelling unit itself. Owning instead of renting was of overriding importance. After tenure, both the amount of indoor and outdoor space and the way it was perceived in relation to family needs had a strong influence on housing satisfaction. Privacy from neighbors was also critical, particularly among persons living in multifamily dwelling units. Among homeowners, perceptions that the home was a good financial investment were important, and among both owners and renters perceived construction quality influenced satisfaction.

Neighborhood characteristics had less influence on housing satisfaction than did characteristics of the dwelling. The most important neighborhood attributes were the perceived attractiveness of the immediate neighborhood and maintenance levels. Upkeep of the neighborhood and building exteriors was particularly important to the satisfaction of persons living in multifamily housing. Density in the abstract had very little influence on housing satisfaction; but persons who perceived their neighborhoods as crowded, noisy, or lacking in privacy were less satisfied with their homes. Obviously, neighborhood design can have a strong influence on housing satisfaction and can overcome negative influences of higher densities.

Although satisfaction with the community as a place to live was associated with satisfaction with the home, the availability of neighborhood and community facilities and satisfaction with them had less influence on housing satisfaction than either dwelling unit or neighborhood factors. One aspect of the institutional organization of the community, however, was strongly associated with housing satisfaction. Persons who were more satisfied with the overall performance of homes associations tended to be more satisfied with their homes as places to live.

Housing Satisfaction in New and Conventional Communities

Only minor differences were apparent in the housing satisfaction of new and conventional community respondents. As shown in table 9-6, there were no significant differences in respondents' satisfaction with single-family detached and townhouse ownership units or rental townhouses. While new community respondents were significantly more likely to be satisfied with rental apartments, the difference in satisfaction was not exceptionally large. New community development has not resulted in greater housing satisfaction than is characteristic of conventional suburban development because new communities have not had a marked influence on the major factors contributing to satisfaction.

As noted above, when housing tenure was held constant, the major contributors to housing satisfaction were characteristics of the dwelling unit. Table 9-6 clearly shows that new communities have not produced housing that has induced greater than usual satisfaction with financial and cost factors, indoor space, outdoor space and privacy, or construction of the home. Thus, it is not surprising that overall housing satisfaction levels were so similar in new communities and conventional communities.

The somewhat greater satisfaction with rental apartments in new communities was mainly due to the greater satisfaction with various attributes of the immediate neighborhood. New community apartment dwellers were significantly more likely than those living in conventional community apartments to give high ratings to their immediate neighborhoods' appearance, upkeep and maintenance, lack of crowding and quiet, reputation, safety, and to places near their apartments for children's outdoor play. Although single-family homeowners living in new communities also gave significantly higher ratings to a number of neighborhood attributes— attractiveness, maintenance, convenience, places for outdoor play, and friendliness—these did not result in higher overall satisfaction with the home. They were possibly offset by conventional community respondents' greater satisfaction with housing costs and construction quality. In the case of ownership and rental townhouses, fewer differences were apparent in respondents' ratings of their immediate neighborhood. New community residents tended to be somewhat more satisfied with the lack of crowding, privacy, quiet, and maintenance of rental townhouses, but ratings of ownership townhouse neighborhoods were similar in both settings.

Paradoxically, the attributes with which new community respondents were generally more satisfied than those living in conventional communities—community facilities and services—had the least effect on housing satisfaction. For example, new community single-family homeowners gave significantly better ratings to community planning, public schools, recreational facilities, shopping facilities, and health facilities, but these advantages in favor of new communities were not reflected in greater housing satisfaction. This was also the case for the availability of the neighborhood facilities which are shown in table 9-6. Although new community respondents were more likely than conventional community respondents to live in neighborhoods with elementary schools, parks and playgrounds,

Table 9-6
Comparison of Housing Satisfaction and Contributing Elements in New and Conventional Communities

	Percent of Respondents[a]							
	Ownership				*Rental*			
	Single-family Detached		*Townhouse*		*Townhouse*		*Apartment*	
Satisfaction Indicators	NC	CC	NC	CC	NC	CC	NC	CC
Satisfaction with dwelling unit								
Completely satisfied	44	42	43	50	24	22	23[b]	19
Satisfied	45	47	45	42	55	59	52[b]	46
Neutral or dissatisfied	11	11	12	8	21	19	25	35[b]
Satisfaction with dwelling unit characteristics								
Financial factors								
Better investment than alternatives considered	70	72	71	70	NA	NA	NA	NA
Cost better than previous dwelling	40	49[b]	31	65[b]	31	29	29	35
Indoor space								
Enough space for families' needs	79	79	77	79	73	65	60	63
Layout and space better than previous dwelling	75	78	58	82[b]	57	61	57	53
Outdoor space								
Enough space for families' needs	82	80	86	86	67	55	75[b]	66
Enough privacy	65	65	73	81	51	38	27	33[b]
Construction								
Better than previous dwelling	48	55[b]	33	60[b]	45	39	39[b]	28
Satisfaction with immediate neighborhood								
Attractiveness								
Attractive[c]	47[b]	42	55	52	44	34	39[b]	29
Appearance[d]	68	68	63	71	60	54	60[b]	47
Density								
Lack of crowding[e]	39	41	41	39	36[b]	17	24[b]	18
Privacy[e]	53	52	58	49	48[b]	23	43	37
Quiet[e]	42	43	48	53	40[b]	22	35[b]	20

	Percent of Respondents[a]							
	Ownership				Rental			
	Single-family Detached		Townhouse		Townhouse		Apartment	
Satisfaction Indicators	NC	CC	NC	CC	NC	CC	NC	CC
Maintenance[c]	52[b]	47	52	60	50[b]	19	46[b]	33
Convenience[c]	54[b]	46	60	55	50	44	53	61[b]
Safety[c]	52	53	55	48	39	44	42[b]	35
Places for child's play[c]	37[b]	33	41	32	37	22	36[b]	16
Social factors								
Friendliness[c]	47	45	53[b]	35	36	32	31[b]	17
Homogeneity[c]	23	24	29[b]	20	16	7	16	13
Reputation[c]	69	67	75	67	63	61	54[b]	45
Satisfaction with community								
Community planning[d]	77[b]	55	81[b]	64	71	52	69[b]	48
Health and medical services[d]	25[b]	21	23	22	22[b]	8	28	25
Public schools[d]	50[b]	47	37	40	34	31	39	34
Recreational facilities[d]	62[b]	49	68[b]	43	67[b]	38	63[b]	58
Shopping facilities[d]	39[b]	33	35	30	37	49	51	58
Homes association[e]	21	14	23	44[b]	11	IC	8	IC
Objective factors								
Appearance								
Foundation planting exists	98	99	97	99	93	87	95	95
Underground utilities exist	67[b]	46	92	98	64	66	76[b]	66
Maintenance								
Exteriors well kept up	94	93	99	99	92[b]	73	89[b]	66
Lawn and property well kept up	91[b]	87	96	94	90[b]	74	86[b]	70
Street well maintained	98	96	99[b]	93	98[b]	86	96[b]	77
Street Design								
Cul-de-sac street	28	26	34	45	24	13	17	36[b]
Curved through street	47[b]	40	34	37	32	51	32	36[b]
Straight through street	25	34[b]	32[b]	22	44	36	51[b]	28

Table 9-6 (cont.)

	Percent of Respondents[a]							
	Ownership				Rental			
	Single-family Detached		Townhouse		Townhouse		Apartment	
Satisfaction Indicators	NC	CC	NC	CC	NC	CC	NC	CC
Neighborhood facilities available								
Elementary school	47[b]	27	45[b]	8	35	26	44[b]	20
Park or playground	75[b]	54	70[b]	42	64	48	61[b]	38
Swimming facility	36[b]	22	67	82[b]	65	65	89	86
Tennis courts	23[b]	15	43[b]	24	43	54	41	42
Convenience store	29	46[b]	37[b]	18	37	44	44	62[b]
Gasoline service station	12	31[b]	25	30	21	43[b]	33	60[b]

[a]NC = New communities
CC = Conventional communities
IC = Insufficient number of cases (less than ten)
NA = Not applicable
[b]Significant difference at 0.05 level of confidence.
[c]Highest rating on five-point scale.
[d]Better than previous community.
[e]Highest rating on seven-point scale.

swimming facilities, and tennis courts, the availability of these facilities made only a minor contribution to their housing satisfaction.

Figures for other objective characteristics of new and conventional community homes and neighborhoods are also reported. The greater proportion of new community dwellings served by underground telephone and electric wires was reflected in subjective perceptions of the attractiveness of the immediate neighborhood. New community single-family homes and apartments were more likely than those in conventional communities to have buried wires and were also more likely to be rated as attractive by respondents. A similar parallel was apparent for indicators of exterior building and yard maintenance. That is, interviewers' ratings of upkeep were reflected in respondents' own perceptions of their immediate neighborhoods, which were judged to be better kept up in new community single-family and apartment neighborhoods than in the conventional communities.

Housing satisfaction among individual new and conventional communities is illustrated in figure 9-3, which shows the proportions of respondents who were completely satisfied with single-family detached ownership units and rental apartments.[g] It can be readily seen that housing

---

[g]These two housing alternatives covered over 80 percent of the new community respondents.

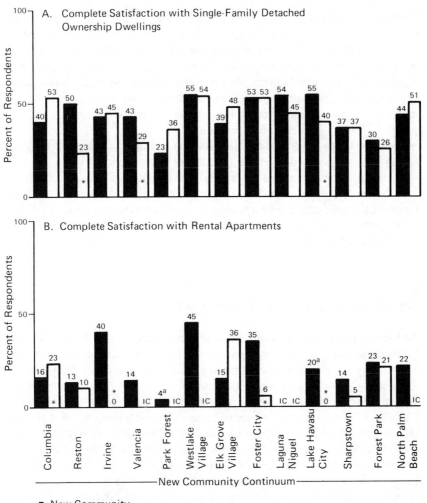

A. Complete Satisfaction with Single-Family Detached Ownership Dwellings

B. Complete Satisfaction with Rental Apartments

■ New Community
□ Conventional Community
* Statistically Significant Difference
IC Insufficient Number of Cases
  (less than ten)

[a]Rental townhouses and duplexes.

Figure 9-3. Residents' Satisfaction with Single-family Homes and Apartments

satisfaction had little to do with a new community's place on the new community continuum. Since community characteristics did not strongly influence satisfaction levels, this was to be expected. For single-family homes, housing satisfaction was highest in the three new communities with the highest median home values—Reston, Westlake Village, and Foster City—and in two new communities—Lake Havasu City and Laguna Niguel—with dispersed development patterns that led to higher than average perceptions of outdoor space and privacy. The lowest satisfaction with single-family detached homes was expressed by respondents who lived in the older new communities, and, in particular, Park Forest, Forest Park, and Sharpstown, where median home values were low and a greater proportion of small homes had been built.

Satisfaction with rental apartments was strikingly higher than average for apartments located in Irvine, Westlake Village, and Foster City. Most of these apartments were in extremely well designed projects with meticulous landscaping and grounds maintenance and a variety of recreational amenities. Satisfaction with apartments in other new communities did not vary greatly from the average—23 percent completely satisfied—for all new community respondents.

Implications for Future New Communities

The findings discussed in this chapter have a number of implications for future new community development. Although housing satisfaction is of crucial importance in new community marketing and in residents' overall satisfaction with new communities as places to live, this was not an area where new community development surpassed conventional suburbs. Clearly, if new communities are to be market successes, developers must pay greater attention to delivering housing value—particularly more space and better designed and constructed homes for the money. Developers' previous attention to neighborhood design and community facilities is reflected in residents' satisfaction with these community features, but they cannot be substituted for housing value without sacrificing dwelling unit satisfaction.

Of course, this creates a basic dilemma. If new community planners and developers are to provide both a better environment and more home for the money, housing prices can only be escalated so that the developer's housing products are within the financial means of a narrower segment of the market and the possibilities of achieving socially heterogeneous populations are diminished. Unfortunately, it is easier to state the problem than to find a solution. One answer may be public assumption of the costs of producing a high quality environment. However, this raises serious problems of equity unless the public sector devotes its resources to environmental improvements in both new and conventional communities.

Another means of maintaining reasonable housing costs and at the same time not scrimping on environmental quality is to raise the density of new community development. It has been shown here that if properly designed, higher density development need not result in diminished housing satisfaction, particularly if higher density ownership units rather than rental units are provided.

10 Recreation and Leisure

New communities are at the forefront of the growing environmental movement in the housing industry. In place of home builders' traditional emphasis on housing value and the immediate neighborhood, community builders design and market a total living environment. Recreation and leisure play leading roles in their image of the good community.

An excursion through developers' colorful brochures and other advertising materials leaves little doubt that recreational opportunities and enhanced leisure are major advantages to be gained by living in a new community. The Reston master plan is advertised as a design for living, working, and playing. In California, Westlake Village was planned to provide residents with the "enjoyment and recreation of a weekend resort." At Irvine "villageness" means "Sharing village shops and recreation centers, parks and bicycle paths. . . . And you can be a part of it." To the north, Foster City residents "race their sailboats on the lagoons, lakes and canals; their children swim, play and fly kites in the neighborhood beach parks. . . . And all around them on this 'Island of Blue Lagoons' is a wonder world of water." To the southwest recreation is "Big as the Great Outdoors at Lake Havasu City, Arizona. . . the West's fun land!" While at North Palm Beach in Florida, it's "The Water. To some it's a playground. For sailing and fishing and sunning and swimming. To some it's simply the serenity of a stroll along a moonlit shore."

Organizing for Recreation

Behind the four-color pictures of children walking down a forest path and adults sunning by a pool lies the enormous task of actually putting together a recreational service system. In the usual pattern of suburban growth and development urban facilities and services have typically been provided in stages. Basic facilities and services—transportation, water and sewer systems, and police and fire protection—have always come first. Only after the passage of some years and only if funds were left over after the "basics" were provided have communities turned to social amenities such as parks, open space, and recreational facilities.

New community development requires two departures from the conventional pattern of establishing recreational services. First, the distinction

217

between basic public services and social amenities in ordering priorities is relatively meaningless in the new communities context. Each is viewed as an integral and essential part of the new community environment and as necessary for economic and social success. Second, new community development embraces the concept of preservicing. This means that a variety of recreational facilities are put in place and are available for use before each cohort of residents occupies a new section of housing.

Departing from traditional approaches to social service delivery challenges the ingenuity of both planners and developers. New communities are typically initiated on the peripheries of metropolitan areas far from existing urban service systems. Local government is rarely able to plan, build, and maintain the full array of recreational amenities and services required by large-scale community development. On the other hand, few developers initially have the skill, experience, or organizational capacity to initiate the full range of recreational amenities and services needed to make a new community functional.

During the initial stages of a new community's development and potentially throughout the development process two public institutions which predate the new community may make significant contributions to its recreational resources. These institutions are county government and local school districts. However, neither governmental institution has a consistent record of support for new community recreation.

County Participation: A Mixed Record

As subdivisions of state governments many counties are not legally authorized to provide urban-type services, including recreational services. Where counties have become interested in open space and recreation their efforts are most often devoted to the development of regional parks and recreational facilities. The regional bias of county interest in outdoor recreation has produced some benefits for new communities. Irvine, Laguna Niguel, Sharpstown, and Forest Park have county regional parks and Elk Grove Village and Park Forest benefit from county forest preserves. Nevertheless, many county recreational officials view with disdain the more intimate open space and neighborhood recreational facilities that characterize new community master plans and are unable to materially support them.

Financial and political factors also limit county involvement in providing recreational resources in new communities. Many counties, particularly those in rural areas, have limited financial resources for outdoor recreation. For example, in 1973 the operating expenditures of the Columbia Association were over ten times those of the entire Howard County

Park and Recreation Department. Inadequate financing also plagues many urban counties. Recreational expenditures in Reston for 1973 were over half as large as those of the Fairfax County Recreation Department, although the latter served a population over 20 times as large as that of Reston. Thus, county governments often find it financially impossible to fund extensive recreational resources in new communities. The financial crunch is further compounded by the political problem, mentioned repeatedly in this book, of providing higher levels of service in only a portion of a county's jurisdiction. Whatever money is available for recreation must be spent evenly over the entire county.

In spite of the limitations of most counties there are some important exceptions. Los Angeles County provides relatively high quality recreational services throughout its jurisdiction. As a result, it has been able to provide and operate neighborhood parks in both Valencia and Westlake Village. The use of special county service areas and taxing districts provides another way for counties to increase their participation in new community recreational service systems. This approach has been used by Los Angeles County to maintain the pathway system in Valencia and by Orange County in providing various recreational and open space services in Irvine and Laguna Niguel.

Support from Local School Districts

New communities have had somewhat greater success in securing support for the recreational system from local school districts. In every new community studied one or more community schools was used by residents for outdoor recreation. Fifty-six percent of the schools with gymnasiums, 75 percent of those with multipurpose rooms, and 80 percent of those with outdoor recreational facilities were available for community use. During the previous year over a fifth of the persons interviewed in new communities had actually taken advantage of these facilities.

In a number of new communities schools have been designed in conjunction with neighborhood or community parks and recreational centers. This joint use of facilities conserves land and reduces the number of trips residents must make. Community school programs, which offered both educational and recreational activities for local residents, were operated at 58 percent of the schools serving the study new communities. Sixty percent of the new community recreational organizations surveyed reported the existence of cooperative programs with local schools. Finally, community colleges and universities provided another source of recreational opportunities. Colleges in Columbia, Valencia, and Irvine were all used to some extent for community outdoor recreation.

Notwithstanding the widespread use of schools in new community recreational systems, several factors limit the role they can potentially play in providing recreational services. One limiting factor is state legislation. In only a few states, including California, Minnesota, Illinois, New York, and Ohio, are school boards authorized to conduct community school programs financed by the school district. Most states only go so far as to allow school districts to let agencies other than the school board make use of school facilities for noneducational purposes. Second, school officials are not uniformly in favor of recreational use of school plants, since excess wear and tear and decreased efficiency of the school program may result. Third, recreationists are also not universally in favor of school-run recreational programs. Their opposition stems from fear of a regimented educational bias, fear that funds for recreation may be harder to obtain, fear that school programs will favor children at the expense of adults, and the simple fact that many recreational activities are not suitable for school grounds and buildings.

A more fundamental problem in using schools as a component of a new community's recreational system has been the lag in school construction in many new communities. Among the study new communities more than half of the high school students, almost half of the middle school students, and over a quarter of the elementary school students were bussed to schools in adjacent communities. In school districts with declining enrollments at existing schools, such as in the districts serving Reston and Foster City, there has been strong voter resistance to financing new school construction rather than bussing children to existing schools. This attitude, as well as other uncertainties surrounding the timing of school construction, can play havoc with a community plan that designates elementary and secondary schools as neighborhood and community recreational centers.

The Communities' Dilemma

Because surrounding governmental units and school districts have not been able to assume full financial and operating responsibility for new community open space and recreational systems, developers and residents have had to establish internal governmental structures to provide recreational resources. Sharpstown was annexed to the city of Houston. A portion of Westlake Village was annexed to the city of Thousand Oaks and to the Conejo Park and Recreation District. Elk Grove Village was incorporated as a village. When the village government was unable to provide satisfactory recreational services, residents incorporated the Elk Grove Village Park District. Five new communities incorporated and established municipal park departments and/or recreation commissions, including

Forest Park, Foster City, Irvine, North Palm Beach, and Park Forest. Two new communities, Foster City and Lake Havasu City, have used multipurpose special districts to aid in providing recreational opportunities for residents.

Although these governmental units have had varying degrees of success, they have all suffered from the same financial problems that beset new community developers during the early years of development. That is, "facilities must be provided for anticipated demand at a time when property values and economic activity do not produce sufficient revenue to support such expenditures" (Advisory Commission on Intergovernmental Relations 1968, p. 91). As a result, new communities that established governmental mechanisms to provide recreational resources had to wait until their populations grew and tax bases were adequate to support bond issues for recreational land acquisition and capital improvements. For example, Forest Park waited 16 years, Elk Grove Village, 10 years, Foster City and Irvine, 7 years, North Palm Beach, 5 years, and Westlake Village, 4 years after initial residential settlement before proceeding with bond referenda. Governments' inability to finance open space acquisition and recreational facilities during the early years shifts the burden of preservicing to the developer. If the developer is unable or unwilling to assume this burden, the result can only be an underdeveloped recreational system not much different from that which occurs in the normal course of suburban expansion.

The Developers' Dilemma

Because local governments have difficulty providing recreational resources in new communities, developers have become increasingly involved in this public service. From a developer's point of view the provision of recreational resources in new communities should have three characteristics (Institute of Government 1971).

First, the method of providing recreational resources should maintain for as long as necessary developer control of the quality of facilities and the timing of their provision. Ideally, open space and recreational facilities should be provided prior to residential sales in each development increment and should be of high enough quality to be an asset in marketing the community. Without developer control it is impossible to insure that each of these objectives is met.

Second, the method of providing resources should allow the costs of open space and recreational facilities and programs to be shared by the residents of a new community. This is essential to the long-run profitability of a developer's new community venture. In addition, to maintain reasonable residential price levels during the early years of development when there are few residents with whom to share early heavy capital costs, repayment of costs should be deferred as long as possible.

Third, the method of providing resources should be acceptable to the residents so that resident discontent (and resulting adverse publicity) is kept to a minimum.

Unfortunately, all of these goals conflict. The more developers monopolize control of the recreational system the harder it is to share costs and maintain residents' satisfaction. If cost sharing is maximized through arrangement for public provision of facilities and services, control is sharply diminished and quality may be impaired. If maximum resident satisfaction is sought, developers may have to choose between the demands of existing residents and the imperative of providing a product that will appeal to prospective residents.

Evolving Developer Approaches

Developers of early new communities, including Park Forest, Sharpstown, North Palm Beach, Forest Park, and Elk Grove Village, chose to give up maximum control in favor of sharing costs of the recreational system. Thus, they fostered early incorporation of their communities and municipal or special district provision of recreational areas and facilities. Given the greater interest in housing value and less emphasis on environmental quality by consumers during the 1950s and early 1960s, this was probably a rational course of action.

Developers of new communities initiated since 1960 have generally sought to achieve a balance among the three characteristics sought in providing recreational resources. This became more feasible after the automatic homes association concept gained widespread acceptance among FHA and local governmental officials and among consumers. As used in Columbia and Reston, communitywide homes associations allow their developers to control the character of the entire open space and recreational service system while sharing costs with the residents. An alternative use of homes associations has characterized California new communities. In these communities developers have tended to maximize their control over the provision of neighborhood amenities through developer provision of facilities and dedication to neighborhood homes associations, but to share costs of communitywide facilities with public agencies.

In addition to using homes associations as tools for providing recreational amenities and services, new community developers have increasingly opted to provide recreational facilities as revenue producing "profit centers." For example, developers have owned and operated or leased golf courses in Columbia, Irvine, Laguna Niguel, Lake Havasu City, Reston, Sharpstown, Valencia, and Westlake Village. AVCO Community Developers, Inc. owned a tennis club and a beach club in Laguna Niguel. McCulloch Properties, Inc. built a bowling alley, movie theater, and marina in Lake Havasu City. Westlake Village's developer owned a tennis club. The Newhall Land and Farming Company operated a number of recreational enterprises in and adjacent to Valencia, including Magic Mountain family ride park, a public riding stable, and a family recreation park for dune buggies and motorcyclists.

Providing Recreational Resources: How Effective Have New Communities Been?

In spite of the many obstacles to be overcome in organizing recreational systems, new communities as a whole have been quite successful in providing recreational resources. New community performance was evaluated on the basis of eight measures of resource availability. These included recreational and open space acreage, recreational sites, variety of facilities, adequacy of facilities in comparison with national standards, accessibility of facilities, recreational personnel, recreational programs, and annual operating expenditures for recreational services.

Recreational and Open Space Acreage

Preserving open space and providing land for recreational facilities is supposed to be one of the major public benefits from new community development. The success of new communities in realizing this goal is readily apparent. Private new communities had an average of 406 acres per 10,000 population in open space and recreational land uses versus an average of 216 acres per 10,000 population in the paired conventional communities. As shown in figure 10-1, new communities that contributed most to this advantage were Lake Havasu City, Valencia, Laguna Niguel, and Elk Grove Village. Lake Havasu City is the site of the very extensive Lake Havasu State Park. Laguna Niguel has several extensive recreational land uses, including a county regional park, county beach park, and golf course. Elk Grove Village lies adjacent to the Ned Brown Forest Preserve, owned by the Cook County Forest Preserve District, while Valencia includes three golf courses provided by the developer.

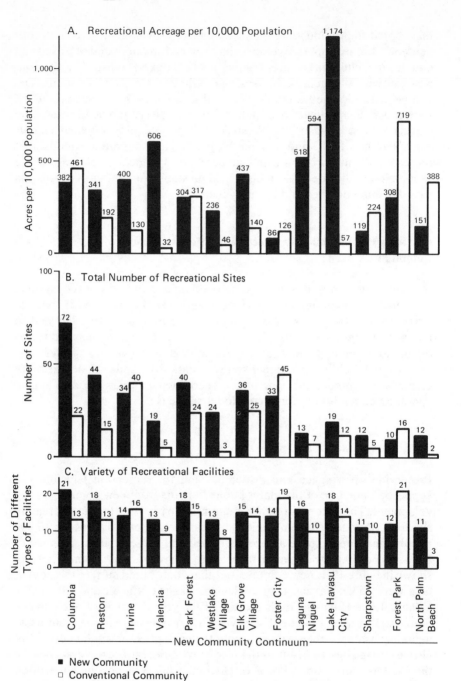

Figure 10-1. Recreational Resources in New Communities and Paired Conventional Communities

The community-by-community comparison included in figure 10-1 shows that many of the conventional communities were also successful in providing recreational and open space land. In fact, for 7 of the 13 paired comparisons shown the conventional communities preserved somewhat more land per capita. The most notable conventional community in this regard was Sharonville, the community paired with Forest Park. Sharonville encompasses a large county regional park and includes a stream valley open space system acquired by the town government. Dana Point/Capistrano Valley, which was paired with Laguna Niguel, was in second place among the conventional communities. As noted in chapter 4, this community contains the Dana Point Harbor and Marina and the Doheny State Park and Beach.

In many cases lands to be committed to open space and recreational uses were spelled out in agreements between new community developers and local officials or in land dedication requirements contained in local ordinances. For example, in securing new town zoning from Howard County, Columbia's developer agreed to devote a minimum of 20 percent of the acreage in the new town zone to permanent open space land uses, 50 percent of which was to be available for public use. In Reston 40 percent of the master planned acreage is designated for various common uses. Elk Grove Village requires dedication of 10 percent of developer-owned land, while dedication requirements in North Palm Beach are 5 percent of tracts of 40 acres or more. In California new communities developers are required to dedicate land based on projected population. This requirement ranges from nine acres per thousand population in Westlake Village (half for schools and half for recreation) to two and one-half acres per thousand population in Valencia and Laguna Niguel.

Although new community developers have contributed to open space preservation, recreational professionals were not uniformly happy with the amount and type of land that had been set aside. A common complaint among professionals was that developers often dedicated land that was unsuitable for recreational use. They admitted that open space had been preserved, but saw little benefit in terms of land for recreational facilities and programs. Moreover, some professionals pointed out that since open space can include ravines, lakes, and golf courses in communities where "percent of development acreage" guidelines are used, there may be relatively little space actually available for general community recreational use. Resolution of this problem may be difficult. The more specific local development codes are about the types of acreage to be dedicated, the less site design flexibility is left to planners and developers. This flexibility is considered to be one of the major advantages of planned unit and new community development since it allows greater sensitivity to the natural environment and encourages innovative site design (So, Mosena, and Bangs 1973).

Recreational Sites and Facilities

Measures of total open space and recreational acreage can be somewhat misleading, as recreational professionals were quick to point out, since they do not indicate the uses of such land. This dimension of recreational resources was evaluated by gathering information on the actual number of sites used for recreation, the variety of types of recreational facilities offered, and the quantity of different facilities available in each community.

On a per capita basis new communities provided over twice as many recreational sites as their paired conventional communities. As shown in figure 10-1, the absolute number of recreational sites was greater in 10 of 13 study new communities than in their paired conventional communities. Figure 10-1 also shows that new communities generally provided a greater variety of recreational facilities than conventional communities. In this case 10 of the study new communities were superior again to their paired conventional communities.

Quantitative data were gathered for 21 different types of recreational facilities. For 10 of the facility types new communities provided from 2 to 7 times the number per capita that were provided in the paired conventional communities. These facilities included tot lots, walking paths, bicycle trails, fishing lakes, boating facilities, swimming facilities, recreational centers, arts and crafts rooms, teen centers, and playing fields. The conventional communities were superior for two of the 21 facility types— basketball courts and baseball diamonds.

Another way to gauge the recreational resources of new communities is to compare recreational facilities provided with minimal national standards. Table 10-1 shows that with the exception of arts and crafts rooms new communities have more than met accepted minimal standards. Swimming facilities, community recreational centers, golf courses, and gymnasiums were each provided at over twice the minimal standard. In contrast the conventional communities failed to meet national minimal standards for four of the facilities compared.

Recreational professionals were asked to name their communities' greatest needs for recreational areas and facilities. They gave a wide variety of answers, but there were a number of clear favorites. Many professionals felt there was a need for new or expanded neighborhood or community recreational centers or multipurpose buildings (Columbia, Reston, Park Forest, Elk Grove Village, Irvine, Westlake Village, and Lake Havasu City), a town hall with meeting facilities (Reston and North Palm Beach), a teen center (Elk Grove Village), or a senior citizens' center (Westlake Village). A need for regional recreational parks was seen in Sharpstown, Valencia, and Westlake Village. Additional neighborhood parks were called for in Reston and North Palm Beach.

Table 10-1

Comparison of Recreational Sites and Facilities Provided in New and Conventional Communities with Selected Minimal Standards

Facility		Number of Sites/Facilities Per 10,000 Population			
			New Communities	Conventional Communities	
	Minimal Standard	Number	Adequacy (%)	Number	Adequacy (%)
Indoor facilities					
Arts and crafts rooms	3.3[a]	3.0	91	1.3	39
Gymnasiums	1.0[a]	2.1	210	2.1	210
Community recreation centers	0.5[b]	1.8	360	0.6	120
Teen centers	0.5[b]	0.7	140	0.1	20
Outdoor facilities					
Baseball-softball diamonds	5.0[b]	8.0	160	10.6	212
Golf courses	0.2[a]	0.7	350	0.5	250
Parks with benches	2.0[c]	2.6	130	2.3	115
Playgrounds	5.0[d]	5.0	100	4.8	96
Swimming pools/ beaches	0.7[b]	5.3	757	2.5	357
Tennis courts	5.0[b]	7.5	150	7.7	154
Tot lots	5.0[e]	8.0	160	2.4	48

Sources:

[a]National Recreation Association 1965a.
[b]National Recreation Association 1965b.
[c]Butler 1959.
[d]Meyer and Brightbill 1956.
[e]Lackawanna County Planning Commission 1963.

Other facilities, which recreational professionals often felt were needed, included playing fields, especially lighted fields, swimming pools and beaches, tennis courts, gymnasiums, arts and crafts facilities, and nature study centers. A survey of articles appearing in local newspapers in the study new communities also showed widespread citizen interest in bicycle trails and walking paths.

Professionals in the conventional communities indicated many of the same types of needs as those working in new communities, though they placed greater emphasis on the need for additional parks and open space.

Accessibility of Recreational Facilities

The accessibility of recreational facilities to potential users is a key factor in gauging the adequacy of a community's recreational resources and is supposed to be one of the primary advantages of new community development. Locating facilities close to users is designed to increase use, promote sociability among neighborhood residents, and reduce the need for many intracommunity vehicular trips.

There are a number of ways to measure accessibility. Table 10-2 compares the study new and paired conventional communities using three types of indicators. The first indicator shows the proportion of respondents who had various recreational facilities within their neighborhoods, the area within one-half mile of their homes not crossed by a major street or geographical barrier. New community residents were significantly more likely than residents of conventional communities to find all but golf courses and tennis courts in their neighborhoods. The most common neighborhood recreational facilities in both settings were playgrounds for children under 12 and swimming facilities. Walking paths were available in the neighborhoods of about a third of the new community respondents, while about a fourth of the respondents in both new and conventional communities had neighborhood tennis courts.

Road distances to the nearest recreational facilities provide a second indicator of accessibility. New communities were superior to conventional communities for each of the facilities compared in table 10-2. The median resident in both settings had the least distance to travel to playgrounds and swimming facilities.

A third way to gauge accessibility is to examine how far people actually went to participate in recreational activities. Since all respondents did not participate in recreational activities, the median distance to facilities used cannot be compared directly with the median distance to the nearest facility, which was calculated over all respondents. Nevertheless, it is obvious that people do not always use the closest facility. For example, new community residents tended to go much farther to play golf and tennis than would have been necessary had participants uniformly used the closest available golf course or tennis court. Most people used the streets and sidewalks running past their homes for walking rather than traveling to the nearest walking path in a park or open space corridor. Thus, while the median distance to the nearest new community walking facility was almost 5,000 feet, the median distance actually traveled to begin walking for pleasure was less than 50 feet. With the exception of walking, however, new community residents uniformly traveled less distance to participate in recreational activities than the residents of conventional communities.

Table 10-2
Accessibility of Recreational Facilities

	New Communities			Conventional Communities		
	Percent with Facility in Neighborhood	Median Distance (ft.)		Percent with Facility in Neighborhood	Median Distance (ft.)	
Facility		Nearest Facility[a]	Facility Used[b]		Nearest Facility[a]	Facility Used[b]
Golf course	2	10,500	20,300	1	11,900	31,700
Playground for children under 12	61	2,100	2,000[c]	49	2,700	2,100[c]
Swimming facility	39	3,900	4,600	33	5,000	6,200
Tennis court	25	4,600	7,300	24	4,900	7,600
Walking path	34	4,800	<50[d]	15	7,900	<50[d]

[a]Road distance to the nearest facility was measured for all respondents, regardless of whether they reported actually using the facility.
[b]Road distance to the facility used was measured for only those respondents who reported that they had actually used the facility during the previous year.
[c]Respondents who lived farther from a playground were less likely to use such a facility than those who lived closer. Hence, the median distance to the playground used (measured only for users) was less than the median distance to the nearest facility (measured for all respondents).
[d]The short distances traveled to begin walking occurred because more than half of the respondents began walking from their homes, using sidewalks and/or streets, rather than traveling to the nearest walking facility in a park or open space corridor.

Recreational Personnel, Programs, and Expenditures

Recreational facilities provide places for people to go and equipment to use for their recreational pursuits. For many of these pursuits, very little supervision and leadership are required. Nevertheless, many people want opportunities to engage in a variety of activities that, by their very nature, must be organized. Children need places to play that are protected and activities that are guided. Young adults need to acquire new skills, and adults often want to pursue hobbies and engage in other activities that require organization and leadership. To offer these opportunities the recreational system must provide leadership personnel who can organize programs and activities for a community's residents.

Most of the recreational organizations serving the study new and conventional communities had relatively small staffs with 10 or fewer persons employed full-time. Overall, new communities provided 55 full- and part-time employees per 10,000 population, more than double the recreational personnel employed in the paired conventional communities. For 10 of the 13 new community-conventional community paired comparisons, the new community had a larger number of recreational employees.

In addition to their paid staffs, many recreational organizations made extensive use of volunteers. In some organizations volunteers were active primarily in specific types of programs, most notably baseball and softball leagues, arts and crafts programs, and festivals and special events. Elsewhere, volunteers were involved in all aspects of an organization's work, from planning and management to advertising and coaching, and in some cases, such as Reston, took primary responsibility for the entire recreational program. This was particularly true of voluntary and homes associations, but several public agencies also gave far-reaching responsibilities to volunteers. Volunteers also played an important role in administrative and supportive activities, such as fund raising, service on boards and committees, distribution of literature, and in maintenance, clean-up, and environmental work. Altough sometimes overlooked, volunteers were an essential aspect of recreational leadership in both new and conventional communities.

The availability of 21 supervised recreational programs was checked in each of the study communities. Baseball was the only activity offered in more conventional than new communities. In terms of popularity the most frequently found programs in new communities were, first: arts and crafts and gymnastics—12 communities; second: softball, tennis, and volleyball—11 communities; and third: basketball, field trips, and swimming—10 communities. Programs offered in less than a third of the study new communities included boating, bowling, camping, ice skating, and track. Among new communities the greatest variety of programming for children was offered in Lake Havasu City, Park Forest, Foster City, and Reston. For adults the greatest variety of programming was offered in Reston, Irvine, and Park Forest.

The total operating expenditures for recreational services of the 13 new communities was $5,692,000 ($26 per capita) in 1972-73, more than double the $2,865,000 ($10 per capita) expended in the paired conventional communities. However, per capita operating expenditures varied among individual new communities. The greatest financial effort for recreational services was made by Columbia, which expended $52 per capita for this purpose. Other new communities spending $25 or more per capita for recreational services included Laguna Niguel ($48), Reston ($41), Irvine ($39), and Foster City ($25). In contrast, four new communities—North Palm Beach, Park Forest, Sharpstown, and Valencia—spent less than $15 per capita on recreational services.

Recreational Institutions and Resource Effectiveness

Communitywide homes associations proved to be the most effective vehicles for providing recreational resources. They were more effective than recreational systems centered on decentralized homes associations, municipalities and special districts, and counties and state parks on six of eight indicators evaluated: recreational sites per capita, variety of recreational facilities, adequacy of facilities, accessibility of facilities, recreational personnel per capita, and community recreational expenditures per capita.

Recreational systems centered on neighborhood homes associations and municipalities/park districts tended to be about equal in their ability to marshall recreational resources. The neighborhood homes association approach to providing recreational resources was somewhat more effective in terms of open space acreage, recreational sites, adequacy of facilities, and recreational expenditures, but was notably less effective in terms of the variety of facilities provided, accessibility of facilities, and number of recreational programs and personnel. This reflects a basic weakness of neighborhood associations in tapping communitywide resources and providing a wider variety of facilities than those initially constructed by developer/builders (which tend to be restricted to swimming pools, tennis courts, open space buffers, and club houses).

Only one new community, Irvine, had an extensive system of neighborhood homes associations and a municipal government that encompassed the entire community. However, because the community was incorporated for only a short period before field work for this study was undertaken, the effectiveness of this combination could not be fully evaluated.

Recreational systems in which county or state agencies played the major roles tended to be the least effective in providing resources. They ranked last on five of the eight effectiveness measures evaluated. County and state centered recreational systems were more effective than municipality-park district recreational systems in terms of open space and recreational acreage; somewhat more effective than neighborhood homes associations in the variety of facilities offered; and somewhat more effective than both communitywide and neighborhood homes associations in the number of recreational programs offered.

Children's Outdoor Play

Child play areas are one of the most ubiquitous features of modern new communities. A visitor to any of these communities is sure to be delighted by the care and attention that has been lavished on abstract climbing sculptures and other features of the tot lots and playgrounds that dot the landscape. Do children find them equally fascinating?

When asked where their children usually play outdoors, an overwhelming proportion of new community parents said their own or a neighbor's yard. Streets and parking lots ranked second with undeveloped open space following close behind. Parks and playgrounds were said to be the usual place of play for only 9 percent of the new community parents' children and for only 4 percent of the children of conventional community parents. Irvine (31 percent), Reston (21 percent), and Foster City (16 percent) children were the most likely to usually play at a park or playground.

Although parks and playgrounds were not the places where children played most often, these facilities were used from time to time. Thirty-eight percent of the new community parents and 33 percent of the conventional community parents who knew of a nearby park or playground said their children played there at least once a week. Variation in usage among new communities paralleled variation in the accessibility of community parks. New communities with more accessible park and playground facilities had a greater proportion of children who played at them. For example, 61 percent of the children with a park or playground within one-eighth mile of home played there once a week or more often. Park usage also tended to be proportionately greater (58 percent once a week or more) among children living in townhouses, who generally have limited yard space for outdoor play.

Parents tended to be satisfied with places near their homes for children's outdoor play. Three fourths of the new community parents and two thirds of the conventional community parents rated such places as either excellent or good. New communities that received lower than average ratings—Laguna Niguel, Forest Park, Sharpstown, and Lake Havasu

City—all had parks and playgrounds that were significantly less accessible than the entire sample of new communities.

Recreation for Young Adults

Almost a quarter of the households living in new communities had one or more young adult members in the 14 to 20 age bracket. Satisfying this group's recreational and leisure needs is one of the most challenging and least well met aspects of recreation in new communities.

New communities tended to pay more attention to young adults' recreational needs than did conventional communities. However, young adults' awareness of teen centers and after-school recreational activities and programs was equivalent. Less than half of the young adults in both settings knew of community teen centers; two thirds were aware of after-school programs.

Of those young adults who knew of available teen recreational centers only 20 percent living in new communities and 15 percent living in the conventional communities claimed to use them at least once a week. Low usage was accompanied and probably caused by young adults' low regard for these facilities. Two thirds of the new community young adults rated available teen centers as average, below average, or poor. Ratings in the conventional communities were only slightly better. Less than half of the young adults in both settings said they were happy with organized recreational activities and programs. Even more disturbing, about 40 percent could not rate teen activities because they had never participated in them. Finally, less than half of the young adults in both settings felt there were enough good places in their communities to get together with friends.

Although young adults tended to be overwhelmingly satisfied with some specific types of recreational facilities—over 80 percent reported they were satisfied with facilities used for their favorite activities, bicycling, swimming, and walking—they had a low regard for new community recreational facilities as a whole. In contrast to generally high ratings by their parents, over two thirds of the young adults living in new and conventional communities said facilities were average or below. Over a third were neutral or dissatisfied with the ways in which they spent their leisure time.

To provide one indication of what might be done to improve this situation young adults were asked to name the kinds of places and facilities that were needed in their communities. Apparently new communities have done an adequate job of providing indoor and outdoor sports facilities for young adults. Only 8 percent wanted more indoor and only 14 percent more outdoor recreational facilities. In contrast a relatively large proportion of young adults in conventional communities (28 percent) wanted more outdoor facilities. Rather than sports facilities a relatively large proportion (26 percent) of new community young adults expressed a need for teen centers and an equal proportion wanted more cultural, entertainment, and shopping facilities in their communities, including theaters, places for dances and parties, shopping malls, fast food places, and libraries.

Some of these facilities—teen centers and libraries—can be provided fairly early in the new community development process, but the entertainment and meeting places young adults desire often require a large population for their support and may be some time in coming. In the meantime new communities may find it advantageous to provide organized weekend transportation services to cultural and entertainment facilities in the surrounding region.

Adults' Favorite Out-of-Home Activities

Community recreational systems should accommodate people's favorite out-of-home activities. On the whole new communities have done this rather well in comparison with conventional communities.

The number of different activities people like to do outside of their homes almost defies description. Over 50 categories of out-of-home activities were mentioned by new community residents, 30 by 1 percent or more of the respondents. Nevertheless, there are a number of clear favorites. Eleven activities accounted for 71 percent of the responses. In order of the number of persons who mentioned them, these were: golf, swimming, gardening, walking and hiking, bowling, tennis, boating, fishing, bicycling, arts and crafts, and playing cards. There was little difference in the favorite activities of new and conventional community residents.

The ability of community recreational systems to accommodate people's favorite activities can be gauged by looking at where they went to participate—within the community or somewhere else. For each of the top ten favorite activities except gardening, which most people did in their own yards, new community residents were more likely to participate in their own communities than were residents of the conventional communities. However, as can be seen in table 10-3 the advantage in favor of new communities was statistically significant only for boating, swimming, and tennis.

Another way to look at how well new communities have taken care of people's favorite activities is to examine the number of communities that provided one or more facilities designed for each activity. All of the study new communities had facilities for swimming and tennis, and 12 of the 13 had places other than sidewalks for walking and hiking. Eleven of the 13

Table 10-3
Where People Go for Their Favorite Activities

	Percent Who Usually Participate Within Community[a]	
Favorite Activity	New Communities	Conventional Communities
Gardening	97	100
Bicycling	92	81
Swimming	78[b]	59
Tennis	74[b]	55
Walking and hiking	72	69
Arts and crafts	51	43
Golf	47	39
Boating	45[b]	13
Bowling	19	15
Fishing	17	13

[a]Includes only respondents who cited each activity as their favorite.
[b]Difference from conventional communities statistically significant at 0.05 level of confidence.

had golf courses and facilities for arts and crafts, and a majority (8) had bodies of water for boating and fishing. Only 6 communities, however, had special facilities for bicycling; only 3 had a bowling alley; and only 1 new community provided community garden plots.

Although much gardening takes place in individual yards, the increasing proportion of multiunit housing in new communities precludes opportunities for gardening for a significant proportion of their population. Provision of public gardening space would probably be a highly beneficial recreational service. Only three new communities—Elk Grove Village, Lake Havasu City, and Sharpstown—had bowling alleys, possibly because of the working class overtones associated with this sport. Nevertheless, together with tennis, bowling ranked fifth among new community residents' favorite activities and thus should probably receive more attention in the design and development of recreational systems.

In spite of new communities' advantage in providing for favorite out-of-home activities, their residents were no more satisfied with the facilities they used for these activities than were residents of the conventional communities. In fact, the only activities for which there was a 10 percent or greater difference in satisfaction levels were walking and fishing. Twelve percent more new community residents were satisfied with the place used for walking, while 10 percent more conventional community residents were satisfied with the place used for fishing. Neither difference is statistically significant. Thus, it appears that regardless of whether a community provides facilities for their favorite activities residents will find a place to participate that suits their needs. Bowling and fishing were the only favorite activities where less than three fourths of the new or conventional community residents were satisfied with the facilities they most often used.

Designing for Maximum Participation

In addition to accommodating residents' favorite out-of-home activities, recreational facilities in new communities should be designed to encourage participation in outdoor activities. To this time new community recreational systems have not resulted in rates of adult participation in activities such as golf, swimming, tennis, bicycling, or walking and hiking that are very different from conventional communities.[a] Participation rates in each of these activities were somewhat higher in new communities than in conventional communities, but aggregate differences ranged from a high of only 7 percent for golf to a low of 2 percent for participation in tennis.

In the past recreational planners have focused on accommodating projected demand. To gauge demand they have paid particular attention to the population characteristics of the community (see Barasch 1974), since it has been clearly established that participation rates vary with age, race, sex, income, and other personal attributes. These relationships were confirmed among the residents of the 13 study new communities. For example, participation in golf and swimming was significantly higher among whites, males, persons under age 25 and over age 65, college graduates, and persons with family incomes of $25,000 or more than among the general population. What also needs to be considered, however, is how the characteristics of facilities provided affect participation. By influencing the character of recreational facilities planners can induce greater participation in recreational activities than is usual in conventional communities.

To check this possibility selected characteristics of golf, swimming, and tennis facilities were measured and related to the frequency of their use by new community residents. This analysis clearly showed that better, more accessible recreational facilities induced greater participation than lower quality facilities that were less accessible to users.

In the case of golf 25 percent of the variation in frequent participation (50 or more times annually) was explained by golfers' personal characteristics, their satisfaction with the golf course they used most often, and objective characteristics of golf courses used. Golf course characteristics

---

[a] Participation rates were 10 percent or more above the average for all 13 new communities in the following cases: bicycling (Elk Grove Village and Irvine); golf (none); swimming (Columbia, Irvine, Lake Havasu City, and Valencia); tennis (Irvine); and walking and hiking (Columbia, Reston, and Valencia).

that were most associated with greater participation included private ownership of the course, availability of a club house and bar, location in the user's own community, availability of a driving range at the course, night lighting, and generous landscaping.

Objective characteristics of swimming facilities accounted for the majority of the variation in frequent participation in swimming that could be explained. Swimmers' personal characteristics were much less important. Swimming facility characteristics most associated with greater participation included location (frequent participation was almost 20 percent greater than average for swimming facilities within one-quarter mile of users), ownership by a homes association, outdoor pool or lake beach, heated water, adjacent clubhouse, and longer operating season.

Like golf and swimming, frequent participation in tennis was also associated with the characteristics of the tennis courts players used most often. Frequent participation was higher among tennis players who used a court within one-eighth mile of their homes and dropped steadily with increasing distance. Participation was high among those tennis players who used courts that were open 12 or more hours per day, required payment of a use fee, and that had correspondingly more elaborate facilities, including lighted courts, pro shop and locker room, club house, and a bar. Participation was also higher at tennis facilities that were generously landscaped and well maintained.

In addition to facilities that made participation easier and more enjoyable, greater participation tended to be induced by the sociability aspect of outdoor recreation. Frequent participation in golf, swimming, and tennis was greater at facilities that offered organized social activities for users. On the other hand, organized sports activities, such as tournaments, had no effect on rates of frequent participation.

In sum, these results show that recreational planners can influence the amount of participation in outdoor activities that takes place in a community. Although new community development has not yet resulted in greater than usual participation, careful attention to the location and design of facilities in the future can produce more active new communities.

Residents' Overall Evaluations of the Recreational System

The superiority of new communities in providing recreational resources is reflected in residents' evaluations of the recreational system as a whole. New community residents were significantly more likely than residents of conventional communities to: (1) believe that community recreational facilities were better than those in the communities where they had previously lived; (2) rate facilities as excellent or good; and (3) be satisfied with community expenditures for outdoor recreation.

Sixty-three percent of the new community respondents felt recreational facilities were better than in their previous communities compared with 49 percent of the conventional community respondents. Figure 10-2 shows that this tended to be consistently true across new communities. With the exception of Forest Park each new community's residents were more likely than residents of their paired conventional community to feel that recreational facilities were better. In nine cases the difference was statistically significant. Columbia and Westlake Village residents were those who saw the greatest improvement in recreational facilities by moving to a new community and were also those most likely to give better ratings in comparison with their paired conventional communities.

Seventy-seven percent of the new community respondents rated recreational facilities in their communities as excellent or good. Only 62 percent of the conventional community residents rated facilities that highly. Again, figure 10-2 shows that the advantage was overwhelmingly in favor of new communities. Residents of seven new communities gave significantly higher ratings to community recreational facilities than residents of their paired conventional communities. From their residents' perspectives Columbia, Westlake Village, and North Palm Beach had the best facilities, though Irvine, Reston, Elk Grove Village, and Valencia were not far behind.

Many residents were also satisfied with community expenditures for outdoor recreation. Overall, 66 percent of the new community residents and 60 percent of the conventional community residents thought expenditures were adequate. In only two cases, Forest Park and Sharpstown, did new community residents indicate a significantly greater need for recreational expenditures than residents of their paired conventional communities. It should be noted that Forest Park and Sharpstown ranked next to last and last in terms of recreational resource availability.

Recreational systems in new communities have succeeded in satisfying most segments of the population. Men and women were equally likely to rate facilities as excellent or good. Elderly residents age 65 or older gave somewhat higher ratings (82 percent) than younger residents (76 percent). In the five new communities with subsidized housing 83 percent of both subsidized housing and nonsubsidized housing residents rated facilities above average. Black residents were slightly less likely than white residents (67 percent versus 75 percent) to rate facilities as excellent or good in the five new communities where special subsamples of black residents were obtained. Residents of single-family houses, townhouses, and apartments, and owners and renters did not rate facilities differently, nor did residents who had lived for varying lengths of time in new communities. In

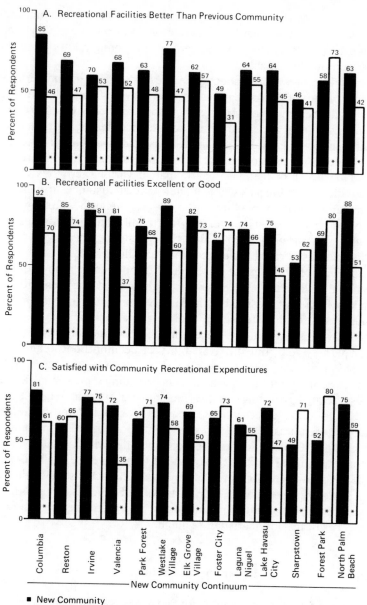

Figure 10-2. Residents' Evaluations of Recreational Facilities in New Communities and Paired Conventional Communities

fact, the only clearly disaffected group living in new communities was young adults. Compared with excellent or good ratings from 77 percent of the adult respondents, only 32 percent of the young adults rated recreational facilities that highly.

Comparison of various aspects of recreation in new communities with residents' ratings of the recreational system provides some clues as to how ratings might be improved. In the first place residents who participated more in recreational activities tended to rate facilities higher than nonparticipants. Inducing greater participation, as discussed earlier, should improve residents' evaluations of the recreational system. Second, residents who had to travel less distance to participate in various activities also rated the recreational system as a whole higher. Critical distances from facilities used include: park or playground, under one-eighth mile; swimming facilities and tennis courts, under one-fourth mile; and golf courses, under two miles. People who lived within these distances of the recreational facilities they used rated facilities as a whole highest.

Regardless of whether they used them or not people who had various recreational facilities available in their neighborhood (the area within one-half mile of home not crossed by a major street or natural barrier) tended to rate the recreational system as a whole highly. Facilities that were most associated with higher ratings were neighborhood and teen centers and an interior path system, but the availability of neighborhood tennis, swimming, and picnic facilities also was associated with higher overall ratings. Finally, the community's overall effort in providing recreational resources was also related to ratings of the recreational system. Highest ratings tended to go to those recreational systems with higher per capita annual operating expenditures and with more community recreational and open space land per 10,000 residents. New communities with a greater variety of outdoor recreational facilities also tended to receive the highest ratings.

The association of a number of objective characteristics of the recreational system with residents' ratings shows that residents' evaluations are not an arbitrary or random phenomenon. More and better recreational facilities result in more satisfied residents.

Leisure Satisfaction: A Disconcerting Finding

Recreational facilities are usually not viewed as ends in themselves, but as means of enabling individuals to make personally productive and enjoyable use of their leisure time. Thus, it is somewhat disconcerting that while recreational resources were better and the recreational system was rated much higher in new than in conventional communities, differences in leisure satisfaction were minimal. Seventy-two percent of the new community residents said they were satisfied with the ways they spent their spare time versus 66 percent of the conventional community residents. Complete satisfaction with the use of leisure time was almost identical in these two settings—31 percent of the new community and 30 percent of the conventional community residents were completely satisfied. Finally, there were no new communities in which residents were significantly more satisfied with the use of their leisure than were residents of their paired conventional communities.

Equally disconcerting is the fact that neither the adequacy of community recreational resources nor residents' ratings of the recreational system were associated with leisure satisfaction. For example, Foster City ranked first in terms of leisure satisfaction, but ranked seventh on recreational resources and twelfth in terms of residents' ratings of recreational facilities as excellent or good. Columbia and Reston, which ranked first and second in terms of resources, and first and fourth in terms of overall ratings, ranked last and next to last in terms of residents' satisfaction with the use of their leisure time.

Thus, it appears that the next frontier for recreation in new communities must be a broader conception of leisure. At present recreation is largely thought of in terms of outdoor facilities and athletic activities. To increase leisure satisfaction and the quality of life new communities need to provide for nonathletic forms of leisure, including various entertainment facilities, and to pay greater attention to leisure time programming. In computer terminology new communities have done well in providing the hardware (outdoor facilities), but must now begin to concentrate on the software (personnel and programs), which can enable people to grow and achieve satisfying lives.

11

Health and Medical Care

In contrast to the considerable amount of attention devoted to recreation, health and medical care has been on the periphery of new community developers' interests. This may be a reflection of residents' general lack of concern for health matters. New community residents rarely moved to a community because of health and medical care facilities and services, even when they were readily available. Health care was a relatively insignificant aspect of their quality of life or the factors residents felt were important in making their communities good places to live. Few respondents cited health care as a major community problem and the availability of facilities had little influence on the use of health care services. Nevertheless, as balanced and self-contained residential settlements, new communities have been expected to provide basic health care resources.

Community-based Health Care

It has often been suggested that the community is a key sphere in which to address problems in the delivery of health care. For example, the Task Force on Organization of Community Health Services recommended the development of local mechanisms to assess health needs and to determine objectives, "because it is in the local community that the citizen both encounters the threats to his health and seeks the protection and services he requires" (1967, p. 15). The National Commission on Community Health Services (1966) proposed that all programs related to city planning provide for the availability and accessibility of comprehensive health and welfare services. Emphasis on the placement of health resources in the community reflects the desirability of readily available sources of care. What people want, according to Robert M. Heyssel, is "guaranteed accessibility to medical care in time of need" (1971b, p. 137). However, planning for community health care need not be limited to questions of accessibility. The community approach may also contribute solutions to many health care problems, including adequacy of care, efficiency of delivery, comprehensiveness of services, consumer participation in health care planning, and the development of health maintenance organizations.

In the new community context, Harold Herman and Michael I. Joroff (1967) have emphasized opportunities offered by new communities to integrate medical facilities with other community services as a means of encouraging their use. Planners involved in the Minnesota Experimental

City Project (1969) have described extensive possibilities for innovations in health care that can be more easily tried in a new community setting. A local government viewpoint was expressed by Mayor Pryor of the city of Irvine, who noted, "If we as a city are really planning a 'New Town' then health care has to be a significant part of that effort" (*Irvine World News,* June 21, 1973).

Health Care and the Developer

Because of the disjointed character of health care delivery in the United States, new community developers have a unique opportunity, and, some might say, a basic obligation to attend to the health care needs of their residents. The imperative of developer involvement, as well as the obstacles in the way of attaining better social services, were summarized by Burnham Kelly as follows:

The redundancy and *ad-hoc*-ery of the agencies and organizations representing the public interest in community social facilities decisions in the United States is such that the subsequent success of any large project depends largely upon the negotiating skills and inventiveness of the developer. At one extreme, he may be so encumbered by the forest of regulations, standards, and "current practices" that his project loses character and quality. At the other extreme, he may succeed in raising the standards of service for local agencies, in combining services in new patterns, in taking full benefit of all available governmental sources of financial aid, and in bringing to his development the interest and support of private institutions and foundations as well (1974, p. 37).

While the opportunities for effective developer action are present and the community benefits are potentially great, developers have varied in their inclinations to become involved in this often frustrating service field.

Three approaches have characterized new community developers' attention to community health care. One approach consists of minimal developer activity—usually through designation of appropriate sites for doctors' offices and other health-related facilities. At a second level of involvement, developers may, in cooperation with outside health institutions, embrace individual projects, such as the construction and staffing of medical office buildings or advocacy of private hospital projects. A third approach is characterized by a deep developer commitment to meet community health needs and participation in a variety of health care planning and service delivery activities.

Responding to the Market

In a few new communities, including Park Forest, North Palm Beach, and Sharpstown, developers left community health care entirely to the entrepreneurial instincts of doctors and surrounding institutions. Because the developers had assembled lucrative markets, health care providers were responsive to the need for health care in North Palm Beach and Sharpstown. These communities ranked first and second in terms of the number of general practitioners per capita. Developer indifference, however, was not always counterbalanced by the initiative of doctors and other health care providers. Although Park Forest was the oldest new community studied and had ample time to attract fee-for-service practitioners, it ranked well below both state and regional averages of physicians per capita.

Since private initiative cannot always be counted upon to meet a new community's needs for health care services, a number of developers have taken positive actions to encourage doctors to locate in their communities. For example, doctors were actively recruited by the developers of Forest Park and Lake Havasu City; in the latter case, the developer subsidized the community's first doctor until his practice was well established. In other new communities, such as Reston, Elk Grove Village, Foster City, Westlake Village, Irvine, and Laguna Niguel, developers built or cooperated in the construction of medical office buildings and clinics that provided attractive space for fee-for-service medical practitioners.

A number of developers have also become directly involved in community hospital projects, though their efforts have sometimes not been successful. The Centex Corporation donated ten acres (of a 40-acre site) for the Alexian Brothers Hospital in Elk Grove Village. The Newhall Land and Farming Company donoted land and staff time to aid in the planning and construction of the $6.5 million Henry Mayo Newhall Memorial Hospital in Valencia, which was scheduled for completion in 1975. This nonprofit institution provides 100 beds and an adjacent medical services complex. In Westlake Village, American-Hawaiian Steamship Company helped a local group secure licensing approval for a proprietary community hospital in the face of strong opposition from surrounding hospitals. Robert P. McCulloch donated land for two community hospitals in Lake Havasu City and attempted to resolve conflicts between competing groups, which led to the eventual construction of both hospitals.

At Irvine the developer has worked for a number of years to plan and secure approval of a 133-acre hospital and medical center complex to be operated by the Western World Medical Foundation of Newport Beach. To facilitate the lowest possible cost for medical care, The Irvine Company agreed to donate an 18-acre site for a 162-bed hospital and to sell the remainder of the acreage for the $400 million medical complex at residential land price levels (one-fifth the price of the proposed site in alternative industrial land uses). Profits from the medical complex were to be used by the foundation to increase hospital services and reduce its operating costs. However, this ambitious undertaking has been stalled by a series of controversies involving nearby hospitals and the medical school at the University of California at Irvine.

Gulf-Reston, Inc. also actively supported an ill-fated community hospital proposal. In this case, a 125-bed general hospital to be built and operated by a proprietary corporation, Beverly Enterprises, was denied state certification when it was opposed by the Reston Community Association, Fairfax County Hospital Association, and a nearby county. The issues involved in this and other new community hospital proposals are discussed below.

Beyond the Market to Comprehensive Planning

Of the 13 privately developed new communities, Columbia's developer and planners have demonstrated the greatest commitment to securing community health care resources. According to the developer,

Health care was determined as a public service to be available to *all* residents. The emphasis in care was on prevention of illness rather than cure, and applied to physical and mental health. In fact, the consideration of all aspects of a family's well being demanded the cooperation of the people-serving agencies, and the specialists within such agencies (American City Corporation 1973a, n.p.).

Health planners were among the diverse group of professionals whose ideas helped give direction to Columbia's growth, and at an early stage of the planning process a relationship was formed with the John Hopkins Medical Institutions of Baltimore. That relationship led to the development of the Columbia Medical Plan, a comprehensive prepaid group practice medical program organized and planned by The Johns Hopkins University, The Johns Hopkins Hospital, and Connecticut General Life Insurance Company. The purpose of the program, which commenced operation less than two years after Columbia's opening, is to make available quality medical care at reasonable cost and to insure the accessibility of and continuity of care 24 hours a day.[a]

The Rouse Company not only gave enthusiastic support to the plan—by providing space for its clinic, donating land for the recently completed Howard County General Hospital (formerly the Columbia Medical Center), and providing assistance in problems of zoning—but also discouraged competing forms of medical practice in the community by not providing

[a] Prepaid group practice medical plans were active in two other new communities, but in each case their availability was not a result of developer initiatives. Over 20 percent of the Foster City respondents were members of the Kaiser Foundation Health Plan, which had a clinic and hospital in nearby Redwood City. Beginning in the spring of 1974, Reston residents could participate in the Georgetown University Community Health Plan through membership in the Reston Community Association. The University operated the Reston-Georgetown Medical Center out of offices located in Reston's Hunters Woods Village Center.

office space designed for fee-for-service physicians. However, in the last few years this policy has changed, in part, because less than half of Columbia's population enrolled in the group practice Medical Plan. Office space has been made available in the village centers for private physicians, and The Rouse Company has taken an interest in projects outside of the Medical Plan, such as community mental health and the location of a county health office and a nursing home in Columbia.

Professionals' Opinions of Health Planning

Health care professionals serving each new community were asked whether they felt adequate attention had been given to the provision of health care services, facilities, and programs in new community planning. In five new communities—Elk Grove Village, Lake Havasu City, Park Forest, Valencia, and Westlake Village—a majority of the professionals thought initial health care planning was sufficient.

In eight other communities, however, health professionals were more critical of the developers' attention to planning. In many cases, including Sharpstown, Laguna Niguel, North Palm Beach, and Forest Park, professionals felt consideration of health care had been mostly lacking in initial community plans, though this was not always viewed as a problem. In the Sharpstown area some professionals felt health care should be left to private initiative and the working of the free enterprise system. In the case of Forest Park, it was argued that planning was a regional concern and that the community was too small an area to address citizens' health care needs.

In a number of cases health care professionals acknowledged specific developer efforts to secure some health care resources, but felt that planning for a wide range of community health care needs had been ignored. For example, a private physicians' group in Columbia thought that The Rouse Company had been too zealous in promoting the Columbia Medical Plan, to the detriment of other forms of care. Columbia's developer was censured by others for not devoting enough resources to establishing an effective social service structure and for giving only lip service to community mental health needs. Gulf-Reston, Inc. was said to have taken a "passive reactionary" stance toward health care, that is, the developer was said to react to outside proposals for meeting various community health care needs, but not to initiate such proposals. The Irvine Company's efforts to provide medical office space and its support of the Western World Medical Foundation hospital proposal were acknowledged. Nevertheless, some professional respondents were critical of the timing of health resources provision, while others expressed concern over the proposed hospital's effect on the chronic overbedding problem, which was mounting in Orange County.

Health care planning for new community development is often hindered by two related problems: First, as real estate entrepreneurs, new community developers are not necessarily the most appropriate agents to engage in such planning. Health care is not their area of expertise and there is little incentive in terms of consumers' market behavior to devote company staff time and funds to community health care. There is no evidence that the market success of a new community venture is affected one way or the other by the health resources available in the community. Even in Columbia, with its well publicized Medical Plan, only 3 percent of the respondents cited health and medical services as one of the three most important reasons for moving there.

Second, the highly decentralized, free-enterprise character of health care delivery in the United States discourages preplanning at the community level. Regional health planning councils, where they existed, were of little help to developers in assessing community health care needs and organizing a program of health care services. County public health agencies lacked the funds, and often the inclination, to engage in health care planning at the community level. Medical societies were mostly concerned with the placement of doctors and were not in a position to offer comprehensive advice about health services. Existing health care institutions, such as hospitals, were sometimes interested in establishing branches in new communities, but more often than not their chief concern was in protecting the integrity of their service areas by discouraging the provision of additional and competing hospital facilities. In sum, institutions that could promote health care planning at the community level are almost completely absent in many suburban locations. When this situation is combined with developers' natural disinclination to become involved in areas with which they are not familiar, the low level of attention to comprehensive community health care planning should not be surprising.

Physicians' Services

Most new community residents' basic point of contact with the health care delivery system comes when they seek the services of a physician or a dentist. The availability of doctors in a community is one indicator of the adequacy of primary health care. Another is residents' actual health care seeking behavior—the distances they traveled to secure primary care, the number of times they thought they needed care but did not seek help, and their rate of use of and satisfaction with their personal doctors.

Availability of Primary Care Physicians and Dentists

The ratio of primary care physicians to population has commonly been used to gauge the adequacy of health care available to a region or community. According to H.K. Schonfield, J.F. Heston, and I.S. Falk (1972), for example, there is a need for 133 primary care physicians (general practitioners, internists, and pediatricians) per 100,000 population. This is far above the national average of physician availability, which in 1970 stood at 82 primary care physicians per 100,000 population (adjusted to include osteopaths and obstetricians/gynecologists).

As shown in figure 11-1, most new communities met neither of these standards. Only North Palm Beach and Sharpstown had more than 133 primary care physicians per 100,000 population. These two new communities, together with Westlake Village and Laguna Niguel, exceeded the national average of primary care physician availability. In contrast, four new communities—Irvine, Valencia, Foster City, and Forest Park—had fewer than one fourth the national average of 82 primary care physicians per 100,000 population. In the other new communities, physician availability was somewhat better, but still fell far below the number of doctors required to meet community needs adequately. It should be noted that the availability of primary care physicians was not much better in the conventional communities. Only four conventional communities exceeded the national average, but six had more physicians per capita than their paired new communities. Less than half of the new communities and conventional communities equaled or exceeded the national average of dentists per 100,000 population.

The shortage of physicians was noted by health care professionals serving almost all the new communities. Health professionals also pointed out that this problem would become more acute as the communities continued to grow and develop, but that there were a number of possible solutions. For example, a hospital official serving Irvine believed that there was a need for "front line" physicians to screen patients and refer them to appropriate types of practitioners. Reston recently attracted national attention with a "Patients and Partners" program, sponsored by Georgetown University, in which residents were trained to provide much of their own basic care. Health surveys conducted in Elk Grove Village and Park Forest recommended that their municipal governments become involved in recruiting physicians.

Analysis of the relationship between physician availability and other community characteristics suggests other means of improving the availability of primary care. Among the study new communities, larger primary-care-physician-to-population ratios were associated with communities that were older, had hospitals, and in which medical office facilities were highly rated by health professionals. Although developers can do little to speed up the maturation process that results in the accumulation of physicians, they can provide better office space and can encourage the construction of community hospitals in order to attract more doctors to the community.

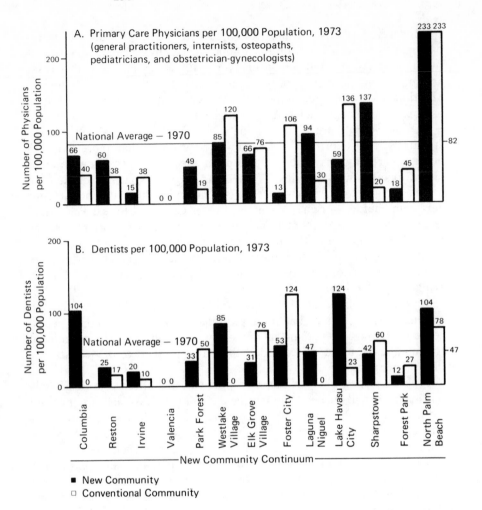

Figure 11-1. Doctors and Dentists Practicing in New and Conventional Communities

Accessibility to Doctors and Distances Traveled to Receive Care

New and conventional community respondents both tended to live within a short distance of the nearest primary care physician. Among new communities, the median road distance to the nearest general practitioner was just over a mile (6,800 feet), while conventional community respondents had to travel only slightly farther (8,800 feet). Most respondents, however, did not use the closest physician. The median aerial distance to the doctor used most often was over five miles (28,400 feet) for new community respondents and over seven miles (38,000 feet) for respondents who lived in the conventional communities. The only exceptions to the tendency of residents to travel relatively far for care were Lake Havasu City and its paired conventional community, Kingman. Because both are freestanding communities, respondents had little choice of doctors beyond those available in their own community.

Among new community residents, the distance traveled to obtain care was not associated with the distance to the nearest general practitioner and was only weakly (but negatively) associated with the number of primary care physicians practicing in their communities. Thus, people seem to have a high tolerance for inconvenience when it comes to finding a doctor who they feel meets their needs. This suggests that developers might be able to postpone the provision of primary care health services without creating major hardships for residents if ample health care resources are available in the surrounding region.

Residents' Use of Physicians' Services

New community development has not resulted in greater than average use of physicians' services. A majority of the respondents in both the new and conventional communities reported they had a regular doctor or clinic they went to, and that they had had a routine checkup during the past year. As shown in figure 11-2, there were only minimal differences between each new community and its paired conventional community.

There were also few differences in the median number of visits made to see doctors, other than dentists, in their offices or clinics during the previous year. However, the emphasis on preventive care by the Columbia Medical Plan and the plan's policy of charging only nominal fees for doctors' visits was apparent. The median number of visits to doctors by Columbia respondents was far greater than any other new community, and was exceeded only by respondents living in Tequesta (the conventional community paired with North Palm Beach), where the median age of respondents was over 60.

Objective indicators of the adequacy of community health resources had no influence on the number of times respondents had been to see doctors during the previous year.[b] Instead, the critical factor influencing use of a doctor or clinic was respondents' own assessment of the status of their health. People visited doctors more frequently if they felt their health

---

[b] Variables tested in relation to the number of doctors' visits included: (1) number of primary care physicians practicing in community; (2) number of specialists practicing in community; (3) availability of neighborhood medical facilities; (4) availability of hospital in community; road distances to nearest (5) general practitioner, (6) hospital, and (7) public health clinic; and (8) aerial distance to the town where regular medical care was obtained.

252

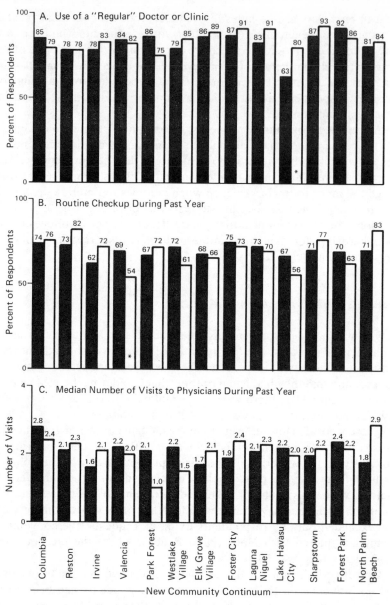

A. Use of a "Regular" Doctor or Clinic

B. Routine Checkup During Past Year

C. Median Number of Visits to Physicians During Past Year

New Community Continuum

■ New Community
□ Conventional Community
* Statistically Significant Difference

Figure 11-2. Use of Physicians' Services

was poor. Also, women tended to make more visits than men, as did respondents' who had a regular doctor or clinic.

The importance of personal health assessment suggests that one reason the availability and accessibility of health resources did not influence utilization behavior was because physicians' services were geared to the treatment of problems; people sought curative treatment when they needed it regardless of where it was located. However, respondents were motivated to visit doctors for preventive as well as curative health care services. For example, respondents with a regular source of care visited doctors more often not because they were less well—there was little association between having a regular source of care and personal health assessments—but because they sought preventive services. People with their own doctor or clinic were more likely to have had a checkup in the past year than those without a regular doctor or clinic.

Because an interest in preventive care influenced respondents to seek physicians' services, an important question is whether increased availability of health resources encouraged individuals to have checkups or to arrange for regular sources of care. The evidence suggests that it did not. Having a regular source of care was not associated with the number of family physicians per 100,000 community residents or to the distance to the nearest general practitioner. Similarly, the likelihood of having had a checkup during the previous year was also not influenced by the ratio of physicians to population or by the distance to the nearest general practitioner. Thus, regardless of respondents' motivations—whether for curative or preventive health care services—the availability and location of health resources had little impact on the frequency of visits to doctors. This again suggests that developers may have a great deal of flexibility in both the timing and location of primary health care resources without adversely affecting utilization rates. Further, there is no indication that the provision of neighborhood health care services, as suggested by the American Public Health Association (1948), has any influence on the use of health care services, at least among the relatively affluent residents of suburban new and conventional communities.

Difficulties Experienced in Obtaining Medical Care

Asked whether they had ever really wanted to see a doctor in the past year but did not for some reason, between 6 percent and 25 percent of the new community respondents, depending on the community, reported that this was the case. Three new communities with higher proportions of doctors to population—Westlake Village, North Palm Beach, and Laguna Niguel— had the lowest proportion (11 percent or less) of respondents who reported not having seen a doctor when such a need was felt. On the other hand, Sharpstown had both a high physician-to-population ratio and a high proportion of respondents (19 percent) who failed to see a doctor. In addition to Sharpstown, the highest incidence of failing to see a doctor when desired occurred in Lake Havasu City (21 percent), Columbia (22 percent), and Valencia (25 percent).

The most common reasons given for failure to see a doctor were inconvenience and the length of time it took to get to a physician. However, comparisons of characteristics of the community health care system and reported incidences of failure to see a doctor indicated that there was little association between them. In the case of respondents' personal characteristics, lower income (under $10,000 a year), female, and younger respondents reported slightly greater difficulties than others.

Respondents who had a regular doctor or clinic were asked whether, on their last visit, they had been annoyed by problems in arranging the appointment, problems in arranging transportation to get there, the way they and other patients were treated, or the cost of the visit. Less than 15 percent of the new community respondents reported having any of these difficulties, though some problems were more frequent in a few communities. For example, 19 percent of the Columbia respondents, and 18 percent in Elk Grove Village, reported difficulties in arranging doctors' appointments. However, there was no association between reported difficulties in making appointments and either objective characteristics of the health care system or respondents personal characteristics, including their education, length of residence in a community, or the number of hours per week the head of household worked.

The problem mentioned most frequently was cost, particularly in Westlake Village and Valencia, where 23 percent and 16 percent of the respondents complained of the cost involved in obtaining medical care. Again, however, there was no relationship between factors that might be expected to create cost problems, such as lower income and lack of health insurance, and the reported incidence of such problems.

Hospital Care: How Much Is Enough?

No health-related matter has been the subject of as much interest in new communities as hospital care. This interest is due not only to the continuing attention focused on hospital care throughout the country, but also to the geographic locations of many of these communities. Because they are outlying developments with few established sources of health care, they naturally rely on hospitals as facilities offering a number of types of care at one location.

Availability of Hospital Care

As of the spring of 1973 only 3 of the 13 new communities had hospitals—Elk Grove Village and Westlake Village each had one community hospital and Sharpstown had two. West San Mateo, Foster City's paired conventional community, also had two hospitals, and Fountain Valley and Kingman, the conventional communities paired with Irvine and Lake Havasu City, had one hospital each. Availability of a hospital was related to both the age of the community and its population—older communities with larger populations were more likely to have attracted such a facility.

Hospitals were in the planning or construction stage of development in a number of other new communities. Two community hospitals were under development in Lake Havasu City, both of which had begun operation by 1975. A hospital was opened in Columbia in July of 1973, and one was scheduled for completion in Valencia in 1975. Two additional hospitals were planned for Sharpstown, and hospital proposals were pending in Reston and Irvine. In Foster City, an attempt to secure a branch of the Peninsula Hospital in the community was turned down after a preliminary feasibility study showed that Foster City was adequately served by the two hospitals in San Mateo. Similarly, North Palm Beach, Laguna Niguel, and Park Forest were served by hospitals in immediately adjacent communities and no efforts had been made to obtain additional hospital facilities.

Overall, the accessibility of the nearest hospital facility was somewhat better in the new communities than in the conventional communities—the median new community resident lived about a mile and a half closer to the nearest hospital (14,800 feet versus 22,200 feet). Also, as shown in figure 11-3, hospital construction that was underway in Columbia and Lake Havasu City, and pending in Reston and Irvine, would increase the accessibility of hospital care in those new communities with the least convenient hospital facilities.

Residents' and Professionals' Perceptions of the Adequacy of Care

New community residents who were familiar with a hospital serving their community were asked whether they would recommend the use of that facility. While only about two thirds of the respondents knew of a hospital serving their community, over 90 percent of those who did said they would recommend its use to others. This enthusiasm for available hospital facilities, however, was not universal. In particular, more than a third of the Valencia and paired community respondents indicated they would not recommend the use of nearby hospitals. This may explain the Newhall

256

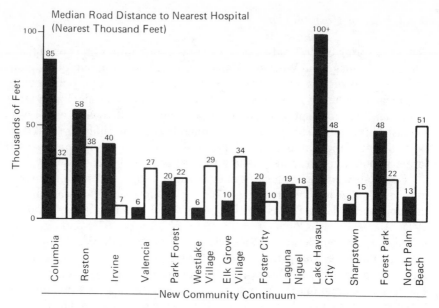

Figure 11-3. Accessibility of Hospital Care

Land and Farming Company's strong support of the Henry Mayo Newhall Hospital in Valencia, considering that the average Valencia resident lived just over a mile from the nearest existing hospital facility.

Health professionals were much less favorably inclined toward available hospital facilities than were new community residents. In five of the 13 new communities—Valencia, Elk Grove Village, Forest Park, Columbia, and Reston—a majority of the health professionals interviewed thought hospital care facilities were inadequate. In the case of a sixth new community—Lake Havasu City—opinion was evenly divided. In addition, health care professionals were very concerned about the proprietary ownership of some hospitals that had been proposed for construction and the whole process by which hospitals were planned and built.

Are Community Hospitals the Answer?

Earlier it was noted that construction of a community hospital can serve as an effective vehicle for attracting doctors to new communities. Additionally, it is shown below that the availability of hospital care was related to new community residents' evaluation of community health care facilities and services. Because of these advantages, many communities have eagerly promoted hospital construction. Their efforts have been substantially aided by groups of doctors seeking to control their own places of work, large central city hospitals seeking to expand to the suburbs, and proprietary hospital institutions seeking to expand their businesses. As a result, many areas are beginning to suffer from overbedding, and competition among existing and proposed hospitals has produced severe controversies in a number of new communities.

For example, when the Columbia Medical Center was built, primarily to provide hospital care facilities for members of the Columbia Medical Plan, it was the first hospital to be constructed in Howard County. A controversy soon arose, however, when two other groups, Bon Secours and Lutheran Hospital, both of Baltimore, proposed the construction of additional hospitals in the county. The Columbia Medical Center changed its name to the Howard County General Hospital and argued that it should expand from 59 beds to 180 beds and serve as the only county hospital. Needless to say, this was not well received by the competing hospital sponsors or other sections of the county where their hospitals were to be constructed.

The Irvine Company's sponsorship of the Western World Medical Foundation hospital was denied certification by the California State Health Planning Council when arguments arose between the hospital's sponsors and doctors associated with the University of California at Irvine's Medical School, who wanted a teaching hospital of their own in Irvine. In addition, a 1973 report by the Orange County Health Planning Council indicated that nearby Santa Ana had an excess of 1,000 hospital beds and a new hospital would not be needed in Irvine before 1982. This conclusion was heatedly disputed by Irvine city officials.

In Lake Havasu City, two groups—one seeking to build a nonprofit hospital and one seeking to build a proprietary institution—approached the developer to donate land for their hospitals. Efforts to mediate their differences and to join forces in the construction of one hospital failed, so that both the 54-bed Lake Havasu City Medical Center Hospital and 34-bed Lake Havasu Community Hospital were built on adjacent sites in the community. A court suit aimed at stopping construction of the Medical Center Hospital failed, when the judge hearing the case ruled that there was no accepted method for determining when a community's hospital needs have been met. Arizona State hospital plans indicated that only 40 hospital beds would have been needed in Lake Havasu City through 1980.

Gulf-Reston, Inc.'s proposed Beverly Enterprises hospital ran into stiff opposition from the Fairfax County Hospital Association, which operated the existing county general hospital, and from neighboring Loudoun

County, whose board of supervisors felt that a new hospital in Reston would encroach on the service area of the Loudoun Memorial Hospital. In February 1974 Beverly Enterprises was denied a certificate of need by the state, and an Ambulatory Care Center-Emergency Service System proposed by the Hospital Association was accepted in its place. This facility is to be included in the proposed county governmental subcenter to be built in Reston.

In Houston, the lack of a strong regional authority for health planning resulted in a spurt of hospital construction centered in the Sharpstown area. With two hospitals in Sharpstown, two more are planned. One is an expanded replacement of the existing Memorial Hospital, which will be converted to a long-term care facility. The second is a result of dissension among doctors at the Sharpstown General Hospital, located across the street from one of the planned hospitals, and the desire of those doctors to control their own facility. Nevertheless, Sharpstown General is undertaking an expansion program of its own. In the suburbs northwest of Chicago, a hospital proposed for Hoffman Estates was approved by the Illinois Hospital Licensing Board just six months after approval was granted to the Rush-Presbyterian-St. Luke's Medical Center branch hospital in neighboring Schaumburg, the conventional community paired with Elk Grove Village. The Hoffman Estates project was opposed by two area hospitals, one of them the Alexian Brothers Hospital in Elk Grove Village, on the grounds of overbedding. Similarly, the construction of the Westlake Hospital was strongly opposed by the Los Robles Hospital in nearby Thousand Oaks on the grounds that it was already meeting the area's hospital needs.

The experiences of these communities illustrate a basic dilemma in the provision of hospital facilities in new communities. Hospital construction has been a favored means of involvement in health matters by new community developers and brings with it a number of health care services for the community. But the activities of developers in support of hospital projects, in communities such as Reston, Irvine, and Westlake Village, may exacerbate the widespread problems of excessive hospital beds and duplication of services. Because most new communities are satellites of metropolitan areas rather than freestanding entities, it is rarely necessary for them to have hospitals of their own if adequate emergency service is available to transport residents to existing health care institutions. Alternatives to hospital construction might include emergency care stations, county-operated health clinics, clinics operated in conjunction with health maintenance organizations, and counseling centers for emotional problems. It may be the absence of such facilities that, in the past, has led residents to view a local community hospital as essential to the well-being of the community.

Emergency Service

Much of the emphasis in debates over hospital building has revolved around emergency care and the view that it should be readily accessible to residents. In addition, many health professionals serving the study communities stated that one of the greatest health care needs was emergency treatment facilities. However, there were only three new communities—Irvine, Laguna Niguel, and Lake Havasu City—in which a majority of the health care professionals thought that existing emergency care was inadequate.[c]

Professionals' evaluation of emergency ambulance service was generally based on their perceptions of the nature of the organization providing the service and its cost, rather than the location from which the service originated. They were more likely to view emergency service favorably if it was provided by public fire departments rather than by private companies or funeral homes. Since private service was more expensive, professionals' assessments were also linked to cost.

In spite of their favorable views toward emergency ambulance service, many health professionals saw room for improvement. Respondents in Columbia, Irvine, and Foster City felt service was too slow and noted that ambulance crews had difficulty finding locations (one of the disadvantages of convoluted street patterns that promote traffic and pedestrian safety). Improved ambulance service was also recommended by health care study groups in North Palm Beach, Elk Grove Village, and Park Forest.

Although ambulance crews received some sort of emergency care training in virtually every community in the study, the lack of adequate training was a widespread deficiency noted by professionals. In Palm Beach County, for example, members of ambulance crews had only eight to ten hours of Red Cross training. Another problem area noted by professionals was that of cooperation with hospitals. This was a potential difficulty in every new community, since none of the systems serving them was provided by a hospital.

Other Health and Social Services

If physicians' services, hospital care, and ambulance service represent the areas of health care requiring the most immediate attention, they hardly exhaust the health needs that must be considered in new community development. For example, one of the most neglected aspects of health

---

[c] In November 1973, six months after the professional survey, the city of Irvine initiated an emergency transportation service that was available to residents at no charge.

care in new communities and conventional communities is that group of activities broadly described as "social services." Health professionals in a number of communities noted problems of stress and anxiety among community residents. Yet, services designed to provide assistance in these and other areas of health care, including help with emotional problems, family and marital counseling, assistance with drug and drinking problems, family planning, health care for children, and prenatal care, were often perceived by residents as unavailable. For example, less than 50 percent of the new and conventional community respondents felt that help with emotional problems was available to residents of their communities. Even though professionals displayed greater familiarity with such services than did residents, many professionals also regarded the absence or inadequacy of some of these services as the major health-related problems facing the community.

On the whole, health professionals viewed social services less favorably than any other area of health care. In eight new communities, including Columbia, Elk Grove Village, Forest Park, Foster City, Lake Havasu City, Laguna Niguel, North Palm Beach, and Valencia, half or more of the professionals interviewed said that social service programs were inadequate. The conventional communities fared no better—in nine of the 13 communities health professionals felt improvements were needed.

Professionals' concerns should not be taken to mean that social services were completely lacking in new communities. They were not. For example, the Columbia Park and Recreation Association provided residents with a listing of a wide range of services available in and around Howard County, including 16 agencies providing some form of counseling. The Elk Grove Village-Schaumburg Townships Mental Health Center, initiated with financial help from Elk Grove Village's town government, had a staff of 12 counselors and a part-time psychiatrist who together averaged more than 400 sessions with clients per week. The Woodburn Center for Community Mental Health operated an outreach station in Reston. In other communities health and social service programs included community mental health and counseling, alcoholism and drug treatment, rehabilitation and other services for the physically handicapped, child development, prenatal care, health education, mental retardation, family counseling, nutrition education, venereal disease, and immunization programs.

Although many of these programs were offered by public agencies or were supported by public funds, many others were run by church groups or voluntary associations. Several health professionals, moreover, commented on the sources of care received in these areas by community residents. As with primary physician care, the orientation of residents in affluent suburban areas is to seek help from private sources on a fee-for-service basis.

The variety of sources from which services were offered compounded problems of coordination that have yet to be solved in many of the study new communities. Health professionals often described services as "fractured" and called for more effective service delivery systems. Of greater concern to professionals, however, was simply the inadequate level of services being offered. By far the greatest number of comments had to do with emotional care. Strong feeling was also expressed concerning the need for education and treatment programs for alcoholism and drug abuse. Other service areas requiring attention were numerous, but the general flavor of health professionals' comments regarding general needs for health and social programs is illustrated by a partial list: adoption services, abortion referral, youth programs and youth centers, family and marital counseling, family planning, rehabilitation, home health care, suicide prevention, augmented social work programs, and programs for prenatal and child health care. As one Columbia respondent stated, "There is a need for an all-purpose social service program which would include advocacy, referral, jobs, a friendship exchange, and liaison with governmental agencies."

One way in which developers can play a useful role in the social service system is through organizing and providing an information and referral service. Residents' relatively low perceptions of the availability of many services is one indication of this need. In addition, residents' groups in several communities, including Columbia, Elk Grove Village, and Park Forest, have placed a high priority on improving information and referral so that gaining entry into the health care and social service system is made as easy as possible.

Public Health Facilities

Facilities offering public health services were not only absent from most of the study new and conventional communities, but were also quite distant from them. Only Park Forest and the conventional communities of Sharonville, West San Mateo, and Kingman had public health facilities or programs located within the community. For all new communities the median distance to the nearest public health clinic was over seven miles (37,000 feet). Conventional community residents had to travel even farther for public health services, the median distance to the nearest facility being over nine miles (47,600 feet).

Health professionals had divided opinions as to whether existing public health facilities were of any use to new community residents. In six new communities, half or more of the professionals interviewed thought such facilities were of value to residents, while in seven communities a majority of the professionals thought public health facilities were of no use.

In explaining their reasons, some respondents stated that existing public health facilities were the only available sources of care for the community, or the only sources of care serving low- and moderate-income residents. Several pointed out that people use public facilities for only certain types of care—most commonly immunization, and, less frequently, social services. Among respondents stating that public sources of care were not useful, two explanations predominated: (1) because such services were geared to lower income people, residents of the study communities reputedly considered them to be inappropriate for their use or believed that they were ineligible for public services; and (2) public health facilities were too far away or too difficult to reach. Others were critical of the quality of the facilities, which were described as poorly equipped, or disapproved of their methods of dispensing care, observing that clinics "treat categories of diseases, not people."

The combination of large distances to public health facilities and the sometimes negative attitudes toward them, especially in new communities, means that these facilities cannot be considered a significant health resource for community residents. This situation contributes to the lack of variety in the types of health care available in new communities, with few alternatives to traditional fee-for-service practice. It may also contribute to the lack of diversity in the populations of these communities, since few residents, other than those who have the means and inclination to rely on private sources for most of their health needs, can find low-cost sources of care in the community.

Health Maintenance Programs: The Columbia Experience

Although new communities have not yet established an outstanding record in the provision of health care services, the Federal Health Maintenance Organization (HMO) Act of 1974 (PL 93-222) may stimulate more comprehensive approaches to health care by making grants available for feasibility studies, planning, and initial development of health maintenance organizations. Because of the likelihood of increased developer interest in this approach to community health care, it is useful to look briefly at the experience of the Columbia Medical Plan—the first HMO organized in conjunction with new community development.

As noted earlier, the Columbia Medical Plan offers comprehensive health services to persons living in and near Columbia. Members may enroll either through employer groups or through special groups such as the Columbia Park and Recreation Association. Premium rates vary, depending upon the group involved and benefits selected. In 1975 those selecting the "high" option paid from $25.25 per month for a single person to $81.90

per month for a family of three or more persons. A slight additional charge was made for each visit to the plan's clinic. In 1970, approximately 45 percent of Columbia's residents were enrolled; in 1973, 37 percent of the household survey respondents reported that they were members of the plan.

The percentage of Columbia respondents subscribing to the plan varied substantially by income. Subscription rates were fairly high for those eligible for medical assistance payments (over 30 percent of the respondents with incomes under $5,000 were members), but fell sharply for respondents with incomes between $5,000 and $9,999—less than 15 percent were plan members. For respondents with incomes of $10,000 or more, the rate of plan membership rose steadily with increasing income.

Membership in the Columbia Medical Plan did not vary greatly by race, but did vary by family life cycle. Membership was lower among the youngest and oldest respondents, and among single-person households and couples than among households consisting of three or more persons. Similar findings were reported by Clifton Gaus (1971). Gaus also showed that families moving to Columbia from within the Baltimore-Washington area were less likely to join the plan than those moving from outside the area, possibly because the former group found it easier to retain their previous physicians.

If some Columbia residents chose not to join the plan because they retained family physicians elsewhere, it was nevertheless the case that a far greater proportion of subscribers to the plan than nonsubscribers reported having a regular doctor or clinic, by a margin of over 20 percent. However, in spite of nearly unanimous reports of a regular doctor or clinic by plan members, and the plan's emphasis on preventive care, the proportion of plan members who had had a routine checkup during the previous year did not differ significantly from nonplan members.

The mean number of visits to a physician during the previous year was about 20 percent higher among members of the Columbia Medical Plan than among other Columbia respondents. M.L. Peterson (1971) reported even more dramatic differences from a comparison of visits by plan members and national averages for a population of comparable income, age, sex, and race (an average of 8.0 versus 4.6 visits annually). Peterson also reported that hospital use was lower than national averages and that 40 percent of the physician visits by Medical Plan members were for well-person care, suggesting that the plan's emphasis on preventive care was effective.

Although use of physicians' services was greater for members of the Columbia Medical Plan, obtaining those services was not always accomplished without difficulty. Among the Columbia respondents with a regular doctor or clinic, more than twice as many plan as nonplan members reported problems arranging appointments and in the way they were treated during their last visit. However, fewer plan members were dissatisfied with the cost of the treatment they received.

Overall, Columbia residents who belonged to the Medical Plan rated health care in the community much higher than those who did not belong—three times as many gave excellent ratings. Columbia health professionals generally felt that the Medical Plan was serving its enrollees well, but their comments were laced with qualifying remarks and indications of problem areas.

The comments of some of the professionals pointed to limitations in the suitability of the Columbia Medical Plan for many residents. Several professionals felt the plan worked well for those who could afford it and that as a self-selected group they were bound to be satisfied. In addition to the frequently mentioned obstacle of cost, residents' lack of awareness of the plan, the fact that many already had personal physicians, and a preference for fee-for-service practice were cited as reasons why the plan was unlikely to serve as a source of care for the entire community. The plan was also faulted for not making special provisions for low- and moderate-income residents.

Several doctors who held positions with physicians' organizations stated that the Medical Plan competed unfairly with private practice and lured the best-paying patients away from private practitioners; however, doubts were expressed that the plan would be able to compete as successfully with fee-for-service practice once office facilities and opportunities were available in Columbia for private doctors.

Writing in 1972, William F. Towle, the administrator of the Columbia Hospital and Clinics, identified the adjustment of physicians to an unfamiliar role in a health maintenance organization as one of the issues that had yet to be faced. By the time of the health professional survey in the spring of 1973, most respondents felt that physician participation in the Medical Plan had been successful from the point of view of the doctors involved and that doctors had become accustomed to working with a health maintenance organization. Respondents representing private physicians' groups indicated that the advantages the plan held for staff doctors were shorter hours, less reponsibility, and the opportunity to improve private practices on the side.

While the health professional interviews were designed to elicit comments regarding the experience of physicians and patients with a community-based prepaid health plan, it is apparent that the Columbia Medical Plan has had to contend with difficulties not discussed in these interviews. Robert M. Heyssel (1971a), for example, described problems involved in attempting to market the plan through a multiplicity of employers working with a multiplicity of insurers. William F. Towle (1972) pointed out the difficulties of developing effective working relationships among a hospital, a private physicians' group, insurance carriers, and consumer groups. At the same time, the Columbia Medical Plan has had the advantage, particularly in its early years, of operating in a captive market, in which residents of a new, somewhat isolated community had few alternatives to a prepaid plan that was being encouraged by the developer.

In sum, based on the Columbia experience, new communities seem to be particularly appropriate settings in which to establish prepaid health plans. The community-based health maintenance organization is an attractive way to provide comprehensive health services in locations where few other sources of care are available. The absence of competing forms of care may increase the chances of successful operation of the HMO. But the real lesson of Columbia's experience is not that plans such as the Medical Plan should be the exclusive source of health care in the area, but that they should be designed to be available to all members of a balanced community who wish to join and use them. The unhappiness resulting from developer actions that, until recently, tended to exclude fee-for-service practice suggests the advisability of providing options for more than one type of service where prepaid plans are introduced. Moreover, much of the value of a prepaid plan is lost if it fails to serve all members when needed, as appeared to be the case in Columbia, or if, as was also the case, the cost of membership tends to exclude a significant portion of the community.

Residents' Evaluations of Community Health Care

On an aggregate level, new community residents tended to give somewhat higher ratings to community health care facilities and services than did residents of the paired conventional communities. For example, 25 percent of the new community respondents versus 20 percent in the conventional communities reported that health and medical services were better than in their previous communities, a difference that is small but statistically significant. About two thirds (65 percent) of the new community respondents rated health care facilities and services in their communities as excellent or good, significantly more than the 54 percent of the conventional community respondents who rated facilities and services that highly. Finally, about three fourths (74 percent) of the new community respondents were satisfied with community expenditures for public health facilities, although in this case they were no more satisfied than residents of the conventional communities, where 74 percent of the respondents also indicated that expenditures were adequate.

An examination of residents' evaluations in individual communities reveals that most of the advantage in favor of new communities is contributed by relatively few communities. As shown in figure 11-4, in only four cases—Columbia, Elk Grove Village, Sharpstown, and North Palm Beach—were new community residents significantly more likely than residents of the paired conventional communities to think that health care was better than in the communities from which they had moved. There were no new communities in which a majority of the respondents thought health care was better. In fact, overall, as many new community respondents thought their move to a new community had given them poorer health and medical services than those who thought services were better than where they had lived before.

The same situation applies to residents' absolute ratings of health care facilities and services. Comparisons of individual new communities with their paired conventional communities showed that in four cases, including three new communities at the upper end of the new community continuum, conventional community respondents gave significantly higher ratings to health care in their communities. The overall advantage in favor of new communities was contributed by three new communities—Westlake Village, Laguna Niguel, and North Palm Beach—where respondents gave strikingly higher ratings to community health care than did respondents in their paired conventional communities. Although differences in ratings from their paired conventional communities were not significant, respondents in two other new communities—Elk Grove Village and Sharpstown—were also highly satisfied with health care facilities and services.

Respondents living in only two new communities were significantly more likely than respondents living in their paired conventional communities to be more satisfied with community expenditures for public health facilities. In contrast, respondents who lived in six conventional communities indicated significantly higher satisfaction with public health facility expenditures than respondents in their paired new communities.

Residents' evaluations of health care facilities and services in those new communities that received the lowest ratings will probably improve when health facilities under construction at the time of the household survey are completed. For example, community health care received very low ratings in Valencia and Lake Havasu City, but both communities had hospitals under construction at the time of the survey. Similarly, the improvement in emergency care and opening of another medical building in Irvine, extension of a prepaid health plan to Reston, and hospital construction and improvements in fee-for-service doctors' facilities in Columbia should also result in better ratings of community health care facilities and services.

In order to gain a better understanding of factors associated with residents' evaluations of health care in their communities, ratings were compared with characteristics of the community and health care delivery system, residents' perceptions of the system, and the way they used it.

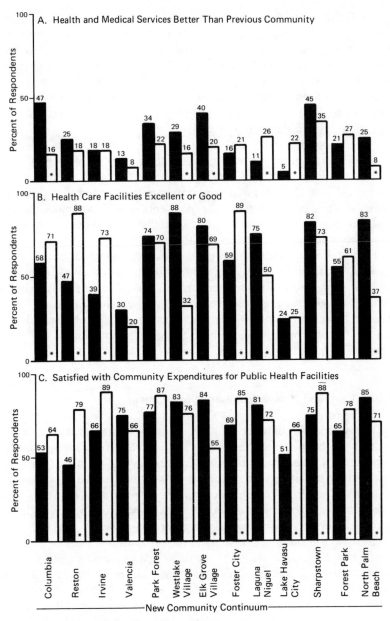

Figure 11-4. Residents' Evaluations of Health Care Facilities and Services

Among all the variables considered, the new community's location and population had the highest associations with absolute ratings of the quality of community health care. New communities with larger populations, and those which were located in more established areas closer to metropolitan central business districts, tended to receive the highest health care ratings. These communities were more likely to have attraeted health care resources and were more likely to have a greater variety of resources easily accessible in the surrounding area.

Among community health care resources, those most strongly associated with respondents' ratings were the availability of hospital care and dental care in the community and the number of medical specialists that were practicing there. In addition, communities tended to receive higher ratings if a higher proportion of respondents perceived emotional care as available in the community and if a higher proportion of health professionals rated social services as adequate.

Finally, health care ratings were associated with patterns of health care use in the community. New communities tended to receive lower ratings if a higher proportion of respondents had failed to see a doctor when they wanted to during the preceding year. On the other hand, higher ratings were given to those communities where a higher proportion of respondents had had an annual checkup and where a higher proportion of respondents reported they had a regular doctor or clinic.

Health Care and New Community Development

Deficiencies in planning for health care in new communities, inadequacies in available health resources, and relatively low resident satisfaction in comparison with other community services point to the need for developer involvement in this service system. It would be a mistake to assume that all problems in a field as complex as health care can be solved on a community level or that developers should bear full responsibility for solving them. But the developer, as the single entity in control of a tract of land large enough to be called a community, is in a unique position to influence events. The need for such action is likely to be great, since new communities tend to be isolated from existing facilities and often lack resources of their own, at least in the initial stages of development. Moreover, the developer is likely to have made claims concerning the creation of a "community," a concept that implies the presence of basic services.

The heightened responsibilities of the developer are matched by heightened opportunities. In the large areas under development, he is clearly the prime mover of events. The contacts developers necessarily have with public bodies and private institutions place them in a position to facilitate health projects. On the other hand, while new community developers have an appropriate role to play in health care planning, their focus should not be restricted solely to the community. Instead, developers and planners should tie their communities into the regions in which they are located, rather than attempt to build all needed health facilities in their community. Developers can also play a useful role in improving information and referral, which would, in effect, bring resources in the surrounding region "closer" to community residents.

While resisting the temptation to plan for the community as an isolated unit that is separate from its surroundings, developers do need to consider locating certain types of resources within the community. Because conditions differ in each community, it is impossible to establish one firm set of priorities for all communities. However, there appear to be certain clear areas of need. These include: attention to emergency service with well trained personnel; more primary care physicians; more sources of assistance for emotional problems; more public health facilities; a greater range of social services; more health and social programs designed—in terms of costs, training of personnel, and problems emphasized—with lower income residents, the elderly, and teenagers in mind. Finally, the development of health maintenance organizations and community-based clinics to support them also offers a promising way of providing health care to new community residents.

12 Schools

The educational system has often been viewed as a critical component of new community development. Parents have traditionally expected their communities to provide good schools. Educational professionals have looked to new communities as potential laboratories for equally new educational systems and ideas. New community planners have used schools to provide a focus for community cultural and recreational activities and to reinforce neighborhood identity. New community developers have been concerned with the influence of school availability on the marketability of land and housing. This broad-based interest sets the stage for an examination of school development processes and outcomes in new communities.

School Development Processes

New community development typically occurs within existing suburban and rural school districts. The characteristics of these districts, their staffs, and methods of financing the development of educational systems limit the ability of new communities to serve as vehicles for new, different, or better approaches to the provision of schools or education of children than have generally characterized suburban development in the United States. The major challenge of educational development in new communities has instead been actually getting schools constructed on time to serve the educational needs of children who occupy each new increment of housing. New community developers' participation in school development processes have often been essential in successfully meeting this challenge.

The Setting: School Districts Serving New Communities

The provision of schools is the responsibility of the school districts within whose jurisdictions new communities are developed. As a result, the educational accomplishments of a new community are less dependent on the hopes and plans of the developer or residents than on the ability of an existing school district to serve the needs of a rapidly developing, large-scale residential community. School districts' responses to new community development have been constrained by a series of factors related to the organization and financing of local educational systems.

271

Development Within Existing School Districts. One of the facts of life in new community education is the location of communities within existing school districts. Furthermore, none of the study communities was developed within a school district whose boundaries corresponded with those of the new community, and in only two cases (Irvine and Lake Havasu City) did new community development result in the organization of a new school district to achieve this end.

Three new communities—Columbia, North Palm Beach, and Reston—were built within the bounds of large countywide school systems, and one—Sharpstown—within a large citywide system. Two new communities—Forest Park and Laguna Niguel—were served by unified (primary and secondary schools combined) suburban school districts, while six communities—Elk Grove Village, Foster City, Lake Havasu City, Park Forest, Valencia, and Westlake Village—were served by more than one district.

With the exception of the school districts serving Irvine and portions of the population in Lake Havasu City and Park Forest, students generated by new community development represented only a small portion of the total enrollment of their parent school districts.

Development within existing school districts meant that the fate of new community schools could not be controlled by the developer or the residents, particularly during the early stages of the development process. For example, new community residents comprised only 26 percent of the membership of the school boards that served them. The only districts controlled by new community residents were the new unified district serving Irvine, one of the two districts serving Lake Havasu City, and two of the five school districts serving Park Forest.

The use of school districts with a broad clientele and an inability to control school board policy has led to one of the general "rules" applying to school development in most new communities. As stated by Evans Clinchy,

The rule is simply that *no new community can be singled out for special, privileged treatment if it in any way appears that this will work to the detriment of schools, teachers, parents, or children in the rest of the district.* Such special treatment is simply not politically acceptable either in rural or urban areas, and it just isn't going to happen. This can perhaps best be summed up as a "non-golden rule"—Do not do unto the new town what you would not do for all others in your district (1972, p. 14).

In fact, 18 of the 25 school districts serving the study new communities followed the nongolden rule by not allowing significant variation from districtwide policies among individual schools.

The most notable examples of school districts that allowed individual schools to vary from districtwide policies were in Columbia, Laguna

Niguel, and Valencia. The development of Columbia led to the upgrading of the entire Howard County School System (see Hovet 1971). Because Columbia's schools were all new, open-space, team-teaching facilities, some variation between schools inside the new community and those serving the rest of the county was inevitable. Also, Wilde Lake High School was developed in Columbia as a model high school for the entire Howard County system. The Capistrano Unified School District, which served Laguna Niguel, developed modern open-space schools and allowed considerable variation in teaching methods and approaches among new and older, more traditional schools in the district. This also characterized the approach of the Newhall Elementary School District, which developed a modern park-school in Valencia.

Although each of these districts, and to a lesser extent four other districts, allowed major variations in policy among district schools, they did not apply this approach solely to the new communities they served. Thus, efforts to provide better educational systems in new communities apparently must be accompanied by efforts to upgrade the entire school district, as in Columbia, or must aim for major improvements on a school-by-school basis, as was done in the districts serving Laguna Niguel and Valencia.

School District Staff. Another factor that has limited the capacity of school districts to do something different, and hopefully better, in developing new community school systems has been the lack of attention among many school districts to school planning and to research and development. For example, 11 of the 25 school districts serving the study communities had fewer than 10 professional employees assigned to their superintendents' offices. Only half of the districts (13 of 25) had assigned even 1 professional to school planning on a full-time basis, and only 9 of the districts had 1 or more persons assigned to full-time research. As a result, school districts' thinking about the educational system and new schools tended to be incremental and based on past experiences and approaches. Even if school districts were inclined to make radical departures from past practices, their capacity to do so was often sharply curbed by a lack of professional manpower and technical expertise.

In fact, most school districts were not even philosophically inclined to make radical changes from their past ways of developing and administering the educational system. Keith Goldhammer has written,

Through the coalition of educators and school board members a bureaucratic structure has been established which can be, and generally is, highly resistant to change. Innovation and experimentation are rewarded neither by the authority structure of the schools nor by the educational establishment itself (1968, p. 91).

Only three of the 25 new community school superintendents described their districts' approaches to education as highly innovative. These districts included the Howard County School System, serving Columbia, and the Newhall Elementary School District, serving Valencia, both of which were mentioned above with regard to variation in school policy among district schools, and one of the four school districts serving Elk Grove Village.

Although one might suppose that new community development would encourage a greater degree of innovation among school districts, this has not occurred. A higher proportion of school superintendents serving the conventional communities than those serving new communities (17 percent versus 12 percent) classified their districts' approaches to education as highly innovative.

School Finance. A final factor inhibiting school districts' capacity to respond to new community development is school finance. As Clinchy has noted, the inability of school districts to plan and develop different approaches to education in new communities, "is not at all helped by the near total absence of federal and state financial assistance, either to the developers or, most especially, to the local school districts" (1972, p. 40). In addition, heavy dependence on local property taxes and the need to go to the voters to pass school bond referendums to finance new construction severely inhibited the long-range planning of educational systems and encouraged a case-by-case or school-by-school approach to developing new community educational systems.

Between 1968 and 1973, the 25 school districts had held a total of 46 school bond referendums. Most districts were successful in passing their bonds, since they were serving newly developing areas with a shortage of schools, but problems in financing new construction were mounting. Bond referendum failures were reported in districts serving North Palm Beach, Reston, Sharpstown, and Westlake Village. In addition, school superintendents of districts serving Forest Park, Foster City, Laguna Niguel, and Park Forest reported that they were experiencing difficulties in financing new school construction.

A contributing factor to school districts' financial problems has been rigid state debt limitations that specify the maximum ratio of debt to assessed value that districts can assume. For example, among school districts serving the study new communities, state laws limited the debt of California districts to 5 or 10 percent (unified districts) of assessed valuation, while the maximum debt of Illinois school districts was 6 to 12 percent; Virginia districts, 18 percent; and Arizona districts, 10 percent of assessed valuation. During the initial years of development of a new community and in school districts undergoing rapid residential growth, increases in assessed valuation are often far behind the explosive need for new school construction. For many school districts the question of providing an innovative and qualitatively better system of education in new communities was academic, given the difficulties they were experiencing in even getting needed schools built.

Planning for New Community Schools

Although plans for each new community specified sites for elementary, middle, and high schools, education was a central element in the planning of only one community—Columbia. As described by the developer,

Early in the deliberation as to what would be most important in the design and development of a good city, the school became focal. . . .

Education was considered fundamental to the good city (American City Corporation 1973, p.2).

As noted in chapter 4, the developer assembled an advisory group of behavioral scientists, economists, and others to meet with Columbia's planners on a regular basis and to explore new ideas as to how the community should be developed. One of the advisory group members was Christopher Jencks, who was education editor of *New Republic* magazine and subsequently became a member of the faculty of the School of Education at Harvard. In April 1964, Jencks submitted a report that proposed various ideas for the role of education in the development of Columbia. The report was subsequently expanded to outline a comprehensive set of alternatives for Columbia's schools and was submitted to the Howard County School Board in June 1964.

The school board then embarked on its own planning program for the development of Columbia's schools and brought in its own outside experts. In July 1966, the report of these experts, which included Jencks' earlier suggestions for an ungraded system with team teaching and multiage grouping of students, was issued. This report and a subsequent report to the school board on the administrative organization of the school system formed the basis of an application to the U.S. Office of Education under Title III to establish model schools in Howard County. Subsequently, grants were received for model elementary and middle schools, though neither was to be located in Columbia (which later received a model high school). Although the developer's original concepts for education in Columbia were modified by the Howard County Board of Education and, in part, extended to the county as a whole, there is no doubt that the developer's attention to public education provided a stimulus for the achievement of a modern, innovative school system in Columbia. In addition, the development of Columbia's school system was greatly assisted by the state's assumption of the capital costs of new school construction.

The master plans of the other new communities all made reference to public schools, but generally limited their attention to estimates of the number of schools needed at full development and designation of their location. Educational programming and curriculum matters were not considered to be an appropriate topic of developer concern. The one innovation contained in a number of new community plans, including those of Columbia, Elk Grove Village, Forest Park, Park Forest, Reston, Sharpstown, Valencia, and Westlake Village, was the combination of educational and recreational facilities at one location through the development of park-schools.

From Plans to Schools: Some Common Problems

The experiences of six new communities illustrate some of the problems that have arisen in translating development plans into completed schools. All of the problems were financial ones, but each manifested itself in a different way.

Impact of State Debt Limitation Laws. As noted above, state laws that limit the bonded indebtedness of school districts can play havoc with the timing of school construction in new communities. For example, the Greenhills-Forest Park City School District prepared a long-range plan for school facilities, but tempered its recommendations by noting,

The proper interpretation of this data to the school-community and the need for annual bond issues bring a great challenge to us. If we are to meet this challenge, herculean efforts must be made by the board of education, administration, staff, and particularly the school-community (1968, p. 1).

Among other problems, the district noted that even though it maintained its indebtedness at the legal maximum, it would fall short of meeting projected needs for new schools.

The situation in Irvine was even more disquieting. The Irvine Unified School District was formed by a vote of the residents in June 1972 from portions of the San Joaquin Elementary School District and Tustin Union High School District. It began with 1,400 more students than it had space for in existing schools, but in November of the same year Irvine voters approved a $50 million bond issue. This sum was expected to finance the construction of 17 schools, the projected school needs in Irvine through 1982, and to give the district great flexibility in planning for future schools. However, it did not solve the district's financial problems, since the state debt limitation of 10 percent of assessed valuation prevented the sale of all of the bonds required to finance needed schools.

In 1974, Irvine voters approved a $44 million loan from the state to finance school construction costs in excess of funds that could be raised under the 10 percent debt limitation. Even this money did not solve Irvine's problems since state approval of new school construction took up to two years. In a rapidly growing new community, such as Irvine, this meant that school building was constantly behind current enrollments; schools were crowded; and school plans were exceedingly difficult to implement.

Impact of Rapid Growth and Lag in Property Tax Receipts. Typically, property taxes are not collected until the year after a family moves to a new home. This lag can cause serious problems for school districts, which must serve students from the moment they move in. Because of this problem and the difficulties experienced in constantly going to the voters with new bond issues, some school districts have attempted to restrict new growth, while others have tried to ease their financial burdens by asking developers to subsidize various aspects of the school development process. The developer, of course, is in a poor position to resist such demands. For example, one and a half years of litigation between the American-Hawaiian Steamship Company and the Valley Oaks School District over the price of land for the first elementary school in Westlake Village resulted in a corresponding delay in completion of the school. As shown below, most developers yielded to school districts' requests and either donated land or sold it at below market rates.

Another outcome of rapid growth is competition between different areas of a school district for new school construction. Since a new community initially has few residents (and few voters), it may be at a political disadvantage in such competition. Some districts, however, have tried to develop rational approaches to the allocation of new schools and to involve the citizenry in these decisions. A notable example is the Capistrano Unified School District's Growth Advisory Committee, which was organized to consider growth-related problems faced by the district and to recommend school construction priorities. This was beneficial to Laguna Niguel, which had secured the construction of only one elementary school through 1973, but was designated as the site for an additional elementary school and a junior high school to be completed by the 1975-76 school year.

Impact of Declining School Enrollments. As important as the absolute amount of residential growth is its distribution. Where new communities are developed in school districts that have already experienced a wave of growth, residents of previously settled portions of the district—who have already secured schools to meet their needs—may resist bond issues for school construction in other portions of the district where growth is still occurring.

The original Foster City master plan, as well as the 1972 General Plan adopted by the city of Foster City, specified the location of a high school, two junior high schools, and five elementary schools in the community. One junior high school and two elementary schools were built; but then the populations of the San Mateo City School District and San Mateo Union High School District, which served Foster City, stabilized and school enrollments dropped at schools outside Foster City, even though students generated by Foster City's development were steadily rising. Noting this phenomenon, the San Mateo City School District's *School Facilities Study* stated,

Thus a major question faces this school community. Will we continue to bus Foster City to available space in schools losing population in the San Mateo areas, or will schools be built in the new residential areas in Foster City? This is a question the board and community must decide (1973, p. 20).

The school district recommended converting one elementary school in Foster City to a permanent structure (students were housed in 27 portable buildings) and building a third elementary school, which would have been immediately filled by students who were being bussed to schools outside of the community. However, because bond issues would be required for these improvements, and a majority of the district's residents lived outside of Foster City, prospects were not bright for further elementary school construction.

In the case of the proposed Marina High School in Foster City, the San Mateo Union High School District would have had to close one or more existing high schools to justify its construction. Whether the district's residents would pass a bond issue to support building a new high school while high schools closer to them were abandoned became increasingly unlikely.

The goals for the development of Reston included provision of "educational facilities as an integral part of the community plan—easily accessible to both children and adults." The master plan for Reston designated 15 sites for elementary schools, as well as two intermediate-high school sites. However, in 1972 and again in 1974 the maturing population served by the Fairfax County public schools voted down large bond issues that would have insured construction of more than the four elementary schools that had been built in Reston. In early 1975, these schools were 850 students over capacity; intermediate and high school students were still being bussed to schools in neighboring Herndon; and the county school system was forced to seek an emergency $2.9 million loan from the Virginia State School Authority to build an additional elementary school.

The Developer's Role

Although education has traditionally been a public function in the United States, and most developers would just as soon not be involved in school construction beyond the designation of school sites and design of architectural motifs, they have rarely been able to maintain such a limited role.

For example, in a number of communities developers' staffs played a major part in calculating and updating projections of future school-age populations (Elk Grove Village, Foster City, Lake Havasu City, and Sharpstown). In several communities developers participated in the establishment of design objectives for new schools (Columbia, Reston, and Valencia).

From the viewpoint of school districts, one of the most important areas of developer involvement was in providing land for new schools. In eight new communities, developers donated (or sold at nominal costs) sites for new school construction (Columbia, Elk Grove Village, Foster City, Lake Havasu City, Laguna Niguel, Park Forest, Reston, and Westlake Village). In three other new communities, land was sold to school districts at below market value (Irvine, Sharpstown, and Valencia).

In two cases, new community developers played an instrumental role in the formation of new school districts. The Irvine Unified School District was formed with the active support of The Irvine Company. Lake Havasu City's developer formed Common School District No. 25 to provide primary education there. Beginning in 1964 with just 39 students, the district grew steadily to a 1973 enrollment of 1,420 students housed in two elementary schools and a junior high school. In addition, the developer played a large part in persuading the Mohave County Union High School District to build a high school in Lake Havasu City, rather than bus students to far-distant schools in other parts of the county.

Finally, a number of developers have been forced actually to participate in financing school construction. When the Irvine Unified School District found it impossible to match the pace of school construction to the pace of residential development, The Irvine Company planned, financed, and built an "instant" elementary school, which it leased to the district. Gulf-Reston, Inc. aided in the construction of Lake Anne Elementary School when financial overruns occurred in building the school and proposed to build schools in Reston for the Fairfax County public schools under a lease-purchase arrangement. Westlake Village's developer, American-Hawaiian Steamship Company, bought the bonds of the Valley Oaks School District when it had difficulty marketing them, and later financed and constructed a portable elementary school, which it at first leased and has since donated to the district.

The most unique and far-reaching developer commitment to the public schools occurred in Park Forest. Believing that developers have a moral obligation to make schools available along with their houses, American Community Builders, Inc. established a school development process that at one time resulted in one half of the company's working capital being tied up in aid to the educational system.

When construction began on Park Forest, the contemplated development acreage was served by six elementary school districts and three high school districts, none of which could afford or wanted to be involved in the rapid growth anticipated for the community. Concentrating on one of the elementary school districts, which Park Forest residents soon dominated, the developer established a cooperative school construction process. A nonprofit school foundation was formed to construct new schools. The foundation was governed by representatives of both the developer and school district. The developer then loaned the foundation funds for new school development and the foundation contracted with the school district to provide schools. The district in turn agreed to operate the completed schools and to repay the foundation for their construction (but not for interest or the land) when its tax base permitted it to issue bonds. American Community Builders also provided operating subsidies for the district until tax revenues and state school assistance were available.

School superintendents tended to be highly pleased with developers' contributions to the educational process. Eight of the 20 superintendents who were willing to evaluate developers' efforts said they were "very helpful" and "highly beneficial." Nine other superintendents said that developers had been "helpful" and that their contributions to the educational process were "generally beneficial." Only three of the 20 superintendents felt that new community developers had had little or no effect on education and were not helpful.

Superintendents were asked to specify the reasons for their ratings. Most had to do with the cooperativeness of the developer and the excellent channels of communications that had been established. Superintendents of the districts serving Irvine, Park Forest, Sharpstown, and Valencia approved of planned community development and the opportunities it provided for better school siting. In Columbia, Elk Grove Village, Laguna Niguel, Lake Havasu City, and Valencia, superintendents pointed to developer school site donations. Howard County's school superintendent also noted that the development of Columbia forced the county to undertake a self-evaluation of its educational system, while the superintendent of Lake Havasu City's elementary school district noted that the developer had taken an active part in the educational life of that community.

Superintendents who were disappointed in the developers' role in the educational process complained that education had not been given high enough priority in community planning (one of four districts serving Elk

Grove Village); that the developer had an ambivalent attitude regarding the location of school sites (one of three districts serving Westlake Village); and that the developer had not established close enough contacts with the school district (one of two districts serving Foster City).

Effects of New Communities on Educational Programs

In addition to the obvious impact of new community development on the financial status of school districts and the strains imposed on their capacity to build new schools, new community development has had some effect on the characteristics of school districts' educational programs.

Three types of impacts were noted by the 13 school districts that reported changes that had occurred. Superintendents of school districts serving Columbia and Valencia indicated that new community development in their districts was the major stimulus for the adoption of more innovative educational programs. The superintendent of the Howard County schools reported that Columbia's development also provided the impetus for renovating old schools in the county and for allowing greater community use of schools.

A second change attributable to new community development has been the broadening of school curriculums. In these cases new community development did not stimulate new approaches to education, but by increasing the number of students served by a district, it allowed more types of courses to be offered. This result was reported by the superintendents of districts serving Elk Grove Village, Forest Park, Laguna Niguel, and Lake Havasu City.

A third type of change stimulated by new community development was the orientation of school districts' educational programs. In these cases in-migration of more educated and higher status residents to the new community led to a demand for more academically oriented curriculums. This type of change was reported in the high school districts serving Lake Havasu City and Valencia and by two of the districts serving Park Forest, which had previously served predominantly rural, farm-oriented populations.

New communities that apparently had no impact on the educational programs of school districts—Foster City, North Palm Beach, Reston, Sharpstown, and Westlake Village—were generally located in larger school districts that could more easily absorb new students along with students generated from other urban growth in their jurisdictions. In these cases, new community development was not large enough, relative to the entire area served, to cause the districts to reconsider their educational programs.

New Community Schools

The question is whether new community development, with all of the problems developers have encountered, has produced different educational results than have occurred in the conventional communities. The outcomes of school development processes may be evaluated from both objective and subjective perspectives. Objective factors considered first include the availability and accessibility of the public schools constructed to serve new communities and conventional communities, characteristics of school facilities and programs, school-community relations, and the degree of racial integration.

Availability of Schools

In spite of the best efforts of many new community developers, the conventional communities had been somewhat more successful in constructing schools. As shown in figure 12-1, for 8 of the 13 paired comparisons, the conventional communities had more elementary and intermediate schools per 100,000 community residents. High schools were in operation in 7 new and 9 conventional communities.

Among the new communities, school construction efforts were most successful in Columbia, Elk Grove Village, and Park Forest. In addition to the developer's concern for the educational system in Columbia, state financing of new construction greatly assisted the school building process in that community. Park Forest's unique school building program has been noted above. In Elk Grove Village, the rapid rise in the tax base attributable to the success of the Centex Industrial Park provided sufficient tax resources to finance an extensive school-building program.

School districts were best able to accommodate the elementary school needs of new communities. Seventy-five percent of the new community children were able to attend an elementary school within their own community. In contrast, only 54 percent of the intermediate school and 41 percent of the high school students attended public schools in their communities.

School sites and plants, including size, design capacity, and number of students enrolled were similar in the new communities and conventional communities. There was also little difference shown in various indicators of overcrowding. Schools in six new communities and six conventional communities employed double shifts or delayed starts. In 10 new communities and 10 conventional communities temporary classrooms were in use at one or more community schools. The average number of students per classroom was also nearly identical—29 among the new and 28 among the conventional communities.

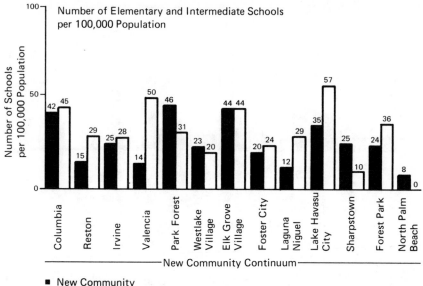

Figure 12-1. Availability of Elementary and Intermediate Schools

Accessibility of Schools

Although the number of elementary and middle schools per capita tended to be greater among the conventional communities, new community developers' attention to school siting resulted in somewhat better accessibility in these communities. The median new community resident lived 3,200 feet from the nearest elementary school and about 8,200 feet from the nearest intermediate school. Among conventional community residents, the figures were 5,200 feet and 9,100 feet, respectively. However, as shown in figure 12-2, the difference between each new community and its paired conventional community was frequently very slight. In six cases new community residents tended to live closer to the nearest elementary school, while in five cases the conventional community residents lived closer. In two cases they were tied.

In eight communities, new community residents tended to live closer to the nearest intermediate school, but the accessibility of high schools was somewhat better in the conventional communities. Median distance to the nearest new community high school was 12,600 feet versus 9,300 feet in the conventional communities. The residents of eight conventional communities tended to live closer to the nearest high school.

One goal of neighborhood design in many new communities has been to place elementary schools within walking distance of students. As noted in

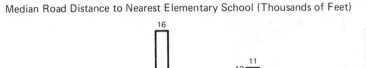

Median Road Distance to Nearest Elementary School (Thousands of Feet)

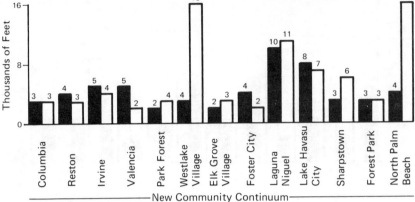

■ New Community
□ Conventional Community

Figure 12-2. Accessibility of Elementary Schools

chapter 9, new community respondents were somewhat more likely than those living in the conventional communities to have an elementary school located within their neighborhood (35 percent versus 24 percent). New community students were also more likely to walk or bicycle to school. Among those attending public elementary schools that were located within their communities, 68 percent of the students typically walked or bicycled. This was true for only 46 percent of the conventional community elementary school students. Among students attending all types of schools, 43 percent walked or bicycled to schools serving new communities versus 34 percent in the case of the conventional communities. Thus, the parts of the educational system over which developers had the most control, school siting and location, did result in some improvement over conventional community development.

New Communities as Laboratories for Innovation

As illustrated by the data summarized in figure 12-3, new community schools have generally been no more innovative in their approaches to education than those serving the conventional communities. This is not to say that schools serving new communities have not adopted many of the ideas that are currently in vogue among educators. Many of them have, but not in greater numbers than was typical of the conventional suburban areas.

Average Number of Six Features Used in Schools (automated learning, media-learning center, open space school plan, teachers' aides, team teaching, ungraded classes)

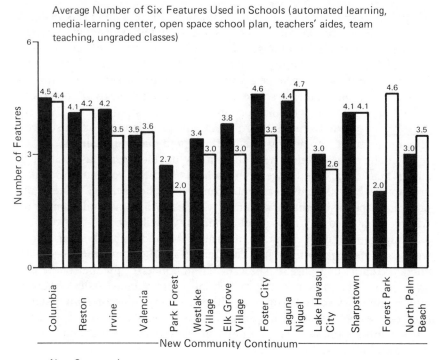

- ■ New Community
- ☐ Conventional Community

Figure 12-3. Use of Innovative Concepts in Community Schools

Eighteen percent of the principals of both new community and conventional community schools rated their educational programs as "highly innovative." However, the new community principals represented schools in only 5 of the 13 communities—Columbia (4 of 7 schools), Elk Grove Village (1 of 7), Reston (1 of 3), Sharpstown (3 of 4), and Valencia (1 of 1). Principals of elementary schools serving the other new communities viewed their educational appoaches as more conservative.

Principals of intermediate and high schools were less likely to rate their educational programs as highly innovative. Only 1 of 11 new community intermediate school principals and 1 of 7 high school principals characterized their programs in those terms.

School-Community Relations

Public schools are increasingly being viewed as community resources that can serve a number of functions in addition to education. Recreational uses of the schools were noted in chapter 10. In addition, public schools have begun to initiate community school programs that offer residents a variety of academic and leisure-interest courses and activities. Since school plants are not in session for a large part of the time, they offer convenient settings for the activities of various community groups—from newly formed churches who may meet in schools' multipurpose rooms to various recreational organizations who may use gymnasiums and athletic fields. Conversely, schools may enrich their educational programs by taking students off campus to use community institutional and cultural facilities.

To determine whether new community development has resulted in closer than usual ties between the schools and the community, school principals were asked about parents' concern for their schools' educational programs, the availability of community school programs, and whether the schools ever used any nonschool community facilities.

New community elementary, intermediate, and high school principals were each more likely than their counterparts in the conventional communities to report that parents showed "great concern" for the school program. However, new community schools were somewhat less likely to offer community school programs, although every new community had at least one school where such a program was available. Most new community schools also allowed various nonschool groups to use the schools when they were not in session.

School use of community facilities for educational purposes varied as much among individual schools as among new communities and conventional communities. Overall, 56 percent of the new community elementary school principals said they had used community facilities, versus 44 percent of the conventional community elementary school principals. One or more elementary schools used community facilities in every new community except North Palm Beach and Valencia. Middle and high schools were somewhat more likely to have used community facilities, though in the case of high schools the conventional community schools were those most likely to have done so.

Integration of Community Schools

The goal of population diversity in new communities carries with it the related goal of improving educational opportunities for minority students. Two indicators of the integration experience of new community and conventional community schools are summarized in figure 12-4. The first is the proportion of minority (black, Mexican American, American Indian, and Oriental) students attending schools in both settings. The second is parents' perceptions of racial conflict and hostility in the schools attended by their children.

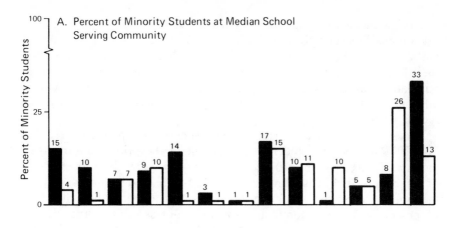

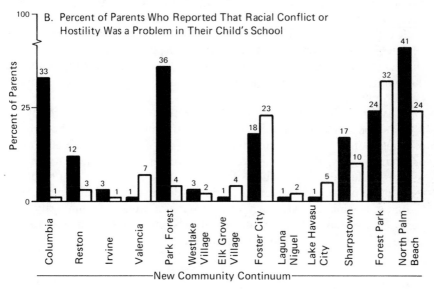

Figure 12-4. Integration Experience at Community Schools

Median minority enrollments of 5 percent or more of the student body characterized schools serving 10 new communities and 8 conventional communities. Minority students came from both the resident populations of these communities and, in the case of Park Forest and North Palm Beach, from neighboring communities from which they were bussed in an effort to achieve greater racial balance.

As figure 12-4 indicates, in many communities integration has not been achieved without some problems. One of the most serious, at least from the perspectives of parents, was racial conflict and hostility in the schools. This was particularly true in the four new communities—Columbia, Park Forest, Forest Park, and North Palm Beach—with the largest proportions of black students. In each case, 24 percent or more of the parents reported their concern about such problems. New communities whose minority populations were primarily composed of Mexican Americans and Orientals, such as the California communities, experienced fewer problems of racial conflict.

In a number of cases new community school principals indicated that both minority groups students (37 percent of the principals) and their parents (22 percent of the principals) were dissatisfied with various aspects of the schools. In the case of minority students, the most common problems mentioned were general feelings of racial tension and prejudice; their lack of power in schools dominated by middle-class whites; the lack of minority-oriented programs, activities, and minority teachers; and, in a few cases, difficulties of inner-city students in adjusting to middle-class values.

It was noted of minority parents, on the other hand, that they tended to be much more concerned with their children's progress in school than was characteristic of the white majority. In some cases, principals also reported that militant black parents carefully monitored the schools for signs of racial prejudice.

Most schools in both the new and conventional communities were taking steps to alleviate various problem situations. As a Columbia school principal noted, the most important step was to admit that problems were occurring. Activities designed to insure greater racial tranquility in the schools included the formation of human relations councils and committees; hiring black and Mexican American administrators, counselors, and teachers; organizing extracurricular activities designed for minority students; and simply holding frequent rap sessions with the students to improve communications and understanding.

Children's Attitudes and Performance

In 11 of the 13 new communities 50 percent or more of the parents reported that their children liked going to school "very much." However, as shown in figure 12-5, there was little difference between new and conventional communities on this indicator of school performance. In only two cases—Columbia and Foster City—were new community parents significantly more likely than parents in their paired conventional community to say that their children liked going to school.

Children's performance in school also tended to be very similar. Overall, school principals reported that 74 percent of the new community and 76 percent of the conventional community elementary school children were

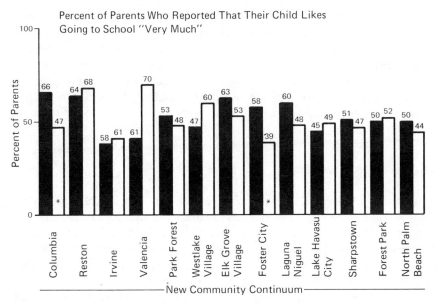

Figure 12-5. Children's Attitude Toward School

reading at grade level. In the case of middle schools, 5 percent more new community students were reading at grade level (73 percent versus 68 percent). Students' performance in Foster City, Columbia, Reston, and Forest Park tended to be somewhat above the average for all new communities.

Two measures of high school performance were obtained from the high school principals—drop-out rates and the proportion of students who went on to college among the previous year's graduates. On both measures new community high school students did slightly better than students who attended high schools serving the conventional communities. For example, 66 percent of the new community high school students versus 62 percent of the conventional community students were reported to have gone on to college. The drop-out rate for new community high schools was 1.7 percent; for conventional community high schools, it was 3.8 percent.

Residents' and Parents' Overall Evaluations of the Schools

Although new community residents and parents tended to give high ratings to the schools in their communities, their evaluations were not very much

290

different from those of conventional community residents. Forty-six percent of the new community respondents and 45 percent of those living in the conventional communities thought the schools were better than those of their previous communities. Seventy-nine percent and 80 percent, respectively, of the parents rated their children's schools as excellent or good.[a] A slightly larger proportion of conventional community respondents, 70 percent versus 66 percent, were satisfied with community expenditures for schools.

Community Comparisons

Aggregate similarities in evaluations of the schools are reflected in the individual community comparisons illustrated in figure 12-6. In only four cases—Columbia, Reston, Elk Grove Village, and North Palm Beach—were new community residents more likely than residents of their paired conventional community to think that community schools were better than those of their previous communities. There were no significant differences in parents' ratings of the quality of their children's schools, and satisfaction with community school expenditures were evenly divided. In three cases—Irvine, Westlake Village, and Elk Grove Village—new community residents were those most satisfied with expenditure levels. However, for three other paired comparisons—Columbia, Reston, and Foster City—conventional community residents were those most satisfied. In the seven other paired communities, differences were not statistically significant.

Residents' attitudes toward community expenditures for the schools reflected difficulties noted earlier in school financing and construction, and also deficiencies in school availability (compare figure 12-1 with figure 12-6C). For example, Reston, Foster City, and Laguna Niguel each had problems with new school construction; each ranked well below average in the number of community schools per 100,000 population; and their residents were least satisfied with the level of community expenditures for the schools. North Palm Beach, where only one elementary school site was indicated on the community master plan, also had a much lower than average proportion of residents who were satisfied with school expenditures. This occurred in spite of the fact that it had an older population that in other situations might have been expected to be less concerned with school matters.

Elk Grove Village was the top-rated new community on all three indi-

---

[a] In households with school-age children, parents were asked to rate the school of one randomly selected child (if more than one school-age child was present). Respondents who did not have children in school were not asked to rate community schools, though they were asked to compare them with schools in their previous communities and to indicate their satisfaction with expenditures for the schools.

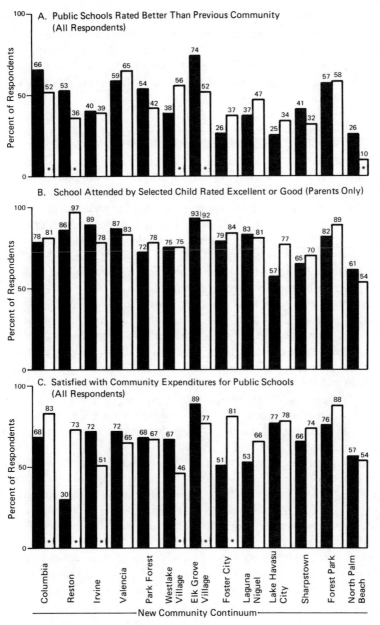

Figure 12-6. Residents' Evaluations of the Schools

cators of residents' satisfaction with the schools. As noted earlier, Elk Grove Village had a relatively high ratio of schools per 100,000 population (figure 12-1) and the most accessible elementary schools among the study new communities (figure 12-2). Even more noteworthy, per capita educational operating expenditures there were the highest of any new community studied.

Factors Associated with Perceptions of School Excellence

For all the study new communities, a number of characteristics of the schools and the school districts in which they were located were associated with residents' ratings. For example, in the case of elementary schools, parents were significantly more likely to rate schools as excellent if school district expenditures per pupil were higher.[b] Whereas 38 percent of the new community parents rated their child's school as excellent, 57 percent of those whose children attended a school in a district spending $1,200 or more per pupil annually gave excellent ratings.

Parents were particularly unhappy with school districts with more innovative approaches to education and districts that had racial bussing programs. For example, while 58 percent of the parents of elementary school children rated schools as excellent in districts whose superintendents said their approach to education was traditional, only 28 percent gave excellent ratings to elementary schools in districts characterized by their superintendents as highly innovative. Only 24 percent of the parents in districts with bussing programs to achieve racial balance and only 12 percent of those with children in schools with black enrollments of greater than 15 percent gave ratings of excellent.

Although new community planners have paid particular attention to the accessibility of elementary schools, there was little association between measures of road- and time-distance to school or students' typical mode of travel to school and parents' evaluations.

Parents' concern for racial hostility and other disruptions of the educational process were reflected in their evaluations of the excellence of their children's elementary schools. Only 16 percent of the parents whose children attended schools where the school principal reported the existence of disciplinary problems rated such schools as excellent, compared with excellent ratings by 41 percent of the parents whose children attended schools without severe disciplinary problems.

Parents' satisfaction with smaller class size was apparent. For example, 52 percent of the parents whose children attended a school with less than 25

---

[b] This and the following analyses were performed with data from 461 parents whose children attended 52 new community elementary schools.

students per classroom rated such schools as excellent. On the other hand, schools with temporary classrooms in use—an indicator of crowding problems—received lower ratings (26 percent excellent) than schools without them (42 percent excellent).

Fifty-three percent of the parents with children attending schools whose principals said their programs were "neither innovative nor traditional" rated such schools as excellent. Lower ratings were given to schools with programs that, according to the school principals, were innovative or traditional. There was little association between parents' evaluations of the schools and schools' use of progressive educational concepts, such as automated learning, open space school plans and team teaching, ungraded classes, pass-fail grading, or the availability of media-learning centers.

Finally, schools with better community relations tended to receive a higher proportion of excellent ratings. Only 13 percent of the parents whose children attended an elementary school where the principal said parents' concern for the school was average rated such schools as excellent, in comparison with 40 percent who gave excellent ratings to schools where parents' concern was rated as above average. Parents' ratings were also significantly higher for schools that had sponsored various community activities during the previous year.

Improving the School Development Process

To this time developers' involvement in the educational systems of new communities has often been erratic, and the results, with the possible exception of somewhat better elementary and intermediate school accessibility, have been little different from those of conventional suburban development. Clearly, if new communities are to provide vehicles for better educational opportunities than are characteristic of conventional suburbs, new approaches to new community education are required. Potential areas in which new community school development processes can be improved include: (1) initial planning of schools; (2) design and location of school plants; (3) organization for the provision of schools and educational services; and (4) financing of school systems.

School Planning

With the exception of Columbia, school planning for new communities has usually not proceeded beyond the construction of the physical plants required to house students and the design of the next school to be built.

Greater attention should be given in the initial planning of a new community to the community's impact on the entire school system, to educational methods and processes as well as physical design, and to the involvement of parents and students in the planning process. This will not occur until new community developers pay greater attention to educational planning. Also local school districts must be provided with adequate financial resources to hire professional personnel who can think creatively about the future of the district and how new community development can be used as a positive influence on the educational process.

School Plants

The ability of school districts to provide schools on time in new communities and to provide qualitatively different and better schools than usual has been constrained by the felt need of school districts (and state legislation) to build traditional school houses. When schools have to be built in a hurry to accommodate a burgeoning school population, this can lead to shortsighted school designs and serious problems in financing school construction. As an alternative, developers and school districts should give greater attention to interim solutions to the need for new schools.

As demonstrated by Irvine's "instant school," attractive schools in temporary buildings can be constructed. This would allow time for greater attention to, and greater parent participation in, the design of permanent school facilities. Attention should also be given to other interim school development alternatives, such as converting existing structures in the community to temporary schools, and using commercial buildings as schools.

A number of new communities have begun to integrate their schools more closely with other community functions and services. The development of schools in conjunction with neighborhood and community parks is a notable example. School districts are also increasingly providing adult education and community school programs and allowing community groups to use school facilities after school hours and during vacation periods. However, most schools are still located in their own separate buildings, and are often far removed from buildings housing other community-service organizations.

The next step in integrating schools and schooling with the surrounding community could be closer physical integration of facilities. Schools could be grouped with other community-service functions, such as preschool education, day care, recreational facilities, health care, shared-use religious facilities, and some types of shopping in separate buildings on the same site, thus allowing for shared parking, joint use of recreational facilities, and savings in user transportation costs. Alternatively, these and other functions might be housed in the same physical structures, with each function sharing in the cost of the building. Both of these alternatives would save school districts and developers money from decreased site acquisition costs, as well as in overall construction and maintenance costs.

Achieving more rational development of school facilities will require developers to become more intimately involved in the school development process. Use of interim school buildings in new communities will be much easier to achieve if developers actually finance the design and construction of facilities (which some developers are already doing) and lease them to school districts. Development of multiple-use facilities cannot be achieved by school districts acting on their own. Developers must take the lead in demonstrating the need for better approaches to school construction, convincing school boards of this need, and formulating new institutions, such as nonprofit community service corporations, to implement new ideas.

As with better planning, this requires money. To expect developers, who are already burdened with huge front-end costs and heavy debt service, to finance new approaches to building schools is unreasonable, though it is reasonable to expect them to share in such costs. State and federal help will probably be needed if new communities are to live up to their potential as vehicles for better schools.

Organizational Structures

Even if developers were willing to pay closer attention to educational planning and even if state and federal aid were available to developers and school districts, the present administrative structure for providing educational services in new communities is not conducive to new educational approaches. School districts usually have much wider responsibilities than a new community's schools. They have difficulty in treating only a portion of their jurisdiction differently from the remainder of their service area. They are bound by numerous state laws that restrict their freedom of action; and given the conventional mores of the educational profession, districts may resist joint planning of educational facilities and integration with other community functions. For all of these reasons there is a clear need to invent a new administrative structure for the provision of community services in new communities.

As a minimum, state and local authorities should give strong consideration to forming new school districts whose boundaries would be coterminous with those of each new community. Beyond this, attention should be given to matching a comprehensively planned new community with an organization that can comprehensively implement such plans. The development of new community authorities, as discussed at the conclusion of chapter 8, seems to be a promising approach. Such authorities could be empowered to provide all necessary community services, including educational services, and should be allowed to preservice community facilities by incurring far greater debt than is currently allowed by most state debt limitation laws. In addition, state and federal guarantees of authority bonds should be provided to insure their marketability.

Financing School Development

Underlying most of the previous discussion has been the need to provide a better means of financing school development processes in new communities. Most local school districts are tied to local property taxes as a means of paying for school construction and operation. This method of financing has been attacked on a number of grounds. As a means of financing public services in new community development, as well as services in any fast-growing area, it is clearly inadequate. Population growth and the demand for services far outrun the capacity of the tax base to provide needed revenues. Given the uncertainties of commercial and industrial location decisions, it is doubtful that new community development can succeed if residential occupancy is tied to the pace of such development and the growth of the tax base. It is also not feasible to expect new community developers to assume the lion's share of the costs of public service delivery. For one, developers' debt service costs are far greater than those of public agencies. In addition, land prices can absorb only a limited amount of public service infrastructure costs before they become uncompetitive with conventional subdivisions whose developers are not expected to shoulder the burden of providing public facilities and services.

In short, if new communities are to realize the opportunities offered by large-scale development for improved educational service delivery, the state and federal governments must assume a share of the front-end costs, particularly during the early years of development. If state and/or federal aid is not forthcoming, it has been shown in this chapter that new communities are not likely to achieve better educational systems than are characteristic of conventional suburbs.

13 Shopping Facilities

The goal of preservicing in new community development—where homes and facilities are provided simultaneously—implies that residents' shopping needs are accommodated at all stages of the community development process. This represents a sharp departure from the usual pattern of suburbanization. Typically, the people have come first. When an adequate population base has been established, the stores have followed. It also presents new community developers with a problem.

According to the manager of commercial leasing for The Irvine Company,

> The dilemma we and our potential commercial tenants face is pretty elementary, like which comes first, the chicken or the egg? Except the question here is, which comes first, the houses or the shops? If we have the houses but no shops nearby, the houses could lose their value. If we have the shops but no houses, then the shopkeepers could lose their shirts (Roach 1973).

Preservicing shopping facilities is thus not an easy task. But it is a necessary one. If satisfactory shopping facilities are not provided early in new communities, opportunities for their later development may be lost, simply because the competition will have captured or diluted the market through the construction of nearby shopping centers.

The Hierarchy of Shopping Facilities

Since the end of World War II, commercial establishments have been increasingly grouped in centers. In contrast to shopping districts or the strip commercial areas common in many parts of the country, where a miscellaneous collection of stores stand on their own separate lots, the shopping center is a unified commercial development that is designed, constructed, and operated by a single owner. This offers many advantages to both merchants and consumers. Merchants benefit from the assemblage of complementary stores that reinforce each other and increase the total amount of traffic. In addition, through center development it is easier to provide adequate parking and to create an attractive environment that may contribute a competitive edge over other merchants serving the same market. Consumers benefit from the convenience of stores grouped together, with a consequent reduction in the number of automobile trips they must make, and from the opportunities provided to shop in a pleasant environment that satisfies not only the need to buy goods and services but also the need to socialize and communicate with others.

Beginning with small neighborhood centers consisting of a supermarket, a drug store, and a few service stores, shopping centers have become increasingly elaborate. The regional center concept originated during the early 1950s. Initially, regional centers consisted of 1 or 2 department stores as anchors at each end of a group of from 30 to 50 specialty shops facing each other along an open mall. During the 1960s, the closed mall concept became popular, with 2 or 3 department stores interconnected by an arcade lined with specialty shops and service stores. Ever larger malls have been built, some rising to 3 levels and including up to 5 major department stores. Most recently, multifunctional centers have been proposed. These centers will combine the shopping opportunities provided by large regional centers with other functions, such as offices, hotels, governmental facilities, entertainment, residential apartments, and various institutional and cultural facilities.

As shopping centers evolved, three distinct types emerged: neighborhood, community, and regional. The type of center is determined by its function, its major tenant, and the corresponding market area it serves.

Neighborhood centers are designed to provide the convenience goods a family needs for daily living. The major tenant is usually a supermarket, which requires a minimum of 5,000 people within a six-minute drive to be marginally viable. In most cases a population of 12,000 people without competing centers already in existence is recommended before a supermarket and neighborhood center can be established. Other tenants in a neighborhood center include convenience goods stores, such as drugs, liquors, and sundries, and personal services, such as laundry, dry cleaning, hair styling, and shoe repair.

Community shopping centers are typically built around both a supermarket and a junior department store or large variety store. They provide a greater choice and depth of goods and services than are available at neighborhood centers and require a greater trade area—usually 40,000 or more people within a radius of three to five miles of the center. Because community centers contain features that are found in both smaller neighborhood centers and larger regional centers, they are said to be vulnerable to competition.

Regional centers are the largest type of shopping center. They usually include over 300,000 square feet of gross leasable area and provide a full range of merchandise, including food, apparel, furniture and home furnishings, and a variety of personal services. They are usually designed to serve a trade area of 150,000 or more people and occupy sites averaging 50 acres and up. All regional centers are anchored by one or more full-line department stores. The drawing power of the department store and greater depth and variety of goods and services offered extends the radius of a regional center's trade area to 10 or 15 miles or more, though competition from other regional centers may reduce the effective market area.

Developer Approaches to Community Shopping Needs

New community developers' interest in commercial and retail facilities stems from the important roles they can play in making the community a financial success and a good place to live. As noted by Decision Sciences Corporation (1973, p. 1), shopping facilities may serve four functions in new community development: First, they may provide a critical source of revenue for the developer, either from the sale of commercial sites to shopping center developers or through the leasing of facilities constructed by the developer. Second, shopping facilities generate a secondary source of employment within the community. Third, they make living in the community more convenient, thereby enhancing its attractiveness. Fourth, they add interest to the design of the community and provide a focal point and logical location for many other community facilities and activities.

Shopping Facilities and New Community Design

For the new communities studied, every development plan designated sites for shopping facilities. However, the types of centers to be developed, and their functions, varied from one new community to another.

A number of new communities, including Columbia, Elk Grove Village, Foster City, Laguna Niguel, Sharpstown, and Westlake Village, have developed small neighborhood centers that are usually anchored by a convenience food store. Such centers have been located at the periphery of neighborhoods along major streets, as well as in interior locations adjacent to neighborhood elementary schools and recreational facilities. They were designed to meet families' needs for day-to-day shopping items, and, in the case of Columbia, were viewed as serving an important social function.

For example, the Columbia Work Group recommended that neighborhood convenience stores act as social gathering places and as community service centers. In addition to commercial services, the stores were to act as receiving points for deliveries into the neighborhood, as a communications link out from the neighborhood, and would also perform some managerial and caretaker functions. The Work Group recognized that if these functions were to be performed effectively, the store proprietor had to be more than a businessman. He would also have to function as a neighborhood confidant. He would have to be tolerant of children and adolescents and be able to deal with school personnel; and he would have to be capable of monitoring the overall physical and social performance of the neighborhood center (Slidell 1972, p. 25).

Neighborhood and community shopping centers anchored by major supermarkets were the most frequent types of centers developed in new communities. The size of the centers depended on their intended functions in the community and the population available for their support. In Columbia and Reston, for example, shopping centers (some in enclosed malls) were developed as part of more complex multifunction village centers. In addition to a supermarket, they included a number of commercial services—automobile service stations, banks, drug stores, dry cleaners, restaurants, beauty salons, barber shops, liquor stores, and a variety of specialty stores. Additional functions that were often grouped in village centers included doctors' offices and other professional services, community meeting rooms and the offices of various voluntary social service organizations, religious facilities, post offices, branch library facilities, recreational facilities, and, in Columbia, village association offices. Intermediate and high school sites were also nearby.

In other new communities, less attention was given to grouping shopping and other community services in integrated centers. Instead, these functions tended to be segregated, with neighborhood and community shopping centers limited solely to retail and commercial facilities and services. However, there were some exceptions. Religious facilities shared parking with a neighborhood shopping center (village center) in Valencia. Medical offices and office buildings were grouped with shopping centers in Irvine, Laguna Niguel, Westlake Village, Foster City, Elk Grove Village, and Park Forest. A community center, park, and homes association offices were located adjacent to a convenience center in Westlake Village. Postal facilities were included in shopping centers in Foster City, Sharpstown, and Elk Grove Village.

In every new community except Lake Havasu City, Elk Grove Village, and North Palm Beach, where shopping needs were to be met by neighborhood and community shopping centers and districts, initial master plans reserved sites for town centers designed to provide regional-serving shopping. The most notable of these regional center proposals were developed for Columbia, Irvine, and Valencia.

Downtown Columbia was planned to include a regional mall, office buildings, a hotel-motel complex, restaurants, theaters, and a 40-acre town center park and music pavilion. These facilities were to be located near the center of Columbia adjacent to Lake Kittamaqundi, with a town plaza, outdoor cafes, and boat moorings along the lake shore. The regional shopping center—called the Columbia Mall—was to include between 1.8 million and 2.2 million square feet of retail selling space to be developed in three phases. When completed, the mall development would include five major department stores, one minor department store, and over 300 shops on a 70-acre site.

Plans for Valencia's town center, to occupy a 93-acre site in the heart of the community, were developed in 1963 by the firm of Victor Gruen Associates. At that time Valencia was projected to grow to a city of 250,000 persons. To serve this population, Gruen proposed a multifunctional center developed according to a platform principle. The entire center was to be built on a single base structure. Service, public transportation, and parking were to be provided in underground levels, with various income-producing uses, public uses, and pedestrian plazas and arcades occupying the superstructures that rose overhead. The development program called for 14.15 million square feet of building space allocated to retail facilities and services (2.5 million square feet), offices, apartments, governmental buildings, cultural functions, entertainment functions, hotels, and institutional uses.

The Irvine Company has also proposed the construction of a multifunction regional business and commercial complex to be known as the Irvine Center. Located south of the presently developed sections of the community at the junction of the San Diego and Santa Ana freeways, the Irvine Center will occupy a 470-acre site. The first phase of the project, to be opened in the summer of 1977, will include a regional shopping center with three to four department stores, 100 retail shops, a hotel, and what Irvine planners have called a "City Room." The City Room is a 100,000 square-foot section of the center to be devoted to entertainment, recreation, and cultural functions. It is expected to operate 24 hours a day. Later phases of the Irvine Center will include business and finance centers and residential apartments.

The Irvine Center is the second multifunction regional commercial complex to be developed by The Irvine Company. The city of Irvine is presently served by the Newport Center, located to the west of the community in Newport Beach on a site overlooking the Pacific Ocean. Fashion Island, the first phase of the development, is a regional shopping center with four major department stores linked by a series of open plazas. The second phase includes office buildings, financial institutions, high-rise apartments, medical facilities, and entertainment.

Making It Happen: Successes and Failures

The status of shopping center development in the 13 new communities, as of the spring of 1973, is summarized in table 13-1. It can be readily seen that not all new communities were equally successful in their development. Factors that have worked against the provision of shopping centers have included the economics of their development and external developments, which have diluted the market.

Since the population base in the early stages of new community development is not adequate to support a full range of shopping, developers must choose either inconveniencing the residents until a positive cash flow from residential sales allows them to carry the first centers or constructing the first centers and absorbing the deficits incurred in their operation. Alternatively, developers may sell sites to supermarkets, but foodstore chains have often resisted building facilities until the market was ready.

Because of the importance of establishing the credibility of their new communities, most developers built initial neighborhood shopping centers at the same time as residential construction was undertaken. Typically, rents were greatly reduced for the first several years of the centers' existence, until villages or neighborhoods grew sufficiently for merchants to operate at a profit. Developers also used several other strategies to make their first centers a success. In some cases, such as Laguna Niguel and Valencia, shopping centers were built at the edge of the new community so that they could include the residents of neighborhood subdivisions and communities in their trade areas. In others, such as Columbia, Irvine, Elk Grove Village, and Sharpstown, developers staged the construction of centers, expanding facilities as the population grew and could support a wider variety of stores. In still others, developers exercised less discrimination in tenant selection, accepting anyone who was willing to pioneer in their centers, regardless of whether the merchandise or services offered were what the residents most wanted or needed at the time.

The difficulty in establishing a viable structure of shopping facilities in new communities is illustrated by the following interview with Lee Shur, vice president for marketing of Gulf-Reston, Inc.,

'Before the population was here,' said Shur in a telephone interview with *the Reston Times,* 'we had to take what we could get' (in the way of tenants for commercial space). Now, with more freedom to pick and choose, he says the plaza's landlord, Gulf Reston Inc. is beginning to implement a plan for a balanced and viable situation. 'We're working on tailoring our centers to what the people really want,' he says, 'not just leasing space to who's beating down our doors' (*The Reston Times,* April 10, 1975).

In other cases, however, developers have been more aggressive in assuring that needed shopping facilities were provided. In the case of Lake Havasu

Table 13-1
New Community Shopping Centers

New Community	Number of Centers by Type[a]				Total
	Neighborhood	Community	Regional	Other	
Columbia	0	3	1	3	7
Reston	0	2	0	0	2
Irvine	2	0	0	1	3
Valencia	1	0	0	0	1
Park Forest	1	1	1	3	6
Westlake Village	1	1	0	1	3
Elk Grove Village	2	2	0	1	5
Foster City	1	1	0	1	3
Laguna Niguel	2	0	0	1	3
Lake Havasu City	2	0	0	1	3
Sharpstown	2	1	1	10	14
Forest Park	1	0	0	0	1
North Palm Beach	0	4	0	0	4

[a]The following criteria were used to define types of centers: neighborhood, 10-19 stores and services; community, 20-49 stores and services; regional, 50 or more stores and services, including one or more department stores; other, less than 10 stores, including convenience centers and specialty centers.

City, the developer went to small towns in California and Arizona to see what types of commercial facilities were available at various stages of development and compared these with the establishments that had opened in the community. When a deficiency was noted, the developer tried to recruit a merchant who would supply the service. If this failed, the developer built the facility, including Lake Havasu City's first shopping center, theater, and bowling alley, and sold them at cost to entrepreneurs willing to assume their operation.

Developers' problems in providing shopping centers were matched by those of their first tenants. While chain stores have often been able to weather the slow sales experienced during the early years of a new community shopping center's existence, smaller merchants may have a harder time. Reported difficulties at Columbia's convenience stores and the Columbia Mall illustrate this situation.

Originally, Columbia's planners expected that each neighborhood in the community would be served by a small "Mom and Pop" store, whose proprietor would serve both commercial and social functions. However, when the first neighborhood was built, it became obvious that a very small store run by an individual was not financially feasible to operate. Therefore, the Mom and Pop concept was dropped in favor of operation by the WaWa chain of convenience stores.

The WaWa's, however, were financial failures because neighborhood density was not adequate for their support and few people walked to the centers for day-to-day items. Once residents got in their cars, it was just as convenient to travel to the village center supermarkets, which were open until midnight. To solve this problem, the WaWa's were allowed to sell specialty foods, but this attracted traffic from outside of the neighborhood and violated the principle of limiting traffic on neighborhood streets designed solely for residential use. By 1973, only one WaWa was operating in Columbia, along with two "7-11" convenience stores (all of which were reported to be losing money), and their provision in later neighborhoods was being reevaluated. Needless to say, the social function of the neighborhood store was dropped when chainstore operation of the convenience centers was adopted.

An April 1, 1974 article in the trade journal *Clothes* highlighted some of the difficulties experienced by merchants in large regional shopping centers developed during the early phases of new community development. Opening in August 1971 with two department stores and 102 specialty shops, many merchants in the Columbia Mall reportedly had a number of problems. According to *Clothes,* "In addition, a nothing-before noon, Saturday-and-sale survival syndrome prevails; the pervasive mood is gloom and doom; and most store managers seem to be biding their time, awaiting the transfers that they are hoping for" (p. 33).

The reasons for the slow sales experienced by some of the mall's tenants were reported to stem from the lack of an adequate population (81,000 versus a recommended 150,000) in its primary trading area; the tendency of about a quarter of Columbia's residents (see table 13-2) to go elsewhere to shop; and the division of its anchor department stores' primary markets between the Baltimore and Washington metropolitan areas, which hurt store recognition and increased advertising costs. Another problem, which may also be endemic to new towns that do not provide much low-cost housing, was the lack of availability of sales help in Columbia. Since a full-time saleswoman could not afford to live in Columbia on her salary alone, mall merchants were said to rely on part-time help from housewives and students and, as a result, experienced very high turnover rates.

In concluding, *Clothes* warned its readers to be wary of locating in a new community shopping center, as follows:

The lesson to be learned from Columbia is to leave the solution of the world's social, philosophical and political problems to St. Augustine. The developer is only a businessman. Retailers who allow themselves to be swept into a fantasy world will find themselves on the primrose path to penury. Those who allow themselves to be befuddled by grandiose visions of a grand tomorrow will only end up waiting for Godot (p. 37).

It should be noted, however, that the merchants' problems may not have been shared by the developer. According to the general manager of the Howard Research and Development Corporation, the Columbia Mall was an economic success and expansion plans were well underway.

Unless regional centers are opened at an early stage, the potential for full implementation of a new community's town center may be sharply circumscribed by events beyond the developer's control. In addition to Columbia, regional centers were operating in Park Forest and Sharpstown. Park Forest's Plaza Shopping Center was begun early in the development process and initially provided 300,000 square feet of retail space. However, this proved inadequate and by the early 1960s the plaza was dying. It was revived when the developer gave Sears, Roebuck & Company land that had been reserved for high-rise apartments and subsequently expanded the center to 800,000 square feet, which enabled it to compete successfully with other large shopping centers in the region. Ground was broken for the Sharpstown Center in January 1960, six years after the first residents moved to the community. Occupying a 77-acre site, the Sharpstown Center includes over one million square feet of air conditioned shopping space, two major department stores, and a civic auditorium. In 1973, a $9 million project was initiated to double-deck and renovate the center.

The success of Columbia, Park Forest, and Sharpstown in building and operating regional centers contrasts sharply with some notable failures. For example, a regional shopping center proposed for Forest Park had to be dropped when the 912,000-square-foot Tri-County Shopping Center opened in neighboring Springdale. Westlake Village began development of its town center with the opening of Westlake Plaza—a community-level shopping center that was to be adjacent to a regional center with three department stores. Although one department store took an option on the site (reportedly at a reduced price), it decided to locate the proposed store in Warner Ranch (another new community) and the option lapsed. As a result, the Janss Corporation was able to foreclose further development of Westlake Village's regional center by developing a large shopping center (designed to include six department stores) several miles to the north in Thousand Oaks.

In Foster City, the 135-acre town-center site remained vacant nine years after initial residential settlement of the community. In this case, Foster City's planners were overly optimistic in assuming that a new regional center could compete with the established 1.1 million-square-foot Hillsdale Shopping Center, located just three miles to the west in San Mateo. Similarly, although Reston residents had to travel some nine miles to the nearest regional shopping center, which included three department stores and well over 100 specialty shops, Tysons Corner Center effectively limited the potential for region-serving commercial development in Reston.

Additionally, Reston's inability to use fully the Dulles Airport access road restricted the capacity of the town-center site to serve some 75,000 residents living outside the community, as specified in Reston's master plan.

Valencia's proposed town center still remains viable, although as of 1973 the slow development of the community had not allowed Gruen's innovative plan to be implemented. One problem with the Valencia megastructure proposal, however, should be noted. It is most efficient to build the entire base of the structure at one time. But, if the developer waits until the market is available to support such an immense undertaking, substantial inroads to the center's trade area may occur through the development of competing regional centers outside of Valencia.

Finally, The Irvine Company was able to postpone construction of a regional center in the city of Irvine until ten years after initial residential settlement. The proposed Irvine Center remained financially viable because The Irvine Company controlled an extremely large amount of land, so that consumers in the northern sections of Irvine had to travel some distance to the nearest competing center. Nevertheless, a more central location for the proposed Irvine Center was ruled out by development of the South Coast Plaza regional shopping center north of Irvine in Costa Mesa, and The Irvine Company's own Newport Center development to the west.

Shopping Facilities in New and Conventional Communities

In order to determine whether new community development had led to the provision of more adequate shopping facilities than characterize conventional suburban communities, the availability and accessibility of shopping facilities in these two settings were compared, along with consumers' shopping behavior.

Availability of Shopping Facilities

The number of shopping centers located in the new communities and conventional communities and the number of individual shopping and service establishments were strongly correlated with the size and affluence of a community's trade area. Communities located in the more established surroundings, which were closer to metropolitan central business areas and which had both larger populations and higher median family incomes, tended to have the most shopping centers and a larger number of commercial establishments. On the other hand, because of the dependence of commercial centers and establishments on the market area, it is understandable why the majority of new communities did not have a greater number of shopping centers or establishments than the conventional communities. See figure 13-1.

Accessibility of Shopping Facilities

By contrast, the greater attention to land use planning that characterizes new community development has led to better accessibility of centers to the consumers they serve. Both new and conventional community residents tended to live within accepted travel distances of the nearest neighborhood and community shopping center and of the nearest regional center, but in both cases the new community residents tended to live much closer to the nearest center. For example, the median road distance to the nearest neighborhood or community shopping center was 4,900 feet for new community residents versus 7,200 feet for conventional community residents. Respondents living in 9 of the 13 new communities were closer to such a center than respondents living in their paired conventional communities. See figure 13-2. Median road distance to the nearest regional shopping center was 26,800 feet versus 30,500 feet, respectively, with respondents in 7 new communities tending to live closer to a regional center than respondents who lived in the paired conventional communities.

The greater accessibility of shopping facilities serving new community residents was reflected in respondents' travel behavior. That is, new community respondents traveled about 20 percent less distance (median distances of 20,300 feet versus 27,200 feet) to the shopping centers or malls they used most frequently. Since the shopping centers used by a majority of the respondents were regional malls, median distances to the centers used and to the nearest regional center were similar.

New community residents with a regional center located within their community or a short distance from it, such as the respondents who lived in Columbia, Park Forest, Foster City, Sharpstown, and Forest Park, tended to make the shortest trips to shopping centers. In contrast, respondents living in Valencia and Laguna Niguel were distant from the nearest regional center and tended to travel over 15 miles to the shopping centers they used most often.

Comparison of figures 13-2B and 13-2C reveals three anomalies: First, rather than shopping at the nearest regional shopping center, which was located in Thousand Oaks, Westlake Village respondents tended to journey to the much larger Topanga Plaza in the San Fernando Valley. Second, since a regional shopping center was not located in Lake Havasu City or Kingman, respondents tended to use smaller centers and shopping districts located within their own communities, rather than traveling to the nearest

308

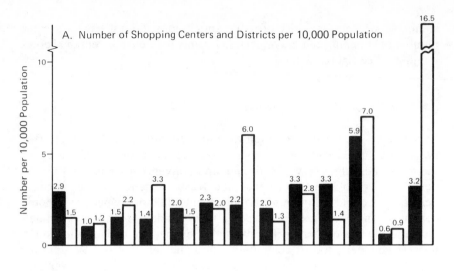

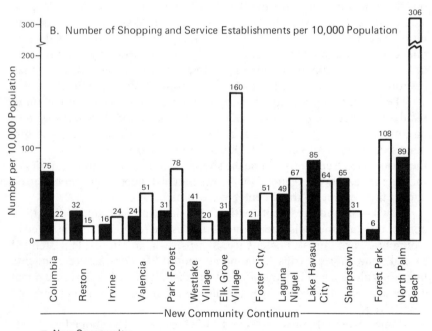

Figure 13-1. Availability of Shopping Facilities in New and Conventional Communities

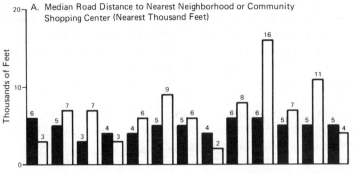

A. Median Road Distance to Nearest Neighborhood or Community Shopping Center (Nearest Thousand Feet)

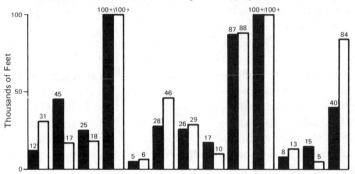

B. Median Road Distance to Nearest Regional Shopping Center (Nearest Thousand Feet)

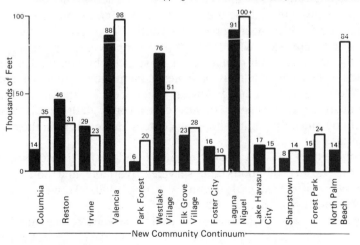

C. Median Road Distance to Shopping Center Used Most Often (Nearest Thousand Feet)

New Community Continuum

■ New Community
□ Conventional Community

Figure 13-2. Accessibility of Shopping Facilities

regional shopping facilities, which were located in Las Vegas. Third, close to half of the North Palm Beach residents opted to do most of their shopping at the center located within their own community, rather than travel to Palm Beach Mall regional shopping center located eight miles to the south in West Palm Beach.

Shopping Centers Used Most Frequently. Major shopping centers used by new community respondents and the three reasons mentioned most often for the choice of a center are summarized in table 13-2. In a majority of the new communities, respondents chose to shop at very large regional centers (for 8 of the 13 new communities, the shopping center used most often contained one million or more square feet of retail selling space) and generally cited the same reasons for their choice.

For 10 of the 19 shopping centers listed, the largest proportion of respondents mentioned the convenience of the center's location as one of the 3 most important reasons for shopping there. In 9 cases, the variety of goods was mentioned most frequently, while the attractiveness of a center's stores, as a second reason, was mentioned 8 times. Other factors that sometimes attract people to a shopping center, including parking, hours open, prices, cleanliness, availability of places to sit and rest, and opportunities to meet friends, were mentioned less frequently as reasons for shopping at particular centers.

As shopping centers and malls have blossomed across the nation, they have increasingly replaced the urban street corner and suburban drive-in restaurant as a favorite meeting place for youth. Young adults in the 14 to 20 age bracket were asked where they went to shop. Not surprisingly, they went to the same regional centers used most often by adults. The only exceptions were young adults living in new communities, such as Laguna Niguel, Westlake Village, and Valencia, which were located many miles from the nearest regional center. In these cases, young adults tended to use neighborhood and community shopping centers located right in their own communities.

Two of the three reasons most often cited by adults for their choice of a center—the variety of goods and services available and convenient location—were also frequently given by young adults. However, while adults often mentioned the attractiveness of stores, this characteristic of shopping centers was not important to youth. Instead, young adults frequently mentioned that shopping centers were good places to meet or shop with their friends.

Among individual new communities, the social function of regional centers was most noticeable for the Columbia Mall, where meeting with friends was mentioned most frequently by young adults as an important reason for going to the mall. The shopping center as a place to meet with friends ranked in second place among young adults who most often shopped at the Plaza in Park Forest, Woodfield Mall in Schaumburg, University Park Shopping Center in Irvine, the Plaza in Westlake Village, Old Orchard Shopping Center in Valencia, and at the Hillsdale Shopping Center in San Mateo. Thus, for residents in a number of new communities, malls and shopping centers served a social function, augmenting teen centers and other activity places availblable to suburban youth.

Mode of Travel to Shopping. Although about half of the young adults walked to shopping centers located within their communities, adults seldom walked to engage in shopping of any kind. Among all of the new community respondents only 6 percent usually walked to a convenience store; 3 percent reported walking to a supermarket; and 2 percent often walked to a shopping center. Walking was even less prevalent among conventional community respondents, where only 4 percent walked to a convenience store and less than 1 percent walked to either the supermarket or shopping center they used most often.

Where shopping facilities were designed in conjunction with surrounding residential areas, the proportion of respondents who walked to a center showed a dramatic increase. For example, 17 percent of the respondents who reported shopping at the Safeway supermarket at Lake Anne Village Center in Reston said they typically walked to the store. This center is surrounded by high-density townhouses and a high-rise apartment building. Other stores that attracted a higher than average proportion of walkers included the Pantry Pride supermarket in North Palm Beach (12 percent), the Food Giant at the Sharpstown Center (12 percent), and the Bazaar supermarket in Westlake Village (16 percent). In contrast, less than 5 percent of the respondents reported walking to any of the supermarkets in Columbia, which were located in multifunction village centers about a mile away from the average Columbia resident.

Shopping Within the Community

"Shop at Home" has been a popular slogan with chambers of commerce and local merchants associations across the country. While the merchants obviously have their own self-interest at heart, the ability of a community to retain shoppers is an indication of the extent to which community shopping facilities meet residents' needs. Additionally, in those states with local sales taxes or that rebate a portion of local sales tax receipts to local governments, "shopping at home" can provide an important source of revenue.

Figure 13-3 compares the proportion of new community and con-

Table 13-2
Shopping Centers Used Most Often by New Community Residents

| New Community | Shopping Center | | Percent of Respondents | Most Frequent Reasons Given for Choice of Center | | |
	Name	Sq. Ft. in Buildings		First	Second	Third
Columbia	Columbia Mall	630,000	76	Location	Attractiveness	Variety
Reston	Tysons Corner	1,500,000	82	Location	Variety	Attractiveness
Irvine	South Coast Plaza	1,200,000	58	Variety	Location	Attractiveness
	Fashion Island	1,000,000	37	Variety	Attractiveness	Location
Valencia	Northridge Fashion Center	1,500,000	45	Variety	Attractiveness	Hours open
	Old Orchard	87,300	28	Location	Parking	Variety/hours open (tied)
Park Forest	Park Forest Plaza	900,000	93	Location	Variety	Parking
Westlake Village	Topanga Plaza	954,100	37	Variety	Attractiveness	Location
	Conejo Village Mall	450,000	21	Variety	Location	Hours open/attractiveness (tied)

City	Mall	Size		Reason 1	Reason 2	Reason 3
Elk Grove Village	Woodfield Mall	1,700,000	67	Location/Variety (tied)	Attractiveness	Hours open
Foster City	Grove	106,000	23	Location	Hours open	Variety
Laguna Niguel	Hillsdale	1,100,000	63	Location	Variety	Hours open
	Fashion Island	1,000,000	39	Variety	Attractiveness	Location
	South Coast Plaza	1,200,000	37	Variety	Attractiveness	Location
Lake Havasu City	Crystal Plaza	NR	39	Parking	Variety	Friendly service
Sharpstown	Sharpstown Center	1,000,000	89	Location	Variety	Parking
Forest Park	Tri-County	912,000	91	Location	Variety	Attractiveness
North Palm Beach	Twin City Mall	350,000	47	Location	Variety/parking (tied)	Hours open
	Palm Beach Mall	1,000,000	45	Variety	Attractiveness	Parking

NR = Not reported.

314

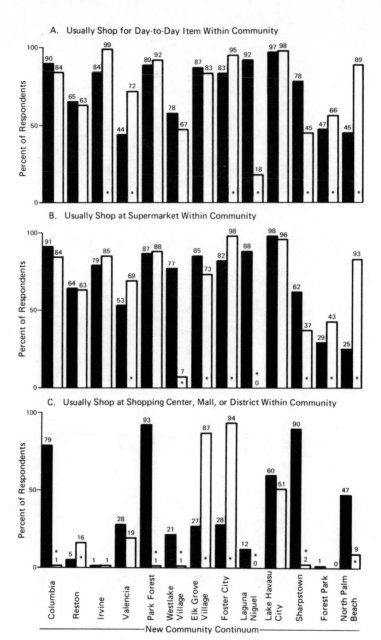

Figure 13-3. Shopping Within Community

ventional community respondents who reported that they usually shopped for day-to-day items at a supermarket, and at a shopping center or mall located within their own community. As a rule, residents in both settings were much more likely to shop for day-to-day items and at supermarkets within their own communities than they were to use community shopping centers (other than for day-to-day and food items).

New communities in which 75 percent or more of the respondents shopped within the community for both day-to-day items and at supermarkets included Columbia, Irvine, Park Forest, Westlake Village, Elk Grove Village, Foster City, Laguna Niguel, and Lake Havasu City. New communities that had a lower proportion of respondents who usually shopped within the community had few supermarkets—Forest Park, North Palm Beach, and Valencia had but one supermarket each—or had a number of competing markets in close proximity to the community (Reston and Sharpstown).

The only new communities where a majority of the respondents usually shopped at a shopping center in the community—Columbia, Park Forest, and Sharpstown—each had a regional shopping center, or, as with Lake Havasu City, were isolated from competing centers. This was also true of the conventional communities. Both Schaumburg, paired with Elk Grove Village, and West San Mateo, paired with Foster City, had large regional centers, while the community paired with Lake Havasu City, Kingman, was similarly isolated.

Although relatively few new communities had regional centers that induced residents to shop within the community, the new community respondents were more likely than those living in the conventional communities to use a shopping center located within their own community. Six new communities retained a significantly higher proportion of the respondents at community shopping centers than their paired conventional communities. In contrast, only three conventional communities—those paired with Reston, Elk Grove Village, and Foster City—could make the same claim.

Residents' Overall Evaluations of Community Shopping Facilities

Residents' evaluations of the quality of community shopping facilities offer another perspective on their adequacy. Forty-one percent of the new community respondents thought that shopping facilities were better than those in the communities from which they had moved. Thirty-one percent of the respondents rated shopping facilities as about the same as those of their previous communities, while 28 percent said they were not as good. A somewhat lower proportion of respondents who were living in the conventional communities (36 percent) reported that the move to their communities resulted in better shopping facilities than those where they had previously lived. Thirty-two percent said facilities were about the same, and the same proportion reported that shopping was not as good as in their former communities.

A slight, but statistically significant, difference in ratings of the absolute quality of shopping facilities was also apparent. In this case, 67 percent of the new community respondents said shopping facilities available to people living in their communities were excellent or good. Sixty-two percent of the respondents rated facilities that highly in the conventional communities.

Community location and population characteristics and characteristics of community shopping facilities were compared to residents' evaluations. The strongest associations were those related to the accessibility of regional shopping centers. New and conventional community residents gave higher ratings to shopping facilities in their communities when they lived closer to the nearest regional center, closer to the center they used most often (which was usually a regional center), and when regional centers were located within their communities. Residents' evaluations of the shopping center they most often used—whether they liked or disliked shopping there—were also related to overall evaluations of community shopping facilities, but the association was not as strong as that with the accessibility of centers.

A second set of strong associations was found between evaluations of shopping facilities and characteristics of communities that were indicative of the presence of a major market for shopping facilities. Residents were more likely to say that facilities were better than their previous communities and to rate facilities as excellent or good if their community was located closer to the metropolitan central business district and if the area surrounding the community was more fully developed. Also, shopping was rated more highly in communities with larger populations and, to some extent, in older communities. There was also a positive, but weaker, association between the median income of residents and their evaluations of shopping facilities.

The availability and accessibility of neighborhood and community shopping centers and of supermarkets was strongly associated with evaluations of shopping facilities, but had less influence on ratings than access to regional centers. Among these variables, the best predictors of shopping facility ratings were the distance traveled to the supermarket respondents used most often, the relative accessibility of the nearest supermarket, and the number of supermarkets available in the community. In addition to accessibility, residents who said they liked shopping at the supermarket used most often were more likely to rate community shopping facilities highly. The number and accessibility of neighborhood and community shopping facilities in a community had somewhat less effect on ratings than supermarket accessibility and evaluations.

Indexes were computed of the access characteristics of shopping centers (pedestrian-vehicular separation, traffic control, and landscaped entrances), parking facilities (marked spaces, location markers, bicycle racks, and landscaping of parking areas) and building exteriors and grounds (covered loading areas, benches, landscaping, fountains or sculptures, and child-play facilities). However, none of these indexes was associated with residents' ratings of the quality of the shopping facilities in their communities.

In addition, there was no association between a community's rank on the new community continuum and shopping ratings. This was to be expected, given the strong associations between ratings and the accessibility of region-serving shopping centers whose availability was, in turn, highly dependent on the characteristics of the market and the number of competing centers in the surrounding region.

The preceding discussion provides a basis for interpreting residents' evaluations of shopping facilities in particular new communities and conventional communities. As shown in figure 13-4, in comparison with shopping facilities in their previous communities, respondents in only three new communities—Columbia, Park Forest, and Sharpstown—were significantly more likely than respondents in their paired conventional communities to feel that facilities were better in their present community. These were the only three whose developers had constructed regional shopping centers within their communities.

Shopping facilities in six new communities—Columbia, Park Forest, Elk Grove Village, Sharpstown, Forest Park, and North Palm Beach—were rated as excellent or good by 75 percent or more of the respondents. As noted above, three of these communities contained regional shopping centers. However, the high ratings given to Forest Park, Elk Grove Village, and North Palm Beach show that regional centers do not have to be located within a new community for shopping facilities to be rated very highly, if they are located nearby or if there is a wide choice of establishments within the community. The median road distance Forest Park respondents traveled to the attractive Tri-County Shopping Center in neighboring Springdale was less than three miles. Elk Grove Village residents had to travel only about five miles to the Woodfield Mall, which is reported to be the largest regional center in the United States. Although North Palm Beach residents did not live in as close proximity to a regional center, their community had the largest number of shopping and service establishments per capita among the study new communities (see figure 13-1).

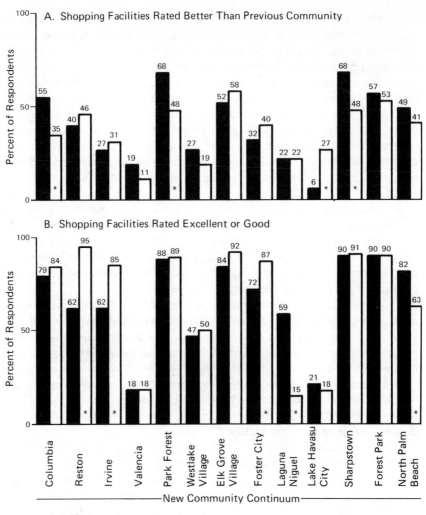

Figure 13-4. Residents' Evaluations of Shopping Facilities

The Need for Public Involvement

Although shopping facilities have generally been the responsibility of the private sector, the preceding discussion clearly shows that new communities cannot consistently provide better shopping opportunities than conventional suburban developments or even meet their own design objectives for viable town centers unless steps are taken to overcome two major problems: The first is the natural conflict between the new community goal of preservicing shopping facilities and the need for an adequate population base to generate customers and revenues to pay for the operation of shopping centers and to keep center merchants in business. The second is the difficulty in assuring that town center development remains viable until the population base in the new community and the surrounding region is large enough to justify the construction and operation of a regional shopping center. The development of regional centers is important to the financial viability of new community projects, since they enhance the value and development potential of surrounding property, and, as shown above, to new community residents' satisfaction with community shopping facilities.

Both of these problems may be ameliorated through greater public involvement in shopping center development. Previous research has established that residents favor the location of public facilities, such as post offices, municipal offices, and community social service agencies, in shopping centers (see "How Shopping Malls Are Changing Life in the U.S.," 1973). Multifunctional centers have been successful in Columbia and have been proposed in other new communities. As noted in the preceding chapter, commercial space might even be used for temporary schools. This would allow the development of such space prior to the time when its commercial use would be financially viable and when permanent educational facilities would be constructed. By serving both private-sector and public-sector functions, such centers provide a basis for public participation in their financing and development.

This would reduce developers' front-end costs and, through public participation in the operation of centers, the drain on cash flow involved in operating shopping centers when revenues from commercial tenants are still too low to cover operating costs and debt-service payments. The cash that is freed through public participation in financing shopping center development might be used to offset merchants' rents during the first years of a center's operation when the market is still thin.

To maintain the viability of new community town centers and protect them from competing regional shopping center development, it could be advantageous for the states or regional councils of government to regulate the location and timing of major shopping center development through a permit system. If such agencies wished to promote new community development, first priority could be given to regional center development in new communities that met other criteria related to accessibility, site conditions, and environmental impact. For example, after the requisite population to support a regional shopping center had been achieved, new community developers could be given one year in which to develop an acceptable regional center proposal. If they failed to do so, then sites located in other settings would be considered for such a center. This would increase the certainty of land value appreciation, which plays a key role in determining the financial feasibility of new community projects; it would correspondingly lessen the tremendous financial risk involved in new community development; and it would stimulate the design and provision of multifunctional centers, carefully integrated with overall needs of the regional community.

In sum, although new communities have not consistently provided superior shopping opportunities for their residents, new community development can make this possible if the public sector takes a more active part in the development process.

14 Transportation and Travel

One of the most pervasive criticisms of less planned suburban development since World War II has been that it fosters major inefficiencies in travel. Frequently used community facilities are often inconvenient to residents and to each other, and suburban residents living toward the urban fringe face longer automobile commutation trips over congested roads, usually without public transportation alternatives. The appeal of a balanced new community lies, in part, in its approach to these problems of metropolitan travel.

The Goal of Easy Access and Movement

A central premise of new community development has been that through comprehensive planning better relationships can be attained among many of the key variables that influence travel behavior. These variables include the convenience of facilities and services, the availability of alternative modes of transportation, the amount and location of employment opportunities and the match between employment wage profiles and community housing prices.

Conveniently located facilities have been expected to have three effects: First, having a facility of a given type nearby is expected to be associated with higher rates of use of the facility and, presumably, greater enjoyment of the activity involved. Second, the availability of facilities and services that are sufficient to meet most of the necessary and the discretionary activity needs of residents is expected to increase marketing appeal and subsequent reports of residents' satisfaction with the community as a whole. Finally, conveniently located facilities are expected to lead to reduced use of the automobile. In the context of past and possible future fuel shortages, the possibility that residence in new communities might be associated with less fuel consumption becomes an issue of considerable interest.

Another means of reducing automobile travel is to provide alternative modes of travel within the community. Rapid, convenient, and inexpensive mass transit linking homes with activity centers and employment areas may make the whole community readily available to all residents, particularly youth and elderly persons who may not have access to automobiles. Other benefits that have been attributed to mass transit include an enhanced sense of community and greater communications among residents. In addition to community transit, provision of walking paths and bicycle trails offers other alternative modes of travel that may divert residents from their cars and, in turn, result in fuel and energy savings.

Since previous research has established that the journey to work can account for up to one third of all vehicle trips (see Svercl and Asin 1973, p. 78), the availability of employment opportunities in the community may do much to reduce commutation and aggregate automobile mileage. Of course, merely providing jobs is not enough. Housing prices must be within the means of those employed in the community, so that employees have the opportunity, at least, of living and working in the same place.

This chapter looks first at the extent to which new communities and conventional communities have achieved the preconditions of easy access and movement by examining the accessibility characteristics of selected facilities, availability of alternative transportation modes, and the amount of employment and match between employee wage and housing price profiles. Next, residents' travel behavior is considered in terms of the journey to work, use of mass transit, walking, and automobile ownership and mileage. Finally, residents' subjective perceptions of the ease of getting around their communities and satisfaction with community expenditures for public transportation are examined.

Accessibility of Facilities and Services

In each of the preceding chapters on community facilities and services it was noted that improved accessibility was one of the major beneficial outcomes of new community development. These data are summarized in table 14-1. The median distance to the nearest facility was less for residents in the 13 new communities for 13 of the 15 facilities considered. These included each of the 5 recreational facilities examined, 2 of 3 types of schools, as well as 3 of the 4 types of shopping facilities, and all 3 of the health-oriented facilities. Conventional community residents tended to live closer to a high school and, by a margin of a little over 100 yards, to a convenience store.

Of course, the provision of readily accessible facilities will have little influence on travel if residents do not use them. Therefore, in addition to the measurements of the nearest facilities, map-based road-distance calculations were also made to facilities named by respondents as those they had most often used. As shown in table 14-1, in most cases new community residents were able to make use of a closer facility than were conventional community residents. The exceptions were the high school (new commu-

Table 14-1
Accessibility of Facilities and Services

Facility	Median Road Distance (Ft.)			
	Nearest Facility		Facility Used	
	New Communities	Conventional Communities	New Communities	Conventional Communities
Recreation				
Playground for children under 12	2,100	2,700	2,000	2,100
Swimming facility	3,900	5,000	4,600	6,200
Tennis court	4,600	4,900	7,300	7,600
Bicycling-walking path	4,800	7,900	<50	<50
Golf course	10,500	11,900	20,300	31,700
Health Care				
General practitioner/internist	6,800	8,800	28,400[a]	38,000[a]
Hospital	14,800	22,200	[b]	[b]
Public health clinic/facility	37,000	47,600	[b]	[b]
Education				
Elementary school	3,600	5,200	3,400	6,400
Intermediate school	8,200	9,100	7,600	10,500
High school	12,600	9,300	15,000	8,200
Shopping				
Convenience store	4,400	4,000	4,300	4,600
Supermarket	4,700	5,600	7,200	11,200
Neighborhood/community shopping center	4,900	7,200	{ 20,300	27,200 }
Regional shopping center	26,800	30,500		

[a]Aerial distance from respondents' communities to communities in which doctor/clinic was located.
[b]Because of the relatively low frequency of hospitalization and use of public health clinics, data on facilities used and their distances from respondents' homes were not determined.

nity students went almost twice the distance traveled by conventional community students) and hiking and walking. In the latter case, the majority of respondents in each setting reported—quite logically—that walking as a recreational activity usually originated at their homes, hence the uniformly low median distances (less than 50 feet) for that activity.

In most cases the median distance to the facility used approximated that of the nearest facility. For two facilities, however, tennis courts and supermarkets, the median distance to the facility used most often was about 50 percent farther than the nearest. In the case of golf, the median was close to twice that of the nearest golf course, and the median distance to the doctor or clinic used was over four times the median distance to the most convenient general practitioner or internist. For these four activities, therefore, and particularly golfing and visiting a doctor, it is apparent that road distance alone had a limited impact on the decisions of many residents in selecting destinations and facilities.

Transportation Modes

New community development has taken advantage of existing transportation facilities, particularly limited access highways, and, by clustering housing units and aggregating facilities in logical centers, has created the potential for effective community transit systems. On the other hand, with the exception of the Howard Research and Development Corporation (Columbia), few developers have become involved in the development or operation of transit services. For example, Raymond L. Watson, president of The Irvine Company, might have been representing the views of a number of private developers when he responded to a question concerning the company's role in providing rapid transit services,

That is a public sector issue, regionally and locally. It is already being responded to in part by the Orange County Transit District. They are off to a good start. It is also a prime responsibility of the city in their master planning. As a company, we pledge to work with the public agencies to accommodate their planning. But it is clearly their initiative, not ours. We don't have the access to federal funds that they do. What the company can do—the limits of our responsibility—is to make sure there is a place in our land use plans for transportation alternatives. By the way we arrange land uses, we can accommodate transportation systems (1973).

The availability of transportation alternatives in new and conventional communities is summarized in figure 14-1. Of the 6 facilities and services inventoried (freeway interchanges, taxis, community bus service, intercity bus service, commuter bus service, and commuter railway), no more than 4 were present in any of the new communities during the spring of 1973. Nevertheless, 7 of the 13 new communities had more transportation facilities and services than their paired conventional communities. There were 3 cases in which a new community and its paired conventional community were tied, and in 3 cases the conventional community had more facilities and services.

The Key Role of Highway Access

The development of a number of new communities became financially feasible undertakings when the extension of limited access highways and

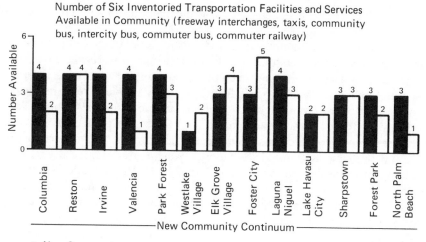

Figure 14-1. Transportation Facilities and Services

freeways made the development site accesssible to large metropolitan populations. In chapter 4 it was noted that Frank Sharp donated land to the Texas Highway Department in order to insure passage of Houston's Southwest Freeway (U.S. 59) through his property. The presence of U.S. 99 and its upgrading to freeway status (Golden State Freeway—I-5) in 1963 was one of the major stimuli for the development of Valencia.

Irvine is served by no less than five existing and proposed freeways. Originally, the Irvine Ranch was traversed by one of California's major north-south highways (U.S. 101). It was converted to a full freeway in 1958 and is now part of Interstate Route 5. Three other major freeway routes were included for future construction in the 1959 California Freeway and Expressway System—the San Diego Freeway (I-405); Newport Freeway (California Route 55); and Corona Del Mar Freeway (California Route 73). Since then, the Laguna Freeway (California Route 133) has also been planned across Irvine land. The increase in accessibility brought about through major road construction projects made development of the Irvine properties inevitable.

Other new communities served by major limited access highways include: Columbia (Columbia Pike—U.S. 29); Westlake Village (Ventura Freeway—U.S. 101); Foster City (Bayshore Freeway—U.S. 101 and J. Arthur Younger Freeway—California Route 92); and Forest Park (Circle Freeway—I-275). Although it is not traversed by a freeway, Elk Grove Village lies in close proximity to the Northwest Tollway, which connects to the John Fitzgerald Kennedy Expressway to the Loop in Chicago, and

North Palm Beach is bisected by U.S. 1, the major north-south route along the east coast of Florida.

The only new community that was a major loser in the fight to secure freeway access was Reston. When the first homes were placed on the market in 1964, the major approach to the community was over a six-and-one-half mile stretch of Virginia Route 7, a hilly two-lane rural highway. Although Route 7 was upgraded to four lanes between 1967 and 1969, repeated efforts by the developer to gain access to the Dulles Airport Access Freeway, which bisected Reston and linked the airport to the Capital Beltway (I-395) and the George Washington Memorial Parkway leading into Washington, met with failure. The Federal Aviation Administration agreed to allow construction of an interchange that would give Reston residents access to the outbound lanes to the airport, but not access to the inbound lanes, which would have greatly reduced travel times to Washington and the inner suburbs on the Virginia side of the Potomac River.

Community Transit

Columbia was the only new community that consciously included a community transit system in its initial planning. A transit right-of-way was integrated into the land use plan in order to link the downtown area to each of the proposed seven villages, some of the neighborhood centers, and almost all of the commercial and employment areas of the community.

As originally conceived, small buses were to run with five- to ten-minute headways along the separate roadways, which were to be within a three-minute walk of 40 percent of the population. However, this concept proved to be impractical. In 1968, the Columbia Park and Recreation Association secured financial assistance from the Urban Mass Transit Administration and commissioned the Bendix Corporation to investigate the feasibility of a new-concept transit system for Columbia and to assist with an interim transit demonstration program.

The first phase report of the transit study concluded that implementation of Columbia's land use plan would generate enough demand to sustain systems operating with automated vehicles on exclusive rights-of-way through Columbia or manually driven buses operating on roadways. The automated system would offer the best service—17 miles of track with 46 off-line stations—but also would entail the greatest investment risk with a capital cost of $34.5 million in 1970 dollars. Also, a grant of 53 to 69 percent of the capital and land costs would be required to cover those costs that could not be financed from revenues (Columbia Park and Recreation Association 1970).

The interim transit demonstration program in Columbia, named Co-lumBUS, began with two fixed schedule buses providing service to developed neighborhoods. Initially, the buses operated 17 hours per day at 30-minute intervals, but this was cut back to 13 hours per day every 60 minutes and then to 11 hours per day. During the first two years of ColumBUS's operation, when the population of Columbia rose from 1,000 to 9,000 people, ridership never exceeded 100 passengers a day and the transit system was becoming an embarrassment to the developer. According to one report,

Lack of operational control, poor schedule adherence, a low level of promotion, plus relatively few major destinations, added to the transit system's problems. Virtually every resident of Columbia had experienced or heard a "horror story" concerning Columbia transit (Bartolo and Navin 1971).

Although the Columbia transit system was termed a token solution to community transit needs by another major developer (Watson 1973b), ridership grew as Columbia expanded. In August 1972, some 9,000 passengers were carried on the system, and when the Columbia Association inaugurated its "Package Plan," which allowed use of all the association's services for a fixed annual fee, ridership grew even more, climbing to 19,326 passengers in August of the following year.

Nevertheless, the ColumBUS experience indicated the need for a transit system in Columbia that could compete more effectively with the automobile. This led to the inauguration on January 14, 1971 of a demand-activated transportation system known as Call-a-Ride. With this system a person desiring transportation called a central dispatcher who arranged a pick-up time and routed a vehicle to the person's home. Columbia's Call-a-Ride operation was the country's first purely demand-activated transit system that was able to accommodate persons from dispersed locations and deliver them to dispersed destinations. It was an overnight success, averaging between 250 and 300 passengers a day after its first month in operation (versus some 50 passengers a day carried by ColumBUS at that time).

One other Columbia mass transit experiment, however, ended in failure. This system, called "Easy Rider," was a neighborhood express bus service designed to pick up passengers during morning and evening rush hours and deliver them to their places of employment. In spite of a large promotional campaign, ridership never surpassed 35 passengers a day and the Easy Rider service was terminated after a 7-month trial.

The availability of community and intercity transit services in other new communities is summarized in table 14-2. Eight of the 13 new communities and 5 of the 13 paired conventional communities had some form of community transit service available. Intercity service was available to 9 new and 6

Table 14-2
Bus Service

| New Community | Type of Service | | Percent of Respondents Who Reported a Bus Stop Within a Ten-minute Walk of Home |
	Community	Intercity	
New communities	8/13	9/13	43
Conventional communities	5/13	6/13	22
Columbia	Yes	Yes	88
Reston	Yes	Yes	94
Irvine	Yes	Yes	58
Valencia	Yes	Yes	55
Park Forest	Yes	Yes	71
Westlake Village	No	No	4
Elk Grove Village	No	Yes	28
Foster City	No	No	23
Laguna Niguel	Yes	Yes	28
Lake Havasu City	No	Yes	15
Sharpstown	Yes	No	88
Forest Park	No	Yes	49
North Palm Beach	Yes	No	26

conventional communities. With the exception of the Columbia transit systems noted above and a small minibus service operated with volunteer drivers by Reston's Common Ground Foundation, transit services were usually offered by regional and metropolitan carriers originating service from outside of the new communities.

Another indication of the availability of transit services is provided by the proportion of respondents, also shown in table 14-2, who reported that a bus stop was within a ten-minute walk of their homes. It is noteworthy that almost twice as many new community respondents as conventional community respondents (43 percent versus 22 percent) thought that a bus stop was available. However, the variation among new communities was as great as that between new communities and conventional communities. A majority of the respondents living in 6 of the 13 new communities—Reston, Columbia, Sharpstown, Park Forest, Irvine, and Valencia—reported that a bus stop was within a ten-minute walk of their homes. At the other end of the scale, only 4 percent of those living in Westlake Village and 15 percent in Lake Havasu City were aware of a bus stop that close to their homes.

Since completion of the field research in the spring of 1973, a number of new communities have taken steps to improve community transit services. Using federal revenue-sharing funds, Elk Grove Village initiated a dial-a-ride service in March 1974. However, the service did not include pick-ups or destinations in the Centex Industrial Park and local merchants were successful in defeating an effort to extend service to the Woodfield Mall in neighboring Schaumburg.

The city of Foster City secured $176,638 from the Metropolitan Transit Commission to plan a community bus service, which began operations in October of 1975. Irvine's city government inaugurated a free summer bus service in 1974, which reportedly carried 500 passengers a day. Avco Community Developers, Inc. provided a minibus service during the summer to transport children to the beach. A beach bus service was also subsidized by the Thousand Oaks city government, which served a portion of Westlake Village. Finally, Elk Grove Village, Park Forest, and Westlake Village were served by demand-activated bus programs designed to take senior citizens from their homes to shopping and entertainment facilities, though none of these programs originated from the new communities.

Commuter Service

Prior to the gasoline shortages experienced in the winter of 1974, express transit services designed to carry residents to employment areas were a rarity in new communities and conventional communities. Only two new communities—Reston and Foster City—had commuter bus service and only one new community—Park Forest—had a commuter rail terminal within the community. In addition, Foster City and Elk Grove Village were in close proximity to commuter rail terminals located in nearby communities. In the conventional communities, commuter bus service was provided to two communities and commuter rail service to one community.

The most notable effort to provide a community-based commuter service occurred in Reston. As reported above, highway access to Reston was severely restricted. Even so, a relatively high proportion of the residents (42 percent of the employed household heads in 1973) commuted to work in Washington, D.C. In the summer of 1966 the developer began to explore the possibility of establishing an express bus service to Washington during the morning and evening rush hours. By the fall of 1966, the developer agreed to subsidize the experimental operation of an express bus; however, only about seven commuters per day were served and the service was abandoned after two weeks (Bain 1969).

Although the developer subsequently lost interest in the provision of a commuter bus service, resident interest mounted as the community continued to grow. During January 1968, after the Reston Community Association had been organized and had decided to concentrate its attention on transportation, plans for an express service were drawn up by the association's Transportation Committee. When initial advanced ticket sales were not sufficient to guarantee that the service would break even, Gulf-Reston, Inc. agreed to cover losses, up to a maximum of $150, during an experimental two-week trial. The experiment was a success and a regular corps of express bus riders soon emerged. A highlight of the service was a Friday afternoon social hour with drinks on the return trip home.

With financial backing from both Gulf-Reston and WV&M Coach Company, a second express bus was soon added and ridership began to mount. By the end of its first year in operation the service had four buses and was averaging about 1,300 passengers a week. The Reston Commuter Bus, Inc. is now an established community institution, whose valuable services have been recognized by Fairfax County. When bus charter costs were raised and threatened the financial viability of the operation in the fall of 1974, the county agreed to provide a $45,000 six-month operating subsidy.

Concurrent with the gasoline shortage in the winter of 1974, interest in express commuter buses increased in several new communities. In Columbia, a Columbia-Washington Commuter Bus Association was formed and provided 13 scheduled round trips by the end of the year. In January 1974, a shuttle service between Elk Grove Village and two commuter rail stations was initiated on a six-month trial basis underwritten by the village government. During the same month, Avco Community Developers, Inc., completely subsidized a commuter bus from Laguna Niguel to Santa Ana, Anaheim, Newport Beach, and Los Angeles for a period of two weeks. After that time the developer covered costs above fare revenues until the demise of the experiment in May, when rider interest waned with renewed gasoline supplies, and scheduled service to Laguna Niguel was begun by the Orange County Transit District.

Walking Paths

A number of new communities have attempted to ease walking to facilities and services by developing attractive internal path systems (walkways behind homes rather than adjacent to the street) and grade-separated crossings where paths intersected with streets and highways. The most complete path systems were available in Columbia, Reston, and Valencia, where walking paths were designed to connect homes with neighborhood and village centers. Several other new communities, including Irvine, Westlake Village, Foster City, and Laguna Niguel, had path systems in several neighborhoods, but had also developed neighborhoods without internal paths. In most cases, they did not provide grade-separated crossings at path-street intersections. Among the older new communities and Lake Havasu City, internal path systems were not developed. In contrast with the availability of path systems in seven new communities, only three of the conventional communities had one or more neighborhoods with paths.

Overall, new community respondents were significantly more likely than conventional community respondents (98 percent versus 90 percent) to have access to a sidewalk or path. However, for 10 of the 13 paired comparisons differences were not statistically significant. In fact, virtually all of the respondents living in 9 of the new and 9 of the conventional communities had a sidewalk or path in front of, adjacent to, or behind their homes. The advantage in favor of new communities was mostly due to the greater availability of sidewalks in Forest Park than in Sharonville and in North Palm Beach than in Tequesta.

The increasing popularity of bicycling has also been felt in new communities. Columbia, Reston, and Valencia, with their extensive internal path systems, have been able to accommodate safely the mounting participation in this form of transportation and outdoor recreation. Four other new communities—Elk Grove Village, Irvine, Laguna Niguel, and Park Forest—have established official bicycle routes with appropriate signing. The most ambitious of these efforts has been undertaken by the city of Irvine. There, a 108-mile, $9 million bikeway system is under development, which will connect all major activity centers in the community. Fourteen miles of bikeways had been completed by the end of 1974.

Employment Self-sufficiency

Employment self-sufficiency, the condition where residents live and work in the same community, has long been viewed as a desirable objective of new community development. The primary advantages claimed for self-sufficiency include reduced costs of commuting, enhanced community identity, and greater interest of residents in their places of work. Additionally, attraction of industrial development to new communities, regardless of where employees presently live, has been viewed as a desirable means of increasing housing demand and the pace of development, and of providing the tax base necessary to finance many community facilities and services.

However, the concept of employment self-sufficiency has also had its critics. Self-containment becomes more likely the farther new communities are located from existing concentrations of employment. Such communities may result in reduced commuting costs, but only at the price of unstable local economic conditions and lack of adaptability to changing economic circumstances that characterize many small towns. What is more, few developers have been interested in freestanding communities. Instead, new communities tend to be located at the fringe of large metropolitan regions and within commuting range of major employment concentrations.

As a result, William Alonso has predicted that new community development may lengthen, rather than shorten, commuting distances (Alonso 1970b, p. 45). In addition, James A. Clapp (1971, p. 259) has suggested that the notion of self-containment is slightly anachronistic, since "In the modern metropolis people are more footloose, they move more frequently (or the job rotation policies of their companies require them to), and they have less attachment to a particular local community and its institutions."

Great Britain has had extensive experience with a conscious policy of creating self-contained new communities. To achieve this goal, most British new towns were developed with a balance between the number of employment opportunities in the community and the number of employed residents. However, after studying eight new towns in the London area, A.A. Ogilvy concluded that, ". . . it is doubtful whether any of the new towns can be called self-contained, even in respect of employment. Large numbers of new town residents travelled out to work in other areas, and large numbers of new town jobs were filled by people who lived elsewhere. . . ." (1968, p. 52). Nevertheless, the degree of employment self-sufficiency attained was rather high (at least in comparison to new communities in the United States). Among the eight new towns studied by Ogilvy, the proportion of employed residents who worked in the communities ranged from a low of 39 percent in Hatfield to a high of 86 percent in Stevenage. For five of the eight new towns, however, over two thirds of the employed residents worked in their home communities.

If new communities in the United States are to meet this degree of employment self-sufficiency, several conditions must be met: First, employment self-sufficiency is likely to be achieved in freestanding new communities, where residents have little choice of employment in the surrounding region. Second, where employment opportunities exist in large numbers in the surrounding region, as they do in all new communities located in metropolitan areas, the new community must establish a substantial employment base, with at least as many job opportunities located in the community as there are employed residents. Third, housing and employment must be interrelated, so that persons employed in the community can afford to also live there.

Of the 13 study new communities, only one—Lake Havasu City—met the freestanding criterion. The other 12 new communities are all located on the peripheries of large metropolitan areas and are all within commuting range of a vast array of job opportunities.

Only six new communities—Irvine, Westlake Village, Valencia, Lake Havasu City, Elk Grove Village, and Columbia—had as many or more jobs located in the community as there were employed residents. Two of these communities—Irvine and Elk Grove Village—had three to four times the number of jobs as employed residents, while Columbia had about one and one-half times as many jobs. In the other three cases, jobs and residents were approximately in balance. Among the remaining new communities, the estimated proportion of employed residents to jobs ranged from two and one-half employed residents per job in Laguna Niguel to five employed residents per job in Foster City, Forest Park, and North Palm Beach, and ten employed residents per job in Park Forest.

Although systematic data on the wages and salaries associated with jobs in new communities were not collected, it is apparent that housing prices and rents are often beyond the means of many employees. This conclusion was affirmed by studies in the two new communities with the largest employment bases. For example, a survey of employees in the Centex Industrial Park in Elk Grove Village, conducted in 1971, indicated that about 10 percent of the Park's 23,000 employees wanted to live in Elk Grove Village, but felt that they could not afford the community's housing prices and rents. A preliminary report issued by the city of Irvine's Planning Department, based on a survey of 393 manufacturing firms in the Irvine Industrial Complex, showed that only 14 percent of the persons working in Irvine could afford to live there.

In sum, most of the preconditions required for employment self-sufficiency and reduced commutation to work did not characterize the privately developed new communities. Only 1 of the 13 new communities was freestanding; many had yet to develop sufficient ratios of jobs to residents to allow residents to work in the community if they so desired; and housing prices and rents were often beyond the means of blue-collar and clerical workers employed in the communities.

Do New Community Residents Travel Less?

Having examined the accessibility of facilities and services, alternative transportation modes available, and employment characteristics of the study communities, the question remains whether the general advantages in favor of new communities were reflected in residents' travel behavior. Several types of travel behavior data were collected, including the time-distance and mode of travel to work, use of buses, mode of travel to shopping and schools, automobile ownership, and annual mileage driven.

The Journey to Work

As suggested by the previous discussion, relatively few new community (14 percent) or conventional community (16 percent) employed household heads lived and worked in the same community. Among the new communities, Lake Havasu City stands alone—both literally and in terms of the proportion (94 percent) who work within the community. See figure 14-2. Of course, Lake Havasu City is freestanding and residents had few employment opportunities located outside of the community.

Among the new communities located within metropolitan areas, the three with the highest ratios of jobs to employed heads of household had the highest proportion of residents working in the community—Columbia, 23 percent; Irvine, 17 percent; and Elk Grove Village, 16 percent. Since each of these communities had excess of 15,000 jobs, it is probably unreasonable to expect new communities in the United States to achieve greater employment self-sufficiency without a closer match between the incomes of employees and new community housing prices. Even then, the variety of employment opportunities in metropolitan areas may make self-sufficiency an unattainable goal. In this regard, it is revealing that in the five new communities where subsidized housing residents were interviewed, a lower proportion of the subsidized housing employed household heads (26 percent) than employed household heads living in nonsubsidized housing (29 percent) both lived and worked in the new communities.

Figure 14-2 also summarizes the length of time it took residents to travel to their places of work. The median trip times for new community (24.8 minutes) and conventional community (25.3 minutes) employed household heads were almost identical. Median trip times were, predictably, the lowest in Lake Havasu City. Trip times also tended to be lower among some of the older new communities, such as Sharpstown, Forest Park, and North Palm Beach, where industrial development had accumulated in the immediately surrounding regions, and in Irvine, which was well served by freeways and had a higher than average proportion of residents who actually worked within the community.

Data from the Nationwide Personal Transportation Study (Svercl and Asin 1973) show that in contrast with the 25-minute median trip times characteristic of new community residents, the median for a national cross section of the population was 15 minutes, with a median of 17 minutes for persons living in households with incomes over $15,000. Data on the distance to work yield similar results. For example, in the nation as a whole the median distance to work was just over 7 miles, compared with over 11 miles per trip among residents of the 13 new communities. Another study that focused on residents living in over 30 SMSAs reported 5.6 miles as the

335

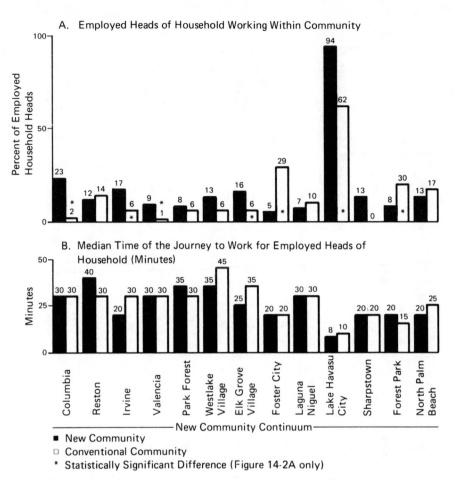

Figure 14-2. Location of Employment and Travel Time to Work

median distance to work for suburban residents, which was comparable to the national cross sectional results and, again, considerably less than that found for new communities (see Lansing and Hendricks 1967).

With the exception of 2 of the 13 new communities where three fourths of the residents went to work by car, the automobile was the overwhelming choice of over 90 percent of the residents as a means of travel to work. There was virtually no differences between the new communities and conventional communities on mode of travel to work.

As shown in table 14-3, however, the availability of the Reston Commuter Bus and a rail transit terminal in Park Forest was reflected in notably lower dependence on the automobile in both of these communities. On the

Table 14-3
Mode of Journey to Work of Head of Household

	Percent of Employed Heads of Household			
New Community	Car or Car Pool Only	Part Car and Part Public	Public Transportation Only	Walk or Bicycle
New communities	94	2	2	2
Conventional communities	94	1	2	3
Columbia	93	1	4	1
Reston	75	3	19	3
Irvine	96	0	0	4
Valencia	99	0	0	1
Park Forest	73	17	8	2
Westlake Village	98	2	0	0
Elk Grove Village	93	4	1	2
Foster City	92	2	5	1
Laguna Niguel	97	1	0	2
Lake Havasu City	95	0	0	5
Sharpstown	96	0	1	3
Forest Park	98	0	0	2
North Palm Beach	96	1	0	3

other hand, the availability of express commuter bus service in Foster City and the close proximity of Foster City and Elk Grove Village to commuter rail stations in neighboring communities were not reflected in much lower than usual dependence on the automobile.

Data from the Nationwide Personal Transportation Study are again available for comparative purposes. For persons in households with incomes over $15,000, the NPTS figures show dependence on the automobile to be less striking than found in 11 of the 13 new communities. Nationwide, 80.8 percent of the employed persons at this income level traveled to work by car, 11.8 percent went part or all of the way on public transport, and 3.5 percent walked (Svercl and Asin 1973, p. 65).

Although the number of persons who drove to work was high no matter how far the trip, at the extremes of the distance distribution (under 1 mile and 15 miles or more) there was a clear decrease in automobile use. For distances up to 1 mile, while 92 percent still traveled only in a car or car pool, 3 percent walked and 5 percent bicycled to work. For the longer distance trips to work, 10 percent used public transportation for part or all of the trip, while 88 percent traveled by car.

Use of Buses

The use of buses was significantly higher among new community respondents than among respondents living in conventional communities, but the proportion who reported ever using a bus was very low in both settings. Only 8 percent of the new and 4 percent of the conventional community respondents reported that they or members of their family had ever used a bus in their community. Frequent use of community buses—5 to 7 days a week—was even less common. Two percent of the new community respondents and 1 percent of those living in the conventional communities said they or members of their family used a bus that often.

If respondents who were not aware of a bus stop within a ten-minute walk of their homes are excluded from consideration, the proportion of bus riders improves somewhat, but the advantage in favor of new communities disappears. Among just those respondents who were aware of a nearby bus stop, 19 percent of those living in new communities and 20 percent of those living in conventional communities reported that they had used the bus at one time or another.

As shown in figure 14-3, the two new communities with community-based transit systems—Columbia and Reston—had by far the greatest transit patronage. Even more impressive was the fact that 20 percent of the Reston respondents reported that their families used a bus five to seven days a week, a percentage roughly equivalent to the ridership reported on the Reston Commuter Bus. With the exception of Columbia, where more than a third of the families rode a bus (but only 6 percent did so regularly), ridership on the metropolitan and regional transit systems available in other new communities was clearly the activity of a small minority. In 9 of the 13 new communities, in fact, 1 percent or less of the respondents said their families rode the buses on a daily basis.

Finally, it should be noted that neither new community nor conventional community respondents indicated much interest in the location of a bus stop within their neighborhood. For example, only from 4 percent of the Irvine respondents to 15 percent of the Elk Grove Village respondents indicated that a bus stop was one of the three facilities they would most like to have within one-half mile of their homes. Even in Elk Grove Village, however, having a bus stop was only the tenth most frequent mention (out of 23 possibilities), and in the 13 new communities as a whole, having a bus stop ranked fourteenth in frequency of mentions. Included by two to three times as many respondents were a library, supermarket, swimming pool, and a quiet place to walk and sit. It is also instructive to note that new community residents were as likely to want a gas station (10.9 percent) within their neighborhoods as a bus stop (10.2 percent), though these responses were secured prior to the gas and energy shortages, which gained national attention beginning in the winter of 1974.

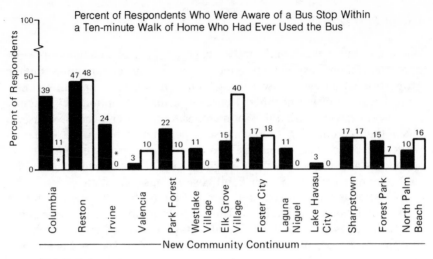

Figure 14-3. Use of Buses

Modes of Local Travel

Data were collected on respondents' usual mode of travel to shopping and their children's usual mode of travel to school. As reported in chapter 13, with several notable exceptions, both new and conventional community respondents overwhelmingly used their cars to travel to convenience stores, supermarkets, and shopping centers. On the other hand, new community children were most likely to have walked or bicycled to school (43 percent) rather than take a school bus (34 percent) or drive (23 percent). Conventional community children were most likely to take a school bus (45 percent), and were less likely to have walked or bicycled to school (34 percent) or to have driven (21 percent).

Cross-sectional comparative data from the Nationwide Personal Transportation Study (Beschen, Jr. 1972, p. 9) provide evidence that differences between the new communities and the national mode-to-school data are slight. Nationwide, slightly fewer children went to school by car (16 percent), while slightly more (38 percent) used a school bus. Finally, in the national sample 42 percent walked or bicycled to school versus 43 percent among the new community children.

Supplemental tabulations were calculated to see if residents were more likely to walk to shopping or schools in communities that provided walking-pathway systems. The usual means of getting to various types of shopping sites was uninfluenced by the presence of pathways, though in an earlier study, John B. Lansing, Robert W. Marans, and Robert B. Zehner (1970) did find that residents in Columbia and Reston, which had internal path systems, were more likely to walk to shop than residents of less planned communities.

Striking differences emerged in the case of trips to school, however. In new communities with no walking-pathway systems, only 22 percent of the children walked to school. In communities with provisions for even one walkway, the percentage walking to school rose to 29 percent, and in communities with two or more pathways, the proportion went to 49 percent, more than double the no-path situation.

Automobile Ownership and Annual Mileage

One of the key consequences of living in new communities with better access to facilities and services is supposed to be reduced dependence on the automobile and a reduced amount of miles driven in a year. Based on a 1969 survey of households living in Columbia, Reston, and a group of less planned communities, Lansing, Marans, and Zehner (1970) found that residents of the new communities had somewhat lower rates of car ownership, but were driving about as many miles in a year as residents of the less planned areas. The authors concluded, however, that as new communities mature and begin to provide a fuller complement of neighborhood and community facilities, a relative decrease in automobile travel might become evident.

A similar conclusion was reached in a recent study, *The Costs of Sprawl,* by the Real Estate Research Corporation (1974). In a report that investigated the relative costs of a range of development patterns—from low-density suburban sprawl to higher density planned residential environments—the authors estimated that by being able to walk to stores and services families in planned settings could use half the gasoline required in traditional sprawl areas. Neither the new communities data on shopping and the journey to work nor the Lansing, Marans, and Zehner (1970) findings suggest that such marked reductions in mileage will actually occur to that degree in nonhypothetical situations, but the possible economies are important in the context of energy crises and shortages.

Automobile Ownership. According to 1972 data on national rates of auto ownership, 79.5 percent of the households in the United States own at least 1 car, and 30.2 percent own 2 or more, for an average of 1.15 cars per household. In suburban areas outside of SMSA central cities (a classification close to most of the study communities) 87.3 percent own cars and 38.7

own 2 or more. The average rate of ownership in these areas is 1.34 cars per household. Finally, in the income group most comparable to that of the study communities, $15,000-25,000, 96.5 percent of the families own cars and 58.4 percent own at least 2. These families average 1.69 cars, a number that is only slightly less than that found in the study new communities (1.74 cars per household) and below that found in conventional communities (1.81 cars per household).

As expected, rates of ownership tended to be highest in the southern California communities. Families in Valencia and Laguna Niguel, for instance, averaged over 1.8 cars. At the other end of the scale—and the only new community where more than half (53 percent) of the families owned less than 2 cars—Park Forest families averaged only 1.49 cars per household.

The rate of car ownership in new communities was strongly associated with the number of miles driven during the previous year by families and with four other variables. Families with higher incomes, those living in single-family homes or townhouses, those with an employed spouse, and those with more teenagers in the household all tended to own more cars. Somewhat weaker associations were found between car ownership and the presence of children in school, and with fewer cars per family, living in elevator and walk-up apartments. Car ownership was not associated with the length of the head's journey to work. Finally, none of the measures of accessibility to facilities and services (see table 14-1) was strongly related to automobile ownership rates.

Car ownership was also associated with the mode of the head's journey to work. For example, households living in Park Forest where the head used only public transit (commuter trains) to go to work averaged 1.3 automobiles. When the head used a combination of automobile and rapid transit modes to get to work, auto ownership averaged 1.52. But, automobile ownership among households whose head went to work entirely by car was 1.58. Similarly, commuter bus riders in Reston averaged 1.22 cars per household, while nonriders averaged 1.70. Thus, while car ownership in new communities was not much different from ownership in conventional communities, if future new communities can divert employed residents from their automobiles to commuter trains or buses, reduced automobile ownership and reduced annual automobile mileage should result.

Annual Mileage. According to the Nationwide Personal Transportation Study, families with incomes of $15,000 and over drove an average of 24,410 miles per year in 1969-70 (Goley, Brown, and Samson 1972). Motor Vehicle Manufacturers Assocation (1972) data indicate that annual miles driven per vehicle increased approximately 4 percent from 1969 to 1972, a rate that can be used to adjust the NPTS figure upward to an estimated 1972

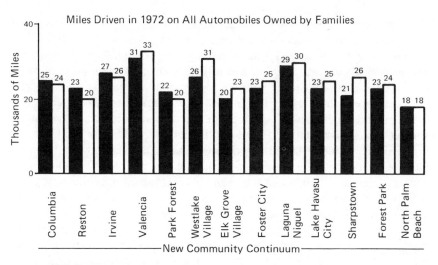

Figure 14-4. Annual Automobile Mileage Per Family, 1972

annual miles per year of 25,400. In the aggregate, new community families drove an average of 23,900 miles in 1972 versus an average of 25,700 miles driven by conventional community families.

The 7.5 percent fewer miles per year driven by new community families was mainly a result of the 5,000 miles per year less driven by families in Westlake Village and Sharpstown than by their counterparts living in the paired conventional communities of Agoura/Malibu Junction and Southwest Houston. See figure 14-4. The six other new communities in which families drove somewhat less than families living in their paired conventional communities included Valencia, Elk Grove Village, Foster City, Laguna Niguel, Lake Havasu City, and Forest Park, although in these cases differences of only 1,000 to 3,000 miles a year were found. Annual mileage was greatest among families living in the two most isolated (other than Lake Havasu City) new communities in the study—Valencia and Laguna Niguel—where families averaged 31,000 and 29,000 miles per year.

Factors that were associated with higher annual mileage included higher family income, living in a single-family detached home, distance to the head's place of work, presence of teenagers in the household, presence of an employed spouse in the household,[a] and greater distances to the

[a] Consistently lower rates of driving in new communities than in the conventional communities remained when comparisons were made controlling for family income, household size, dwelling type, and employment status of the head and spouse. However, it should be noted that differences in mileage among various demographic groups living in new communities and conventional communities were much greater than differences between these two settings.

shopping center used by families and to the school attended. Also, as noted above, automobile ownership rates were strongly associated with mileage driven. As with their association with automobile ownership, accessibility to various facilities and services had little influence on the number of miles driven during the preceding year.

There are two sides to the influence (or lack thereof) of access to facilities and miles driven. On the one hand, convenient facilities mean shorter trips to use them and a greater likelihood that the trips will be via a nonvehicular mode of travel. On the other hand, convenient, high quality facilities can encourage greater participation (see chapter 10) and thereby generate a greater number of trips (and miles) than would otherwise have occurred. For example, although the mean distances to golf, swimming, and tennis facilities were somewhat shorter in new than in conventional communities, somewhat greater participation in these activities meant that on the average, new community residents traveled slightly (although insignificantly) more over a year's time to participate in them—264.1 miles versus 258.1 miles.

It was also possible to test Lansing, Marans, and Zehner's (1970) hypothesis that as Columbia and Reston matured and acquired additional facilities, annual mileage driven would drop. When the present mileage data are adjusted to parallel the sample design of their 1969 study (they did not interview apartment dwellers), the annual mileage in Columbia did not drop, but rose from 21,700 in 1969 to 25,100 in 1973, an increase of 15.7 percent. Similarly, Reston residents' mileage rose from 20,900 to 24,500 miles per year, an increase of 17.2 percent. Nevertheless, mileage in a conventional community common to both studies—Norbeck-Wheaton—rose even more over the same period, from 19,700 to 26,900 miles per family, an increase of 36.5 percent. The implications of such a large percentage difference in the rate of increase are that the planning that underlies new community development and the availability of community transit systems can dampen increasing use of automobiles as communities mature.

Residents' Evaluations of Travel and Public Transportation

Figure 14-5 summarizes new and conventional community residents' evaluations of the ease of getting around their communities in comparison with the communities from which they had moved and their satisfaction with community expenditures for public transportation.

In the case of residents' ratings of the ease of getting around their communities, the new communities were rated better than respondents' previous communities significantly more often (48 percent versus 35 percent) than were the conventional communities. This pattern of responses

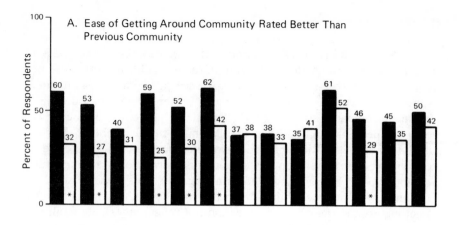

A. Ease of Getting Around Community Rated Better Than Previous Community

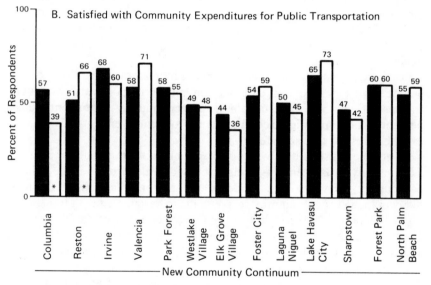

B. Satisfied with Community Expenditures for Public Transportation

- ■ New Community
- ☐ Conventional Community
- * Statistically Significant Difference

Figure 14-5. Residents' Evaluations of Travel and Public Transportation

was true in 11 of the 13 paired comparisons, though differences were statistically significant in only 6, including 5 of the 6 new communities at the upper half of the new community continuum.

The greatest contrast between individual new communities and their paired conventional communities, that between Valencia and Bouquet Canyon, can be attributed to the presence of both community bus and taxi service in Valencia, in addition to a developed internal path system, and their complete absence in Bouquet Canyon. Since residents in Columbia, Reston, and their paired conventional communities each had a number of locally oriented transportation services, it could be inferred that the planning that went into the physical layout of roads and facilities in those new communities, rather than the mere existence of services, was a salient aspect of the ratings. In addition, a much higher rate of bus ridership in Columbia compared to Norbeck-Wheaton (39 percent ever rode a bus versus 11 percent) suggests that the Columbia residents found their ColumBUS (and Call-a-Ride) particularly useful means of getting around the community. Bus ridership in Reston and West Springfield was comparable and appeared to be largely due to commuter bus use.

Comparison of accessibility data with respondents' ratings of the ease of getting around their communities did not reveal any single facility or group of facilities that stood out as a key determinant of the ratings. Nevertheless, modest associations were evident between higher ratings and better access to supermarkets, and to a lesser extent, better access to elementary and middle schools, tennis courts, golf courses, and convenience stores.

In the aggregate, the leading contender for greater community spending among both new and conventional community respondents was public transportation. Some 47 percent of the new community respondents and 45 percent of the conventional community respondents were not satisfied with expenditures for this service.

Since the household survey took place at the time the issue of beginning a community bus system was being discussed in Elk Grove Village, it is not particularly surprising that residents of that community were the least likely of the new commuiunity respondents to be satisfied with transportation expenditures and to want to see more money spent on this service. Irvine, which had excellent freeway access, had residents who were most satisfied with community expenditures for public transportation and least interested in greater expenditures.

Among the variables considered in the analysis of transportation and travel, the factor most associated with satisfaction with community expenditures for public transportation was the rating of the ease of getting around the community. Of those who rated their present new community as better than their previous community, 57 percent were satisfied with community expenditures for public transportation. Of those who rated the community worse, on the other hand, only 41 percent were satisfied. Having a bus stop nearby was also associated with greater satisfaction. Fifty-seven percent of those with a bus stop within a ten-minute walk of their home were satisfied with transportation expenditures versus 46 percent of those without a bus stop. The journey to work variables, automobile ownership, and use of buses were less associated with satisfaction with community expenditures for public transportation.

The Future of Travel in New Communities

In summary, transportation and travel has been one of the more successful aspects of new community development, at least in comparison with conventional suburban communities. New community residents were more likely to live closer to a variety of community facilities, to have access to mass transit services (with the exception of commuter services), to accumulate significantly less annual family automobile mileage, and to give higher ratings to the ease of getting around their communities. Nevertheless, the wide variation found among new communities and the strong relationship between travel behavior and household demographic and employment characteristics indicate that new community development does not automatically produce these benefits.

While community design and the provision of transit facilities can have a significant, direct effect on travel behavior over and above that had by the demographic composition of the community, the composition variables will continue to have the greatest impact. Insofar as community design can influence housing costs and dwelling unit mix, however, it will have an important indirect effect on travel behavior. In essence, the data show a clear relationship between residence in higher density housing, smaller household size, lower incomes, lower automobile ownership, and lower annual rates of automotive travel.

Changes in travel behavior approaching the magnitude of those suggested in the Real Estate Research Corporation's study (1974), where new community families were projected to be able to use as little as half the gasoline of persons in suburban sprawl areas, will be possible only if higher density, facility-intensive areas in new communities are able to attract those three-or-more-person families now oriented toward a low-density, single-family home life-style. Until that time, increased density in new community development will continue to attract those somewhat less affluent, smaller households in the metropolitan area who, on average, would not have been particularly automobile dependent in any case. Even for those families, however, as well as for most other groups, residence in a new community can bring about less dependence on the automobile than in conventional suburban areas.

15 The Social Life of New Communities

In addition to housing and service systems, an important component of community development is the emergence of social networks and social ties among the residents. A number of aspects of new community development have led to heightened expectations regarding community social life. New community planners have frequently been interested in facilitating contacts among the residents and in enhancing community identity. Community plans, which designate a variety of facilities—commercial, educational, religious, and recreational—in close proximity to residential areas, are intended, in part, to increase the frequency of informal meetings and interaction among residents and to encourage family-oriented activities. These results have also been expected from the provision of better community transportation facilities, availability of neighborhood and community meeting rooms, presence of community newspapers, which allocate part or all of their coverage to local events, and the use of developer-organized homes and community associations.

The creation of wholly new communities has also been associated with an aura of adventure and experimentation. While for some residents this situation could lead to direct attempts to become involved in community planning and development decisions (see chapter 7), almost all residents would share in a greater awareness of their community than normally experienced in more conventional suburban areas. This sense of community and shared experiences may further encourage participation in neighborhood and community social activities.

This chapter examines four aspects of the social life of new communities in comparison with less planned conventional communities. The topics considered include: (1) residents' perceptions that they belong to and are a part of community activities; (2) satisfaction with family life and the community as a place to raise children; (3) perceptions of neighbors and neighborhood social contacts; and (4) participation in community voluntary organizations.

The Sense of Belonging

A direct indication of the strength of residents' identification with their communities is how much they feel a part of what happens there. Residents living in the new communities and conventional communities were asked whether they agreed or disagreed with the statement: "I don't feel much a part of what goes on in this town." Those who said that they disagreed or disagreed strongly are considered to have a greater sense of belonging to and identity with their communities than those who agreed with the statement.

There was little overall difference in the proportions of new community (51 percent) and conventional community (50 percent) respondents who indicated that they felt a part of the activities that took place in their communities. The sense of belonging to the community was strongest in communities whose residents were most involved in community social networks. A higher proportion were likely to say they felt a part of community life where more respondents thought that it was easy to make new friends in the community, frequently visited friends living in the community, and where a higher proportion of community residents participated in political activities and voluntary civic and social organizations.

The sense of belonging was also enhanced by a number of community characteristics. For example, the sense of belonging was greater in communities whose developers made greater use of automatic membership homes and community associations. People were more likely to feel a part of community life if their community was relatively isolated from surrounding development and smaller (in terms of population). The existence of more shopping and commercial facilities and of a local newspaper was associated with enhanced perceptions of belonging. People were also more likely to feel a part of community life in those communities where a higher proportion of respondents thought it was easy to get around the community and safe for women and children to be out alone at night. By and large these characteristics and perceptions should tend to foster and support the formation of local social ties that in turn lead to a greater sense of belonging to the community.

Individual community comparisons are illustrated in figure 15-1. In the new communities the proportion of respondents who reported that they felt a part of community life ranged from a low of 42 percent in Forest Park to a high of 64 percent in Lake Havasu City. New communities at the upper half of the new community continuum tended to have slightly higher than average proportions of residents who felt a part of community life, while those at the lower half of the continuum, with the exception of isolated Lake Havasu City and Laguna Niguel, had slightly lower than average proportions of respondents who felt they belonged. The two new communities at the top of the new community continuum—Columbia and Reston—were the only two whose residents were significantly more likely to feel a part of community life than residents living in their paired conventional communities. Both Columbia and Reston had communitywide

349

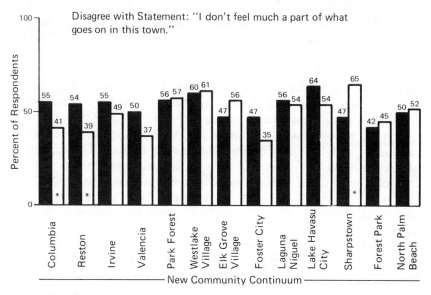

Figure 15-1. Sense of Belonging to Community

and neighborhood cluster automatic homes associations, community newspapers, transit systems, and conveniently located facilities and services that should have enhanced opportunities for the development of social networks.

Family Life and the Community as a Place to Raise Children

One reason people commonly give for moving from cities to suburban areas is to find a better place to raise their children and improve their family life generally. As already noted (see chapter 6), the most frequently reported reason for moving to new communities was the belief that they would be good places to raise children. This section examines respondents' satisfaction with their family life and their perceptions of how well their communities have turned out as places to raise children.

Respondents who agreed strongly or agreed somewhat with the statement, "All things considered, I am very satisfied with my family life—the time I spend and the things I do with members of my family," make up the group considered to be satisfied with their family life. Overall, satisfaction with family life was very close in the new communities and the conventional communities. Fifty-six percent of the new community respondents were satisfied versus 58 percent of the conventional community respondents.

Among the 13 paired comparisons illustrated in figure 15-2, there were no significant differences between individual new communities and the paired conventional communities in reported satisfaction with family life. In contrast with the sense of belonging to the community, which was somewhat higher among communities at the top of the new community continuum, satisfaction with family life tended to decrease with greater adherence to the new community concept. For example, less than half the Columbia and Reston respondents indicated that they were satisfied with their family life, while in Laguna Niguel, Lake Havasu City, Forest Park, and North Palm Beach, which ranked toward the bottom of the new community continuum, three fifths of the respondents were satisfied.

It is not surprising that satisfaction with family life tended to be lower in communities where a higher proportion of household heads and their spouses were both employed. It is surprising, however, that the availability of leisure facilities was associated with lower, rather than higher, satisfaction with family life. For example, satisfaction with family life tended to be lower in communities where a higher proportion of respondents were aware of nearby child play areas and rated them highly, where a relatively large number of recreational opportunities, particularly for tennis and swimming, were available, and where a higher proportion of respondents were aware of a bus stop within a ten-minute walk of home. Thus, the mere presence of facilities is not enough to insure that households will enjoy a satisfying family life.

Several other factors were associated with respondents' satisfaction with their family life. The proportion of respondents who were satisfied with their family life tended to be higher in communities where the median education of respondents was lower, where a higher proportion of respondents reported that they could find the church and religious activities they desired within their community, and where a higher proportion of respondents rated neighborhood safety and homogeneity highly.

Satisfaction with family life and satisfaction with the community as a place to raise children were negatively associated with one another. That is, communities that were rated highly as places to raise children tended not to be those in which residents were most satisfied with their family life. This may be because when children can safely leave their own homes and participate in various activities in the neighborhood and community, parents are less apt to feel obligated to organize and participate in family activities.

Two measures of residents' evaluations of their communities as places to raise children were obtained. Residents were asked to compare their

351

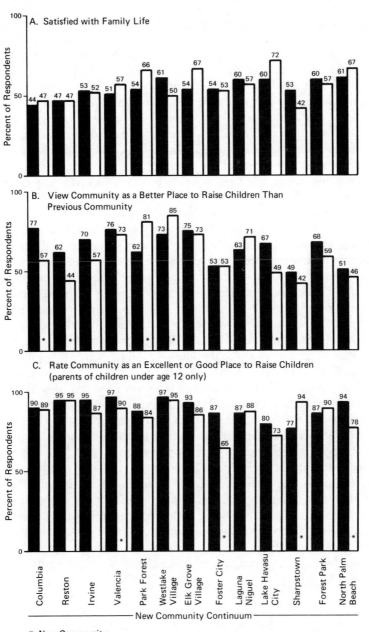

Figure 15-2. Family Life and the Community as a Place to Raise Children

present community as a good place to raise children with the communities from which they had moved. In addition, those with children under age 12 living in their households were asked to rate the community as a place to raise children in that age group. Overall, there was little difference in the ratings given to new and conventional communities as places to raise children. Sixty-four percent of the new community respondents, versus 61 percent of the conventional community respondents, thought that their present community was a better place to raise children than the communities from which they had moved. Ninety percent of the new community parents, versus 87 percent of the conventional community parents, rated their communities as excellent or good places to raise young (under age 12) children.

New communities that were most likely to be rated as better places to raise children than respondents' previous communities tended to have more acreage per capita devoted to recreational facilities and open space. Also, communities tended to be viewed as better places to raise children if a higher proportion of respondents felt that safety from crime was better than in their previous communities, and if schools, nieghborhood appearance, and the type of people living in the neighborhood were rated as better. In addition to the presence of highly rated neighborhood parks and playgrounds, communities with a higher proportion of cul-de-sac streets and with a higher proportion of homes served by neighborhood and community centers tended to receive a higher proportion of ratings as better places to raise children than communities with lower proportions of respondents served by cul-de-sac streets and community centers.

By far the most important factor underlying parents' ratings of the community as an excellent or good place to raise young children was the availability of a highly rated park or playground near their homes. Less strongly related factors included living in a community generally rated as better than the previous community in terms of recreational facilities, overall community planning, and opportunities for participation in community life. Communities with a higher proportion of cul-de-sac streets tended to receive proportionately more excellent or good ratings as places to raise young children. This was also true of communities with a higher than average amount of neighboring (neighbors chatting or visiting with one another often).

Perceptions of Neighbors and Neighborhood Contacts

Respondents were asked several questions about their neighbors, including how they viewed the friendliness of neighbors, how easy it was to call on their present neighbors in time of need as compared with the neighbors where they lived before, and what types of contact, if any, they had with their immediate neighbors. In most cases there was little difference between the responses of new and conventional community residents on any of these items. See figure 15-3.

Satisfaction with the friendliness of neighbors was most strongly associated with perceptions of neighborhood privacy. It appears that when neighbors have adequate privacy they are less likely to intrude on each other's lives and are more likely to develop friendly relationships. Respondents were also more likely to perceive their neighbors as friendly in those communities where a higher proportion of residents rated neighborhood homogeneity highly, where they judged the community as a whole as one in which it was easy to make new friends, and where a higher proportion of respondents rated community recreational facilities as better than those of their previous communities.

Respondents were more likely to feel it was as easy to call on neighbors in time of need as in their former communities when the community had facilities that made contacts with neighbors easier. For example, the factor most strongly associated with finding it relatively easy to call on neighbors was the availability of a neighborhood park or playground. Also, people tended to find it easier to call on neighbors when they lived in communities with more transportation facilities, where they had greater access to neighborhood paths and trails, and more facilities available within their neighborhoods.

To find out about residents' actual neighboring activities, respondents living in the new and conventional communities were asked whether they frequently visited in each other's homes with their nearest neighbor, frequently chatted with their neighbor in the yard or on the street, occasionally chatted with their neighbor in the yard or on the street, or if they hardly knew their neighbors. As illustrated in figure 15-3C, a majority of the respondents in each type of community indicated they either often visited with their neighbors or frequently chatted with them. As with perceptions of the neighbors as friendly and as easy to call on in time of need, there was little difference in actual neighboring activity between new community and conventional community residents.

As might be expected, people were likely to have closer contacts with their neighbors in communities where a higher proportion of the residents thought their neighbors were friendly. Also, neighboring was somewhat more prevalent in communities with more active social life generally. Communities characterized by somewhat closer contacts among neighbors tended to be those where a higher proportion of residents had joined voluntary organizations and a higher proportion of respondents said they frequently visited with their friends. Several community design characteristics were also associated with closer contacts among neighbors. A some-

354

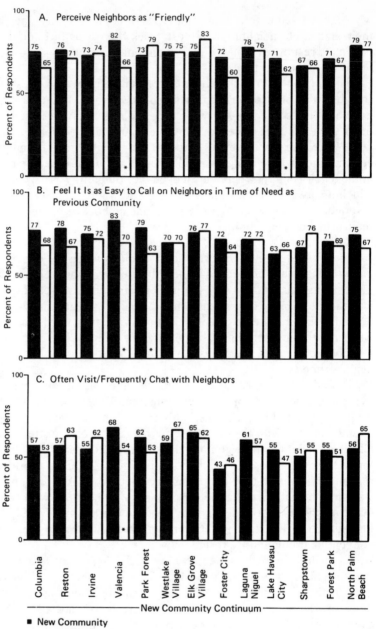

Figure 15-3. Perceptions of Neighbors and Neighborhood Social Contacts

what higher proportion of respondents tended to report close contacts in communities with lower average cluster density, with internal path systems, and with a higher proportion of households served by cul-de-sac streets. These are all factors community planners have expected would promote closer social contacts among the residents.

Participation in Community Organizations

New community residents were much more likely than the residents of the conventional communities to report that opportunities for participation in community life were better in their present community than in the communities from which they had moved. Fifty-nine percent of the new community respondents thought opportunities for participation were better versus only 47 percent of the conventional community respondents.

As shown in figure 15-4, perceptions of opportunities for participation in community life generally followed the new community continuum. Over 70 percent of the respondents living in the three new communities at the top of the continuum—Columbia, Reston, and Irvine—rated opportunities for participation as better. In each case a significantly higher proportion of new community than conventional community respondents felt this way about their community. In most of the new communities at the lower part of the new community continuum, including Foster City, Laguna Niguel, Lake Havasu City, Sharpstown, and North Palm Beach, barely more than half, and in Sharpstown, just over a third, of the respondents felt their move had resulted in improved opportunities for community participation.

A number of other community characteristics were associated with the proportion of respondents who viewed opportunities for participation in community life as better than those in their previous communities. For example, perceptions of opportunities for participation in community life tended to be higher in communities with local newspapers, a larger number of community facilities within one-half mile of respondents' homes, an internal path system and pedestrian-vehicular separation, shopping facilities grouped in centers, and available neighborhood and community centers with meeting rooms. In terms of community social life, opportunities for participation were more likely to be viewed as better than the previous community in those communities where higher proportions of respondents interacted frequently with their neighbors and thought the type of people living in their neighborhoods were better than in their previous communities.

Surprisingly, however, residents' actual rates of membership in social organizations and clubs and membership in clubs that met in their own communities bore little resemblance to their perceptions of opportunities

356

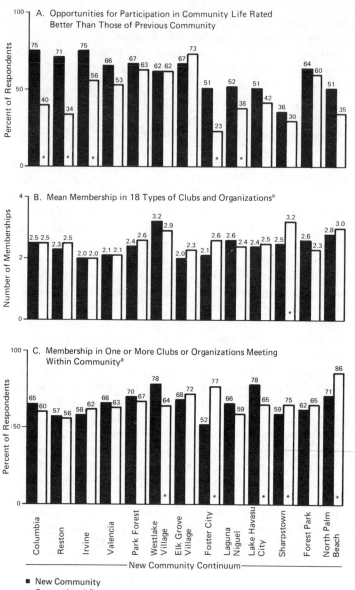

A. Opportunities for Participation in Community Life Rated Better Than Those of Previous Community

B. Mean Membership in 18 Types of Clubs and Organizations[a]

C. Membership in One or More Clubs or Organizations Meeting Within Community[a]

New Community Continuum

■ New Community
□ Conventional Community
* Statistically Significant Difference

[a]Does not include automatic membership homes and community associations.

Figure 15-4. Participation in Social Clubs and Organizations

for participation in community life. New community and conventional community respondents were shown a list of 18 types of clubs and organizations and asked: "Please look at each of the groups on the list and tell me which of these organizations you yourself belong to. Are there any others that aren't on this list?" Then, for each type of club or organization mentioned, respondents were asked: "Does the (Type of Organization) meet or hold its activities here in this community?"

In each of the communities a sizable proportion of the respondents belonged to more than one type of organization. The mean number of organizational memberships (excluding automatic homes and community associations) ranged from a low of 2.0 organizations per respondent in Irvine and Elk Grove Village to a high of 3.2 organizations per respondent in Westlake Village. As shown in figure 15-4B, there was little difference in organizational memberships between each new community and its paired conventional community.

Figure 15-4C summarizes the proportion of respondents who belonged to one or more types of club or organization that met within the community. In this case, the range was from a low of 52 percent of the respondents living in Foster City to 78 percent of those living in Westlake Village and Lake Havasu City. New community respondents were no more likely than conventional community respondents to belong to a community-based organization. As has been reported in an earlier study (Zehner 1974), there was little association between the overall degree of community planning or adherence to the new community concept and actual rates of participation in community organizations. There was also little association between membership in automatic homes or community associations and participation.

To determine whether new community residents were substituting informal social contacts for membership in organized groups, the association between the frequency of contacts with neighbors, friends, and relatives and organizational participation was calculated. In general, communities with higher than average rates of participation in informal social contacts also tended to have higher rates of participation in formal organizations. Thus, there was no indication that new community respondents substituted informal contacts for participation in organized groups. There was also no indication (see Zehner 1974) that new community respondents substituted recreational participation for participation in community organizations. In sum, while new community development may have presented more opportunities for participation in community life (residents' perceptions tended to confirm this supposition), there was no evidence to suggest that the extent of social participation in organized groups in new communities was very different from that found in less planned conventional communities.

Implications for New Community Development

Herbert J. Gans (1967) has noted that the community, and especially its physical component, may have little influence on social life. For example, based on his studies of Levittown, Gans noted,

Plans and policies aimed at changing people's behavior can therefore not be implemented through prescribing alterations in the physical community or by directives aimed at builders; they must be directed at the national sources and agents which bring about the present behavior (Gans 1967, p. 289).

The data presented in this chapter tend to confirm Gans' hypothesis that the physical environment does not have a strong influence on social behavior and perceptions. Although new community planners have often attempted to design communities so as to increase social contacts and neighborhood and community participation, there was relatively little difference between new and conventional communities in the sense of belonging to the community, satisfaction with family life and with the community as a place to raise children, interaction with neighbors, or membership in social clubs and organizations.

Nevertheless, the physical environment should not be viewed as totally irrelevant simply because new community developers have not yet succeeded in inducing greater social satisfaction or participation. Several physical characteristics of new communities and conventional communities were associated with residents' perceptions of their communities and the extent of social participation. For example, the use of neighborhood and community homes associations tended to promote a sense of belonging to the community. Residents tended to be happier with the community as a place to raise children when highly regarded neighborhood parks were available, their homes were located on cul-de-sac streets (which increased traffic safety), and they felt safe from criminal activities. Interaction with neighbors and perceptions that neighbors were friendly were heightened when neighborhood privacy was adequate; when residents felt the neighborhood was socially homogeneous; and when facilities that increased the potential of meeting neighbors, such as parks, playgrounds, transportation facilities (particularly internal path systems), and more neighborhood facilities, were available. Location on a cul-de-sac street also was associated with increased interaction among neighbors. On the whole, community planning variables had little influence on the extent of membership in voluntary clubs and organizations. People living in more highly planned communities with more neighborhood facilities, paths, newspapers, meeting rooms, and other features that had been designed, in part, to increase community participation and interaction among residents were more likely to feel that opportunities for participation were better than were residents who lived in communities without these features.

16 Community Livability

Much of what has been written about new communities suggests that the new community is, or should be, a more rewarding environment in which to live than less comprehensively planned conventional suburban development. Various aspects of the new community environment, from housing to social life, were examined in the preceding chapters. Here the focus shifts to an overall assessment of new communities as places to live.

Residents' satisfaction with new community livability is examined from four perspectives: The first centers on perceptions of improvements gained from the move to a new community. Second, residents' overall ratings of their communities as excellent or good places to live are considered, together with the reasons given for their ratings. Third, perceptions of community problems are identified and compared to the problems facing residents of the paired conventional communities. The chapter then concludes with residents' prognoses of their communities as places to live in five years and their recommendations for community improvements.

Comparisons with the Previous Community

A majority of the new community respondents rated 7 of 19 community attributes as better in their present new communities than in the communities from which they had moved. Five of these 7 attributes—the community as a good place to raise children, layout and space of the dwelling and lot, appearance of the immediate neighborhood, nearness to the outdoors and natural environment, and community planning—were also among the most frequently given reasons for moving to new communities. Thus, new community residents tended to perceive improvements in those aspects of their communities that received the highest priority in their moving decisions.

Two other features—recreational facilities and opportunities for participation in community life—were less important in residents' moving decisions, but were viewed by a majority of the respondents as better in their new communities than in the communities from which they had moved. Recreational service systems, as reported in chapter 10, were one of the most outstanding aspects of new community development. Community participation, on the other hand, was not much greater in the new than

359

Table 16-1
Comparison of Present Community with Previous Community on 19 Community Attributes

	Percent of Respondents			
	Reason for Moving to Community		Believe Community Is Better Than Previous Community	
Housing and Community Characteristics	New Communities	Conventional Communities	New Communities	Conventional Communities
Good place to raise children	31	33	64	61
Convenience to work	30	29	40	40
Layout and space of the dwelling and lot	28	37[a]	69	71
Appearance of the immediate neighborhood	26	26	65	62
Nearness to the outdoors and natural environment	26	29	61	60
Cost of buying (and financing) the dwelling or renting	24	28[a]	37	47[a]
Overall planning that went into community	23[a]	7	75[a]	53
Climate	21	22	46	46

Public schools	15	15	46	45
Recreational facilities	12[a]	6	63[a]	49
Type of people living in the neighborhood	12	14	45	42
Shopping facilities	9	7	41[a]	36
Construction of the dwelling	7	10[a]	45	50[a]
Ease of getting around the community	7	7	48[a]	36
Safety from crime	6	6	48	48
Opportunities for participation in community life	5	3	59[a]	47
Finding a job in the community	4	4	26	26
Cost of living in the community	2	3	18	20
Health and medical services	2	1	25[a]	20

[a]Difference between new communities and conventional communities is statistically significant at the 0.05 level of confidence.

in the conventional communities. Nevertheless, a majority of the respondents in every new community except Sharpstown thought that opportunities for participation were better than in their former communities.

New community respondents were not the only ones to perceive improvements over their previous communities. As shown in table 16-1, among the seven features that were mentioned most often as reasons for moving to conventional communities, the conventional community respondents were just as likely as new community respondents to feel that their present communities were better than the communities from which they had moved. There were only two significant differences in perceptions of improvements in key community characteristics. New community respondents were significantly more likely to have rated planning as better in their present communities, while the conventional community respondents were significantly more likely to have rated the cost of buying or renting as better. In sum, while new community development has tended to satisfy the objectives residents expressed in their moving decisions, it has had no greater success in this regard than conventional suburban development.

Among those features that were less important in residents' moving decisions, new communities had a decided edge in perceptions of improvements gained from the move. New community respondents were significantly more likely than conventional community respondents to have rated recreational facilities, shopping facilities, ease of getting around their communities, opportunities for participation in community life, and health and medical services as better than in their former communities. The only factor in the conventional communities' favor was perceptions that construction of the dwelling was better than in the previous community.

Comparisons between individual new communities and their paired conventional communities are summarized in figure 16-1. For 9 of the 13 paired comparisons, the new community respondents were significantly more likely to have given "better" ratings to more community characteristics. In 3 instances conventional community respondents rated more of the 19 characteristics as "better" significantly more often than their paired new community respondents, and in 1 case there was no difference in the number of characteristics that were most often rated as "better."

If one looks at the total number of potential differences in ratings (19 community characteristics times 13 paired comparisons), in these terms there appears to be much less difference between the ratings of new and conventional communities. Of the 247 possible differences, new communities received a significantly higher proportion of "better" ratings for 26 percent of the paired comparisons. The conventional communities received a significantly higher proportion of "better" ratings for 11 percent of the paired comparisons, but for 63 percent of the comparisons there were no significant differences in ratings.

Columbia was the only new community whose residents were signifi-

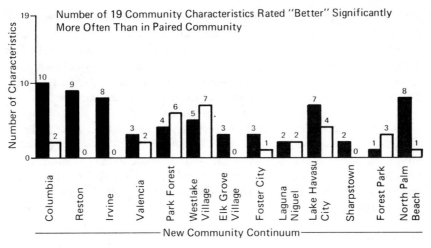

Figure 16-1. Rating of Community in Comparison with Communities from Which Residents Had Moved

cantly more likely than residents of its paired conventional community to have given "better" ratings to more than half (10) of the 19 community characteristics. Only 2 of these 10 differences, however, were for community characteristics that were among the 8 major reasons residents gave for moving to new communities. Two other new communities at the top of the new community continuum—Reston and Irvine—also fared well in comparison with their paired conventional communities. Reston (9 community characteristics rated as "better" significantly more often—4 of which were among the top 8 characteristics given as reasons for moving to new communities) ranked second among the 13 new communities. Irvine was tied with North Palm Beach for third (8 community characteristics rated as "better" significantly more often than in the paired conventional communities—with 4 and 3 of the differences, respectively, occurring in the characteristics that were among the top 8 reasons for moving to new communities). The advantage in favor of new communities was much less impressive for the other 9 paired comparisons illustrated in figure 16-1.

Residents' Overall Evaluations of New and Conventional Communities

In addition to comparative ratings of particular community attributes, respondents were also asked to indicate their satisfaction with the community as a whole and to indicate the reasoning behind their community ratings. To insure that residents were all responding to the same definition of the community, they were asked to examine an area outlined on a map that corresponded to the main boundaries of the community involved. The question used was: "I'd like to ask you how you feel now about this area as a place to live—I mean the area outlined on the map (show map). From your own personal point of view, would you rate this area as an excellent place to live, good, average, below average, or poor?"

Later in the interview respondents were given a second chance to express a summary evaluation of their community. In this case the question was phrased in terms of their willingness to recommend the community as a place to live: "If a close relative or friend asked you if they should consider moving to this community, would you tell them that this would be a particularly good community to move to, that it's pretty much like other communities around here, or that they could probably do better somewhere else?"

Both overall community evaluations are summarized in figure 16-2. In both cases new community respondents indicated that they were highly satisfied with the livability of their communities. They also gave significantly higher ratings to their communities than their paired conventional community respondents. However, the margins of difference were not large. Ninety percent of the new community respondents versus 86 percent of the conventional community respondents rated their communities as excellent or good places to live. Eighty-one percent of the new community respondents versus 75 percent of the conventional community respondents said they would recommend their community as a particularly good place to move to.

Residents' overall ratings were not associated with the new community continuum. Seven new communities—Reston, Irvine, Valencia, Westlake Village, Elk Grove Village, Laguna Niguel, and North Palm Beach—were rated as excellent or good places to live by over 90 percent of the respondents. The overall advantage in favor of new communities was primarily contributed by Irvine, Valencia, and Lake Havasu City, which were rated as excellent or good places to live by significantly higher proportions of respondents than their paired conventional communities. In the other ten cases differences in overall ratings were not statistically significant.

New community residents were somewhat less likely to recommend their communities as particularly good places to which to move than they were to rate them as excellent or good places to live. In this case, only three new communities—Reston, Valencia, and Westlake Village—received such recommendations from 90 percent or more of the respondents. Also, less than 80 percent of the respondents said they would recommend Park Forest, Lake Havasu City, Sharpstown, and Forest Park as particularly good communities. On the other hand, the difference in ratings between

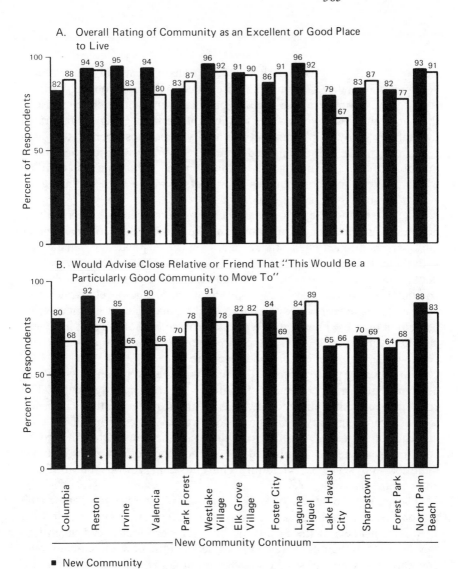

A. Overall Rating of Community as an Excellent or Good Place to Live

B. Would Advise Close Relative or Friend That "This Would Be a Particularly Good Community to Move To"

- New Community
- Conventional Community
- * Statistically Significant Difference

Figure 16-2. Residents' Overall Evaluations of Their Communities

new communities and conventional communities was more widely distributed. For 5 of the 13 paired comparisons illustrated in figure 16-2—Reston, Irvine, Valencia, Westlake Village, and Forest City—the new community respondents were significantly more likely to have given their community a high recommendation.

Reasons for Community Ratings

To explore the reasons underlying evaluations of new and conventional community livability, respondents were asked to elaborate on their ratings. Apparently, people are able to focus on whatever positive characteristics their communities have in order to substantiate their generally favorable evaluations of overall community livability. The most frequently given types of response are summarized in table 16-2. With two exceptions—the mentions of overall planning of new communities and the lack of crowding in the conventional communities—residents living in both settings gave similar reasons for ¡ sitive evaluations.

The quality of the environment, including perceived lack of crowding, nearness to nature and the outdoors, and the attractiveness of the community, was mentioned most often as a reason for respondents' satisfaction with the livability of their communities. Environmental factors were particularly noteworthy aspects of the appeal of the southern California new communities, which were located on the urban fringe in relatively undeveloped areas. Seventy-six percent of the Laguna Niguel respondents, 63 percent in Irvine, 62 percent in Westlake Village, and 56 percent in Valencia cited various aspects of the environment as reasons for rating these communities as excellent or good places to live.

Close behind perceptions of the quality of the environment were perceptions that various community facilities were conveniently located. The convenience of shopping facilities was given most frequently as a reason for positive community evaluations, followed by perceptions of the convenience of recreational facilities, schools, and, less often, health care. In addition, respondents mentioned the convenience of a variety of other facilities and services, including churches and various cultural and entertainment activity places.

The quality of community facilities and services ranked third among the reasons given for rating communities as excellent or good places to live. However, aspects of the quality of facilities were mentioned much less frequently than their convenience. Residents of the new and conventional communities were most likely to mention the quality of community schools, and somewhat less often, the quality of recreational facilities and shopping facilities.

The frequency with which respondents mentioned the convenience and quality of community facilities and services varied among the study communities. For example, characteristics of the schools were mentioned most often by the respondents living in four new communities—Elk Grove Village, Forest Park, Park Forest, and Sharpstown—which had well established school plants. Shopping facilities were mentioned most frequently

Table 16-2
Reasons Most Frequently Given for Rating Community as an Excellent or Good Place to Live

Reasons for Positive Ratings	Percent of Respondents[a]	
	New Communities	Conventional Communities
Quality of the environment		
Lack of crowding	16	23[b]
Nearness to nature and		
the outdoors	15	16
Attractiveness	15[b]	11
Convenience of facilities		
Shopping	11	9
Recreation	6	6
Schools	5	3
Health care	1	1
Other (church, cultural,		
entertainment, etc.)	16	15
Quality of facilities		
Schools	8	9
Recreation	5	3
Shopping	4	6
Health care	1	0
Other (church, cultural,		
entertainment, etc.)	2	2
Type of people living in		
community		
Friendliness	10	10
High social status	8	9
Planning of community	12[b]	4
Streets and transportation	9	8
Convenience to work/employment		
opportunities	4	4
Safety		
Lack of crime	3	2
Safe streets	1	1
Social programs and citizen		
participation	4	4
Children (nice, good for		
teens, etc.)	3	3
Police and fire protection	3	2

[a]Responses add to more than 100 percent because some respondents mentioned more than one reason for rating their communities as excellent or good places to live.

[b]Difference between new communities and conventional communities is statistically significant at the 0.05 level of confidence.

by Sharpstown and Park Forest residents. Both of these communities contained regional shopping centers. Recreational facilities were mentioned most often by Valencia respondents, while health care facilities were mentioned most by Sharpstown respondents.

Eighteen percent of the new community respondents cited the type of people living in their communities as the reason for their satisfaction. By type of people they meant the friendliness of people living in the community and also the high social status of community residents. North Palm Beach respondents and those living in Forest Park, Park Forest, Sharpstown, and Valencia were most likely to mention characteristics of the population as reasons for their communities' livability.

The character of community planning was mentioned by 12 percent of the respondents. Planning was most often mentioned by persons who were living in new communities that ranked toward the top of the new community continuum. For example, 24 percent of the Valencia respondents, 22 percent in Reston, 21 percent in Irvine, 17 percent in Westlake Village, and 15 percent in Columbia mentioned planning as one of the reasons for rating these communities highly.

A number of other reasons were given for positive overall community evaluations. These included streets and transportation, convenience to work, safety, and, less often, social programs and citizen participation, the character of the children living in the community, and the quality of police and fire protection.

Although respondents mentioned a variety of reasons for their positive community evaluations, the quality of the environment and convenience of facilities clearly stood out as the key bases for community livability. These two factors received over half of all the mentions of reasons for respondents' ratings and were mentioned by a sizable proportion of the respondents living in each of the study new communities.

Correlates of Satisfaction with Community Livability

Satisfaction with community livability varied somewhat among persons with different personal characteristics and among those living in different types of housing. Overall, however, personal and housing characteristics accounted for only about 6 percent of the variance in livability ratings.

Family income was moderately associated with community satisfaction. As households' family incomes increased, they tended to be increasingly likely to rate their communities as excellent or good places to live. Nevertheless, 84 percent of the new community respondents with below average incomes (under $10,000) rated their communities that highly. The proportion of respondents who gave their communities excellent or good ratings increased to 89 percent of those with average incomes ($10,000-$14,999), 90 percent with above average incomes ($15,000-$24,999), and to 95 percent of the affluent respondents with family incomes of $25,000 or more.

There was also a moderate association between respondents' life cycle-family type and community satisfaction. The most satisfied respondents were single persons age 40 and over without children living in the household (94 percent gave excellent or good ratings to their communities). Married couples over age 40 without children living in the household were also highly satisfied (90 percent excellent or good), as were married couples with children (91 percent excellent or good). Somewhat lower ratings were given by younger respondents without children in their households—84 percent of the single persons under age 40 and 85 percent of the younger married couples rated their communities as excellent or good places to live. Satisfaction with community livability did not vary significantly with other personal characteristics of the respondents, including sex, marital status, education, and race.

Among housing characteristics, tenure had the strongest influence on ratings of the community as a place to live—owners (91 percent gave excellent or good ratings) were significantly more satisfied with the livability of their communities than were renters (84 percent excellent or good ratings). Because of the association between tenure and housing type, respondents who were living in apartments were somewhat less likely to rate their community as highly as were respondents who were living in townhouses and single-family detached homes. Among both owners and renters respondents who lived in more expensive dwelling units gave higher overall ratings to their communities than respondents who lived in less expensive homes.

In chapter 9 it was noted that housing density was not systematically associated with respondents' satisfaction with their homes. This was also true of their ratings of the community as a place to live. There was no significant association between density and satisfaction with community livability.

Respondents' satisfaction with community livability was also compared to ratings of their homes, immediate neighborhoods, and the community service systems discussed in the preceding chapters. The results of this analysis show that the three factors with a statistically significant influence on overall ratings were respondents' evaluations of the immediate neighborhood, recreational facilities, and their homes. Of less importance in overall evaluations of community livability were ratings of health care facilities, schools, homes associations, ease of getting around the community, religious facilities, and shopping facilities.

A third set of factors examined in relation to overall community evaluations was the availability of various community facilities. Like personal and housing characteristics, these variables explained very little—about 4 percent—of the variance in overall ratings. In general, communities which had more types of facilities tended to be older communities with larger populations. These communities often lacked the environmental features that were associated with community satisfaction, so that the variety of community facilities available not only did not explain much of the variance in overall ratings, but the associations were not in the expected direction. That is, new communities with a greater variety of community facilities tended to receive lower rather than higher ratings as places to live.

In combination, the three sets of variables—personal and housing characteristics, subjective ratings of housing and community facilities and services, and the variety of facilities and services actually available—explained 28 percent of the variance in livability ratings. Seventeen percent of the variance was accounted for by respondents' satisfaction with the immediate neighborhood, evaluation of community recreational facilities, and satisfaction with their homes. Tenure, family income, and dwelling unit value explained another 5 percent of the variance, and the remaining 6 percent of the variance explained was accounted for by other personal characteristics, evaluations of other community attributes, and the variety of services and facilities available.

Reasons respondents gave for rating their communities highly and the various factors associated with livability ratings help explain why there was only a 4 percent difference in the proportion of new community respondents and conventional community respondents who rated their communities as excellent or good places to live. First, from the residents' perspectives the sources of community satisfaction were virtually identical in both settings. Of the key reasons respondents gave for their ratings—quality of the environment and convenience of facilities—only the latter tended to be rated more highly by new community respondents. As shown in table 16-1, there were no significant differences in the proportions of respondents who thought that the appearance of their immediate neighborhoods or nearness to the outdoors and natural environment were better in their present communities than in the communities from which they had moved. A significantly higher proportion of new community respondents, however, rated the ease of getting around the community as better than their previous communities.

Among the three items that were most strongly associated with overall community ratings—evaluations of the immediate neighborhood, recreational facilities, and the dwelling unit—only recreational facilities were rated significantly higher by new than by conventional community respondents. Housing satisfaction was virtually identical in new and conventional communities, as were ratings of the immediate neighborhood as a good place to live.

Table 16-3
Community Problems Most Frequently Mentioned

Community Problems	Percent of Respondents[a]	
	New Communities	Conventional Communities
Quality of the environment		
Increasing density/crowding	20	24[b]
Ugliness/poor maintenance	5	3
Lack of natural open space	3	11[b]
Schools		
More schools needed	14[b]	8
Poor quality of existing schools	5	6
Recreational facilities		
More facilities needed/ existing facilities are inconvenient	6	5
Poor quality of existing facilities	3	2
Lack of facilities for children	3	4
Cost of living (including taxes)	11	9
Police, fire, and other public services	11	12
Transportation and street maintenance	10	17[b]
Teenagers (primarily drug use)	9	9
Developer and local officials	9	8
Poor planning/plans not followed	7	8
Safety from crime	6	8

[a]Responses add to more than 100 percent because some respondents mentioned more than one community problem.
[b]Difference between new communities and conventional communities is statistically significant at 0.05 level of confidence.

Community Problems

In addition to asking residents to evaluate their communities as places to live (table 16-2), they were also asked to name the most important issues or problems facing the community as a whole. The community problems most frequently mentioned are summarized in table 16-3.

Again, concerns about the quality of the environment were foremost in residents' minds. In particular, about one fifth of the new community respondents mentioned increasing density and crowding as an important problem. Although the density of respondents' immediate neighborhoods was not statistically associated with evaluations of new community livability, higher density of the community as a whole and its effects on the environment were obviously viewed by many respondents as a threat to their communities' livability.

Difficulties with school construction and educational programs reported in chapter 12 were reflected in respondents' assessments of community problems. The need for more schools was the second most frequently mentioned problem in new communities. A lower proportion of respondents, however, were concerned about the quality of community schools.

A number of other problems were mentioned. These included concerns about community recreational facilities, the cost of living and taxes, police protection, fire protection, transportation and street maintenance, teenagers and drug use, the behavior of the developer and local officials, and safety from crime. With some exceptions, including significantly greater concern with the lack of natural open space and with transportation and street maintenance, conventional community residents perceived about the same array of problems as new community residents.

The types of problems residents mentioned varied from one new community to another. For example, as shown in table 16-4, although increasing density and crowding were mentioned as problems by 10 percent or more of the respondents in ten new communities, they were mentioned by a quarter or more of those living in Laguna Niguel (51 percent); North Palm Beach (33 percent); Reston (26 percent); and Irvine (25 percent). With the exception of North Palm Beach, where increasing condominium apartment construction was opposed by many residents, lack of crowding and nearness to the outdoors were the most common reasons respondents gave for rating these communities as excellent or good places to live. Obviously, many residents felt these aspects of their communities' livability were threatened by the increasing proportion of townhouses and rental apartments that were being built.

Concern for the provision of schools was greatest in those new communities noted in chapter 12 where school construction had fallen far behind initial expectations. Almost a third of the Reston and Foster City respondents mentioned that the need for more schools was a major community problem. The need for additional schools was also noted by more than 10 percent of the respondents in Forest Park, Irvine, Laguna Niguel, North Palm Beach, Valencia, and Westlake Village.

A variety of other public facilities and services were viewed as major problems in some new communities. The need for more recreational

Table 16-4

Community Problems Mentioned by 10 Percent or More of the Respondents in Each New Community

Community and Problems	Percent of Respondents Who Mentioned Problem
Columbia	
Cost of living too high	16
Excessive crime	13
Excessive developer control	12
Social planning and citizen participation	12
Increasing density/crowding	11
Reston	
Need for more schools	32
Increasing density/crowding	26
Master plan not being followed	12
Drugs	11
Irvine	
Increasing density/crowding	25
Need for more schools	14
Lack of low-income housing	11
Valencia	
High taxes	25
Need for more schools	19
Need for more shopping facilities	18
Need for more recreational facilities	11
Increasing density/crowding	10
Park Forest	
Race relations	33
Quality of the schools	18
Need for more recreational facilities	14
Drugs	13
Teenagers' behavior	13
Westlake Village	
Increasing density/crowding	19
Need for more schools	17
Need for more recreational facilities	11
Elk Grove Village	
Increasing density/crowding	17
Poor public services (police, fire, etc.)	12
Foster City	
Need for more schools	32
High taxes	24
Increasing density/crowding	16
Need for more recreational facilities	11

Table 16-4 (cont.)

Community and Problems	Percent of Respondents Who Mentioned Problem
Laguna Niguel	
Increasing density/crowding	51
Need for more schools	25
Need for more recreational facilities	17
Encroachment on natural environment	10
Lake Havasu City	
Need for more health care facilities	34
Lack of employment opportunities	23
Cost of living too high	19
Poor public services (police, fire, etc.)	17
Need for more shopping facilities	15
Character of local politics	11
Sharpstown	
Increasing density/crowding	23
Poor public services (police, fire, etc.)	20
Drugs	18
Quality of the schools	14
Poor street maintenance	13
Lack of public transportation	12
Forest Park	
Need for more schools	21
Race relations	13
Need for more recreational facilities	12
Drugs	12
High taxes	12
North Palm Beach	
Poor public services (police, fire, etc.)	40
Increasing density/crowding	33
Need for more recreational facilities	18
Need for more schools	14

Note: As discussed in the preceding chapters, some of these problems have been addressed by construction of needed facilities and/or inauguration of new programs since the household survey was conducted in the spring of 1973.

facilities was mentioned by 10 percent or more of the respondents in seven new communities. Limited shopping facilities were viewed as problems in Lake Havasu City and Valencia. Although the lack of health care facilities was the most frequently mentioned community problem facing Lake Havasu City, it was probably alleviated by the subsequent construction of two community hospitals. Other community services, including police protection, fire protection, and garbage collection were a major concern of North Palm Beach respondents (mentioned by 40 percent), and were also viewed as problems in Elk Grove Village, Lake Havasu City, and Sharpstown.

Residents' concerns about some community problems stemmed from unique situations in particular new communities. For example, Columbia was the only new community where more than 10 percent of the respondents were concerned with excessive developer control. It may be recalled from the discussion in chapter 8 that the major community institution in Columbia—the Columbia Park and Recreation Association—was controlled by the developer. Reston, where Gulf-Reston, Inc. succeeded Robert E. Simon, Jr. as the developer, was the only new community in which more than 10 percent of the respondents cited the developer's deviation from the community master plan as a serious problem. Freestanding Lake Havasu City, where residents had to rely on employment opportunities located within the community, was the only new community in which more than 10 percent of the respondents mentioned the lack of employment opportunities as a problem. Park Forest and Forest Park, where black in-migration had increased markedly since 1970, were the only new communities where more than 10 percent of the respondents were concerned with the character of race relations. Finally, the young, highly educated population of Columbia indicated the greatest concern with the status of social service programs and citizen participation.

Residents' Prognoses for the Future

The fact that new communities were facing many of the same problems as less planned conventional suburban communities was not unexpected. With the exception of Park Forest, each of the study communities was at an intermediate stage of development, and, as noted in the preceding chapters, developers have had to contend with a number of difficulties in providing, or negotiating for the provision of, many community services. Nevertheless, the existence of more extensive community planning and centralized direction of the development process might be expected to give new communities an edge in resolving problem situations and in evolving into much more desirable places to live than less planned conventional suburbs. To see whether the residents shared this belief, respondents were asked whether in five years they thought their communities would be better places to live, about the same, or not as good.

Five Years from Now

Less than a majority—37 percent—of the new community respondents thought their communities would be better places to live in five years. This proportion was only slightly, but significantly, greater than the 33 percent of the conventional community respondents who were similarly optimistic

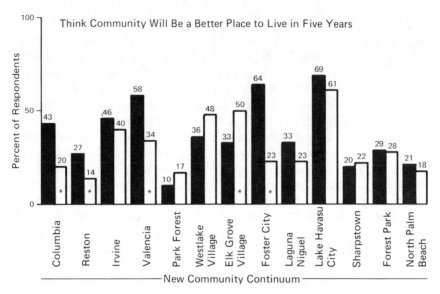

Figure 16-3. Residents' Prognoses for Community Improvement

about their communities' futures. The most frequent response in both settings—40 percent of the new and 42 percent of the conventional community respondents—was that the community would be about the same. Finally, 23 percent of the new and 25 percent of the conventional community respondents thought their communities would be worse places in which to live.

There was greater variation in optimism about the future among the study new communities than there was between new and conventional communities. As illustrated in figure 16-3, residents' prognoses about their communities' future were not associated with the new community continuum. On the other hand, there was some association between the stage of community development and residents' optimism. Residents who were living in older new communities, such as Park Forest, Sharpstown, Forest Park, and North Palm Beach, were generally less likely than others to think their communities would be better places to live in five years.

In four new communities—Laguna Niguel, Park Forest, Reston, and Sharpstown—a higher proportion of the respondents thought that their community would be a worse place to live in five years than thought that it would be better. Sharpstown and Park Forest were the two oldest new communities in the study and had gone furthest toward achieving their

target populations. Residents could see little prospect of additional community services, and once new sections of these communities were beginning to show the effects of age. For example, the concluding section of Park
Forest's 1972 Comprehensive Plan summary discussed the need to consider redevelopment of a portion of the community. Obviously, over time
older new communities must become renewing communities if they are to
remain as highly desirable and livable residential environments. In Reston
and Laguna Niguel, on the other hand, the prospect of additional community facilities and services was evidently less encouraging to many residents than the negative implications of increased density and the increased
population.

With the exception of these four new communities, new community
residents were generally much more likely to think their communities
would improve over time than they were to think that they would become
worse places in which to live. The margin of difference in the proportion of
respondents who perceived improvements over those who thought things
would get worse ranged from a low of 7 percent in Westlake Village to
between 19 percent and 22 percent in Columbia, Irvine, and Elk Grove
Village to over 40 percent in Valencia, Foster City, and Lake Havasu City.

Making New Communities Better Places to Live

New community residents suggested a wide variety of improvements that
they thought would increase community livability. These changes are
summarized in table 16-5, which shows the percent of respondents who
offered each suggestion and the number of new communities in which
improvements were suggested by 10 percent or more of the respondents.

The most frequently mentioned type of improvement was the provision
of more and better community facilities. Recreational facilities—
mentioned by 20 percent of the respondents—topped the list of suggested
improvements. In addition, respondents in a number of communities
thought that the addition of more shopping facilities and more schools
would improve community livability. Relatively few respondents, on the
other hand, indicated that improvements in street patterns, provision of
bicycle routes, or additional health care facilities would make their communities better places in which to live.

The concern many respondents expressed for increasing population
and density was reflected in suggestions for improving community livability. For example, almost a fifth of the respondents thought that continued
growth of their new communities should be controlled and that higher
density development (townhouses and apartments) should be limited. This
strong sentiment for limited growth, if translated into more restrictive

Table 16-5
Suggested Improvements to Make the New Community a Better Place to Live

Suggested Improvement	Percent of Respondents Who Suggested Improvement[a]	Number of New Communities in Which Improvement Was Suggested by 10 Percent or More of Respondents
Improve community facilities		
Recreational facilities	20	12
Shopping facilities and commercial services	12	8
Schools	9	5
Streets and bicycle routes	5	1
Health care facilities	3	0
Maintain quality of the environment		
Limit and control growth/ reduce density	19	10
Protect natural areas from development	5	2
Improve maintenance of building exteriors and private yards	5	0
Improve maintenance and appearance of public and common open space	3	0
Improve public services		
Public transportation	5	2
Police protection	3	0
Other services (fire protection, garbage collection, water and sewer, etc.)	2	0
Change behavior of developer and local authorities		
Adhere to community master plan	5	1
Increase citizen participation	3	0
Improve local government	2	0
Improve developer-citizen relations	1	0
Change social character of community		
Encourage residents to care about their community	3	1
Recruit different type of resident	2	0
Improve race relations	1	0

Suggested Improvement	Percent of Respondents Who Suggested Improvement[a]	Number of New Communities in Which Improvement Was Suggested by 10 Percent or More of Respondents
Increase amount of development		
Provide more employment opportunities	2	1
Increase pace of development	1	0
Increase tax base through industrial and commercial development	1	1
Reduce cost of living		
Lower taxes	1	0
Reduce prices in general	1	0
Other responses		
Don't know what could be done	6	0
No improvements are needed— community is a good place to live	6	0
No improvements are possible— the situation is hopeless	2	0

[a]Responses add to more than 100 percent because some respondents mentioned more than one type of improvement.

zoning requirements, could be disastrous for the financial feasibility of many new community ventures. It also presents new community residents with a hard choice, though few residents may realize that they cannot have the best of both worlds. The provision of improved community facilities and services depends, in part, on the accumulation of an adequate supporting population. New community residents want the facilities and services, but many do not want the increased population density that is a necessary prerequisite for their provision. The only solution to this problem may be to inform the residents fully of a new community's anticipated population and the location of future high density development, and/or to remove control of population density from local government.

Increasing density also has implications for new community marketing. Because new communities are often located at the edge of or beyond the developing urban fringe during the initial years of development, developers have used the pastoral character of their communities' surroundings as an aide in marketing. In fact, as shown in table 16-1, just over a quarter of the new community respondents as a whole chose their communities, in part, because of the nearness to the outdoors and the natural environment. Over half of the respondents moved to Lake Havasu City, Laguna Niguel, and

Westlake Village because of the proximity of the natural environment, and between 25 percent and 50 percent chose Reston, Irvine, Valencia, and Columbia for this reason. Having moved to a new community because of its natural surroundings, it is understandable that residents would seek to preserve this valued feature by limiting population growth. While extolling the virtues of a "City in the Country," developers might diminish residents' adverse reactions to continued development by apprising them fully about future development plans before and after they have occupied homes in the new community and by making clear the association between population growth and improved facilities and services.

Better community facilities and maintenance of the quality of the environment accounted for over half of the respondents' suggestions for making their communities better places to live. However, other suggestions were also made. Some respondents pointed to the need for improved public services, including better public transportation and police protection. Changes in developers' and local officials' behavior were mentioned. Under this heading were suggestions that deviations from the master plan be eliminated; that citizen participation in community governance be increased; that local government operate in a more honest and aboveboard fashion, and that the developer improve his relations with the citizenry.

Aspects of the social character of the community were infrequently mentioned. The few that were included residents' perceptions of the need to get people to care about what was occurring in the community, suggestions that the population composition of the community should change, and statements about the need for improved race relations.

Not surprising in view of their concern with increasing density, few respondents suggested that increased or accelerated development would make their communities better places to live. Respondents' concern about the availability of jobs was centered in Lake Havasu City, where 15 percent indicated that this improvement was needed. Although many respondents wanted improved community facilities and public services, only 1 percent indicated that an improved tax base would lead to improved community livability. Again, major interest in this aspect of community development came from Lake Havasu City, where 10 percent of the respondents mentioned the need for commercial and industrial development to improve the tax base. Lake Havasu City respondents were also those most in favor of an accelerated pace of development, though this suggestion was also put forward by a higher than average proportion of Foster City and Valencia respondents, probably because of their concern—shown in table 16-4— about high taxes. Residents of these two communities were also those most likely to state that lower taxes would make their communities better places to live.

Implications for New Community Development

The reasons residents gave for moving to new communities, the improvements they achieved as a result of the move, and the statistical correlates of their overall community ratings suggest that four factors are key elements of community livability. These include satisfaction with: (1) the dwelling unit; (2) the immediate neighborhood; (3) the proximity of the natural environment and countryside; and (4) the convenience of community facilities, particularly recreational facilities. In general, new communities have met these conditions for a livable environment. An overwhelming proportion of the residents rated each new community as an excellent or good place to live.

At the same time, however, residents' satisfaction with new communities was only marginally greater than that expressed by the residents of conventional suburban communities. The reason for the similarity in ratings is that new communities have yet to improve on many of those aspects of the home and environment that are most important in residents' choice of a community and that are most associated with perceptions of community livability. As shown in chapter 9, dwelling unit satisfaction was nearly identical in both settings, as were residents' perceptions of the key factors associated with neighborhood livability—appearance and upkeep. Clearly, the character of the dwelling unit and the immediate neighborhood must be given top priority if future new community development is to result in markedly better community livability than that offered by conventional suburban growth.

Although community facilities were not often mentioned as key factors in the decision to move to a new community, and, with the exception of recreational facilities, were not strongly associated with livability evaluations, they were mentioned as reasons for rating communities highly, or as major community problems when they were unavailable, inconvenient, or of poor quality. They were frequently among residents' suggestions for making their communities better places to live. New community residents were most concerned with recreational facilities, shopping facilities, and schools. Transportation and health care were less often viewed as aspects of community livability, though transportation facilities and services were occasionally viewed as major community problems and elicited the greatest support for increased community expenditures. As discussed in the preceding chapters, there are a variety of ways for effectively providing these service systems through new community development.

17 The Quality of Life in New Communities

A popular premise of the new community movement has been the expectation that residents will find the nature of their lives improved significantly through the new community experience. In essence, new communities are believed to provide and arrange a better physical environment so as to foster more opportunities for personally satisfying encounters by the individual and the family.

Implicit in this reasoning is the assumption that factors amenable to manipulation by community planners are, in fact, important components in residents' evaluations of the overall quality of their lives. It also assumes that there is a more or less direct link between objective characteristics of communities and residents' subjective perceptions of life quality. Recent research has cast doubt on both of these assumptions.

Robert W. Marans and Willard Rodgers (1972, p. 102) found that both housing satisfaction and satisfaction with community livability were positively associated with the quality of life as perceived by respondents from a national sample. However, in comparison with respondents' evaluations of other attributes of their lives, housing and community satisfaction were relatively unimportant. They ranked eighth and tenth, respectively, among ten life domains. Instead, assessments of overall life quality depended on satisfaction with leisure activities, family life, work, friendships, and marriage (also see Frank M. Andrews and Stephen B. Withey 1974a; 1974b).

The research of both Marans and Rodgers (1972) and James R. Murray (1974) indicates that a number of factors may intervene between objective characteristics of the environment and residents' expressions of satisfaction. In the first place, people differ in their perceptions of various attributes of community characteristics and the values they place on these attributes. For example, psychophysical studies have shown that individuals do not often "correctly" perceive their environments, though they do systematically translate physical characteristics into subjective images. Second, the standards a person uses in judging an attribute influence how it is assessed. Such standards could include a person's expectations prior to moving to a community, the desired or ideal value of the attribute, or the perceived character of the attribute in relation to a person's past experience or perception of its character in other settings. Finally, a person's emotional state at the time an evaluation is given may influence satisfaction levels. Because of these intervening variables, the relationship between objective characteristics of the environment and subjective expressions of satisfaction with the quality of life may be rather weak.

Even though previous studies have minimized the impact of community and environmental factors on perceptions of overall life quality, it was hypothesized that if any population were likely to respond to environmental characteristics, it would be those persons who had moved into planned new communities. To delineate the relationship between the community and subjective perceptions of life quality, residents were asked, first, what they felt were the key determinants of their quality of life; second, in these terms whether moving to their present community had improved the quality of their lives; and third, how satisfied they were with a series of life domains and with life as a whole.

Residents' Perspectives on the Quality of Life

Polls and household surveys have posed a variety of questions asking people to define what they felt their happiness and life satisfaction most depended upon (see Hazel F. Erskine 1973). Although responses have varied somewhat with the phrasing of particular questions, several types of factors are mentioned with regularity. These include satisfaction with aspects of life that are clearly interpersonal in nature—family, marriage, and friendships—as well as others with less of a social dimension, such as one's job, health, and economic security. References to aspects of residential communities and/or environmental quality (other than occasional references to housing) are virtually absent from the responses elicited.

In order to give new and conventional community respondents an opportunity to say in their own words what they saw as the most important determinants of their quality of life, they were asked at the very start of the interview: ''There's quite a bit of talk these days about the overall 'quality' of people's lives. What does the phrase 'quality of life' mean to you—that is, what would you say are the main things the overall 'quality' of your own life depends on?''

Responses to the question are summarized in table 17-1. The results show that residents living in new communities and conventional communities mentioned virtually the same factors as contributors to their quality of life. Most frequently mentioned was economic security. Beyond that, family life, personal strengths (such as honesty, fortitude, and intelligence), and friendships were mentioned by over 20 percent of the respondents. Living in an attractive physical environment was the fifth most frequent factor in both new and conventional communities—mentioned by 18 percent and 16 percent of the residents in those areas, respectively. The quality and accessibility of community facilities and services ranked

Table 17-1
Residents' Perceptions of Factors Contributing to Their Quality of Life

Contributing Factors	Percent of Respondents[a]	
	New Communities	Conventional Communities
Economic security	34	32
Family life	27	30
Personal strengths/values	23	23
Social relationships (other than family)	20[b]	16
Physical environment (attractive, spacious, close to nature, etc.)	18	16
Contentment/well-being/happiness	17	15
Job satisfaction	16	19[b]
Leisure/recreational activities	16[b]	13
Health	15	14
Religious values	11	11
Being a good parent	10	12
Quality and accessibility of community facilities and services	8[b]	4
Housing	8	9

[a]Responses add to more than 100 percent because some respondents mentioned more than one contributing factor.
[b]Statistically significant difference at 0.05 level of confidence.

eleventh among new community respondents (mentioned by 8 percent) and thirteenth among conventional community respondents (mentioned by 4 percent).

The mentions centering on the physical environment and community facilities and services suggest that new community residents hold somewhat different views of the quality of life than those indicated by the results of previous national studies. However, while new community residents were more likely to mention the physical environment, vis-à-vis the results of previous studies, they were no more likely to do so than the residents of the less planned, paired conventional communities. On the other hand, the availability and quality of community facilities and services, though not often mentioned, were cited more frequently by new community respondents than by respondents in either previous national studies or by respondents living in the paired conventional communities.

The importance residents attached to both the character of the physical environment and the quality and convenience of community facilities and services varied among the new communities. See figure 17-1. Although differences were not necessarily statistically significant, for 9 of the 13 paired comparisons, new community residents were more likely than resi-

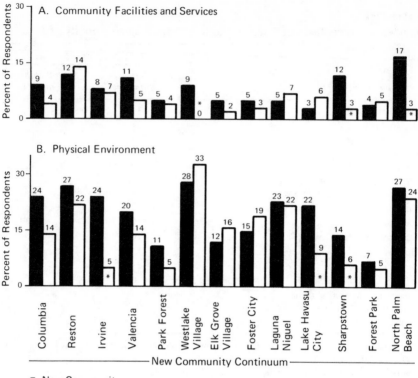

Figure 17-1. Community Facilities and the Physical Environment as Determinants of the Quality of Life

dents of the conventional communities to perceive community facilities and services, and, for 10 of the paired comparisons, the quality of the physical environment as key determinants of their quality of life. In short, from new community residents' perspectives, factors that can be influenced by community planning and new community development are not infrequently viewed as important aspects of their quality of life.

The Effect of Moving to the Present Community on the Quality of Life

Since many new community residents felt that access to the natural environment and the quality of community facilities were better in their present new communities than the communities from which they had moved, it is not surprising that the move was also associated with perceptions of an improved quality of life. In fact, two thirds of both the new community respondents and the conventional community respondents said their life had been improved by the move.

Among the new communities, the favorable responses were most frequent in Elk Grove Village (76 percent perceived improvements in the quality of their lives) and in Westlake Village (75 percent perceived improvements). At the lower end of the scale, less than 60 percent of the respondents in Forest Park and Sharpstown were as impressed with the consequences of their move to those communities. As shown in figure 17-2, perceptions of an improved quality of life were not associated with a new community's place on the new community continuum.

Although comparisons of new communities with their paired conventional communities show no differences that quite attain statistical significance, the new communities that did best on this basis (with from 8 to 11 percent more favorable responses) were Columbia, Reston, Irvine, and North Palm Beach. Residents living in the conventional communities were more positive about improvements in their quality of life by about the same margin in the cases of Lansing (paired with Park Forest) and Kingman (paired with Lake Havasu City). The highest proportion (81 percent) of people who felt their lives had improved lived in the Agoura/Malibu Junction conventional community that was paired with Westlake Village.

In addition to identifying differences in perceived improvements in the quality of life across communities, it is also important to: (1) identify variation in such perceptions among new community residents; and (2) determine whether perceptions of improvements in some community characteristics are more associated with perceptions of improvements in life quality than others.

As has been found in other quality of life analyses (e.g., Marans and Rodgers 1972, and Andrews and Withey 1974a), residents' personal and housing characteristics did not account for much of the variation in perceptions of improvements in the quality of life. However, some statistically significant differences among respondents were apparent. For example, about 5 percent more women than men (69 percent versus 64 percent) thought the move to a new community had led to improvements in their quality of life. Married persons were about 12 percent more likely to see improvements than nonmarried persons (68 percent versus 56 percent). Persons with family incomes under $10,000 were less likely (61 percent) to feel their quality of life had improved than persons with average incomes (65 percent), above average incomes (70 percent), or affluent respondents (65 percent). Also, new community residents below age 35 were more likely to report that their quality of life had improved (69 percent) than were residents age 65 and over (60 percent). Black residents, however, were just

388

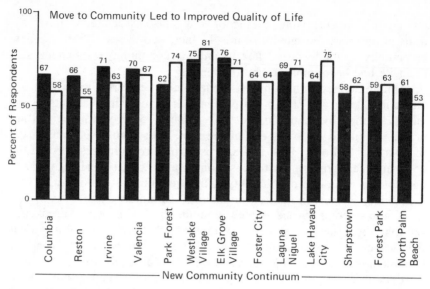

- New Community
- Conventional Community
- Statistically Significant Difference[a]

[a]None at the 0.05 level of confidence in this figure.

Figure 17-2. Residents' Perception of Improvement in Quality of Life After Moving to Present Community

as likely as white residents to feel that their quality of life had been improved, and there was little difference in such perceptions among respondents with varying amounts of formal education.

There were also some statistically significant differences among persons living in different types of housing. Owners were more likely to see their quality of life improved by the move to a new community than were renters (69 percent versus 58 percent). Related to tenure, improvement was reported by a higher proportion of persons living in single-family detached homes (69 percent) than by those living in townhouses (64 percent) or apartments (58 percent). Higher housing cluster density, however, was not uniformly associated with less frequent perceptions of improvement in the quality of life. While only 59 percent of the respondents living in relatively high-density situations (10 or more units per acre) indicated that their quality of life had improved, a similar proportion—63 percent—of those living in low-density environments (less than three dwelling units per acre) reported the same result. Reported improvements in the quality of life were highest (70 percent indicated improvement) among respondents who were living in medium-density housing (four to five dwelling units per acre).

Residents' perceptions that various aspects of their communities were better than the communities from which they had moved were summarized in table 16-1 of the preceding chapter. Perceived improvements in the community as a place to raise children and of the type of people living in the neighborhood (particularly the perceived friendliness of neighbors) were most strongly associated with perceived improvements in the quality of life. Better recreational facilities, neighborhood appearance, layout and space and construction of the home, and opportunities for participation in community life were important, but less so. These results help explain why new community residents were no more likely than conventional community residents to perceive improvements in their quality of life. As shown in table 16-1, there were no significant differences in the proportions of new and conventional community respondents who perceived improvements (over their former communities) in the community as a good place to raise children, type of people living in the neighborhood, neighborhood appearance, or layout and space of the home. Of the top seven housing and community attributes associated with reported improvements in the quality of life, only recreational facilities and opportunities for participation in community life were rated better than the previous community significantly more often by new community respondents.

Residents' Satisfaction with Their Lives as a Whole

In addition to asking respondents whether the move to their present community improved their quality of life, information was also obtained about satisfaction with life as a whole and about the satisfaction people derive from various aspects (domains) of their lives, such as work, leisure, standard of living, family, and the like. This portion of the study was designed to parallel a pioneering investigation of the quality of life in the nation, which was being conducted by Angus Campbell, Phillip E. Converse, and Willard L. Rodgers at The University of Michigan.[a]

Both the present study and the Campbell-Converse-Rodgers investigation gauged people's overall assessment of the quality of their lives by responses to the question: "We have talked about various parts of your life; now I want to ask you about your life as a whole. How satisfied are you with your life as a whole these days?" The respondents were asked to answer using a seven-point scale ranging from "completely satisfied" to "completely dissatisfied."

New community residents tended to be highly satisfied with their lives. Only 12 percent of the respondents placed themselves on the neutral or dissatisfied part of the seven-point scale (responses four through seven). In

[a] Initial results from the Campbell-Converse-Rodgers study are summarized in "Measuring the Quality of Life in America" (1974).

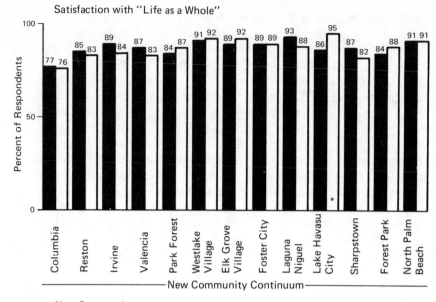

Satisfaction with "Life as a Whole"

■ New Community
□ Conventional Community
* Statistically Significant Difference

Figure 17-3. Residents' Overall Life Satisfaction

contrast, 31 percent said they were completely satisfied with their lives (response one), while another 57 percent were satisfied (responses two and three). However, the distribution of responses in new communities was virtually identical to that of the conventional communities where 31 percent of the respondents were completely satisfied, 55 percent were satisfied, and 13 percent were neutral or dissatisfied with their lives as a whole.

In comparison with responses to the same question obtained by Campbell, Converse, and Rodgers from a 1971 national cross-section sample, both new and conventional community respondents were somewhat more likely to report complete satisfaction with their lives. For example, among persons with family incomes of $17,000 and up (the category most comparable to the new and conventional community samples), 26 percent of the 1971 national cross-section respondents indicated complete satisfaction with their lives versus 31 percent of both the new and conventional community respondents. About the same proportion of respondents, however, indicated that they were neutral or dissatisfied with their lives (11 percent of the 1971 national cross-section respondents, 12 percent of the new community respondents, and 13 percent of the conventional community respondents).

The highest proportions of satisfied (response categories one, two, or three) new community respondents were in Laguna Niguel (93 percent), followed closely by Westlake Village (91 percent), North Palm Beach (91 percent), and Irvine, Elk Grove Village, and Foster City (89 percent each). As illustrated by figure 17-3, residents' satisfaction with their lives was not associated with the new community continuum. Also, there was only one case in which there was a significant difference in reports of satisfaction between a new community and its paired conventional community. The Kingman respondents were more satisfied with their lives than were respondents living in Lake Havasu City.

Various groups of new community residents found their lives significantly less satisfying than others. Among all new community respondents, 88 percent indicated that they were satisfied with their lives. However, this was true for only 69 percent of the new community nonmarried respondents, 76 percent of those with below average incomes (under $10,000), 80 percent of the black respondents,[b] and 84 percent of those who rented and of those were living in apartments.

On the other hand, women were as satisfied with their lives as men. In fact, a higher proportion of women (35 percent) than men (27 percent) reported that they were completely satisfied. Age had little influence on satisfaction versus dissatisfaction with life, but there were rather striking differences in complete satisfaction among different age groups. The proportion of completely satisfied respondents increased with increasing age—from 26 percent of the respondents under age 35 to 40 percent of those who were 65 years old or older. Also, while there was little variation in satisfaction versus dissatisfaction among respondents with different amounts of formal education, complete satisfaction did vary. Respondents with less formal education were more likely to report complete satisfaction with their lives than those with more formal education.

As with people's overall satisfaction with their lives as a whole, these results are very similar to those reported by the Campbell-Converse-Rodgers study at The University of Michigan. (See "Measuring the Quality of Life in America," 1974.) Thus, it does not appear that new community development has led to very different life satisfaction—either for the population as a whole or for particular population groups—than is characteristic of people in the nation as a whole.

---

[b]In new communities with relatively large concentrations of blacks, including Columbia, Reston, Park Forest, and Forest Park, differences between the proportions of white and black respondents who were satisfied with their lives were not statistically significant. Because black respondents were concentrated in communities where the proportion of respondents who were satisfied with their lives was lower than other new communities, they appeared to be less satisfied than white respondents. This difference disappears when community by community differences are controlled.

Components of Life Satisfaction

Assessments of ten life domains—many of which parallel the factors respondents mentioned as determinants of their quality of life—are summarized in table 17-2.[c] Respondents' satisfaction with various aspects of their lives varied from one domain to another. Satisfaction with marriage drew the highest rating among new community respondents. Respondents also tended to be satisfied with their communities, neighborhoods, personal health, family life, dwelling units, standard of living, and jobs, all of which received positive evaluations from between 85 percent and 90 percent of those interviewed. The least satisfaction was expressed with the use of leisure time and with housework.

Although residents tended to be satisfied with each of these aspects of their lives, the distribution of residents who gave the most positive responses on each scale (shown in parentheses in table 17-2) indicates that in many cases a number of persons saw room for improvement. For example, a majority of the respondents gave the most positive rating possible to only three life domains—marriage, the neighborhood, and family life. Less than a third of the respondents were highly satisfied with the use of their leisure time and housework, which again ranked at the bottom for the ten life domains.

A significantly higher proportion of new community respondents than conventional community respondents gave positive evaluations to four of the ten domains—community, personal health, standard of living, and use of leisure time. In each case, however, the difference was not large.

For most of the life domains there was a sizable range in positive responses across new communities. Laguna Niguel residents, who were most satisfied with their lives as a whole, proved to be the most satisfied with four aspects of their lives. They gave the highest ratings to the use of leisure time (80 percent were satisfied), marriage (tied with Elk Grove Village, 95 percent), the community (96 percent), and their neighborhood (tied with Westlake Village, 94 percent).

Westlake Village residents, who were tied with North Palm Beach residents for second place in terms of satisfaction with life as a whole, gave the highest ratings to three aspects of their lives—their dwelling unit (93 percent were satisfied), neighborhood (tied with Laguna Niguel, 94 percent), and job (93 percent). Other new communities where residents were particularly satisfied with some aspects of their lives included Foster City (health, 94 percent); North Palm Beach (standard of living, 94 percent);

---

[c]Willard Rodgers of the Survey Research Center at The University of Michigan provided advice on the salient life domains to include in the household survey interview schedule when it was being prepared during the summer and fall of 1972. These items were drawn from his work on the Campbell-Converse-Rodgers study.

Table 17-2
Satisfaction with Ten Life Domains

Life Domains	Percent Giving Positive Evaluations[a]			
	New Communities		Conventional Communities	
Marriage[b]	93	(64)	93	(66)
Community livability[c]	90[d]	(49)[d]	86	(42)
Neighborhood livability[c]	89	(59)	90	(57)
Personal health[b]	88[d]	(50)[d]	84	(45)
Family life[e]	87	(56)	88	(57)
Dwelling unit[b]	86	(39)	85	(39)
Standard of living[b]	86[d]	(38)	82	(36)
Job[b]	85	(43)	83	(41)
Use of leisure time[b]	72[d]	(31)	65	(29)
Housework[e]	71	(31)	69	(31)

[a]The percent of respondents who gave the most positive responses on each scale are shown in parentheses.
[b]Seven-point scale.
[c]Five-point scale.
[d]Difference between new communities and conventional communities is statistically significant at the 0.05 level of confidence.
[e]Four-point scale.

Lake Havasu City (family life, 92 percent); and Forest Park (housework, 79 percent).

Although respondents in new communities differed from one another in their satisfaction with various life domains, they did not often differ from respondents in the paired conventional communities. Of 130 possible differences (10 life domains times 13 paired comparisons), new community residents were significantly more satisfied for only 9 percent of the paired comparisons. The biggest differences in satisfaction were with community livability (respondents in 3 new communities gave significantly higher ratings), personal health (respondents in 2 new communities gave significantly higher ratings), and standard of living (respondents in 2 new communities gave significantly higher ratings). The conventional community residents were significantly more satisfied with various life domains for only 4 percent of the paired comparisons. For 87 percent of the comparisons, however, differences in satisfaction were not statistically significant.

Differences in overall life satisfaction among various groups of new community residents were paralleled by differences in satisfaction with life domains. For example, with the exception of marriage and family life, respondents with lower family incomes tended to be significantly less satisfied with each of the other domains than more affluent respondents. As might be expected, income had the strongest effect on satisfaction with standard of living. While 79 percent of the respondents with below average incomes and 81 percent of those with average incomes were satisfied with their standard of living, satisfaction increased to 87 percent of those with above average incomes and to 93 percent of the affluent respondents.

Along with income, age had the most consistent association with life domain satisfaction. Younger respondents were significantly more satisfied with their health than older respondents, but for each of the other life domains as respondents' ages increased so did their satisfaction. The association between age and satisfaction was strongest for satisfaction with the standard of living and with the dwelling unit, both of which reflect the improved economic circumstances of more mature households.

Although the women's liberation movement has drawn increasing attention to the problems of women in our society, those living in new communities tended to be more satisfied with various aspects of their lives than were men. Men were significantly more likely to report satisfaction with their health, but women were significantly more satisfied with their standard of living, jobs (if they were employed), family life, use of leisure time, dwelling units, and immediate neighborhoods. The only aspects of their lives where men and women were equally satisfied were marriage and community livability.

Black respondents living in new communities tended to be more satisfied than whites with their homes and immediate neighborhoods, but were somewhat less satisfied with their standard of living and use of leisure time. There were no significant racial differences in community satisfaction or satisfaction with health, the job, marriage, or family life.

The lower satisfaction with life indicated by renters and persons living in apartments was accompanied by lower satisfaction with several life domains. In particular, these persons were less satisfied with their homes, the livability of the immediate neighborhoods and of the community as a whole, and, reflecting their lower family incomes and tendency to be single, with their standard of living and family life.

Satisfaction with Life Domains and Overall Life Satisfaction

The statistical relationships between respondents' satisfactions with various life domains and their satisfaction with life as a whole in many respects paralleled respondents' own reports of the factors that contributed to their life quality (see table 17-1). Economic security was mentioned most frequently as a determinant of the quality of life, while respondents' satisfaction with their standard of living had the strongest association with their reported overall life satisfaction. The character of family life was the second most frequently mentioned contributor to the quality of life; satisfaction with family life had the third strongest influence on life satisfaction. Other life domains that were highly associated with life satisfaction included satisfaction with the use of leisure time, with the job, and with marriage.

Respondents' satisfaction with aspects of the physical environment had less influence on their overall satisfaction with life than satisfaction with those domains that were more personal in nature or that reflected their economic well-being. In the strength of their influence on overall life satisfaction, among the ten life domains considered, satisfaction with the dwelling unit ranked seventh; satisfaction with the livability of the immediate neighborhood ranked ninth; and satisfaction with overall community livability ranked tenth.

Improving the Quality of Life in New Communities

Since the quality of life depends on many factors that cannot be greatly influenced by community planning and adjustments in the physical environment, there are obviously limits to the extent to which new community development should be or can be expected to produce a better quality of life than could be experienced in other settings. Nevertheless, the fact that over a quarter of the new community respondents as a whole, and over a third of the respondents in some new communities, mentioned the quality of the environment and community facilities as key determinants of their quality of life suggests that planners and developers should not dismiss this subject as irrelevant to their endeavors or as something that is beyond their influence.

Analyses of factors associated with perceived improvements in the quality of life after moving to new communities and of overall life satisfaction indicate a number of ways in which planners and developers can improve residents' perceptions of the quality of life in new communities. However, because people with different personal and family characteristics and people living in different types of housing have different needs, the same actions will not be relevant to the perceived quality of life of all residents.

For example, to improve the quality of life of the residents of single-family neighborhoods, many of whom either had children living in their households or were anticipating child rearing, actions could be taken to improve perceptions that the neighborhood and community are good places to raise children. These might include giving particular attention to the safety of streets, provision of a variety of recreational facilities in close proximity to homes, and increased recreational programming for children.

In the case of townhouse residents, the data indicate that planners should pay particular attention to recreational facilities, which were highly associated with perceptions of improved life quality upon moving to new communities, and to improving people's satisfaction with the use of their leisure time, which was highly associated with townhouse residents' satisfaction with their lives as a whole. Since the availability of recreational facilities was not highly related to leisure satisfaction, planners should give as much attention to recreational programming and the establishment and functioning of community institutions offering rewarding outlets for people's discretionary time as they currently do to recreational facilities.

Among apartment dwellers, perceptions of an improved quality of life after the move were highly associated with perceived improvements in the microenvironment—particularly, the friendliness of people in the neighborhood, neighborhood appearance, and the layout and space of the dwelling. Overall satisfaction with life among apartment residents was highly associated with satisfaction with family life. By designing projects with these values in mind, apartment dwellers' perceptions of the quality of their lives, which tended to be much lower than those of other new community residents, might be significantly improved.

Analysis of the associations between community characteristics and perceived improvements in the quality of life gained from the move to new communities and between life domains and overall life satisfaction highlight concerns of particular importance to other groups of new community residents. For example, key variables affecting the quality of life of men and women differed. The quality of life perceptions of men were strongly affected by their perceptions of neighborhood appearance, while women were influenced more by the friendliness of neighbors. Job satisfaction was particularly important to men, while women's satisfaction with their lives was strongly influenced by their satisfaction with the use of their leisure time. Older residents' (age 65 or more) quality of life perceptions were more dependent on the layout and space of their homes, cost of living in the community, and satisfaction with the use of their leisure time than was the case for younger persons. In comparison with white persons, black residents' quality of life perceptions were more dependent on their perceptions of opportunities for participation in community life and satisfaction with their dwelling units.

In sum, by being sensitive to the needs expressed by various groups in the community, planners and developers can have a positive influence on residents' perceptions of their quality of life. Although new community development has not yet resulted in life quality perceptions that are much different from those of conventional community residents, closer attention to key community characteristics is more likely to have this effect.

**Part V
Federally Assisted New
Communities and the Target
Populations**

18 Federally Assisted New Communities: Two Case Studies

With the passage of federal new communities legislation in 1968 and 1970, Congress and the Department of Housing and Urban Development (HUD) opened a new chapter in new community development in the United States. Through public-private partnership the pace of new community development was to be significantly expanded. New communities for the first time were viewed as keystones in an emerging national urban growth policy. Equally important, in exchange for federal backing of their long-term debt and various other forms of assistance (see chapter 3), new community developers and the communities they created were expected to contribute to the accomplishment of a broad range of economic, social, environmental, and governmental objectives that were sometimes present, but rarely emphasized, in wholly private new community ventures.

In order to insure the orderly growth of undeveloped suburban areas, plans for federally assisted new communities were to be consistent with existing regional and metropolitan growth objectives. To reduce economic and racial polarization in the nation, new communities were to provide a substantial amount of housing for low- and moderate-income families and were to be open to all people, regardless of race, religion, sex, or ethnic origin. All forms of environmental pollution were to minimized; sensitivity to the natural environment was to be stressed; and development was to be guided by the highest standards of design quality. What is more, federally assisted new communities were viewed as laboratories for testing new solutions to long-standing domestic problems. These were to include not only technological advances but also innovations in the design of social service delivery systems and new forms of government.

In contrast to the physical design emphasis of new communities begun in the 1950s and 1960s, the federally assisted new communities of the 1970s were to consider and plan for virtually every aspect of community life. As stated by HUD Assistant Secretary Samuel C. Jackson,

They are communities whose creators are sensitive not only to the need for diversity and innovation in the physical planning sense, but in social planning as well. This is as it should be; in the final analysis, social questions are the really important ones, for the final measure of new communities is not convenience or reduction in urban sprawl for their own sake but the quality of life they sustain (1972, p. 7).

In sum, the federal new communities program was designed to produce nothing short of a new generation of new communities. These communities

399

would provide opportunities for advancement in every facet of the community building process and bring about a more humane and livable urban environment.

Concept and reality, unfortunately, do not always coincide. The federal new communities program was begun with very high aspirations, but delivered few resources to assist in their realization. The paucity of federal support and crippling effects of the national economic recession, which began in 1973, combined to produce a struggle for survival among the new generation of new communities participating in the federal program. Quite naturally, attention within the federal bureaucracy and the new communities industry has shifted away from the goals of the program to more pressing concerns for the economic viability of assisted projects. In the long run, however, continuance of the federal presence in the new community development will depend on more than financial considerations. Federally assisted new communities not only must survive as financially sound undertakings, they must also produce benefits that could not be readily achieved through conventional suburban growth.

Because federally assisted new communities are in the initial phases of development, it is still too early to determine whether, or to what extent, they will accomplish the objectives of the new communities program. Nevertheless, a first reading on their performance is possible, if it is kept in mind that both objective conditions and residents' responses to their living environments will change during successive stages of development.

Two federally assisted new communities—Jonathan, Minnesota, and Park Forest South, Illinois—were selected for a baseline evaluation. Among the 17 new communities that are eligible to receive federal loan guarantees and/or other assistance under the provisions of the 1970 Urban Growth and New Community Development Act (see table 18-1), these two were furthest along in terms of planning and development when the sample communities were chosen in 1972. Because only two communities are examined—no other federally assisted new communities had an adequate population from which to gauge residents' responses—there are limitations on the generalization of Jonathan's and Park Forest South's experience to the entire federal new communities program. Nevertheless, they do provide an early empirical picture of the benefits from the program and benchmarks for comparison with future surveys of these two and other federally assisted new communities.

The Communities and Their Residents

Origins and Planning

Jonathan is located in rural Carver County 25 miles southwest of downtown Minneapolis within the Twin Cities Metropolitan Area. The planning area

Table 18-1
New Community Projects Approved by the Department of Housing and Urban Development as of January 1, 1974

New Community	Guarantee Commitment Date	Amount	Project Agreement Date	Projected[a] Dwellings	Population
Jonathan, Minn.	2/70	$21,000,000	10/70	15,000	50,000
St. Charles Communities, Md.	6/70	24,000,000	12/70	25,000	75,000
Park Forest South, Ill.	6/70	30,000,000	3/71	37,000	110,000
Flower Mound, Tex.	12/70	18,000,000	10/71	18,000	64,000
Maumelle, Ark.	12/70	7,500,000	12/71	14,000	45,000
Cedar-Riverside, Minn.	6/71	24,000,000	12/71	13,000	30,000
Riverton, N.Y.	12/71	12,000,000	5/72	8,000	26,000
San Antonio Ranch, Tex.	2/72	18,000,000	NS	29,000	88,000
The Woodlands, Tex.	4/72	50,000,000	8/72	47,000	150,000
Gananda, N.Y.	4/72	22,000,000	12/72	17,000	56,000
Soul City, N.C.	6/72	14,000,000	NS	13,000	44,000
Radisson, N.Y.	8/72	NA	NA	5,000	18,000
Harbison, S.C.	10/72	13,000,000	NS	6,000	23,000
Roosevelt Island, N.Y.	12/72	NA	NA	5,000	18,000
Shenandoah, Ga.	2/73	40,000,000	NS	23,000	70,000
Newfields, Oh.	10/73	32,000,000	11/73	13,000	40,000
Beckett, N.J.	10/73	35,500,000	NS	20,000	60,000

Source: Comptroller General of the United States 1974, p. 54.
NS = Project Agreement not signed as of January 1, 1974
NA = Not applicable—loan guarantee not requested

[a]Based on Project Agreement and does not reflect subsequent revisions.

for the community encompasses 8,166 acres of rolling hills interspersed with wooded areas along a ravine system that runs through the property. The site and surrounding region has historically been used for agricultural purposes. Jonathan is located a short distance north of the farm-center community of Chaska, which has over 5,000 residents.

The community traces its origin to the vision of the late Henry T. McKnight, a former Minnesota state senator with interests in downtown real estate, land development, and cattle ranching. McKnight was noted for his concern for natural resource development and conservation and, as a state senator, was author of the Minnesota Omnibus Outdoor Recreation Act. In the winter of 1964-65 he visited several English new towns and Reston and Columbia in the United States. McKnight saw the potential of new community development as an alternative to conventional suburban growth and, upon his return to Minneapolis, began intensive study for a new community in the Twin Cities area. After consideration of three potential sites for the community, land north of Chaska—some of which was already owned by the McKnight family—was selected because of the availability of water, sewer, and other public utilities, its excellent access to existing and proposed transportation facilities, and McKnight's contacts with local officials.

In 1966 the Ace Development Corporation (subsequently to become the Jonathan Development Corporation) was formed to manage the development process and the Carver Company was organized to spearhead land acquisition. Architect-Planner Benjamin H. Cunningham was hired to work on plans for physical development and the firm of Robert Gladstone and Associates was retained to conduct market analyses and a financial roughout.

Between 1965 and 1970, when a Project Agreement with the Department of Housing and Urban Development was signed, the concept for Jonathan evolved through three stages. As originally envisioned, the community was to be developed on about 3,000 acres in two upper and middle-income residential villages with two golf courses, a commercial center, and a research and industrial park. However, on the basis of a financial analysis and development program prepared by Gladstone in 1966, the scope of the project was expanded to encompass 4,800 acres with a target population of 41,300 persons after a 20-year development period.

By early 1969, a sophisticated development strategy had evolved. To insure long-term financing of the proposed new community venture, the plan was submitted to the Department of Housing and Urban Development as part of Jonathan's application for a federal loan guarantee under Title IV of the 1968 Housing and Urban Development Act. The project area was expanded to 6,000 acres (and subsequently in the Project Agreement with HUD to over 8,000 acres), projected population was increased to approximately 50,000, industrial acreage was expanded from 500 acres to 1,989 acres (an increase of from 10 percent of the development site to 24 percent), and a commitment was made to provide over 6,500 housing units for low- and moderate-income families. Major adjustments in the plan were subsequently made in a 1972 revision of the 1970 General Development Plan approved by the Department of Housing and Urban Development, including reduction of the projected population at full development to 44,000.

The design concept for Jonathan is shaped by the existing road system and a 1,700-acre open space grid (21 percent of the site) following the natural ravines and drainage courses through the property. Within the matrix of highways and open space, five villages, each to house approximately 7,000 persons in a variety of housing types, are planned. Village centers are to be designed to provide for daily living, including shopping, post offices, municipal services, and elementary schools. The town center is to serve as a regional multifunctional center with major retail, medical, office, and entertainment facilities. In addition, some 15,000 persons will reside in apartments in the town center area. Adjacent to the town center is to be a learning center, which will contain facilities for higher education—colleges, business, and vocational schools—the central community library, major audio-visual centers, auditoriums, and athletic areas. Most of these facilities are to be jointly used by the proposed educational institutions and the community at large. Finally, four industrial centers are planned, the first occupying a 250-acre site immediately adjacent to the town center. The revised plan (New Communities Services, Inc. 1972) is to be implemented over a 20-year period, at the end of which time Jonathan is projected to have 44,000 residents housed in 16,286 dwelling units (40 percent low density and 60 percent medium density) and an employment base of over 23,000 jobs.

Because Minnesota law discourages the creation of new incorporated municipalities, Jonathan's developers decided at an early date to annex to the city of Chaska. In 1967 Chaska adopted a new city plan that corresponded with the proposed Jonathan development, Jonathan was announced to the public, and subsequently was annexed to the city. Reasons given for annexation to Chaska included the ability to use municipal bonding capacity to finance sewer and water trunk systems, roads, and other municipal facilities; the extension of existing municipal services, such as police and fire protection, to the development site; and protection of the new community and surrounding area through municipal zoning. In addition, Chaska is eligible to receive federal funds for open space and various public facilities to be developed in Jonathan. For its part, the city of Chaska had earlier annexed a portion of the Jonathan development site in 1963 (prior to the proposal to build a new community), and was further protecting its sphere of influence from adverse annexation by the neighboring community of Chanhassen.

Park Forest South is located in Will County 32 miles south of the Chicago Loop and immediately south of Park Forest. Park Forest South's emergence as a full-scale new community venture, like Jonathan, took several years to unfold. The idea for the community originated with the late Nathan Manilow, who was one of the principal partners involved in the building of Park Forest. When Park Forest's development company, American Community Builders, Inc., disbanded in 1959, Manilow retained control of the Park Forest Plaza shopping center through his solely owned company, Park Forest Properties. In the mid-1960s Nathan Manilow and his son Lewis saw the potential for the expansion of Park Forest to a community of some 60,000 residents and began to assemble the necessary acreage to the south in Will County.

By 1966, 1,300 acres had been acquired by Park Forest Properties and the Manilows began to map out a development strategy. The initial acreage was adjacent to a small bankrupt subdivision called Wood Hill. In order to free themselves from zoning and subdivision control by Will County and to provide a foundation for the development of municipal services, they suggested that the residents of Wood Hill incorporate as a village. Through a contract zoning procedure allowed under Illinois law, they could then prezone and annex the adjacent acreage owned by Park Forest Properties. After acquiring the privately owned utility company that provided water and sewer service to the Wood Hill residents, the Manilow organization spent the remainder of 1966 and the first half of 1967 in developing plans for their proposed new community and in convincing the residents of its feasibility.

In June 1967, the 250 families living in the Wood Hill subdivision voted to incorporate as the Village of Park Forest South. The new village encompasses 100 acres. The Manilows then retained the firm of Carl L. Gardner and Associates to develop a comprehensive plan for the village and to prepare zoning and subdivision regulations. When these were completed, the Manilows requested annexation of 1,200 acres of adjoining land, which had been prezoned for a large planned unit development. This was accomplished on January 26, 1968 in exchange for a promise by the Manilows to support village fire protection and police services.

Park Forest South's development then proceeded on three fronts. To bolster the firm's financial base, additional equity participation in the venture was sought. In 1968 Mid-America Improvement Corporation (owned by Illinois Central Industries, Inc.) became a partner in the new community and in 1969 United States Gypsum Urban Development Corporation (owned by the United States Gypsum Company) was recruited. Each company took a 25 percent interest in the Park Forest South Development Company, with the Manilow Organization, Inc. acting as managing partner. Second, to generate the long-term capital required to develop a full-scale new community, assistance was sought from the Department of Housing and Urban Development under Title IV of the 1968 Housing and Urban Development Act. Third, to improve the image of the community, construction was begun on new single-family homes to round out the old Wood Hill project, and ground was broken for the community's first apartment development, even though the comprehensive plan required by HUD was still being prepared.

The development plan for Park Forest South was formalized in the Project Agreement signed with HUD on March 17, 1971. There it was agreed that Park Forest South would house a projected population of 110,000 persons at the completion of a 15-year development period. The planning area covered 8,291 acres, about half of which was then owned by the Park Forest South Development Company (New Community

Enterprises, Inc. was formed to develop the community). On this acreage some 35,000 housing units were to be constructed (69 percent rental and condominium apartments and 31 percent single-family detached units and townhouses), including an estimated 4,500 units to be constructed with assistance from federal low- and moderate-income housing programs.

Highlights of the development plan included the 753-acre campus of Governors State University, Governors Gateway Industrial Park, and a multifunctional town center. These three elements were to be connected by the "Main Drag"—a three-mile linear strip development containing major commercial, recreational, and municipal facilities served by a rapid transit system. Other commercial and institutional facilities were to be provided in a number of neighborhood centers designed to serve day-to-day needs. Rapid transit service to Chicago was to be initiated through an extension of the Illinois Central Gulf commuter rail line when 3,000 dwelling units had been constructed. A major hospital and medical complex with close connections with the university were planned. Almost 900 acres of major open space were to be provided, together with a more intimate open space network and path system running through individual neighborhoods. Finally, Park Forest South was expected to provide an employment base of over 28,000 jobs, giving most residents an opportunity to live and work within the same community if they so desired.

Status of Development

From the very beginning the pace of development in Jonathan and Park Forest South fell far behind the schedules projected in their project agreements with the Department of Housing and Urban Development. During 1971 and 1972 Jonathan achieved only 65 percent of its residential land sales projections and Park Forest South attained about 75 percent of its projections. These were still boom years for the national economy. When mortgage money began to dry up in 1973, builders' housing sales faltered and the inventory of developed land ready for home construction mounted in each community. As a result, land sales fell even further behind projected rates. By late in 1974 both new communities had defaulted on interest payments due on their federally guaranteed debentures. Jonathan subsequently dissolved its development staff and began searching for a buyer. To cover a $1 million interest loan payment made by the federal government in March of 1974, the three major partners in the development of Park Forest South injected $5 million in additional capital into the venture, buying 700 acres from their own company (with a long-term sell-back option). Both communities were seeking approval of additional federally guaranteed loans.

In spite of the severe financial problems they were experiencing, by 1973 Jonathan and Park Forest South had established a nucleus for further residential, commercial, and industrial growth. Some 420 dwelling units were occupied in Jonathan by 1,500 residents. Park Forest South had a population of 3,200 residents living in 1,310 dwelling units. Industrial development was proceeding apace. By the end of 1973, 45 firms had located in Jonathan, providing an employment base of 1,080 jobs. In Park Forest South, 925 persons were employed by 34 firms.

To provide a basis of comparison with less planned conventional suburban development, Jonathan and Park Forest South were matched with nearby communities that were beginning to experience rapid residential growth. The village of Chanhassen merged with Chanhassen Township in 1967 (at the same time Chaska was annexing Jonathan) to form a community of 16,000 acres. Located directly adjacent to Jonathan's northeast and eastern planning boundaries, Chanhassen's population had increased to 5,100 residents by the end of 1972. New development was occurring in apartment projects located near a small downtown core, and in a series of scattered subdivisions. Richton Park was located directly north of Park Forest South and adjacent to the western boundary of Park Forest. By the end of 1972 it had accumulated some 4,800 residents and had attracted a number of new residential projects. These included a large subdivision of single-family detached homes marketed under the FHA Section 235 subsidized home ownership program, as well as conventional single-family subdivisions, townhouses, and apartments.

Housing. The status of development of Jonathan, Park Forest South, and their paired conventional communities is summarized in table 18-2. The federally assisted communities provided a somewhat broader range of housing types, but housing costs, though lower in Jonathan than in Chanhassen, were somewhat higher in Park Forest South than in Richton Park. These differences are directly attributable to the availability of subsidized housing in each community.

Jonathan's developer, Henry T. McKnight, was firmly committed to the new town goal of population balance and had decided to provide some housing priced within the means of moderate-income families even before he decided to participate in the federal new communities program. By 1973 two subsidized housing projects had been completed. Farmhill Townhouses is a 96-unit rental project built under the FHA Section 236 program. Neighborhood 5 is an FHA Section 235 project consisting of 52 single-family ownership units. Neither project met with resistance from Chaska city officials or from the residents of Jonathan or Chaska who were living in nonsubsidized housing. The residents' acceptance of housing for moderate-income families was a direct result of the marketing of Jonathan

Table 18-2
Status of Development, 1973

Indicator	Jonathan	Chanhassen	Park Forest South	Richton Park
Population (1972)	1,500	5,100	3,200	4,800
Housing				
Dwelling units (total, 1972)	420	1,645	1,310	1,661
Tenure (percent of respondents)				
Own	52	59	68	66
Rent	48	41	32	34
Housing types (percent)				
Single-family detached	44	59	49	62
Townhouse/duplex	24	0	12	14
Apartment	32	41	39	24
Housing costs				
Median home value	$33,500	$40,600	$30,600	$25,300
Median rent	$145	$163	$206	$191
Neighborhood development				
Density (mean dwelling units per acre)				
Cluster	6.3	7.4	7.6	5.6
Neighborhood	1.9	4.3	3.1	4.8
Facilities (percent of respondents with facility within one-half mile of dwelling unit)				
Community center	67	0	85	14
Convenience store/supermarket	29	59	10	18
Elementary school	47	65	25	69
General practitioner/internist	29	0	0	9
Internal path system	100	0	84	0
Neighborhood/community shopping center	0	35	0	25
Park/playground	100	73	93	70
Swimming facility	23	7	38	47
Teen center	69	0	28	0
Tennis courts	43	7	29	39
Recreation				
Recreation and open space acreage	201	98	671	23
Recreational sites	20	9	14	6
Variety of recreational facilities (number of types)	18	16	16	7

Table 18-2 (cont.)

Indicator	Jonathan	Chanhassen	Park Forest South	Richton Park
Access to facilities (median road distance to nearest—feet)				
Golf course	8,600	21,800	10,400	15,600
Park/playground	500	2,000	1,200	1,600
Swimming facility	4,200	6,100	4,300	12,300
Tennis courts	3,600	13,200	3,300	11,100
Health care				
Medical practitioners (number)				
General practitioners/ internists	3	0	0	2
Obstetricians/gynecologists	0	0	0	0
Pediatricians	0	0	0	0
Dentists	3	1	0	3
Access to facilities (median road distance to nearest—feet)				
General practitioner/ internist	3,700	23,000	12,100	3,800
Hospital	44,100	32,400	33,900	27,300
Schools				
Schools in community (number)				
Elementary	0	1	1	2
Middle	0	1	0	0
High	0	0	0	1
Access to schools (median road distance to nearest—feet)				
Elementary	3,900	2,000	4,100	2,000
Middle	17,900	50,400	12,200	11,300
High	9,900	42,600	12,200	4,200
Shopping				
Facilities (number)				
Convenience stores	1	0	1	2
Supermarkets	0	1	0	2
Other establishments	6	27	6	63
Access to facilities (median road distance to nearest—feet)				
Convenience store or supermarket	3,600	2,400	4,500	3,800
Supermarket	17,000	2,400	15,300	4,200
Neighborhood/community shopping center	17,100	2,700	21,400	3,700
Regional shopping center	100,000+	50,400	19,700	10,400

as a community for all types of people. For example, one brochure distributed to prospective residents stated,

The plan is that it will be a balanced community in all respects. The federal government has initiated major programs to assist persons in lower income brackets to rent or buy proper housing for their families. Some of the homes and apartments in Jonathan qualify for the federal purchase or rental assistance programs (Jonathan Development Corporation, n.d.).

When asked about the effects of housing for moderate-income families on their neighborhoods, less than 10 percent of the Jonathan respondents thought that their neighborhoods would be harmed by the nearby location of housing for either white or black moderate-income families. In contrast, almost 20 percent of the respondents interviewed in neighboring Chanhassen felt that housing for moderate-income white families would harm their neighborhoods and more than a third perceived harm to their neighborhood from moderate-income black families. Subsidized housing, of course, had not been constructed in Chanhassen.

Under the terms of its Project Agreement with the Department of Housing and Urban Development, Park Forest South Development Company was to provide 500 units of housing for low- and moderate-income families in Park Forest South by the end of 1973. However, the developer secured HUD approval of a delay in meeting this commitment so that the character of the community could be established before subsidized housing was introduced. By the fall of 1973, no subsidized housing existed in the community, though in August of that year a proposal was approved by the Illinois Housing Development Authority to convert 46 units in a previously unoccupied mid-rise apartment building from market-rate to subsidized rents under the FHA Section 236 program.

The major attempt to initiate subsidized housing in Park Forest South was defeated by the village residents and their elected village trustees. In the fall of 1972, New Community Enterprises submitted an application to the Illinois Housing Development Authority for a multifamily planned unit development (PUD 1-9) that would contain a mixture of market-rate and subsidized apartment units, and also informed the village Board of Trustees and Planning Commission of its proposal. After initial approval by the board, plans became stymied when the village held up further approval at the behest of a citizen committee—Save Our Forest Trees (SOFT). SOFT claimed that valuable woods would be destroyed by the construction of the proposed 450-unit complex. PUD 1-9 became a major issue in Park Forest South—petitions were circulated, funds were raised to support SOFT's efforts, and a study of the site by a group at Governors State University was commissioned. In the election for three seats on the village Board of Trustees the following April, all candidates went on record favoring the preservation of the woods. After the election, the village board proposed that a park be created on the PUD 1-9 site. New Community Enterprises agreed to sell the property and also to supply the matching funds that would enable the village to receive a grant from the Bureau of Outdoor Recreation in order to acquire the PUD 1-9 site for a park.

Fifteen percent fewer Park Forest South than Jonathan respondents (81 percent versus 96 percent) felt that housing for moderate-income white families would not harm their neighborhoods, while 19 percent fewer (75 percent versus 94 percent) felt that way about moderate-income black families. In contrast to the significantly more tolerant attitudes in Jonathan than in Chanhassen, there was no difference in attitudes toward income integration between Park Forest South and Richton Park respondents. In short, by delaying implementation of the Project Agreement, New Community Enterprises may have established the character of Park Forest South at the cost of an economically balanced community.

Neighborhood Development. Initial residential construction in Jonathan and Park Forest South was occurring at densities that were very close to those expected to characterize the communities at the completion of the development process. For example, at full development net residential density in Jonathan was to be 6.4 dwelling units per acre. Jonathan's (equivalent cluster) density was 6.3 units per acre at the end of 1972. Similarly, in comparison with a projected final net residential density of 7.8 units per acre, cluster density in Park Forest South stood at 7.6 units per acre after the first three years of residential development. Given the residents' resistance experienced in some nonfederally assisted communities when higher density housing was introduced at later stages of the development process, Jonathan and Park Forest South were probably wise to build at higher densities during the first stages of development. Because residents were made aware of the types of future development programmed for the communities, they were less likely to view high density housing as a threat to their neighborhoods. For example, when Jonathan and Park Forest South respondents were asked whether they would oppose townhouse and apartment construction within their neighborhoods, they were significantly less likely to indicate opposition than the respondents who were living in nonfederally assisted new communites.

Jonathan residents were much more likely than the residents of Chanhassen to have a variety of amenities available in their neighborhoods (the area within one-half mile of their homes). Neighborhood path systems, a community center, and a teen center were easily accessible to the residents of Jonathan, but were totally absent from Chanhassen neighborhoods. Jonathan residents also had better access to a general practitioner, park or playground, swimming facilities, and tennis courts. Park Forest South residents, on the other hand, had greater access to neighborhood community centers, parks and playgrounds, walking paths, and to a teen center than residents of Richton Park, but were less likely to live within one-half mile of a convenience store or supermarket, elementary school, general practitioner, shopping center, or available swimming facilities and tennis courts.

Community Facilities. The record of the federally assisted new communities is also mixed in terms of the provision of community facilities. As was true of nonfederally assisted new communities, both Jonathan and Park Forest South provided considerably more recreational and open space land, recreational sites, and recreational facilities than their paired conventional communities. Greater difficulties, however, were experienced with facilities that required a substantial supporting population and/or public participation in their provision.

Schools are one example. Because of its slower than anticipated population growth, Jonathan's planners had not begun detailed discussions with officials of Minnesota Independent School District 112 about the character of public schools in the community. As a result, questions regarding the number and size of school sites, design enrollments, physical design objectives, and the timing and financing of school construction had not been raised with the school district, and Jonathan was viewed as having little effect on the educational system. Although school officials were sympathetic with the concepts for Jonathan's development, they felt too much emphasis was being placed on technological gadgetry (such as Jonathan's proposed community information system) at the expense of some hard thought by the Jonathan Development Corporation and the Department of Housing and Urban Development about the character and financing of the schools that would be needed. When the household survey was conducted in 1973, Jonathan students attended schools in Chaska and Chanhassen.

In Park Forest South, on the other hand, schools have been a major concern of the developer, the residents, and Crete-Monee School District 201U. However, relationships among these three groups have often been quite rocky. When the initial plans were being laid for Park Forest South, schools within walking distance of residential clusters were viewed as important elements in the development of the community. However, while the planners scheduled the construction of 24 elementary schools, five middle schools, and three high schools, they did not determine how these schools were to be built or what types of educational programs would be offered. These matters were viewed as the responsibility of the Crete-Monee school district. The school district, however, did not begin to revise its 1960 school development plan until 1972, several years after the construction of Park Forest South had gotten underway. As a result, initial school decisions were made on an incremental, case-by-case basis.

The first such decision occurred before the Village of Park Forest South approved the new community's first master plan in January 1968. Lewis Manilow wanted to have an elementary school in operation when the first residents moved to Park Forest South and agreed to donate the site. The school district, however, had serious financial problems. No new school bonds could be issued until property values in the district rose to a point where bonded indebtedness was less than 12 percent of assessed valuation (as prescribed by Illinois debt limitation laws). Park Forest South's development would not have produced the necessary increase in valuation until some 18 months after the first residents had occupied their homes. In order to expedite school construction, Manilow proposed to build the school and lease it to the board at a rate just high enough to cover his interest costs. After a long delay, the school board agreed to accept the offer, but it was January 1972—three years after the first residents moved to the new community—that Hickory Elementary School began operation.

Although the district has now paid for the school, this came only after a serious conflict over the rent charged by New Community Enterprises— the district was to pay an annual rent of 8.5 percent of the capital costs of the school, but claimed it was being charged 22 percent. Through the efforts of the Park Forest South village board the conflict was resolved when New Community Enterprises agreed to lower the rent charged if the difference between the old and new rental rate went into an escrow account for new school construction.

In September 1972, the voters of the school district passed a bond issue that included funds for the construction of a middle school in Park Forest South. Passage of the bonds was opposed by all areas of the district outside of Park Forest South. Through the effort of a Joint Planning Committee (composed of citizens, the developer, village representatives, and representatives of Governors State University) formed in 1973, plans for the school were revised to include a number of joint community-educational uses of the facility. This, however, did not resolve continuing conflicts that were occurring between the school board, New Community Enterprises, and the village Board of Trustees.

Earlier, growing out of dissatisfaction with the amount of recreational land adjacent to Hickory Elementary School, the village Board of Trustees had required developer donations of recreational sites adjacent to new schools as a condition for annexation of additional land scheduled for development. When a golf course was developed on a site scheduled (but not immediately needed) for an elementary school, the village board accepted a cash donation in lieu of the recreational portion of the school site and placed it in escrow for use in the purchase of middle and high school sites (New Community Enterprises had agreed to donate elementary school sites). Therefore, before the proposed middle school could be constructed, the village board had to release these and other funds it was holding in escrow for school site acquisition.

After ten months of discussion about an appropriate site, when a preannexation agreement for the proposed school site came up for board approval, it discovered that a clause in the agreement between the school board and developer had been inserted requiring the annexation of 120 acres of developer-owned land around the school site and approval of development plans that had never gone before the Planning Commission. The village Board of Trustees balked at approving the preannexation agreement and construction of the school was further delayed. In fact, it was March of 1974, after adjacent developer-owned land had been separated from the school site annexation proposal, that the village agreed in principle to annex the 17-acre site for the planned Deer Creek Junior High School and to release escrow funds so that the school district could purchase the land and proceed with construction.

In addition to difficulties with schools, both Jonathan and Park Forest South have experienced (or face) a number of potential problems with health care and shopping facilities. In the case of Jonathan, the potential problem of acquiring community health services before an adequate population was present was resolved by renting space in the first village center for the establishment of a satellite branch of the Lakeview Clinic (group practice), which had its headquarters in the nearby city of Waconia. Future difficulties could be expected, however, when Jonathan attempted to implement its proposal for a community hospital. The administrators of the two hospitals that were presently serving Jonathan—St. Francis Hospital in Shakopee and Ridgeview Hospital in Waconia—indicated that their facilities would adequately serve Jonathan and that they would strongly oppose a new hospital. In addition, little attention had been given to other forms of health care that might be needed in the community. Although Jonathan's Project Agreement spoke of a communitywide plan for health services and preventive medicine, as of 1973, such planning was not expected to get underway for a couple of years.

In contrast to Jonathan's pragmatic approach to health care, but lack of planning, health care planning had occupied a central role in the development of Park Forest South. A key feature of Park Forest South's proposed health care delivery system is to be a 180-bed, short-term general hospital with related mental health and ambulatory care facilities and services. After a number of years of discussion with potential hospital sponsors, Lewis Manilow secured a commitment from Rush-Presbyterian-St. Lukes Medical Center of Chicago to own and operate a branch hospital in Park Forest South and to extend the Center's prepaid comprehensive health plan to the community. In July 1972 plans for the construction of the proposed hospital and medical center in Park Forest South were announced to the public and target completion dates of 1975 for the first phase medical center and early 1976 for the entire hospital complex were established.

Although New Community Enterprises donated 40 acres of the proposed hospital site and Rush-Presbyterian-St. Lukes Medical Center agreed to underwrite approximately $8 million in construction costs, Hill-Burton funds were needed to finance the remaining portion of the $10,470,000 cost of the hospital. To be eligible for the federal funds, approval of the Park Forest South hospital had to be obtained from the Will-Grundy-Kankakee Comprehensive Health Planning Council located in Joliet, the county seat of Will County. An application was submitted in October 1972 and 11 months later, in September 1973, the proposed hospital was rejected by the Health Planning Council on the grounds that a hospital was not needed in Park Forest South. Since the council had not adopted a comprehensive health plan for its region at the time of the negative hospital decision, reasons for rejection of the hospital proposal were apparently based on opposition by existing medical interests in the area. Regardless of the reason, since Medicare, Medicaid, and Blue Cross-Blue Shield coverage would not be extended to the hospital without the approval of the regional health planning council, the decision effectively removed the kingpin of Park Forest South's health plan. As an interim solution to the new community's health care needs, Rush-Presbyterian-St. Lukes Medical Center proposed to open a limited medical service center on the first floor of an apartment building in mid-September 1974.

Jonathan and Park Forest South adopted relatively similar approaches to the problem of providing shopping services during the early years of development when the population would not be adequate to support even a modest neighborhood center. As part of the initial construction undertaken in each community, convenience shopping centers were built. In Jonathan, this took the form of a first-phase portion of the Village One Center, which also provided space for the development staff and a public information display. In Park Forest South, a freestanding convenience center was built at the entrance to the community and the developer provided an express minibus service to the Park Forest Plaza regional shopping center. In both cases a convenience store/mini-supermarket was the major commercial tenant in the community. As land sales and home construction lagged in Jonathan and Park Forest South, plans for additional shopping facilities were delayed, and prospective tenants shied away from pioneering in communities whose future growth was uncertain. In Park Forest South, a major supermarket backed away from its commitment to occupy space in the first increment of the town center, which was originally scheduled to open in the fall of 1974. In Jonathan, the community's convenience store went out of business in early 1975. It later reopened under new management.

In sum, the experiences of Jonathan and Park Forest South suggest that federally assisted new communities will be plagued by the same problems as the nonfederally assisted new communities discussed in the preceding chapters. While more than adequate recreational facilities were provided through private market mechanisms (and assistance from federal open space and recreation grant programs), the early provision of schools, health care, and shopping was much more difficult. What is more, as the experience of Park Forest South demonstrates, the mere existence of a committed developer and extensive long-range planning do not guarantee solutions. Instead, they may be costly delusions—costly to the developer, in terms of the time, money, and manpower expended, and costly to the residents, in terms of inadequate community services until the community matures. Clearly, if the federally assisted new communities are to be a new generation of new communities, federal assistance in the provision of community facilities is mandatory.

The Residents

The people who moved to Jonathan and Park Forest South were in a number of respects similar to those who moved to the nearby paired conventional communities. They were most likely to have moved from another metropolitan suburb, to be young, and to have children living in their households. See table 18-3. Although Jonathan had attracted a significantly higher proportion of central city residents than Chanhassen, differences between Park Forest South and Richton Park in this regard were not statistically significant. Jonathan had also attracted a significantly higher proportion of divorced, separated, and widowed persons with children than either Chanhassen, Park Forest South, Richton Park, or the nonfederally assisted new communities. This seems to be due to the relatively high proportion of subsidized housing in Jonathan and the attraction of the new community to persons seeking to establish a new start in life.

The availability of subsidized housing in Jonathan and Richton Park is reflected in the socioeconomic characteristics of the residents. For example, 40 percent of the respondents in Jonathan had family incomes of under $10,000 a year compared with 19 percent of the Chanhassen respondents. While a majority of the Richton Park respondents had family incomes below $15,000 per year, Park Forest South respondents tended to have above average incomes. In fact, the median family income in Park Forest South ($16,800) was little different from that of the respondents of nonfederally assisted new communities ($17,500). As noted earlier, by delaying the provision of subsidized housing, Park Forest South reduced the possibility that its population profile would meet the federal objective of

Table 18-3
Population Characteristics

Characteristic	Percent of Respondents			
	Jonathan	Chanhassen	Park Forest South	Richton Park
Location of previous residence				
Central city of metropolitan area	29[a]	15	20	26
Metropolitan suburb	49	65[a]	72	70
Same community	4	6	5	6
Another suburb	45	59[a]	67	64
Outside of metropolitan area	22	20	8	4
Life cycle characteristics				
Age of head of household				
Under 40	84	77	74	78
40-54	11	21	19	12
55 or older	5	2	7	10
Median age	28	31	32	29
Household composition				
Unmarried adults without children	15	15	12	18
Unmarried adults with children	14[a]	5	2	6
Married couples with children	53	63	62	51
Married couples without children	18	17	24	25
Socioeconomic characteristics				
Education (household head)				
High school graduate or less	38	31	26	46[a]
Some college/college graduate	42	36	54	45
Graduate/professional training	20	33[a]	20[a]	9
Occupation (household head)				
Professional or managerial	52	61	48	39
Other white collar	23	20	25	18
Blue collar	25	19	27	43[a]
Family income (1972)				
Under $10,000	40[a]	19	12	20
$10,000-$14,999	25	31	25	46[a]
$15,000-$24,999	29	34	50[a]	25
$25,000 or more	6	16[a]	12	9
Median family income	$11,800	$15,000	$16,800	$12,700

	Percent of Respondents			
Characteristic	Jonathan	Chanhassen	Park Forest South	Richton Park
Race				
White	97	100	90	99[a]
Black	2	0	10[a]	1
Other	1	0	0	0

[a]Difference statistically significant at 0.05 level of confidence.

income balance, at least during the first stage of the development process.

The social class indicators, education and occupation, suggest that even Jonathan has not attracted a predominantly working class population, in spite of the high proportion of residents with below-average family incomes. Seventy-five percent of the Jonathan household heads held white-collar jobs (52 percent held professional, technical, or managerial positions), and 62 percent had attended college. There was no significant difference in the occupational status of Jonathan and Chanhassen household heads, though Chanhassen household heads were significantly more likely to have had some graduate or professional training. In comparison with the households living in Richton Park, those living in Park Forest South were significantly more likely to have more than a high school education and to be working in a white collar occupation.

Finally, Jonathan had attracted few nonwhite households, but did match the Twin Cities metropolitan racial profile. Park Forest South had attracted a significantly higher proportion of black residents than Richton Park and was one of the few suburbs south of Chicago with a racially mixed population (10 percent black at time of household survey).

Recent estimates of Park Forest South's black population have been in the range of 18 to 20 percent of the total population. While Park Forest South was achieving the racial integration goals of the federal new communities program, this was a source of marketing concern for the developer, given the conservative outlook of the south suburbs of Chicago. Blacks were reportedly being directed to Park Forest South by area realtors, which was said to discourage white in-migration. However, Park Forest South's relatively large black population may create the potential for black identity and a political voice in this community, which, outside of Columbia and Reston, the black residents have not attained in new communities in the United States.

The Pioneers: What Attracts Residents During the Early Years

Community characteristics that attracted residents to the federally assisted new communities were in some respects similar to those reported earlier (see chapter 6) for nonfederally assisted new communities that were in later stages of the development process. Nearness to the outdoors and natural environment, the community as a good place to raise children, and community planning were again important considerations in the moving decisions of a number of households. Community facilities, with the exception of recreational facilities in Jonathan, were again relatively unimportant.

There were also some noteworthy differences in the reasons residents gave for moving to Jonathan and Park Forest South, in comparison with the nonfederally assisted new communities, with each other, and with their individual paired conventional communities. First, in comparison with the older nonfederally assisted new communities, residents of Jonathan and Park Forest South were much more likely to have been attracted by both the nearness of the outdoors and natural environment and perceptions of the communities as good places to raise children. This is understandable, since both Jonathan and Park Forest South are located in semirural areas and are surrounded by large tracts of undeveloped land.

As shown in table 18-4, residents were more likely to have been attracted to Jonathan than to Park Forest South by characteristics of the environment—the nearness to the outdoors, perceptions of the community as a good place to raise children, overall planning that went into the community, and recreational facilities. Park Forest South, on the other hand, was more likely than Jonathan to have attracted residents because of characteristics of housing and the immediate neighborhood. By contrast, people may have moved to Jonathan in spite of its housing, since it was not viewed by many residents as a key aspect of the community's appeal. The character of housing in Jonathan may also account for the very slow sales pace. A majority of the market tends to focus on characteristics of the house and the immediate neighborhood, before attending to characteristics of the community and environment beyond the neighborhood.

Differences in factors comprising the appeal of Jonathan and Park Forest South were greater than those between each new community and its paired conventional community. Residents were significantly more likely to have moved to Jonathan than to Chanhassen because of community planning and the availability of recreational facilities. Chanhassen residents, on the other hand, were more likely to have cited convenience to work, layout and space of the dwelling and lot, and appearance of the

Table 18-4

Reasons for Moving to Jonathan and Park Forest South

Reasons for Moving to Community	Percent of Respondents			
	Jonathan	Chanhassen	Park Forest South	Richton Park
Nearness to the outdoors and natural environment	56	49	36[a]	14
Good place to raise children	49	39	35	23
Overall planning that went into community	34[a]	3	21[a]	6
Cost of buying (and financing) the dwelling or renting	29	25	38	47
Convenience to work	27	45[a]	29	35
Recreational facilities	22[a]	3	9	11
Layout and space of the dwelling and lot	15	27[a]	41	29
Appearance of the immediate neighborhood	14	26[a]	22	14
Type of people living in the neighborhood	11	16	16	18
Opportunities for participation in community life	8	7	9[a]	1
Cost of living in the community	7	3	3	4
Finding a job in the community	6	12	5	8
Ease of getting around the community	6	4	4	7
Safety from crime	5	2	8	10
Public schools	3	10	8	22[a]
Construction of the dwelling	2	7	5	7
Shopping facilities	2	6	2	10[a]
Health and medical facilities	1	0	0	0
Climate	1	2	0	2

[a]Difference statistically significant at 0.05 level of confidence.

immediate neighborhood as reasons for their housing choice. Compared to households that had moved to Richton Park, Park Forest South households were more likely to have been attracted by their community's nearness to the outdoors and natural environment, community planning, and opportunities for participation in community life. Richton Park households more often cited the public schools and shopping facilities.

All of these differences are understandable in terms of the characteristics of each community. The greater sophistication of planning in new
communities is obvious. While both Jonathan and Chanhassen were surrounded by large expanses of undeveloped land, as was Park Forest South,
Richton Park was bounded on two sides by mature communities. As a
result, residents were less likely to move there to gain access to the natural
environment. Schools and shopping facilities, however, were more accessible to Richton Park than to Park Forest South residents, and, accordingly, played a larger role in residents' moving decisions.

Comparisons of respondents' ratings of their present new communities
in relation to the communities they had moved from provide an indication
of the trade-offs that are involved in the move to new communities in the
initial stages of development. Over two thirds of the respondents who had
moved to Jonathan and Park Forest South thought the overall planning of
their community, layout and space of their homes, and opportunities for
participation in community life were better than the communities from
which they had moved. Over two thirds of the Jonathan respondents and
between one half and two thirds of those living in Park Forest South also
thought their community was better in terms of the appearance of their
immediate neighborhood, nearness to the outdoors and natural environment, and as a place to raise children. Finally, a majority of the Jonathan
respondents, but less than a majority in Park Forest South, rated recreational facilities, the type of people living in their neighborhood, ease of
getting around the community, and safety from crime as better than their
former communities.

The major factor residents gave up in achieving these gains was the
quantity and convenience of shopping facilities—a majority of both the
Jonathan and Park Forest South respondents thought shopping was worse
than in their former communities. Employment was the only other community characteristic that both Jonathan and Park Forest South respondents
tended to feel was worse, rather than better, than their former communities. In both communities more respondents (but not a majority) thought
their convenience to work and the job opportunities available in the community were worse than thought they were better than where they had
formerly lived.

A majority of the Park Forest South respondents thought the cost of
housing was worse than where they had lived before. On the other hand,
reflecting generally lower housing costs and the availability of subsidized
housing, a higher proportion of respondents thought housing costs were
better in Jonathan than in their former communities than thought they were
worse (46 percent versus 29 percent, respectively). Similarly, while many
more Park Forest South respondents thought health and medical services

were worse than those of their former communities than thought they were better (37 percent versus 11 percent), just the opposite was true of Jonathan. More than a third of the Jonathan respondents rated health and medical services as better than their former communities, but only a sixth thought that these services were worse.

Over time, improvements should be realized in each of the areas in which Jonathan and Park Forest South did not rate well in comparison with their residents' previous communities. Park Forest South can be expected to provide a broader range of housing prices, in keeping with its Project Agreement with the federal government, and health care, shopping, and employment opportunities will begin to accumulate as each community matures.

Residents' Responses to the Communities

Although Jonathan and Park Forest South were young communities in which a number of physical improvements could be expected to occur as the development process proceeded, they provided the primary living environment for a total of some 5,000 people. The ways in which these people respond to the environment provide an indication of how well new communities can meet people's needs in early stages of the development process. Residents' responses also provide information that can be used in later design and development decisions in these two communities and in the initial planning of future federally assisted new community projects.

Planning and Governance

Thirty-four percent of the Jonathan respondents and 21 percent of those living in Park Forest South moved to these communities because of the character of community planning. In each community, over two thirds of the respondents said that they were aware of neighborhood development plans when they occupied their homes.[a] Many residents—87 percent of the Jonathan respondents and 65 percent of Park Forest South respondents— thought that neighborhood development plans had been followed.

However, while federal regulations required that the Jonathan Development Corporation and New Community Enterprises, Inc. provide

[a] In this regard, Jonathan and Park Forest South residents were similar to residents of nonfederally assisted new communities that were in relatively early stages of the development process. As noted in chapter 7, however, residents' concern with planning when they moved to new communities diminished as development proceeded and the character of the neighborhood and community became more established.

residents with an opportunity to comment on planning decisions, many citizens felt ill-informed about plans for future development and powerless to affect decisions that might seriously harm their neighborhoods. Thirty-two percent of the Jonathan respondents and 38 percent of the Park Forest South respondents felt that they had not been adequately informed about future development. Few residents in either community (15 percent in Jonathan and eight percent in Park Forest South) listed the developer as their most reliable source of information. When asked whether they could do anything about a development decision that would (hypothetically) harm their neighborhood, only about a third (36 percent of the Jonathan respondents and 30 percent of those living in Park Forest South) felt they could do something that would have more than a limited chance of success. These figures are comparable to those obtained in nonfederally assisted new communities and in the conventional communities. They suggest that federal citizen participation requirements and federal oversight of the new community development process have not produced very different developer-citizen relations than are typical of developing suburbs in the United States, either within or outside of new communities.

This is not to say that residents were unhappy with the character of community planning. As was true of the nonfederally assisted new communities in comparison with their paired conventional communities, Jonathan respondents were much more likely than those living in Chanhassen (84 percent versus 36 percent) to rate community planning as better than that of the communities from which they had moved, as were Park Forest South respondents in comparison with those living in Richton Park (70 percent versus 39 percent rated planning as better than their former communities). Residents of Jonathan, Park Forest South, and the nonfederally assisted new communities gave similar reasons for their perceptions of better planning. In each case the quality and convenience of recreational facilities was mentioned most often, followed by the organization of land uses. In contrast with the residents of Park Forest South and the nonfederally assisted new communities, however, Jonathan respondents also considered the preservation of the natural environment as a key reason for rating planning highly.

In sum, new community residents—whether they lived in federally or nonfederally assisted new communities—tended to be highly pleased with the quality of community planning, although residents often did not feel capable of influencing community development decisions. Achievement of this federal objective may be extremely difficult. The Jonathan Development Corporation and New Community Enterprises, Inc. both held citizen forums to inform residents about development decisions, and in both communities, development could not proceed without the formal approval of a municipal government. The fact that greater than usual citizen confidence in their ability to influence the character of development was not forthcoming in Jonathan and Park Forest South indicates that broad-based citizen participation in the planning of federally assisted new communities will not occur until basic reforms occur in the character of the planning and development process. Unless residents actually collaborate in and help make planning decisions, they are not likely to feel that they can have an effective role in shaping their community's future.

Residents' attitudes about their ability to influence planning decisions carried over to their perceptions of municipal government. Less than one third of the Jonathan and Park Forest South respondents thought that Chaska city and Park Forest South village officials usually did what a majority of the citizens wanted. Barely a majority (52 percent in each community) felt that local governmental affairs were carried on in the open, rather than "behind closed doors." However, as was also the case among the residents of nonfederally assisted new communities, distrust of local officials was accompanied by relatively high rates of participation in local politics. Jonathan residents had taken part in an average of 2.1 local political activities during the previous year (among 10 types of political activities they were questioned about). Park Forest South residents had taken part in 2.4 local political activities on the average. Although political cynicism and participation tended to be about equal in Jonathan and Chanhassen, Park Forest South residents were significantly more cynical about local officials and significantly more likely to participate in local politics than the residents of Richton Park.

In general, residents' satisfaction with expenditures for public services was significantly greater in Jonathan and Chanhassen than in Park Forest South and Richton Park. Of seven public services residents were asked about, Jonathan respondents were significantly more satisfied than those living in Chanhassen with expenditures for outdoor recreation, and were significantly less satisfied with expenditures for public transportation. There were no differences in their evaluations of expenditures for public health, schools, police protection, fire protection, or community upkeep and maintenance. Compared to Park Forest South residents, however, those living in both Jonathan and Chanhassen were significantly more satisfied with community expenditures for public health facilities, recreational facilities, schools, police protection, and community upkeep and maintenance. Richton Park residents were significantly more satisfied than those living in Park Forest South with expenditures for schools, police protection, and public transportation. There were no instances in which Park Forest South residents were significantly more satisfied with public service expenditures than the residents of Richton Park.

As gauged by residents' responses to community public service expenditures, Jonathan Development Corporation's decision to annex to the city of Chaska worked out much better than Nathan and Lewis Manilow's decision to incorporate Park Forest South as a new village at the start of the development process. Whereas Chaska had an established service system, public services had to be started from scratch in Park Forest South. Difficulties in funding public services during the start-up phase of new community development were anticipated in the federal new communities legislation. Provision was made for public service grants for a three-year period to enable communities to get basic services off to a good start. However, as noted in chapter 3, this section of the legislation was never implemented. In the absence of anticipated federal aid, and without an adequate tax base to fund essential services, Park Forest South's village government had to struggle to make ends meet. Quite naturally, it looked to the developer to fund what in other cases would be viewed as purely public functions. For example, in March 1974 the village trustees asked New Community Enterprises to provide an aerial platform for the fire department, communications equipment for use by the police and fire departments, various repairs to a main village road, and a new public works vehicle. New Community Enterprises had earlier agreed to pay the village manager's and village planner's salaries pending the receipt by the village of revenues from other sources. Although over the years the developer had complied with many of the village's requests for aid, there were occasions when this was not possible. As a result, some friction and distrust occurred.

Even in Jonathan, the city of Chaska was not able to assume all of the public functions associated with new community development. Because Chaska showed no interest in operating Jonathan's greenway system and other recreational amenities, the Jonathan Development Corporation established a communitywide automatic homes association (the Jonathan Association). Jonathan respondents tended to be highly satisfied with services performed by the Jonathan Association—over three fourths said they were satisfied with architectural controls, maintenance of common property, and the provision of recreational facilities and social activities. However, when asked to rate overall association performance, 55 percent said they were neutral or dissatisfied. As was true of the communitywide associations in Reston and Columbia, the primary reason appeared to be residents' dissatisfaction with developer control of the association.

New Community Enterprises attempted to establish a communitywide automatic homes association modeled after the Columbia Association. However, although covenants establishing the New Town Park and Recreation Association in Park Forest South were recorded, the association was never activated because the village Board of Trustees objected to sharing control over the community recreational system with a strong quasi-governmental organization. Since the village was in no position to operate an extensive recreational system—recreational expenditures by the village in 1972 were less than $1 per capita—New Community Enterprises operated some facilities as commercial enterprises, allowed free use of others, and established two automatic membership recreation associations to operate the two neighborhood recreational complexes it had constructed. From the residents' perspective, this solution was not very satisfactory. Park Forest South had one of the lowest rated recreational service systems of any of the new communities studied. Only 45 percent of the respondents there were satisfied with the level of community recreational expenditures, 34 percent less than in Jonathan and 21 percent less than the average for 13 nonfederally assisted new communities.

In summary, residents' responses to planning and governance in the federally assisted new communities did not appear to be much different from the responses of residents living in nonfederally assisted new communities. Although residents had a high regard for community planning, they did not feel confident of their ability to influence development decisions, were suspicious of local officials and the developer, and, in general, were no more nor less satisfied with public services than the residents of less planned conventional communities at the same stage of development.

Housing and Neighborhood Evaluations

Residents' satisfaction with their homes and the livability of the immediate neighborhood had strong influences on their evaluations of overall community livability. It was shown in chapter 9 that housing and neighborhood evaluations were in turn strongly influenced by ownership or rental of the dwelling unit. Owners tended to be consistently more satisfied than renters, regardless of the type of housing. This was also true of the federally assisted new communities. In both Jonathan and Park Forest South owners tended to be more satisfied with the livability of their homes and immediate neighborhoods than renters.

Satisfaction with ownership housing units in Jonathan, Park Forest South, and their paired conventional communities is summarized in table 18-5. Housing satisfaction in the two federally assisted new communities was equivalent and generally somewhat lower than in the nonfederally assisted new communities. Compared to the paired conventional communities, Jonathan homeowners were no more satisfied with their dwellings than were Chanhassen homeowners; Park Forest South owners, on the other hand, were significantly more likely to be satisfied with single-family detached homes, but not townhouses, than the residents of Richton Park.

The greater satisfaction of single-family homeowners in Park Forest South (versus those living in Richton Park) stemmed from greater satisfaction with the indoor space of their homes, privacy, construction quality,

Table 18-5
Residents' Evaluations of Ownership Housing

Percent of Respondents (Homeowners Only)

Satisfaction Indicator	Single-family Detached				Townhouses				Condominium Apartments			
	J	C	PFS	RP	J	C	PFS	RP	J	C	PFS	RP
Satisfaction with dwelling unit												
Completely satisfied	35	35	28	33	IC	IC	46	37	IC	IC	17	IC
Satisfied	55	51	59[a]	33	IC	IC	48	56	IC	IC	83	IC
Neutral or dissatisfied	10	14	13	33[a]	IC	IC	6	7	IC	IC	0	IC
Satisfaction with dwelling unit characteristics												
Financial factors												
Better investment than alternatives	63	73	69[a]	39	IC	IC	55	34	IC	IC	40	IC
Cost better than previous dwelling	44	42	35	77[a]	IC	IC	35	33	IC	IC	36	IC
Indoor space												
Enough space for family's needs	78	82	74	69	IC	IC	100	100	IC	IC	100	IC
Layout and space better than previous dwelling	71	82	78	71	IC	IC	94	76	IC	IC	66	IC
Outdoor space												
Enough space for family's needs	86	89	76	87	IC	IC	80	81	IC	IC	100	IC
Private area available	49	51	42	31	IC	IC	35	66[a]	IC	IC	50	IC
Construction												
Better than previous dwelling	62	71	54	38	IC	IC	53	39	IC	IC	33	IC

Satisfaction with livability of immediate neighborhood												
Completely satisfied	65	67	37	33	IC	IC	55[a]	24	IC	IC	50	IC
Satisfied	29	29	60	57	IC	IC	39	56	IC	IC	42	IC
Neutral or dissatisfied	6	4	3	10	IC	IC	6	20	IC	IC	8	IC
Satisfaction with neighborhood characteristics												
Attractiveness												
Attractive[b]	56	58	33	17	IC	IC	39	30	IC	IC	67	IC
Appearance better than previous community	81	69	58	43	IC	IC	64	53	IC	IC	75	IC
Density												
Lack of crowding[b]	46	35	32	19	IC	IC	13	40[a]	IC	IC	17	IC
Privacy[b]	45	39	41	38	IC	IC	35	57	IC	IC	50	IC
Quiet[b]	46	42	41	42	IC	IC	36	42	IC	IC	67	IC
Social factors												
Friendliness[b]	64	47	46	47	IC	IC	68[a]	24	IC	IC	33	IC
Homogeneity[b]	24	21	30	27	IC	IC	23	24	IC	IC	33	IC
Reputation[b]	62	78	48[a]	25	IC	IC	55	40	IC	IC	42	IC
Safety[b]	78	72	48	46	IC	IC	68	55	IC	IC	75	IC
Maintenance[b]	64	72	39	31	IC	IC	52	30	IC	IC	28	IC
Convenience[b]	43	51	28	33	IC	IC	23	49	IC	IC	34	IC

J = Jonathan; C = Chanhassen; PFS = Park Forest South; RP = Richton Park

IC = insufficient number of cases (less than ten)

[a]Difference statistically significant at 0.05 level of confidence.

[b]Highest rating on five-point scale.

and the potential for a good return on their housing investment. Park Forest South homeowners also tended to be more satisfied with the attractiveness, lack of crowding, reputation, and maintenance of the immediate neighborhood. Many of these advantages were tied to the price of the housing in these two communities. Single-family detached homes in Richton Park were significantly less expensive than those in Park Forest South, which was also reflected in residents' evaluations of the cost of buying in relation to their previous communities. As noted above, many of the single-family detached homes in Richton Park were marketed under the FHA Section 235 subsidy program, while dwellings in Park Forest South were all sold and financed at market rates.

Satisfaction with overall neighborhood livability was similar among Jonathan and Chanhassen single-family homeowners, and among single-family homeowners living in Park Forest South and Richton Park. Park Forest South townhouse owners, however, gave much higher ratings to the livability of their immediate neighborhoods than did Richton Park townhouse owners. This difference was mainly due to Park Forest South townhouse owners' greater satisfaction with neighborhood attractiveness, friendliness, safety, and maintenance.

Jonathan homeowners' perceptions of neighborhood livability were somewhat better than those of the residents of nonfederally assisted new communities, while Park Forest South homeowners tended to be less satisfied. In comparison with homeowners in Park Forest South, those living in Jonathan gave higher ratings to neighborhood attractiveness and appearance, lack of crowding, friendliness of neighbors, reputation, safety, maintenance, and convenience. The two areas in which both Jonathan and Park Forest South performed poorly compared to the responses of homeowners living in nonfederally assisted new communities were privacy and convenience. Residents' dissatisfaction with privacy may stem, particularly in Jonathan, from the prohibition of fenced yards and the placement of community greenways and paths along the back lot lines of homes. Dissatisfaction with convenience, of course, stems from the relative lack of many community facilities and services during the early stages of the development process.

Evaluations of rental housing in Jonathan and Park Forest South are summarized in table 18-6. Although differences were not statistically significant, Jonathan and Park Forest South renters tended to be more satisfied with their apartments and immediate neighborhoods than were renters living in their paired conventional communities. Jonathan fared particularly well in comparison with Chanhassen in terms of residents' perceptions of outdoor space and privacy, neighborhood attractiveness, quiet, convenience, and the friendliness of neighbors.

In comparison with renters living in Richton Park, those living in Park Forest South gave somewhat higher ratings to the layout and space, pri-

Table 18-6
Residents' Evaluations of Rental Housing

	Percent of Respondents							
	Townhouses				Apartments			
Satisfaction Indicator	J	C	PFS	RP	J	C	PFS	RP
Satisfaction with dwelling unit								
Completely satisfied	22	IC	IC	IC	18	20	27	19
Satisfied	49	IC	IC	IC	50	40	47	52
Neutral or dissatisfied	29	IC	IC	IC	32	40	26	29
Satisfaction with dwelling unit characteristics								
Financial factors								
Cost better than previous dwelling	72	IC	IC	IC	16	52[a]	11	29
Indoor space								
Enough space for family's needs	69	IC	IC	IC	52	69	62	84
Layout and space better than previous dwelling	68	IC	IC	IC	58	62	51	39
Outdoor space								
Enough space for family's needs	73	IC	IC	IC	96[a]	69	78	94
Private area available	28	IC	IC	IC	56[a]	19	31	23
Construction								
Better than previous dwelling	32	IC	IC	IC	37	28	43	29
Satisfaction with livability of immediate neighborhood								
Completely satisfied	34	IC	IC	IC	43	39	36	26
Satisfied	47	IC	IC	IC	37	35	48	45
Neutral or dissatisfied	19	IC	IC	IC	20	27	16	29
Satisfaction with neighborhood characteristics								
Attractiveness								
Attractive[b]	19	IC	IC	IC	41[a]	19	49	35
Appearance better than previous community	50	IC	IC	IC	76[a]	39	45	42
Density								
Lack of crowding[b]	15	IC	IC	IC	43	38	25	26
Privacy[b]	19	IC	IC	IC	39	31	50	35
Quiet[b]	13	IC	IC	IC	41[a]	19	42	23
Social factors								
Friendliness[b]	38	IC	IC	IC	45[a]	19	29	29
Homogeneity[b]	16	IC	IC	IC	16	12	11	23
Reputation[b]	30	IC	IC	IC	51	50	54	39

Table 18-6 (cont.)

| | Percent of Respondents | | | | | | | |
| | Townhouses | | | | Apartments | | | |
Satisfaction Indicator	J	C	PFS	RP	J	C	PFS	RP
Safety[b]	67	IC	IC	IC	55	54	54	55
Maintenance[b]	31	IC	IC	IC	37	35	59	45
Convenience[b]	50	IC	IC	IC	49	35	32	45

J = Jonathan; C = Chanhassen; PFS = Park Forest South; RP = Richton Park
IC = Insufficient number of cases (less than ten)
[a]Difference statistically significant at 0.05 level of confidence.
[b]Highest rating on five-point scale.

vacy, and construction quality of their rental apartments, and to the attractiveness, privacy, quiet, reputation, and maintenance of the immediate neighborhood. None of these differences, however, was statistically significant.

The only townhouse apartments in the federally assisted new communities were located in an FHA-236 subsidized project in Jonathan. Although residents' evaluations differed for particular aspects of their apartment and neighborhood, residents who lived in subsidized rental units in Jonathan were about as satisfied with their homes as those who lived in nonsubsidized housing. Residents of the subsidized townhouses were generally more satisfied than residents of nonsubsidized apartments with the cost of renting, indoor space of their units, and neighborhood safety. Residents of the nonsubsidized rental units were happier with construction quality, outdoor space and privacy, and the attractiveness, lack of crowding, privacy, quiet, and reputation of their neighborhood. Overall ratings of the dwelling unit and neighborhood, however, were not significantly different.

Apartment renters living in Jonathan and Park Forest South gave similar evaluations to their dwellings and neighborhoods as renters who were living in nonfederally assisted new communities. There was no difference in renters' overall evaluation of their apartments as a place to live, or in their evaluations of indoor space, construction quality, or neighborhood homogeneity and reputation. Jonathan and Park Forest South apartments were rated somewhat higher than apartments in the nonfederally assisted new communities in terms of outdoor space, privacy, quiet, and safety. For the other measures summarized in table 18-6, ratings of apartments in the nonfederally assisted new communities tended to fall in between those given to apartments in Jonathan and Park Forest South.

In summary, housing satisfaction tended to be as high or higher in Jonathan and Park Forest South as in their paired conventional communities. Jonathan homeowners, however, tended to be much happier with their neighborhoods than homeowners in Park Forest South. Differences in satisfaction among apartment renters were not as great. Renters in Jonathan were somewhat more satisfied than those in Park Forest South with outdoor space, lack of crowding, and the friendliness and convenience of their neighborhoods. Park Forest South renters, on the other hand, were more satisfied than those living in Jonathan with indoor space, privacy, and maintenance of the immediate neighborhood. Evaluations of rental units in these two federally assisted new communities were generally equivalent to those given rental units in nonfederally assisted new communities. Satisfaction with ownership units, however, while equivalent in Jonathan, was lower in Park Forest South than in the nonfederally assisted new communities.

Community Facility Evaluations

Because the federally assisted new communities were in the start-up stages of development, residents' evaluations of community facilities have to be viewed with some caution. As development proceeds and more facilities are provided, residents' opinions should improve.

The ratings residents gave to various community facilities and services (see table 18-7) parallel the earlier discussion of developer efforts to organize community service systems. For example, the Jonathan Development Corporations's attention to health care and recreation paid off in residents' assessments of these facilities that were generally higher than those given health care and recreation in Chanhassen and assessments of health care and recreational facilities given by the residents of nonfederally assisted new communities. On the other hand, lack of attention to schools and the difficulty in providing shopping facilities before an adequate base population was present were reflected in ratings of these service systems. They were no different in Jonathan than in Chanhassen and were significantly lower than ratings received by the nonfederally assisted new communities.

The problems of governance and plan implementation in Park Forest South were clearly reflected in residents' ratings of community facilities and services. For each of the service systems summarized in table 18-7, Park Forest South received significantly lower ratings than those given to facilities and services in the more developed nonfederally assisted new communities. On the other hand, Park Forest South residents were generally no more unhappy with community service systems than the residents of nearby Richton Park. Compared to Richton Park, Park Forest South

Table 18-7
Residents' Evaluations of Community Facilities and Services

	Percent of Respondents			
Service System Ratings	*Jonathan*	*Chanhassen*	*Park Forest South*	*Richton Park*
Health care				
Better than previous community	36[a]	18	11	13
Excellent or good	73[a]	50	48[a]	24
Satisfied with community expenditures for public health facilities	68	68	44	47
Recreation				
Better than previous community	82[a]	40	49	39
Excellent or good	94[a]	51	56[a]	35
Satisfied with community expenditures for outdoor recreational facilities	80[a]	63	45	38
Schools				
Better than previous community	33	27	34	45
Excellent or good	68	71	68	78
Satisfied with community expenditures for public schools	67	66	53	69[a]
Shopping				
Better than previous community	22	24	18	49[a]
Excellent or good	39	48	52	71[a]
Transportation				
Ease of getting around community better than previous community	59	48	22	31
Convenience to work better than previous community	33	51[a]	27	47[a]
Satisfied with community expenditures for public transportation	21	77[a]	40	63[a]

[a]Difference statistically significant at 0.05 level of confidence.

health care and recreational facilities received a significantly higher proportion of excellent or good ratings. Richton Park residents, on the other hand, gave somewhat better ratings to shopping facilities, schools, and transportation facilities.

Jonathan's relatively compact development resulted in highly satisfactory ratings of the ease of getting around the community. However, because of their rural locations, residents living in both new communities were not overly happy with convenience to work and were often dissatisfied with community expenditures for public transportation.

Early in the development process, the Jonathan Development Corporation decided to stress industrial expansion as a means of stimulating home sales and residential occupancy. By the end of 1973, in fact, there were almost twice as many persons working in Jonathan as households who lived in the community. As a result, 20 percent of the respondents both lived and worked in Jonathan, a figure that is comparable to communities, such as Columbia, Elk Grove Village, and Irvine, that had much larger employment bases. The reason for Jonathan's success in capturing a relatively high proportion of the community labor force is that housing was priced within the means of employees working there. In the case of Park Forest South, the number of households exceeded the number of jobs in the community and housing prices were beyond the means of many blue-collar workers. As a result, only 10 percent of the respondents both lived and worked in Park Forest South.

The Unfinished Community: Residents' Views of the Present and the Future

Reflecting the similar ratings given to housing, the neighborhood, and recreational facilities, Jonathan respondents were just as likely as the residents of the more fully developed nonfederally assisted new communities to rate their community as an excellent or good place to live. Ninety-one percent of the Jonathan respondents rated their community that highly, while 84 percent reported that they would recommend Jonathan to friends and relatives as a particularly good community to which to move. It should be noted, however, the Chanhassen residents were also highly enthusiastic about the livability of their community—87 percent rated Chanhassen as an excellent or good place to live, though a significantly lower proportion of residents than in Jonathan (69 percent) gave their community the highest recommendation as a place to which to move.

The overall livability of Park Forest South received lower ratings than either Jonathan or Chanhassen—only 77 percent of the Park Forest South respondents rated the community as an excellent or good place to live and only 66 percent said they would recommend the community to friends and relatives as a particularly good place to which to move. Nevertheless, Park Forest South received significantly higher livability ratings than Richton Park, where less than two thirds of the respondents thought the community was an excellent or good place to live and only 37 percent said they would give it the highest recommendation to friends and relatives. In short, although Park Forest South did not rate well in comparison with new communities in other parts of the nation, it was highly competitive in its market area with conventional community development. It is also noteworthy that the community livability ratings received by Park Forest South were not significantly different from those received by Park Forest, the older more mature nonfederally assisted new community located adjacent to Park Forest South's northern boundary.

Residents' prognoses of community livability in five years are summarized in table 18-8. Fifty-five percent of the residents living in Jonathan and Park Forest South felt their community would become a better place in which to live, while only about a fifth of those living in each community thought that community livability would diminish. Optimism for the future was not limited to the new communities. Fifty percent of the Chanhassen respondents and 52 percent of those living in Richton Park thought their conventional communities would be better places in which to live in five years.

Table 18-8 also summarizes a variety of suggestions residents offered for improving community livability. It is not particularly surprising that the most frequently mentioned improvement in both Jonathan and Park Forest South was the addition of more shopping facilities and commercial services. Both communities, it may be recalled, had minimal shopping facilities as of spring 1973. Three other suggestions were made by 10 percent or more of the Jonathan respondents. These included limiting the growth of Jonathan (which may actually be achieved through economic slowdown of the development venture), improvements in public transportation, and adherence to the community master plan. Concern for the integrity of the master plan in Jonathan was mentioned in another context. When residents were asked to name the major problems facing their community, deviations from the master plan by the Jonathan Development Corporation constituted the second most frequently mentioned problem. Poor communication between the developer and the citizens was the problem most often mentioned.

In Park Forest South, over 10 percent of the respondents suggested limiting or controlling the growth of the community. Residents there were also concerned with protecting natural areas from development.[b] In contrast to the Jonathan respondents, those living in Park Forest South were much more concerned about the availability of recreational facilities and

[b] New Community Enterprises had previously withdrawn from proposed development in Thorn Creek Woods between Park Forest South and Park Forest, when this became a regional environmental issue, and was not able to keep its low- and moderate-income housing commitment with the Department of Housing and Urban Development when residents objected to proposed development of moderate-income housing in another wooded section of the community.

schools. New Community Enterprises' problems with these service areas were discussed above. The failure to build schools on time in Park Forest South was the most frequently mentioned community problem, followed by concern over the density of the community, poor communication between residents and the developer, and the need for more recreational facilities.

Implications for the Federal New Communities Program

Although the early experience of Jonathan and Park Forest South should not be used as a basis for evaluating the federal new communities program as a whole, the implications of the findings for the federal program cannot be ignored.

Jonathan and Park Forest South exemplify the extent of commitment to balanced development required of participants in the federal program. Goals for community service systems, industrial development, low- and moderate-income housing, and environmental protection that are contained in their project agreements with the Department of Housing and Urban Development far surpass even the most advanced nonfederally assisted new communities. On the other hand, development experience in Jonathan and Park Forest South and residents' responses to these communities do not suggest that the accomplishments of federally assisted new communities are likely to be very different from those achieved by new communities that are not participating in the federal program.

The reason for this expectation is straightforward. The federal new communities program has required that developers devote a considerable amount of attention to environmental and community service system planning. However, there is little evidence that such planning provides a commensurate return to the developer for the resources invested. These are public functions. Requirements for public planning by the private sector can be expected to result in perfunctory efforts, as was the case for educational and health care planning in Jonathan, or to so divert the developer from the fundamental task of producing a marketable product, as in Park Forest South, that the new community venture faces financial ruin. As often as not, both results may occur. If the federal new communities program is to produce a truly new generation of new communities, some means must be found to match the private sector's capacity to design and produce high quality housing and neighborhood environments with an improved capacity of the public sector to plan for and provide equally high quality community service systems.

The need for better performance from the public sector was clearly anticipated in the Urban Growth and New Community Development Act of

436

Table 18-8
Residents' Prognoses for the Future

Prognoses/Recommendations	Percent of Respondents			
	Jonathan	Chanhassen	Park Forest South	Richton Park
Expectations for the community as a place to live in five years				
Community will be a better place in which to live	55	50	55	52
Community will be about the same	24	25	25	23
Community will not be as good a place in which to live	21	25	20	25
Recommendations for making the community a better place in which to live[a]				
Improve community facilities				
Shopping facilities and commercial services	20	18	23	7
Recreational facilities	8	19	24	22
Streets and bicycle routes	4	2	3	16
Schools	3	5	11	6
Health care facilities	2	1	5	3
Maintain quality of the environment				
Limit and control growth/reduce density	13	31	21	7
Protect natural areas from development	5	8	11	1
Improve maintenance of building exteriors and private yards	3	2	2	6
Improve maintenance and appearance of public and common open space	0	1	1	2

Improve public services

Public transportation	11	3	5	4
Other services (police, fire, etc.)	5	3	5	6
Change behavior of developer and local authorities				
Adhere to community master plan	10	9	7	1
Improve local government	0	2	4	7
Improve homes association performance	7	4	7	1
Improve developer-citizen relations	3	2	6	0
Increase amount of development				
Increase pace of development	5	2	1	1
Provide more employment opportunities	4	1	1	1
Increase tax base through industrial and commercial development	2	8	1	1
Change social character of community	6	6	7	9
Reduce taxes and cost of living	1	4	2	2
Other responses				
Don't know what could be done	4	2	6	19
No improvements are needed—community is a good place to live	8	7	5	5
No improvements are possible—the situation is hopeless	1	0	1	2

[a]Responses add to more than 100 percent because some respondents mentioned more than one type of improvement.

1970. Section 715 of the act authorized public service grants to enable local governments and school districts to provide services during the first three years of development when the lag between demands generated by residential development and increases in the tax base are most acute. This section of the act was never funded. Funding of Section 718, which provided supplemental grants to the federal share of existing categorical grants-in-aid programs, was limited to $25 million and was terminated in 1973. Section 719 of the act was to provide technical assistance to developers and public agencies, but was never funded. Finally, Section 720 of the Title VII legislation was designed to provide special planning grants for public service planning in new communities, but it also was never funded. Thus, public agencies that served Jonathan and Park Forest South were no better equipped to respond to new community development opportunities and problems than agencies serving nonfederally assisted new communities.

Not only has a variety of federal assistance promised by the Title VII legislation been lacking, but there has also been very little coordination between the New Communities Administration in the Department of Housing and Urban Development and local agencies attempting to serve federally assisted communities. Public officials serving both Jonathan and Park Forest South reported that they have had minimal contacts with federal new community administrators.

In short, while the federal new communities program promised to close the gap between the rhetoric of the new communities movement and the realities of community development in the United States, the degree of commitment from the federal government has never lived up to the potential of the program. Until this occurs, federally assisted new communities will provide only marginally better living environments than nonfederally assisted new communities. On the other hand, significantly more income and racial integration can be expected in the federally assisted new communities than are characteristic of new suburban growth. Whether this level of accomplishment justifies continued federal participation in new community development (at recent levels of assistance) is a moot question until the experiences of target populations—subsidized housing residents, blacks, and the elderly—currently living in new communities are examined. This topic is addressed in chapter 19.

19 Experiences of Target Populations

The rationale for policies of income, racial, and age integration in new communities is based on two suppositions. One is that new communities provide mechanisms for demonstrating that housing can be designed, grouped, and distributed in such ways as to reduce middle-class hostility to integration. As shown in chapter 5, in those cases where income and racial integration have occurred, new communities appear to be serving this function. A second supposition underpinning support for balanced new community development is the belief that new communities offer a means for improving the housing, neighborhoods, and community facilities available to disadvantaged groups in our society. The experiences of target populations living in new communities—subsidized housing residents, blacks, and elderly persons—are summarized in this chapter.

Subsidized Housing Residents

By early 1974, subsidized housing units had been constructed in 5 of the 13 nonfederally assisted new communities and in Jonathan and Park Forest South—the two federally assisted communities that were studied. Selected characteristics of these housing projects are summarized in table 19-1.

With the exception of a 300-unit townhouse complex in Columbia, subsidized housing projects were each located on one site. Columbia experimented by locating its first project on five sites in two villages, but did not follow this practice with later subsidized housing developed in the community. Nevertheless, only three of the subsidized housing projects in the sample new communities were isolated from the rest of the community: FHA Section 235 single-family detached subdivisions in Forest Park and Jonathan and a large planned unit development (PUD) in Park Forest. Reston had the only concentration of several projects in one area of the community—three garden apartment complexes in the Village of Hunters Woods. However, the three projects are within walking distance of the new U.S. Geological Survey facility in Reston and are located near a very expensive neighborhood composed of single-family detached homes.

With these exceptions, there does not appear to be a pattern of isolation or concentration of subsidized housing across the seven new communities. The tendency is for each project to be situated on one site, but not isolated

Table 19-1
Subsidized Housing Projects in New Communities

Community	Number of Units	Subsidy Program	Initial Occupancy	Percent Minority Population	Spatial Location and Design
Columbia	300	FHA 221(d)3	1969	30	Townhouse apartments on five sites in two villages
	10	FHA 235	1970	NR	Single family; scattered; one village
	108	FHA 236	1971	48	Garden apartments; one site; near village center
	12	FHA 235	1971	NR	Townhouses; in project of 156 units
	100	FHA 236	1973	35	High-rise apartments; across from village center
Reston	198	FHA 221(d)3	1969	17	Garden apartments; nine buildings; one site
	138	FHA 202	1971	2	High-rise apartments; elderly; near village center
	240	FHA 236	1973	20	Garden apartments; 14 buildings; one site
	200	FHA 236	1974	NR	Garden apartments; 12 buildings; one site
	50	Turnkey	1974	NR	Garden apartments; one site
Park Forest	106	FHA 213	1971	2	High-rise apartments; elderly; near town center
	248	IHDA[a]	1973	10	High-rise apartments and townhouses; 372 units; mixed-income PUD; isolated
Lake Havasu City	64	FHA 235	1969	0	Single family; 50 percent of subdivision
Forest Park	201	FHA 235	1971	10	Single family; entire subdivision; isolated
Jonathan	55	FHA 235	1971	0	Single family; entire subdivision; isolated
	96	FHA 236	1971	3	Townhouse apartments; one site
Park Forest South	46	IHDA[b]	1974	NR	High-rise apartment building in four-building complex

Note: Projects as of December 1973. NR = Not reported

[a]Illinois Housing Development Authority; 66 percent of units financed under FHA Section 236 program.
[b]Illinois Housing Development Authority; 78 percent of units financed under FHA Section 236 program.

from other housing. This pattern is consistent with the recommendations of Herbert J. Gans (1973), who observed that if new communities are to pursue a policy of class integration, it should best be done on a community level, with homogeneity on the block level maintained.

Resident Heterogeneity

The data summarized in table 19-2 indicate the extent of resident heterogeneity in new communities with subsidized housing. Three categories of respondents are represented—higher income residents living in nonsubsidized housing in five new communities, residents of subsidized housing in the same five new communities, and residents of subsidized housing in two conventional communities. The five new communities— Columbia, Forest Park, Jonathan, Lake Havasu City, and Reston—had occupied subsidized housing at the time of the household survey in the spring of 1973. A special subsample of 274 subsidized housing residents was obtained in these communities.[a] For comparative purposes, subsidized housing residents were interviewed in two conventional communities, including residents living in a FHA Section 235 single-family detached subdivision in Richton Park, Illinois (located adjacent to Park Forest and Park Forest South), and the residents of three FHA Section 236 rental apartment projects near Laurel, Maryland, located 17 miles northwest of Washington, D.C., in Prince George's County.[b]

In many respects, the nonsubsidized housing residents in the five new communities with subsidized housing had similar characterisitics to residents of new communities without subsidized housing. Age, occupation, income, and family composition were nearly identical. However, the communities with subsidized housing had attracted residents with somewhat more formal education and had also attracted more black residents.

---

[a] The special subsidized housing subsample included: Columbia (61 respondents); Forest Park (53 respondents); Jonathan (55 respondents); Lake Havasu City (47 respondents); and Reston (58 respondents).

[b] Although these projects were chosen to be representative of suburban subsidized housing in the vicinity of the sample new communities, comparative data to establish this fact firmly were not available. Therefore, some caution should be exercised in generalizing the comparisons presented in this chapter to all suburban subsidized housing located outside of new communities.

To maintain the comparability of the conventional community subsidized housing sample with subsidized housing in new communities and other conventional communities, interviews conducted in a FHA Section 235 single-family detached subdivision in Chicago Heights, Ill., were not included in the analyses reported in this chapter. These interviews were deleted because: (1) the all-black occupancy of the subdivision was not comparable to the FHA Section 235 single-family detached subdivisions in new communities; and (2) the relatively high rate of home abandonment in the subdivision was not comparable to subsidized housing projects in either new communities or suburban conventional communities.

Table 19-2

Characteristics of Residents Living in Nonsubsidized and Subsidized Housing in Five New Communities and Two Conventional Communities

	Percent of Respondents		
	Five New Comunities [a]		Two Conventional Communities [b]
Characteristic	Nonsubsidized Housing	Subsidized Housing	Subsidized Housing
Housing tenure and type			
Own	77[c]	42	32
Single-family detached	86	100	100
Townhouse/duplex	13	0	0
Apartment	1	0	0
Rent	23	58[c]	68
Single-family detached	13	5	3
Townhouse/duplex	39	45	59
Apartment	48	50	38
Life cycle characteristics			
Age of head of household			
Under 35	48	64[c]	83[d]
35-54	38[c]	30[d]	13
55 or older	14[c]	6	4
Household composition			
Unmarried adults without children	13[c]	4	6
Unmarried adults with children	3	20[c]	12
Married couples with children	58	67[c]	70
Married couples without children	26[c]	9	12
Socioeconomic characteristics			
Education (household head)			
High school graduate or less	29	67[c]	66
Some college or college graduate	38[c]	30	33
Graduate or professional training	33[c]	3	1
Occupation (household head)			
Professional or managerial	62[c]	24	22
Other white collar	15	18	24
Blue collar	23	59[c]	54
Family Income (1972)			
Under $10,000	16	62[c]	52
$10,000-$14,999	26	26	35
$15,00-$24,999	40[c]	10	11
$25,000 or more	18[c]	2	2

	Percent of Respondents		
	Five New Comunities[a]		Two Conventional Communities[b]
Characteristic	Nonsubsidized Housing	Subsidized Housing	Subsidized Housing
Race			
White	93[c]	82	80
Black	6	17[c]	20
Other	1	1	0

[a]Five new communities with subsidized housing subsamples include: Columbia, Forest Park, Jonathan, Lake Havasu City, and Reston.

[b]Two conventional communities with subsidized housing samples include: Laurel, Maryland, and Richton Park, Illinois.

[c]Difference between subsidized housing and nonsubsidized housing new community respondents statistically significant at 0.05 level of confidence.

[d]Difference between subsidized housing new community respondents and subsidized housing conventional community respondents statistically significant at 0.05 level of confidence.

This combination of income and racial integration is significant, since it has been noted that "the most difficult kind of residential balance to achieve is integration of both racial and economic groups" (Fava 1970, p. 14).

The residents of subsidized housing in new communities represented a distinctly lower status group than nonsubsidized housing residents. They held much lower status jobs, earned less than half the annual income (with larger families), had less formal education, and more than six times the proportion of households with children living in the home and a single, divorced, separated, or widowed household head. It has been suggested that lower status "families with emotional and social problems that are visible to their neighbors," be screened and discouraged from settling in new communities (Gans 1973, p. 149). From the data presented in table 19-2 it cannot be determined whether the subsidized housing residents in the five new communities had problems. However, the data do demonstrate that subsidized housing new community residents do not differ significantly in social status from subsidized housing residents living in conventional communities.

Why Subsidized Housing Residents Moved to New Communities

With the exception of the cost of housing, subsidized housing residents moved to new communities for about the same reasons as nonsubsidized housing residents. See table 19-3. Nearness to the outdoors and natural

Table 19-3
Subsidized Housing Residents' Reasons for Moving to New Communities and Perceived Improvements Gained from the Move

	Percent of Respondents					
	Reason for Moving			Improvements Gained		
	New Communities[a]		Conventional Communities[b]	New Communities[a]		Conventional Communities[b]
Community Characteristic	Nonsubsidized Housing	Subsidized Housing	Subsidized Housing	Nonsubsidized Housing	Subsidized Housing	Subsidized Housing
Housing						
Construction of the dwelling	4	4	3	43	43	44
Cost of buying or renting	15	46[c]	68[d]	26	55[c]	59
Layout and space	18	16	12	67	65	61
Community facilities						
Health and medical services	1	3	4	26	35[c,d]	19
Public schools	13	13	17	46	59[c,d]	37
Recreational facilities	19[c]	12[d]	3	71	74[d]	37
Shopping facilities	5	5	12	36	42[c]	42

Physical environment

Appearance of immediate neighborhood	16[c]	10	15	62[c]	51	44
Climate	17	12[d]	1	32	33[d]	5
Nearness to outdoors	39	46[d]	10	69	71[d]	46
Community planning	34[c]	17[d]	2	79	78[d]	42

Social environment

Good place to raise children	36	44[c]	25	71	67[d]	44
Participation in community	8	7	3	66	69[d]	51
Safety from crime	5	7	5	48	44[d]	30
Type of people in neighborhood	12	11	9	48[c]	32	33

Work/transportation/living costs

Finding a job in community	7	7	10	28	45[c,d]	25
Convenience to work	26	24	36	42	54[c]	44
Ease of getting around community	7	6	11	56	60[d]	32
Cost of living in community	1	7[c]	19[d]	12	27[c]	25

[a] Five new communities with subsidized housing subsamples include: Columbia, Forest Park, Jonathan, Lake Havasu City, and Reston.

[b] Two conventional communities with subsidized housing samples include: Laurel, Md., and Richton Park, Ill.

[c] Difference between subsidized housing and nonsubsidized housing new community respondents statistically significant at 0.05 level of confidence.

[d] Difference between subsidized housing new community respondents and subsidized housing conventional community respondents statistically significant at 0.05 level of confidence.

environment, the community as a good place to raise children, and convenience to work were important to both groups. As would be expected,
three times the proportion of subsidized housing residents as nonsubsidized housing residents mentioned the cost of buying or renting as a factor
in their moving decision. Since they were more likely to have children
living in their households, it is also not surprising that subsidized housing
residents placed somewhat more emphasis on the community as a place to
raise children than did nonsubsidized housing residents. On the other hand,
subsidized housing residents, like lower income residents in general, were
less concerned with the character of community planning than were more
affluent residents of the same new communities.

Compared to subsidized housing residents who were living in the conventional communities, where cost factors and convenience to work were
of overriding importance in the choice of a home, those living in new
communities were attracted by a broader array of community characteristics. They were significantly more likely than the conventional community residents to have moved to their communities because of the character
of recreational facilities, nearness to the outdoors, community planning,
and, reflecting the aviiailability of subsidized housing in Lake Havasu City,
the climate.

A majority of the subsidized housing respondents reported that their
move to a new community had resulted in improvements in 11 of the 19
community characteristics summarized in table 19-3. In contrast, a majority of the subsidized housing residents who had moved to the conventional
communities reported improvements in only 3 of the 19 characteristics—
the cost of buying or renting, the layout and space of their home, and
participation in community life. A quarter or more new than conventional
community subsidized housing residents perceived improvements in recreational facilities, nearness to the outdoors and natural environment,
overall community planning, and ease of getting around the community.
Between 20 percent and 25 percent more new than conventional community subsidized housing residents saw improvements in the public schools,
the community as a place to raise children, and ease of finding a job in the
community. In short, households perceived improvements in many more
community characteristics as a result of their move to new communities
than did households who moved to subsidized housing in the conventional
communities.

In a number of cases subsidized housing residents were also more likely
to perceive improvements over their former communities than new community residents who were not living in subsidized housing. Differences
that were statistically significant included the cost of buying or renting,
health and medical services, public schools, shopping facilities, ease of

finding a job in the community, convenience to work, and the cost of living in the community. In contrast, the only factors for which nonsubsidized housing residents were more likely to perceive improvements were two aspects of the immediate neighborhood—the type of people living there and neighborhood appearance.

Subsidized Housing Residents' Satisfaction with Housing and the Immediate Neighborhood

Nonsubsidized housing residents' greater satisfaction with housing and neighborhood characteristics are elaborated in table 19-4. In the case of single-family detached subdivisions, nonsubsidized housing residents gave significantly higher ratings than subsidized housing residents to the livability of their homes and immediate neighborhoods and to the adequacy of indoor space, neighborhood appearance, lack of crowding, privacy, quiet, safety, maintenance, convenience, and reputation. In the case of rental apartments, nonsubsidized housing residents gave significantly higher ratings to overall neighborhood livability, outdoor privacy, neighborhood attractiveness, quiet, and reputation. For both types of housing, subsidized housing residents gave better ratings to the cost of buying or renting.

In sum, while new community development offered subsidized housing residents a better community than they could achieve in other suburban locations, price constraints on housing and federal regulations governing housing and neighborhood design resulted in housing satisfaction that was distinctly lower than that of the nonsubsidized housing residents of new communities and not much different from that of subsidized housing residents living in conventional communities. What is more, the strikingly lower ratings given to the reputation of the immediate neighborhood suggests that new community development has not succeeded in diminishing the stigma attached to residence in subsidized housing projects.

The data summarized in table 19-4 also facilitate comparisons between the two major types of subsidized housing available in new communities—ownership single-family detached homes subsidized under the FHA Section 235 program and rental apartments subsidized under the FHA Section 221(d)3 and Section 236 programs. In general, there was much less difference in the housing and neighborhood evaluations of single-family and apartment subsidized housing residents than was true of nonsubsidized housing residents. This seems to be primarily due to the rather low ratings given to subsidized single-family detached units in comparison with nonsubsidized single-family housing. The primary advantages in favor of the new community subsidized single-family ownership homes

Table 19-4

Subsidized Housing Residents' Evaluations of Housing and the Immediate Neighborhood

	Percent of Respondents					
	Single-family Detached (Own)			Apartments (Rent)		
	New Communities[a]		Conventional Communities[b]	New Communities[c]		Conventional Communities[d]
Housing and Neighborhood Characteristics	Nonsubsidized Housing	Subsidized Housing	Subsidized Housing	Nonsubsidized Housing	Subsidized Housing	Subsidized Housing
Dwelling unit						
Completely satisfied with dwelling	44[e]	20	34	14	18	21
Better investment than alternatives	58[e]	45	32	NA	NA	NA
Cost better than previous dwelling	28[e]	54[e]	78[f]	20	52[e,f]	30
Enough indoor space	84[e]	62	63	54	64	71
Enough outdoor space	83	80	88	75	71	70
Outdoor privacy available	51	44[f]	19	39[e]	22	18
Construction better than previous dwelling	55	49	32	31	44	61

Immediate neighborhood[a]

Completely satisfied with overall livability	56[e]	31	34	43[e]	28	12
Attractive	47[e]	16	15	32[e]	16	18
Uncrowded	56[e]	15	17	19	11	12
Private	58[e]	29	37	36	37	32
Quiet	49[e]	19	37	34[e]	13	21
Friendly	52	44	48	31	37	24
Good reputation	63[e]	35	24	50[e]	18	21
Safe	61[e]	46	49	31	23	18
Well kept up	55[e]	29	29	33	24	32
Convenient	57[e]	42	32	45	49	32
Homogeneous	26	18	29	13	11	12

NA = Not applicable to rental housing

[a] Three new communities with subsidized housing single-family detached subsamples include: Forest Park, Jonathan, and Lake Havasu City.

[b] Single-family detached subsidized housing sample in Richton Park, Ill.

[c] Two new communities with subsidized housing rental apartment subsamples include: Columbia and Reston.

[d] Rental apartment subsidized housing sample in Laurel, Md.

[e] Difference between subsidized housing and nonsubsidized housing new community respondents statistically significant at 0.05 level of confidence.

[f] Difference between subsidized housing new community respondents and subsidized housing conventional community respondents statistically significant at 0.05 level of confidence.

[g] Highest rating on five-point scale.

over subsidized rental apartments were in evaluations of outdoor yard space, the availability of privacy from neighbors, reputation of the neighborhood, and safety of the neighborhood. Overall evaluations of dwelling unit and neighborhood livability, however, were nearly identical. Because of this, there does not appear to be a strong case in terms of residents' livability perceptions for one or the other type of subsidized housing in new communities.

Satisfaction with Community Facilities and Overall Community Livability

The similarity of new community and conventional community subsidized housing residents' evaluations of their homes and neighborhoods was not matched by their evaluations of community facilities and overall community livability. As illustrated in table 19-5, subsidized housing residents living in new communities tended to give higher ratings to health care, recreational facilities, schools, ease of getting around the community, and to overall community livability.

Table 19-5
Subsidized Housing Residents' Evaluations of Community Facilities and Overall Community Livability

	Percent of Respondents		
	Five New Communities[a]		Two Conventional Communities[b]
Indicator	Nonsubsidized Housing	Subsidized Housing	Subsidized Housing
Health care			
Better than previous community	26	35[c,d]	19
Excellent or good	50	51	44
Satisfied with expenditures for public health facilities	47	45	40
Recreation			
Better than previous community	71	74[d]	37
Excellent or good	83[c]	73[d]	31
Satisfied with community expenditures for outdoor recreational facilities	65	62[d]	25

| | Percent of Respondents | | |
| | Five New Communities[a] | | Two Conventional Communities[b] |
Indicator	Nonsubsidized Housing	Subsidized Housing	Subsidized Housing
Schools			
Better than previous community	46	59[c,d]	37
Excellent or good	76	76	75
Satisfied with community expenditures for public schools	58	58	62
Shopping			
Better than previous community	36	42[c]	42
Excellent or good	60[c]	43	51
Transportation			
Ease of getting around community better than previous community	56	60[d]	32
Convenience to work better than previous community	42	54[c]	44
Satisfied with community expenditures for public transportation	46	43	31
Overall community livability			
Excellent or good	86[c]	79[d]	53
Would recommend community to a friend or relative as a particularly good place to which to move	78[c]	71[d]	35
Community will be a better place to live in five years	45	41	39

[a]Five new communities with subsidized housing subsamples include: Columbia, Forest Park, Jonathan, Lake Havasu City, and Reston.

[b]Two conventional communities with subsidized housing samples include: Laurel, Md., and Richton Park, Ill.

[c]Difference between subsidized housing and nonsubsidized housing new community respondents statistically significant at 0.05 level of confidence.

[d]Difference between subsidized housing new community respondents and subsidized housing conventional community respondents statistically significant at 0.05 level of confidence.

Compared to nonsubsidized housing residents living in the same new communities, subsidized housing residents gave somewhat higher overall ratings to health care, shopping, and convenience to work in comparison with their previous communities. On the other hand, they gave significantly lower ratings to the excellence of recreational and shopping facilities and to overall community livability. The lower ratings given to community shopping and recreational facilities were due solely to the lower satisfaction with these facilities of subsidized housing residents living in Forest Park. The FHA Section 235 subsidized single-family project in Forest Park was located at the edge of the community some distance from community shopping and recreational facilities. In addition, the major community recreational facility, a swimming center operated by a nonprofit community club, was priced beyond the means of subsidized housing residents.

The somewhat lower ratings given by subsidized housing residents to overall community livability was due to the relatively low livability ratings given to Columbia and Reston; in the three other new communities (Forest Park, Jonathan, and Lake Havasu City) differences in livability ratings given by subsidized housing and nonsubsidized housing residents were not statistically significant. Twenty nine percent fewer Columbia subsidized housing than nonsubsidized housing respondents (54 percent versus 83 percent) rated Columbia as an excellent or good place to live. Seventeen percent fewer Reston subsidized housing than nonsubsidized housing respondents (78 percent versus 95 percent) rated Reston as an excellent or good place to live. The greater dissatisfaction of subsidized housing residents in these two new communities was not due to differential perceptions of the quality of community facilities and services, which tended to receive similar ratings from both groups of respondents. Instead, subsidized housing residents rated community livability lower because they were much less likely to be satisfied with their homes and neighborhoods. In both new communities 20 percent more nonsubsidized housing than subsidized housing residents were satisfied with their homes and twice the proportion of nonsubsidized housing as subsidized housing residents rated neighborhood livability highly. Both of these factors, of course, are tied more to FHA standards for subsidized housing (and the cost constraints imposed on such housing) than to the design decisions of new community planners.

When they were asked what could be done to make their communities better places in which to live, the responses of subsidized housing and nonsubsidized housing residents were generally similar. Both types of new community residents most often suggested improvements in recreational facilities and programs. Other improvements suggested by 10 percent or more of the subsidized housing and nonsubsidized housing respondents included improved shopping facilities, limitations on future growth and increased density, and changes in the social character of the community (particularly the hope that people would be friendlier and show more interest in the community).

Social Integration

Occasional concern has been expressed that lower income residents living in the midst of affluent, high social status communities may achieve the benefits of superior community facilities and services funded by their more affluent neighbors at the cost of extreme social isolation (see, for example, Gans 1973). However, subsidized housing residents living in new communities did not appear to be at all isolated. They had more interaction with friends and relatives than their higher income neighbors or respondents living in the conventional communities. The lower status subsidized housing residents also did not see their higher income neighbors as hostile. Over 80 percent reported that it was "easy to make new friends in the community" and that it was not "harder to call on neighbors in time of need" than in their previous places of residence. Finally, there was only a 7 percent difference between new community subsidized housing residents (49 percent) and nonsubsidized housing residents (56 percent) who felt a part of what went on in their communities.

Thus, from the perspective of subsidized housing residents, new communities appear to offer physical, social, and economic advantages without the undesirable side effects many have feared.

Black Residents

In its 1974 report, *Equal Opportunity in Suburbia,* The United States Commission on Civil Rights wrote,

Despite a plethora of far-reaching remedial legislation, a dual housing market continues today in most metropolitan areas across the United States. Inadequate enforcement by Federal agencies and circumvention or, at best, lip-service adherence by local authorities, builders, real estate agents, and others involved in the development of suburban communities have helped to perpetuate the systematic exclusion of minorities and low-income families. The result has been the growth of overwhelmingly white, largely affluent suburbs, and the concurrent deterioration of central cities, overburdened by inordinately large and constantly increasing percentages of poor and minority residents (The United States Commission on Civil Rights 1974, p. 64).

As reported in chapter 5, new community development has often perpetuated the exclusion of racial minorities from suburban areas. Just over 3 percent of the population of 13 nonfederally assisted new communities

were black. Black households represented 1 percent or less of the population of 5 of the 13 communities. In 8 of the 13 new communities, residents
were significantly more antagonistic to neighborhood integration by
moderate-income black families than to integration by moderate-income
white families.

Nevertheless, racial integration has long been an important goal of new
community proponents. In urging federal support of new community development, the American Institute of Planners (1968, p. iii) recommended
that, "This nation should launch a massive drive to create integrated new
communities . . . for the same reason that it is already working simultaneously to enrich the ghetto and build an integrated society—to create a
single nation undivided by racial strife." Racial integration was included as
one of the goals of Title IV of the 1968 Housing and Urban Development
Act and of the Urban Growth and New Community Development Act of
1970, which provided federal assistance for new community development,
in part, to "increase for all persons, particularly members of minority
groups, the available choices of locations for living and working, thereby
providing a more just economic and social environment" (Section 710 (f)).

Remarkably, however, there has been little heard from blacks about the
desirability of racially integrated new communities. For example, Sylvia F.
Fava (1974, p. 112) has noted ". . . the virtual absence of informed input
by or about blacks during the crucial years when the new communities
provisions of the 1968 and 1970 Housing Acts were passed, the initial
guidelines set, and the first communities accepted for eligibility under these
Titles. A review of the literature to 1971 revealed that the Niagara of
material on the social goals of new communities, including racial integration, was mainly rhetoric and wishful thinking."

In the absence of informed black opinion on the subject, some have
even questioned whether many black households would want to live in
predominantly middle-income, white new communities. According to
Gans (1973, p. 144), "Although discussions of new-town planning generally
take only the first perspective, assuming that new towns are so desirable
that minority people will automatically come to them and live where the
majority population wants them to live, this assumption is by no means
warranted, particularly in an era when some blacks have sought to achieve
racial equality through voluntary self-segregation." After surveying existing data on black attitudes toward living in integrated neighborhoods, Fava
concluded,

The pool of blacks interested in living in New Towns under these circumstances is
relatively limited and is particularly limited among low-income and newly-urban
blacks. If new towns are to achieve a significant racial balance, a strategy must be
devised in the context of and with the cooperation of various segments of the black
population (Fava 1974, p. 119).

The following section reports on the experiences of black pioneers who have already settled in new communities.

Characteristics of Black Residents of New Communities

Although racial integration is limited in new communities, some communities have begun to achieve a degree of racial balance. Columbia and Reston, whose developers have pursued open marketing policies, have achieved national recognition as successfully integrated new communities. In the spring of 1973, 19 percent of the Columbia households and 4 percent of those living in Reston were black. Through in-migration of black families into previously all-white neighborhoods, both Forest Park (9 percent black) and Park Forest (6 percent black) have achieved a relatively greater amount of racial integration then was usual in new communities. Black in-migration has also characterized the early development of federally assisted Park Forest South, where 10 percent of the households were black.

Special subsamples of black households to supplement black respondents who fell into the regular household survey samples were obtained in each of these new communities.[c] For comparative purposes, black residents were also interviewed in two suburban communities with large black populations living in predominantly black single-family detached residential subdivisions. These two included the Carmody Hills subdivision bordering Seat Pleasant, seven miles from downtown Washington, D.C.,in Prince George's County, Maryland; and a predominantly black subdivision in Markham, Illinois, 22 miles south of Chicago's Loop.[d]

Gans (1973, p. 149) has suggested that racial integration in new communities will be more feasible when there are no class differences between racial groups. As shown in table 19-6, this is precisely what has occurred. Black persons living in new communities differ in very few respects from nonblacks. About two thirds of the black household heads had at least some college education (though a slightly higher proportion of blacks than nonblacks had not attended college); a majority were employed in professional or managerial positions (though, again, a somewhat higher proportion of black household heads were employed in blue-collar occupations); and family income in 1972 tended to be somewhat higher for blacks than for nonblacks. Further, black residents were living in the same pro-

[c] The distribution of the 290 black respondents included: Columbia (99 respondents); Reston (43 respondents); Park Forest (29 respondents); Park Forest South (39 respondents); and Forest Park (80 respondents).

[d] These subdivisions were chosen to be representative of housing opportunities available to black families in the vicinity of the sample new communities. Nevertheless, caution should be exercised in generalizing the comparisons presented in this chapter to all conventional suburban communities providing housing for black residents.

Table 19-6

Characteristics of Black and Nonblack Residents Living in Five New Communities and Two Conventional Communities

	Percent of Respondents		
	Five New Communities[a]		*Two Conventional Communities*[b]
Characteristic	*Nonblack*	*Black*	*Black*
Housing Tenure and Type			
Own	67	71	100[c]
Single-family detached	81	83	100[c]
Townhouse/duplex	18	15[c]	0
Apartment	1	2	0
Rent	33	29[c]	0
Single-family detached	6	3	0
Townhouse/duplex	24	24[c]	0
Apartment	70	73[c]	0
Life cycle characteristics			
Age of head of household			
Under 40	66	71[c]	48
40-54	24	26	41[c]
55 or older	10[d]	3	11[c]
Household composition			
Unmarried adults without children	14[d]	6	6
Unmarried adults with children	4	7	13
Married couples with children	62	76[c,d]	65
Married couples without children	21[d]	11	16
Socioeconomic characteristics			
Education (household head)			
High school graduate or less	26	34[d]	61[c]
Some college or college graduate	42[d]	34	30
Graduate or professional training	32	32[c]	9
Employment status			
Only household head employed	61[d]	35	39
Both head and spouse employed	33	61[d]	51
Only spouse employed	1	1	2
Neither head nor spouse employed	5	3	8
Occupation (household head)			
Professional or managerial	61	57[c]	30
Other white collar	19[d]	13	12
Blue collar	20	30[d]	58[c]

| Characteristic | Percent of Respondents | | Two Conventional Communities[b] |
| | Five New Communities[a] | | |
	Nonblack	Black	Black
Family income (1972)			
Under $10,000	14	15	16
$10,000-$14,999	25[d]	16	22
$15,000-$24,999	44	44	48
$25,000 or more	17	25[c,d]	14

[a]Five new communities with black subsamples include: Columbia, Forest Park, Park Forest, Park Forest South, and Reston.

[b]Two conventional communities with black samples include: Seat Pleasant, Md., and Markham, Ill.

[c]Difference between nonblack and black new community respondents statistically significant at 0.05 level of confidence.

[d]Difference between black new community respondents and black conventional community respondents statistically significant at 0.05 level of confidence.

portions in ownership and rental housing and in single-family detached, townhouse, and apartment dwellings as nonblack residents of the five new communities.

In contrast with nonblack households, blacks living in new communities tended to be somewhat younger, somewhat more likely to have children living in the household, and were much more likely to have both the household head and spouse employed.

Although a majority of the black households in the two conventional communities had above average family incomes, they differed in a number of respects from the black families who had settled in new communities. In particular, conventional community black household heads tended to be older, were more likely to have ended formal education with high school graduation, were more likely be working in blue-collar occupations, and to have somewhat lower annual incomes. These differences remained after differences in tenure (owning versus renting) between new community and conventional community black residents were controlled.

New community black households also differed in one other respect from both nonblack households living in new communities and black households who had moved to the two conventional communities. They were much more likely to have moved from a metropolitan central city (Chicago, Baltimore, or Washington, D.C.).

Why Black Residents Moved to New Communities

Six factors were mentioned by 20 percent or more of the black respondents as reasons for having selected a home in a new community. See table 19-7. In order of the frequency they were mentioned, these included: the community as a good place to raise children, overall community planning, the public schools, nearness to the outdoors and natural environment, appearance of the immediate neighborhood, and layout and space of the dwelling and lot. With the exception of the public schools, each of these factors was also mentioned by 20 percent or more of the nonblack respondents as reasons for moving to a new community.

Possibly because they were more likely to have been moving from a central city, black respondents were much more concerned than nonblacks with child-related community characteristics (schools and the community as a place to raise children) and with safety from crime. On the other hand, they were much less concerned than nonblacks with the cost of buying or renting and convenience to work.

The reasons black households gave for moving to new communities also differed from black households' reasons for moving to the two conventional suburban cummunities. Those moving to the conventional communities were more likely to have given aspects of the dwelling (construction quality, cost, and layout and space) as reasons for their choice. They were less likely to have selected their communities because of the character of community planning, the quality and convenience of community facilities, convenience to work, or the quality of the community as a place to raise children (though the latter factor was also an important consideration in their housing choice).

As shown in table 19-7, black households who had moved to new communities were more likely to have improved more aspects of the residential package than nonblack households who had moved to the same new communities and black households who had moved to the conventional suburban communities. The advantage of new over conventional communities for black households was greatest for perceptions of improvements in community planning (36 percent more new community black respondents than conventional community black respondents saw improvement over their former communities). Other sizable differences in favor of new communities included perceived improvements in: recreational facilities (30 percent difference); the community as a good place to raise children (25 percent difference); safety from crime (24 percent difference); ease of getting around the community (17 percent difference); public schools (16 percent difference); and shopping facilities (15 percent difference). However, achieving these benefits involved some costs. Black residents of new communities were significantly less likely than black residents of the conventional communities to feel that the cost of housing and the cost of living were better than the communities from which they had moved.

Black Residents' Satisfaction with Housing and the
Immediate Neighborhood

Compared with nonblack new community single-family homeowners, black homeowners were significantly more satisfied with the livability of both their homes and neighborhoods. As shown in table 19-8, greater black housing satisfaction extended to a number of aspects of their immediate neighborhood, including attractiveness, lack of crowding, privacy, quiet, and neighborhood reputation. In the case of rental apartments, however, there were virtually no differences in housing and neighborhood satisfaction between black and nonblack residents.

Differences in satisfaction between black homeowners living in new and conventional communities were as great as those between black and nonblack new community residents; however, because of the lower number of respondents involved, there were fewer statistically significant differences. In general, black homeowners living in new communities were somewhat more likely to be satisfied with their homes and much more likely to be satisfied with neighborhood livability and various neighborhood attributes than black homeowners living in the conventional communities. Neighborhood attributes that received significantly higher ratings in new communities included lack of crowding, reputation, safety, maintenance, and convenience.

In addition to asking respondents to rate their homes and neighborhoods, they were asked which three neighborhood facilities they would most prefer within one-half mile of their homes. Those most preferred by new community black respondents included a private medical clinic or public health clinic (mentioned by 26 percent), a teen center (26 percent), supermarket (25 percent), indoor movie theater (23 percent), playground (21 percent), library (20 percent), and bowling alley (20 percent). Compared to nonblacks living in the same five new communities, black respondents were significantly more likely to prefer health care facilities, day care center or nursery school, movie theater, teen center, and bowling alley within their neighborhoods. They were significantly less likely to want a quiet place to walk and sit, a convenience store, post office substation, and tennis courts in their neighborhoods. In designing new communities planners should take into account these and other variations in preferences among various population groups.

Black Residents' Satisfaction with Community Facilities
and Overall Community Livability

Evaluations of community facilities and overall community livability are

460

Table 19-7
Black Residents' Reasons for Moving to New Communities and Perceived Improvements Gained from the Move

	Percent of Respondents					
	Reason for Moving			Improvements Gained		
	New Communities[a]		Conventional Communities[b]	New Communities[a]		Conventional Communities[b]
Community Characteristic	Nonblack	Black	Black	Nonblack	Black	Black
Housing						
Construction of the dwelling	3	5	17[c]	44	52[d]	62
Cost of buying or renting	32[d]	15	32[c]	34[d]	27	70[c]
Layout and space	28	22	56[c]	69	82[d]	90[c]
Community facilities						
Health and medical services	1	1	1	28	27	24
Public schools	17	27[c,d]	15	51	66[e,d]	50
Recreational facilities	10	9[e]	2	64	63[e]	33
Shopping facilities	9	7[e]	2	47	54[e]	39

Physical environment						
Appearance of immediate neighborhood	20	23	31	58	71[d]	73
Climate	1	<1	<1	18	21	22
Nearness to outdoors	27	24	24	60	77[d]	74
Community planning	28	31[c]	6	80	83[c]	47
Social environment						
Good place to raise children	35	55[c,d]	37	64	83[c,d]	68
Participation in community	9	12	6	70	66	60
Safety from crime	5	14[d]	19	40	66[c,d]	42
Type of people in neighborhood	15	18	13	47	42	46
Work/transportation/living costs						
Finding a job in community	4	2	0	30	25	24
Convenience to work	32[d]	18[c]	6	36	33	27
Ease of getting around community	7	4	3	47	44[c]	27
Cost of living in community	3	1	5	15	11	29[e]

[a] Five new communities with black subsamples include: Columbia, Forest Park, Park Forest, Park Forest South, and Reston.

[b] Two conventional communities with black samples include: Seat Pleasant, Md., and Markham, Ill.

[c] Difference between black new community respondents and black conventional community respondents statistically significant at 0.05 level of confidence.

[d] Difference between nonblack and black new community respondents statistically significant at 0.05 level of confidence.

Table 19-8
Black Residents' Evaluations of Housing and the Immediate Neighborhood

	Percent of Respondents				
	Single-family Detached (Own)			Apartments (Rent)	
	Five New Communities[a]		Two Conventional Communities[b]	Five New Communities[a]	
Housing and Neighborhood Characteristics	Nonblack	Black	Black	Nonblack	Black
Dwelling unit					
Completely satisfied	31	44[c]	36	19	15
Better investment than alternatives	61	72[c,d]	59	NA	NA
Cost better than previous dwelling	41	34	71[d]	27	22
Enough indoor space	77	81	89	58	73
Enough outdoor space	82	86	87	73	80
Outdoor privacy available	46	47	58	33	24
Construction better than previous dwelling	50	60	64	35	52[c]

Immediate neighborhood[e]

Completely satisfied with livability	53	63[c]	43	37	41
Attractive	39	57[c]	45	32	38
Uncrowded	39	59[c,d]	32	17	26
Private	45	57[c]	48	39	48
Quiet	38	59[c]	50	30	41
Friendly	47	47	38	30	34
Good reputation	57	74[c,d]	44	42	42
Safe	49	55[d]	25	35	35
Well kept up	50	61[d]	42	34	45
Convenient	52	60[d]	38	47	40
Homogeneous	20	18	25	13	9

NA = Not applicable

[a]Five new communities with black subsamples include: Columbia, Forest Park, Park Forest, Park Forest South, and Reston.

[b]Two conventional communities with black samples include: Seat Pleasant, Md., and Markham, Ill.

[c]Difference between nonblack and black new community respondents statistically significant at 0.05 level of confidence.

[d]Difference between black new community respondents and black conventional community respondents statistically significant at 0.05 level of confidence.

[e]Highest rating on five-point scale.

summarized in table 19-9. In general, black residents were as satisfied as nonblacks with their communities, and were considerably more satisfied than black residents of the suburban conventional communities. Differences between blacks and nonblacks living in the five new communities were greatest for satisfaction with community expenditures for public health facilities—black respondents were considerably less satisfied with current expenditure levels. As noted above, black residents were also more interested than nonblack residents in neighborhood public and private medical clinics. However, there was little difference in evaluations of community health care and medical services, either in relation to the respondents' previous communities or in their ratings of the excellence of facilities and services.

New community black residents were also somewhat less satisfied with the excellence of community recreational facilities than nonblack residents. This tendency was most notable in Columbia and Forest Park, where 12 percent and 17 percent fewer black than nonblack respondents rated facilities as excellent or good. In part, blacks' lower satisfaction may stem from the unavailability of facilities for their favorite out-of-home activities. For example, compared to nonblacks, black respondents were much more likely to mention bowling and basketball as their favorite activities. New communities as a whole have not done well in supplying facilities for either of these activities. Ninety-four percent of the black respondents typically traveled outside of their communities to participate in bowling and 42 percent went outside of the community to participate in basketball. Although over 80 percent were satisfied with the bowling facilities they typically used, less than a majority of the black respondents were satisfied with basketball facilities. Finally, blacks expressed greater interest than

Table 19-9
Black Residents' Evaluations of Community Facilities and Overall Community Livability

Indicator	Percent of Respondents		
	Five New Communities[a]		Two Conventional Communities[b]
	Nonblack	Black	Black
Health care			
Better than previous community	28	27	24
Excellent or good	57	56[c]	22
Satisfied with community expenditures for public health facilities	58[d]	43	68[e]

| | Percent of Respondents | | |
| | Five New Communities[a] | | Two Conventional Communities[b] |
Indicator	Nonblack	Black	Black
Recreation			
Better than previous community	64	63[c]	33
Excellent or good	75[d]	67[c]	26
Satisfied with community expenditures for outdoor recreational facilities	61	56	67[c]
Schools			
Better than previous community	51	66[c,d]	50
Excellent or good	77	81[c]	64
Satisfied with community expenditures for public schools	59	54	54
Shopping			
Better than previous community	47	54[c]	39
Excellent or good	74	74[c]	52
Transportation			
Ease of getting around community better than previous community	47	44[c]	27
Convenience to work better than previous community	36	33	27
Satisfied with community expenditures for public transportation	54[d]	46	66[c]
Overall community livability			
Excellent or good	84	86[c]	48
Would recommend community to a friend or relative as a particularly good place to which to move	73	84[c,d]	35
Community will be a better place to live in five years	32	43[c,d]	20

[a]Five new communities with black subsamples include: Columbia, Forest Park, Park Forest, Park Forest South, and Reston.

[b]Two conventional communities with black samples include: Seat Pleasant, Md., and Markham, Ill.

[c]Difference between black new community respondents and black conventional community respondents statistically significant at 0.05 level of confidence.

[d]Difference between nonblack and black new community respondents statistically significant at 0.05 level of confidence.

nonblacks in various community entertainment facilities, which also tended to be lacking in many new communities.

Compared with black respondents living in the suburban conventional communities, black persons living in new communities tended to give higher ratings to community health care, recreational facilities, schools, shopping facilities, the ease of getting around their communities, and overall community livability. These differences occurred both in the aggregate comparisons summarized in table 19-9, as well as when each new community was compared with the conventional community in its metropolitan area. The only exception was the equivalent ratings given to the schools by Columbia black parents and Seat Pleasant black parents. As shown by the differences in community livability ratings, however, which were higher in each new community than in either of the two conventional communities, new communities have provided highly satisfying living environments for their black residents.

When new community black and nonblack residents were asked what could be done to make their communities better places in which to live, only two major differences in their recommendations were apparent. Black residents were somewhat more likely (22 percent versus 14 percent) to suggest that the residents of their communities could be friendlier, could care more about the community, and that race relations could be improved. They were also more likely (12 percent versus 6 percent) to feel the need for improved recreational programs for young adults. These two factors were also the two recommendations that black residents most frequently gave for improving life in their communities.

Social Integration

Although information was not obtained about black residents' contacts with nonblacks in new communities, blacks appear to be about as well integrated into community life as their nonblack neighbors. A significantly higher proportion of black respondents than nonblack respondents (63 percent versus 52 percent) said they felt a part of what went on in their communities. Three fourths of the black respondents (versus just over 80 percent of the nonblack respondents) thought that it was easy to make new friends in their communities. Finally, two thirds of the black respondents (versus just over three fourths of the nonblack respondents) reported that it was no harder to call on their neighbors in time of need than in their former communities. For all of these measures—calling on neighbors, making new friends, and feeling a part of the community—new community black residents indicated a higher degree of social integration than the black residents of the two suburban conventional communities.

In sum, at least for black persons who chose to move to and live in affluent, predominantly white communities, minority status in the community did not appear to have created special hardships. Whether black attitudes would change were the proportion of blacks living in new communities much larger than the 19 percent living in Columbia, or whether these findings apply to less affluent and less socially mobile black households, of course, cannot be deduced from the experiences of black persons now living in new communities. The data do show, however, that new communities have provided highly desirable living environments for those black households with middle and upper middle incomes and some college education who, in any event, are likely to be the first of their race to move in great numbers to suburban locations (see Fava 1974).

Elderly Residents

As of the 1970 census, there were just over 20 million persons age 65 and over in the United States. Elderly persons comprised nearly 10 percent of the population. By the year 2000 the elderly are expected to increase to 28.8 million persons, or about 11.5 percent of the population. Since the elderly, as a group, have needs that are distinctly different from the general population that is likely to settle in new communities (see Lawton and Byerts 1973), it is important to determine the extent to which new communities are meeting their requirements in comparison with conventional suburban environments.

One of the most widely debated issues in planning for the elderly is whether older persons should live primarily in proximity to other older persons (age segregation) or in age mixtures approximating those of the general population (age integration). Although current federal policy rejects large-scale age segregation in new communities (apartment buildings designed and inhabited exclusively by elderly persons are acceptable), most studies of this question have indicated that the elderly are happier in age-segregated living situations. For example, Rostow has noted,

. . . the prevailing wisdom was that the best way to revitalize old people was to mix them up with a lot of young people. It sounded good, but unfortunately it was the surest way to alienation and isolation. Having their own community gives older people an insulation from an outside world that demeans, rejects, and degrades them. They profit from it in many ways. It may not sound very nice, but it's an unfortunate fact of life. (Quoted in Cherry and Cherry, 1974, p. 86. © 1974 by The New York Times Company. Reprinted by permission.)

Similarly, Gans (1973, p. 157) has written "all the available evidence indicates that in a postindustrial society, cultural and other differences between age groups are widening; consequently, such groups have little interest in living together."

The availability of a limited number of age-segregated retirement new communities in the United States offers the opportunity to compare the living experiences of older persons (age 65 and over) residing in age-integrated new communities and age-segregated retirement community environments. In order to pursue this comparison, residents were interviewed in two retirement communities—Rossmoor Leisure World in Laguna Hills, California, and Sun City Center, south of Tampa, Florida.[e] In comparison with the age-integrated new communities and conventional communities, which had developed relatively few facilities and programs specifically for older persons. Rossmoor Leisure World and Sun City Center were planned and developed with the needs of the elderly specifically in mind.

In 1972, Rossmoor Leisure World had approximately 15,000 residents living in 9,028 garden and duplex condominium apartments. The community was surrounded by walls and had security guards to regulate access. A minibus system provided transit service to all parts of the community and to adjacent shopping and health facilities. A major community institution, the Leisure World Foundation, had established an Office of Medical Administration, which supervised health care facilities and services. These included a medical center, home support services with nurses and doctors on 24-hour call, ambulance service, weekly television series dealing with personal health, maintenance of residents' medical records, and assistance to residents in completing health insurance forms. In 1974, the Saddleback Community Hospital began operation at a site adjacent to the community. In addition to golf courses, swimming pools, and tennis courts (which are also offered in age-integrated new communities), Rossmoor Leisure World provided for its residents numerous arts and crafts facilities with instructors, boccie, lawn bowling, shuffleboard courts, stables, library, garden plots (since the community consisted entirely of apartments), and a movie theater. Numerous clubs and social organizations had been formed around residents' leisure interests, previous occupations, and home states.

Sun City Center is located 26 miles south of Tampa in Hillsborough County, Florida. In contrast with the apartments of Rossmoor Leisure World, Sun City Center's 3,000 (1972) residents lived almost entirely in single-family detached homes. The community was begun in 1962 by the Del E. Webb Corporation, but slow home sales led to the sale of the undeveloped land in Sun City Center to W/G Devolopment Corporation in 1972. Future plans call for the conversion of Sun City Center to a retirement

[e] Interviews were completed with 104 Rossmoor Leisure World residents and 100 residents of Sun City Center. These are compared with responses from 153 elderly (age 65 and over) new community residents and 95 elderly residents who were living in the paired conventional communities.

village surrounded by a much larger age-integrated balanced new community. Because of its smaller size, Sun City Center lacked many of the facilities available at Rossmoor Leisure World. Nevertheless, in 1972 it provided a large multifunctional recreational center with craft rooms, lawn bowling, and a swimming pool, an 18-hole golf course, tennis courts, four fishing lakes, a theater, small medical center with two doctors, neighborhood shopping center, library, and a resident-operated ambulance and emergency squad. Many facilities, services, and social programs were provided in Sun City Center by the community's automatic homes association, the Sun City Center Civic Association, and by the voluntary Home Owners Association. In addition, over 50 social clubs and civic groups were active.

Characteristics of Elderly Residents

Because elderly persons (age 65 and over) are much less residentially mobile than younger households, it is not surprising that the elderly comprised only 4 percent of the sample households from 13 nonfederally assisted new communities and only 2 percent of those living in the 13 paired conventional communities.[f] Until these communities have had a greater opportunity to mature, they are not likely to accumulate elderly persons proportionate to the nation as a whole. In addition, elderly persons were not evenly distributed among the new communities. Over half of the respondents who were 65 years old or older lived in 3 new communities located in warmer climates: Lake Havasu City, Arizona; Laguna Niguel, California; and North Palm Beach, Florida.

Selected characteristics of elderly respondents living in new, paired conventional, and two retirement communities are summarized in table 19-10. Compared with older persons in the United States as a whole, those living in all three settings tended to be much more affluent and were somewhat less likely to be living with their spouses. For example, in 1970 only 17 percent of the elderly married couples in the nation, and even fewer unmarried elderly persons, had family incomes of $10,000 or more. In contrast, 62 percent of the new community elderly households, 56 percent of the elderly households living in the conventional communities, 51 percent of those living in Rossmoor Leisure World, and 63 percent of the households in Sun City Center received $10,000 or more in annual income. While 77 percent of the elderly persons in the nation were living with their spouses in 1970, only 65 percent of the households in the new communities, 71 percent in the conventional communities, 64 percent in Sun City Center,

---

[f]Only one of the 407 persons interviewed in the federally assisted new communities—Jonathan and Park Forest South—was 65 years old or older.

Table 19-10

Characteristics of Elderly Residents Living in New Communities, Conventional Communities, and Retirement Communities

Characteristic	Percent of Elderly Respondents			
			Retirement Communities	
	New Communities	Conventional Communities	Rossmoor Leisure World	Sun City Center
Housing tenure and type				
Own	77	95[a]	100[b]	100[b]
Single-family detached	50	56	0	100[b]
Townhouse/duplex	22[a]	3	19	0
Apartment	28	41	81[b]	0
Rent	23[a]	5	0	0
Single-family detached	6	0	0	0
Townhouse/duplex	18	50[a]	0	0
Apartment	76	50	0	0
Life cycle characteristics				
Age of head of household				
Under 65	5	3	0	1
65-74	45	42	61[b]	78[b]
75 or older	50	55	39	21[b]
Household composition				
Unmarried adults without children	34	29	41	36
Unmarried adults with children	1	0	0	0
Married couples with children	4	1	0	0
Married couples without children	61	70	59	64

Socioeconomic characteristics

Education (household head)				
High school graduate or less	46	47	35	36
Some college or college graduate	38	38	48	50
Graduate or professional training	16	15	17	14
Employment status				
Only household head employed	17	13	9	3[b]
Both head and spouse employed	8	7	0[b]	0[b]
Only spouse employed	5	1	0	0
Neither head nor spouse employed	70	79	91[b]	97[b]
Occupation (household head)				
Professional or managerial	58	63	73[b]	64
Other white collar	22	17	16	21
Blue collar	20	20	11	15
Family income (1972)				
Under $10,000	38	44	49	37
$10,000–$14,999	31[a]	16	35	24
$15,000–$24,999	24	19	10	35
$25,000 or more	8	21[a]	6	4
Race				
White	96	99	100	99
Black	4	1	0	1
Other	<1	0	0	0

[a]Difference between elderly respondents living in new communities and conventional communities statistically significant at 0.05 level of confidence.
[b]Difference between elderly respondents living in new communities and elderly respondents living in Rossmoor Leisure World/Sun City Center statistically significant at 0.05 level of confidence.

and 59 percent in Rossmoor Leisure World consisted of married couples.

In general, there were relatively few differences in the characteristics of elderly households living in new, conventional, and retirement communities. Elderly persons living in new communities were the most likely to be renting their homes. They also had somewhat lower annual incomes than elderly persons living in the paired conventional communities (69 percent versus 60 percent had average or below-average incomes). Residents of the two retirement communities, as might be expected, were more likely to be retired than elderly residents living in the new communities and the paired conventional communities. Nevertheless, 70 percent of the new community elderly and almost 80 percent of the elderly respondents in the conventional communities lived in households where the household head was retired. Finally, new communities had attracted a small proportion of elderly black households (4 percent). Black households comprised only 1 percent of the elderly population living in the conventional communities and Sun City Center. No black households were living in the Rossmoor Leisure World sample housing clusters.

In sum, both new communities and retirement communities have tapped the growing market of relatively affluent older Americans who are looking for improved living environments and are willing to make the adjustments required by a change in residence at later stages of their life cycle. Although new community housing is often priced beyond the means of many elderly families, several communities have taken steps to insure that housing is available within the means of the less affluent elderly. A 138-unit high rise apartment building subsidized under the FHA Section 202 program was located in the Lake Anne Village Center in Reston. A high-rise apartment building sponsored by the Cook County Housing Authority was built in Park Forest. Also, housing projects designed for elderly persons with limited means were under consideration in Forest Park and Park Forest South. As these and other elderly housing projects are completed, the goal of age balance in new communities, as well as income and racial balance, may come closer to being realized.

Why Elderly Households Moved to New Communities

There were no significant differences in the reasons elderly households gave for moving to age-integrated new communities and conventional communities. However, there were a number of differences in the appeal of these communities and the two retirement communities.

As shown in table 19-11, the key reasons for the move to a new community (mentioned by 20 percent or more of the elderly households) were: (1) climate (mentioned by 44 percent of the households); (2) near-

Table 19-11
Elderly Residents' Reasons for Moving to Communities and Perceived Improvements Gained from the Move

	Percent of Respondents							
	Reason for Moving				Improvements Gained			
Community Characteristic	NC	CC	RLW	SCC	NC	CC	RLW	SCC
Housing								
Construction of the dwelling	7	9	1	2	35	30	16[a]	33
Cost of buying or renting	11	15	6	5	31	46[b]	16[a]	38
Layout and space	25	35	6[a]	12[a]	57	46	28[a]	45
Community facilities								
Health and medical services	9	8	36[a]	3	23	13	72[a]	21
Recreational facilities	14	21	30[a]	32[a]	53	45	84[a]	84[a]
Shopping facilities	23	16	1[a]	1[a]	43	34	38	19[a]
Physical environment								
Appearance of immediate neighborhood	26	27	22	46[a]	61[b]	39	45[a]	52
Climate	44	54	40	62[a]	65	71	70	89[a]
Nearness to outdoors	36	37	15[a]	19[a]	58	47	55	48
Community planning	12	5	23[a]	30[a]	68[b]	39	61	73
Social environment								
Participation in community	7	4	11	20[a]	49[b]	32	63	57
Safety from crime	12	5	62[a]	19	51	43	87[a]	82[a]
Type of people in neighborhood	16	20	10	37[a]	41[b]	20	38	50
Work/transportation/living costs								
Finding a job in community	0	1	0	0	18	25	6[a]	15
Convenience to work	5	5	2	0	23	32	10[a]	23
Ease of getting around community	18	16	11	2	49	41	66[a]	75[a]
Cost of living in community	1	2	7	4	19	19	13	31

NC = New communities; CC = Conventional communities; RLW = Rossmoor Leisure World; SCC = Sun City Center

[a]Difference between elderly respondents living in new communities and elderly respondents living in Rossmoor Leisure World/Sun City Center statistically significant at 0.05 level of confidence.

[b]Difference between elderly respondents living in new communities and conventional communities statistically significant at 0.05 level of confidence.

ness to the outdoors and natural environment (36 percent); (3) appearance of the neighborhood (26 percent); (4) layout and space of the dwelling and lot (25 percent); and (5) the availability of shopping facilities (23 percent). Compared to the general population of new communities, elderly households were much more likely to be attracted by the climate, shopping facilities, and ease of getting around the community (mentioned by 18 percent of the elderly households). As would be expected, new community elderly residents were much less concerned with convenience to work, the community as a place to raise children and the schools. Surprisingly, they were also much less concerned with the cost of buying or renting. It seems likely that elderly households had accumulated substantial personal assets so that the purchase or rental of a new home was not a major financial burden.

A number of the features of the retirement communities are reflected in the reasons elderly households gave for moving to them. For example, compared to the new communities, elderly households were much more likely to have moved to Rossmoor Leisure World because of the health and medical services there, recreational facilities designed for the elderly, safety from crime provided by an extensive security system, and the overall planning of the community. Sun City Center residents were significantly more likely to have been attracted by the community's recreational facilities, climate (many had moved from the Midwest), community planning, appearance of immediate neighborhood, type of people living in the neighborhood, and community planning. New community elderly residents, on the other hand, were more likely than the residents of either Rossmoor Leisure World or Sun City Center to have moved because of community shopping facilities, the layout and space of their homes, and nearness to the natural environment.

Table 19-11 also summarizes elderly residents' perceptions of improvements gained by their move. Although new and conventional community elderly respondents mentioned about the same reasons for moving to their communities, new community elderly residents were more likely to believe they had made improvements in their living situations over their former communities. These differences were most notable for the appearance of the immediate neighborhood, community planning, participation in community life, and satisfaction with the type of people living in the neighborhood. The conventional community elderly respondents were somewhat more likely to believe that the cost of housing was better than in their previous communities.

Compared to elderly persons who had moved to new communities, those who had moved to Rossmoor Leisure World were much less likely to perceive improvements in the construction, cost, and layout and space of their dwellings and appearance of the immediate neighborhood. Since

Rossmoor Leisure World was an apartment community, residents' lack of enthusiasm about their homes and immediate neighborhoods is understandable. On the other hand, the facilities at Rossmoor designed specifically for the elderly are reflected in residents' perceptions of improvements over their previous communities. Compared to new community elderly residents, those living in Rossmoor Leisure World were much more likely to feel that they had gained improvements in health and medical services, recreational facilities, safety from crime, and ease of getting around the community.

Since Sun City Center consisted almost entirely of single-family detached homes, it is not surprising that there were no significant differences from new communities in perceptions of improvements in housing or neighborhood characteristics. Along with Rossmoor Leisure World residents, however, Sun City Center residents were more likely than elderly persons living in new communities to perceive improvements in recreational facilities, safety from crime, and ease of getting around the community. They also were more likely to believe that the cost of living was better than in their former communities, but were less likely to see improvements in shopping facilities (only a small neighborhood center was located in the community and residents had to travel many miles to the nearest regional shopping center).

Elderly Residents' Satisfaction with Housing and the Immediate Neighborhood

In general, there was little difference in the housing and neighborhood satisfaction of new community and conventional community elderly single-family homeowners, though elderly occupants of condominium apartments in the conventional communities tended to be more satisfied with their homes and neighborhoods than condominium owners in the new communities. Both retirement community single-family homeowners (Sun City Center) and condominium apartment owners (Rossmoor Leisure World) tended to be more satisfied than elderly residents in either the new communities or the conventional communities. See table 19-12. Compared with younger residents, however, the elderly living in new communities were generally as satisfied or more satisfied with the livability of their homes and neighborhoods.

Compared with single-family detached homes occupied by older households in new communities, homes and neighborhoods in Sun City Center scored particularly well in terms of factors of key importance to the elderly, including neighborhood quiet, friendliness, homogeneity, safety,

Table 19-12
Elderly Residents' Evaluations of Housing and the Neighborhood

	Percent of Respondents					
	Single Family (Own)			Apartments (Own)		
Housing and Neighborhood Characteristics	New Communities	Conventional Communities	Sun City Center	New Communities	Conventional Communities	Rossmoor Leisure World
Dwelling unit						
Completely satisfied	67	64	88[a]	32	66[b]	74[a]
Better investment than alternatives	58	66	64	66	75	66
Cost better than previous dwelling	27	34	36	51	57	16[a]
Enough indoor space	97	95	97	88	81	85
Enough outdoor space	98[b]	83	97	91	96	99
Outdoor privacy available	82	78	71	39	62	71[a]
Construction better than previous dwelling	44	32	35	47[b]	21	15[a]
Immediate neighborhood[c]						
Completely satisfied with livability	66	71	86[a]	75	80	85
Attractive	61	52	98[a]	58	77	88[a]
Uncrowded	45	54	83[a]	45	64	32
Private	71	60	88	54	84[b]	81
Quiet	53	37	95[a]	58	56	71
Friendly	57	61	85[a]	54	84	75
Good reputation	69	75	98[a]	74	96[b]	90[a]
Safe	61	50	97[a]	70	69	90
Well kept up	56	57	95[a]	62	92[b]	81
Convenient	60	60	74	62	84	82
Homogeneous	30	37	59[a]	34	67[b]	56

[a]Difference between elderly respondents living in new communities and elderly respondents living in Sun City Center/Rossmoor Leisure World statistically significant at 0.05 level of confidence.

[b]Difference between elderly respondents living in new communities and conventional communities statistically significant at 0.05 level of confidence.

[c]Highest rating on five-point scale.

and maintenance. Sun City Center residents also gave their neighborhoods higher ratings for attractiveness and reputation. In the case of condominium apartments, elderly residents living in both the conventional communities and Rossmoor Leisure World were more satisfied than new community elderly persons with their dwellings, and, to a lesser extent, with neighborhood livability. Nevertheless, Rossmoor Leisure World scored well behind new community condominium apartments on several counts, including cost, layout and space, and construction quality. Privacy, however, was judged to be much better in the retirement community. Rossmoor Leisure World condominium apartment residents were more satisfied than new community residents with most aspects of the immediate neighborhood around their apartments, though only differences in ratings of attractiveness and neighborhood reputation were statistically significant.

Preferences for neighborhood facilities were generally similar in the new and conventional communities. Elderly residents in both settings most frequently mentioned their desire for a neighborhood supermarket (39 percent of the new community elderly and 50 percent of the conventional community elderly). Other facilities mentioned by more than 20 percent of the new community elderly respondents included a library (37 percent), post office substation (32 percent), quiet place to walk and sit (25 percent), drug store (25 percent), and bus stop (24 percent). Compared to younger persons living in new communities, the elderly were much less interested in neighborhood recreational facilities, such as swimming pools and tennis courts, and facilities for children, such as playgrounds and teen centers.

Elderly residents of the retirement communities were interested in about the same neighborhood facilities as new community elderly residents. The only exception was that retirement community residents were less interested in a neighborhood bus stop, but were much more interested in neighborhood health facilities. Forty-four percent of the Rossmoor Leisure World respondents and 36 percent of those living in Sun City Center said that a private medical clinic was one of the three facilities they most wanted in their neighborhoods. In contrast, only 10 percent of the elderly new community respondents were interested in a clinic. Possibly because of their affluence, neither retirement community nor new community elderly respondents were interested in a public health clinic, which was mentioned as a preferred neighborhood facility by 13 percent or less of the respondents in each setting. Sun City Center residents, but not those in Rossmoor, were highly interested in having a bowling alley in their neighborhood. Rossmoor Leisure World residents, on the other hand, were much more interested than Sun City Center residents (38 percent versus two percent) in a quiet place to walk and sit (probably because of the high concentration of apartments in Rossmoor).

Elderly Residents' Satisfaction with Community Facilities
and Overall Community Livability

As shown in table 19-13, elderly residents living in new communities tended to give higher ratings to community health care and recreational facilities than elderly residents living in the conventional communities. However, there was little difference in elderly residents' satisfaction with shopping facilities, transportation and ease of getting around the community, or overall community livability. Compared to younger residents of the new communities, elderly residents tended to be somewhat more satisfied with community facilities, while ratings of overall community livability were equivalent for both groups.

Rossmoor Leisure World residents tended to be more satisfied with health care, recreational facilities, the ease of getting around the community, and public transportation than new community elderly residents. Their ratings of overall community livability, however, were not significantly higher. Sun City Center residents were more satisfied than new community elderly residents with community recreational facilities and the ease of getting around the community, but were less satisfied with shopping facilities and health care. Sun City Center residents were highly pleased with overall community livability, with 100 percent of the respondents saying they would recommend the community to friends and relatives as a particularly good place to live.

Only two improvements were recommended by more than 10 percent of the new community elderly respondents as ways to make their communities better places in which to live. Twenty-three percent of the elderly residents of new communities thought continued growth should be limited and greater steps taken to protect the natural environment. Thirteen percent thought that the provision of additional shopping facilities would improve community livability. These improvements were also mentioned frequently by elderly persons living in the conventional communities. Rossmoor Leisure World and Sun City Center were the only two communities studied in which more than 20 percent of the respondents reported that their communities were excellent places in which to live and that no improvements were needed. Nevertheless, a number of respondents did have suggestions to make. In Rossmoor Leisure World, 22 percent of the respondents recommended that continued growth of the community be limited and 13 percent wanted to see more shopping facilities. Thirty percent of the Sun City Center residents thought that the addition of more shopping facilities would improve community livability, while 21 percent mentioned the need for more health care facilities, and 10 percent suggested additional recreational facilities.

Social Integration

Based on three indicators of social integration, the age-segregated retirement communities appear to provide more opportunities for social contact and the avoidance of social isolation than age-integrated new communities. For example, while 61 percent of the new community elderly respondents reported that it was not harder to call on neighbors in time of need than in their former communities, 80 percent of the Rossmoor Leisure World respondents and 87 percent of those living in Sun City Center indicated it was not harder to call on neighbors. Eighty-six percent of the elderly persons in Rossmoor Leisure World and 93 percent of those living in Sun City Center said they felt it was easy to make new friends in these communities, compared with 74 percent of the new community elderly respondents. Finally, while less than a majority (43 percent) of the new community elderly said they felt a part of what went on in their communities, 65 percent of the Rossmoor Leisure World and 82 percent of the Sun City Center respondents said they felt a part of their community life.

Summary

Although population balance does not characterize the current profile of residents living in new communities, the preceding data suggest that this is a highly desirable goal, which should continue to be emphasized in the federal new communities program.

Low- and moderate-income residents of subsidized housing and black residents were both more likely to improve the quality of facilities and services available to them by moving to new communities than were white middle-class residents. They also tended to be more satisfied with their living environments than subsidized housing residents and black households living in conventional suburban communities. These findings clearly indicate that there is ample justification for federal policies aimed at encouraging population balance in new communities. Compared with other suburban locations, new communities provide more satisfactory living environments for these target populations without the social isolation that many have feared.

However, the data also show that if new communities are to optimize their response to the needs of black and low- and moderate-income residents, more attention must be given to housing characteristics and community facilities of concern to these groups. In particular, subsidized housing residents were much less satisfied with the livability of their homes and neighborhoods than other new community residents and in some commu-

Table 19-13
Elderly Residents' Evaluations of Community Facilities and Overall Community Livability

| | | | *Percent of Elderly Respondents* | |
| | | | *Retirement Communities* | |
Indicator	*New Communities*	*Conventional Communities*	*Rossmoor Leisure World*	*Sun City Center*
Health care				
Better than previous community	23	13	72[b]	21
Excellent or good	73[a]	47	92[b]	58[b]
Satisfied with community expenditures for public health facilities	87	79	98[b]	57[b]
Recreation				
Better than previous community	53	45	84[b]	84[b]
Excellent or good	82[a]	66	99[b]	94[b]
Satisfied with community expenditures for outdoor recreational facilities	92[a]	78	94	86
Shopping				
Better than previous community	43	34	38	19[b]
Excellent or good	74	67	84	27[b]

Transportation

Ease of getting around community better than previous community	49	41	66[b]	75[b]
Convenience to work better than previous community	23	32	10[b]	23
Satisfied with community expenditures for public transportation	60	57	77[b]	67

Overall community livability

Excellent or good	92	89	98	93
Would recommend community to a friend or relative as a particularly good place to move	82	79	86	100[b]
Community will be a better place to live in five years	27	21	12[b]	45[b]

[a]Difference between elderly respondents living in new communities and conventional communities statistically significant at 0.05 level of confidence.
[b]Difference between elderly respondents living in new communities and elderly respondents living in Rossmoor Leisure World/Sun City Center statistically significant at 0.05 level of confidence.

nities were dissatisfied with available shopping and recreational facilities. Black residents indicated a need for greater attention to public health facilities and to recreational facilities, such as those for bowling and basketball, that are of greater interest to black than nonblack residents. One obvious problem, however, is the attainment of a population of blacks and low- and moderate-income residents sufficiently large, so that it becomes economically feasible to provide facilities geared to their tastes and needs.

Elderly residents living in new communities were somewhat more satisfied with their housing, neighborhoods, and community facilities than were younger families. However, the data do not support the contention, currently embodied in federal new community policy, that age-integrated environments are most desirable for the elderly. In fact, elderly residents living in age-segregated retirement communities, who were demographically similar to new community elderly residents, gave much higher ratings to attributes of their neighborhoods and communities. They also tended to be less isolated and to feel more attached to their communities. These findings suggest that planners and developers would be justified in providing for age-segregated neighborhoods and villages as component sections of otherwise age-integrated new communities. In addition, attention should be given to extending federal support to full-scale age-segregated retirement communities in order to make available the choice of this type of living environment to a broader segment of the elderly population of the United States.

Part VI

New Communities at the Crossroads

20 The Future of New Communities U.S.A.

. . . When it comes to new towns, the image is the message. This is why they hold such profound fascination for planners, architects, and interested laymen. The new town is to these people what "being born again" is to a Baptist preacher; a second chance, redemption, to live a new life unencumbered by the sins of the past.

Unfortunately new towns must be developed in the matrix of reality (Alonso and McGuire 1973, p. 253).

This book has been about the reality of new community development in the United States. It has traced the efforts of myriads of individuals and institutions seeking to produce better communities, documented their successes and failures, and indicated how community development influences people's lives. The results have undoubtedly disappointed many observers who have expounded the virtues of new communities over conventional forms of suburban expansion. The results, however, show that while new communities have encountered their fair share of problems, the promise of new community development is by no means a chimera. Behind the image is the real potential for more rational patterns of urban growth, more effective community service systems, and more livable residential environments.

The reality of new communities is in fact many realities. New communities under development in the United States share some common elements. They are large. They are planned (though sometimes to varying degrees). Their growth has been guided by a unified development organization. Beyond this, new communities differ—in the motivation and social consciousness of their developers, regional contexts for development, stage and pace of growth, and governmental structure. These and other differences make generalization difficult and even somewhat risky. The shining success of one new community may be the faltering stepchild of another.

Nevertheless, common threads run throughout the new community experience. These form the basis for the conclusions about the strengths and weaknesses of existing new community development that follow. Because new community development is, in many respects, in its infancy in the United States, the potential for significant improvements in the processes and outputs of community development remains strong. This chapter presents the research team's conclusions, based on the study findings, about: (1) needed state new community policies; (2) federal participation

485

in new community development; (3) the planning, design, and implementation of new community development programs; and (4) needed additional research. The chapter then concludes with a brief consideration of alternative futures for new community development in the United States.

What New Communities Are Doing Best

The outputs of new community development processes were in many respects superior to those of conventional community growth. The advantages in favor of new communities included: (1) better land use planning and access to community facilities; (2) reduction in automobile travel; (3) superior recreational facilities; (4) enhanced community livability; and (5) improved living environments for low- and moderate-income households, blacks, and the elderly.

Orderly growth and the careful arrangement of land uses have been keystones of the new community concept since the first large-scale community development projects emerged after World War II. Based on objective measures, and from the residents' perspectives, better land use planning is a major benefit of new community development. Compared with conventional suburban communities, new communities provided an increased choice of housing types for purchase or rent. Neighborhoods were designed with more amenities and with greater attention to the provision of safe modes of access to them. A variety of community facilities and services—from elementary schools to doctors' offices—were more conveniently located. Almost without exception, new community residents rated the planning of their communities more highly than the residents of conventional communities.

Major transportation and travel benefits resulted from new community development. New communities provided more alternative modes of travel than conventional communities. New community residents gave higher ratings to the ease of getting around their communities. They were also less likely to use their automobiles. New community residents drove 7.5 percent fewer miles, on average, than conventional community residents, a significant saving in light of the nation's diminishing energy resources.

Centralized direction of the community development process and the use of new forms of community governance enabled new communities to provide better recreational services than conventional suburban communities. In turn, more abundant recreational resources were reflected in residents' evaluations. Recreational facilities and services were rated much higher in new communities than in conventional communities.

Community planning, convenience of facilities, and the generally high quality of new community environments contributed to very high resident assessments of overall community livability. In addition, new community residents were more likely than the residents of conventional communities to rate their communities as excellent or good places to live and to say that they would advise others that their communities were particularly good places to which to move.

Finally, although only a few new communities made significant progress in achieving income, class, and racial balance, new communities provided highly desirable living environments for target populations. Low- and moderate-income residents of subsidized housing were more likely to improve the quality of facilities and services available to them by moving to new communities than were nonsubsidized housing new community residents. They also tended to be more satisfied with their living environments than subsidized housing residents living in conventional communities. Black residents of new communities rated a number of aspects of their homes, neighborhoods, and communities as highly as nonblack residents and were more satisfied with their living environments than black residents of conventional suburban communities. Elderly residents of new communities were generally more satisfied with their living environments than younger residents or elderly persons living in conventional communities. However, older persons living in retirement new communities that were specifically designed with the needs of the elderly in mind tended to be even more satisfied and experienced significantly less isolation from the mainstream of community life.

What New Communities Are Doing Well—But Often Not Better Than Conventional Communities

For a variety of reasons—many of which were beyond the control of developers—there were a number of aspects of community development in which the performance of new communities was little different from that of conventional communities. These included: (1) satisfaction of many of the key goals families hoped to achieve in moving to new and conventional communities; (2) evaluations of housing and neighborhood livability; (3) residents' social perspectives and participation in community life; (4) satisfaction with the quality of life; (5) the provision of some community services; and (6) community governance.

New and conventional community residents gave similar reasons for their choice of a community, and in both settings were likely to feel that their move led to improvements over their previous communities. Perceptions of improvements were equivalent for: (1) the community as a good place to raise children; (2) convenience to work; (3) layout and space of the dwelling and lot; (4) appearance of the immediate neighborhood; and (5) nearness to the outdoors and natural environment.

Both new community and conventional community residents tended to be attracted by characteristics of the home and immediate environment around the home. Satisfaction with the overall livability and various characteristics of the home were similar. Although overall neighborhood livability was also rated the same in new communities and conventional communities, new community residents were more satisfied with some aspects of their neighborhoods. This was particularly so in new community rental apartment neighborhoods, which were rated more highly than conventional community apartment neighborhoods in terms of appearance, privacy, quiet, safety, maintenance, and places for children's outdoor play.

New community development generally had much less impact on social perceptions and participation than many planners had anticipated. Community identity, satisfaction with family life and the community as a place to raise children, neighboring, and participation in community organizations were not much different in new communities than in conventional communities. Although the availability and quality of facilities had a moderately strong effect on participation in recreational activities, participation rates were only marginally higher in new communities than in conventional communities. Finally, residents' perceptions of their quality of life—both in terms of improvements gained from the move to a new community or conventional community and in terms of overall life satisfaction—were equivalent in both settings.

New communities have had particular difficulties with community service systems that are highly dependent on the presence of a substantial market for their financial support or that entail political approvals or support from local governments The disjointed character of health care delivery in the United States, developers' unfamiliarity with social services and lack of interest in aspects of community development that are not self-supporting, and political difficulties in securing approval of health care projects resulted in often inadequate health care and social service facilities and programs in new communities. This situation, however, was no better in conventional suburban communities, where health care facilities and services were even less accessible than in new communities. Inadequate health care resources were reflected in residents' attitudes. A sizable proportion of new community and conventional community residents felt that health and medical services were not as good in their present communities as where they had lived before.

Based on perceptions that families want public schools that are easily accessible to their homes, many new community developers contributed to the provision of schools—through donations of staff time, land, and funds for school construction. Based on their experiences with both new community and more conventional forms of urban development, school officials often recognized the advantages to the educational system from the advanced planning that was possible in new communities. Nevertheless, the outcomes of school development processes were similar in new and conventional communities. Although new community schools tended to be more conveniently located than schools in conventional communities, there was little difference in terms of the availability of schools, degree of crowding, use of innovative techniques, community school programs, student performance, parents' perceptions of their children's attitudes toward school, and parents' overall evaluations of the schools.

New communities have been caught between the financial risk involved in premature shopping center development and the risk of losing opportunities to competing centers outside of the new community if shopping centers are delayed too long. As a whole, new communities were doing little better than conventional communities in providing shopping and commercial services. Shopping facilities tended to be somewhat more accessible to users, but the per capita number of establishments was similar. Compared with conventional community residents, those living in new communities were somewhat more likely to patronize a shopping center within their own community, but were somewhat less likely to shop for convenience items and at supermarkets in the community. Although residents of some new communities rated shopping facilities better than the residents of conventional communities, the advantage in favor of new communities was small.

Finally, new communities often did not succeed in centralizing the provision of public services. User satisfaction with services and political participation in planning and governance decisions were similar in new and conventional suburban communities. Local governments serving new communities faced the same problems as governments serving any rapidly developing suburban area. They were called on to make substantial "front-end" investments in public facilities and services before property values and economic activity produced sufficient revenues to support such expenditures. The developer faced the same problem—initial capital outlays far exceeded initial revenues in new community development—but the developer was not limited by often rigid state debt limitation laws that circumscribed debt financing by local government. The new community political problem was further compounded by the number of competing and politically independent jurisdictions that tended to serve new community development sites. Each jurisdiction pursued its own interests, which were not necessarily those of the new community, and answered to its own constituency. While new community development offered the opportunity for installing superior public service systems, many local governments found it politically impossible to favor one section of their jurisdiction over another.

Some of the limitations experienced in new community development in the United States may be overcome as new communities embrace more aspects of the new community concept and as developers incorporate more public objectives into their development programs. In particular, Columbia stands out for the breadth and depth of its attention to population balance, innovation in governance, planning for the provision of better educational, recreational, health care, and transportation service systems, and the development of a variety of shopping facilities at an early stage of community development. At the same time, however, Columbia residents often thought community expenditures for public services were not adequate and shared other new community residents' cynicism about the developer and local officials. Columbia residents were not overly satisfied with housing, neighborhood, and community livability, and were no more likely to be satisfied with their quality of life than other residents of new and conventional communities. Irvine and Reston, along with Columbia, generally subscribed to more aspects of the new community concept than other privately developed new communities. However, like Columbia, they also had a mixed record.

Can Public Policy Make a Difference?

New community development, while producing substantial benefits, has fallen short of achieving the full potential of the new community concept for solving urban problems and making possible a better life. In some cases, such as social and political participation, satisfaction with family life, and with the quality of life as a whole, this gap is probably due to unrealistic expectations about the degree of influence of the physical environment on people's activities and personal satisfactions. Clearly, these expectations have to be trimmed back.

Given the weak influence of community characteristics on satisfaction with housing and neighborhood livability, it is also unreasonable to expect that new communities will uniformly improve on these aspects of community development. In fact, given the importance of housing and neighborhood characteristics in families' selection of a new home, the key will be to maintain a competitive position with conventional development, while at the same time producing a better overall community environment.

In many cases, however, including population balance, education, health care, recreation, shopping, transportation, and other public-private community services, the gap between concept and reality can be traced to a variety of factors subject to change through public policy. These principally include: (1) the private sector's limited ability to assume public sector responsibilities without a corresponding increase in cash flow; (2) the inability of local governments to overcome the debilitating effects of continuing decentralization with accompanying fragmentation of public service responsibilities and insufficient financial capacity; (3) the lack of priority received by new communities in metropolitan planning, state public investment decisions, and the allocation of federal grants-in-aid funds and new capital improvements.

Implications for State and Local Governments

At this writing the Council of State Governments is exploring the role of state government in new community development. A number of states have individually examined their policies toward new communities and some states have already enacted legislation to aid and regulate new community ventures. Full realization of the potential of the new community concept and the federal new communities program will require an even greater state commitment to the objectives of new community development and to formulating and implementing strategies for overcoming the weaknesses of local government.

For example, although the federal new communities program calls for the achievement of population balance in new communities, in the absence of state directives for nonexclusionary land use policies, local governments may, and actually have, discouraged the development of low- and moderate-income housing in new communities. While new community development is predicated on the balanced phasing of growth, local governments may, and have, reneged on commitments toward planned allocations of land uses and densities so as to threaten the financial viability of new community projects. If private investors' enthusiasm for new community development is to be renewed and the social objectives of the federal new communities program are to be uniformly realized, state assumption or monitoring of the administration of land use controls in new communities may be essential. Whether the states are ready to assume this responsibility, however, is a question yet to be answered.

The key to successful governance of new communities lies in improving the tools for financing community services and in developing a system of shared power for the expenditure of funds. If new communities are to provide superior public services while at the same time keeping housing prices at reasonable levels, long-term financing of public facilities at moderate rates of interest is required. Because general-purpose governments—counties and municipalities—often have limited debt carrying capacity and are politically constrained from giving favored treatment to new communities, developers have been forced to turn to special districts to finance some facilities, while loading the costs of others onto land prices and forming homes associations to maintain them.

One promising alternative to the currently unsatisfactory modes of governing new communities may be the formation of transitional new community authorities. Created by joint action of state governments and new community developers, authorities would centralize governmental powers for a new community development site and would be authorized to issue bonds sufficient to cover the capital and initial operating costs of the public infrastructure required by the development program. Local governments, of course, are the creatures of the states. Any reorganization or reform of local governmental structure, such as the proposed new community authorities, will require, at the least, new state legislation, and, in some cases, revisions in state constitutions. Achieving positive results in many cases will involve a herculean effort.

Additional state policy revisions are needed. They include modifying state debt limitation laws, so that local government can play a more effective role in preservicing new communities, and revising state school development regulations to allow for community use of school facilities and participation of educational officials in the planning, financing, and construction of shared-use facilities. Public participation in financing and operating centers that include both commercial and public facilities should be encouraged, together with state or metropolitan regulation of regional shopping center location and development. Both of these innovations would require changes in most states' planning and land use regulation enabling statutes.

Implications for the Federal New Communities Program

The mixed performance of the 13 nonfederally assisted new communities and of the two federally assisted new communities studied indicates that federal participation in new community development is needed. Privately developed new communities are not likely to achieve population balance and cannot be expected to give attention to the full variety of community service systems called for in the new community concept and federal new community standards. At the same time, it seems clear that if the federal new communities program is operated solely as a loan guarantee program, assisted new communities will stand little better chance of fully achieving federal new community standards than new communities developed without federal assistance.

Whether under these circumstances the level of public benefits forthcoming is adequate to justify the federal presence in the new communities field is a difficult question. The benefits from successful income, class, and racially balanced communities, together with the significant benefits from new community development enumerated above, argue for resumption of the federal new communities program, particularly if the costs of new community development, as suggested by reports from the Real Estate Research Corporation (1974) and James Lee Short (1973), are no greater than those incurred in conventional suburban development.

If the full intent of the 1970 Urban Growth and New Community Development Act is to be realized, however, more than a loan guarantee program seems necessary. The federal new communities program raised development standards and required, as a prerequisite for federal assistance, that developers follow the lead of Columbia in planning for a variety of community functions that in other development contexts are assumed by the public sector. Project agreements between new community developers and the Department of Housing and Urban Development call for developer attention to a number of community and public services whose provision adds little to the market appeal of new communities or to developers' cash flow. A variety of assistance programs were included in the federal new communities legislation to enable developers to take on this added burden and to lessen the negative impact of new community development on affected local governments. However, as described in chapter 18, few of these programs were ever implemented. As a result, developers have had difficulties meeting the federal expectations contained in their project agreements. Public agencies, such as those serving Jonathan and Park Forest South, were little better equipped to respond to new community development opportunities and problems than agencies serving nonfederally assisted new communities and conventional suburbs. In sum, if service system performance in federally assisted new communities is to be significantly better than that of conventional suburban development, key provisions of the federal new communities legislation, or their equivalent, must be implemented. These include: public service grants to enable local governments and school districts to provide services during the initial development period; technical assistance to developers and public agencies; and grants to augment the planning capabilities of local governments.

In addition, administration of the federal new communities program should take into account an important lesson revealed by the development of Jonathan and Park Forest South. Public officials serving both communities complained that they had had minimal contact with federal new community administrators. To insure that federal aid is made available to local governments and developers in a timely and effective manner, the Department of Housing and Urban Development might station a project liaison officer at each new community site with adequate administrative support in Washington.

It is difficult to predict whether these policy initiatives will be sufficient to insure that federally assisted new communities do not suffer the same shortfalls as have been experienced by nonfederally assisted new communities. Much will depend on the location of newly assisted projects, the severity of local governmental financial problems, and the sophistication of existing local governments and community service institutions. However, even when conditions are most conducive to the provision of "new-community level" services, such as when development is undertaken in an urban county, a variety of local political factors may limit the capacity of governmental units to take advantage of the opportunities new communities provide for qualitatively better services than have previously been offered.

In many cases the establishment of new community authorities would substantially improve the capacity of local government to serve as an effective partner with the developer in realizing the goals of the federal new communities program. If and when a comprehensive reevaluation of the 1970 Urban Growth and New Community Development Act is undertaken, careful thought should be given to how the federal government can foster state and local initiatives to establish new governmental structures for new communities. One obvious step in this direction would be to guarantee not only the debt instruments of developers, but to guarantee also the bonds of local governments/new community authorities so that they are as capable as developers in meeting the front-end costs imposed by new community development. Guarantees could be made contingent on state establishment of mechanisms for regulating and assisting new community development and state approval of local governmental new community investment programs.

Improvements in the performance of future federally assisted new communities may also be obtained through the application of planning and design standards and criteria in screening proposed new community development projects prior to their approval for federal assistance, and through the establishment of a program for monitoring the performance of social, physical, and environmental systems in assisted new communities. The following section focuses on key variables that influenced the performance of new communities in meeting residents' needs and which should be incorporated into the suggested evaluation and monitoring programs.

Guidelines for Planning New Community Development Projects

The results of this study have a number of implications for the planning, design, and implementation of new community development projects. The 13 nonfederally assisted and two federally assisted new communities evaluated in the research provided an invaluable testing ground for alternative design and program approaches to the provision of housing, neighborhoods, community facilities, and governmental mechanisms. By taking into account the experiences of these communities, developers, planners, and other professionals involved in the development process should be better able to produce new communities that are responsive to the needs of all of their residents.

The suggestions offered here are intended as guidelines and not as directives. They are based on analyses of data collected at one point in time in new communities that were in intermediate stages of development and from populations that were predominantly white and middle class. In addition, the guidelines are not intended to serve as cookbook solutions to very complex design and development problems. Rather they point to important factors that should be considered in new community planning and development. Their application will depend on the imagination and skill of the many professionals and public officials who contribute to planning and development decisions and may vary depending on the unique set of circumstances that characterize individual development programs.

Population Composition

The federal new communities program calls for the production of new communities that are integrated in terms of the race, income, and age of residents. The achievement of racial and income integration is a feasible goal, particularly if federal or state subsidies for low- and moderate-income housing are available.

There appears to be a sufficiently large number of households in most market areas who are willing to live in integrated communities so that integration will not slow the pace of new community development. New communities should achieve racial and income integration early in the development process. Early integration will result in the recruitment of a tolerant population that is less likely to oppose increasing integration. Integration will be more likely to succeed if residents are informed of integration goals from the start of development and are consulted on the design and location of lower priced housing.

Racial integration of average ($10,000-$14,999) and above-average ($15,000 or more) income black families should engender less opposition by new community residents than integration by moderate ($5,000-$9,999) or low (under $5,000) income white or black families. Moderate-income white families will be much more readily accepted than moderate-income black families or low-income white or black families. Opposition to low-income families will be much less for retired white and black families than for working families. Successfully integrating low-income white and black working families in new communities will be extremely difficult.

Less opposition to income integration was voiced by persons living in rental units and lower priced ownership units. These factors should be considered in locating lower priced housing. People who lived closer to subsidized housing voiced less opposition to income integration than those who lived farther away, suggesting that contact with lower income families reduces opposition. To maximize this effect and to increase the acceptance of continued income integration, lower priced housing should be scattered throughout the community rather than being concentrated in one location.

Low- and moderate-income families and black families are attracted to new communities for many of the same reasons as more affluent families and white families. In advertising the community to appeal to lower income households, the cost of housing, proximity to the outdoors, community as a place to raise children, and appearance of the neighborhood should be emphasized. In advertising the community to appeal to black households, emphasis should be placed on the community as a good place to raise children, community schools, community planning, and nearness to the outdoors. Also, the marketing of single-family detached homes should stress layout and space of the home, while the marketing of townhouses and rental apartments should stress convenience to employment areas and leisure facilities.

Because the elderly are less residentially mobile than younger households, achieving age-integrated new communities at an early stage of the development process will require special efforts to attract older persons. There appears to be a market for neighborhoods, villages, and even whole communities designed specifically for and inhabited solely by older persons. Features that are important to the elderly and that may be used to attract elderly persons who are in the housing market include: easy access to community facilities and services, including some form of community transit; recreational and leisure facilities; safety from crime; health and medical services; appearance of the neighborhood; and nearness to the outdoors and natural environment. Also, the elderly are attracted to new communities with warmer climates.

Housing and Neighborhood Design

Residents' satisfaction with the livability of their homes depends on a variety of characteristics of the home, neighborhood, and community, and how these characteristics are perceived and interpreted.

The most important factors influencing housing satisfaction are characteristics of the dwelling unit itself. For all dwelling unit types—single-family detached homes, townhouses, and apartments—owners tend to be consistently more satisfied than renters. This suggests that new community developers should give particular attention to devices for making home ownership available to a wide spectrum of community residents. This may be more feasible with the increasing market acceptance of ownership townhouses and apartments.

After tenure, both the amount of indoor and outdoor space and the way it is perceived in relation to family needs has the strongest influence on satisfaction with housing livability. Satisfaction increases steadily with the number of rooms per person. Families who perceive they have too little indoor space for their needs are less satisfied and are more likely to consider moving than families who perceive indoor space to be adequate. Outdoor space is also important, as is adequate privacy from neighbors. Maintenance of the building and grounds has some influence on the housing livability evaluations of single-family detached homeowners and is of critical importance to the satisfaction of townhouse owners and apartment renters.

Housing livability is influenced by site planning, particularly by characteristics of the immediate neighborhood. The relative influence of various neighborhood characteristics on residents' livability evaluations varies by dwelling unit type. Characteristics of the immediate neighborhood that promote contentment with the livability of single-family detached ownership units, in probable order of importance, are: (1) attractiveness; (2) privacy; (3) maintenance; (4) homogenity of resident characteristics; and (5) lack of crowding. For ownership townhouses key factors, in probable order of importance, are: (1) attractiveness; (2) convenience; (3) maintenance; (4) safety; and (5) privacy. For apartment renters key factors, in probable order of importance, are: (1) maintenance; (2) attractiveness; (3) privacy; (4) safety; and (5) convenience. Although some of these factors are correlated with housing density, density per se is not an important predictor of satisfaction with housing livability.

Street design and placement of utilities also have some influence on livability evaluations. Owners of single-family detached homes tend to be more satisfied with livability if their homes are located on cul-de-sac streets. Cul-de-sac locations, however, are associated with lower rather than higher livability evaluations among townhouse and apartment dwellers. Livability evaluations tend to be higher if telephone and electric utility lines are placed underground.

Closer ties with neighbors is associated with the livability evaluations of owners and, to a lesser extent, renters. Interaction with neighbors and perceptions that neighbors are friendly tend to be enhanced when privacy from neighbors is adequate; when residents feel that the immediate neighborhood is socially homogeneous; when the neighborhood is served by a cul-de-sac street; and when facilities which increase the potential for neighborhood interaction, such as parks, playgrounds, and paths, are present.

The ten most frequently preferred facilities within one-half mile of the home, in order of the proportion of respondents who mentioned them, are: (1) library; (2) supermarket; (3) quiet place to walk and sit; (4) outdoor swimming pool; (5) playground; (6) post office substation; (7) private medical clinic or public health clinic; (8) teenage recreation center; (9) drug store; and (10) indoor movie theater. Many of these facilities can be provided in multifunction neighborhood or village centers, which should be developed as early as possible in the community development process.

Community Facilities and Services

Recreational Facilities and Services. Recreational facilities contribute to contentment with housing livability, promote social interaction among neighbors, and have a strong influence on residents' satisfaction with overall community livability. In designing recreational service systems, the needs of children, young adults, and adults must be considered, as well as those of various population target groups.

The availability of child play areas close to home is associated with parents' evaluations of the community as a good place to raise children, which, in turn, is strongly associated with the market appeal of the community. The provision of totlots and playgrounds is most important in the design of townhouse and apartment projects where children lack individual yard space for outdoor play. The use of parks and playgrounds tends to be much higher among apartment and townhouse children than among children living in neighborhoods of single-family detached homes. Maximum use of totlots and playgrounds occurs when they are located within one-eighth mile of children's homes. Use drops off sharply with increasing distance to childplay facilities.

Meeting young adults' recreational and leisure needs is one of the most challenging and least adequate aspects of new community recreational service systems. Teen centers provided for young adults are often disliked and tend to be infrequently used. Particular care must be exercised in the design and staffing of such centers. Young adults like informal meeting places. They also like to congregate at shopping centers and commercial recreational facilities. Benches for sitting and informal socializing should be available for young adults at shopping facilities, path intersections, and other locations where pedestrian traffic is high. Inexpensive dining faciliiities, such as quick-food restaurants and coffee shops, should be developed as early as possible in new communities. Young adults also appreciate the early availability of a library. During the first years of new community development, when the provision of many commercial facilities is not economically feasible, weekend transportation services to cultural and entertainment facilities in the surrounding region should be provided.

Facilities should be provided for adults' favorite out-of-home activities. The ten activities adults most prefer, in approximate rank order, are: (1) golf; (2) swimming; (3) gardening; (4) walking and hiking; (5) bowling; (6) tennis; (7) boating; (8) fishing; (9) bicycling; and (10) arts and crafts. Favorite out-of-home activities of women include playing cards, while fishing and boating are less popular among women. Favorite out-of-home activities of black persons include basketball and going to movies. Favorite out-of-home activities of lower income residents include baseball and softball.

There is a need for both decentralized and centralized recreational facilities and centers in new communities. Frequent participation in outdoor activities, such as swimming and tennis, can be maximized by locating smaller, less elaborate facilities within one-eighth mile of prospective users. However, there is also a demand for quality recreational facilities, such as pools with heated water, adjoining club houses with restaurants and bars, and facilities with active social programs. To accommodate this demand and to maximize satisfaction with the community recreational system, a major community recreational complex, including golf course, lighted tennis courts, heated swimming pool, and clubhouse and locker facilities, should be included in the community development program.

Health and Medical Care Facilities and Services. Because of the highly decentralized, free-enterprise character of health care delivery in the United States, developer attention to this service system is essential in new community development.

The frequency of use of both preventive and curative health care services is not influenced by the location of health care facilities. If adequate health care resources are available in the surrounding region, first priority should be given to insuring that emergency transportation is adequate and to information and referral services.

If the new community is relatively isolated, so that health care resources in the surrounding region are inaccessible or inadequate, early attention to the provision of health care facilities and services is necessary. Priority should be given to securing the services of primary care physicians and dentists and to emergency transportation to hospitals. Doctors are attracted to new communities by the size and affluence of the population and by the availability of office facilities designed specifically for medical practice. Medical-dental centers should be constructed as early as possible in the community development process.

Development of a community hospital will serve as a means to attract physicians to the community and will also increase residents' satisfaction with the health care system. A community hospital with out-patient and mental health services may serve as the core of the community health care system. Proposals for community hospitals should be carefully coordinated with regional health care needs and resources to avoid overbedding and duplication of services.

New communities are desirable locations for group practice health maintenance plans and organizations. If a health maintenance organization is to serve as the central element in a new community health care system, user costs must be within the means of moderate-income residents. A low-cost basic plan with discretionary extra services priced separately may meet this need. Because a number of residents will prefer traditional doctor-patient relationships and some will prefer to use health care services only when the need is felt, a health maintenance organization cannot serve as the sole source of community health care. An HMO should be accompanied by facilities for fee-for-service physicians.

Health care planning should begin at the earliest possible point in the development process. Developers should seek advice from local medical societies and should bring surrounding health care institutions, such as hospitals and county health departments, into the planning process. Plans should be coordinated with those of regional comprehensive health planning councils.

Educational Facilities and Services. The planning and development of new community schools will be more effective if school district and community boundaries are coterminous. Negotiation for the formation of a separate new community school district, or, alternatively, for a new community authority empowered to provide educational services, should begin at the start of the community planning and development process.

Close and congenial working relationships between the developer and the personnel and officials of existing school districts are essential for the early and successful development of educational facilities. The probable need for developer donations of staff time and consultant expertise to the school district, as well as school sites and financial aid in school construction, should be considered in the calculation of cash flow and other financial projections for new community development programs.

Alternatives to the traditional school house should be considered in school planning. The use of interim portable schools would provide adequate time for planning and arranging financing for permanent school structures and would increase the potential for parent participation in the school planning process. Initial school occupancy of commercial buildings is another possibility. Grouping educational, community, and commercial functions in integrated neighborhood and village centers would provide savings in site acquisition costs and user transportation costs.

The interconnection of homes and schools by paths that are located away from streets and that have grade separations at major path-street crossings encourages walking to schools.

Parents' ratings of the quality of new community schools are associated with a number of factors that should be considered in school siting, design, and operation. Parents tend to be happier with the schools when their children can walk to school; however, distance from schools per se is not associated with higher ratings. Smaller elementary schools (under 600 students) tend to draw higher ratings from parents, as do schools with fewer students per classroom (under 25).

Increasing racial integration of the schools is associated with lower parent ratings. Given the racial and income integration goals of the federal new communities program and the likelihood of substantial minority populations in federally assisted new communities, racial conflict and adjustment problems in the schools should be anticipated. Programs designed to lessen racial tensions, such as the employment of minority teachers and counselors, formation of human relations councils and committees, and the provision of educational and extracurricular activities designed for minority students, should be initiated as soon as new schools open. In addition, majority and minority parents should be involved in initial school facility and program planning.

The use of progressive educational programs has little effect on parents' evaluations of new community elementary schools. However, more parents are likely to feel that their children's schools are too innovative than feel that the schools are not innovative enough. The adoption of new educational techniques should be accompanied by programs that are designed to show parents why the techniques are being used and their advantages over more traditional approaches.

Schools should strive to keep parents and other community residents interested in educational and extracurricular activities. Schools with better community relations are rated more highly by parents than those where parents and citizens are less involved in the educational process.

Shopping Facilities. The staged development of shopping centers offers one means of overcoming the dual problem of an inadequate market during the early years of the development process and dilution of the market by competing shopping centers located outside of the new community. Residents' evaluations of community shopping facilities are associated with the availability and convenience of supermarkets. A supermarket should form the anchor for neighborhood and village shopping centers, whose construction should begin as soon as possible after development of the community gets underway.

Inasmuch as most people prefer to drive to shopping centers, the development of small neighborhood convenience centers to encourage walking should be undertaken with caution. Larger neighborhood and village centers which combine commercial functions with other community facilities and services are more useful to new community residents. Community functions that can be successfully combined with a supermarket in a neighborhood or village center include medical-dental buildings with doctors' offices, intermediate and high schools, religious facilities, postal facilities, branch libraries, major community and commercial recreational facilities, social service agencies, and governmental offices.

Shopping centers should be designed to accommodate young adults' needs for places to gather and socialize with their peers. This may be accomplished by the provision of inexpensive eating facilities and meeting places.

If market conditions are favorable, developers should make every effort to develop a regional shopping center within the new community. Regional centers increase the attractiveness of the community to prospective residents, provide a source of secondary employment, and are strongly associated with residents' evaluations of the quality of community shopping facilities. Key bases of the appeal of regional centers to shoppers include, principally, their convenience, the variety of goods and services offered, and the attractiveness of the stores and shops. Other factors, such as price levels of goods and services, hours open, friendliness of service, cleanliness, and parking, are less important in the choice of a center at which to shop. The inclusion of major cultural and entertainment facilities at regional centers should increase traffic and the appeal of the center to community residents.

Transportation Facilities and Services. New community development creates the potential for more effective community transit systems. Developers should coordinate community planning with metropolitan transportation and transit agencies to insure that this potential is realized in land use and neighborhood design decisions.

New communities may increase the proportion of employed residents working in the community by recruiting major employers and by providing housing that is within the means of persons employed in the community. In addition, use of the automobile for commutation to work may be substantially reduced if commuter bus or rail service is available. Community-based commuter services have been successful in new communities and their formation should be encouraged by the developer.

Although few new community residents walk to facilities other than schools, walking, hiking, and bicycling are preferred recreational activities. Participation in these activities is greater when internal path systems which do not parallel the streets are available and when the community has a bicycle trail system.

Use of bus services tends to be greater for community-based transit systems than for systems originating outside of the community. In addition, demand-activated community transit systems have been successful in new communities. Developers and local governments should give careful consideration to the potential for community-based transit systems and to the creation of financing mechanisms that can withstand initial operating losses during the first year(s) of transit system operation.

The location of community facilities (particularly shopping facilities and schools) in close proximity of users can result in modest reductions in annual household automobile mileage. In addition, automobile usage can be significantly reduced if a greater proportion of employed residents can be induced to work in the community and/or to use public transportation to travel to work. Further reductions in household automobile mileage are possible if households who are used to leading automobile-intensive life styles, such as more affluent residents of single-family detached homes with young adults living in the household, can be induced to own fewer automobiles and to use other transportation modes.

Community Governance

The critical need for improved methods of governing new communities was stressed earlier in this chapter. Major reforms in governmental arrangements are needed to insure that the provision of public facilities and services is coordinated with the community master plan and development program; that the goal of preservicing public facilities is realized; that financing of the capital costs of facilities is efficient and equitable; and that quality facilities and services are equally available to all community residents. As noted above and described in greater detail in chapter 8, the formation of new community authorities has a number of potential advantages. A major disadvantage, however, is the need for state enabling legislation and active state participation in various aspects of the development process. Both may be difficult to secure.

Among existing governmental arrangements that have been devised for new community development, the most effective appears to be the combination of neighborhood homes associations and municipal government used in Irvine. The homes associations provide a means for maintaining neighborhood open space and recreational facilities that is responsive to residents' wishes and that encourages residents to participate in decisions that influence the livability of their homes and neighborhoods. Municipal government serves as a vehicle for the provision of community-level facilities and services and for citizen participation in decisions regarding the allocation of resources among competing demands. Other advantages of municipal government include eligibility to receive federal and state aid, lower financing costs for capital improvements, the relative ease of entering into intergovernmental contracts for service production and delivery, and the ability of residents to deduct local taxes from their income in computing Federal personal income taxes.

Because the tax base may not be adequate to support a municipal government during the first years of the development process, it may be necessary to form a communitywide homes association to operate major community facilities and amenities. If this is necessary, the Columbia Park and Recreation Association provides the best existing model of a communitywide quasi-governmental approach to new community governance. A key feature of the Columbia Association, direct association financing of the capital costs of facilities and amenities, is made possible because association dues are secured by a permanent lien on all taxable property that takes precedence over purchase money mortgages. The security this provides has enabled the association to finance the capital costs of facilities and amenities through borrowing rather than loading their costs onto home prices. However, the Federal Housing Administration (FHA) has never repeated its approval of the precedence of association assessments over purchase money mortgages so that the Columbia Association financial system may be difficult to replicate. Other key features of the Columbia Association include the coverage of commercial and industrial property in the association assessment base, assessment schedules based on county property tax appraisals rather than flat rates, and the allocation of voting rights to renters as well as property owners.

The major disadvantage of communitywide homes associations, resident discontent with developer control, may be minimized if developers open up the planning process and encourage residents to participate in decisions about the type and design of community facilities to be provided in new villages and neighborhoods. Resident participation should also be encouraged in the formulation of operating policies. This may be accomplished by establishing resident advisory committees that parallel major association functions. In addition, actual control of the operation of some facilities should be transferred to the residents at an early point in the development process. One way of doing this would be to establish a federal homes association structure, including a communitywide association to provide and operate major community facilities and a series of neighborhood associations to maintain neighborhood open space and to operate neighborhood recreational facilities. Control of the neighborhood associations could be transferred to the residents when about half of the units in a neighborhood had been sold.

The Need for Additional Research

This study has produced the most significant and comprehensive set of information ever collected for new community development in the United States. At the same time, it has revealed the need for continuing research on the processes and outcomes of large-scale development. Five areas of research appear to be particularly promising in terms of their potential long-term benefits. These include research on: (1) new community governance; (2) industrial location and employment; (3) population target groups; (4) costs and benefits from smaller scale planned unit development; and (5) changes in development outputs and residents' responses to them over time.

New community development has been characterized by the innovation of a variety of new governmental arrangements for the provision of public facilities and services. The partial evaluation of governmental arrangements reported in this volume determined the following: how well they have satisfied residents' desires for public services; residents' attitudes about the responsiveness of local officials; and the extent that new community residents actually participated in local politics. It was noted, however, that a complete determination of the most effective approaches to governing new communities would, of course, include consideration of the full costs of providing local public services.

Future research should be aimed at evaluating the productivity of alternative governmental arrangements for new communities, including consideration of both units of physical-program outputs and benefits obtained per dollar expended. Attention should also be given to the effects of alternative governmental arrangements on: (1) the costs of financing land acquisition and capital improvements; (2) the distribution of costs and benefits from governmental activities among community residents; (3) the character of intergovernmental relations and ease of forming cooperative agreements for the production and delivery of services; (4) the extent of citizen participation in the production of services and in decisions regarding the allocation of resources; (5) innovation in the production and delivery of services; and (6) the ability to adapt to changes in the pace of development.

Industrial development and growth in the employment base are essential if new communities are to realize a rapid pace of residential development, reduce commutation by having residents live and work in the same community, and secure a tax base that is adequate to finance necessary community facilities and services. Additional information is needed on two fronts. First, the relative attractiveness of new community environments to different types of industries is required if industrial recruitment efforts are to be most effective. Second, much more information is needed about adjustments in place of residence in response to changes in the place of employment. In particular, just how attractive are new community living environments to persons actually working in new communities (as opposed to the residents' perspectives revealed in this volume) and how much of a lag occurs between a change in employment and a change in residence? Answers to both of these questions would make possible better estimates of the degree of employment self-sufficiency that can be reasonably expected to occur in new communities.

The research summarized in this book suggests that new communities offer highly desirable living environments for various target populations, including low- and moderate-income residents of subsidized housing, blacks, and the elderly. This conclusion is based on comparisons of the responses of target populations living in new communities with those of persons living in a limited number of conventional communities. For example, black residents of integrated new communities and predominantly black conventional subdivisions were interviewed. Information is needed on the responses of black persons living in integrated conventional suburbs and black persons living in central cities. Similarly, the research conclusions could be strengthened by information on the responses of low- and moderate-income residents to a greater variety of conventional residential environments. Conclusions regarding age-segregation of elderly persons are based on the results of interviews in two middle-class retirement communities. A number of other types of age-segregated environments for the elderly should be examined, including smaller scale retirement villages and less affluent retirement communities and villages in various sections of the nation. Also, much could be learned from elderly persons residing in age-segregated living situations, such as apartment complexes designed for the elderly, located within otherwise age-integrated new communities.

Inasmuch as residents' evaluations of overall community livability are highly dependent on characteristics of the home, neighborhood, and recreational facilities, it may be possible to achieve some of the benefits of new communities in smaller scale planned unit developments that entail less front-end capital, management expertise, and risk than full-scale new communities. Research is needed on the potential benefits, in relation to development costs, that may be forthcoming from planned unit development at various scales and how such development can be most effectively encouraged by federal, state, and local governments.

The research results presented in this book are for the most part based on data collected at one point in time. Information is needed on the temporal stability of residents' responses to their living environments and on the magnitude of change in environmental conditions that is necessary to produce a significant change in residents' responses. This would require periodic monitoring of a sample of new communities and of a panel of new community residents.

Baseline data are summarized in this book for two federally assisted new communities. A monitoring system should be established for these two communities and extended to other communities participating in the federal new communities program. This would make possible a continuous evaluation of program outputs and would provide one means for each new community to learn from the experiences of other program participants.

A number of other promising areas for research on new communities should also be mentioned. This study has focused on suburban new communities. Additional information is needed on the development processes and outputs of new-towns-in-town and on freestanding new communities. The question of the proper location of new communities and their place in a national urban growth policy was not covered in the present study. A complete evaluation of new community development in the United States will also require information on the relative impact of new communities and conventional communities on the natural environment, the costs of new community development in comparison with incremental suburban expansion, and a broader consideration of various community institutions and of various community service systems.

The research reported in this book should stimulate interest in the additional studies that are needed. Application of the research findings can lead to better public and private development decisions and eventually to better communities.

Alternative Futures

Even in the absence of expanded assistance from the states and the federal government, new communities are being planned and built in the United States, and continue to follow a better approach to new urban growth than conventional suburban development. Although the new communities will not have a major impact on metropolitan expansion—too few will be built to accommodate more than a fraction of anticipated suburban population gains—they may be expected to demonstrate significant improvements in the ways in which rural land is converted to urban use. Innovations tested in new communities are likely to be applied in other development contexts so that, overall, the quality of community service systems and the livability of the urban environment in the United States are enriched.

Spontaneous new communities—areas of rapid growth though incremental development—will continue to occur in metropolitan regions that are still experiencing substantial in-migration. With improved planning and a greater commitment of public resources toward the preservation of open space and provision of public services, they may offer a means of achieving some of the benefits of new communities without the enormous financial risks that have slowed community building in an adverse economy. In addition, smaller scale new communities, ranging from developments of several hundred acres to villages of more than a thousand acres will be built. These small-scale new communities will encompass many of the benefits from improved environmental planning and a broader range of residential amenities that characterize full-scale new communities. However, neither spontaneous new communities nor planned unit developments offer a total approach to urban growth problems.

After all is said and done, only full-scale new communities have the potential for a quantum improvement in the form and processes of community development. The findings of this study open the way toward understanding the necessity for strengthening public-private partnerships needed to translate the new community concept into the new community reality.

Appendixes

Appendix A
Methods of the Study

Information presented in this book is based on data gathered in a sample of 36 communities. Seventeen are new communities, including 13 communities developed by the private sector without federal assistance, 2 communities that are participating in the federal new communities program, and 2 communities specifically designed for the elderly. The nonfederally assisted new communities are: Columbia, Md., Reston, Va., and North Palm Beach, Fla., on the East Coast; Forest Park, Oh., Elk Grove Village, Ill., and Park Forest, Ill., in the Midwest; Sharpstown, Tex., and Lake Havasu City, Ariz., in the Southwest; and in California, Foster City, outside San Francisco, and Valencia, Westlake Village, Irvine, and Laguna Niguel, in the Los Angeles area. The federally assisted new communities are Jonathan, Minn., and Park Forest South, Ill., 2 of the first 3 new communities to be approved for assistance under Title IV of the Housing and Urban Development Act of 1968. The retirement new communities include Rossmoor Leisure World, Laguna Hills, Calif., and Sun City Center, Fla.

In order to evaluate new communities in comparison with less planned traditional modes of urban development and to control for contextual factors, such as climate, data were gathered in a sample of conventional communities. Each of the nonfederally assisted and federally assisted new communities was paired with a significantly less planned conventional community that was otherwise similar to the new community in terms of the age, price range and type of housing available, and location. Because the conventional communities did not have sufficient black and low- and moderate-income populations for comparison with the new communities, information was gathered in four additional conventional communities. These included two suburban communities with subsidized housing and two suburban communities with predominantly black residential areas. Further information on the characteristics of the study nonfederally assisted new communities and the paired conventional communities is provided in chapter 4. Characteristics of the federally assisted new communities and paired conventional communities are summarized in chapter 18, while chapter 19 summarizes the characteristics of the two retirement communities.

Four types of data were collected for the study. These included: (1) residents' responses obtained through a household survey; (2) professional evaluations obtained through a series of surveys with professional personnel serving the study communities; (3) developer decision data obtained during two waves of developer decision studies; and (4) objective community characteristic data obtained from public records and site observations in each of the 36 sample communities.

Resident response data were gathered during the period Februay-May 1973 using structured home interviews with a sample of 5,511 households including a basic household sample and additional subsamples of subsidized housing and black households (which had been selected to assure adequate representation of low- and moderate-income and black households). In addition 974 self-administered questionnaires were obtained from young adults (ages 14-20) living in the sampled households.

The professional surveys were conducted from March to July 1973. They resulted in a total of 577 structured interviews with presidents and directors of community associations and with professional personnel responsible for the operation of educational, health care, and recreational facilities in the 36 sample communities. Separate surveys were conducted with school superintendents and school principals.

Developer decision data were obtained in structured and unstructured interviews with developers, their planning and design staffs, consultants, public officials, and others involved in planning and development decisions in the 13 nonfederally assisted and two federally assisted new communities selected for the research, as well as in correspondence with new community developers. The field work for the first wave of the decision studies was largely concurrent with that for the professional personnel surveys and the household survey, running from March to August 1973. The field work for the second wave, which was limited to the 10 sample new communities that began active residential development after 1960 in order to reduce or eliminate problems of recall and staff turnover, was conducted in July and August of 1974.

The number and distribution of household, professional personnel, and developer decision study interviews are summarized in table A-1.

Data on objective community characteristics in the 36 sample communities were obtained from public records and observation of sites. This field work was done concurrently with that for the professional personnel surveys and served as an aid to respondent selection for some of those surveys.

The specific procedures used in the selection of samples and respondents for the various surveys outlined here, and in conducting the field work and recording all four types of data gathered, are described in the remainder of this appendix.

The Household Survey

Selecting the Sample Households and Respondents

The universe sampled for the household survey included family heads and their spouses living in the 36 sample communities. The sample was selected in such a manner that every head or spouse who had moved into his or her dwelling before January 1, 1973 had a known probability of selection. The method of selecting the household sample was as follows.

Visits were made to all 36 sample communities between mid-October 1972 and mid-January 1973 to identify all occupied dwellings on large-scale maps showing lot lines for each community. These maps, with the location and number of occupied dwellings delineated, were used to outline clusters of five, six, or seven dwellings. The number of units to be included in a cluster was chosen after considering projected field costs and the number of clusters needed to generate a household sample representative of the sample communities. The eventual analysis of housing clusters was considered in delineating sample clusters. Accordingly, the clusters were outlined so as to include dwellings that faced one another across a street or common court. Dwellings strung out in a row were rarely defined as clusters.

For apartment buildings where the location of individual dwellings was unknown, the total number of units in the building was divided into a designated number of five-, six-, or seven-dwelling clusters. For buildings containing fewer than ten apartments, two or three neighboring buildings were grouped together and clusters were designated for all units in the group. Where the location of apartments within a building was known it was possible to cluster these units directly as in the procedure described above.

After clusters were defined for a community, a probability sample of clusters was selected. The samples in paired conventional communities that had more than one type of dwelling unit available were stratified by dwelling unit type (single-family detached houses, townhouses, or apartments) so that the proportion of selected clusters of each dwelling type approximated the proportions of dwelling unit types found in the paired new community. Overall, the selection of sample clusters was designed to obtain 200 interviews in each of the 13 nonfederally assisted new communities and 2 federally assisted new communities, and 100 interviews in each of the paired conventional communities, the conventional communities used to obtain interviews with subsidized housing and black residents, and the retirement new communities.

Subsample of New Community Households Occupying Subsidized Housing. Five of the sample new communities (Columbia, Forest Park, Jonathan, Lake Havasu City, and Reston) had FHA 235 (owner) and/or 221(d)3 or 236 (rental) subsidized housing occupied at the time of the sampling process. In each of these communities the sampling frame was divided into two strata, one of subsidized housing units and one of nonsub-

Table A-1
Household Survey, Professional Personnel, and Decision Study Interviews

	Basic Sample	Subsidized Housing	Black	Young Adult	Total
		Number of Interviews			
		Household Survey			
		Subsamples			
13 nonfederally assisted new communities	2,619	219	131	577	3,546
13 paired conventional communities	1,321	NA	NA	264	1,585
Federally assisted new communities and paired conventional communities					
Jonathan, Minn. (NC)	152	55	NA	12	219
Chanhassen, Minn. (CC)	100	NA	NA	18	118
Park Forest South, Ill. (NC)	200	NA	19	28	247
Richton Park, Ill. (CC)	101	NA	NA	4	105
Retirement communities					
Rossmoor Leisure World, Calif.	104	NA	NA	NA	104
Sun City Center, Fla.	100	NA	NA	NA	100
Two subsidized housing conventional communities[b]	187	NA	NA	28	215
Two black conventional communities	203	NA	NA	43	246
Nonfederally assisted new communities and paired conventional communities					
Columbia, Md. (NC)	213	61	37	30	341
Norbeck-Wheaton, Md. (CC)	123	NA	NA	28	151
Elk Grove Village, Ill. (NC)	199	NA	NA	59	258
Schaumburg, Ill. (CC)	102	NA	NA	14	116
Forest Park, Oh. (NC)	202	53	51	68	374
Sharonville, Oh. (CC)	115	NA	NA	30	145
Foster City, Calif. (NC)	176	NA	NA	26	202
West San Mateo, Calif. (CC)	93	NA	NA	19	112
Irvine, Calif. (NC)	202	NA	NA	37	239
Fountain Valley, Calif. (CC)	102	NA	NA	15	117
Laguna Niguel, Calif. (NC)	208	NA	NA	37	245
Dana Point, Calif. (CC)	105	NA	NA	34	139
Lake Havasu City, Ariz. (NC)	209	47	NA	68	324
Kingman, Ariz. (CC)	93	NA	NA	15	108
North Palm Beach, Fla. (NC)	202	NA	NA	43	245
Tequesta, Fla. (CC)	111	NA	NA	15	126

			Number of Interviews			
			Professional Personnel Surveys			
Homes and Community Associations	*School Superin- tendent*	*School Prin- cipal*	*Health*	*Recreation*	*Total*	*Developer Decision Studies*
48	25	114	58	34	279	150[a]
NA	21	86	48	29	184	NA
1	1	4	3	2	11	12
NA	1	3	3	1	8	NA
3	1	3	4	1	12	11
NA	2	6	3	1	12	NA
6	0	0	4	2	12	NA
2	0	0	3	1	6	NA
NA	3	18	9	4	34	NA
NA	3	6	7	3	19	NA
8	1	15	8	3	35	15
NA	1	12	2	2	17	NA
3	4	15	3	2	27	9
NA	2	13	3	2	20	NA
NA	1	8	3	2	14	15
NA	1	5	5	4	15	NA
2	2	5	4	3	16	14
NA	2	4	4	3	13	NA
11	1	6	6	3	27	14
NA	3	13	5	2	23	NA
5	1	5	5	2	18	6
NA	1	4	5	2	12	NA
NA	2	4	3	3	12	10
NA	2	3	3	3	11	NA
NA	1	6	4	3	14	8
NA	1	2	4	1	8	NA

Table A-1 (cont.)

	Basic Sample	Subsidized Housing	Black	Young Adult	Total
		Number of Interviews			
		Household Survey			
		Subsamples			
Park Forest, Ill. (NC)	200	NA	16	37	253
Lansing, Ill. (CC)	64	NA	NA	14	78
Reston, Va. (NC)	197	58	27	49	331
West Springfield, Va. (CC)	95	NA	NA	19	114
Sharpstown, Tex. (NC)	203	NA	NA	45	248
Southwest Houston, Tex. (CC)	108	NA	NA	26	134
Valencia, Calif. (NC)	202	NA	NA	33	235
Bouquet Canyon, Calif. (CC)	103	NA	NA	21	124
Westlake Village, Calif. (NC)	206	NA	NA	45	251
Agoura/Malibu Junction, Calif. (CC)	107	NA	NA	14	121
Total	5,087	274	150	974	6,485

NC = New community
CC = Conventional community
NA = Not applicable

[a]Includes eight interviews covering regional areas (e.g., Orange County, Calif.), not allocated to a specific community.

sidized housing units. Separate random probability cluster samples were drawn from each stratum in the manner described above. Selection of clusters was designed to produce 50 interviews with households occupying subsidized housing, and 200 interviews with households occupying non-subsidized housing, in each of the five communities.

Subsample of New Community Black Households. In each of the five sample new communities known to have more than 100 resident black households (Columbia, Forest Park, Park Forest, Park Forest South, and Reston) a special subsample of black households was selected to supplement those falling into the regular cluster samples. Lists suitable for use as sampling frames were not available in all five of the communities. Therefore, sampling frames were constructed by referrals from the random sample respondents, using their responses to question 141 in the interview schedule. (See p. 559 of the household survey interview schedule in appendix B.) Addresses generated by this question were listed and duplications were eliminated. The five resulting lists were used as the sample frames from

Homes and Community Associations	School Superin-tendent	School Prin-cipal	Health	Recreation	Total	Developer Decision Studies
			Number of Interviews			
		Professional Personnel Surveys				
NA	5	24	4	1	34	12
NA	2	5	3	2	12	NA
5	1	6	7	4	23	21
NA	1	5	5	2	13	NA
NA	1	7	3	2	13	6
NA	1	7	3	2	13	NA
4	2	6	4	2	18	5
NA	2	5	4	2	13	NA
10	3	7	4	4	28	7
NA	2	8	2	2	14	NA
60	57	240	142	78	577	173[a]

[b]Includes Laurel, Md., and Chicago Heights, Ill. The project in the latter community was not included in the analysis in chapter 19 because the population characteristics (100 percent black) were not comparable to those of the subsidized housing projects in the new communities. In its place a single-family detached subsidized housing project in Richton Park, Ill., which was more suitable for comparative purposes, was used in the analysis.

which simple random samples of addresses were drawn, aimed at producing 50 additional interviews with black households in each of the five communities.

It should be noted that because it is a referral sample, this subsample of black households does not constitute a random sample representative of the population of black family heads and their spouses in these communities. However comparison of black subsample respondent characteristics and attitudes with those of black respondents from the random sample in the five communities indicated that the two groups were very similar. Therefore, responses from the black subsample were included with those of random sample blacks in the analysis presented in chapter 19 to increase the reliability of estimates for new community blacks without introducing substantial sampling error. Data obtained from referral interviews are not included in community totals presented in other chapters.

Subsample of New Community and Conventional Community Young Adults. The universe for the young adult subsample included all persons 14 through 20 years olds (other than family heads and their spouses) who were found to be living in sample dwellings. If one such young adult was found at a sample dwelling, this person was selected for the young adult sample. If two or more were found, the interviewer selected one of these at random using a random selection table stamped on the young adult questionnaire. Thus choice of young adult respondents was specified for interviewers rather than left to their discretion.

Designation of the Household Survey Respondent. The prospective respondent was randomly designated as either the head of the family residing at the address or the spouse of the family head for each address in the regular cluster sample, the subsidized housing subsample, and the black subsample prior to assignment of addresses to interviewers. The head was designated as the respondent for half of the addresses sampled in each community; the spouse was designated respondent for the remaining half. Interviews were allowed only with the designated respondent except where the spouse was designated and there was no spouse of family head living in the household. In such situations the interview was to be taken with the family head. If a household was occupied by more than one family unit, the head or spouse of the head of each family unit was to be interviewed.

These procedures left no freedom to interviewers in the choice of respondents. The dwellings at which interviews were to be taken and the individuals to be interviewed within the dwellings were specified.

Interviewing Methods

Interviewers were instructed to ask questions using the exact wording appearing in the questionnaire. When probing was necessary to obtain full answers to open-end questions, interviewers were to use nondirective probes (such as, "How do you mean?" or "Could you tell me more about that?") to avoid influencing the responses.

When recording responses to open-end questions, interviewers were to write the actual words spoken as nearly as possible and to indicate when they had probed for additional information. Recording of responses to closed-end questions simply required checking the appropriate precoded response in most cases.

In situations where the respondent could not be contacted on the first call at a sample household, interviewers were required to call back at the household up to six times in order to obtain the interview. These call-backs were to be made at different times of day and on different days of the week to maximize the chance of a contact. Addresses at which the designated individuals refused to be interviewed were generally reassigned to a second interviewer who contacted the individuals and attempted to persuade them to be interviewed.

No substitutions for sample households or sample respondents were allowed. The addresses of sample households (including apartment designations) were listed for each cluster, and the proper respondent (head or spouse of head) was designated for each address listed prior to assignment of clusters to interviewers. Interviewers were required to interview the designated individuals at the addresses listed.

When an eligible young adult was selected at a sample household, the interviewer was to leave a self-administered questionnaire with or for this person and to make one call-back at the household by appointment to pick up the completed questionnaire. If the questionnaire had not been completed at the time of the call-back, the young adult respondent was asked to mail the completed questionnaire to the field office in a self-addressed postage-paid envelope provided for this purpose.

Reliability of the Data

Sample surveys, even though properly conducted, are liable to several kinds of errors. These include response errors, which arise in the reporting and processing of the data; nonresponse errors, which arise from failure to interview some individuals who were selected in the sample; and sampling errors, which arise from the choice by chance of individuals for the sample who may make the sample unrepresentative of the population from which it was drawn. Some evaluation of each of these types of error is necessary for the proper interpretation of any estimates from survey data.

Response Errors. Such errors include inaccuracies in asking and answering questions in the interview, recording responses, coding the recorded responses, and processing the coded data. They can be reduced by thoroughly pretesting field procedures and instruments, training interviewers and coders, and exercising quality controls throughout the data collection, coding, and editing phases of the research process.

The questionnaires and field procedures used in the household survey were pretested in the autumn of 1972.[a] Pretesting was carried out in Crofton, Md., a planned suburban community in the Washington, D.C., metropolitan area, with respondents similar to the populations in the sam-

---

[a] The field and coding operations for the household survey were conducted by The Research Triangle Institute, Research Triangle Park, North Carolina. Members of the research team monitored all phases of these operations.

ple. Analysis of pretest interviews resulted in some revisions, such as the rewording of questions to make their meaning more clear to respondents and interviewers.

Interviewer training included a question-by-question review of the household interview instrument, the taking of a practice interview, and discussion of this interview with the interviewer's supervisor. Supervisors reviewed interviewers' work with them throughout the field period.

The coding operation involved two procedures. Responses to closed-end questions were scored directly on the household interview and young adult questionnaire forms, which had been printed so that the scored responses could be machine read directly from the forms onto computer tape. Responses to open-end questions were hand coded onto coding forms and keypunched from these forms. Coders were trained as to the codes and coding conventions used prior to the beginning of this work. Hand coding was checked by coding 10 percent of the interviews and questionnaires twice and comparing the two codings for discrepancies. Errors found were corrected.

Data tapes were checked for inconsistencies and incorrect codes and indicated corrections were made.

Nonresponse Errors. Some proportion of the sample in any survey fails to respond, usually because of refusals or the failure of the interviewers to contact potential respondents in spite of repeated attempts. In the random sample for the 36 communities (including the subsidized housing sample) there was a total of 7,626 addresses at which there was an eligible respondent after elimination of those addresses whose occupants had moved in on January 1, 1973 or later, as well as addresses that were vacant, commercial establishments, and others at which no one lived permanently. Interviews were obtained with the selected respondent at 5,361 of these addresses—an overall response of 70.3 percent. Response rates varied somewhat from community to community.

Because response rates were lower than anticipated (80-85 percent overall), a study was conducted to assess the extent to which nonrespondents differed systematically from respondents. First, response rates were computed by dwelling unit type and found to differ. Households living in higher density housing were somewhat underrepresented. Since residents in higher density areas tend to have fewer children, for example, and were thought likely to view the community and its facilities from a different perspective than residents of single-family detached homes, interviews in each of the 36 communities were weighted to give responses from residents of each of the three dwelling unit types a weight proportional to that of the dwelling unit type in the community's original sample.

In addition, a survey of nonrespondents was conducted to gather basic demographic and attitude data.[b] Analyses of these data in comparison with household survey data revealed no significant differences between respondent and nonrespondent households for 8 of 13 demographic items (including race, income, marital status, and employment status). For 5 of 7 community and quality of life rating items there were no significant differences between respondents and nonrespondents (including their overall rating of community livability, ratings of schools and recreational facilities, and satisfaction with life as a whole). The major differences that occurred between respondent and nonrespondent households included age of the head of household, length of residence, and ratings of health care and shopping facilities. Since most differences could be explained by the length of time that elapsed between the original survey and the nonrespondent follow-up survey, it is estimated that the lower than expected response rates obtained for the original household survey do not bias the study findings.

Sampling Errors. If all family heads or their spouses living (as of January 1, 1973) in new and conventional communities fitting the inclusion criteria given in chapter 4 had been interviewed, the percentages and other values reported in the text would be population values. Because a sample of persons was interviewed in a sample of communities the reported statistics are estimates of the population values. Any distribution of individuals selected for a sample will differ by chance somewhat from the population from which it was drawn. If more than one sample were used under the same survey conditions, the estimates from one sample might be larger than the population value for a given variable while the estimates from another sample were smaller. The magnitude of random variability of sample statistics from population values (sampling error) can be calculated for any sample providing it is known exactly how and with what probability the sample was selected.

Sampling errors associated with observed differences in percentages between subgroups (e.g., between individual new communities and their paired conventional communities) indicate the minimum size of a percentage difference required for the difference to be considered statistically significant, that is, for it to reflect a true difference between the subgroups in the population rather than chance variation because of sampling. Estimates of average sampling errors based on experiences with other studies in urban areas were adjusted for the clustering in the sample to estimate the statistical significance of percentage differences. Conservative estimates of the sampling error in the sample have been used.

---

[b] The nonrespondent follow-up survey, involving telephone interviews and mailback questionnaires, was carried out during February and March of 1974 by Chilton Research Services of Radnor, Pennsylvania.

Combining the Samples: Weighting

Before combining the nonfederally assisted new community and paired conventional community samples to produce estimates presented in this report, cases were weighted by factors that include adjustments for each community's probability of selection and expected number of interviews in the community (200 for new communities, 100 for less planned suburban conventional communities, and 50 for subsidized housing subsample). Cases in the five communities have subsidized housing subsamples (Columbia, Forest Park, Jonathan, Lake Havasu City, and Reston) have also been weighted to adjust for oversampling of households in subsidized housing in the community. In addition, each case is weighted by the proportion of its dwelling unit type (single-family detached, townhouse/rowhouse, or apartment) in the original sample for its community to adjust for differential response rates among the three dwelling unit types.

Data presented for combined nonfederally assisted new communities and combined paired conventional communities are weighted to make all the adjustments listed above: each community's probability of selection, dwelling unit type, disproportionate selection of subsidized housing, and expected number of interviews. Data presented for individual communities exclude the weight for the community's probability of selection. Weights for subsidized housing have been applied only for the five new communities with a subsidized housing subsample.

The Surveys of Professionals

General Interviewing Methods

A different questionnaire was constructed for each type of community service system under consideration: one for professionals engaged in the provision of recreational facilities and programs; one for professionals involved in health care faciliites and services; one for officers of community associations; and two for educational administrators (one for school district superintendents and the other for school principals). These questionnaires were pretested in Forest Park and Sharonville, in February 1973, and were revised on the basis of the pretest.

The interviews were structured and generally required about an hour for administration, which was done by appointment with the respondent. Interviewers were instructed to ask the questions exactly as worded and in the order presented in the questionnaire. Interviewing was carried out primarily by members of the study team. Each interview was taken with specific reference to a particular new community or conventional community. Some professionals (e.g., county health officials) had responsibility for facilities or services in more than one sample community. In such cases separate questionnaires were filled out for each community involved. Table A-1 shows the number of interviews obtained in each community for each professional survey.

Choosing the Respondents for the Various Surveys

The overall procedure for choosing respondents was to determine which organizations had responsibility for the facilities and services connected with a given type of service system in a community, generally in connection with completion of the Community Inventory described below, and then to locate and attempt to interview executive personnel with knowledge of the planning and provision of the facilities and services in the community. The precise procedures for selecting professional respondents were as follows:

School Superintendent and School Principal Professional Surveys. Interviews were sought with the superintendent or assistant superintendent of every school district serving the 36 sample communities, as well as the principal of every public school attended by children in the communities. A number of the communities were served by more than one district. Some of the districts served more than one of the communities in the sample. In the latter situation separate interviews were taken for each sample community in the district as described above.

Health Professional Survey. Health was conceptualized broadly in this study to include mental as well as physical health and related social services. A judgmental sample of respondents considered to be most knowledgeable about such health matters was identified in each community. Most health professionals interviewed were officials of county or community health offices, officers of county medical societies, or hospital administrators. The breakdown of professional health respondents by affiliation was as follows:

Hospital or hospital association	51
County health department	21
County medical society	17
Community health agency or community health plan	12
Private medical clinic	6
Community social service agency	5
Health planning council	5

Visiting nurse association	4
Group medical practice	3
New community developer's staff	3
Regional health agency	3
Other	12
Total	142

Recreational Professional Survey. Interviews were sought with recreational directors (or persons in equivalent positions) of every major organization providing recreational facilities or services in each of the 36 sample communities. So as to insure that a significant provider of such facilities and services was not omitted, each respondent was asked the following question as part of the interview:

Before we conclude, could you help us to identify any other persons or organizations involved in providing recreational services for the people of (name of community)? Whom else would you recommend that we interview? (Q. 46)

The breakdown of interviews by affiliation of respondent is as follows:

Municipal recreation departments	20
County recreation departments	19
Park and recreation districts	17
Community (homes) associations[c]	7
Volunteer recreation associations	5
Other county agencies	3
Other municipal agencies	2
School districts	2
State recreation agencies	2
New community developer staff	1
Total	78

Community (Homes) Association Survey. Automatic community or homes associations (i.e., those to which residents automatically belong when they purchase a home or sign a lease) have responsibility for public services and amenities in many new communities in the United States. Such associations exist at various levels in new communities. Associations may draw membership from and provide services to an entire new community, a village or neighborhood within the community, or a single townhouse cluster within a neighborhood. Interviews were sought with the presidents and executive directors of all community and neighborhood or village level

[c] Although most homes associations provide some recreational facilities and services, only those with a full-time, paid recreation staff participated in the recreation survey. In addition, the homes association survey described below included several sections focusing on association recreational facilities and programs.

automatic associations in the ten sample new communities where such associations were in existence. These communities included: Columbia, Elk Grove Village, Foster City, Irvine, Jonathan, Laguna Niguel, Park Forest South, Reston, Valencia, and Westlake Village. In addition, homes association interviews were conducted in the two retirement new communities, Rossmoor Leisure World (Laguna Hills) and Sun City Center.

The Developer Decision Studies

Wave One: Provision of Low- and Moderate-income Housing

Data on the developer decision to build or not to build housing for low- and moderate-income families, on the implementation of the decision, and on selected decision factors were gathered in structured interviews in the 13 nonfederally assisted new communities and 2 federally assisted new communities. Subsidized housing for low- and moderate-income families existed, was under construction, or was planned in 7 of these communities (Columbia, Forest Park, Jonathan, Lake Havasu City, Park Forest, Park Forest South, and Reston).[d] The remaining 8 communities (Elk Grove Village, Foster City, Irvine, Laguna Niguel, North Palm Beach, Sharpstown, Valencia, and Westlake Village) had none, either existing or planned, when the Wave One Decision Study was initiated in the fall of 1972.

Selection of Respondents. It was decided that all those who had a formal role in decisions that influenced housing policies in each of the communities would be interviewed: the developer; appropriate local governmental officials, (mayors, city council members, city, county and regional planning officials, and housing commissioners); FHA officials; and, for the two federally assisted communities in the sample (Jonathan and Park Forest South), HUD New Community Administration officials. Lists were also drawn up of others who could influence these formal decision makers: consultants; community association officers; fair housing organizations; realtors; mortgage bankers; builders of market-rate and subsidized housing; sponsors of subsidized housing; and various ad hoc groups. In the course of the interviews with the above-mentioned participants, names of

[d] In five of these seven communities (Columbia, Forest Park, Jonathan, Lake Havasu City, and Reston) FHA 235 (owner) and/or FHA 221(d)3 or 236 (rental) subsidized housing existed and was occupied at the time of the fieldwork. Subsidized housing subsamples for the household survey were selected in these communities. Such housing was not yet completed in Park Forest or Park Forest South.

others who had been involved with subsidized housing policies in each of the communities were solicited. This process yielded 161 interviews with key participants in the 15 new communities:

Developers and their representatives	23
Sponsors of subsidized housing	10
Builders of subsidized housing	9
Builders of nonsubsidized housing	7
Local government officials	37
Federal Housing Administration (FHA) officials	11
Mortgage bankers	12
Realtors	12
Fair housing organization officials	15
Managers of subsidized housing	11
HUD new community liaison officer	1
Black leaders (other than above categories)	3
Housing market analysts	2
Other	8
Total	161

The questionnaires were pretested in Februay 1973. All interviews were conducted by a member of the study team by appointment with the respondents.

Wave Two: Provision of Community Services and Update on the Communities

In July and August of 1974 a series of informal interviews were conducted by members of the study team with the developers of the ten sample communities where active development began after 1960. The purpose of these interviews was to determine what actions developers had taken in providing community services, especially those that seemed particularly successful or problematic in their own communities on the basis of preliminary analysis of the household survey data. Additional objectives were to obtain developers' interpretations of their residents' responses to the household survey and to learn what changes had occurred in the communities after completion of the household survey and other data collection procedures in the spring of 1973.

This second wave of the developer decision studies was limited to the sample communities that began active residential development after 1960 in order to reduce or eliminate problems of recall and staff turnover. The ten communities included in this wave were: Columbia, Foster City, Irvine, Jonathan, Laguna Niguel, Lake Havasu City, Park Forest South, Reston,

Valencia, and Westlake Village. Although the developers of the five sample new communities begun in the 1940s and 1950s (Elk Grove Village, Forest Park, North Palm Beach, Park Forest, and Sharpstown) were not included in the second wave of interviews, letters soliciting reactions to the findings of the household survey were sent to them as well as to various institutional officials, such as mayors, city councilmen, city managers, planning directors, and leaders of homes associatons in their communities.

Developer interviews were based on a series of community profiles that summarized residents' evaluations of various aspects of the community. Prior to the interview the developer was sent copies of the profile for his community, which showed the new community residents' responses in comparison with the responses from residents of the paired conventional community and with the combined responses of residents of the 13 nonfederally assisted new communities in the sample. In addition, a document summarizing the strengths and weaknesses of each community, as revealed by the household survey, was prepared for discussion during the interview. Twelve interviews were conducted, including two each in Irvine and Westlake Village and one each in the remaining eight new communities.

The interviews themselves were informal and unstructured. Respondents were the developer (i.e., president of the development corporation) and those members of his staff whom he asked to participate. The interviews were arranged by prior appointment and conducted in the developers' offices. They took from 90 to 120 minutes to complete. Each interview was taped.

The Community Inventories and Map Measurements

The Community Inventories

Community level data were collected in the community inventories. The inventory in each sample community was made concurrently with the field work for the professional personnel surveys in that community. The inventory served both as a listing of facilities and services available in the community upon which selection of professional respondents could be based and as an independent data set. Information collected in each inventory included; (1) location and population data for the sample community and for the county and SMSA in which it was located; (2) a listing of all automatic community (homes) associations in the community; (3) a listing of school districts and the public schools serving the community together with inventories of selected characteristics of the schools; (4) characteristics of community, county, and special district governments; (5) a listing of sources of primary health care within the community and hospitals serving the community; (6) housing mix available in the community and selected characteristics of townhouse and apartment complexes in which sample clusters had yielded interviews; (7) a listing of recreational organizations and facilities serving the community together with selected characteristics of the listed facilities; (8) locations of religious congregations available within the community; (9) locations of all supermarkets and stores for convenience shopping within the community, and of shopping centers, malls, or areas serving the community, as well as selected characteristics of the identified shopping centers, malls, or areas; (10) availability of transportation services to the community; and (11) availability within the community of selected child care, commercial, cultural, entertainment, health care, and recreational facilities. This information was gathered from public records, questioning of knowledgeable persons, and observation at the identified sites. Because of the complexity of the data on health care and recreational facilities and services, summary forms were prepared for each community for each of these content areas and included in the community inventory. Data for a community's summaries were taken from the relevant professional surveys and from the community inventory.

All facilities of the types listed, those existing within a sample community and also those outside the community that were viewed by professional respondents as serving the community (including schools and hospitals) or were mentioned by household survey respondents as those usually used for a given activity (including shopping and recreational faciliites), were inventoried and located on maps. Hospitals and schools outside the community that were mentioned by professionals were transferred directly from professional interviews to community inventories and their locations noted on maps. Shopping and recreational facilities outside the community mentioned by household survey respondents were obtained from listings of responses to appropriate questions from approximately half of the household interviews taken in each community. Facilities or sites mentioned by two or more respondents that were located within the same SMSA as the community were located on maps and were usually inventoried.[e]

Map locations of the various facilities and sites were transferred to plat maps of the sample communities so that map measurements could be made.

---

[e] To help the study team locate these facilities respondents were asked for the name of the facility, the names of the streets of the intersection nearest the facility, and of the community in which it was located. Since respondents could not always remember precise names and intersection locations, not all facilities they mentioned could be found. However, the fact that a number of respondents in a community often used a given facility and some could give the name and location precisely helped in determining which facilities were used by those who could remember only the name or only the location. Thus, a high proportion of the facilities used by the respondents was located.

Map Measurements and Computations

Two phases of map measurements were carried out. The first was designed to measure accessibility of facilities and services for household survey respondents and to provide data descriptive of their neighborhoods. The second was to measure accessibility of these respondents to facilities they used most frequently. The procedures used were the same for both phases.

Preparation of Maps. Two maps were used for each community: a plat map of the community showing property lines and a regional map of the area within which the community was found. The location of all household survey sample clusters, which had yielded interviews for the community, were shown on the community plat map.[f] The locations of facilities found in the community inventory were marked on the map. Inventoried facilities lying outside the community were located and marked on the regional map. For the phase-two measurements, any facilities mentioned by household survey respondents that had not already been located on a map were added to the appropriate map. Virtually all such additions involved facilities outside the community and, therefore, additions to the regional map.

Facility location markers were placed on the maps at the location of the building containing or associated with the facility if such a building existed and its location was known. Otherwise they were placed at the center of the parcel containing the facility with two exceptions: (1) markers locating path or trail systems were placed at all publicly available entrances to the system; and (2) markers locating golf courses were placed at the street entrance to the course if the location of the clubhouse was not known. Markers locating shopping centers, malls, or districts were placed at the center of the cluster of buildings.

On community plat maps, color-coded boundaries for areas served by different school districts and automatic homes associations were shown. In addition, boundaries were drawn around areas having subdivision or neighborhood names.

Distance Measurement Procedures. The initial procedures for phase one, and the only procedures for phase two, were those associated with measuring distances from sample clusters to particular facilities.

For phase one, road distances were measured from the center of each sample cluster to the center of the marker locating the nearest available facility for each of 15 given types. Distances were measured in inches (to the nearest fraction of an inch shown on the map-measuring wheel used),

---

[f]The community plat maps used were the same as those used in selecting the household survey sample. Therefore, they showed the location of all housing in the community that had been occupied as of the fall of 1972, as well as the location of clusters sampled for the survey.

and converted to feet in accordance with the scale of the map. All distances measured in phase one were road distances, and were measured along the shortest street route from the sample cluster to the marker locating the facility. When two or more available facilities were equidistant from a cluster, the facility accessible by the route that could accommodate the largest amount of traffic (i.e., arterial streets rather than residential and local streets) took precedence. Where a cluster was adjacent to a facility, the straight-line distance from the center of the cluster to the center of the marker was used.

In considering which facility of a given type was closest to the cluster, only facilities available to the cluster were considered. Facilities operated by community (homes) associations (including community, village, neighborhood, townhouse complex, and apartment complex associations) were considered available only to clusters located within the association boundaries shown on the maps. Public facilities were considered available to all clusters, as were facilities where residents could pay for use if they wished. The latter included commercial facilities and those operated by private membership groups other than community associations (e.g., country clubs).

For phase two (distances to facilities used by household respondents) the same procedures were used as for phase one with two exceptions: (1) it was necessary to locate the facility of a given type each respondent said he or she used most often rather than the facility nearest the cluster; and (2) aerial (straight-line) distances were used consistently for two types of measurements rather than road distances. In this phase distances were measured for the following types of facilities about which respondents had been asked in the household interview: school attended by a child in the household; regular doctor or clinic; park or playground usually used by a child under 12 in the household; golf course, swimming facility, tennis court, bicycle path, walking or hiking path, convenience store, supermarket, and shopping center usually used by the respondent; and the town where the family head was employed.

Aerial (straight-line) distances were measured from the center of the respondent's community to the center of the community where the facility was located for the regular doctor or clinic and the town where the family head was employed. This was done because of the expense and difficulty involved in precisely locating the enormous variety of facilities of these types used by individual respondents.

Road distance was measured from the center of a respondents' sample cluster to the facility usually used for the other types of facilities listed above.

Other Computations (Phase One Only). A number of characteristics of household respondents' neighborhoods were computed or otherwise determined from the maps. In this study neighborhood was conceptualized in two ways, as macro-neighborhood and micro-neighborhood (housing cluster). Characteristics related to each concept were measured for each sample cluster that had yielded household interviews.

The macro-neighborhood was defined as the area within a half-mile radius of a given sample cluster and within distinct boundaries such as major highways, freeways, undeveloped land, bodies of water, or the community boundary as defined by the sample frame. To determine the macro-neighborhood of any given cluster on a map, a transparent, circular overlay with a radius of one-half mile by the scale of the map was placed on the map with its center on the center of the cluster. Then a number of measurements were made. First, the existence of certain faciliites located on the map, including some types other than those to which distances had been measured, within the macro-neighborhood was recorded.[g] Next, the number of sides on which the macro-neighborhood had distinct boundaries such as those noted in the definition of the concept was recorded. Finally the housing density was computed (number of units per acre). The plat maps had been marked to show all housing occupied as of the fall of 1972 as part of the sampling procedures, so determination of the number of units in the neighborhood was a straightforward matter of counting. The number of square inches in the area was determined through use of a gridded transparent overlay. This number was converted to acreage according to the scale of the map, and density was computed.

The micro-neighborhood was defined as the sample cluster itself for clusters of single-family detached housing. For sample clusters from apartment or townhouse complexes, the entire complex was defined as the micro-neighborhood; its perimeter was the external lot lines of the complex. Housing density of the micro-neighborhood was computed using procedures similar to those involved in the computation of macro-neighborhood density. In addition, the following were recorded for the micro-neighborhood: (1) whether it bordered on water, golf course, or other open space of five acres or more; (2) design of the intersecting of immediately adjacent street; (3) for townhouse and apartment complexes only, the land use immediately in front of and behind the units in the cluster; and (4) the automatic community association(s) and school district(s) serving the cluster.

One worker did the measurements for all sample clusters in a commu-

---

[g] These included: elementary school; nursery school or day care center; convenience store or supermarket; park or playground; neighborhood or community center; church or synagogue; library; private medical facilities; public health facilities; internal path system; swimming facilities; tennis courts; bar or tavern; billiard parlor; bowling alley; gas service station; movie theater; laundromat; picnic area with tables; post office; restaurant; roller skating rink; ice skating rink; and teen center.

nity for at least one phase of the work on that community. Measurements were independently checked for at least 10 percent of the clusters in each community. Where consistent errors were found, all such measurements for all clusters in the community were checked and corrected.

The household survey interview schedule is reproduced in appendix B. All other survey instruments are filed at the Center for Urban and Regional Studies of The University of North Carolina at Chapel Hill.

I. D. NUMBER

**A NATIONAL STUDY OF
ENVIRONMENTAL PREFERENCES
AND THE QUALITY OF LIFE**
JANUARY – APRIL 1973

	OFFICE USE ONLY

| Supporting Agency | National Science Foundation
Research Applied to National Needs
Division of Social Systems and Human Resources
Research Grant Number GI–34285 |
|---|---|

Research Organization	Center for Urban and Regional Studies, University of North Carolina at Chapel Hill	Field Work Subcontractor	Research Triangle Institute Research Triangle Park, North Carolina

A. Sample Cluster Number: _____–_____   B. Sample Line Number: _____

C. Street Address:_____

D. City or Town: _____

E. Respondent Designated on Cluster Listing Sheet: ◯ Head   ◯ Spouse

F. Hello, I'm _____ representing the Research Triangle Institute, a not-for-profit national research organization and the University of North Carolina. We are conducting a survey about the attitudes, preferences, living conditions, and activities of people in a number of communities across the United States. Since your household falls into our sample in this community, I would like to ask you a few questions. All the answers you give will be strictly confidential and will be used only in statistical tables where your name can in no way be connected with your answers. Of course, no one is required to participate, but I hope very much that you will, and I think you'll find it interesting.

G. Before we start, however, I need to know if you and your family have moved to this address since the first of the year (1973) or if you've been living here longer than that.
◯ SINCE FIRST OF YEAR - - THANK RESPONDENT AND TERMINATE INTERVIEW
◯ "LONGER THAN THAT" - - CONTINUE WITH HOUSEHOLD LISTING

H. Time is now: _____

I. Good. Now first, I need some information about the people who live here with you. I don't need the names, just the relationships of the people who live here. Let's start with the adults. What is the age of the head of household? (PAUSE. OBTAIN ALL INFORMATION ABOUT HEAD OF HOUSEHOLD AND CONTINUE WITH OTHER HOUSEHOLD MEMBERS.) Have we missed anyone -- a roomer, someone who lives here but who is away right now?

IF HEAD AND SPOUSE ARE LIVING IN A HOUSEHOLD, INTERVIEW PERSON INDICATED ON CLUSTER LISTING SHEET (AND TRANSFERRED TO ITEM E ABOVE). IF HEAD IS NOT NOW MARRIED, OR SPOUSE IS NOT LIVING IN HOUSEHOLD, INTERVIEW HEAD.

ADULTS

All Persons:
* 21 or Older
  or
* Married, any Age
  or
* Under 21 and
  Living Away From
  Parents

List All Adults By Relation to the Head	Sex	Age	Marital Status	Indicate R "X"
1. Head of Household				
2.				
3.				
4.				

NCS Trans-Optic S388C-321

List All Children By Relation to the Head	Sex	Age	* In School? (Circle)	Indicate Child Selected With "X"
1.			Y N	
2.			Y N	
3.			Y N	
4.			Y N	
5.			Y N	

* "IN SCHOOL" DOES NOT INCLUDE NURSERY SCHOOL OR COLLEGE. INDICATE CHILD SELECTED FOR SCHOOL QUESTIONS (Q. 29-38) AFTER REFERRING TO RANDOM SELECTION TABLE BELOW.

RANDOM SELECTION TABLE IF MORE THAN ONE CHILD IN SCHOOL
(FOR QUESTIONS 29-38)

Number of Children In School	Child Selected In Sample
2	_____
3	_____
4	_____
5	_____
6	_____

1. There's quite a bit of talk these days about the overall "quality" of people's lives. What does the phrase "quality of life" mean to you -- that is, what would you say are the main things the overall "quality" of your own life depends on?

_____

_____

1a. Anything else? _____

_____

2. Compared to the last community you lived in, would you say that for you yourself, moving to this community has improved the quality of your life, has made it worse, or hasn't made much difference?

① Improved   ⑤ Worse   ③ Not much difference – Go to Q. 3

2a. How is that?

_____

_____

3. And what year was it you moved to this address?

YEAR: _____

4. Was your previous residence here in this community, or in another part of this metropolitan area, or outside this metropolitan area?

① Outside Metro area   ⑤ Same community
       ③ Same Metro area

4c. What year was it you moved to this community?

Year: _____   ⓪①②③④⑤⑥⑦⑧⑨   (Go to
                         ⓪①②③④⑤⑥⑦⑧⑨   Q. 5)

4a. What city, county, and state was that?

City: _____   County: _____

State: _____

4b. Did you live within the city limits, outside the city in a built up area, outside the city in the open country, or on a farm?

                  ① In city   ② Out – built up   ③ Out – open   ④ Farm

---

5. Just before you moved to this (house/apartment), did you live in a single family house on its own lot, a townhouse or row house, an apartment, or what?

① Single family   ② Townhouse/Row house   ③ Apartment   ④ Other (specify): _____   ⑤   ⑥

6. How many rooms were there in that (house/apartment), not counting bathrooms?

① One   ③ Three   ⑤ Five   ⑦ Seven
② Two   ④ Four   ⑥ Six   ⑧ Eight or more

7. Did you own that place, rent it, or what?

① Own   ② Rent   ③ Other (specify): _____

8. Would you please tell me which of the reasons listed on this card **(HAND CARD A)** were important in your decision to move out of your previous place? (MARK ALL THAT APPLY)

Yes No   Yes No
①   ⑤ Job change or transfer   ①   ⑤ Recent retirement
①   ⑤ Forced moved because of fire, eviction, condemnation, etc.   ①   None of these
①   ⑤ Recent marriage, divorce, separation, or widowhood

9. What (other) factors were important in your decision to move out of your previous place?

_____

_____

9a. Anything else? _____

_____

– 3 –

10. Here is a list of things that people often consider when they move. **(HAND CARD B)** Thinking of what attracted you to this place, could you tell me which three of these factors were most important in your (family's) decision to move to this community (originally)?

11. Now, I'd like you to compare this community to the one you lived in just before you moved here. For each item on CARD B, please tell me if where you're living now is better, not as good, or about the same as where you lived before.

Yes	No		Better	Same	Not As Good
①	⑤ a. Layout and space of the dwelling and lot	a. ①	③	⑤
①	⑤ b. Construction of the place	b. ①	③	⑤
①	⑤ c. Cost of buying (and financing) or renting the dwelling	c. ①	③	⑤
①	⑤ d. Nearness to outdoors and the natural environment	d. ①	③	⑤
①	⑤ e. Appearance of the immediate neighborhood	e. ①	③	⑤
①	⑤ f. Public Schools.	f. ①	③	⑤
①	⑤ g. Health and medical services.	g. ①	③	⑤
①	⑤ h. Shopping facilities	h. ①	③	⑤
①	⑤ i. Recreational facilities.	i. ①	③	⑤
①	⑤ j. Opportunity for participation in community life	j. ①	③	⑤
①	⑤ k. Good place to raise children	k. ①	③	⑤
①	⑤ l. Cost of living in the community	l. ①	③	⑤
①	⑤ m. Safety from crime	m. ①	③	⑤
①	⑤ n. Finding a job here in this community	n. ①	③	⑤
①	⑤ o. Convenience to work; ease of commuting	o. ①	③	⑤
①	⑤ p. Ease of getting around the community	p. ①	③	⑤
①	⑤ q. Climate	q. ①	③	⑤
①	⑤ r. Type of people living in the neighborhood	r. ①	③	⑤
①	⑤ s. Overall planning that went into the community	s. ①	③	⑤
①	⑤ t. Other (specify):	t. ①	③	⑤

12. **Response to Question 11r, "Type of people – neighborhood": (MARK AS 11r ANSWERED)**
① Better -- Continue with Q. 13   ③ Same -- Go to Q. 14   ⑤ Not as good -- Continue with Q. 13

13. When you said that the "type of people living in the neighborhood" was (better/not as good) what, specifically, did you have in mind? (MARK ALL THAT APPLY)

13a. If better:

Yes	No	
①	⑤	Friendly here
①	⑤	Same race as respondent here
①	⑤	Same age, family life cycle here
①	⑤	Same (better) class, income, education, SES level here
①	⑤	Other (specify): _____

13b. If not as good:

Yes	No	
①	⑤	Not as friendly here
①	⑤	Not same race here
①	⑤	Not same age, family life cycle here
①	⑤	Not same (as good) class, income, education, SES level here
①	⑤	Other (specify): _____

14. **Response to Question 11s, "Overall planning -- into community": (MARK AS 11s ANSWERED)**
① Better -- Continue with Q. 15   ③ Same -- Go to Q. 16   ⑤ Not as good -- Continue with Q. 15

15. (And) when you said that the "overall planning that went into the community" was (better/not as good) what, specifically, did you have in mind?

_____

_____

16. At the time you were deciding to move to this community, did you seriously consider moving to another community instead?

① Yes   ⑤ No -- Go to Q. 19

> 16a. Where was that?
>   NAME OF COMMUNITY: _____
>
> 16b. What was the single most important reason you did not move there?
>
> _____

17. **Respondent lives in: (MARK ONE)**
○ Control community; did not mention planned community in Q. 16a -- Continue with Q. 18.

○ Control community; mentions planned community in Q. 16a -- Go to Q. 19.
○ Planned community -- Go to Q. 19.

18. Did you consider moving to (NAME OF PLANNED COMMUNITY)?

① Yes   ⑤ No -- Go to Q. 19

> 18a. What was the single most important reason you did not move there?
>
> _____

19. I'd like to ask you how you feel now about this area as a place to live -- I mean the area outlined on the map **(SHOW MAP)**. From your own personal point of view, would you rate this area as an excellent place to live, good, average, below average, or poor?

① Excellent   ② Good   ③ Average   ④ Below average   ⑤ Poor

   19a. Why do you say that? _____

_____

20. If respondent makes any voluntary comments about the appropriateness of the mapped area, please note them.
① Mapped area too small   ② Mapped area too large   ③ Mapped area wrong shape   ④ Don't understand it

⑦ Other (specify): _____

21. **Household includes: (MARK ONE)**
⑤ No child under 21 -- Go to Q. 39   ③ No children age 12-20 -- Go to Q. 23
① Child(ren) age 12-20 -- Continue with Q. 22

22. From the teenagers' point of view, how would you expect them to rate this community as a place to live -- would they say it was excellent, good, average, below average, or poor?

① Excellent   ② Good   ③ Average   ④ Below average   ⑤ Poor

23. **Household includes: (MARK ONE)**
⑤ No children under 12 -- Go to Q. 28   ① Child(ren) under 12 -- Continue with Q. 24

-- 5 --

24. As a place to raise children under 12, how would you rate this area -- would you say it was excellent, good, average, below average, or poor?

① Excellent   ② Good   ③ Average   ④ Below average   ⑤ Poor

25. How do you feel about the places <u>right near your home</u> for children under 12 to play out of doors -- would you say they are excellent, good, average, below average, or poor?

① Excellent   ② Good   ③ Average   ④ Below average   ⑤ Poor

     25a. Why do you say that? _____

           _____

           _____

26. Is there a park or playground near here where young children can play?

① Yes   ⑤ No -- Go to Q. 27

     26a. Where is that?

               NAME OF PARK OR PLAYGROUND: _____

               NEAREST INTERSECTION: _____

                                           (Street)   (Cross Street)

     26b. About how many minutes would it take a child to walk there from your front door? _____ MINUTES   ⓪①②③④⑤⑥⑦⑧⑨ / ⓪①②③④⑤⑥⑦⑧⑨

     26c. And when the weather is good, do(es) your child(ren) -- those under 12 -- play there every day, several times a week, once a week, once or twice a month, or less often?

         ⑤ Every day   ④ Several times a week   ③ Once a week   ② Once or twice a month   ① Less often

27. When your child(ren) -- those under 12 -- play(s) outdoors where do(es) (they/he/she) usually play? **(HAND CARD C)**

① Your yard/apartment or townhouse grounds   ② Neighbor's yard   ③ Park or playground   ④ Street/parking areas

⑤ Vacant lots   ⑥ Woods or open space away from your yard/apartment grounds

⑦ Somewhere else (specify): _____

28. **ENTER PROPER INFORMATION FROM HOUSEHOLD LISTING ON PAGE 2 FOR SELECTED CHILD. ASK Q. 29 – 38 ABOUT SELECTED CHILD AND SCHOOL THAT CHILD ATTENDS.**

Relationship to Family Head	Sex	Age

⓪ No eligible child -- Go to Q. 39

29. We would also like to know your feelings about different aspects of the schools around here. First, would you tell me the name of the school your (AGE OF CHILD) year old (son/daughter) attends?

NAME OF SCHOOL: _____

30. What town is (NAME OF SCHOOL) in? _____

31. How does your child usually get to that school?

① Walk   ② Bicycle   ③ Car   ④ School bus   ⑤ Other

32. And about how many minutes does it take (him/her) to get there? _____ MINUTES   ⓪①②③④⑤⑥⑦⑧⑨ / ⓪①②③④⑤⑥⑦⑧⑨

33. Here is a list of problems that sometimes come up in schools. (HAND CARD D) For each of the items on the list would you tell me if, in your opinion, it is a serious problem at (NAME OF SCHOOL), somewhat of a problem, or not a problem?

   a) Students disrupting school or causing trouble.
     ① Serious   ③ Somewhat   ⑤ Not a problem

   b) Racial conflict or hostility.
     ① Serious   ③ Somewhat   ⑤ Not a problem

   c) Students using drugs during or after school hours.
     ① Serious   ③ Somewhat   ⑤ Not a problem

   d) Students drinking during or after school hours.
     ① Serious   ③ Somewhat   ⑤ Not a problem

34. Do you think (NAME OF SCHOOL) spends too much time on new kinds of teaching methods and courses, not enough time on that sort of thing, or is it about right?

   ① Too much   ③ About right   ⑤ Not enough

35. Would you say that most of the teachers your child has at that school are excellent, good, average, below average, or poor?

   ① Excellent   ② Good   ③ Average   ④ Below average   ⑤ Poor

36. And how would you rate how well your child is doing in school -- is (he/she) doing well above average, above average, average, below average, or well below average?

   ① Well above   ② Above   ③ Average   ④ Below   ⑤ Well below

37. In general, how do you think your child feels about going to school -- do you think (he/she) dislikes it very much, dislikes it somewhat, likes it somewhat, likes it very much, or doesn't care about it one way or the other?

   ④ Dislikes very much ③ Dislikes somewhat ② Likes somewhat   ① Likes very much   ⑤ Doesn't care

38. All things considered, how would you rate (NAME OF SCHOOL) -- do you think it's excellent, good, average, below average, or poor?

   ① Excellent   ② Good   ③ Average   ④ Below average   ⑤ Poor

39. I have one (more) question about schools. In the last year, have you yourself gone to a local public school - - - - - - - -

   Yes No
   ①   ⑤ To attend a school function (play, open house, athletic event)?
   ①   ⑤ To attend a meeting of the parent–teachers association?
   ①   ⑤ To attend a meeting of some other club or organization?
   ①   ⑤ To make use of any of the school's indoor or outdoor recreation facilities?

40. Now we have some questions about your health and health care. Of course, most people get sick now and then, but overall, how satisfied are you with your own health? (HAND CARD E) Here is a card I'd like you to use to answer this question. If you are completely satisfied with your health, you would say "one." If you are completely dissatisfied, you would say "seven." If you are neither completely satisfied nor completely dissatisfied, you would put yourself somewhere from two to six; for example, four means that you are just as satisfied as you are dissatisfied.

          Completely Satisfied   ①   ②   ③   ④   ⑤   ⑥   ⑦   Completely Dissatisfied

41. Have you had a routine check-up in the past year, that is, since (MONTH) 1972?
① Yes   ⑤ No

42. Do you have routine check-ups as often as you feel you should?
① Yes   ⑤ No

43. Do you have a regular doctor or clinic you go to?
① Doctor   ③ Clinic   ⑤ No -- Go to Q. 44

> 43a. Where is (his/her office/the clinic) located?
>
> NAME OF DOCTOR/CLINIC: _____
>
> NEAREST INTERSECTION: _____ _____   TOWN: _____
>   (Street)   (Cross Street)
>
> 43b. How long does it usually take to get there from here? _____ MINUTES
>
> 43c. The last time you went to that (doctor/clinic), did you find anything annoying or inconvenient about - - - - -
>
> Yes   No
> ①   ⑤ Arranging appointments?
> ①   ⑤ Arranging transportation to get there?
> ①   ⑤ The way you and other patients were treated?
> ①   ⑤ The cost of the visit for treatment received?
>
> 43d. Overall, how satisfied are you with the quality of the medical care you usually receive from that (doctor/clinic)?
> (HAND CARD E) Which number comes closest to how you feel?
> Completely Satisfied   ①   ②   ③   ④   ⑤   ⑥   ⑦   Completely Dissatisfied

44. Altogether, how many different times have you been to see doctors, other than dentists, in their offices or in clinics about your own health in the past 12 months -- that is, since (MONTH) 1972?

                              _____ TIMES

45. And during the last 12 months, did you ever really want to see or talk to a doctor but didn't for some reason?
① Yes   ⑤ No -- Go to Q. 46.

> 45a. The last time that happened, why didn't you?
>
> _____
>
> _____

46. Do you belong to a prepaid medical plan or have any other kind of medical or hospital insurance?

① Yes -- Prepaid plan only   ③ Yes -- Both   ⑤ No -- Go to Q. 47.
② Yes -- Insurance only   ④ Yes -- Not sure/don't know which

> 46a. What is the name of the (plan/insurance)?
>
> NAME(S): _____
>
> 46b. (Does this/Do these) cover your doctor's bills in full, in part, or not at all?
> ① In full   ③ In part   ⑤ Not at all
>
> 46c. (Does it/Do they) cover your hospital expenses in full, in part, or not at all?
> ① In full   ③ In part   ⑤ Not at all

— 8 —

47. Here is a list of services available in many communities. (HAND CARD F) We'd like to know, first, if such services are available in this community or its vicinity, and second, if you would be willing to recommend those that are here as good places to go for help.

	SERVICE AVAILABLE			SERVICE NOT AVAILABLE	DON'T KNOW IF SERVICE AVAILABLE
	Would Recommend	Not Sure	Would Not Recommend		
a. Emergency medical care	①	②	③	⑤	⑥
b. Hospital care	①	②	③	⑤	⑥
c. Family planning	①	②	③	⑤	⑥
d. Prenatal care	①	②	③	⑤	⑥
e. Health care for children	①	②	③	⑤	⑥
f. Dental care	①	②	③	⑤	⑥
g. Convalescent or nursing home care	①	②	③	⑤	⑥
h. Public assistance or welfare services	①	②	③	⑤	⑥
i. Family and marital counseling	①	②	③	⑤	⑥
j. Help with a legal problem	①	②	③	⑤	⑥
k. Help with a drug problem	①	②	③	⑤	⑥
l. Help with an emotional problem	①	②	③	⑤	⑥
m. Help with a drinking problem	①	②	③	⑤	⑥

48. Overall, how good would you say health care facilities and services are for people who live in this community -- excellent, good, average, below average, or poor?

① Excellent ② Good ③ Average ④ Below average ⑤ Poor

49. We are also interested in where people in this area go shopping. First, what about day to day items, such as milk and bread that you need between trips to the supermarket. Where do you usually go for these -- or do you get all that sort of thing at the supermarket?

(Ask 49a–g for convenience store, then ask Q. 50a–g for supermarket, and then ask Q. 51a–g for shopping center used most often.)

○ Supermarket only -- Go to Q. 50

	49. Where do you usually go for day to day items?	50. What supermarket do you usually go to?	51. What shopping center or mall do you use most often?
a. Name of store (shopping center)			
b. Location	Name: _____ Nearest Intersection: _____ ___Street___ ___Cross Street___ Town: _____	Name: _____ Nearest Intersection: _____ ___Street___ ___Cross Street___ Town: _____	Name: _____ Nearest Intersection: _____ ___Street___ ___Cross Street___ Town: _____
c. How often do you usually go there?	① More than once a week ② Once a week ③ 2–3 times a month ④ Less often	① More than once a week ② Once a week ③ 2–3 times a month ④ Less often	① More than once a week ② Once a week ③ 2–3 times a month ④ Less often
d. How do you usually get there?	① Walk ② Bicycle ③ Car ④ Bus ⑤ Taxi ⑥ Other	① Walk ② Bicycle ③ Car ④ Bus ⑤ Taxi ⑥ Other	① Walk ② Bicycle ③ Car ④ Bus ⑤ Taxi ⑥ Other
e. And how many minutes does it take to get there?	⓪①②③④⑤⑥⑦⑧⑨ ⓪①②③④⑤⑥⑦⑧⑨ MINUTES:	⓪①②③④⑤⑥⑦⑧⑨ ⓪①②③④⑤⑥⑦⑧⑨ MINUTES:	⓪①②③④⑤⑥⑦⑧⑨ ⓪①②③④⑤⑥⑦⑧⑨ MINUTES:
f. Would you say you like, dislike, or neither like nor dislike shopping at (NAME OF STORE OR SHOPPING CENTER)?	① Like shopping ③ Neither ⑤ Dislike shopping	① Like shopping ③ Neither ⑤ Dislike shopping	① Like shopping ③ Neither ⑤ Dislike shopping
g. (HAND CARD G) What are the main reasons you go there to shop? (UP TO 3 ITEMS MAY BE CHECKED IN EACH COLUMN)	ⓐ Convenient location ⓑ Variety of goods ⓒ Prices ⓓ Hours open ⓔ Friendly service ⓕ Place to sit and rest ⓖ Cleanliness ⓗ Parking space ⓘ Attractive store ⓙ Place to meet or shop with friends	ⓐ Convenient location ⓑ Variety of goods ⓒ Prices ⓓ Hours open ⓔ Friendly service ⓕ Place to sit and rest ⓖ Cleanliness ⓗ Parking space ⓘ Attractive store ⓙ Place to meet or shop with friends	ⓐ Convenient location ⓑ Variety of goods ⓒ Prices ⓓ Hours open ⓔ Friendly service ⓕ Place to sit and rest ⓖ Cleanliness ⓗ Parking space ⓘ Attractive store ⓙ Place to meet or shop with friends

52. Thinking over everything we've mentioned about shopping facilities, overall, how good would you say they are for people who live in this community -- excellent, good, average, below average, or poor?
① Excellent   ② Good   ③ Average   ④ Below Average   ⑤ Poor

53. We are also interested in what people do in their spare time. What is your favorite type of leisure or recreational activity to do outside the house?
⓪ No favorite activity -- Go to Q. 54
FAVORITE ACTIVITY: _____

53a. About how often did you (ACTIVITY) last year, not counting when you were on vacation? (ACCEPT RANGES)

_____ TIMES   ⓪ ① ② ③ ④ ⑤ ⑥ ⑦ ⑧ ⑨
⓪ ① ② ③ ④ ⑤ ⑥ ⑦ ⑧ ⑨

53b. Where do you go most often?
NAME OF FACILITY: _____

NEAREST INTERSECTION: _____   TOWN: _____
STREET   CROSS STREET

53c. The last time you went (ACTIVITY) there, did you go and (ACTIVITY) by yourself or with someone else? (PAUSE) Who (ACTIVITY) with you? (MARK ALL THAT APPLY)

Yes	No		Yes	No		Yes	No	
ⓐ	ⓐ Self only		ⓒ	ⓒ Child(ren)		ⓔ	ⓔ Friend(s)	
ⓑ	ⓑ Spouse		ⓓ	ⓓ Other relative		ⓕ	ⓕ Other	

53d. Overall, how satisfied are you with that place as a place to (ACTIVITY)? Which number comes closest to how you feel?
CARD E   Completely Satisfied   ① ② ③ ④ ⑤ ⑥ ⑦   Completely Dissatisfied

54. Here is a list of recreational activities. **(HAND CARD H)** I'd like to know which of these you have taken part in within the last year, not counting when you were on vacation. (COMPLETE Q. 54a FOR ALL FIVE ACTIVITIES, THEN COMPLETE b FOR EACH ACTIVITY, THEN COMPLETE c-f FOR EACH ACTIVITY THAT IS NOT R'S FAVORITE.)

	GOLF	SWIMMING
a. Participate?	① Yes ⑤ No	① Yes. ⑤ No
b. Interviewer: (CHECK ONE) If activity is - - - - - - - - -	① Favorite, go to next activity ⑤ Not favorite, complete column	① Favorite, go to next activity ⑤ Not favorite, complete column
c. About how often did you (ACTIVITY) last year, not counting when you were on vacation?	TIMES: ⓪ ① ② ③ ④ ⑤ ⑥ ⑦ ⑧ ⑨ ⓪ ① ② ③ ④ ⑤ ⑥ ⑦ ⑧ ⑨	TIMES: ⓪ ① ② ③ ④ ⑤ ⑥ ⑦ ⑧ ⑨ ⓪ ① ② ③ ④ ⑤ ⑥ ⑦ ⑧ ⑨
d. Where did you go (most often)?	NAME OF PLACE: NEAREST INTERSECTION: _____ STREET CROSS STREET TOWN: _____	NAME OF PLACE: NEAREST INTERSECTION: _____ STREET CROSS STREET TOWN: _____
e. The last time you went (ACTIVITY) there did you go and (ACTIVITY) by yourself or with someone else? Who (ACTIVITY) with you? (MARK ALL THAT APPLY)	Yes No Yes No ①⑤ Self only ①⑤ Other relative ①⑤ Spouse ①⑤ Friend(s) ①⑤ Child(ren) ①⑤ Other	Yes No Yes No ①⑤ Self only ①⑤ Other relative ①⑤ Spouse ①⑤ Friend(s) ①⑤ Child(ren) ①⑤ Other
f. Overall, how satisfied are you with that place as a place to (ACTIVITY)? Which number comes closest to how you feel? **HAND CARD E**	Completely Satisfied ① ② ③ ④ ⑤ ⑥ ⑦ Completely Dissatisfied	Completely Satisfied ① ② ③ ④ ⑤ ⑥ ⑦ Completely Dissatisfied

— 10 —

54. (Continued)

TENNIS	BICYCLING	WALKING AND HIKING
① Yes ⑤ No	① Yes ⑤ No	① Yes ⑤ No
① Favorite, go to next activity ⑤ Not favorite, complete column	① Favorite, go to next activity ⑤ Not favorite, complete column	① Favorite, go to next activity ⑤ Not favorite, complete column
TIMES:	TIMES:	TIMES:
⓪①②③④⑤⑥⑦⑧⑨ ⓪①②③④⑤⑥⑦⑧⑨	⓪①②③④⑤⑥⑦⑧⑨ ⓪①②③④⑤⑥⑦⑧⑨	⓪①②③④⑤⑥⑦⑧⑨ ⓪①②③④⑤⑥⑦⑧⑨
NAME OF PLACE:	NAME OF PLACE:	NAME OF PLACE:
NEAREST INTERSECTION:		NEAREST INTERSECTION:
STREET CROSS STREET		STREET CROSS STREET
TOWN: _____	TOWN: _____	TOWN: _____
Yes No Yes No ①⑤ Self only ①⑤ Other relative ①⑤ Spouse ①⑤ Friend(s) ①⑤ Child(ren) ①⑤ Other	Yes No Yes No ①⑤ Self only ①⑤ Other relative ①⑤ Spouse ①⑤ Friend(s) ①⑤ Child(ren) ①⑤ Other	Yes No Yes No ①⑤ Self only ①⑤ Other relative ①⑤ Spouse ①⑤ Friend(s) ①⑤ Child(ren) ①⑤ Other
Completely Satisfied ① ② ③ ④ ⑤ ⑥ ⑦ Completely Dissatisfied	Completely Satisfied ① ② ③ ④ ⑤ ⑥ ⑦ Completely Dissatisfied	Completely Satisfied ① ② ③ ④ ⑤ ⑥ ⑦ Completely Dissatisfied

— 11 —

55. All things considered, how good would you say the recreational facilities in this community and its immediate vicinity are for the people who live here -- excellent, good, average, below average, or poor?

① Excellent ② Good ③ Average ④ Below average ⑤ Poor

56. We'd like to ask you about other types of leisure activities too. For example, how many different days in the last week did you spend an hour or more:

DO NOT MARK

a. watching television?	_____ DAYS	⓪	①	②	③	④	⑤	⑥	⑦
b. reading a book in your spare time?	_____ DAYS	⓪	①	②	③	④	⑤	⑥	⑦
c. working at a hobby?	_____ DAYS	⓪	①	②	③	④	⑤	⑥	⑦
d. playing cards with friends?	_____ DAYS	⓪	①	②	③	④	⑤	⑥	⑦
e. reading newspapers and/or magazines?	_____ DAYS	⓪	①	②	③	④	⑤	⑥	⑦
f. doing community volunteer work?	_____ DAYS	⓪	①	②	③	④	⑤	⑥	⑦

57. Overall, how satisfied are you with the ways you spend your spare time? (HAND CARD E) Which number comes closest to how you feel?

Completely Satisfied ① ② ③ ④ ⑤ ⑥ ⑦ Completely Dissatisfied

58. We have asked you a number of questions about the facilities and services you've used in the last year or so. Now here is a list of some of these same facilities as well as some new ones we've added. (HAND CARD I) Whether or not you have them now, if you had your choice, which <u>three</u> of these facilities would you most prefer to have in your neighborhood, that is, within one-half mile of your home?

	Yes	No	
a.	①	⑤	Bar or tavern
b.	①	⑤	Billiard parlor
c.	①	⑤	Bowling alley
d.	①	⑤	Bus stop
e.	①	⑤	Convenience grocery store
f.	①	⑤	Day care center
g.	①	⑤	Drug store
h.	①	⑤	Gasoline service station
i.	①	⑤	Indoor movie theatre
j.	①	⑤	Laundromat
k.	①	⑤	Library
l.	①	⑤	Nursery school
m.	①	⑤	Outdoor swimming pool
n.	①	⑤	Picnic area
o.	①	⑤	Playground with swings and slides
p.	①	⑤	Post office substation
q.	①	⑤	Private medical clinic
r.	①	⑤	Public health clinic
s.	①	⑤	Quiet place to walk and sit outdoors
t.	①	⑤	Roller skating rink
u.	①	⑤	Supermarket
v.	①	⑤	Teenage recreation center
w.	①	⑤	Tennis courts

* *

This next section goes better if you fill it out yourself. (HAND R THE SELF—ADMINISTERED QUESTIONNAIRE.) Here are some statements that some people agree with and others disagree with. Please mark each one according to whether you agree or disagree and how strongly. (EXPLAIN BY USING FIRST ONE AS AN EXAMPLE IF NECESSARY. CON—TINUE WITH Q. 59 WHEN SELF—ADMINISTERED QUESTIONNAIRE IS COMPLETED.)

* *

59. A number of people have indicated that one of the more important things about a neighborhood is how well kept up it is. As far as you're concerned, what would the <u>main reason</u> be that a well kept up neighborhood is important? **(CARD J)**

① Helps keep the property values up
② Indicates that the people there would probably be good neighbors
③ Makes the neighborhood look better and more attractive

④ Something else (specify): _____   ⑤   ⑥

60. Sometimes a source of concern for people living in residential areas is the type and the cost of housing going up in their vicinity. If a builder were able to buy up a tract of land within half a mile or so of your home, would you care what kind of housing he built there?

① Yes   ⑤ No -- Go to Q. 61

60a. Would you be opposed to any of the following types of housing being built there? **(HAND CARD K;** MARK ALL THAT APPLY)

Yes	No		○ Opposed to none	Yes	No	
①	⑤	Single family detached homes		①	⑤	Garden apartments
①	⑤	Townhouses or rowhouses		①	⑤	High rise apartments

60b. How about the cost of such housing -- would you object if new homes were sold for: (ASK EACH RANGE)

	Would Object	Would Not Object
1) Under $25,000?	1) ①	⑤
2) $25,000 up to $30,000?	2) ①	⑤
3) $30,000 up to $35,000?	3) ①	⑤
4) $35,000 up to $45,000?	4) ①	⑤
5) $45,000 or more?	5) ①	⑤

60c. What if the housing were rental apartments -- would you object if they rented for - - - - -
○ (RESPONDENT VOLUNTEERS THAT HE/SHE OBJECTS TO ALL RENTAL HOUSING REGARDLESS OF COST: MARK HERE AND GO TO Q. 61.)

	Would Object	Would Not Object		Would Object	Would Not Object
1) Under $150/month?	①	⑤	3) $200-$250/month?	①	⑤
2) $150-$200/month?	①	⑤	4) Over $250/month?	①	⑤

61. If (NAME OF DEVELOPER IF STILL ACTIVE/a builder) were considering locating a facility or type of housing within half a mile or so of your home which in your opinion would seriously damage the residential character of this neighborhood, do you think that there is anything you could do to prevent it?

① Yes   ⑤ No   ⑧ Don't Know

61c. Why is that? _____

_____
(Go to Q. 62)

61a. What could you do? _____

61b. What do you think your chances for success would be -- would you have a:
① very good chance of success,   ② a good chance,   ③ a limited chance, or
                                     ④ no chance at all for success?

62. When you moved to this place, were you aware of any plans for the development of the area around your neighborhood, say, within a half a mile or so of your home?

① Yes   ⑤ No -- Go to Q. 63

62a. Has the area been developed in accordance with these plans?   ① Yes   ⑤ No

— 13 —

63. Since you've been living here, do you think you have been adequately informed about plans for future developments, such as shopping centers, apartment houses and other facilities in the vicinity of your home?
① Yes ⑤ No

64. What has been the most reliable source for the information that you have gotten? **(HAND CARD L)**
① Local newspaper ② Friends/neighbors/family ③ Radio/TV ④ Developer

⑤ Community/homeowners' association ⑥ Other (specify): _____

65. As far as you're concerned, do you think it's a good idea for neighborhoods -- and here I'm thinking of clusters of five or six homes -- to have people of different religious backgrounds or the same religious backgrounds, or doesn't it matter?
① Good if different ⑤ Good if same ③ Doesn't matter

66. And as far as you're concerned, do you think it's a good idea for neighborhoods to have people with quite different levels of education or roughly the same levels of education, or doesn't it matter?
① Good if different ⑤ Good if same ③ Doesn't matter

67. And do you think it's a good idea for neighborhoods to have people of different racial backgrounds or the same racial background, or doesn't it matter?
① Good if different ⑤ Good if same ③ Doesn't matter

68. | **Race of Respondent:** | ⑤ Respondent is black -- Go to Q. 71 |
    | **(MARK ONE)** | ① Respondent is not black -- continue with Q. 69 |

69. If a black family moved into this neighborhood, do you think that that would upset all, most, a few, or none of the families already living here?
④ All ③ Most ② A few ① None

70. Which of the reasons on this card comes closest to how you would feel about it? **(HAND CARD M)** Would you: (READ CATEGORIES)
① a. wish they hadn't moved in and try to encourage them to leave;
② b. wish they hadn't moved in but try to be nice to them anyway;
③ c. not think about their race very much one way or the other and treat them like any other neighbor; or
④ d. go out of your way to make sure they were made to feel a part of the neighborhood?

71. Which of the following statements on this card **(HAND CARD N)** would best describe the relationships you have with your nearest neighbor? (READ CATEGORIES)
① a. Often visit one another in each other's homes, or
② b. Frequent casual chatting in the yard or if you happen to run into each other in the street, or
③ c. Occasional casual chatting in the yard or if you happen to run into each other in the street, or
④ d. Hardly know your neighbors?

72. Next, would you tell me how many of your five or six closest friends live here in this community -- all of them, most of them, one or two, or none of them?
④ All ③ Most ② One or two ① None -- Go to Q. 74

73. How often do you get together with any of these friends -- every day, several times a week, once a week, 2-3 times a month, or once a month or less?
⑤ Every day ④ Several times a week ③ Once a week
② 2-3 times a month ① Once a month or less

74. What about your relatives -- how many of the relatives you feel closest to live in this community -- all of them, most of them, one or two, or none of them?
④ All ③ Most ② One or two ① None -- Go to Q. 76

— 14 —

IDENTIFICATION NUMBER

INTERVIEWER'S NAME _____

SAMPLE CLUSTER NO. _____ — _____ LINE NO. _____

A NATIONAL STUDY OF ENVIRONMENTAL PREFERENCES AND THE QUALITY OF LIFE
JANUARY – APRIL 1973

Sponsoring Agency: National Science Foundation
Research Applied to National Needs
Division of Social Systems and Human Resources
Research Grant Number GI-34285

Research Organization: Center for Urban and Regional Studies, University of North Carolina at Chapel Hill

Field Work Subcontractor: Research Triangle Institute Research Triangle Park North Carolina

SELF-ADMINISTERED SECTION

Please indicate for each of the following sentences whether you agree or disagree with it and how much. Do this by placing a mark in the appropriate circle under the sentence.

1. All things considered, the people who live in this community are pretty much the same.
   ① Agree Strongly   ② Agree Somewhat   ③ Disagree Somewhat   ④ Disagree Strongly

2. I am much more interested in national affairs than I am in local affairs.
   ① Agree Strongly   ② Agree Somewhat   ③ Disagree Somewhat   ④ Disagree Strongly

3. I can live the way I please in this community without social pressures for me to act in particular ways.
   ① Agree Strongly   ② Agree Somewhat   ③ Disagree Somewhat   ④ Disagree Strongly

4. As often as not, I actually enjoy cooking, cleaning, and doing other chores around the house.
   ① Agree Strongly   ② Agree Somewhat   ③ Disagree Somewhat   ④ Disagree Strongly

5. I am able to see my close friends about as much as I want these days.
   ① Agree Strongly   ② Agree Somewhat   ③ Disagree Somewhat   ④ Disagree Strongly

6. I don't believe that public officials care about what people like me think.
   ① Agree Strongly   ② Agree Somewhat   ③ Disagree Somewhat   ④ Disagree Strongly

7. It is quite safe for women and children to be out alone at night in this community.
   ① Agree Strongly   ② Agree Somewhat   ③ Disagree Somewhat   ④ Disagree Strongly

8. It is harder to call on my neighbors in time of need in this community than where I used to live.
   ① Agree Strongly   ② Agree Somewhat   ③ Disagree Somewhat   ④ Disagree Strongly

9. It is worth considerable effort to assure one's self of a good name with important people.
   ① Agree Strongly   ② Agree Somewhat   ③ Disagree Somewhat   ④ Disagree Strongly

NCS Trans-Optic S388A-321   – CONTINUED –

SELF-ADMINISTERED SECTION (Continued)

10. These days a person doesn't really know whom he can count on.
    ① Agree Strongly   ② Agree Somewhat   ③ Disagree Somewhat   ④ Disagree Strongly

11. Despite all the newspaper and television coverage, national and international happenings rarely seem as interesting as events that occur right in the local community in which one lives.
    ① Agree Strongly   ② Agree Somewhat   ③ Disagree Somewhat   ④ Disagree Strongly

12. Most local officials are primarily concerned with looking out for themselves.
    ① Agree Strongly   ② Agree Somewhat   ③ Disagree Somewhat   ④ Disagree Strongly

13. The major advantage of living in a highly planned community is that you don't have to worry that the character of your neighborhood will change for the worse.
    ① Agree Strongly   ② Agree Somewhat   ③ Disagree Somewhat   ④ Disagree Strongly

14. As far as I can tell, black families are treated just as well in this community as anyone else.
    ① Agree Strongly   ② Agree Somewhat   ③ Disagree Somewhat   ④ Disagree Strongly

15. Sometimes politics and government seem so complicated that a person like me can't really understand what's going on.
    ① Agree Strongly   ② Agree Somewhat   ③ Disagree Somewhat   ④ Disagree Strongly

16. People like me are always treated fairly by the police and other law enforcement officers in this community.
    ① Agree Strongly   ② Agree Somewhat   ③ Disagree Somewhat   ④ Disagree Strongly

17. All things considered, I am very satisfied with my family life — the time I spend and the things I do with members of my family.
    ① Agree Strongly   ② Agree Somewhat   ③ Disagree Somewhat   ④ Disagree Strongly

18. The social needs of the citizens are the responsibility of themselves and their families and not the community.
    ① Agree Strongly   ② Agree Somewhat   ③ Disagree Somewhat   ④ Disagree Strongly

19. There doesn't seem to be much connection between what people like me want and what town officials do.
    ① Agree Strongly   ② Agree Somewhat   ③ Disagree Somewhat   ④ Disagree Strongly

20. The raising of one's social position is one of the more important goals in life.
    ① Agree Strongly   ② Agree Somewhat   ③ Disagree Somewhat   ④ Disagree Strongly

21. In spite of what some people say, the lot of the average man is getting worse.
    ① Agree Strongly   ② Agree Somewhat   ③ Disagree Somewhat   ④ Disagree Strongly

22. There are a lot more interesting things to do around this town than there were in the last place I lived.
    ① Agree Strongly   ② Agree Somewhat   ③ Disagree Somewhat   ④ Disagree Strongly

23. I don't feel much a part of what goes on in this town.
    ① Agree Strongly   ② Agree Somewhat   ③ Disagree Somewhat   ④ Disagree Strongly

24. Religious groups in this community are too involved in social concerns and neglect spiritual matters.
    ① Agree Strongly   ② Agree Somewhat   ③ Disagree Somewhat   ④ Disagree Strongly

549

SELF-ADMINISTERED SECTION (Continued)

25. White people have a right to keep black people out of their neighborhoods.
① Agree Strongly ② Agree Somewhat ③ Disagree Somewhat ④ Disagree Strongly

26. Hardly anything to do with local government in this town takes place behind closed doors; everything is pretty much above board.
① Agree Strongly ② Agree Somewhat ③ Disagree Somewhat ④ Disagree Strongly

27. Being a member of a church or synagogue should be part of any well-rounded life.
① Agree Strongly ② Agree Somewhat ③ Disagree Somewhat ④ Disagree Strongly

28. Police and other law enforcement officers in this community are not doing a very good job.
① Agree Strongly ② Agree Somewhat ③ Disagree Somewhat ④ Disagree Strongly

29. It is very easy to make new friends in this community.
① Agree Strongly ② Agree Somewhat ③ Disagree Somewhat ④ Disagree Strongly

30. If a man has an important job, he ought to be very careful about the kind of neighborhood he lives in.
① Agree Strongly ② Agree Somewhat ③ Disagree Somewhat ④ Disagree Strongly

31. Most people around here would like to spend more time with their neighbors.
① Agree Strongly ② Agree Somewhat ③ Disagree Somewhat ④ Disagree Strongly

32. All things considered, how satisfied are you with your marriage? Which number comes closest to how you feel?

Completely Satisfied ① ② ③ ④ ⑤ ⑥ ⑦ Completely Dissatisfied

(○ Not Applicable)

---

33. There has recently been a great deal of talk about building homes for low and moderate income families in suburban areas. We would like to know what you think about putting homes for the following types of families here in this neighborhood, say within a half mile of your home. Please place a mark in the circle which indicates whether you think homes in this neighborhood for each type of family would greatly improve, improve, not effect, harm, or greatly harm your neighborhood.

Homes for:

	Greatly Improve	Improve	Not Effect	Harm	Greatly Harm
a. Retired white families with incomes under $5000 a year	①	②	③	④	⑤
b. White families with incomes under $5000 a year	①	②	③	④	⑤
c. White families with incomes of $5000-$10,000 a year	①	②	③	④	⑤
d. White families with incomes of $10,000-$15,000 a year	①	②	③	④	⑤
e. White families with incomes of $15,000 or more a year	①	②	③	④	⑤
f. Retired black families with incomes under $5000 a year	①	②	③	④	⑤
g. Black families with incomes under $5000 a year	①	②	③	④	⑤
h. Black families with incomes of $5000-$10,000 a year	①	②	③	④	⑤
i. Black families with incomes of $10,000-$15,000 a year	①	②	③	④	⑤
j. Black families with incomes of $15,000 or more a year	①	②	③	④	⑤

34. Below are some words and phrases which we would like you to use to describe this <u>neighborhood</u> as it seems to you. By neighborhood, we mean roughly the area near here which you can see from your front door – that is, the five or six homes nearest to yours around here. For example, if you think the neighborhood is noisy, please put a mark in the circle right next to the word "noisy." If you think it is quiet, please put a mark in the circle right next to the word "quiet." If you think it is somewhere in between, please put a mark where you think it belongs.

YOUR NEIGHBORHOOD

Noisy	O	O	O	O	O	Quiet
Attractive	O	O	O	O	O	Unattractive
Unfriendly people	O	O	O	O	O	Friendly people
Enough privacy	O	O	O	O	O	Not enough privacy
Poorly kept up	O	O	O	O	O	Well kept up
People who are like me	O	O	O	O	O	People who are not like me
Pleasant	O	O	O	O	O	Unpleasant
Convenient	O	O	O	O	O	Inconvenient
Very poor place to live	O	O	O	O	O	Very good place to live
Safe	O	O	O	O	O	Unsafe
Bad reputation	O	O	O	O	O	Good reputation
Crowded	O	O	O	O	O	Uncrowded

DO NOT MARK IN THIS BOX

75. And how often do you get together with any of these relatives -- every day, several times a week, once a week, 2-3 times a month, or once a month or less?
⑤ Every day   ④ Several times a week   ③ Once a week
② 2-3 times a month   ① Once a month or less

76. All things considered, would you like to see your relatives a lot more than you do now, somewhat more than now, about as often as you have been seeing them, or somewhat less often than now?
① A lot more than now   ② Somewhat more than now   ③ About as have been seeing them   ④ Less often than now

77. If a close relative or friend asked you if they should consider moving to this community, would you tell them that this would be a particularly good community to move to, that it's pretty much like other communities around here, or that they could probably do better somewhere else?
① It's particularly good here   ② It's like other communities   ③ Could probably do better

78. In your opinion, what are the most important issues or problems facing the community as a whole at the present time?

_____

_____

78a. Anything else? _____

_____

79. How often do you discuss local government or community policy matters with other people -- would you say several times a week, once a week, once or twice a month or less often than that?
① Several times a week   ② Once a week   ③ Once or twice a month   ④ Less often

80. There are a number of ways people become involved in local community matters. (HAND CARD O) Have you engaged in any of these activities in this community during the past year? Please tell me which ones. (PAUSE) Anything not on the list?
                ○ None

Yes	No	
①	⑤	Written to a local political leader or public official
①	⑤	Written to a local newspaper about a community problem or issue
①	⑤	Attended a meeting or gathering in which local government or community policy matters were a major subject or consideration
①	⑤	Given money to help in a local political campaign or issue
①	⑤	Been a candidate for and/or held local elective office
①	⑤	Spoken to a local political leader or public official
①	⑤	Contributed time in a local political campaign
①	⑤	Contributed time in support of or opposition to a local issue
①	⑤	Served in a local appointive office
①	⑤	Other (specify): _____

81. People have different feelings about the responsiveness of local officials. Which of the following statements do you think best applies to (MOST LOCAL GOVERNMENTAL UNIT) officials in this area? Do you think:
① they do pretty much what the majority of the citizens want, or
② they do what a few of the more influential citizens want, or
③ they tend to do what they themselves think best?
④ (DON'T KNOW)

82. DOES R LIVE IN NEW COMMUNITY OR RETIREMENT COMMUNITY STILL UNDER ACTIVE DEVELOP-MENT? (MARK ONE)

     ① Yes -- Continue with Q. 83   ⑤ No -- Go to Q. 84

83. How about officials of (NAME OF DEVELOPER)? Do you think:
① they do pretty much what the majority of the citizens want, or
② they do what a few of the more influential citizens want, or
③ they tend to do what they themselves think best?
④ (DON'T KNOW)

84. **RESIDENCE OF R: (MARK ONE)**
① Columbia, Md. -- Go to Q. 86   ④ Sun City Center, Fla. -- Go to Q. 86
② Jonathan, Minn. -- Go to Q. 86   ⑤ Other Community -- Continue with Q. 85
③ Reston, Va. -- Go to Q. 86

85. Did you automatically become a member of a group such as a community, homeowners, property owners, townhouse, or condominium association when you moved here?
① Yes   ③ Not sure   ⑤ No -- Go to Q. 98

85a. What is the name of the association(s)?

_____ (Go to Q. 87)

86. Now I have some questions about the (Columbia Park and Recreation Association/Jonathan Association/Reston Homeowners' Association/Sun City Center Civic Association).

87. Here is a list of services such associations often provide for their members. **(HAND CARD P)** Which of the services on this list do you believe your association provides? (PAUSE) Does your association do anything that is not on this list?

88. (ASK FOR EACH SERVICE R BELIEVES IS PRO—VIDED) Are you very satisfied, somewhat satisfied, somewhat dissatisfied, or very dissatisfied with the way your association handles (SERVICE)?

	87. PROVIDES?			88. SATISFACTION			
	NO	DON'T KNOW	YES	VERY SATIS.	SOME SATIS.	SOME DISSAT.	VERY DISSAT.
a. Architectural control	⑤	③	①→ a.	①	②	③	④
b. Maintenance of open space and common facilities	⑤	③	①→ b.	①	②	③	④
c. Provision of recreation facilities	⑤	③	①→ c.	①	②	③	④
d. Representation of residents' views to local government	⑤	③	①→ d.	①	②	③	④
e. Representation of residents' views to developer or builder	⑤	③	①→ e.	①	②	③	④
f. Social activities for members	⑤	③	①→ f.	①	②	③	④
g. Other (specify): _____			①→ g.	①	②	③	④

(IF R LIVES IN COLUMBIA, MD. SAY: "NOW I HAVE SOME QUESTIONS ABOUT YOUR VILLAGE ASSOCIATION.")

89. Do you attend all the meetings of
{ your village association
  the Jonathan Association
  the Reston Homeowners' Association
  the Sun City Center Civic Association
  your association

most of them, a few of them, or none of them?
④ All   ③ Most   ② A few   ① None

90. Have you ever served on a committee or been an officer of that association?

　① Yes　　⑤ No

91. Did you vote in the last election of officers for the association?

　① Yes　　⑤ No

92. How satisfied are you with the amount of voice you have in your association -- would you say you are very satisfied, somewhat satisfied, somewhat dissatisfied or very dissatisfied?

　① Very satisfied
　② Somewhat satisfied
　③ Somewhat dissatisfied
　④ Very dissatisfied

93. Which of the following statements do you think best applies to the officers of your association? Do you think:

　① they do pretty much what the majority of the members want, or
　② they do what a few of the more influential members want, or
　③ they tend to do what they themselves think best?
　④ (DON'T KNOW)

94. How do you feel about the dues and assessments of your association -- do you think they are too high, too low, or just about right?

　① Too high
　③ Just about right
　⑤ Too low

95. **DOES RESPONDENT LIVE IN NEW COMMUNITY OR RETIREMENT COMMUNITY STILL UNDER ACTIVE DEVELOPMENT? (MARK ONE)**

　① Yes -- Continue with Q. 96
　⑤ No -- Go to Q. 97

96. What do you think of the role of (NAME OF DEVELOPER) in your association? Would you say that they generally have too much control over the affairs of the association, generally have too little control, or does it depend more on the issues involved?

　① Too much
　⑤ Too little
　③ Depends

97. Based on your experience, how satisfied are you with the overall performance of your association? (HAND CARD E) Which number comes closest to how you feel?

　　　　Completely Satisfied　①　②　③　④　⑤　⑥　⑦　Completely Dissatisfied

– 17 –

98. Here is a list of other types of clubs and organizations that many people belong to. **(HAND CARD Q)** Please look at each of the groups on the list and tell me which of these organizations you yourself belong to. (PAUSE) Are there any others that aren't on this list?

⓪ Belongs to no organizations -- Go to Q. 102

99. Does the (TYPE OF ORGANIZATION) meet or hold its activities here in this community?

> **MARK AT LEFT EACH KIND OF ORGANIZATION R BELONGS TO, THEN ASK Q. 99 FOR EACH ORGANIZATION MENTIONED.**

	98. Mark if belongs		99. In community?
Yes No		Yes No	
a. ① ⑤	Church or synagogue	a. ① ⑤	
b. ① ⑤	Church-connected group (but not the church itself)	b. ① ⑤	
c. ① ⑤	Charity or welfare organization	c. ① ⑤	
d. ① ⑤	Civic or business group.......................................	d. ① ⑤	
e. ① ⑤	College alumni (alumnae) association	e. ① ⑤	
f. ① ⑤	Country club	f. ① ⑤	
g. ① ⑤	Fraternal lodge or organization	g. ① ⑤	
h. ① ⑤	Hobby club	h. ① ⑤	
i. ① ⑤	Labor union	i. ① ⑤	
j. ① ⑤	Nationality or ethnic club or organization........................	j. ① ⑤	
k. ① ⑤	Parent-teachers association	k. ① ⑤	
l. ① ⑤	Political club or organization..................................	l. ① ⑤	
m. ① ⑤	Professional group or association	m. ① ⑤	
n. ① ⑤	Regular card playing group	n. ① ⑤	
o. ① ⑤	Senior citizens organization...................................	o. ① ⑤	
p. ① ⑤	Sport team or athletic club....................................	p. ① ⑤	
q. ① ⑤	Youth group (Girl Scout leader, Little League manager, etc.)	q. ① ⑤	
r. ① ⑤	Voluntary homeowners, neighborhood, or community association	r. ① ⑤	
s. ①	Other (specify): _____	s. ① ⑤	
t. ①	Other (specify): _____	t. ① ⑤	

100. With which one of the organizations you belong to (including the AUTOMATIC HOMEOWNERS' ASSOCIATION) do you usually spend the most time?

TYPE OF ORGANIZATION: _____

101. How active is this organization in dealing with important issues, problems, or projects facing this community -- would you say very active, somewhat active, or not active at all?

① Very active   ③ Somewhat active   ⑤ Not active at all

102. How many cars or trucks do you have for family use?

① One   ② Two   ③ Three or more   ⓪ None -- Go to Q. 103

> **102a.** In the last twelve months, about how many miles has the car (have the cars) been driven? (ACCEPT APPROXIMATION)
>
> 1st CAR: _____ MILES   2nd CAR: _____ MILES   3rd CAR: _____ MILES
>
> ⓪ⓧ②③④⑤⑥⑦⑧⑨   ⓪ⓧ②③④⑤⑥⑦⑧⑨   ⓪ⓧ②③④⑤⑥⑦⑧⑨
> ⓪ⓧ②③④⑤⑥⑦⑧⑨   ⓪ⓧ②③④⑤⑥⑦⑧⑨   ⓪ⓧ②③④⑤⑥⑦⑧⑨

103. Is there a bus stop within a 10 minute walk of your home?

① Yes   ⑤ No -- Go to Q. 104   ⑨ Don't know -- Go to Q. 104

> **103a.** How often do you or someone in your family use the bus?
>
> ⑤ Daily or almost every day (5-7 days a week)   ② One day a month or less
> ④ 1-4 days a week   ① Never
> ③ 2-3 days a month

104. Here is a list of facilities and services. **(HAND CARD R)** Some we have talked about already, others we have not. For each, I want you to tell me whether you think about the right amount of money is now being spent on the facility or service in this community or whether there should be more money spent, or less money spent than there is now. (ASK Q. 104 FOR ALL ITEMS; <u>THEN</u> GO TO Q. 105)

105. FOR EACH ITEM FOR WHICH R SAID "MORE" IN Q. 104 ASK: Would you be willing to pay more in taxes or assessments to help pay for greater expenditures for (FACILITY OR SERVICE)? (MARK RESPONSE AT FAR RIGHT BELOW)

	104. SPEND				105. TAXES	
	DON'T KNOW	LESS	SAME	MORE	YES	NO
a. Schools	⑧	①	③	⑤➔	a.①	⑤
b. Fire protection	⑧	①	③	⑤➔	b.①	⑤
c. Police protection	⑧	①	③	⑤➔	c.①	⑤
d. Outdoor recreation facilities	⑧	①	③	⑤➔	d.①	⑤
e. Community upkeep and maintenance	⑧	①	③	⑤➔	e.①	⑤
f. Public Health facilities	⑧	①	③	⑤➔	f.①	⑤
g. Teen club or recreation center...................	⑧	①	③	⑤➔	g.①	⑤
h. Building housing for low-income families	⑧	①	③	⑤➔	h.①	⑤
i. Public transportation	⑧	①	③	⑤➔	i.①	⑤
j. Community advertising and promotion	⑧	①	③	⑤➔	j.①	⑤

106. All in all, would you say that your taxes and assessments are too high, too low, or about right to pay for the facilities and services that are needed in this community?
   ① Too high   ③ About right   ⑤ Too low

107. Which of the items on this card **(HAND CARD S)** best describes the employment status of the head of this household?
   ① Employed full time -- Go to Q. 108
   ┌─② Employed part time   ┌─⑤ Retired but still working for pay   ┌─⑦ Student -- not employed
   ├─③ Not employed   ├─⑥ Disabled   └─⑧ Student -- employed
   └─④ Retired

   107a. Is (HEAD) presently looking for full or part-time work?
        ① Yes, full   ③ Yes, part   ⑤ No -- Go to Q. 108

   107b. Would you say there is a good chance or not that (HEAD) will be able to find a job right here in this community or the immediate vicinity?
        ① Good chance   ③ Don't know   ⑤ Not good chance

108. What (is/was) (HEAD'S) <u>main</u> job (when HEAD last worked)? (PROBE CAREFULLY FOR SPECIFIC JOB AND DUTIES)
   ⓪ Never worked -- Go to Q. 116

   MAIN JOB: _____

   108a. What kind of business or industry (is/was) that in? (MAIN JOB)

   BUSINESS OR INDUSTRY: _____

109. Is (HEAD) now working? (MARK ONE)
                        ① Yes -- Ask Q. 110-115   ⑤ No -- Go to Q. 116

110. Where is (HEAD'S) job located? (IF UNKNOWN, PROBE FOR COMPANY NAME AND GENERAL LOCATION)

   CITY OR TOWN: _____

111. Does (HEAD) usually make the entire trip to work by car or in a car pool, usually go part way by car and part way by public transportation, usually make the entire trip by public transportation or usually go some other way?
① Car/car pool ② Part car, part public ③ Public ④ Walk

⑤ Other (specify): _____

112. How many minutes does it usually take (HEAD) to get to work? (ACCEPT APPROXIMATIONS) _____ MINUTES

113. Does (HEAD) have a second job at this time or second source of income from work (HEAD) does, in addition to the one we've just been talking about?
① Yes ⑤ No

114. On the average, about how many hours a week does (HEAD) work altogether? _____ HOURS

115. All things considered, how satisfied is (HEAD) with (his/her) main job? **(HAND CARD E)** Which number comes closest to how satisfied or dissatisfied (HEAD) feels?
Completely Satisfied ① ② ③ ④ ⑤ ⑥ ⑦ Completely Dissatisfied

116. How many years of school did (HEAD) complete?
① 0–8 grades
② 9–11 grades, some high school
③ 9–11 grades, plus vocational training
④ 12 grades, high school graduate
⑤ 12 grades, plus vocational training
⑥ 13–15 years, some college
⑦ 16 years, college graduate
⑧ 17 or more, graduate or professional training

117. **Head has: (MARK ONE)** ⑤ No spouse living at home -- Go to Q. 123
① Spouse living at home -- Continue with Q. 118

118. Which of the items on the card **(HAND CARD S)** best describes the employment status of (SPOUSE OF HEAD)?
① Employed full time -- Go to Q. 120
② Employed part time
③ Not employed
④ Retired
⑤ Retired but still working for pay
⑥ Disabled
⑦ Student -- not employed
⑧ Student -- employed

118a. Is (SPOUSE) presently looking for full or part-time work?
① Yes, full ③ Yes, part ⑤ No -- Go to Q. 119

118b. Would you say there is a good chance or not that (SPOUSE) will be able to find a job right here in this community or the immediate vicinity?
① Good chance ③ Don't know ⑤ Not good chance

119. **Is (SPOUSE) now working? (MARK ONE)**
① Yes -- Continue with Q. 120 ⑤ No -- Go to Q. 122

120. On the average, about how many hours a week does (SPOUSE) work altogether? _____ HOURS

121. All things considered, how satisfied is (SPOUSE) with (SPOUSE'S) main job? **(HAND CARD E)** Which number comes closest to how satisfied or dissatisfied (SPOUSE) feels?
Completely Satisfied ① ② ③ ④ ⑤ ⑥ ⑦ Completely Dissatisfied

122. How many years of school did (SPOUSE) complete?
① 0–8 grades
② 9–11 grades, some high school
③ 9–11 grades, plus vocational training
④ 12 grades, high school graduate
⑤ 12 grades, plus vocational training
⑥ 13–15 years, some college
⑦ 16 years, college graduate
⑧ 17 or more, graduate or professional training

— 20 —

123. Please tell me the letter of the group on this card **(HAND CARD T)** that would indicate about what the total income for you and your family was last year -- 1972 -- before taxes, that is.

Ⓐ Under $5,000   Ⓓ $12,500 — $14,999   Ⓖ $20,000 — $24,999   Ⓙ $40,000 — $49,999
Ⓑ $5,000 — $9,999   Ⓔ $15,000 — $17,499   Ⓗ $25,000 — $29,999   Ⓚ $50,000 and over
Ⓒ $10,000 — $12,499   Ⓕ $17,500 — $19,999   Ⓘ $30,000 — $39,999

    123a. Does that include the income of everyone in the family who was living here in 1972?
        ① Yes   ⑤ No -- Ask for "EVERYONE'S INCOME", make corrections above

124. The things people have -- housing, car, furniture, recreation and the like -- make up their standard of living. Some people are satisfied with their standard of living, others feel it is not as high as they would like. How satisfied are you with your standard of living? **(HAND CARD E)**
        Completely Satisfied ① ② ③ ④ ⑤ ⑥ ⑦ Completely Dissatisfied

125. All things considered, how often do you find that you don't have enough money to do the things you would like because of what it costs just to live here -- fairly often, once in a while, or almost never?
    ① Often   ③ Once in a while   ⑤ Never

126. Do you own this (house/apartment), are you renting it or what?
    ① Owns or buying   ② Rents   ③ Other

    120e. How is that? _____

    (Go to Q. 127)

    126c. **(HAND CARD V)** Could you tell me the letter of the group on this card that would indicate about how much the rent is on this (apartment/house) each month, not including utilities?

    Ⓐ Under $100   Ⓔ $250 — $299   Ⓘ $450 — $499
    Ⓑ $100 — $149   Ⓕ $300 — $349   Ⓙ $500 and over
    Ⓒ $150 — $199   Ⓖ $350 — $399
    Ⓓ $200 — $249   Ⓗ $400 — $449

    126d. All things considered, how good a (landlord/resident manager) would you say you have -- good, neither good nor bad or not very good?
    ① Good   ③ Not good or bad   ⑤ Not good
    ○ R says he/she has no real landlord
    (Go to Q. 127)

126a. **(HAND CARD U)** Could you tell me the letter of the group on this card that would indicate about what the present value of this house/apartment is? What would it bring if you sold it today?

Ⓐ Under $20,000   Ⓓ $30,000 - $34,999   Ⓖ $45,000 - $49,999   Ⓙ $70,000 - $79,999
Ⓑ $20,000 - $24,999   Ⓔ $35,000 - $39,999   Ⓗ $50,000 - $59,999   Ⓚ $80,000 and over
Ⓒ $25,000 - $29,999   Ⓕ $40,000 - $44,999   Ⓘ $60,000 - $69,999

126b. Compared to other homes you considered at the time you were buying, do you think that this home will be a better financial investment, a worse financial investment, or about the same?
    ① Better   ③ Same   ⑤ Worse

127. When was this (house/building) built? (ACCEPT GUESSES)
    YEAR BUILT _____

128. How many rooms do you have in this (house/apartment), not including bathrooms?
    ① One   ③ Three   ⑤ Five   ⑦ Seven
    ② Two   ④ Four   ⑥ Six   ⑧ Eight or more

129. Do you have more space indoors in this (house/apartment) than you and your family need, too little space or about the right amount?
① More than need   ③ About right   ⑤ Too little

130. How do you feel about the amount of outdoor space near your home which members of your family can use for their different activities -- do you have more space than you need, too little space, or about the right amount?
① More than need   ③ About right   ⑤ Too little

131. Do you have a place where you can be outside and feel that you really have privacy from your neighbors if you want it?
① Yes   ⑤ No

132. Now, overall how do you feel about the (house/apartment) as a place to live? **(HAND CARD E)** Which number comes closest to how satisfied or dissatisfied you feel?
Completely Satisfied ① ② ③ ④ ⑤ ⑥ ⑦ Completely Dissatisfied

133. How likely are you to move from this place in the next two or three years? Are you certain to move, will you probably move or do you plan to stay here?
① Certain to move   ② Probably move   ③ Don't know   ④ Plan to stay -- Go on to Q. 134

133a. Why are you thinking of moving?

_____

_____

134. Do you have a religious preference? That is, do you consider yourself Protestant, Roman Catholic, Jewish or something else?
① Protestant   ② Roman Catholic   ③ Jewish   ④ Other (what) _____   ⑤ No preference

135. Is being a member of a church or synagogue an important part of your life?
① Yes   ⑤ No

136. Can you find the kinds of church and religious activities you want in this community?
① Yes   ③ Don't care about that   ⑤ No

137. Generally speaking, do you usually think of yourself as a Democrat, a Republican, an Independent, or what?
① Democrat   ② Independent or other
     Republican

137b. Do you think of yourself as closer to the Democratic Party, the Republican Party or not very close to either party?
③ Closer to Democrat
④ Closer to Republican
⑧ Not close to either
(Go to Q. 138)

137a. Would you call yourself a strong (Democrat/Republican) or not?
① Strong Democrat   ⑤ Not strong Republican
② Not strong Democrat   ⑥ Strong Republican

138. We have talked about various parts of your life; now I want to ask you about your life as a whole. How satisfied are you with your life as a whole these days? **(HAND CARD E)** Which number on the card comes closest to how you feel?

Completely Satisfied ① ② ③ ④ ⑤ ⑥ ⑦ Completely Dissatisfied

139. Finally, what do you think this community will be like in five years? Will it be a better place to live than it is now, not as good, or about the same?

① Better   ③ Same   ⑤ Not as good

139a. Why do you say that? _____

_____

139b. What do you think could be done to make it better?

_____

_____

140. In case we have to get in touch with you to clarify any of these answers which sometimes happens in research of this kind, could I please have your telephone number? Thank you.

TELEPHONE NUMBER: _____   ○ NO PHONE   ○ REFUSED

(ASK Q. 141 ONLY OF RESPONDENTS LIVING IN COLUMBIA, MD.; RESTON, VA.; FOREST PARK, OHIO; PARK FOREST, ILL.; PARK FOREST SOUTH, ILL.)

141. I've been asked to ask you one more thing. When the responses to these interviews are analyzed, we would like to be able to look at the reactions of black people living in (NAME OF COMMUNITY) separately. At this point, however, we can't be sure that the sample of houses that was selected includes enough black respondents. In case we do need to contact more black residents, would you give me the names and addresses of two friends or acquaintances who live in (NAME OF COMMUNITY) who are black? We'd be asking them the same questions I've just asked you. You don't have to give me any information, or course, and I can assure you that we wouldn't mention you to them.

FIRST FRIEND/ACQUAINTANCE   SECOND FRIEND/ACQUAINTANCE

NAME _____   NAME _____

ADDRESS _____   ADDRESS _____

TOWN   ⓪①②③   TOWN _____

TIME IS NOW: _____

THANK RESPONDENT FOR HIS/HER TIME. FILL IN POST-INTERVIEW ITEMS DIRECTLY AFTER LEAVING HOUSEHOLD.

POST INTERVIEW ITEMS

P1. Race of respondent:

① White   ② Black   ③ Oriental   ④ Other (specify): _____

P2. Type of dwelling in which respondent lives:
① Single family detached house
② Duplex
③ Rowhouse; townhouse
④ Walk–up apartment building

⑤ Elevator apartment building
⑥ Store with dwelling above or behind
⑦ House converted to rooms or apartments

Ⓐ Other (specify): _____

P3. Number of floors in respondent's building, not counting basement.

FLOORS _____   ⓪①②③④⑤⑥⑦⑧⑨
⓪①②③④⑤⑥⑦⑧⑨

P4. Floor on which respondent's apartment is found:
(Ⓞ Respondent does not live in apartment)   ◯ Above ground floor
◯ Basement   ◯ 1st (ground) floor   (specify floor): _____

⓪①②③④⑤⑥⑦⑧⑨
⓪①②③④⑤⑥⑦⑧⑨

P5. Respondent's rowhouse or townhouse is:
① At the end of a row   ⑤ Not at the end of a row   (Ⓞ Respondent does not live in rowhouse/townhouse)

P6. Condition of exterior of building:
① Well kept up
② Requires some maintenance -- in need of paint or minor repair
③ Requires extensive maintenance -- in need of major repair, structural deterioration; many minor repairs

P7. Condition of lawn and property:
① Well kept up
② Requires some maintenance -- lawn needs cutting, shrubs need pruning
③ Requires extensive maintenance -- parts (all) of lawn and shrubs need replacement; a lot of litter

P8. Foundation planting (shrubs, bushes) in front of building:
① Exists   ⑤ Does not exist

P9. Sidewalk or pathway in front of, beside, or behind respondent's house/apartment house:
① Exists   ⑤ Does not exist

P10. Utilities in respondent's immediate neighborhood are:
① Underground   ② Overhead behind homes (on back lot line, etc.)   ③ Overhead along street

P11. Curb and gutter in front of respondent's house/apartment house:
① Exists   ⑤ Does not exist

P12. Street serving respondent's house/apartment house:
① In good state of repair   ⑤ Requires some maintenance -- bumps, holes, serious cracks, etc.

P13. I certify that the respondent was informed at the start of the interview of the purpose of the survey and the safeguards being taken to keep his replies confidential and that I obtained the respondent's verbal consent to proceed with the interview.

INTERVIEWER'S SIGNATURE _____

DATE OF INTERVIEW: _____ | _____
Month   Day

LENGTH OF INTERVIEW: _____ MINUTES

TODAY'S DATE	
Mo.	Day

LENGTH OF INTERVIEW (Minutes)

TODAY'S DATE:
⓪⓪⓪⓪
①①①①
②②②②
③③③③
④④④④
⑤⑤⑤⑤
⑥⑥⑥⑥
⑦⑦⑦⑦
⑧⑧⑧⑧
⑨⑨⑨⑨

LENGTH OF INTERVIEW:
⓪⓪⓪
①①①
②②②
③③③
④④④
⑤⑤⑤
⑥⑥⑥
⑦⑦⑦
⑧⑧⑧
⑨⑨⑨

Bibliography

Bibliography

Advisory Commission on Intergovernmental Relations. 1968. *Urban and Rural America: Policies for Future Growth*. A Commission Report (A-32). Washington, D. C.: U.S. Government Printing Office, April.

Alonso, William. 1970a. "The Mirage of New Towns," *The Public Interest*, No. 19 (Spring), pp. 3-17.

_____. 1970b. "What Are New Towns For?" *Urban Studies*, 7 (February), pp. 37-55.

Alonso, William, and McGuire, Chester. 1973. "Pluralistic New Towns," in *Frontiers of Planned Unit Development: A Synthesis of Expert Opinion*, Robert W. Burchell (ed.). New Brunswick, N.J.: Center for Urban Policy Research, Rutgers University, pp. 251-262.

American City Corporation. 1971. *City Building: Experience, Trends & New Directions*. Columbia, Md.: The Corporation, April.

_____. 1972. *The Greater Hartford Process*. Hartford, Conn.: The Greater Hartford Process, Inc.; and Columbia, Md.: American City Corporation, April.

_____. 1973a. "Columbia's Goals and Policies," in *The Columbia Process*, A Workbook Prepared for the Workshop in the Development of a New City, The Urban Life Center, Columbia, Maryland, May 23-25, 1973, Columbia, Md.: The Corporation.

_____. 1973b. "The Schools in the Columbia Development Process" in *The Columbia Process*, A Workbook Prepared for the Workshop in the Development of a New City, The Urban Life Center, Columbia, Maryland, May 23-25, 1973. Columbia, Md.: The Corporation.

American Institute of Architects. 1972. *First Report of the National Policy Task Force*, Second Edition. Washington, D.C.: The Institute, May.

American Institute of Planners, The AIP Task Force on New Communities. 1968. *New Communities: Challenge for Today*. American Institute of Planners Background Paper, No. 2, Muriel I. Allen (ed.). Washington, D.C.: The Institute.

American Public Health Association. 1948. *Planning the Neighborhood*. Chicago: Public Administration Service.

Anderson, James R., Weidemann, Sue, Chenoweth, Richard, and Francescato, Guido. 1974. "Residents' Satisfaction: Criteria for the Evaluation of Housing for Low and Moderate Income Families." Paper presented at the 1974 AIP Confer-In, Denver, Colorado, October.

Andrews, Frank M., and Withey, Stephen B. 1973. "Developing Measures of Perceived Life Quality: Results from Several National Surveys." Paper presented at the Annual Meeting of the American Sociological Association, New York City, August.

_____. 1974a. "Assessing the Quality of Life as People Perceive It." Paper presented at the Annual Meeting of the American Sociological Association, Montreal, August.

_____. 1974b. "Research Topics and Selected Results of the Andrews-Withey Project on Development of Measures of Perceived Life Quality." Ann Arbor, Mich.: Institute for Social Research, The University of Michigan, April.

Apgar, Mahlon, IV. 1971. *Managing Community Development: The Systems Approach in Columbia, Maryland.* New York: McKinsey & Company, Inc.

Babchuk, Nicholas, and Booth, Alan. 1969. "Voluntary Association Membership: A Longitudinal Analysis," *American Sociological Review*, Vol. 34 (February), pp. 31-45.

Bailey, James, ed. 1973. *New Towns in America: The Design and Development Process.* Washington, D.C.: The American Institute Of Architects, and New York: John Wiley & Sons.

Bain, Henry. 1968. *The Development District: A Governmental Institution for the Better Organization of the Urban Development Process in the Bi-County Region.* Working Paper No. 5. Prepared for The Maryland-National Capital Park and Planning Commission. Washington, D.C.: The Washington Center for Metropolitan Studies, November.

_____. 1969. *The Reston Express Bus: A Case History of Citizen Action to Improve Urban Transportation. Improving Transportation in the Washington Metropolitan Area*, Number 2. Washington, D.C.: Washington Center for Metropolitan Studies, August.

Baltimore Regional Planning Council and Maryland State Planning Department. 1963. *Metrotowns for the Baltimore Region—Stages and Measures.* Planning Report No. 2. Baltimore, Md.: The Council.

Barasch, Stephen B. 1974. *Recreational Planning for New Communities.* Jericho, N.Y.: Exposition Press, Inc.

Barker, Michael B. 1966. *California Retirement Communities.* Special Report No. 2. Berkeley, Calif.: Center for Real Estate and Urban Economics, Institute for Urban and Regional Development, University of California.

Bartolo, Robert C., and Navin, Francis P. D. 1971. "Demand Responsive Transit: Columbia, Maryland's Experience With Call-A-Ride." Paper prepared for presentation at Confer-In West, Annual Conference of the American Institute of Planners, San Francisco, October.

Bell, Wendell, and Boat, Marion D. 1957. "Urban Neighborhoods and Informal Social Relations," *American Journal of Sociology*, Vol. 12 (January), pp. 391-398.

Bell, Wendell, and Force, Maryanne. 1956. "Urban Neighborhood Types and Participation in Formal Associations," *American Sociological Review*, Vol. 21 (February), pp. 25-34.

Beschen, Darrell A., Jr. 1972. *Transportation Characteristics of School Children. Nationwide Personal Transportation Study*, Report No. 4. Washington, D.C.: Federal Highway Administration, U.S. Department of Transportation, July.

Bradburn, Norman M., Suchman, Seymour, and Gockel, Galen L. 1970. *Racial Integration in American Neighborhoods, A Comparative Study*. NORC Report No. 111-B. Chicago: National Opinion Research Center, The University of Chicago.

Breckenfeld, Gurney. 1971. *Columbia and the New Cities*. New York: Ives Washburn, Inc.

Brooks, Richard. 1971. "Social Planning in Columbia." *Journal of the American Institute of Planners*, Vol. 37 (November), pp. 373-379.

Bryan, Jack. 1972. "'Main Street' Revisited in Midwest New Town." *Journal of Housing*, Vol. 29 (June 30), pp. 282-289.

Bultena, Gordon L., and Wood, Vivian. 1969. "The American Retirement Community: Bane or Blessing?" *Journal of Gerontology*, Vol. 24 (April), pp. 209-217.

_____. 1970. "Leisure Orientation and Recreational Activities of Retirement Community Residents," *Journal of Leisure Research*, Vol. 2 (Winter), pp. 3-15.

Butler, Edgar W., Chapin, F. Stuart, Jr., Hemmens, George C., Kaiser, Edward J., Stegman, Michael A., and Weiss, Shirley F. 1969. *Moving Behavior and Residential Choice: A National Survey*. National Cooperative Highway Research Program Report 81. Washington, D.C.: Highway Research Board, National Academy of Sciences-National Academy of Engineering.

Butler, George D. 1959. *Introduction to Community Recreation*. Prepared for the National Recreation and Park Association. New York: McGraw-Hill Book Company.

Campbell, Angus. 1971. *White Attitudes Toward Black People*. Ann Arbor, Mich.: Institute for Social Research, The University of Michigan, August.

Caplow, Theodore, and Forman, Robert. 1950. "Neighborhood Interaction in a Homogeneous Community," *American Sociological Review*, Vol. 15 (June), pp. 357-366.

Cherry, Rona, and Cherry, Laurence. 1974. "Slowing the Clock of Age," *The New York Times Magazine*, May 11.

Clapp, James A. 1971. *New Towns and Urban Policy: Planning Metropolitan Growth*. New York: Dunellen Publishing Company.

Clark, Reuben, and Mode, Paul J., Jr. 1971. "The Transfer of Power in New Communities," in *New Community Development: Planning Process, Implementation, and Emerging Social Concerns*, Vol. 2, Shirley F. Weiss, Edward J. Kaiser, and Raymond J. Burby, III (eds.). Chapel Hill, N.C.: New Towns Research Seminar, Center for Urban and Regional Studies, University of North Carolina at Chapel Hill, October, pp. 1-37.

Clawson, Marion. 1960. "Suburban Development Districts: A Proposal for Better Urban Growth," *Journal of the American Institute of Planners*, Vol. 26 (May), pp. 69-83.

Clinchy, Evans. 1972. *New Towns, New Schools*? Working Paper No. 1. New York: Educational Facilities Laboratories, Inc., November.

_____. 1974. *Dollars and Educational Sense: Some Financial and Educational Options for the Provision of Educational Services in New Towns*. Working Paper No. 4. New York: Educational Facilities Laboratories, Inc., January.

"Columbia, Md.: Waiting for Godot," 1974. *Clothes*, Vol. 9 (April 1), pp. 30-37.

Columbia Park and Recreation Association. 1970. *Columbia Transit Program. Phase 1 Final Report, Concept Formulation*. Report on a Mass Transportation Demonstration Project. MD-MTD-2. Columbia, Md.: The Association, April.

Columbia Roles Study Committee. 1972. "Citizen Participation in Columbia: A Study of Roles, Relationships, and Processes in New Town Government." Columbia, Md.: Columbia Park and Recreation Association.

Comey, Arthur C., and Wehrly, Max S. 1939. *Planned Communities*. Part 1 of *Urban Planning and Land Policies*. Vol. II of the Supplementary Report of the Urbanism Committee to the National Resources Committee. Washington, D.C.: U.S. Government Printing Office.

Community Builders' Council of Urban Land Institute. 1960. *The Community Builders Handbook*. The Executive Edition. Washington, D.C.: Urban Land Institute.

Comptroller General of the United States. 1974. *Getting the New Communities Program Started: Progress and Problems*. Department of Housing and Urban Development. Report to the Congress. B-170971. Washington, D.C.: U.S. General Accounting Office.

Conkin, Paul. 1959. *Tomorrow a New World: The New Deal Community Program*. Published for the American Historical Association. Ithaca, N.Y.: Cornell University Press.

Cunningham, Ben H. 1971. "Designing the Environment for a Balanced Community: Jonathan, Minnesota," in *New Community Development: Planning Process, Implementation, and Emerging Social Concerns*. Vol. 1, Shirley F. Weiss, Edward J. Kaiser, and Raymond J. Burby, III (eds.). Chapel Hill, N.C.: New Towns Research Seminar, Center for Urban and Regional Studies, University of North Carolina at Chapel Hill, February, pp. 117-143.

Decision Sciences Corporation. 1973. *Advanced New Community Simulation System (NUCOMS) Retail Model*. Jenkintown, Pa.: The Corporation, October.

Downs, Anthony. 1973. *Opening Up the Suburbs, An Urban Strategy for America*. New Haven, Conn.: Yale University Press.

Education in New Communities Project. 1973. *Schools for New Towns*. Working Paper No. 2. New York: Educational Facilities Laboratories, Inc., May.

Eichler, Edward P., and Kaplan, Marshall. 1967. *The Community Builders*. Berkeley and Los Angeles, Calif.: University of California Press.

Einsweiler, Robert C., and Smith, Julius C. 1971. "New Town Locates in a Municipality: Jonathan Saves Money and Chaska Increases Tax Base," *Planners Notebook*, Vol. 1 (June-July), pp. 1-8.

Erskine, Hazel F. 1973. "The Polls: Hopes, Fears and Regrets." *The Public Opinion Quarterly*, Vol. 37 (Spring), pp. 132-145.

Evans, Henry K. 1965. "Transportation Planning Criteria for New Towns," in *Planned Communities: 5 Reports*. Presented at the 44th Annual Meeting, Highway Research Board. Highway Research Record, Number 97. Washington, D.C.: Highway Research Board of the Division of Engineering and Industrial Research, National Academy of Sciences-National Research Council, pp. 30-51.

Fava, Sylvia F. 1970. "The Sociology of New Towns in the U.S.: 'Balance' of Racial and Income Groups." Paper delivered at the 1970 AIP Confer-In, Minneapolis/St. Paul, Minnesota, October.

_____. 1974. "Blacks in American New Towns: Problems and Prospects," *Sociological Symposium*, No. 12 (Fall), pp. 111-130.

Foer, Albert A. 1969. "Democracy in the New Towns: The Limits of Private Governance," *University of Chicago Law Review*, Vol. 36 (Winter), pp. 379-412.

Fonaroff, Arlene. 1970. "Identifying and Developing Health Services in a New Town," *American Journal of Public Health*, Vol. 60 (May), pp. 821-828.

Fucick, William C. 1975. "The Challenge of Implementing Federally Assisted New Communities." *Public Administration Review*, Vol. 35 (May/June), pp. 249-256.

Gans, Herbert J. 1961. "Planning and Social Life: Friendship and Neighbor Relations in Suburban Communities," *Journal of the American Institute of Planners*, Vol. 27 (May), pp. 134-140.

_____. 1967. *The Levittowners: Ways of Life and Politics in a New Suburban Community*. New York: Pantheon Books, A Division of Random House, Inc.

_____. 1968a. *People and Plans: Essays on Urban Problems and Solutions*. New York: Basic Books, Inc.

_____. 1968b. "Planning for the Everyday Life and Problems of Suburban and New Town Residents," in *People and Plans: Essays on Urban Problems and Solutions*, by Herbert J. Gans, New York: Basic Books, pp. 183-201.

_____. 1973. "The Possibilities of Class and Racial Integration in American New Towns: A Policy-Oriented Analysis," in *New Towns: Why— And for Whom?* Harvey S. Perloff and Neil C. Sandberg (eds.). New York: Praeger Publishers, pp. 137-158.

Gaus, Clifton. 1971. "Who Enrolls in a Prepaid Group Practice: The Columbia Experience," *Johns Hopkins Medical Journal*, Vol. 128 (January), pp. 9-14.

Gliege, John G. 1970. *New Towns: Policy Problems in Regulating Development*. Tempe, Ariz.: Institute of Public Administration, Arizona State University.

Gobar, Alfred. 1973. "Should You Have a Shopping Center in Your Project?" *House & Home*, Vol. 44 (August), pp. 67-69.

Godschalk, David R. 1973a. "New Communities or Company Towns? An Analysis of Resident Participation," in *New Towns: Why–And for Whom?* Harvey S. Perloff and Neil C. Sandberg (eds.). New York: Praeger Publishers, pp. 198-220.

_____. 1973b. "Reforming New Community Planning," *Journal of the American Institute of Planners*, Vol. 39 (September), pp. 306-315.

Godschalk, David R., Balcom, Donald, O'Connor, Terrence, and Wood, Gary. 1972. *New Communities and Large Scale Development: Alternative Policies for North Carolina*. State Planning Report 146.08. Raleigh, N.C.: Office of State Planning, North Carolina Department of Administration, June.

Goldhammer, Keith. 1968. "Local Provision for Education: The Organization and Operation of School Systems and Schools," in *Designing Education for the Future, No. 5, Emerging Designs for Education*,

Edgar L. Morphet and David L. Jesser (eds.). New York: Citation Press.

Goley, Beatrice T., Brown, Geraldine, and Samson, Elizabeth. 1972. *Household Travel in the United States. Nationwide Personal Transportation Study*, Report No. 7. Washington, D.C.: Federal Highway Administration, U.S. Department of Transportation, December.

Greenhills-Forest Park City School District. 1968. *A Long Range Plan to Adequately House Students*. Greenhills, Oh.: The District, November.

Griffin, Nathaniel M. 1974. *Irvine: The Genesis of a New Community*. ULI Special Report. Washington, D.C.: ULI-the Urban Land Institute.

Gruen, Nina Jaffe, and Gruen, Claude. 1972. *Low and Moderate Income Housing in the Suburbs, An Analysis for the Dayton Region*. New York: Praeger Publishers.

Gruen, Victor. 1973. *Centers for the Urban Environment: Survival of the Cities*. New York: Van Nostrand Reinhold Company.

Hanson, Royce. 1971. "Background Paper'" in *New Towns: Laboratories for Democracy*, Report of the Twentieth Century Fund Task Force on Governance of New Towns. New York: The Twentieth Century Fund, pp. 25-73.

_____. 1972. *Managing Services for New Communities*. A Report of the Symposium on the Management of New Communities, Held at Columbia, Maryland, and Reston, Virginia, October 25-28, 1970. Washington, D.C.: The Washington Center for Metropolitan Studies and The New Communities Study Center, Virginia Polytechnic Institute and State University.

Hatley, Rolan M. 1972. *Availability of Public Transportation and Shopping Characteristics of SMSA Households. Nationwide Personal Transportation Study*, Report No. 5. Washington, D.C.: Federal Highway Administration, U.S. Department of Transportation, July.

Hatry, Harry P., and Dunn, Diana R. 1971. *Measuring the Effectiveness of Local Government Services: Recreation*. Washington, D.C.: The Urban Institute.

Hawley, Amos H., and Rock, Vincent P. (eds.) 1973. *Segregation in Residential Areas*. Papers on Racial and Socioeconomic Factors in Choice of Housing. Washington, D.C.: Division of Behavioral Sciences, National Research Council, National Academy of Sciences.

Herman, Harold, and Joroff, Michael I. 1967. "Planning Health Services for New Towns," *American Journal of Public Health*, Vol. 57 (April), pp. 633-640.

Hertel, Miachael M. 1971. *Irvine Community Associations*. A Research Report of the Claremont Urban Research Center. Claremont, Calif.: Claremont Urban Research Center, Claremont Graduate School.

Heyssel, Robert M. 1971a. "Causes of Retarded Growth in Pre-Payment Plans," *Johns Hopkins Medical Journal*, Vol. 71 (January), pp. 4-8.

———. 1971b. "Summary Comments'" in *Audio Proceedings of a Conference on Community-Centered Health Plans*, Sponsored by the American City Corporation, The Urban Life Center, Columbia, Maryland, September 8-10, 1971. Columbia, Md.: The Corporation.

Hovet, Mary Rockwell. 1971. *A Study to Identify and Describe Productive School-Community Relationships in Howard County, Maryland*. Ann Arbor, Mich.: University Microfilms.

"How Shopping Malls Are Changing Life in the U.S.," 1973. *U.S. News and World Report*, Vol. 74 (June 18), pp. 43-46.

Howard, Ebenezer. 1945. *Garden Cities of To-morrow*, F.J. Osborn (ed.). Originally published in 1898 as *To-morrow: A Peaceful Path to Real Reform*; reissued in 1902, with slight revisions, under current title. London: Faber and Faber Limited.

Howes, Jonathan B. 1971. "The Shape of Federal Involvement in New Community Building—1970," in *New Community Development: Planning Process, Implementation, and Emerging Social Concerns*, Vol. 2, Shirley F. Weiss, Edward J. Kaiser, and Raymond J. Burby, III (eds.). Chapel Hill, N.C.: New Towns Research Seminar, Center for Urban and Regional Studies, University of North Carolina at Chapel Hill, October) pp. 163-191.

Hyman, Herbert H., and Wright, Charles R. 1971. "Trends in Voluntary Association Membership of American Adults: Replication Based on Secondary Analysis of National Surveys," *American Sociological Review*, Vol. 36 (April), pp. 191-206.

Institute of Government, The University of North Carolina. 1971. *How Govern Soul City*? Report of Organizational Studies for Region K/New Communities Program (NCP-192). Chapel Hill, N.C.: Institute of Government, The University of North Carolina, September.

Jackson, Mercer L., Jr. 1972. "Housing for Older Americans," *HUD Challenge*, Vol. 3 (July), pp. 4-7.

Jackson, Samuel C. 1972. "New Communities," *HUD Challenge*, Vol. 3 (August), pp. 4-7.

Jonathan Design Group. 1968. *Jonathan*. Chaska, Minn.: Jonathan Development Corporation, November.

Jonathan Development Corporation. 1971. *Jonathan New Town: Design and Development*. Chaska, Minn.: The Corporation, February.

Jonathan Development Corporation. n.d. *Questions and Answers about Jonathan*. Chaska, Minn.: The Corporation.

Jonathan Housing Corporation. 1970. *Jonathan Housing Corporation: A Status Report—March, 1970*. Chaska, Minn.: The Corporation, March.

Kaiser, Edward J., Weiss, Shirley F., Burby, Raymond J., III, and Donelly, Thomas G. 1970. "Neighborhood Environment and Residential Satisfaction: A Survey of the Occupants of 166 Single-Family Homes in Greensboro, North Carolina," *Research Previews*, Vol. 17 (November), pp. 11-25.

Kaplan, Marshall. 1973. "Social Planning, Perceptions, and New Towns," in *New Towns: Why—And for Whom*? Harvey S. Perloff and Neil C. Sandberg (eds.). New York: Praeger Publishers, pp. 130-136.

Keller, Suzanne. 1968. *The Urban Neighborhood—A Sociological Perspective*. New York: Random House.

Kelly, Burnham. 1974. *Social Facilities for Large-Scale Housing Developments*. Ithaca, N.Y.: Center for Urban Development Research, Cornell University, October.

Kirk, Frank A. 1975. "State Policy Issues in New Towns and Large-Scale Developments." *Public Administration Review*, Vol. 35 (May/June), pp. 246-249.

Lackawanna County Planning Commission. 1963. *Recreation and Open Space Plan*. Prepared by Candeub, Cabot and Associates. Scranton, Pa.: The Commission.

Lansing, John B. 1966. *Residential Location and Urban Mobility: The Second Wave of Interviews*. Ann Arbor, Mich.: Survey Research Center, Institute for Social Research, The University of Michigan, January.

Lansing, John B., and Hendricks, Gary. 1967. *Automobile Ownership and Residential Density*. Ann Arbor, Mich.: Institute for Social Research, The University of Michigan.

Lansing, John B., and Marans, Robert W. 1969. "Evaluation of Neighborhood Quality," *Journal of the American Institute of Planners*, Vol. 35 (May), pp. 195-199.

Lansing, John B., Marans, Robert W., and Zehner, Robert B. 1970. *Planned Residential Environments*. Ann Arbor, Mich.: Institute for Social Research, The University of Michigan.

Lansing, John B., Mueller, Eva, with Barth, Nancy. 1964. *Residential Location and Urban Mobility*. Ann Arbor, Mich.: Survey Research Center, Institute for Social Research, The University of Michigan.

Lawton, M. Powell, and Byerts, Thomas O. (eds.) 1973. *Community Planning for the Elderly*. Report prepared for the U.S. Department of Housing and Urban Development by the Gerontological Society. Washington, D.C.: U.S. Department of Housing and Urban Development, September.

Manilow, Lewis. 1971. "New Communities in the Seventies, Part III: Park Forest South, Illinois," in *New Community Development: Planning Process, Implementation, and Emerging Social Concerns*. Vol. 2,

Shirley F. Weiss, Edward J. Kaiser, and Raymond J. Burby, III (eds.). Chapel Hill, N.C.: New Towns Research Seminar, Center for Urban and Regional Studies, University of North Carolina at Chapel Hill, October, pp. 217-241.

Marans, Robert W., and Rodgers, Willard. 1972. "Toward an Understanding of Community Satisfaction." Ann Arbor, Mich.: Institute for Social Research, The University of Michigan, December.

Maryland-National Capital Park and Planning Commission. 1962. . . . on *Wedges and Corridors*. Silver Spring, Md,: The Commission.

McKeever, J. Ross. 1973. *Shopping Center Zoning*. Technical Bulletin 69. Washington, D.C.: ULI-the Urban Land Institute.

"Measuring the Quality of Life in America," 1974. *ISR Newsletter*, Vol. 2 (Summer), pp. 3-8.

Meltzer, Jack. 1953. "Administrative Problems of New Towns," *Planning 1952*. Chicago: American Society of Planning Officials, pp. 77-78.

Metropolitan Fund, Inc. 1970. *Regional New Towns: Alternatives in Urban Growth*. Detroit, Mich.: The Fund, May.

————. 1971. *Regional New-Town Design: A Paired Community for Southeast Michigan*. Detroit, Mich.: The Fund, February.

Meyer, Harold D., and Brightbill, Charles K. 1956. *Recreation Administration: A Guide to Its Practice*. Englewood Cliffs, N.J.: Prentice-Hall, Inc.

————. 1964. *Community Recreation: A Guide to Its Organization*. 3rd Edition. Englewood Cliffs, N.J.: Prentice-Hall, Inc.

Mields, Hugh, Jr. 1971. "The Politics of Federal Legislation for New Community Development," in *New Community Development: Planning Process, Implementation, and Emerging Social Concerns*, Vol. 2, Shirley F. Weiss, Edward J. Kaiser, and Raymond J. Burby, III (eds.). Chapel Hill, N.C.: New Towns Research Seminar, Center for Urban and Regional Studies, University of North Carolina at Chapel Hill, October, pp. 245-261.

————. 1973. *Federally Assisted New Communities: New Dimensions in Urban Development*. A ULI Landmark Report. Washington, D.C.: ULI-the Urban Land Institute.

Millen, James S. 1973. "Factors Affecting Racial Mixing in Residential Areas," in Amos H. Hawley and Vincent P. Rock (eds.), *Segregation in Residential Areas*. Washington, D.C.: Division of Behavioral Sciences, National Research Council, National Academy of Sciences, pp. 148-171.

Miller, Myron, Krauss, Richard, Phillips, Nancy, and Pittas, Michael. 1974. *The Imperative of Planning Together: Educational Planning in*

New Communities. Working Paper No. 5. New York: Educational Facilities Laboratories, Inc., January.

Minnesota Experimental City Authority. 1973. *Minnesota Experimental City: A Summary.* Minneapolis, Minn.: The Authority.

Minnesota Experimental City Project. 1969. *MXC, Minnesota Experimental City, Vol. I. A Compendium of Publications Relating to Socio-Cultural Aspects.* Minneapolis, Minn.: University of Minnesota.

Morrison, Peter A. 1970. *Urban Growth, New Cities, and the "Population Problem."* Report P-4515-1. Santa Monica, Calif.: The Rand Corporation, December.

Motor Vehicle Manufacturers Association. 1972. *1972 Automobile Facts and Figures.* Detroit, Mich.: The Association.

Mueller, Eva, and Gurin, Gerald. 1962. *Participation in Outdoor Recreation: Factors Affecting Demand among American Adults.* Outdoor Recreation Resources Review Commission Study Report 20. Washington, D.C.: U.S. Government Printing Office.

Murray, James R. 1974. "Causes of Satisfaction." Chicago: National Opinion Research Center, The University of Chicago, May 30.

National Advisory Commission on Rural Poverty. 1967. *The People Left Behind.* A Report by the President's National Advisory Commission on Rural Poverty. Washington, D.C.: U.S. Government Printing Office, September.

National Association of Counties. 1964. *County Parks and Recreation: A Basis for Action.* Washington, D.C.: The Association.

National Capital Planning Commission and National Capital Regional Planning Council. 1961. *A Policies Plan for the Year 2000: The Nation's Capital.* Washington, D.C.: U.S. Government Printing Office.

National Commission on Community Health Services. 1966. *Health Is a Community Affair.* Cambridge, Mass.: Harvard University Press.

National Commission on Urban Problems. 1968. *Building the American City.* Report of the National Commission on Urban Problems to the Congress and the President of the United States. Washington, D.C.: U.S. Government Printing Office, December.

National Committee on Urban Growth Policy. 1969. *The New City,* Donald Canty (ed.). New York: Frederick A. Praeger, Inc., Publishers.

National Health Forum. 1970. *Meeting the Crisis in Health Care Services in Our Communities.* Washington, D.C.: The Forum.

National Recreation Association. 1962. *Standards for Municipal Recreation Areas.* Revised Edition. New York: The Association.

_____. 1965a. *Outdoor Recreation Space Standards.* New York: The Association.

————. 1965b. *Standards: Playgrounds, Recreation Buildings, Indoor Facilities*. New York: The Association.

The National Research Bureau, Incorporated. 1974. *Directory of Shopping Centers in the United States and Canada*. Vol. XV, 15th Edition. Burlington, Iowa: The Bureau.

"The Nebulous Art of New Community Management," 1971. *Columbia Today*, Vol. 4 (March), pp. 8-15.

"New Communities," 1972. *HUD Challenge*, Vol. 3 (August), pp. 4-23.

"New Communities Checklist Update," 1974. *Systems Building News*, Vol. 5 (August), pp. 30-32.

New Communities Division, Community Resources Development Administration, U.S. Department of Housing and Urban Development. 1969. "Survey and Analysis of Large Developments and New Communities Completed or Under Construction in the United States Since 1947." Washington, D.C.: The Department, February.

New Community Digest. 1973; 1974. Reprinted from *Systems Building News*, Parts One and Two, June-July 1973; *Update*, August-September 1974. Chicago: Barton-Aschman, Inc.

New Community Services, Inc. 1972. *Jonathan General Development Plan 1972*. Chaska, Minn.: Jonathan Development Corporation, September.

New York State Urban Development Corporation and New York State Office of Planning Coordination. 1970. *New Communities for New York*. New York and Albany, N.Y.: The Corporation and the Office, December.

Nicoson, William J. 1971. "The Role of the Federal Government in New Community Development: Present and Projected," in *New Community Development: Planning Process, Implementation, and Emerging Social Concerns*. Vol. 1, Shirley F. Weiss, Edward J. Kaiser, and Raymond J. Burby, III (eds.). Chapel Hill, N.C.: New Towns Research Seminar, Center for Urban and Regional Studies, University of North Carolina at Chapel Hill, February, pp. 451-480.

Norcross, Carl. 1966. *Open Space Communities in the Market Place*. Technical Bulletin 57. Washington, D.C.: Urban Land Institute, December.

————. 1973. *Townhouses & Condominiums: Residents' Likes and Dislikes*. A Special Report. Washington, D.C.: ULI-the Urban Land Institute.

O'Connell, Daniel W. 1973. "Existing 'New Community' Policy and Legislation in Florida 1973," in *New Communities: A Tool to Implement a Policy for the Management of Growth*, Summary Report of the Environmental Land Management Study Committee's Conference on

New Communities, Miami, July 15-17, 1973, James C. Nicholas (ed.). Tallahassee, Fla.: State of Florida Environmental Land Management Study Committee, pp. 142-146.

Office of the Secretary, Department of Housing and Urban Development. 1971. "Assistance for New Communities: Notice of Proposed Rule Making," *Federal Register*, Vol. 36, No. 148, Saturday, July 31, Section 32.7(d), p. 14208.

Ogilvy, A.A. 1968. "The Self-Contained New Town: Employment and Population," *The Town Planning Review*, 39 (April), pp. 38-54.

Park Forest Properties. 1968. *Village of Park Forest South*. Park Forest, Ill.: Park Forest Properties.

Park Forest South Developers, Inc. n.d. *Park Forest South: New Town of the Seventies*. Park Forest, Ill.: Park Forest South Developers, Inc.

Parsons, Kermit C., Budke, Harriet L., Clemhout, Simone, Farrell, Paul B., Prost, James L., and Roberts, Ernest F. 1973. *Public Land Acquisition for New Communities and the Control of Urban Growth: Alternative Strategies*. Final Report Prepared for New York State Urban Development Corporation. Ithaca, N.Y.: Center for Urban Development Research, Cornell University, March.

Paul, Robert M. 1971. "The New Town Development Process: Public and Private Venture," in *New Community Development: Planning Process, Implementation, and Emerging Social Concerns*. Vol. 2, Shirley F. Weiss, Edward J. Kaiser, and Raymond J. Burby, III (eds.). Chapel Hill, N.C.: New Towns Research Seminar, Center for Urban and Regional Studies, University of North Carolina at Chapel Hill, October, pp. 71-88.

Perry, Clarence A. 1929. *Regional Survey of New York and Its Environs*. Vol. VII. New York: Russell Sage Foundation.

_____. 1939. *Housing for the Machine Age*. New York: Russell Sage Foundation.

Peterson, M.L. 1971. "The First Year in Columbia: Assessments of Low Hospitalization Rate and High Office Use," *Johns Hopkins Medical Journal*, Vol. 128 (January), pp. 15-23.

Pettigrew, Thomas F. 1973. "Attitudes on Race and Housing: A Social-Psychological View"' in Amos H. Hawley and Vincent P. Rock (eds.), *Segregation in Residential Areas*. Washington, D.C.: Division of Behavioral Sciences, National Research Council, National Academy of Sciences, pp. 21-84.

"Project Agreement Between United States of America and Jonathan Development Corporation." 1970. October 8.

"Project Agreement Between United States of America and Park Forest South Development Company." 1971. March 17.

Real Estate Research Corporation. 1974. *The Costs of Sprawl: Environmental and Economic Costs of Alternative Residential Development Patterns at the Urban Fringe: Detailed Cost Analysis.* Washington, D.C.: U.S. Government Printing Office, April.

Redstone, Louis G. 1973. *New Dimensions in Shopping Centers and Stores.* New York: McGraw-Hill Book Company.

Reps, John W. 1965. *The Making of Urban America: A History of City Planning in the United States.* Princeton, N.J.: Princeton University Press.

Roach, Michael S. 1973. "Which Comes First—Homes or Shops? Often Both Do," *Irvine World News*, December 13.

Rossi, Peter H. 1955. *Why Families Move.* Gelncoe, Ill.: The Free Press.

San Mateo City School District. 1973. *School Facilities Study.* San Mateo, Calif.: The District, February.

Schonfield, H.K., Heston, J.F., and Falk, I.S. 1972. "Numbers of Physicians Required for Primary Care," *New England Journal of Medicine*, Vol. 286 (March 16), pp. 571-576.

Scott, Stanley. 1965. "Local Government and the Large New Communities," *Public Affairs Report*, Vol. 6 (June), pp. 1-5.

————. 1967. "The Homes Association: Will 'Private Government' Serve the Public Interest?" *Public Affairs Report*, Vol. 8 (February), pp. 1-4.

Senior, Boris, and Smith, Beverly A. 1972. "The Number of Physicians as a Constraint on Delivery of Health Care: How Many Physicians Are Enough?" *Jounral of the American Medical Association*, Vol. 222 (October 9), pp. 178-182.

Short, James Lee. 1973. *Total New Town Building Costs and Comparisons with Alternative Development.* Ph.D. Dissertation, University of California, Los Angeles. Ann Arbor, Mich.: University Microfilms.

Simon, Robert E., Jr. 1971. "New Communities in the Seventies, Part II: Riverton, New York," in *New Community Development: Planning Process, Implementation, and Emerging Social Concerns.* Vol. 2, Shirley F. Weiss, Edward J. Kaiser, and Raymond J. Burby, III (eds.). Chapel Hill, N.C.: New Towns Research Seminar, Center for Urban and Regional Studies, University of North Carolina at Chapel Hill, October, pp. 195-216.

Sinding, Monica K., under direction of Shirley F. Weiss. 1967. *The Philosophic Basis for New Town Development in America.* Chapel Hill, N.C.: Center for Urban and Regional Studies, University of North Carolina at Chapel Hill, September.

Slidell, John B. 1972. *The Shape of Things to Come? An Evaluation of the*

Neighborhood Unit as an Organizing Scheme for American New Towns. Chapel Hill, N.C.: Center for Urban and Regional Studies, University of North Carolina at Chapel Hill, January.

Small, Robert L., and Sutnar, Radoslav L. 1972. "Public/Private Partnership in the Community Development Process: Rancho San Diego—A Case Study." Paper prepared for presentation at Confer-In 72, American Institute of Planners Annual Conference, Boston, Massachusetts, October 7-11.

So, Frank S., Mosena, David R., and Bangs, Frank S., Jr. 1973. *Planned Unit Development Ordinances*. Planning Advisory Service Report No. 291. Chicago: American Society of Planning Officials, May.

Social Science Panel, Advisory Committee to the Department of Housing and Urban Development, National Academy of Sciences-National Academy of Engineering. 1972. *Freedom of Choice in Housing, Opportunities and Constraints*. Washington, D.C.: National Academy of Sciences-National Academy of Engineering.

Stein, Clarence S. 1957a. *Shopping Centers: Principles of Planning and Possible Income to be Derived from Rental of Stores*. A Report for the Resettlement Administration. Reproduced in Clarence S. Stein, *Toward New Towns for America*. New York: Reinhold Publishing Corporation, pp. 162-165.

_____. 1957b. *Toward New Towns for America*. New York: Reinhold Publishing Corporation.

The Study Team on RHOA Role & Structure. 1972. "Toward New Town Governance." Reston, Va.: The Study Team, January.

Svercl, Paul V., and Asin, Ruth. 1973. *Home to Work Trips and Travel*. *Nationwide Personal Transportation Study*, Report No. 8. Washington, D.C.: Federal Highway Administration, U.S. Department of Transportation, August.

Task Force on Organization of Community Health Services. 1967. *Health Administration and Organization in the Decade Ahead*. Washington, D.C.: Public Affairs Press.

Thibeault, Russell W., Kaiser, Edward J., Butler, Edgar W., and McAllister, Ronald J. 1973. "Accessibility Satisfaction, Income, and Residential Mobility," *Traffic Quarterly*, Vol. 27 (April), pp. 289-305.

Touche, Ross & Co. 1973. *Depreciable Lives of Shopping Centers*. An Independent Study Prepared for the International Council of Shopping Centers. New York: International Council of Shopping Centers.

Towle, William F. 1972. "New City, New Hospital," *Hospitals, Journal of the American Hospital Association*, Vol. 46 (January 16), pp. 46-49, 120.

Trevino, Alberto F., Jr. 1974. "New Communities Program: Performance and Promises," *Update: New Community Digest*, reprinted from *Systems Building News*, August-September, 1974. Chicago: Barton-Aschman, Inc., unpaged.

Twentieth Century Fund Task Force on Governance of New Towns. 1971. *New Towns: Laboratories for Democracy*. Report of the Twentieth Century Fund Task Force on Governance of New Towns. New York: The Twentieth Century Fund.

The United States Commission on Civil Rights. 1974. *Equal Opportunity in Suburbia*. Washington, D.C.: U.S. Government Printing Office, July.

U.S. Congress, House of Representatives, Committee on Banking and Currency. 1970. *The Quality of Urban Life*. Hearings Before the Ad Hoc Subcommittee on Urban Growth, Ninety-first Congress, First and Second Sessions, on The Quality of Urban Life. Washington, D.C.: U.S. Government Printing Office.

_____. 1973. *Oversight Hearings on HUD New Communities Program*. Hearings Before the Subcommittee on Housing of the Committee on Banking and Currency, House of Representatives, Ninety-third Congress, First Session, May 30 and 31, 1973. Washington, D.C.: U.S. Government Printing Office.

U.S. Department of Health, Education, and Welfare, Office of Human Development, Administration on Aging. 1973. *New Facts about Older Americans*. DHEW Publication No. (SRS) 73-20006. Washington, D.C.: U.S. Government Printing Office, June.

U.S. Department of the Interior. Bureau of Outdoor Recreation. 1967. *Outdoor Recreation Space Standards*. Washington, D.C.: U.S. Government Printing Office, April.

Van Arsdol, Maurice, Jr., Sabagh, Georges, and Butler, Edgar W. 1968. "Retrospective and Subsequent Residential Mobility," *Demography*, Vol. 5, pp. 249-267.

Van Beckum, William G., Jr. 1971. "Developer vs. Residents in a California New Town: A Study of the Evolution of Democracy in Foster City." Master of Urban Planning Thesis, University of Oregon, August.

Varady, David P. 1973. "Moving Intentions and Behavior in the Cincinnati Model Neighborhood: The Utility of the Survey Approach in Forecasting Residential Mobility." Paper presented at the Association of Collegiate Schools of Planning, American Institute of Planners Annual Conference, Atlanta, Georgia, October 22.

Vivrett, Walter K., and Wilkinson, George R. 1972. *Development of Jonathan*. Report to the Ford Foundation, Grant #69-0525. Minneapolis, Minn.: School of Architecture and Landscape Architecture, University of Minnesota, September 30.

Watson, Raymond L. 1973a. "Phasing Growth: How Fast? Where Next?" in *New Towns in America: The Design and Development Process*, James Bailey (ed.). New York: Published for the American Institute of Architects by John Wiley & Sons, pp. 87-89.

_____. 1973b. "Some Questions Asked and Answered," *Irvine World News*, September 20.

Weaver, Robert C. 1964. *The Urban Complex*. New York: Doubleday and Company, Inc.

Weiss, E.B. 1971. "Department Stores as New Town Builders." *Stores*, Vol. 53 (December), pp. 42-43.

Weiss, Shirley F. 1973. *New Town Development in the United States: Experiment in Private Entrepreneurship*. Chapel Hill, N.C.: Center for Urban and Regional Studies, University of North Carolina at Chapel Hill.

Werthman, Carl, Mandel, Jerry S., and Dienstfrey, Ted. 1965. *Planning and the Purchase Decision: Why People Buy in Planned Communities*. A Prepublication of the Community Development Project. Berkeley, Calif.: Institute for Urban and Regional Development, Center for Planning and Development Research, University of California, July.

Whyte, William H., Jr. 1956. *The Organization Man*. New York: Simon and Schuster, Inc.

Zehner, Robert B. 1971. "Neighborhood and Community Satisfaction in New Towns and Less Planned Suburbs," *Journal of the American Institute of Planners*, Vol. 37 (November), pp. 379-385.

_____. 1974. "Participation in Perspective: A Look at New Town Involvement"' *Sociological Symposium*, Vol. 12 (Fall), pp. 65-80.

Zehner, Robert B., and Marans, Robert W. 1973. "Residential Density, Planning Objectives and Life in Planned Communities," *Journal of the American Institute of Planners*, Vol. 39 (September), pp. 337-345.

Index

Index

586

Foer, Albert A., 177
Forest Park, Ohio, 4, 18, 49, 70; automobiles in, 371; citizen participation in, 144, 149, 150; development of, 76-77, 161; family income in, 106; governance of, 170; health care delivery in, 245, 247, 249, 256; and highway access, 325; housing in, 190, 192, 196, 213; incorporation of, 159; livability of, 361; path systems in, 331; population balance in, 110-111; problems with, 372; ranking of, 98; recreational facilities in, 221, 225; residents' evaluation of, 364, 365, 366, 387; school systems in, 121, 272, 276, 289; shopping facilities for, 303, 307, 313, 315, 317; social life in, 348, 349, 350, 356; social service programs in, 260; subsidized housing in, 108, 115; transit system in, 328, 335, 337
Foster, T. Jack, 83, 161
Foster City, Calif., 4, 18, 70, 82, 83-84; citizen participation in, 144, 145, 149, 150; development of, 161, 162; family income in, 106; governance of, 170; health care delivery in, 245, 249, 255, 259; and highway access, 325; homes associations in, 164, 178, 179; housing in, 190, 192, 195, 196, 213; livability of, 363; moderate-income housing in, 115; path systems in, 330; problems in, 373, 374; public services in, 171; recreational facilities in, 221, 231, 241; residents of, 139; residents' evaluation of, 365, 380, 391, 393; school districts of, 272, 278; school systems in, 289, 290; shopping facilities for, 299, 300, 303, 307, 313; social life in, 349, 355, 356, 357; social service programs in, 260; transit system in, 329, 335, 337
Foster City Community Association, 150, 162
Fountain Valley, Calif., 91, 255
Future, of new communities, 35-36, 485, 508; residents attitudes toward, 436-437

Gans, Herbert J., 100, 358
Garden city movement, English, 38
Gardening, 234, 499. See also Recreation
Gardner, Carl L., and Associates, 404
Gaus, Clifton, 263
General Electric Co., 51
Godschalk, David R., 136
Goldhammer, Keith, 273
Golfing, 223, 228, 229, 324, 499. See also Recreation
Governance, guidelines for, 503-504; homes

associations, 180, (see also Homes associations); of Jonathan, 421-425; local, 12-13, 175-176; of new communities, 13, 21-22, 155-176, 491; of Park Forest South, 421-425
Government, policies of, 114-116; responsibility of, xx. See also Federal government
Governors Gateway Industrial Park, 405
Governors State University, 405, 409
Grant, Richard D., 83
Grants-in-aid programs, federal, 12, 61, 491
Great Britain, new towns of, 48
Great Depression, 38
Greater Hartford Development Corporation, 55
Groups, special interest, 4
Growth, accommodation of, 40; haphazard pattern of, xxiii; metropolitan, 39, 54; urban, 45. See also Development
Growth policy, xix
Gruen, Victor, associates, 77, 86, 301
Guidelines, for planning new community development projects, 494-504
Gulf Oil Corporation, 51
Gulf-Reston, Inc., 246, 257, 279, 302, 330, 375

Handbooks, for federal programs, 63
Health care delivery, 9, 24, 25, 243-269; facilities for, 10, 499-500; in Jonathan, 413; and new community development, 24-25, 95, 323
Health Maintenance Organization (HMO) Act, federal, 262
Hemmens, George C., 129
Herman, Harold, 243
Herndon, Va., 278
Heston, J.F., 249
Heyssel, Robert M., 243, 264
Highways, 157, 324-326. See also Transportation
Hiking, 236, 499. See also Recreation
Homeowners, black, 107; single family, 34, 209. See also Households
Homes associations, 163-168, 176-180, 231, 358; federal structure of, 504; satisfaction with, 205, 208; survey of, 524-525
Hoppenfeld, Morton, 95
Hospital care, 254-258
Hospitals, community, 256-258, 499-500; and new community locations, 87
Households, black 33, 34, 107, 516-517; with children, 125 (see also Children); mobility of, 118, 130; and new community development, 126, 416; in sub-

About the Contributors

Thomas L. Ashley is a member of Congress from the Ninth District of Ohio. Principal author of most major housing legislation since coming to Congress in 1954, including the Urban Growth and New Community Development Act of 1970, he is a ranking member of the Subcommittee on Housing and Community Development, of the Committee on Banking, Currency and Housing, and a member of the House Budget Committee.

William Nicoson is an urban affairs consultant in Washington, D.C. He was the first director of the Office of New Communities in the U.S. Department of Housing and Urban Development. Mr. Nicoson, a resident of Reston, Virginia, has written extensively about new communities and urban growth policies in the United States.

About the Authors

Raymond J. Burby, III, is senior research associate at the Center for Urban and Regional Studies of The University of North Carolina at Chapel Hill. He was co-principal investigator and deputy project director of the NSF/RANN New Communities Project. He received the M.R.P. and Ph.D. in planning from The University of North Carolina at Chapel Hill. Dr. Burby is the author of numerous articles and monographs including *Planning and Politics: Toward a Model of Planning-Related Policy Outputs in American Local Government*. He is co-editor of *New Community Development: Planning Process, Implementation, and Emerging Social Concerns*.

Shirley F. Weiss is professor of planning at The University of North Carolina at Chapel Hill and associate research director at UNC's Center for Urban and Regional Studies. She was principal investigator and project director of the NSF/RANN New Communities Project. She received the M.R.P. in planning from The University of North Carolina at Chapel Hill and the Ph.D. in economics from Duke University. Dr. Weiss is the author of numerous articles and monographs, including *New Town Development in the United States: Experiment in Private Entrepreneurship*. She is co-editor of *Urban Growth Dynamics in a Regional Cluster of Cities*.

Thomas G. Donnelly is senior research associate at the Center for Urban and Regional Studies of The University of North Carolina at Chapel Hill. He was co-principal investigator of the NSF/RANN New Communities Project. He received the M.A. in statistics from Queen's University and the Ph.D. in mathematical statistics from The University of North Carolina at Chapel Hill. Dr. Donnelly is co-author of *A Probabilistic Model for Residential Growth* and a contributor to the *Communications of the ACM*, among other publications.

Edward J. Kaiser is professor of planning at The University of North Carolina at Chapel Hill and associate research director at UNC's Center for Urban and Regional Studies. He was co-principal investigator of the NSF/RANN New Communities Project. He received the Ph.D. in planning from The University of North Carolina at Chapel Hill. Dr. Kaiser is the author of *A Producer Model for Residential Growth* and co-author of *Moving Behavior and Residential Choice: A National Survey*, as well as many articles on planning and urban growth.

Robert B. Zehner is Fulbright Senior Scholar (1975) and Honorary Visiting Fellow in the School of Town Planning at the University of New South

Wales in Australia. He was co-principal investigator of the NSF/RANN New Communities Project. He received the A.M. and Ph.D. in sociology from The University of Michigan. Dr. Zehner is co-author of *Planned Residential Environments* and *Across the City Line: A White Community in Transition*, as well as articles on neighborhood and community satisfaction.

David F. Lewis is a regional planner with the Centralina Council of Governments, Charlotte, N.C. He was a research associate with the NSF/RANN New Communities Project. Mr. Lewis received the M.R.P. from The University of North Carolina at Chapel Hill.

Norman H. Loewenthal is program coordinator of State Wide Independent Study by Extension, at the University of North Carolina at Chapel Hill. He was a research associate with the NSF/RANN New Communities Project. Mr. Loewenthal received the M.Ed. from The University of North Carolina at Chapel Hill.

Mary Ellen McCalla holds a NICHD traineeship in population and is in the doctoral program in sociology at The University of North Carolina at Chapel Hill. She was a research associate with the NSF/RANN New Communities Project. Ms. McCalla received the M.A.T. from Harvard University.

Barbara G. Rodgers is administrative aide and publications Manager at the Center for Urban and Regional Studies of The University of North Carolina at Chapel Hill. She was research assistant/administrative aide with the NSF/RANN New Communities Project. Ms. Rodgers received the A.A.S. from the Technical Institute of Alamance.

Helene V. Smookler is assistant professor of Political Science at Wellesley College. She was a research associate with the NSF/RANN New Communities Project. Dr. Smookler received the M.A. and Ph.D. in political science from the University of California, Los Angeles. She is a contributing author in *New Towns: Why–And for Whom?*